USA

VS | EE.UU. | США

Alaska

Alaska | Aljaška | Alaszka | Алясі

Southern Canada

Canada du Sud | Südliches Kanada | Zuidelijk Canada | Canada meridionale | Canadá meridional | det sydlige Canada | södra Kanada | Jižní Kanada | Kanada południowa | Dél-Kanada | Южная Канада

GB Contents	I Indice	CZ Obsah	
Motorways and trunk roads	Autostrade e strade di grande comunicazione	Dálnice a hlavní dálkové silnice	2–3
Information	Informazioni	Informace	4
Key map and administrative units	Quadro d'unione con confini amministrativi	Klad mapových listů a administrativní rozdělení	5
Legend	Segni convenzionali	Vysvětlivky	6–8
Maps 1 : 4 000 000	Carte 1 : 4 000 000	Mapy 1 : 4 000 000	10–44
California 1 : 800 000	California 1 : 800 000	Kalifornie 1 : 800 000	46–78
Florida 1 : 800 000	Florida 1 : 800 000	Florida 1 : 800 000	80–91
National parks	Parchi nazionali	Národní parky	94–116
City maps 1 : 20 000 / Urban transit route maps 1 : 100 000	Piante del centro città 1 : 20 000 / Piante di attraversamento urbano 1 : 100 000	Plany středů měst 1 : 20 000 / Průjezdné plány měst 1 : 100 000	118–154
Index of place names 1 : 4 000 000	Elenco dei nomi di località 1 : 4 000 000	Rejstřík sídel 1 : 4 000 000	156–176

F Sommaire	E Índice	PL Spis treści	
Autoroutes et routes de grande liaison	Autopistas y rutas de larga distancia	Autostrady i drogi dalekiego zasięgu	2–3
Informations	Informaciónes	Informacje	4
Carte d'assemblage et circonscription administrative	Mapa índice y unidades administrativas	Skorowidz arkuszy i podział administracyjny	5
Légende	Signos convencionales	Objaśnienia znaków	6–8
Cartes 1 : 4 000 000	Mapas 1 : 4 000 000	Mapy 1 : 4 000 000	10–44
Californie 1 : 800 000	California 1 : 800 000	Kalifornia 1 : 800 000	46–78
Floride 1 : 800 000	Florida 1 : 800 000	Floryda 1 : 800 000	80–91
Parcs nationaux	Parques nacionales	Parki Narodowe	94–116
Plans de centre-ville 1 : 20 000 / Plans de traversée des villes 1 : 100 000	Planos del centro de las ciudades 1 : 20 000 / Mapas con las calles de mayor tránsito 1 : 100 000	Plany centrów miast 1 : 20 000 / Mapy przejazdów miejskich 1:100.000	118–154
Index des localités 1 : 4 000 000	Índice de topónimos 1 : 4 000 000	Skorowidz miejscowości 1 : 4 000 000	156–176

D Inhaltsverzeichnis	DK Inholdsfortegnelse	H Tartalomjegyzék	
Autobahnen und Fernstraßen	Motorveje og hovedveje	Autópályák és távolsági forgami utak	2–3
Informationen	Information	Információ	4
Kartenübersicht und Verwaltungsgliederung	Oversigtskort og forvaltningsindelling	Áttekintő térkép és közigazgatási egységek	5
Zeichenerklärung	Tegnforklaring	Jelmagyarázat	6–8
Kartografie 1 : 4 000 000	Kort 1 : 4 000 000	Térképek 1 : 4 000 000	10–44
Kalifornien 1 : 800 000	California 1 : 800 000	Kalifornia 1 : 800 000	46–78
Florida 1 : 800 000	Florida 1 : 800 000	Florida 1 : 800 000	80–91
Nationalparks	National parks	Nemzeti parkok	94–116
Citypläne 1 : 20 000 / Stadtdurchfahrtskarten 1 : 100 000	Byplaner 1 : 20 000 / Bytransitkort 1 : 100 000	Citytérképek 1 : 20 000 / Áthajtási várostérképek 1 : 100 000	118–154
Ortsnamensverzeichnis 1 : 4 000 000	Navnefortegnelse 1 : 4 000 000	Helységnévmutató 1 : 4 000 000	156–176

NL Inhoud	S Innehållsförteckning	RUS Оглавление	
Autosnelwegen en belangrijke verbindingswegen	Motorvägar och genomfartsleder	Автомагистрали и дороги дальнего сообщения	2–3
Informatie	Information	Информация	4
Overzichtskaart en administratieve indeling	Kartöversikt och förvaltningsindelning	Общий вид карт и административное деление	5
Legenda	Teckenförklaring	Условные обозначения	6–8
Kaarten 1 : 4 000 000	Kartor 1 : 4 000 000	Карты 1 : 4 000 000	10–44
Californië 1 : 800 000	Kalifornien 1 : 800 000	Калифорния 1 : 800 000	46–78
Florida 1 : 800 000	Florida 1 : 800 000	Флорида 1 : 800 000	80–91
Nationale parken	Nationalparker	Национальные парки	94–116
Stadsplattegronden 1 : 20 000 / Stadsoverzichtskarten 1 : 100 000	Stadskartor 1 : 20 000 / Kartor för stadsgenomfarter 1 : 100 000	карты городов 1 : 20 000 / Карты транзитного проезда по городу 1 : 100 000	118–154
Register van plaatsnamen 1 : 4 000 000	Ortnamnsförteckning 1 : 4 000 000	Указатель населённых пунктов 1 : 4 000 000	156–176

ROSSIJA
Bering Sea
Bering Strait
Chukchi Sea
Monday
Sunday
Beaufort Sea
North Slope
Alaska (U.S.)
Aleutian Islands
Fox Islands
Andreanof Islands
Rat Islands
Near Islands
Komandorskie o-va
Alaska Peninsula
Bristol Bay
Norton Sound
Seward Pen.
Gulf of Alaska
Alexander Archipelago
Queen Charlotte Islands
Dixon Entrance
Queen Charlotte Sound
Vancouver Island
Yukon Plateau
Liard Plateau
Coast Mountains
Columbia Mountains
Cascade Range
Coast Ranges
Sierra Nevada
Banks Island
Amundsen Gulf
M'Clure Str.
Wollaston Pen.
PACIFIC OCEAN
Anchorage
Fairbanks
Juneau
Whitehorse
Prince George
VANCOUVER
Victoria
SEATTLE
Tacoma
Spokane
PORTLAND
Eugene
SACRAMENTO
SAN FRANCISCO
SAN JOSE
Fresno
Bakersfield
LOS ANGELES
SAN DIEGO
TIJUANA
Denali Nat. P.
Kluane Nat. Park
Tatshenshini-Alsek Provincial Park
Glacier Bay Nat. P.
Nahanni Nat. Park
Jasper Nat. P.
Yoho Nat. P.
Banff Nat. P.
Kootenay Nat. P.
Waterton Glacier Int'l. Peace P.
Olympic Nat. P.
Redwood Nat. Park
Yosemite Nat. P.
Death Valley N.P.
Kings Canyon N.P.
10
11
12
13
14
15
16
24
32
38
Hawaiian Islands (U.S.)
French Frigate Shoals
Necker I.
Nihoa
Kauai
Niihau
Lihue
Oahu
Honolulu
Molokai
Maui
Kahului
Honokaa
Hilo
Kailua-Kona
Hawaii
Hawaii Volcanoes Nat. P.
PACIFIC OCEAN
44
Turks and Caicos Islands (U.K.)
Caicos Is.
Turks Is.
ATLANTIC OCEAN
Hispaniola
Cap-Haïtien
DAYTI HAITI
PORT-AU-PRINCE
SANTIAGO
D.L. CABALLEROS
REP. DOMINICANA
La Romana
Baní
San Juan
Ponce
Puerto Rico (U.S.)
Virgin Islands (U.S.) (Brit.)
(U.K.) Anguilla
St.-Martin/Sint Maarten (Fr.) (Ned.)
Caribisch Nederland
ST. KITTS AND NEVIS
ANTIGUA AND BARBUDA
St. John's
Montserrat (U.K.)
Guadeloupe (Fr.)
Basse-Terre
Roseau
DOMINICA
Martinique (Fr.)
Fort-de-France
SAINT LUCIA
Castries
Lesser Antilles
Greater Antilles
Caribbean Sea
42

Baffin Bay
Devon Island
Lancaster Sound
Resolute
Arctic Bay
Clyde
Baffin Island
Davis Strait
Kalaallit Nunaat (Dan.)
Nuuk Godthåb
Narsarsuaq
Pangnirtung
Prince of Wales I.
Boothia Peninsula
Gulf of Boothia
Melville Peninsula
Prince Charles I.
Foxe Basin
Repulse Bay
Iqaluit
Lake Harbour
Labrador Sea
Cambridge Bay
Gjoa Haven
Foxe Channel
Cape Dorset
Hudson Strait
Southampton I.
Coral Harbour
Ivujivik
Ungava Bay
Péninsule d'Ungava
Kuujjuaq (Fort-Chimo)
Hebron
Makkovik
Holton
L'Anse aux Meadows
St. Anthony
Island of Newfoundland
Chesterfield Inlet
Baker Lake
Barren Grounds
Hudson Bay
Labrador
Happy Valley-Goose Bay
Churchill Falls
Schefferville
Blanc Sablon
Gander
St. John's
Reliance
Inukjuak (Port Harrison)
Labrador City
Gros Morne N.P.
Corner Brook
Channel-Port-aux-Basques
St.-Pierre et Miquelon (Fr.)
Île d'Anticosti
Pt. Menier
Gulf of St. Lawrence
Sept-Îles
Churchill
Belcher Islands
Péninsule
Matane
Miguasha N.P.
Bathurst
Charlottetown
Fort Severn
Radisson
Manicouagan
Baie-Comeau
Chibougamau
Chicoutimi
New Glasgow
Halifax
Truro
Moncton
Lake Athabasca
Key Lake Mine
Kinoosao
Lynn Lake
Gillam
Winisk
James Bay
Fort Albany
Moosonee
Clay Belt
Matagami
Edmundston
QUÉBEC
Saint John
Bangor
Yarmouth
Bay of Fundy
Gulf of Maine
La Loche
Sandy Lake
Thompson
Flin Flon
Norway House
Webequie
Trois-Rivières
Beauval
Central Patricia
Kapuskasing
Prince Albert
Grand Rapids
Lake Winnipeg
Pine Dock
Red Lake
Nakina
Timmins
MONTRÉAL
OTTAWA
Sherbrooke
Portland
North Battleford
Hudson Bay
Dauphin
Savant Lake
Nipigon
Wawa
Sudbury
North Bay
Pembroke
Montpelier
BOSTON
Providence
Saskatoon
Yorkton
WINNIPEG
Kenora
Isle Royale
Lake Superior
Sault Ste. Marie
Oshawa
Utica
NEW YORK
Statue of Liberty
Independence Hall
PHILADELPHIA
Dinosaur Prov. Park
Regina
Brandon
Portage la Prairie
Thunder Bay
Marquette
Upper Pen.
Lake Huron
Syracuse
Elmira
Scranton
Medicine Hat
Weyburn
Minot
Bemidji
Duluth
Escanaba
Menominee
Lower Pen.
TORONTO
HAMILTON
London
Harrisburg
BALTIMORE
ATLANTIC
OCEAN
Havre
Glasgow
Williston
Grand Forks
Fargo
Fergus Falls
Saint Paul
Big Rapids
Lake Michigan
DETROIT
Lake Erie
Cleveland
Great Falls
Glendive
Bismarck
Jamestown
Minneapolis
Sheboygan
MILWAUKEE
Toledo
Pittsburgh
WASHINGTON D.C.
Monticello
Richmond
Hampton
Virginia Beach
Hamilton
Bermuda (U.K.)
Billings
Miles City
Aberdeen
Mason City
CHICAGO
South Bend
Yellowstone N. P.
Rapid City
Huron
Waterloo
Davenport
INDIANAPOLIS
COLUMBUS
Charleston
Grand Teton N.P.
Buffalo
Sioux Falls
Sioux City
Des Moines
Champaign
Cincinnati
Lexington
Roanoke
Greensboro
Raleigh
New Bern
Casper
Douglas
Omaha
Springfield
Saint Louis
Mt. Vernon
Louisville
Mammoth Cave N.P.
Wilmington
Pocatello
Great Divide Basin
Scottsbluff
North Platte
Hastings
Cheyenne
Evansville
Glasgow
Knoxville
CHARLOTTE
Ogden
Rock Springs
Rocky Mtn. N.P.
DENVER
Hays
Salina
Kansas City
Cahokia Mounds
Cape Girardeau
Clarksville
NASHVILLE
Great Smoky Mountains N.P.
Greenville
Columbia
Georgetown
Charleston
Colorado Springs
Pueblo
Dodge City
Winfield
Springfield
Jonesboro
MEMPHIS
Huntsville
Atlanta
Savannah
Arches N.P.
Canyonlands N. P.
Ponca City
Birmingham
Macon
Brunswick
Mesa Verde N.P.
Durango
Trinidad
Liberal
Tulsa
Little Rock
Greenwood
Tuscaloosa
Montgomery
Albany
JACKSONVILLE
Bryce Canyon N.P.
Page
Taos Pueblo
Stratford
OKLAHOMA CITY
McAlester
Pine Bluff
Dothan
Valdosta
Gainesville
Daytona Beach
BAHAMAS
Chaco Culture N.H.P.
Santa Fe
Las Vegas
Amarillo
Altus
Ardmore
Jackson
Tallahassee
Orlando
Florida
Grand Bahama I.
ALBUQUERQUE
Clovis
Plainview
Wichita Falls
DALLAS
Shreveport
Monroe
Mobile
Apalachee Bay
West Palm Beach
Eleuthera I.
Gallup
Roswell
Lubbock
Baton Rouge
Bayonet Point
St. Petersburg
Sarasota
Fort Lauderdale
Nassau
Mayaguana I.
PHOENIX
Carlsbad
Carlsbad Caverns Nat.P.
Abilene
Waco
Lufkin
Lafayette
New Orleans
Houma
Mississippi River Delta
Naples
Miami
Andros Island
Clarence Town
Abraham's Bay
TUCSON
Odessa
San Angelo
AUSTIN
HOUSTON
Beaumont
Pasadena
Everglades N. P.
Key West
Florida Keys
Straits of Florida
Baracoa
EL PASO
Pecos
Kerrville
Victoria
Freeport
Matanzas
Santa Clara
CUBA
Las Tunas
Douglas
CIUDAD JUÁREZ
Alpine
Gulf of Mexico
Nogales
Casas Grandes
Nuevo Casas Grandes
El Sueco
SAN ANTONIO
Beeville
Corpus Christi
LA HABANA
Cienfuegos
Camagüey
Manzanillo
Pilón
Guantánamo
HAITI
Jérémie
HERMOSILLO
CHIHUAHUA
Delicias
Nueva Rosita
Allende
Nuevo Laredo
Laredo
Isla S. Pedro Mártir
Monclova
S. NICOLÁS D.L.GARZAS
Brownsville
Pinar del Río
Yucatán Channel
Guaymas
Ciudad Obregón
Hidalgo d. Parral
Altiplanicie Mexicana
MONTERREY
Cayman Is. (U.K.)
Georgetown
Savanna-la-Mar
Spanish Town
JAMAICA
Los Mochis
El Fuerte
TORREÓN
San Fernando
Rio Lagartos
CANCÚN
Bahía de Loreto N.P.
Guasave
MÉXICO
Matehuala
Ciudad Victoria
MÉRIDA
Peto
MÉXICO
Islas del Cisne (Hon.)
Constitución
CULIACÁN
Hidalgo
Camino Real
S. LUIS POTOSÍ
Tampico
Península de Yucatán
Campeche
Chetumal
Cabo Pulmo
Mazatlán
La Paz
San José del Cabo
Cabo San Lucas
Acaponeta
AGUASCALIENTES
Tamazunchale
Poza Rica
Escárcega
BELIZE
Belize City
HONDURAS
Colotlán
Frontera

U.S.A.	Discover America LLC www.usatourist.com	+1	**1 Dollar (USD) =** 100 Cents	**0800 222 43 57** American Automobile Association (AAA)	**911**	**911**	**911**
Canada	Canadian Tourism Commission us.canada.travel	+1	**1 Dollar (CAD) =** 100 Cents	**0800 222 43 57** Canadian Automobile Association (CAA)	**911**	**911**	**911**

U.S.A.	**mph**	**20–30**	**55–65**	**70–75**	✓	✓	✓	**0,8 ‰**
Canada	**km/h**	**50**	**80**	**100**	✓	✓	✓	**0,8 ‰** **0,5 ‰** in BC, MB, NB, NL

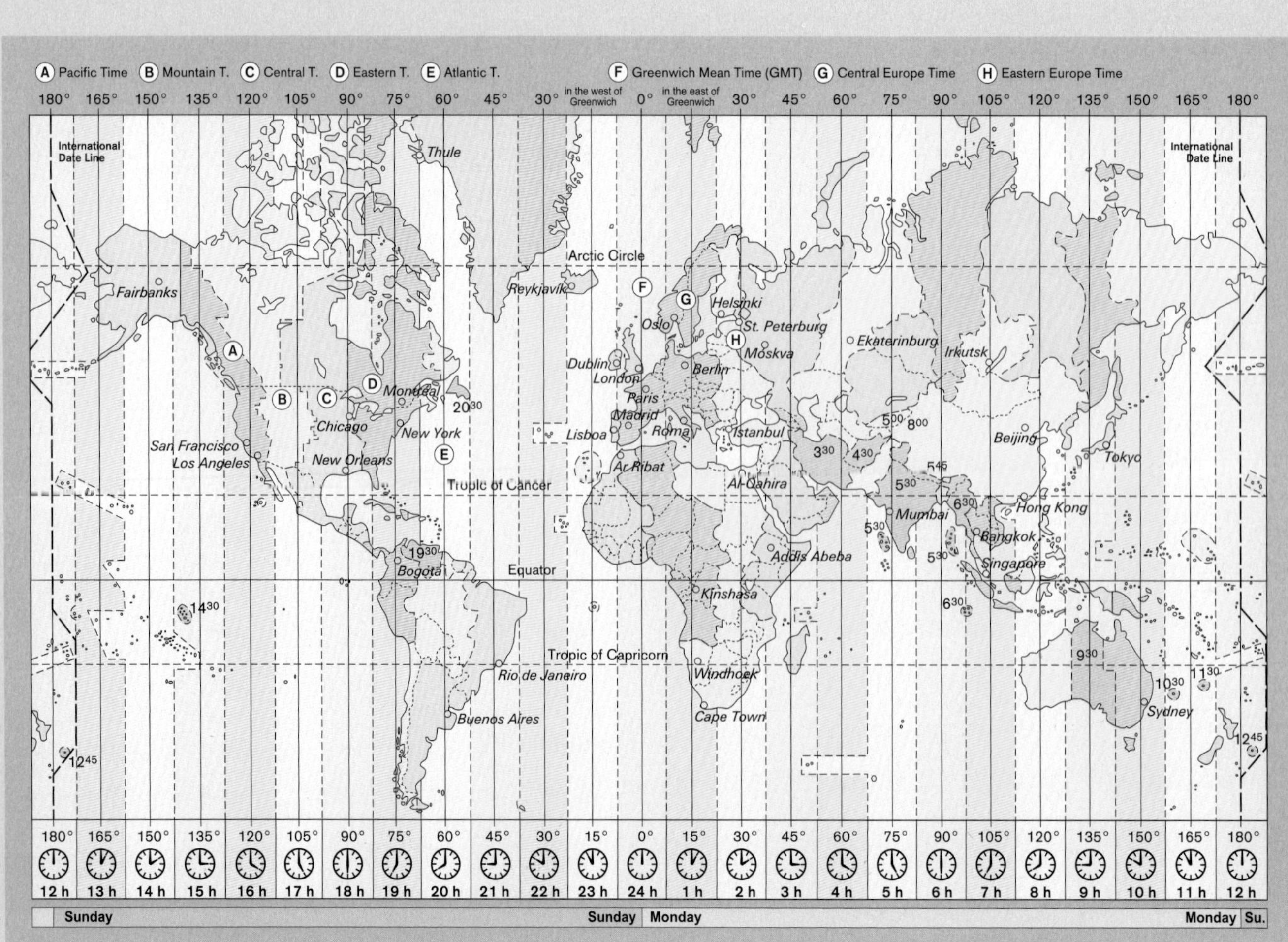

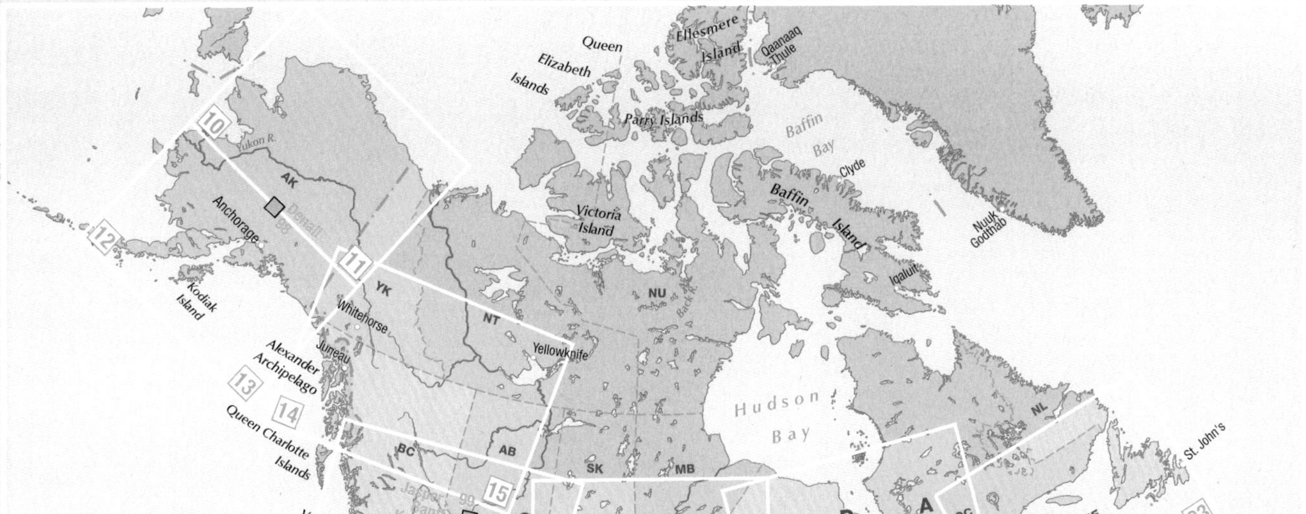

Queen Elizabeth Islands
Ellesmere Island
Qaanaaq Thule
Parry Islands
Baffin Bay
Clyde
Baffin Island
Victoria Island
Nuuk Godthåb
Iqaluit
AK
Denali
Anchorage
Kodiak Island
YK
Whitehorse
NT
NU
Yellowknife
Alexander Archipelago
Juneau
Queen Charlotte Islands
Hudson Bay
NL
St. John's
BC
AB
SK
MB
EDMONTON
CALGARY
120
C A N A D A
QC
PE
Vancouver Island
VANCOUVER
150
154
SEATTLE
WA
Regina
WINNIPEG
Lake Winnipeg
ON
QUÉBEC
NB
Fredericton
NS
Halifax
ME
MONTRÉAL
136
TORONTO
VT
NH
BOSTON
118
MA
CT
RI
NEW YORK
140
NJ
146
PACIFIC OCEAN
Salem
OR
Boise
ID
MT
Bismarck
ND
SD
Pierre
MN
Saint Paul
WI
MI
NY
PA
Yellowstone
Grand Teton
WY
CHICAGO
122
DETROIT
OH
IN
WASHINGTON D.C.
152
MD
DE
SAN FRANCISCO
144
CA
NV
Salt Lake City
Cheyenne
NE
IA
IL
Lincoln
Yosemite
UT
Arches
CO
DENVER
121
Rocky Mountain
KS
MO
KY
WV
VA
Raleigh
NC
Kings Canyon Sequoia
LAS VEGAS
125
Canyonlands
Grand Canyon
U N I T E D   S T A T E S
NASH-VILLE
TN
Great Smoky Mountains
LOS ANGELES
128
AZ
PHOENIX
Santa Fe
NM
OK
OKLAHOMA CITY
Little Rock
AR
MS
AL
Atlanta
GA
SC
Columbia
Hamilton
ATLANTIC OCEAN
Joshua Tree
DALLAS
TX
LA
Jackson
Tallahassee
FL
New Orleans
HOUSTON
131
Fort Myers
130
Fort Lauderdale
135
Miami Beach
134
Miami
Everglades
BAHAMAS
Turks and Caicos Islands (U.K.)
MÉXICO
Gulf of Mexico
MONTERREY
CUBA
SANTIAGO DE CUBA
REP. DOMINICANA
San Juan Puerto Rico
PORT-AU-PRINCE
HAITI
SANTO DOMINGO
JAMAICA
Mérida
GUADALAJARA
106 Death Valley
110 Zion
111 Bryce Canyon
Necker I.
Kaua'i
O'ahu
Hawaii
Maui
Honolulu
10
11
12
13
14
15
16
17
18
19
20
21
22
23
24
25
26
27
28
29
30
31
32
33
34
35
36
37
38
39
40
41
42
43
44

Boise
Oregon
Idaho
Medford
Twin Falls
Snake Riv.
Redding
Nevada
Great Salt Lake
Salt Lake City
Great Basin
Utah
Reno
SACRAMENTO
Carson City
Sierra Nevada
UNITED STATES
144
SAN FRANCISCO
SAN JOSE
Yosemite
Bryce Canyon
Death Valley
St. George
Zion
Kings Canyon / Sequoia
LAS VEGAS
125
Grand Canyon
Bakersfield
California
Flagstaff
Arizona
LOS ANGELES
128
Joshua Tree
PACIFIC OCEAN
Colorado Desert
SAN DIEGO
PHOENIX
TIJUANA
TUCSON
NM
MÉXICO
46
47
48
49
50
51
52
53
54
55
56
57
58
59
60
61
62
63
64
65
66
67
68
69
70
71
72
73
74
75
76
77
78

Columbia
Missouri
Birmingham
Alabama
Atlanta
South Carolina
Georgia
Jackson
Montgomery
Savannah
Sea Islands
UNITED STATES
Cumberland Island
ATLANTIC OCEAN
Mobile
Pensacola
Tallahassee
JACKSONVILLE
Apalachee Bay
Orlando
Florida
St. Petersburg
Lake Okeechobee
Gulf of Mexico
West Palm Beach
131
Fort Myers
130
Fort Lauderdale
Miami Beach
134
135
Miami
Everglades
Florida Bay
Key West
BAHAMAS
LA HABANA
Pinar del Río
CUBA
80
81
82
83
84
85
86
87
88
89
90
91

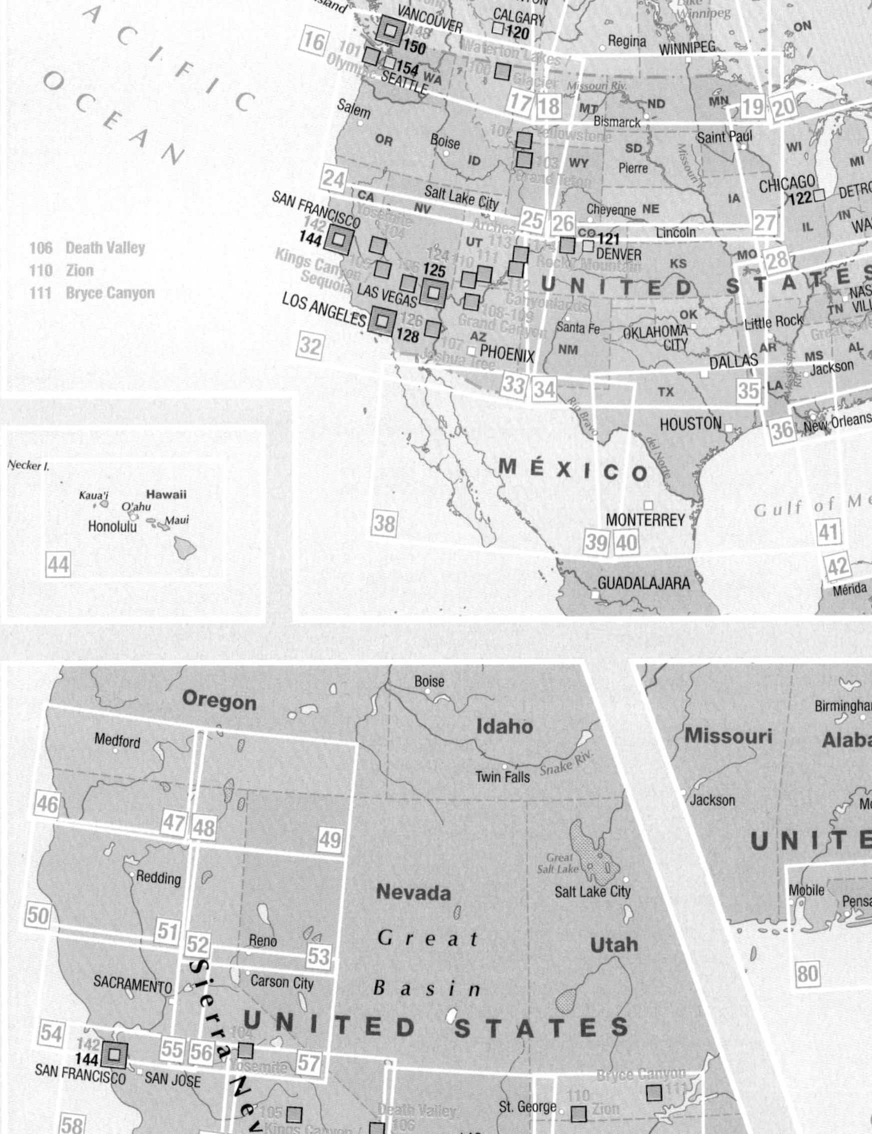

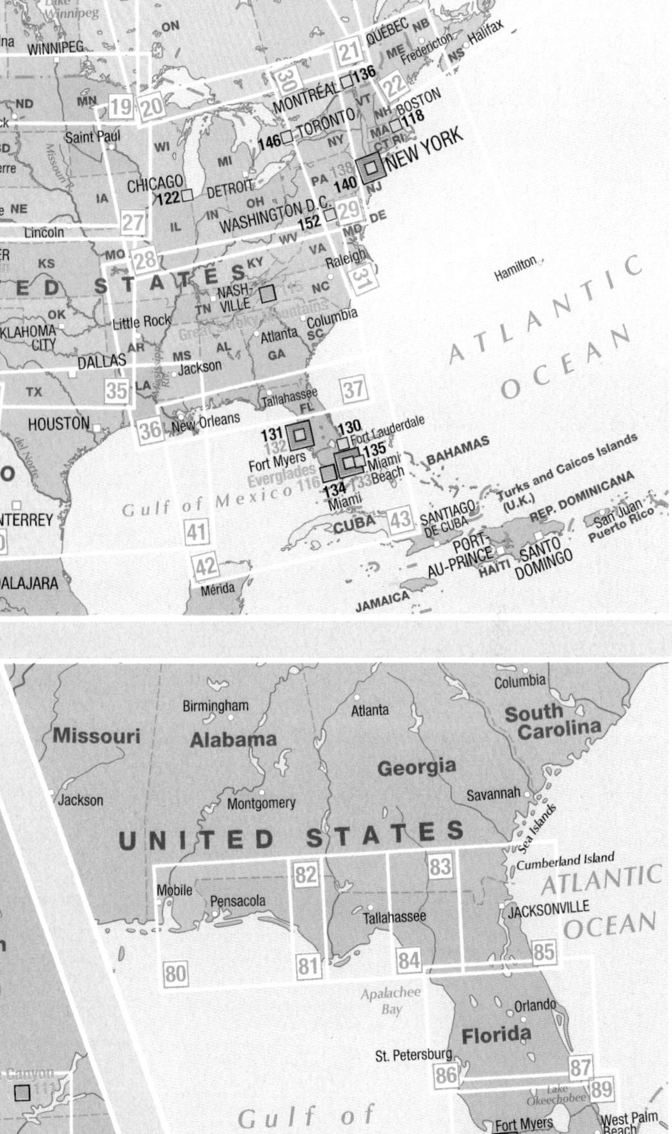

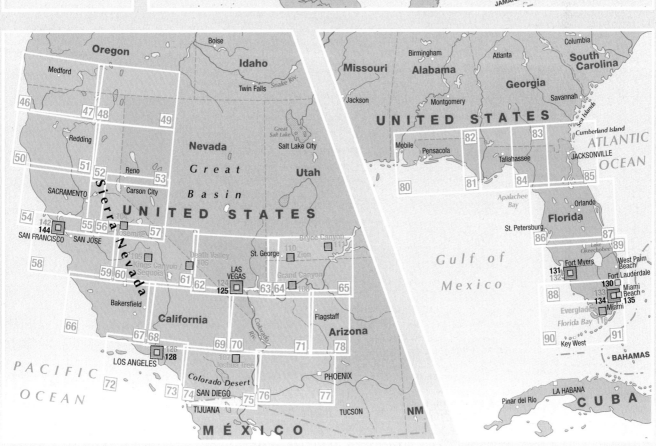

Legend | Légende | Zeichenerklärung | Legenda

TRAFFIC (GB) CIRCULATION (F)		(D) VERKEHR (NL) VERKEER
Motorway · under construction Autoroute · en construction		**Autobahn · in Bau** Autosnelweg · in aanleg
Dual carriageway with motorway characteristics · under construction Chaussée double de type autoroutier · en construction		**Autobahnähnliche Schnellstraße · in Bau** Autoweg met gescheiden rijbanen · in aanleg
Trunk road · under construction Route de grand trafic · en construction		**Fernverkehrsstraße · in Bau** Weg voor interlokaal verkeer · in aanleg
Main road Route principale		**Hauptstraße** Hoofdweg
Secondary road Route secondaire		**Nebenstraße** Secundaire weg
Carriageway · Footpath · Trekking route Chemin carrossable · Sentier · Itinéraire de trekking		**Fahrweg · Fußweg · Trekkingroute** Rijweg · Voetpad · Trekking Route
Distances in miles (USA) / kilometres Distances en lieues (USA) / kilomètre	227 130 97	**Entfernungen in Meilen (USA) / Kilometer** Afstanden in mijlen (USA) / kilometer
Height in metres · Pass Altitude en mètres · Col	1365	**Höhe in Meter · Pass** Hoogte in meter · Bergpas
Main railway · Secondary line railway Chemin de fer principal · Chemin de fer secondaire		**Eisenbahn, Hauptbahn · Nebenbahn** Belangrijke spoorweg · Lokale spoorweg
Car ferry · Shipping route · Car ferry on river Bac pour automobiles · Ligne de navigation · Bac fluvial pour automobiles		**Autofähre · Schifffahrtslinie · Autofähre an Flüssen** Autoveer · Scheepvaartroute · Autoveer over rivieren
Toll station · Filling-station · Road-side restaurant Gare de péage · Poste d'essence · Restaurant		**Mautstelle · Tankstelle · Raststätte** Tolkantoor · Tankstation · Restaurant
Road closed for motor vehicles · Closure in winter Route interdite aux véhicules à moteur · Fermeture en hiver	12-04	**Straße für Kraftfahrzeuge gesperrt · Wintersperre** Gesloten voor motorvoertuigen · Winterafsluiting
Road numbers Numéros de routes	4 75 88 17 127	**Straßennummern** Wegnummers
Important international airport · Airport · Airfield Aéroport international important · Aéroport · Aérodrome		**Wichtiger internationaler Flughafen · Flughafen · Flugplatz** Belangrijke internationale luchthaven · Luchthaven · Vliegveld

OTHER INFORMATION AUTRES INDICATIONS		SONSTIGES OVERIGE INFORMATIE
International boundary · Administrative boundary Frontière internationale · Frontière administrative		**Internationale Grenze · Verwaltungsgrenze** Internationale grens · Administratieve grens
Time zone boundary Limite de fuseau horaire		**Zeitzonengrenze** Tijdzonegrens
National capital Capitale nationale	WASHINGTON D.C.	**Hauptstadt eines souveränen Staates** Hoofdstad van een souvereine staat
Seat of the administration Siège de l'administration	SACRAMENTO	**Verwaltungssitz** Zetel van de administratië
Well · Volcano Puits · Volcan		**Brunnen · Vulkan** Waterput · Vulkaan

PLACES OF INTEREST CURIOSITÉS		SEHENSWÜRDIGKEITEN BEZIENSWAARDIGHEDEN
Of particular interest: culture · nature Particulièrement intéressant: culture · nature	LAS VEGAS *Niagara Falls*	**Besonders sehenswert: Kultur · Natur** Bijzonder bezienswaardig: cultuur · natuur
Place of interest Localité intéressante	Galveston	**Sehenswerter Ort** Bezienswaardige plaats
Of interest: culture · nature Intéressant: culture · nature	*Fort Fisher* *Ozark Wonder Cave*	**Sehenswert: Kultur · Natur** Bezienswaardig: cultuur · natuur
Route with beautiful scenery · Tourist route Parcours pittoresque · Route touristique	*Alaska Hwy*	**Landschaftlich schöne Strecke · Touristenstraße** Landschappelijk mooie route · Toeristische route
National park · Nature park Parc national · Parc naturel		**Nationalpark · Naturpark** Nationaal park · Natuurpark
Prohibited area · Indian reservation Zone interdite · Réserve d'indiens		**Sperrgebiet · Indianerreservat** Afgesloten gebied · Indianenreservaat
Bathing beach · Coral reef Plage · Récif de corail		**Badestrand · Korallenriff** Badstrand · Koraalrif
Point of view · Waterfall · Cave Point de vue · Cascade · Grotte		**Aussichtspunkt · Wasserfall · Höhle** Uitzichtpunt · Waterval · Grot
Monument · Archaeological excavation or ruins · Tower · Lighthouse Monument · Site archéologique ou ruines · Tour · Phare		**Denkmal · Ausgrabungs- oder Ruinenstätte · Turm · Leuchtturm** Monument · Uitgraving of ruïne · Toren · Vuurtoren
Isolated hotel · Refuge · Youth hostel · Camping site Hôtel isolé · Refuge · Auberge de jeunesse · Terrain de camping		**Alleinstehendes Hotel · Berghütte · Jugendherberge · Campingplatz** Afgelegen hotel · Berghut · Jeugdherberg · Kampeerterrein
Ranger station · Parking place Ranger station · Parking	P	**Rangerstation · Parkplatz** Ranger station · Parkeerplaats
Picnic area · Riding Aire de pique-nique · Équitation		**Picknickplatz · Reiten** Picknickplaats · Paardrijden

Segni convenzionali | Signos convencionales | Tegnforklaring | Teckenförklaring

COMUNICAZIONI (I) / TRÁFICO (E)	(DK) TRAFIK / (S) TRAFIK
Autostrada · in costruzione Autopista · en construcción	Motorvej · under opførelse Motorväg · under byggnad
Doppia carreggiata di tipo autostradale · in costruzione Autovía · en construcción	Motortrafikvej med to vejbaner · under opførelse Motortrafikled · under byggnad
Strada di grande comunicazione · in costruzione Ruta de larga distancia · en construcción	Fjerntrafikvej · under opførelse Fjärrtrafikväg · under byggnad
Strada principale Carretera principal	Hovedvej Huvudled
Strada secondaria Carretera secundaria	Bivej Sidoväg
Sentiero carrabile · Sentiero · Percorso per trekking Camino · Senda · Trekking ruta	Mindre vej · Gangsti · Trekking route Körväg · Gångväg · Trekking route
Distanze in miglia (USA) / chilometri Distancias en leguas (USA) / kilómetros 227 130 97	Afstande i mil (USA) / kilometer Avstånd i miles (USA) / kilometer
Altitudine in metri · Passo Altura en metros · Puerto de montaña 1365	Højde i meter · Pas Höjd i meter · Pass
Ferrovia principale · Ferrovia secondaria Ferrocarril principal · Ferrocarril secundario	Jernbanelinie, Hovedjernbanelinie · Sidebane Järnväg, Huvudjärnväg · Mindre viktig järnväg
Traghetto per auto · Linea marittima · Trasporto auto fluviale Transbordador para automóviles · Ruta marítima · Paso de automóviles en barca	Bilfærge · Skibsrute · Bilfærge på flod Bilfärja · Sjöfartslinje · Flodfärja
Stazione a barriera · Area di servizio · Area di ristoro in autostrada Estación de peaje · Estación de servicio · Albergue	Vejafgiftsstation · Tankanlæg · Rastested Vägavgiftstation · Bensinstation · Vägrestaurang
Strada vietata ai veicoli a motore · Chiusura invernale Carretera cerrada para automóviles · Cerrado en invierno 12-04	Vej spærret for motortrafik · Vinterlukning Avstängd väg för motortrafik · Avstängd vintertid
Numeri di strade Números de carreteras 4 75 88 17 127	Vinterlukning Vägnummer
Aeroporto internazionale importante · Aeroporto · Aerodromo Aeropuerto internacional importante · Aeropuerto · Aeródromo	Vigtig international lufthavn · Lufthavn · Flyveplads Viktig internationell större trafikflygplats · Flygplats · Flygfält

ALTRI SEGNI / OTROS DATOS	ANDET / ÖVRIGT
Confine internazionale · Confine amministrativo Frontera internacional · Frontera administrativa	International grænse · Forvaltningsgrænse Internationell gräns · Förvaltningsgräns
Limite di fusio orario Límite del huso horario	Tidszonegrænse Tidszongräns
Capitale di stato sovrano Capital de estado soberano WASHINGTON D.C.	Suveræn stats hovedstad Huvudstad i suverän stat
Sede amministrativa Centro administrativo SACRAMENTO	Forvaltningssæde Förvaltningssäte
Pozzo · Vulcano Fuente · Volcán	Brønd · Vulkan Brunn · Vulkan

INTERESSE TURISTICO / PUNTOS DE INTERÉS	SEVÆRDIGHEDER / SEVÄRDHETER
Di particolare interesse: cultura · natura De interés especial: cultura · naturaleza LAS VEGAS Niagara Falls	Særlig seværdig: kultur · natur Särskilt sevärd: kultur · natur
Localita' di interesse Localidad de interés Galveston	Seværdig by Sevärd ort
Interessante: cultura · natura De interés: cultura · naturaleza Fort Fisher Ozark Wonder Cave	Seværdig: kultur · natur Sevärd: kultur · natur
Percorso pittoresco · Strada turistica Ruta pintoresca · Ruta turística Alaska Hwy	Landskabelig smuk vejstrækning · Turistrute Naturskön sträcka · Turistled
Parco nazionale · Parco naturale Parque nacional · Parque natural	Nationalpark · Naturpark Nationalpark · Naturpark
Zona vietata · Riserva indiana Zona prohibida · Reserva de indios	Spærret område · Indianerreservat Spärrzon · Indianreservat
Spiaggia · Scogliera corallina Playa · Arrecife coralino	Badestrand · Koralrev Badstrand · Korallrev
Punto panoramico · Cascata · Grotta Vista panorámica · Caterata · Cueva	Udsigtspunkt · Vandfald · Hule Utsiktsplats · Vattenfall · Grotta
Monumento · Scavo o rovine · Torre · Faro Monumento · Excavación o ruinas históricas · Torre · Faro	Mindesmærke · Udgravnings- eller ruinsted · Tårn · Fyrtårn Monument · Utgrävnings- eller ruinplats · Torn · Fyrtorn
Albergo isolato · Rifugio · Ostello della gioventù · Campeggio Hotel aislado · Refugio · Albergue juvenil · Camping	Enlig hotel · Bjerghytte · Vandrerhjem · Campingplads Enslig hotell · Fjällstuga · Vandrarhem · Campingplats
Stazione di Ranger · Parcheggio Estación de Ranger · Aparcamiento P	Ranger Station · Parkeringplads Ranger Station · Parkering
Posto di picnic · Equitazione Área de picnic · Equitación	picnic område · Ride Picnic plats · Rida

Vysvětlivky | Objaśnienia znaków | Jelmagyarázat | Условные обозначения

DOPRAVA CZ / KOMUNIKACJA PL		H KÖZLEKEDÉS / RUS Транспорт
Dálnice · ve stavbě Autostrada · w budowie		Autópálya · építés alatt Автомагистраль · строящаяся
Dvouproudá silnice dálnicového typu · ve stavbě Droga szybkiego ruchu · w budowie		Gyorsforgalmi út autópályahoz hasonlóan · építés alatt Скоростная дорога, подобная автомагистрали · строящаяся
Dálková silnice · ve stavbě Droga dalekobieżna · w budowie		Távolsági összekötő út · építés alatt Магистральная дорога · строящаяся
Hlavní silnice Droga główna		Főútvonal Главная дорога
Vedlejší silnice Droga drugorzędna		Mellékút Основная дорога
Zpevněná cesta · Stezka · Trekkingová trasa Droga bita · Droga dla pieszych · Szlak trekkingowy		Földút · Gyalogút · Trekking útvonal Проесжая дорога · Пещеходная дорожка · Поход марщрут
Vzdálenosti v mílích (USA) / kilometrech Odległości w milach (USA) / kilometrach	227 130 97	Távolság mérföldben (USA) / Kilométertávolság Расстояния в милях (США) / километрах
Výška v metrech · Průsmyk Wysokość w metrach · Przełęcz	1365	Magasság méterben · Szoros Высота в метрах · Перевал
Hlavní železnice · Místní železnice Kolej główna · Kolej drugorzędna		Fővasútvonal · Mellékvasútvonal Железная дорога · Железнодорожный паром
Trajekt pro auta · Lodní linka · Říční přívoz pro auta Prom samochodowy · Linia żeglugowa · Prom rzeczny samochodowy		Autószallító komp · Hajózási vonal · Autókomp folyókon Перевозы мащин · Судоходные маршруты · Речный автомобильный паром
Místo výběru poplatků · Čerpací stanice · Motorest Płatna rogatka · Stacja benzynowa · Restauracja		Vámház · Benzinkút · Vendéglő Пункт оплаты · Заправочная станция · Придорожная зона отдыха
Silnice uzavřená pro motorová vozidla · Silnice uzavřená v zimě Droga zamknięta dla ruchu samochodowego · Zamknięta zimą	12-04	Gépjárműforgalom elől elzárt út · Télen elzárt útszakasz Дорога закрытая для автотранспорта · Дорога закрытая зимой
Čísla silnic Numery dróg	4 75 88 17 127	Útszámok Номера дорог
Důležitá mezinárodní letiště · Dopravní letiště · Přistávací plocha Ważny międzynarodowy port lotniczy · Port lotniczy · Lotnisko		Fontos nemzetközi repülőtér · Közlekedési repülőtér · Egyéb repülőtér Важный международный аэропорт · Аэропорт · Аэродром

ZAJÍMAVOSTI / INNE INFORMACJE		LÁTVÁNYOSSÁGOK / Проице знаки
Mezinárodní hranice · Správní hranice Granica międzynarodowa · Granica administracyjna		Nemzetközi határ · Közigazgatási határ Международная граница · Граница провинции
Hranice časového pásma Granica strefy czasowej		Időzónahatár Граница часовых поясов
Hlavní město suverenního státu Stolica państwa	WASHINGTON D.C.	Önálló állam fővárosa Столица суверенного государства
Sídlo správního úřadu Siedziba administracji	SACRAMENTO	A közigazgatás székhelye Административнач столицы
Studna · Sopka Studnia · Wulkan		Kút · Vulkán Колодец · Вулкан

JINÉ ZNAČKY / INTERESUJĄCE OBIEKTY		EGYÉB / Достопримецателбности
Turisticky pozoruhodný: kultura · příroda Szczególnie interesujący: kulturalny · przyrodniczy	LAS VEGAS Niagara Falls	Különleges látványosság: kultúra · természet Особенно достопримечательно: Культура · Природа
Turisticky zajímavá lokalita Interesująca miejscowość	Galveston	Látványos település Достопримечательное место
Zajímavý: kultura · příroda Interesujące: kultura · przyrodniczy	Fort Fisher Ozark Wonder Cave	Látványos: kultúra · Natur Достопримечательно: Культура · Природа
Úsek silnice s pěknou scenérií · Turistická silnice Piękna droga widokowa · Droga turystyczna	Alaska Hwy	Természetileg szép szakasz · Turistaút Путь по особенно красивой местности · Туристическая дорога
Národní park · Přírodní park Park narodowy · Park krajobrazowy		Nemzeti park · Természeti park Национальный парк · Природный парк
Zakázaný prostor · Indiánská rezervace Obszar zamknięty · Reserwat indiański		Zárt terület · Indián reservátum Запрещенный район · Индейкая ресервачия
Pláž · Korálový útes Plaża · Rafa koralowa		Strand · Korallszirt Пляж · Кораловый
Výhled · Vodopád · Jeskyně Punkt widokowy · Wodospad · Jaskinia		Kilátópont · Vízesés · Barlang Обзорная точка · Водопад · Пещера
Pomník · Archeologické naleziště nebo ruiny · Věž · Maják Pomnik · Wykopalisko albo ruina · Wieża · Latarnia morska		Emlékmű · Régészeti asatások és romhely · Torony · Világítótorony Памятник · Расколка или руины · Башня · Маяк
Osamoceně stojící hotel · Horská bouda · Ubytovna mládeže · Kempink Samotnie stojący hotel · Schronisko górskie · Schronisko młodzieżowe · Kemping		Egyedül álló szálloda · Menedékház · Ifjúsági szálló · Kemping Отдалённый отель · Туристская база · Молодежная туристическая база · Кемпинг
Ranger stanice · Parkoviště Ranger stacji · Parking	P	Ranger állomás · Parkolóhely Рейнджеров станция · Парковка
Piknik prostoru · Jezdectví Piknik obszarze · Jazda konne		piknik hely · Lovagol Пикника · Ездить

1:4 000 000 / 1cm = 40km

Photo: Monument Valley Navajo Tribal Park (getty-images/Andrew Gunners)

Lk
Ma
Mb
Mc
Md
Me
Mf
Mg
Mh
Mj
Mk
10
11
12
13
14
15
Chukchi Sea
12h Gr.Time
-9h Gr.Time
International Date Line
Bering Strait
Arctic Circle
Pt. Barrow
Barrow
Tapkaluk Is.
Plover Is.
Walakpa
Tangent Pt.
Pt. Franklin
Atanik
Seahorse Is.
Peard Bay
Tikiklut
C. Simpson
Smith Bay
Kokruagarok
C. Halkett
Harrison
Bay
Wainwright
Alaktak
Mitliktavik
Icy Cape
Akeonik
Atqasuk
Anaktuk
Kangik
Kasegaluk Lagoon
Pt. Lay
North Slope
Brooks
Knifeblade Ridge
Lookout Ridge
Valley of Willow
Umiat
Colville R.
C. Lisburne
Wevok
620
Mt. Hamlet
Corwin
Pt. Hope
Mt. Kelly
961
Timmerkpuk Mt.
1154
Thunder Mt.
1463
De Long Mts.
1529
1515
Feniak L.
Noatak National Preserve
Anaktuvuk Pass
1859
2261
Kivalina
Mulgrave Hills
1080
Noatak
Kanaktok Mt.
1011
Baird Mountains
Gates of the Arctic National Park and Preserve
Endicott M
2290
Schwatka Mts.
Arrigetch Peaks
2682
Cape Krusenstern Nat. Mon.
C. Krusenstern
Igichuk Hills
1311
Kobuk Valley Nat. Park
Sheshalik
Deviation Peak
816
Kotzebue
Nana Mus. of the Arctic
Baldwin Peninsula
Kiana
Mountains
Ambler
Shungnak
Kobuk
Noorvik
Waring
Lookout Mt.
Bettles
Shishmaref
Espenberg
C. Espenberg
Devil Mt.
242
Kotzebue Sound
Selawik
Shekluk Range
Zane Hills
Lockwood Hills
Inalik
Bering Land Bridge Nat. Reserve
Reindeer Station
Elephant Point
1007
1167
Purzell Mt.
Allakaket
Kanuti National Wildlife Refuge
Wales
Brooks Mt.
883
Serpentine Hot Springs
Deering
Kiwalik
Candle
Buckland
Fink Creek
623
Hog Landing
Hughes
Seward Peninsula
Taylor
Aurora
Pt. Spencer
Teller
Koyukuk Nat. Wildlife Refuge
Huslia
Ray Moun
1471
King I.
Bendeleben Mts.
1058
867
Alaska (U.S.)
Pilgrim Springs
Bunker Hill
1136
Kigluaik Mts.
Iron Creek
Casadepaga
Darby Mts.
Traverse Peak
864
Council
Birches
Tanana
Sinuk
White Mountain
Moses Point
Koyuk
Elim
Siedge I.
Dickson
Nome
Bluff
Koyukuk
Nulato
Galena
Nowitna National Wildlife Refuge
C. Nome
Golovin
Norton Bay
Ruby
Rocky Pt.
Golovin Mission
Ungalik
Denbigh
C. Darby
Debauch Mtn.
1106
Shaktoolik
Besboro I.
Kaltag
Bitzshtini Mt.
971
Norton Sound
Khotol Mt.
865
Unalakleet
960
Poorman
Haystack Mt.
1070
Stuart I.
Stebbins
St. Michael
Kaiyuh Mountains
Innoko National Wildlife Refuge
L. Minchumina
Lake Minchumina
Yukon Delta
Kwikpak
Pastol B.
Pikmiktalik
1402
Dishkakat
Cripple
Kuskokwim Mountains
Kantishna
Emmonak
Kotlik
Hamilton
701
1042
437
Von Frank Mtn.
1377
Alakanuk
Kwiguk
New Hamilton
Cloudy Mtn.
1291
Waklarok
Akulurak
366
Ophir
Mt. McKinley
Mt. Foraker
5304
Black
Yukon Delta
Anvik
McGrath
Sterling Landing
Crater Mtn.
1250
Mt. Russell
3557
Krekatok I.
Sand Is.
New Knockhock
396
Shageluk
366
Mountain Village
Scammon B.
Neragon I.
Romanzof
Scammon Bay
714
Askinuk Mts.
Pitkas Pt.
Pilot Sta.
Flat
Farewell
Mt. Dall
2668
Yukon Delta National Wildlife Refuge
Hooper Bay
Chevak
Chakaktolik
Fortuna Ledge
Marshall
800
Stuyahok
Ohogamuit
Crooked Creek
Horn Mts.
1097
595
1285
12
0 20 40 60 80 100km
0 20 40 60miles

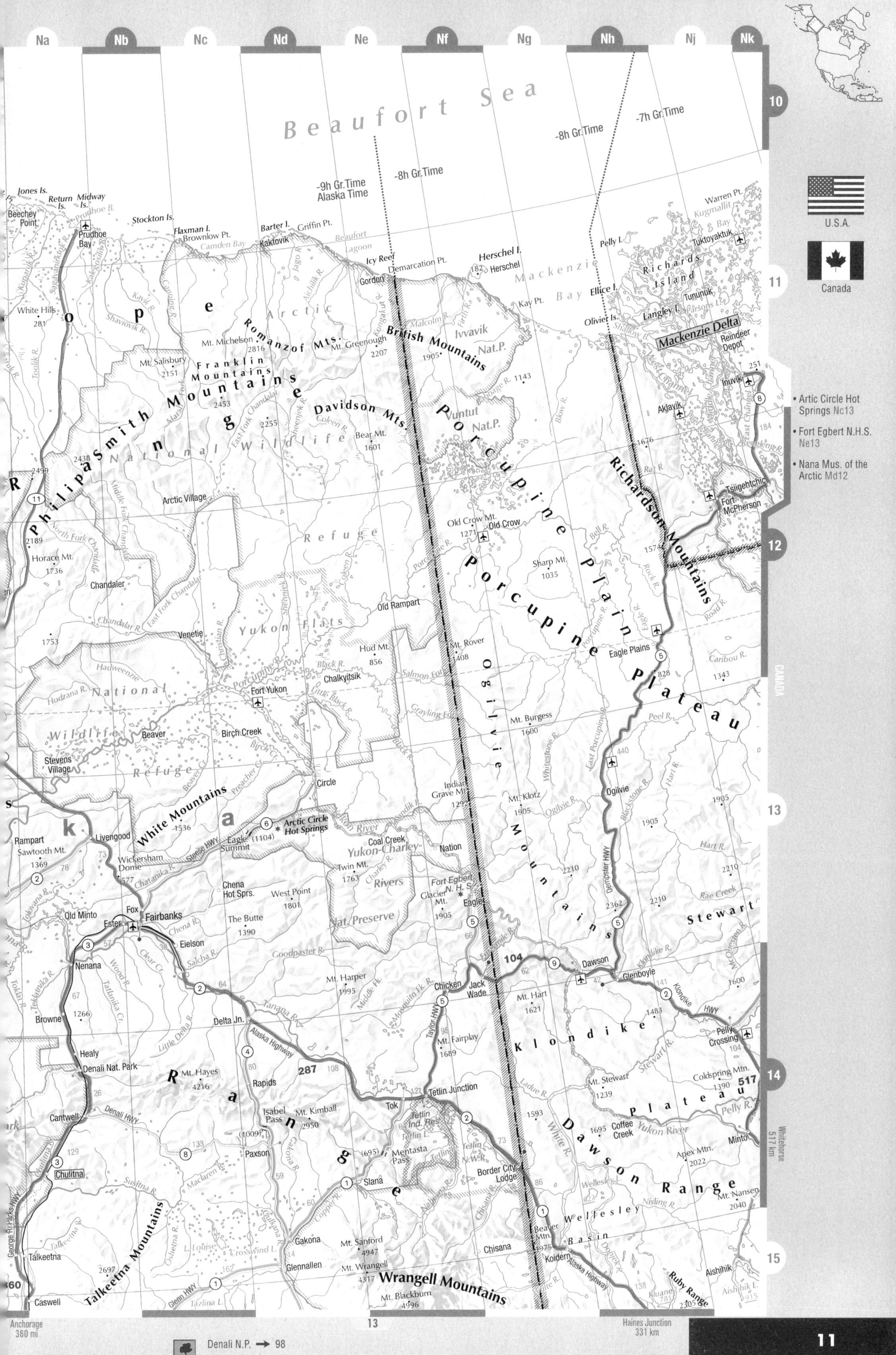

Na
Nb
Nc
Nd
Ne
Nf
Ng
Nh
Nj
Nk
10
11
12
13
14
15
Beaufort Sea
-9h Gr.Time
Alaska Time
-8h Gr.Time
-8h Gr.Time
-7h Gr.Time
U.S.A.
Canada
• Artic Circle Hot Springs Nc13
• Fort Egbert N.H.S. Ne13
• Nana Mus. of the Arctic Md12
Jones Is.
Return Is.
Midway Is.
Beechey Point
Prudhoe B.
Prudhoe Bay
Stockton Is.
Flaxman I.
Brownlow Pt.
Camden Bay
Barter I.
Kaktovik
Griffin Pt.
Beaufort Lagoon
Icy Reef
Gordon
Demarcation Pt.
Herschel I.
Herschel
Mackenzie Bay
Kay Pt.
Pelly I.
Ellice I.
Olivier Is.
Warren Pt.
Kugmallit Bay
Tuktoyaktuk
Richards Island
Tununuk
Langley I.
Mackenzie Delta
Reindeer Depot
Inuvik
Aklavik
Tsiigehtchic
Fort McPherson
Richardson Mountains
White Hills
Arctic
Romanzof Mts.
Mt. Michelson
2816
Mt. Greenough
2207
British Mountains
Ivvavik Nat.P.
Franklin Mountains
Mt. Salisbury
2151
Philip Smith Mountains
Davidson Mts.
Bear Mt.
1601
Vuntut Nat.P.
Porcupine Plain
Porcupine Plateau
National Wildlife Refuge
Arctic Village
Old Crow Mt.
1271
Old Crow
Sharp Mt.
1035
Horace Mt.
1736
Chandalar
Old Rampart
Yukon Flats
Venetie
Hud Mt.
856
Chalkyitsik
Mt. Rover
1408
Ogilvie Mountains
Eagle Plains
Fort Yukon
Beaver
Birch Creek
Stevens Village
Mt. Burgess
1600
Ogilvie
Circle
White Mountains
Arctic Circle Hot Springs
Eagle Summit
Yukon River
Coal Creek
Yukon-Charley-Rivers Nat.Preserve
Nation
Indian Grave Mt.
Mt. Klotz
1905
Rampart
Sawtooth Mt.
1369
Livengood
Wickersham Dome
Steese HWY
Twin Mt.
1763
Chena Hot Sprs.
West Point
1801
Fort Egbert N. H. S.
Glacier Mt.
1905
Eagle
Dempster HWY
Old Minto
Fox
Ester
Fairbanks
The Butte
1390
Eielson
Nenana
Stewart
Dawson
Glenboyle
Mt. Harper
1995
Chicken
Jack Wade
Taylor HWY
Mt. Hart
1621
Klondike
Klondike HWY
Browne
Delta Jn.
Alaska Highway
Mt. Fairplay
1689
Pelly Crossing
Healy
Denali Nat. Park
Mt. Hayes
4216
Range
Rapids
Tetlin Junction
Mt. Stewart
1239
Coldspring Mtn.
1390
Plateau
Cantwell
Denali HWY
Isabel Pass
Mt. Kimball
2950
Tok
Tetlin Ind. Res.
Coffee Creek
Yukon River
Pelly R.
Minto
Paxson
Mentasta Pass
Tetlin N.W.R.
Dawson Range
Apex Mtn.
2022
Chulitna
Slana
Border City Lodge
Wellesley Basin
Mt. Nansen
2040
Talkeetna Mountains
Gakona
Mt. Sanford
4947
Chisana
Beaver Mtn.
Koidern
Talkeetna
Glennallen
Mt. Wrangell
4317
Wrangell Mountains
Ruby Range
Aishihik
George Parks HWY
Glenn HWY
Caswell
Mt. Blackburn
4996
Anchorage
360 mi
13
Haines Junction
331 km
Whitehorse
517 km
CANADA

Denali N.P. → 98

Ma
Mb
Mc
Md
Me
Mf
10
Mg
Mh
14
15
16
17
18
19
Stuart I.
St. Michael
Stebbins
Yukon Delta
Kwikpak
Pastol B.
Pikmiktalik
Emmonak
Kotlik
Hamilton
701
1042
Alakanuk
Kwiguk
New Hamilton
Waklarok
Akulurak
366
Black
Yukon
Delta
396
Krekatok I.
Sand Is.
New Knockhock
Mountain Village
Scammon B.
Neragon I.
C. Romanzof
Scammon Bay
Pitkas Pt.
714
Askinuk Mts.
Pilot Sta.
Fortuna Ledge
Hooper Bay
Chevak
Chakaktolik
Marshall
National
Ohogamuit
Wildlife
Refuge
Hazen B.
Cahkwaktolik
Keyaluvik
Chiftak
Kasigluk
C. Vancouver
452
Nelson I.
Akiachak
Baird Inlet
Tununak
C. Etolin
C. Mohican
Mekoryuk
Nightmote
Bethel
Nash Harbor
Napaiskak
Etolin
Nunivak I.
Chefornak
Tuntutuliak
283
Kinak Bay
Eek
Eek I.
C. Mendenhall
C. Corwin
Kikegtek I.
Kipnuk
Pingurbek I.
Strait
Kwigluk I.
Kwigillingok
Kuskokwim
Bay
Carter Spit
Quinhagak
Explorer Mtn.
812
Platinum
Goodnews Bay
C. Newenham
Calm Pt.
543
Hagemeister Strait
Hagemeister I.
Bering
Sea
Bristol
Bay
1402
Old Woman R.
Innoko
National
Wildlife
Refuge
437
Innoko R.
Anvik
Yukon R.
Anvik R.
Shageluk
366
Flat
Stuyahok
800
Dishkakat
Cripple
Cloudy Mtn.
1291
Ophir
Crater Mtn.
1250
39
McGrath
Sterling Landing
Von Frank Mtn.
1377
Kuskokwim Mountains
South Fork Kuskokwim R.
Crooked Creek
Horn Mts.
1097
595
Kalskag
Aniak
Kuskokwim R.
Pack Trail
Tuluksak
Mt. Plummer
1463
Kilbuck Mountains
Kiokluk Mts.
1211
Nogamut
Taylor Mts.
1091
Stony River
Swift R.
1285
2944
2256
Cairn Mts.
1158
Old Village
Finn Mt.
755
1431
Chikuminuk L.
Mulchatna R.
Chilikadrotna R.
Lake Clark
Nat. Park
and Preserve
L. Clark
Mt. Oratia
1646
Tikchik
Lakes
Nuyakuk L.
Ketok Mtn.
1517
Koliganek
Nondalton
1289
Pile Bay Village
Ahklun Mountains
L. Nerka
L. Beverley
New Stuyahok
Newhalen
L. Aleknagik
Iliamna Lake
Togiak
L. Nunavaugaluk
Aleknagik
Iguigig
Nushagak R.
Kvichak R.
Togiak Bay
Dillingham
Lewis Point
Hallersville
Chenik
1252
High I.
Crooked I.
Walrus Is.
State Game Sanctuary
Nushagak Pen.
Clarks Point
Sugarloaf Mtn.
745
Katmai
Mt. Douglas
2153
Naknek
King Salmon
Etolin Pt.
Kvichak Bay
Nushagak Bay
Cape Constantine
Nat. Park
Mt. Denison
2318
C. Nukshak
Mt. Katmai
2047
King Salmon R.
and Preserve
Steep
Raspberry I.
C. Ilktugitak
Katmay Bay
Uganik I.
Becharof L.
Mt. Peulik
1500
Ugashik Bay
Pilot Point
Ugashik L.
Kanatak
C. Kekurnoi
Portage Bay
Wide Bay
Karluk
1341
C. Ikolik
Island
Mt. Chiginagak
2143
Port Heiden
Aniakchak Crater
C. Providence
Chiginagak Bay
Strogonof Pt.
Low C.
Akhiok
Seal Is.
C. Kunmik
C. Alitak
Ilnik
Geese Is.
Aiaktalik I.
Kumliun
Foggy C.
Sitkinak Strait
488
Sitkinak Is.
Sutvik I.
C. Sitkinak
Chignik Bay
Nakchamik I.
Tugidak I.
Trinity Is.
Veniaminof Vol.
2507
Lagoon Pt.
Walrus I.
Port Moller
Chignik
Castle C.
Aghiyuk I.
Semidi Is.
Perryville
Seal C.
Chowiet I.
Anvak I.
Moffet Pt.
1311
Mt. Dana
Chiachi I.
Paul I.
Jacob I.
Mitrofania I.
Chirikof I.
South C.
Kudiakof Is.
Pavlof Vol.
Cold Bay
2504
Unga Strait
Korovin I.
Kupreanof Pt.
Alaska Marine HWY
Unimak I.
Otter Pt.
C. Mordvinof
1763
Pavlof Is.
Unga I.
696
Sand Point
Alaska
Peninsula
Aleutian Range
Shumagin Islands
King Cove
Andronica I.
Popof I.
561
C. Sarichef
2002
Shishaldin Vol.
2857
False Pass
Deer I.
Wosnesenski I.
Poperechnoi I.
Dolgoi I.
Big Koniuji I.
Fawn Pt.
Nagai I.
Little Koniuji I.
Pogromni Vol.
Unimak Bight
C. Pankof
Simeonof I.
Bird I.
Unimak
Sanak
Cherni I.
Chernabura I.
Sanak I.
Caton I.
Ugamak I.
Tigalda I.
Sanak Islands
Krenitzin Is.
0 20 40 60 80 100km
0 20 40 60miles

Mk
Fairbanks 360 mi
Na
Nb
Fairbanks 287 mi
Nc
11
Nd
Jack Wade 168 mi
Ne
CANADA
Nf
14
15
16
17
18
U.S.A.
Canada
Haines Junction 331 km
• Aniakchak Crater Mf17
• Fort Abercrombie S.H.P. Mj17
• Independence Mine Na15
Denali
National Park
and Preserve
Kantishna
Mt. McKinley
Mt. Foraker 5304
6194
Mt. Russell 3557
Mt. Dall 2668
Petersville
Healy
Denali Nat. Park
Cantwell
Denali HWY
Chulitna
George B. Parks HWY
Talkeetna
Talkeetna Mountains
2697
360
Caswell
Independence Mine
Willow
Houston
Wasilla
Palmer
Chickaloon
Glenn HWY
Matanuska R.
Mt. Marcus Baker 4016
Chugiak
ANCHORAGE
Fire I.
Alexander
Beluga L.
Pt. Possession
Rainbow
Alyeska Resort & Skiarea
Girdwood
Portage
Whittier
Hope
Turnagain Arm
Kustatan
Kenai
Soldotna
127
Moose Pass
Kenai Peninsula
Kenai Mountains
Kalgin I.
Chisik I.
219
Ninilchik
712
2015
Kenai National Wildlife Refuge
Tustumena L.
Woodrow
Seward
Cook Inlet
Sterling HWY
Homer
Kachemak Bay
Kenai Fjords Nat. Park
Aialik Cape
Cape Resurrection
Rugged I.
Ragged I.
Pye Is.
Nuka I.
Gore Pt.
East Chugach I.
Perl I.
Chugach Is.
West Amatuli I.
East Amatuli I.
Barren Is.
Seldovia
Pt. Adam
Elizabeth I.
Alaska Marine HWY
Pt. Banks
Shuyak I.
Afognak Island
Tonki C.
Marmot I.
Marmot Bay
Spruce I.
Fort Abercrombie S. H. P.
Kodiak
Woody I.
Chiniak B.
C. Chiniak
Narrow C.
Ugak I.
Gerdine 3840
1339
1984
Mt. Hayes 4216
Alaska Range
Rapids
Isabel Pass
Mt. Kimball 2950
(1009)
Paxson
Maclaren R.
Susitna R.
Gulkana R.
L. Louise
Crosswind L.
Gakona
Glennallen
Tazlina L.
Tonsina
Chitina
Copper R.
Mt. Sanford 4947
Mt. Wrangell 4317
Wrangell Mountains
Mt. Blackburn 4996
Wrangell- St. Elias
Nat. Park and Preserve
McCarthy
Mt. Bona 5029
Mt. Bear 4520
Chugach Mountains
Valdez
(845) Thompson Pass
1685
Tatitlek
Cordova Peak 2356
Glacier I.
Bligh I.
Naked I.
Esther I.
Perry I.
Culross I.
Prince William Sound
Hawkins I.
Cordova
Alaganik
Knight I.
857
Green I.
888
Hinchinbrook I.
C. Hinchinbrook
Hinchinbrook Entrance
Latouche I.
Latouche
914
San Juan
Evans I.
Montague I.
Montague Strait
Cape Cleare
Middleton I.
Wingham I.
Kayak I.
Cape Saint Elias
Chilkat
Bering Glacier
Bagley Icefield
Mt. Tom White 3274
Mt. Miller 3352
Icy Cape
Pt. Riou
Icy Bay
Guyot Glacier
Malaspina Glacier
Mt. Fairplay 1689
Alaska Highway
287
Tok
Tetlin Junction
Tetlin Ind. Res.
Tetlin L.
Tetlin N.W.R.
Mentasta Pass
(695)
Slana
Nabesna R.
Chisana R.
Chisana
Border City Lodge
Beaver Mtn. 1975
Koidern
Wellesley Basin
Wellesley L.
Ladue R.
White R.
Donjek R.
Mt. Stewart 1239
1593
1695
Coffee Creek
Dawson Range
331
Mt. Constantine 3138
Mt. Steele 5073
Tatshenshini-Alesk Kluane Nat. Park
3848
Mt. Logan 5959
Seward Glacier
Mt. St. Elias 5489
Mt. Augusta 4289
Mt. Cook
Gulf of Alaska
PACIFIC OCEAN

Denali N.P. ➔ 98

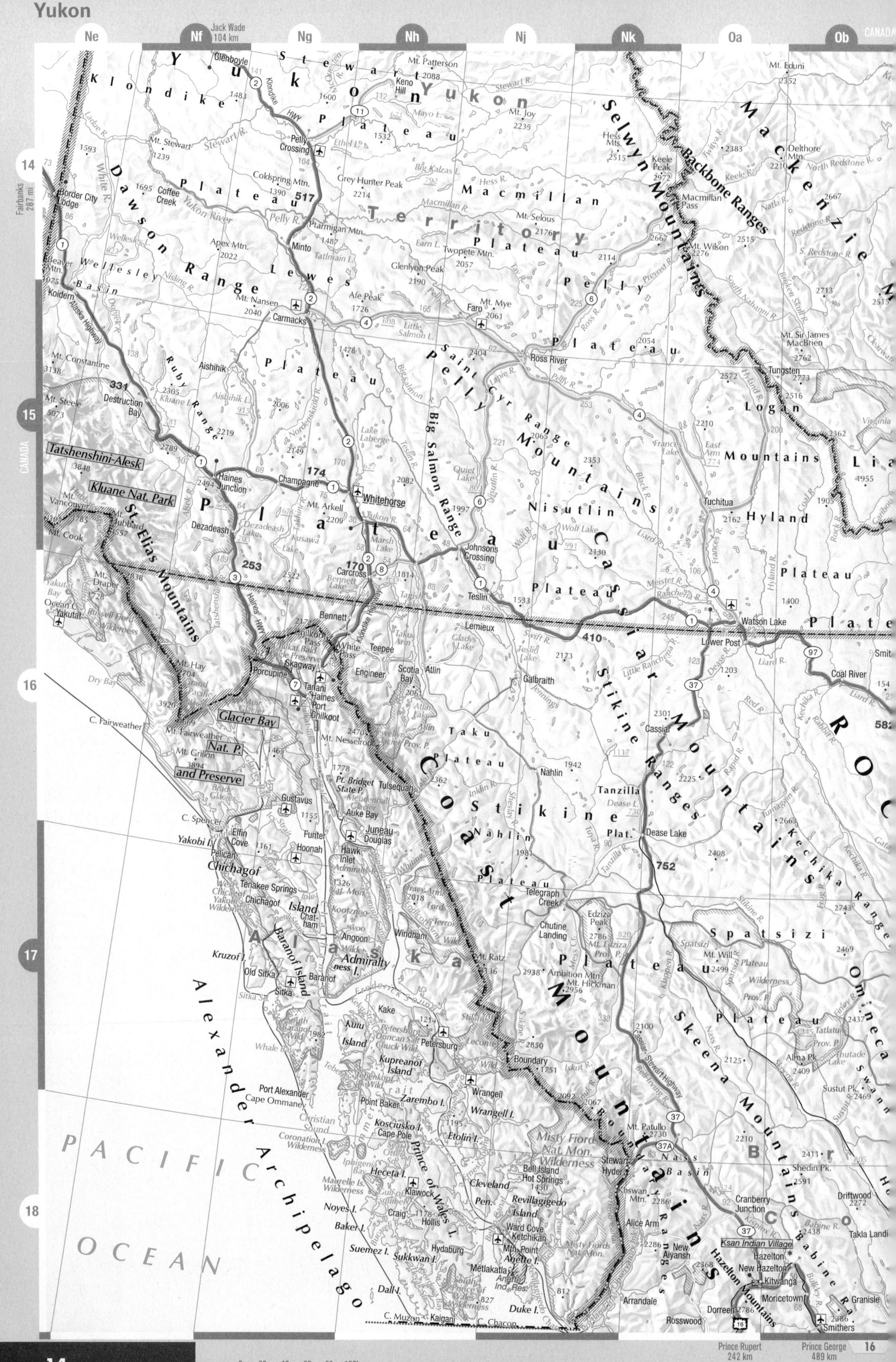
Ne
Nf
Jack Wade
104 km
Ng
Nh
Nj
Nk
Oa
Ob
CANADA
14
15
16
17
18
Fairbanks
287 mi
Yukon Territory
Klondike Plateau
Stewart R.
Glenboyle
Keno Hill
Mt. Patterson
2088
Mayo L.
Mt. Joy
2235
Mt. Stewart
1239
Stewart R.
Pelly Crossing
Ethel L.
Coldspring Mtn.
1390
Grey Hunter Peak
2214
Big Kalzas L.
Hess Mts.
2515
Keele Peak
2972
Macmillan Pass
Selwyn Mountains
Backbone Ranges
Mackenzie Mountains
Mt. Eduni
2352
Delthore Mtn.
2210
North Redstone R.
Border City Lodge
Coffee Creek
Dawson Range
Yukon River
Pelly R.
Macmillan Plateau
Ptarmigan Mtn.
1487
Minto
Tatlmain L.
Mt. Selous
2176
Twopete Mtn.
2057
Glenlyon Peak
2190
Mt. Wilson
2276
Apex Mtn.
2022
Wellesley Basin
Beaver Mtn.
Koidern
Mt. Nansen
2040
Lewes Plateau
Afe Peak
1726
Carmacks
Little Salmon L.
Faro
Mt. Mye
2061
Pelly Plateau
Ross River
South Nahanni R.
Mt. Sir James MacBrien
2762
Tungsten
2773
2516
Logan Mountains
Mt. Constantine
3138
Aishihik
Ruby Range
Aishihik L.
Kluane L.
Destruction Bay
Mt. Steele
5073
Big Salmon R.
Saint Cyr Range
Pelly Mountains
Big Salmon Range
Lake Laberge
Nisutlin Plateau
Quiet Lake
Tatshenshini-Alesk
Kluane Nat. Park
Haines Junction
Champagne
Whitehorse
Mt. Arkell
2209
Mt. Vancouver
Mt. Hubbard
Mt. Cook
St. Elias Mountains
Dezadeash
Dezadeash L.
Kusawa Lake
Marsh Lake
Johnsons Crossing
Wolf Lake
2130
Cassiar Mountains
Tuchitua
Hyland Plateau
East Arm
Frances Lake
Carcross
Bennett Lake
Tagish
Teslin
Teslin L.
Rancheria R.
Watson Lake
Lower Post
Mt. Draper
Yakutat Bay
Ocean C.
Yakutat
Russell Fiord Wilderness
Haines Hwy
Klondike Highway
Bennett
Chilkoot Pass
White Pass
Teepee
Taku Arm
Lemieux
Gladys Lake
Swift R.
Little Rancheria R.
Dease R.
Liard R.
Coal River
Smith
Mt. Hay
Porcupine
Skagway
Tanani
Haines
Port Chilkoot
Engineer
Scotia Bay
Atlin
Atlin Lake
Galbraith
Jennings
Dry Bay
Grand Pacific Glacier
Glacier Bay
Nat. P.
and Preserve
C. Fairweather
Mt. Fairweather
Mt. Grillon
3894
Mt. Nesselrode
Atlin Prov. P.
Taku Plateau
Stikine Ranges
Cassiar
Kechika R.
Rabbit R.
ROC
Pt. Bridget State P.
Tulsequah
Mendenhall Glacier
Gustavus
Auke Bay
Juneau
Douglas
Nahlin
1942
Tanzilla
Dease L.
Dease Lake
Stikine Plateau
Tanzilla Plat.
Kechika Ranges
Turnagain R.
C. Spencer
Elfin Cove
Yakobi I.
Pelican
Chichagof
Funter
Hoonah
Hawk Inlet
Admiralty I.
Nat. Mon.
Tenakee Springs
Chichagof Island
Chatham
Kootznoowoo Wilderness
Angoon
Tracy Arm
Fords Terror
Windham
Coast Mountains
Telegraph Creek
Edziza Peak
2786
Mt. Edziza Prov. P.
Chutine Landing
Spatsizi Plateau
Mt. Will
2499
Spatsizi Plateau Wilderness Prov. P.
Krúzof I.
Baranof Island
Alaska
Admiralty Island
Old Sitka
Baranof
Mt. Ratz
3136
Ambition Mtn.
Mt. Hickman
2956
Omineca Mountains
Sitka
Sitka Sd.
Alexander Archipelago
Kake
Frederick Sound
Kuiu Island
Petersburg
Duncan Salt Chuck Wild.
Le Conte
Kupreanof Island
Boundary
Whale Bay
Port Alexander
Cape Ommaney
Point Baker
Zarembo I.
Wrangell
Wrangell I.
Tatlatui Prov. P.
Alma Pk.
2409
Thutade Lake
Sustut Pk.
2469
Skeena Mountains
Christian Sound
Coronation I. Wilderness
Kosciusko I.
Cape Pole
Etolin I.
Prince of Wales I.
Misty Fiord Nat. Mon. Wilderness
Mt. Patullo
2730
Stewart
Hyder
Nass Basin
Cassiar-Stewart Highway
Bell-Irving R.
Iskut R.
Boundary Ranges
Shedin Pk.
2591
Driftwood
2272
PACIFIC OCEAN
Heceta I.
Maurelle Is. Wilderness
Klawock
Craig
Hollis
Noyes I.
Baker I.
Suemez I.
Sukkwan I.
Hydaburg
Cleveland Pen.
Bell Island Hot Springs
Revillagigedo Island
Ward Cove
Ketchikan
Mtn. Point
Annette I.
Metlakatla
Annette Ind. Res.
Kswan Mtn.
Alice Arm
New Aiyansh
Cranberry Junction
Ksan Indian Village
Hazelton
New Hazelton
Kitwanga
Hazelton Mountains
Babine R.
Babine Range
Takla Landi
Moricetown
Granisle
Smithers
Dall I.
C. Muzon
Kaigani
C. Chacon
Duke I.
Arrandale
Dorreen
Rosswood
Prince Rupert
242 km
Prince George
489 km
16
0 20 40 60 80 100km
0 20 40 60miles

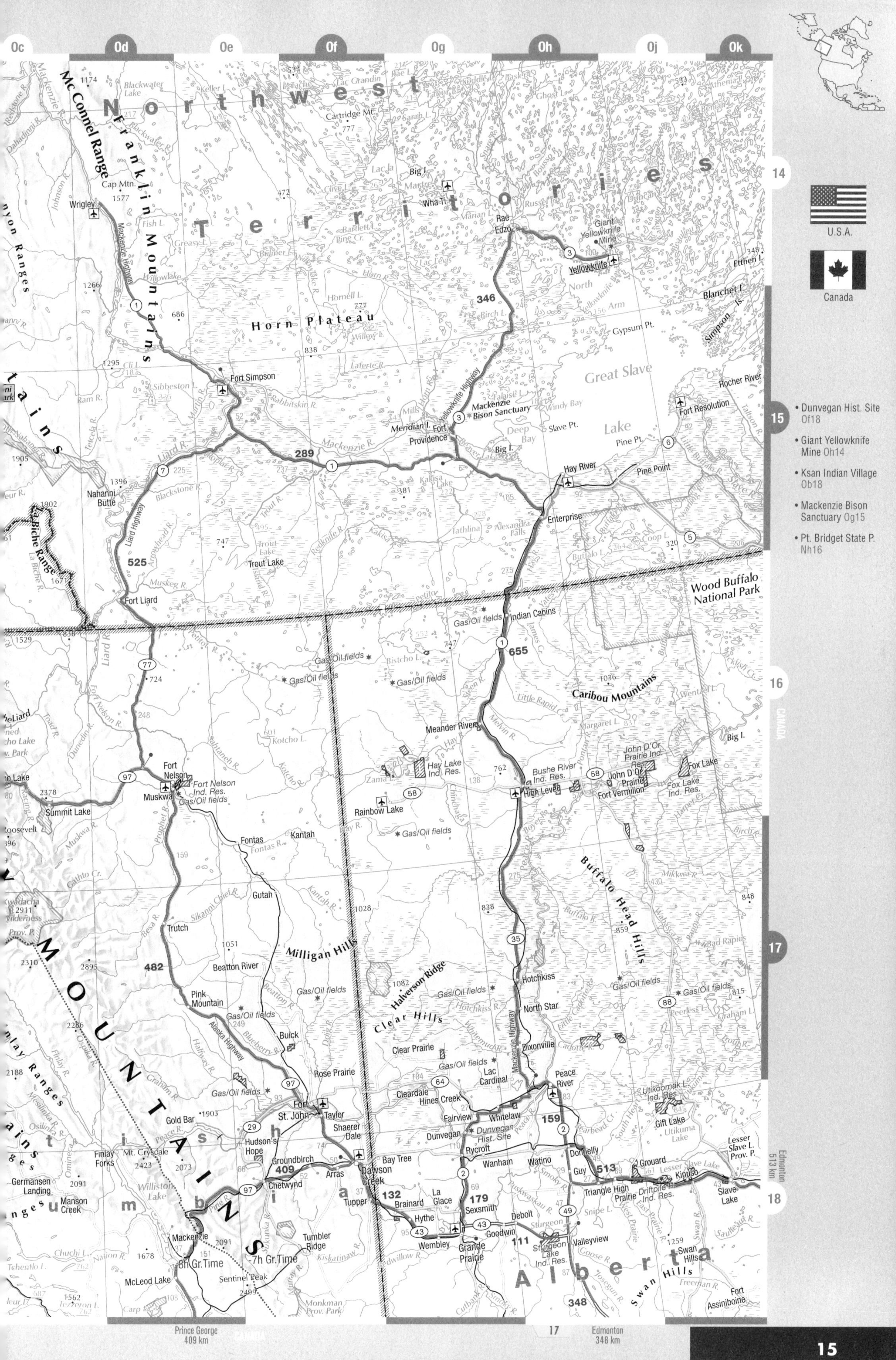

0c
0d
0e
0f
0g
0h
0j
0k
14
15
16
17
18
U.S.A.
Canada
• Dunvegan Hist. Site Of18
• Giant Yellowknife Mine Oh14
• Ksan Indian Village Ob18
• Mackenzie Bison Sanctuary Og15
• Pt. Bridget State P. Nh16
Northwest Territories
Alberta
McConnel Range
Franklin Mountains
Horn Plateau
Great Slave Lake
North Arm
Wood Buffalo National Park
Caribou Mountains
Buffalo Head Hills
Milligan Hills
Halverson Ridge
Clear Hills
MOUNTAINS
Swan Hills
Wrigley
Cap Mtn.
Fort Simpson
Nahanni Butte
Fort Liard
Trout Lake
Fort Providence
Mackenzie Bison Sanctuary
Meridian I.
Rae
Edzo
Wha Ti
Yellowknife
Giant Yellowknife Mine
Hay River
Enterprise
Pine Point
Fort Resolution
Rocher River
Slave Pt.
Gypsum Pt.
Deep Bay
Indian Cabins
Meander River
Hay Lake Ind. Res.
Rainbow Lake
High Level
Bushe River Ind. Res.
Fort Vermilion
John D'Or Prairie
Fox Lake
Fox Lake Ind. Res.
Fort Nelson
Fort Nelson Ind. Res.
Muskwa
Summit Lake
Fontas
Kantah
Gutah
Trutch
Beatton River
Pink Mountain
Buick
Rose Prairie
Fort St. John
Taylor
Hudson's Hope
Gold Bar
Finlay Forks
Mt. Crysdale
Germansen Landing
Manson Creek
Mackenzie
McLeod Lake
Sentinel Peak
Tumbler Ridge
Monkman Prov. Park
Groundbirch
Chetwynd
Arras
Dawson Creek
Tupper
Shaerer Dale
Bay Tree
Brainard
La Glace
Hythe
Wembley
Grande Prairie
Sexsmith
Clear Prairie
Cleardale
Hines Creek
Fairview
Whitelaw
Dunvegan
Dunvegan Hist. Site
Rycroft
Wanham
Watino
Peace River
Lac Cardinal
Dixonville
North Star
Hotchkiss
Donnelly
Guy
Falher
Grouard
Kinuso
Triangle
High Prairie
Driftpile R. Ind. Res.
Utikoomak L. Ind. Res.
Gift Lake
Lesser Slave L. Prov. P.
Slave Lake
Swan Hills
Fort Assiniboine
Valleyview
Sturgeon Lake Ind. Res.
Debolt
Goodwin
Gas/Oil fields
8h Gr.Time
7h Gr.Time
Prince George 409 km
Edmonton 348 km
Edmonton 513 km

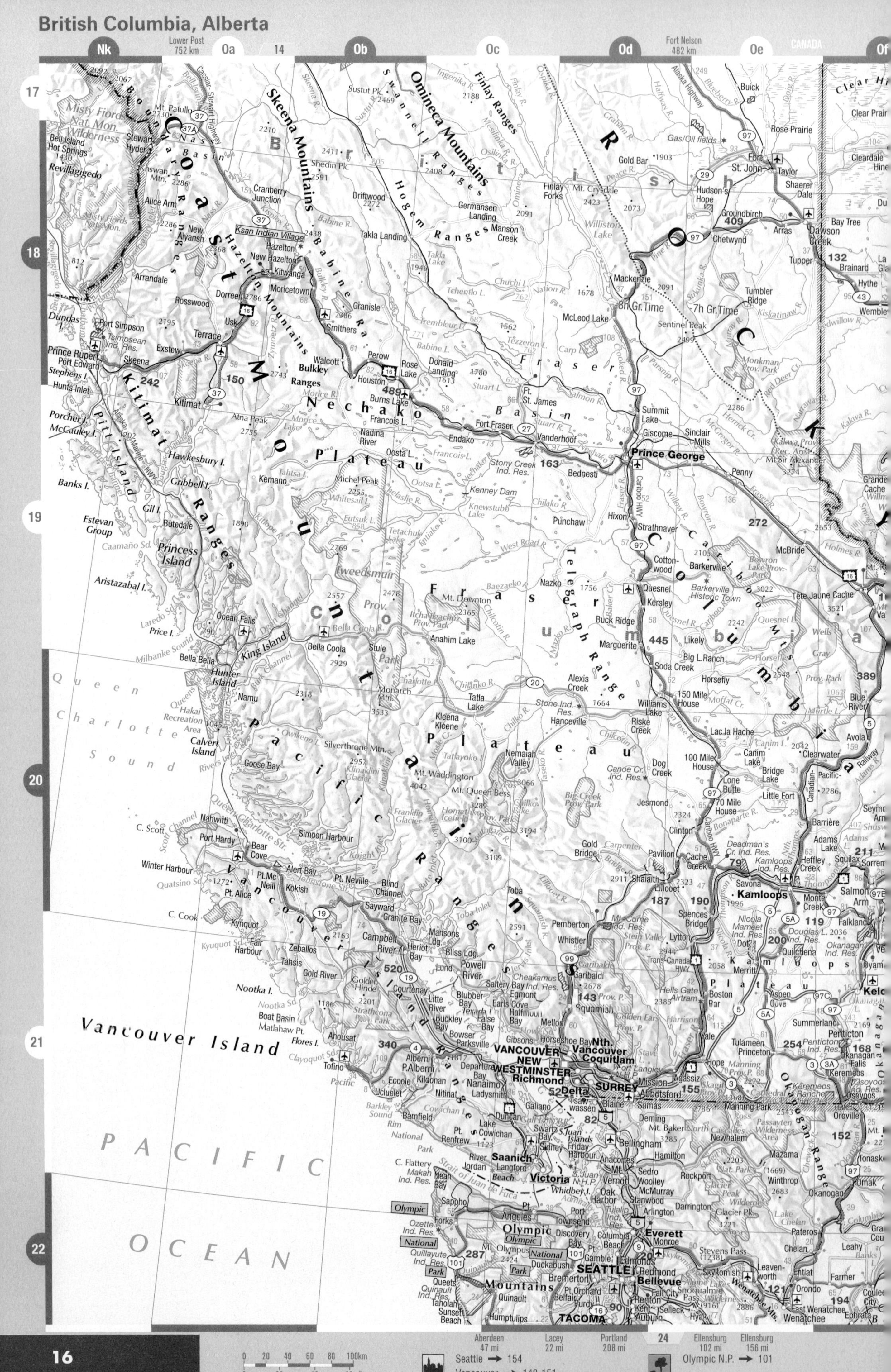
Nk
Lower Post 752 km
Oa
14
Ob
Oc
Od
Fort Nelson 482 km
Oe
CANADA
Of
17
18
19
20
21
22
Misty Fiords Nat. Mon. Wilderness
Bell Island Hot Springs
Revillagigedo
Stewart
Hyder
Mt. Patullo 2730
Boundary Ranges
Nass Basin
Kshwan Mtn.
Alice Arm
New Aiyansh
Cranberry Junction
Ksan Indian Village
Hazelton
New Hazelton
Kitwanga
Moricetown
Smithers
Granisle
Hazelton Mountains
Skeena Mountains
Babine Ra.
Sustut Pk. 2469
Shedin Pk.
Driftwood
Takla Landing
Omineca Mountains
Swannell Ranges
Hogem Ranges
Finlay Ranges
Germansen Landing
Manson Creek
Finlay Forks
Mt. Crysdale
Williston Lake
Gold Bar
Mackenzie
8h Gr.Time
7h Gr.Time
McLeod Lake
Sentinel Peak
Gas/Oil fields
Fort St. John
Taylor
Hudson's Hope
Chetwynd
Groundbirch
Arras
Dawson Creek
Tupper
Buick
Rose Prairie
Clear Prairie
Cleardale
Shaerer Dale
Bay Tree
Brainard
Hythe
Tumbler Ridge
Monkman Prov. Park
Kiskatinaw R.
Rocky Mountains
British Columbia
Arrandale
Rosswood
Dorreen
Usk
Terrace
Exstew
Port Simpson
Tsimpsean Ind. Res.
Dundas I.
Prince Rupert
Port Edward
Stephens I.
Hunts Inlet
Skeena
Kitimat
Kitimat Ranges
Porcher I.
McCauley I.
Pitt Island
Banks I.
Hawkesbury I.
Gribbell I.
Gil I.
Estevan Group
Butedale
Princess Royal Island
Caamaño Sd.
Aristazabal I.
Laredo Sd.
Price I.
Ocean Falls
Milbanke Sound
Bella Bella
King Island
Hunter Island
Namu
Queen Charlotte Sound
Hakai Recreation Area
Calvert Island
Rivers Inlet
Walcott
Bulkley Ranges
Houston
Perow
Rose Lake
Burns Lake
Francois L.
Nechako Plateau
Donald Landing
Ft. St. James
Fort Fraser
Vanderhoof
Endako
Fraser Basin
Nadina River
Oosta L.
Kemano
Michel Peak
Whitesail L.
Tahtsa L.
Stony Creek Ind. Res.
Kenney Dam
Knewstubb Lake
Bednesti
Prince George
Summit Lake
Giscome
Sinclair Mills
Penny
Chilako R.
Punchaw
Hixon
Strathnaver
Cottonwood
Quesnel
Kersley
Barkerville
Barkerville Historic Town
Bowron Lake Prov. Park
Cariboo Mts.
McBride
Tete Jaune Cache
Mt. Sir Alexander
Kakwa Prov. Rec. Area
Grande Cache
Tweedsmuir Prov. Park
Coast Mountains
Fraser Plateau
Telegraph Range
Mt. Downton
Itcha-Ilgachuz Prov. Park
Anahim Lake
Nazko
Baezaeko R.
Buck Ridge
Marguerite
Alexis Creek
Likely
Big L.Ranch
Soda Creek
Horsefly
150 Mile House
Williams Lake
Riske Creek
Hanceville
Stone Ind. Res.
Bella Coola
Stuie
Monarch Mtn.
Charlotte L.
Tatla Lake
Kleena Kleene
Silverthrone Mtn.
Klinaklini Glacier
Mt. Waddington
Mt. Queen Bess
Nemaiah Valley
Chilcotin Plateau
Canoe Cr. Ind. Res.
Dog Creek
Jesmond
Big Creek Prov. Park
Lac la Hache
100 Mile House
70 Mile House
Canim L.
Canim Lake
Bridge Lake
Little Fort
Clearwater
Avola
Blue River
Wells Gray Prov. Park
Goose Bay
Pacific Ranges
Franklin Glacier
Homathko Icefield Prov. Park
Nahwitti
C. Scott
Port Hardy
Bear Cove
Winter Harbour
Quatsino Sd.
Pt.Mc Neill
Alert Bay
Pt. Neville
Kokish
Pt. Alice
C. Cook
Simoon Harbour
Knight Inlet
Blind Channel
Sayward
Granite Bay
Toba
Pemberton
Whistler
Lillooet
Pavilion
Clinton
Cache Creek
Gold Bridge
Shalalth
Kamloops
Savona
Monte Creek
Falkland
Salmon Arm
Sorrento
Squilax
Adams Lake
Heffley Creek
Barriere
Kamloops Ind. Res.
Deadman's Cr. Ind. Res.
Spences Bridge
Lytton
Nicola Mameet Ind. Res.
Douglas L.
Merritt
Quilchena
Okanagan Ind. Res.
Kamloops Plateau
Aspen Grove
Summerland
Penticton
Penticton Ind. Res.
Okanagan Falls
Keremeos
Osoyoos
Oroville
Okanagan Range
Kyuquot
Fair Harbour
Zeballos
Tahsis
Gold River
Campbell River
Heriot Bay
Mansons Ldg.
Bliss Ldg.
Lund
Powell River
Saltery Bay
Egmont
Cheakamus Ind. Res.
Garibaldi
Squamish
Golden Hinde
Strathcona Prov. Park
Nootka I.
Nootka Sd.
Boat Basin
Matlahaw Pt.
Flores I.
Ahousat
Courtenay
Little River
Blubber Bay
Texada I.
Earls Cove
Halfmoon Bay
Buckley Bay
False Bay
Bowser
Parksville
Gibsons
Horseshoe Bay
Vancouver Island
Tofino
Clayoquot Sd.
Pacific Rim National Park
Alberni
P.Alberni
Ucluelet
Ecoole
Kildonan
Nitinat
Departure Bay
Nanaimo
Ladysmith
Barkley Sound
Bamfield
Cowichan L.
Duncan
Lake Cowichan
Pt. Renfrew
River Jordan
Saanich
Langford
Victoria
Sidney
Galiano
Swartz Bay
VANCOUVER
NEW WESTMINSTER
Richmond
Nth. Vancouver
Coquitlam
Fort Langley N.H.P.
SURREY
Delta
Tsawwassen
Blaine
Mission
Abbotsford
Agassiz
Hope
Harrison L.
Hells Gate Airtram
Boston Bar
Yale
Tulameen
Princeton
Manning Prov. P.
Sumas
Deming
Mt. Baker
Bellingham
Hamilton
Sedro Woolley
Anacortes
Mt. Vernon
Rockport
North Cascades
Pasayten Wilderness Area
Newhalem
Mazama
Winthrop
Okanogan
Omak
Tonasket
Glacier Peak Wilderness
Glacier Pk.
Darrington
Arlington
Stanwood
Oak Harbor
Whidbey I.
McMurray
Everett
Monroe
Stevens Pass
Leavenworth
Chelan
Pateros
Entiat
Orondo
East Wenatchee
Wenatchee
Ephrata
C. Flattery
Makah Ind. Res.
Neah Bay
Strait of Juan de Fuca
Sappho
Forks
Pt. Angeles
Port Townsend
Discovery Bay
Olympic National Park
Olympic Mountains
Mt. Olympus
Ozette Ind. Res.
Quillayute Ind. Res.
Queets
Quinault Ind. Res.
Taholah
Sunset Beach
Humptulips
Quinault
Duckabush
Bremerton
Port Orchard
Belfair
Purdy
SEATTLE
Bellevue
Redmond
Renton
Kent
Auburn
Fall City
Snoqualmie Pass
Selleck
Hyak
Skykomish
TACOMA
Edmonds
Columbia Beach
Wenatchee Mts.
Queen Charlotte Str.
PACIFIC OCEAN
Aberdeen 47 mi
Lacey 22 mi
Portland 208 mi
24
Ellensburg 102 mi
Ellensburg 156 mi
0 20 40 60 80 100km
0 20 40 60miles
Seattle → 154
Vancouver → 148-151
Olympic N.P. → 101

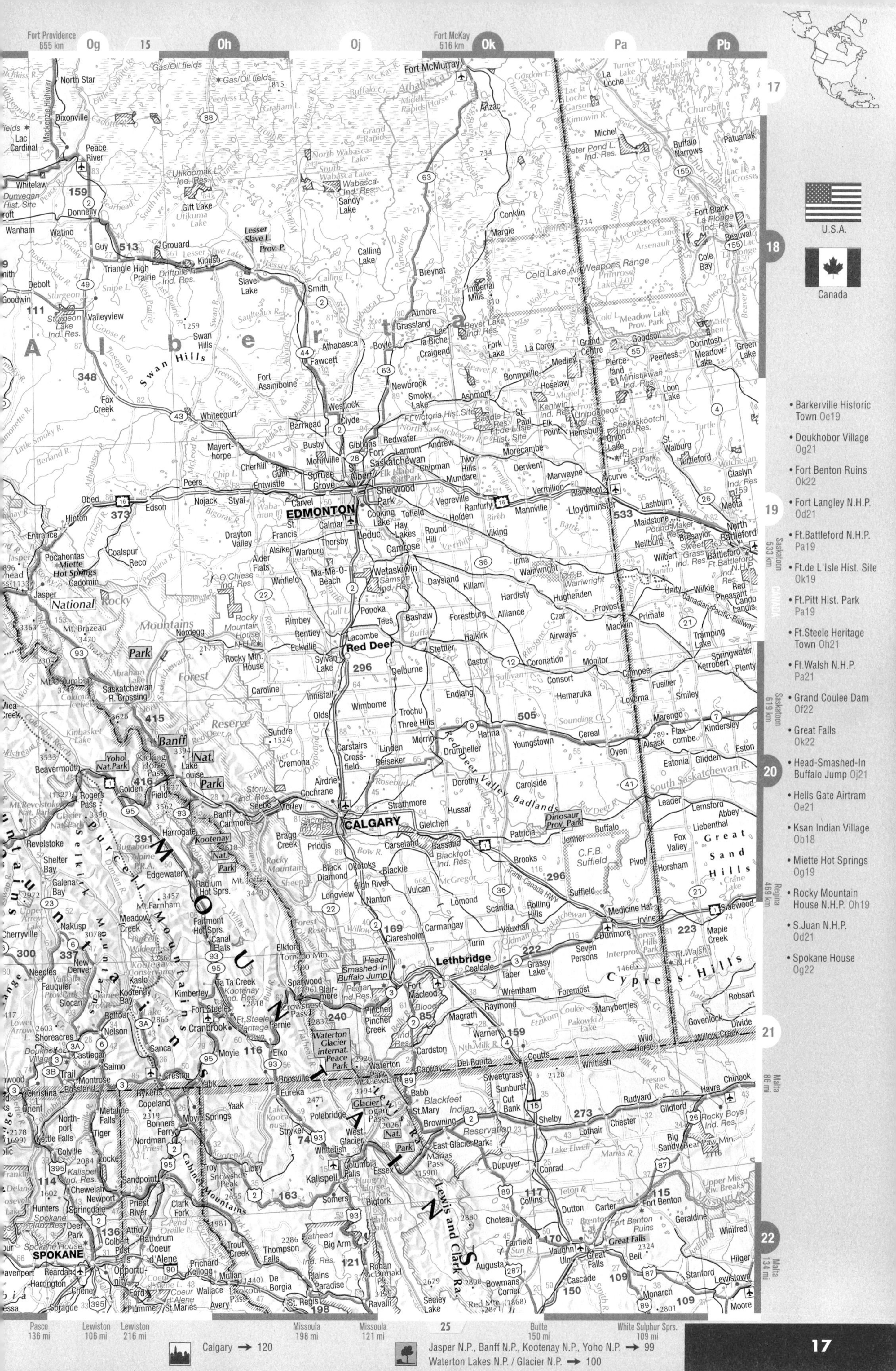
Fort Providence 655 km
Og
15
Oh
Oj
Fort McKay 516 km
Ok
Pa
Pb
17
18
19
20
21
22
U.S.A.
Canada
Saskatoon 533 km
Saskatoon 619 km
Regina 469 km
Malta 86 mi
Malta 134 mi
CANADA
• Barkerville Historic Town Oe19
• Doukhobor Village Og21
• Fort Benton Ruins Ok22
• Fort Langley N.H.P. Od21
• Ft.Battleford N.H.P. Pa19
• Ft.de L'Isle Hist. Site Ok19
• Ft.Pitt Hist. Park Pa19
• Ft.Steele Heritage Town Oh21
• Ft.Walsh N.H.P. Pa21
• Grand Coulee Dam Of22
• Great Falls Ok22
• Head-Smashed-In Buffalo Jump Oj21
• Hells Gate Airtram Oe21
• Ksan Indian Village Ob18
• Miette Hot Springs Og19
• Rocky Mountain House N.H.P. Oh19
• S.Juan N.H.P. Od21
• Spokane House Og22
Alberta
Rocky Mountains
EDMONTON
CALGARY
Red Deer
Lethbridge
Medicine Hat
Fort McMurray
SPOKANE
Great Falls
Jasper National Park
Banff Nat. Park
Yoho Nat.Park
Kootenay Nat. Park
Waterton Glacier internat. Peace Park
Glacier Nat. Park
Cypress Hills
Great Sand Hills
Swan Hills
Lewis and Clark Ra.
Pasco 136 mi
Lewiston 106 mi
Lewiston 216 mi
Missoula 198 mi
Missoula 121 mi
25
Butte 150 mi
White Sulphur Sprs. 109 mi
Calgary → 120
Jasper N.P., Banff N.P., Kootenay N.P., Yoho N.P. → 99
Waterton Lakes N.P. / Glacier N.P. → 100

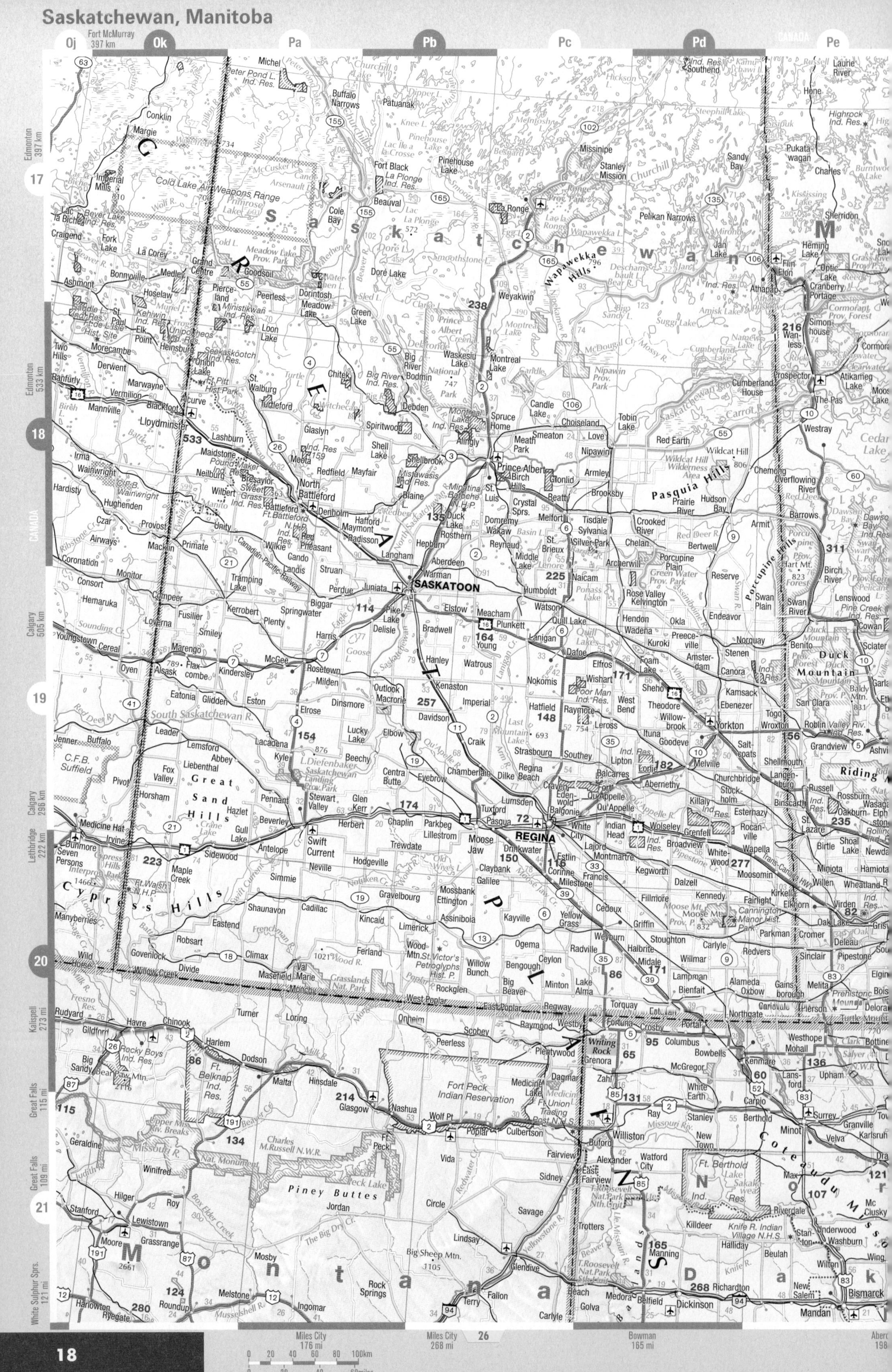
Fort McMurray 397 km
Oj
Ok
Pa
Pb
Pc
Pd
Pe
CANADA
17
18
19
20
21
Edmonton 397 km
Edmonton 533 km
Calgary 505 km
Calgary 296 km
Lethbridge 222 km
Kalispell 273 mi
Great Falls 115 mi
Great Falls 109 mi
White Sulphur Sprs. 121 mi
Michel
Peter Pond L. Ind. Res.
Buffalo Narrows
Patuanak
Conklin
Margie
Cold Lake Air Weapons Range
Primrose Lake
Imperial Mills
Lac la Biche
Craigend
Fork Lake
La Corey
Bonnyville
Medley
Grand Centre
Goodsoil
Meadow Lake Prov. Park
Ashmont
Pierceland
Peerless
Dorintosh
Meadow Lake
Green Lake
St. Paul
Elk Point
Heinsburg
Morecambe
Two Hills
Derwent
Marwayne
Vermilion
Ranfurly
Mannville
Blackfoot
Lloydminster
Lashburn
Maidstone
Neilburg
Wilbert
Irma
Wainwright
Hardisty
Hughenden
Provost
Czar
Airways
Coronation
Consort
Monitor
Hemaruka
Compeer
Fusilier
Loverna
Youngstown
Cereal
Oyen
Alsask
Marengo
Kindersley
Eatonia
Glidden
Eston
Leader
Jenner
Buffalo
C.F.B. Suffield
Lemsford
Liebenthal
Fox Valley
Great Sand Hills
Pivot
Horsham
Hazlet
Medicine Hat
Irvine
Dunmore
Seven Persons
Maple Creek
Sidewood
Cypress Hills
Ft. Walsh N.H.P.
Manyberries
Eastend
Robsart
Govenlock
Wild Horse
Divide
Climax
Willow Creek
Shaunavon
Cadillac
Gull Lake
Antelope
Swift Current
Beverley
Pennant
Simmie
Neville
Hodgeville
Kincaid
Gravelbourg
Val Marie
Masefield
Monchy
Grasslands Nat. Park
Ferland
Limerick
Assiniboia
Wood Mtn.
St. Victor's Petroglyphs Hist. P.
Willow Bunch
Rockglen
Big Beaver
Bengough
Minton
Ceylon
Ogema
Radville
Kayville
Yellow Grass
Weyburn
Halbrite
Midale
Stoughton
Lampman
Bienfait
Estevan
Oxbow
Alameda
Gainsborough
Carlyle
Redvers
Kennedy
Moosomin
Fairlight
Kipling
Dalzell
Broadview
Grenfell
Wolseley
Indian Head
Qu'Appelle
Balgonie
Fort Qu'Appelle
Lumsden
Regina
White City
Moose Jaw
Pasqua
Tuxford
Drinkwater
Claybank
Galilee
Mossbank
Ettington
Milestone
Francis
Corinne
Estlin
Lajord
Montmartre
Kegworth
Fillmore
Griffin
Cedoux
Chaplin
Herbert
Parkbeg
Lillestrom
Trewdate
Chamberlain
Dilke
Strasbourg
Craik
Davidson
Kenaston
Imperial
Hanley
Watrous
Nokomis
Hatfield
Raymore
Lanigan
Young
Plunkett
Elstow
Meacham
Saskatoon
Warman
Aberdeen
Langham
Hepburn
Rosthern
Duck Lake
Wakaw
Domremy
Reynaud
St. Brieux
Naicam
Humboldt
Watson
Quill Lake
Wadena
Kuroki
Foam Lake
Elfros
Wishart
Sheho
Theodore
Yorkton
Melville
Ituna
Goodeve
Southey
Lipton
Balcarres
Abernethy
Esterhazy
Rocanville
Langenburg
Churchbridge
Stockholm
Saltcoats
Kamsack
Canora
Norquay
Sturgis
Preeceville
Stenen
Endeavor
Hendon
Okla
Kelvington
Rose Valley
Porcupine Plain
Archerwill
Tisdale
Sylvania
Melfort
Crystal Spgs.
Birch Hills
Prince Albert
St. Louis
Kinistino
Beatty
Brooksby
Nipawin
Choiseland
Smeaton
Love
Candle Lake
Spruce Home
Meath Park
Armley
Crooked River
Chelan
Bertwell
Reserve
Hudson Bay
Prairie River
Armit
Pasquia Hills
Porcupine Hills
Swan Plain
Swan River
Red Earth
Tobin Lake
Cumberland House
The Pas
Westray
Barrows
Birch River
Lenswood
Bowsman
Benito
Duck Mountain
San Clara
Roblin
Grandview
Russell
Binscarth
St. Lazare
Birtle
Shoal Lake
Rossburn
Oakburn
Riding Mountain
Miniota
Virden
Elkhorn
Kirkella
Oak Lake
Pipestone
Reston
Melita
Cromer
Sinclair
Deleau
Waskesiu Lake
Prince Albert National Park
Montreal Lake
La Ronge
Lac la Ronge Prov. Park
Stanley Mission
Missinipe
Pelikan Narrows
Sandy Bay
Pukatawagan
Southend
Jan Lake
Flin Flon
Creighton
Athapap
Cranberry Portage
Sherridon
Wanless
Cormorant
Atikameg Lake
Big River
Debden
Spiritwood
Shellbrook
Blaine Lake
Mayfair
Redfield
Hafford
Maymont
Radisson
North Battleford
Battleford
Denholm
Wilkie
Red Pheasant
Cando
Landis
Unity
Macklin
Primate
Kerrobert
Tramping Lake
Plenty
Biggar
Perdue
Juniata
Struan
Springwater
Harris
Pike Lake
Delisle
Bradwell
Rosetown
McGee
Milden
Dinsmore
Elrose
Lucky Lake
Beechy
Kyle
Lacadena
Outlook
Macrorie
Elbow
Central Butte
Eyebrow
Stewart Valley
Glen Kerr
Saskatchewan Landing Prov. Park
Hold Lake
Mistawasis Ind. Res.
St. Walburg
Turtleford
Edam
Glaslyn
Meota
Cochin
Loon Lake
Dore Lake
Beauval
Ile-à-la-Crosse
Pinehouse Lake
Cole Bay
Montana
Havre
Chinook
Harlem
Dodson
Malta
Hinsdale
Glasgow
Nashua
Wolf Pt.
Poplar
Culbertson
Fort Peck Indian Reservation
Medicine Lake
Plentywood
Scobey
Peerless
Turner
Loring
Opheim
Rudyard
Gildford
Big Sandy
Rocky Boys Ind. Res.
Ft. Belknap Ind. Res.
Geraldine
Winifred
Roy
Hilger
Stanford
Lewistown
Moore
Grassrange
Piney Buttes
Jordan
Circle
Vida
Fairview
Sidney
Savage
Lindsay
Glendive
Big Sheep Mtn.
Mosby
Melstone
Roundup
Ryegate
Harlowton
Ingomar
Rock Springs
Terry
Fallon
Carlyle
Golva
Beach
Medora
Belfield
Dickinson
Richardton
Mandan
Bismarck
New Salem
Williston
Buford
Alexander
Watford City
East Fairview
Trotters
Killdeer
Manning
Halliday
Beulah
Washburn
Underwood
Stanton
Riverdale
Max
Minot
Surrey
Velva
Granville
Karlsruhe
Berthold
Stanley
New Town
Ft. Berthold Ind. Res.
Ray
Tioga
Zahl
Grenora
Writing Rock
Fortuna
Crosby
Columbus
Bowbells
McGregor
White Earth
Kenmare
Lansford
Upham
Mohall
Westhope
Portal
Northgate
Torquay
Regway
West Poplar
East Poplar
Raymond
Westby
Carpio
Coteau du Missouri
North Dakota
Miles City 176 mi
Miles City 268 mi
Bowman 165 mi
0 20 40 60 80 100km
0 20 40 60miles

26

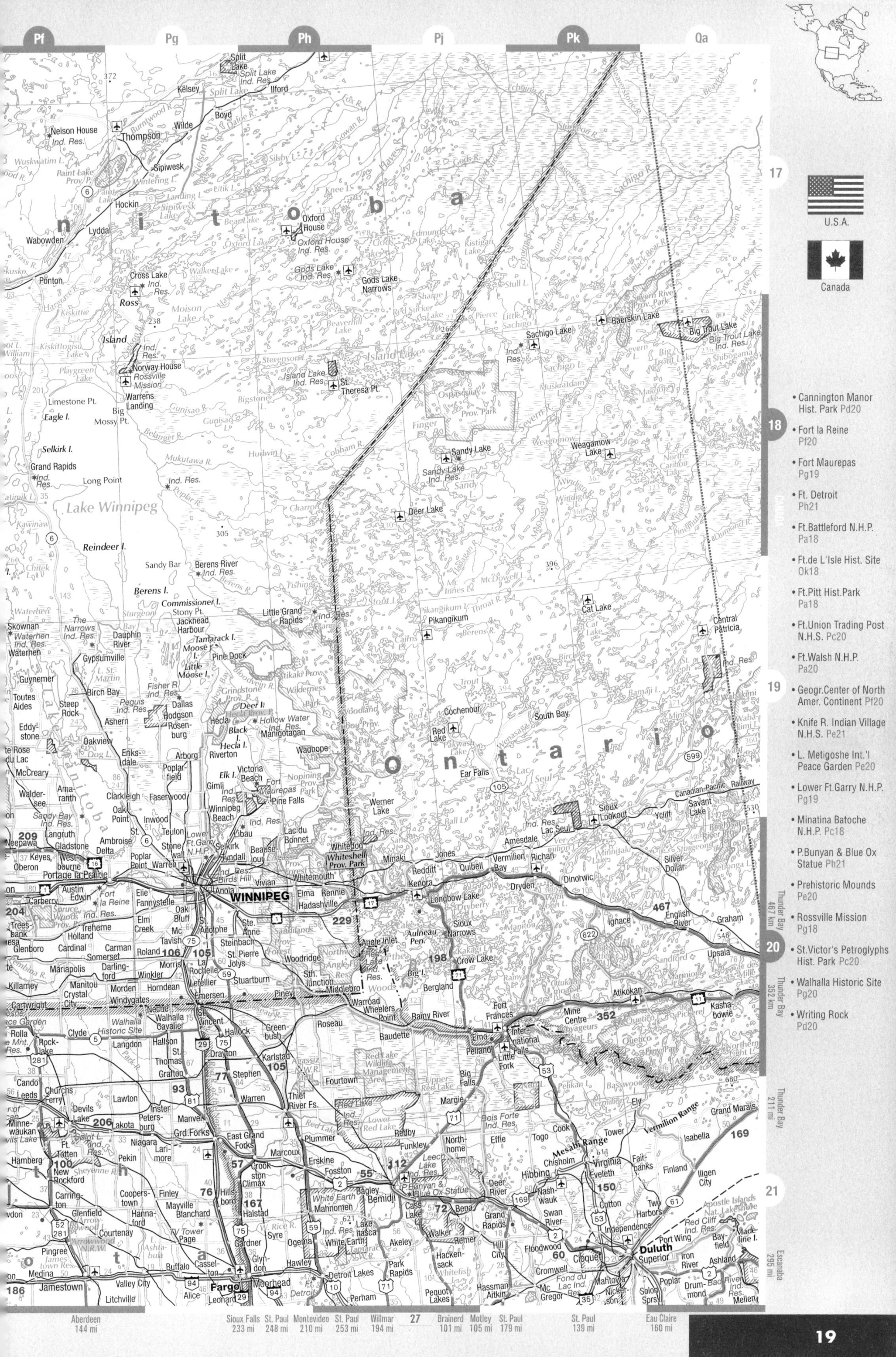
Pf
Pg
Ph
Pj
Pk
Qa
17
18
19
20
21
U.S.A.
Canada
• Cannington Manor Hist. Park Pd20
• Fort la Reine Pf20
• Fort Maurepas Pg19
• Ft. Detroit Ph21
• Ft.Battleford N.H.P. Pa18
• Ft.de L'Isle Hist. Site Ok18
• Ft.Pitt Hist.Park Pa18
• Ft.Union Trading Post N.H.S. Pc20
• Ft.Walsh N.H.P. Pa20
• Geogr.Center of North Amer. Continent Pf20
• Knife R. Indian Village N.H.S. Pe21
• L. Metigoshe Int.'l Peace Garden Pe20
• Lower Ft.Garry N.H.P. Pg19
• Minatina Batoche N.H.P. Pc18
• P.Bunyan & Blue Ox Statue Ph21
• Prehistoric Mounds Pe20
• Rossville Mission Pg18
• St.Victor's Petroglyphs Hist. Park Pc20
• Walhalla Historic Site Pg20
• Writing Rock Pd20
Thunder Bay 467 km
Thunder Bay 352 km
Thunder Bay 211 mi
Escanaba 295 mi
Aberdeen 144 mi
Sioux Falls 233 mi
St. Paul 248 mi
Montevideo 210 mi
St. Paul 253 mi
Willmar 194 mi
27
Brainerd 101 mi
Motley 105 mi
St. Paul 179 mi
St. Paul 139 mi
Eau Claire 160 mi
Manitoba
Ontario
Lake Winnipeg
WINNIPEG
Thompson
Kenora
Fargo
Duluth
Superior
Grand Forks
Bemidji

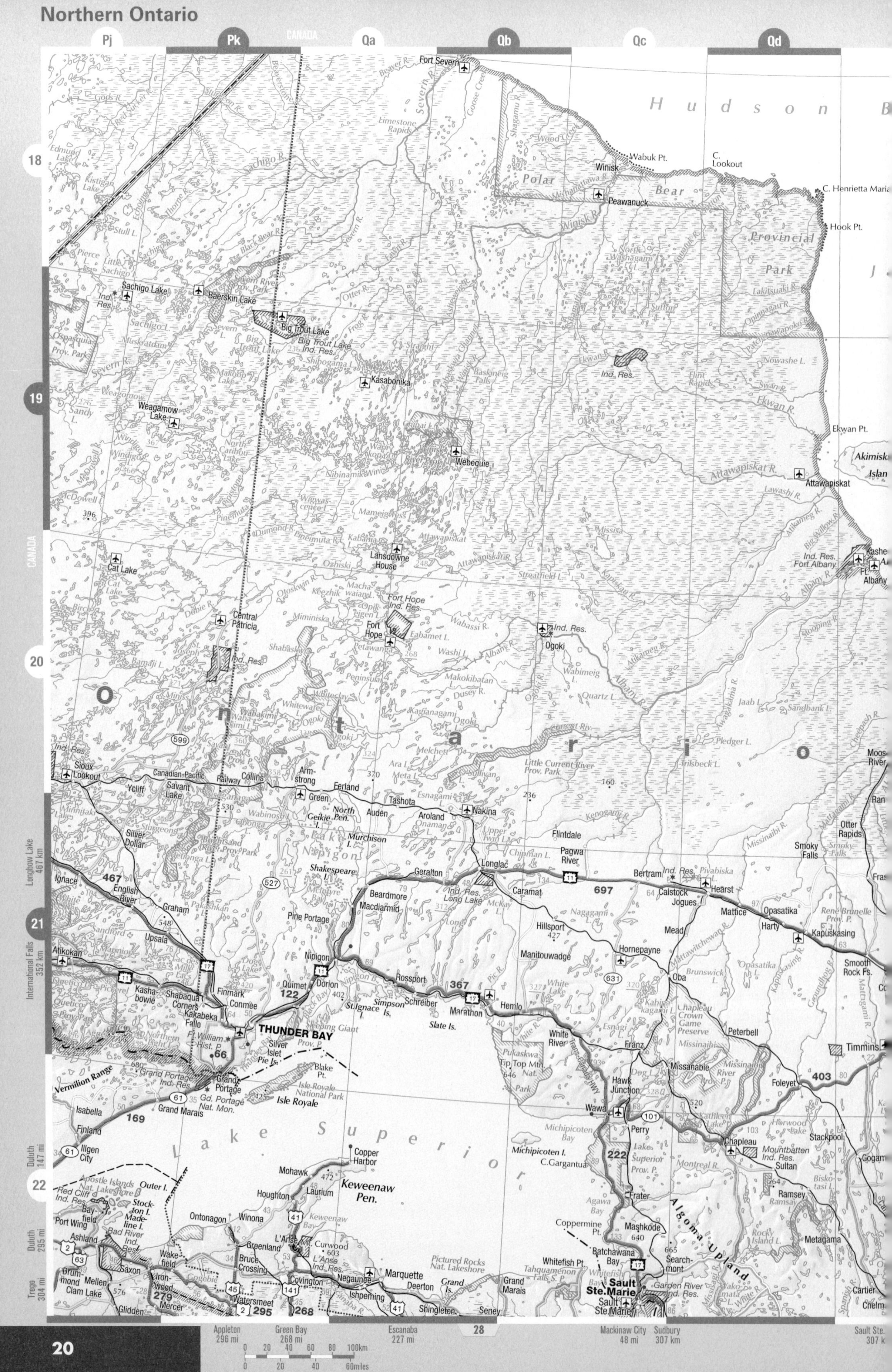

0 20 40 60 80 100km
0 20 40 60miles

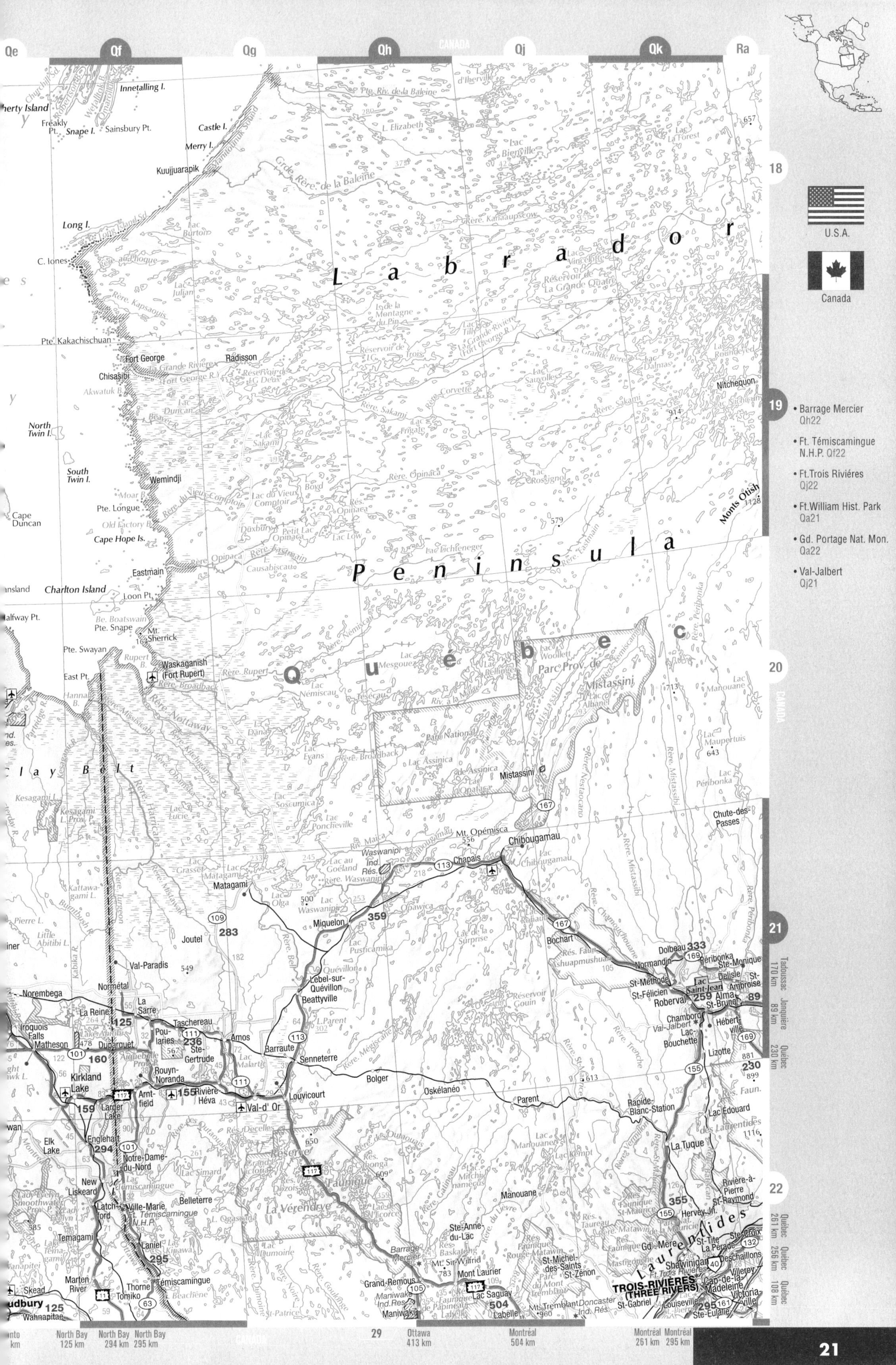
Qe
Qf
Qg
Qh
Qj
Qk
Ra
CANADA
18
19
20
21
22
U.S.A.
Canada
• Barrage Mercier
Qh22
• Ft. Témiscamingue
N.H.P. Qf22
• Ft.Trois Riviéres
Qj22
• Ft.William Hist. Park
Qa21
• Gd. Portage Nat. Mon.
Qa22
• Val-Jalbert
Qj21
Labrador
Peninsula
Québec
Clay Belt
Laurentides
Innetalling I.
Freakly Pt.
Snape I.
Sainsbury Pt.
Castle I.
Merry I.
Kuujjuarapik
Long I.
C. Jones
Pte. Kakachischuan
Fort George
Chisasibi
Radisson
North Twin I.
South Twin I.
Wemindji
Pte. Longue
Cape Duncan
Cape Hope Is.
Eastmain
Charlton Island
Loon Pt.
Pte. Snape
Mt. Sherrick
Pte. Swayan
East Pt.
Waskaganish (Fort Rupert)
L. Elizabeth
Lac Bienville
Lac La Forest
Réservoir de La Grande Quatre
Lac Sakami
Lac du Vieux Comptoir
Lac Mesgouez
Lac Némiscau
Parc Prov. de Mistassini
Lac Mistassini
Lac Albanel
Mistassini
Monts Otish
Nitchequon
Lac Manouane
Lac Maupertuis
Lac Péribonka
Chute-des-Passes
Mt. Opémisca
Chibougamau
Chapais
Waswanipi Ind. Rés.
Matagami
Miquelon
Joutel
Val-Paradis
Normétal
Lebel-sur-Quévillon
Beattyville
Amos
Barraute
Senneterre
Bolger
Oskélanéo
Parent
Louvicourt
Val-d'Or
Rivière-Héva
Rouyn-Noranda
La Sarre
Taschereau
Duparquet
Kirkland Lake
Larder Lake
Arnt-field
Matheson
Iroquois Falls
Englehart
Elk Lake
New Liskeard
Notre-Dame-du-Nord
Latchford
Ville-Marie
Belleterre
Temagami
Laniel
Marten River
Thorne
Témiscamingue
Tomiko
Sudbury
Skead
Wahnapitae
La Vérendrye
Barrage Mercier
Grand-Remous
Maniwaki
Ste-Anne-du-Lac
Mt. Sir Wilfrid
Mont Laurier
Lac Saguay
Labelle
Mt. Tremblant
Doncaster Ind. Rés.
Manouane
St-Michel-des-Saints
St-Zénon
Rapide-Blanc-Station
La Tuque
Lac Édouard
Hervey Jct.
Rivière-à-Pierre
St-Raymond
St-Tite
Ste-Croix
La Pérade
Deschaillons
Shawinigan
Gd. Mère
TROIS-RIVIÈRES (THREE RIVERS)
Cap-de-la-Madeleine
Villeroy
Victoriaville
St-Gabriel
Louiseville
Ste-Eulalie
Bochart
Dolbeau
Normandin
Péribonka
Ste-Monique
Delisle
St-Méthode
St-Félicien
Roberval
Alma
St-Bruno
Ambroise
Chambord
Val-Jalbert
Hébertville
Lac-Bouchette
Lizotte
Lac Saint-Jean
Tadoussac 170 km
Jonquière 89 km
Québec 230 km
Québec 261 km
Québec 256 km
Québec 108 km
North Bay 125 km
North Bay 294 km
North Bay 295 km
Ottawa 413 km
Montréal 504 km
Montréal 261 km
Montréal 295 km
29

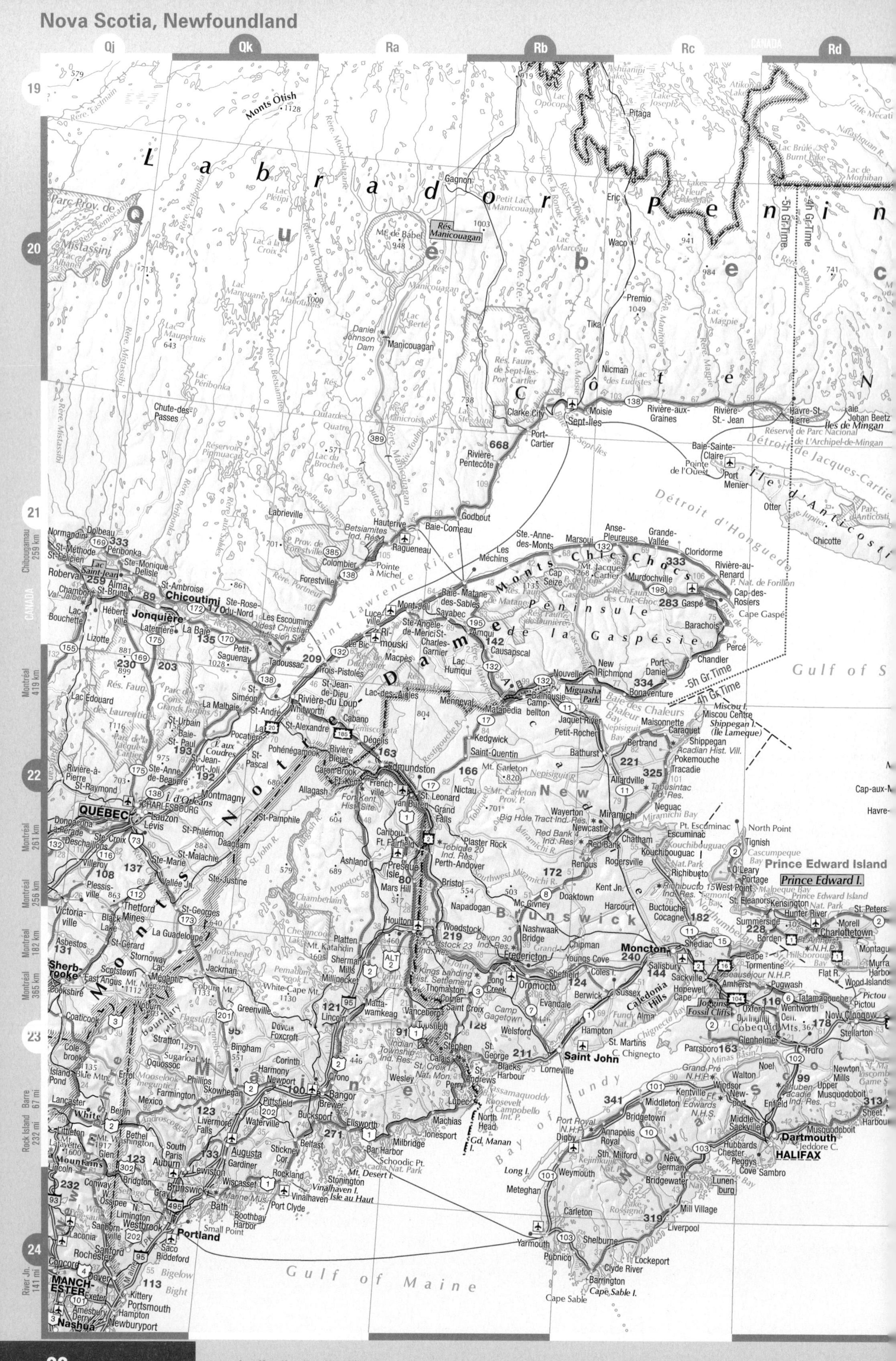
Qj
Qk
Ra
Rb
Rc
Rd
CANADA
19
20
21
22
23
24
L a b r a d o r P e n i n
Q u é b e c
C ô t e N
Monts Otish
Parc Prov. de Mistassini
Rés. Manicouagan
Mt. de Babel
Gagnon
Petit Lac Manicouagan
Lac Plétipi
Lac à la Croix
Lac Manouane
Lac Mistassini
Lac Maupertuis
Lac Péribonka
Daniel Johnson Dam
Manicouagan
Lac Opocopa
Ashuanipi Lake
Atikonak Lake
Lake Joseph
Pitaga
Little Mecatina
Natashquan R.
Lac Brûlé
Burnt Lake
Lac de Morhiban
Lakes Fleur de Lys
Eric
Waco
Premio
Tika
Lac Magpie
Nicman
Lac des Eudistes
Rés. Faun. de Sept-Îles-Port Cartier
Clarke City
Moisie
Sept-Îles
Port-Cartier
Rivière-aux-Graines
Rivière-St.-Jean
Havre-St.-Pierre
Johan Beetz
Îles de Mingan
Réserve de Parc National de L'Archipel-de-Mingan
Détroit de Jacques-Cartier
Baie-Sainte-Claire
Pointe de l'Ouest
Port Menier
Île d'Anticosti
Parc d'Anticosti
Otter
Chicotte
Détroit d'Honguedo
-5h Gr.Time
-4h Gr.Time
Chute-des-Passes
Réservoir Pipmuacan
Lac du Brochet
Outardes Quatre
Manicouagan
Rivière-Pentecôte
Godbout
Baie-Comeau
Hauterive
Labrieville
Betsiamites Ind. Rés.
Ragueneau
Pointe à Michel
Colombier
Forestville
Les Escoumins
Tadoussac
Saint Lawrence River
Ste.-Anne-des-Monts
Les Méchins
Marsoui
Anse-Pleureuse
Grande-Vallée
Cloridorme
Rivière-au-Renard
P. Nat. de Forillon
Cap-des-Rosiers
Cape Gaspé
Gaspé
Murdochville
Monts Chic-Chocs
Péninsule de la Gaspésie
Barachois
Percé
Chandler
Port-Daniel
New Richmond
Bonaventure
Nouvelle
Miguasha Park
Gulf of S
Normandin
Dolbeau
Péribonka
St-Méthode
St-Félicien
Lac Saint-Jean
Roberval
Ste-Monique
Delisle
Alma
St-Bruno
Chambord
Val-Jalbert
St-Ambroise
Chicoutimi
Ste-Rose-du-Nord
Jonquière
Laterrière
La Baie
Hébertville
Lac-Bouchette
Lizotte
Petit-Saguenay
Rés. Faun. des Laurentides
Lac Édouard
La Malbaie
St-Siméon
St-André
Rivière-du-Loup
Trois-Pistoles
Le Bic
Rimouski
Mont-Joli
Baie-Matane
Matane
Sayabec
Amqui
Causapscal
Lac Humqui
Matapédia
Dalhousie
Campbellton
Cabano
Dégelis
Lac-des-Aigles
Menneval
Kedgwick
Saint-Quentin
Mt. Carleton
Bathurst
Jaquet River
Petit-Rocher
Baie des Chaleurs
Chaleur Bay
Maisonnette
Caraquet
Miscou I.
Miscou Centre
Shippegan I. (Île Lameque)
Shippegan
Acadian Hist. Vill.
Bertrand
Pokemouche
Tracadie
Allardville
Tabusintac
Neguac
Miramichi
Miramichi Bay
Newcastle
Red Bank
Chatham
Pt. Escuminac
Escuminac
Kouchibouguac
Rogersville
Richibucto
Kent Jn.
Harcourt
Buctouche
Cocagne
Shediac
Moncton
Salisbury
Sackville
Amherst
Pugwash
Hillsborough
Hopewell Cape
Joggins Fossil Cliffs
Caledonia Hills
Sussex
Alma
Fundy Nat. P.
Hampton
St. Martins
Saint John
Chignecto Bay
C. Chignecto
Parrsboro
Minas Basin
Truro
Glenholme
Cobequid Mts.
Oxford
Springhill
New Glasgow
Stellarton
Pictou
Tatamagouche
Wentworth
Prince Edward Island
Prince Edward I.
North Point
Tignish
Cascumpeque Bay
O'Leary
Portage
West Point
Malpeque Bay
Summerside
Kensington
Borden
Charlottetown
Hunter River
Morell
St. Peters
Montague
Murray Harbour
Wood Islands
Flat R.
Northumberland Str.
Cap-aux-M
Havre-
Edmundston
Clair
St. Leonard
Grand Falls
Plaster Rock
Perth-Andover
Tobique 20 Ind. Rés.
Big Hole Tract Ind. Res.
Red Bank 4 Ind. Res.
Renous
Doaktown
Mc Givney
Napadogan
Bristol
Woodstock
Nashwaak Bridge
Chipman
Fredericton
Oromocto
Gagetown
Welsford
Youngs Cove
Coles I.
Sheffield
Berwick
Evandale
Kings Landing Hist. Settlement
Long Creek
Thomaston Corner
Saint Croix
St. Stephen
St. George
Blacks Harbour
St. Andrews
Lorneville
Bay of Fundy
Campobello I.
Roosevelt Campobello Int. P.
Lubec
Grand Manan I.
North Head
Passamaquoddy Bay
Calais
Vanceboro
Topsfield
Mattawamkeag
Lincoln
Millinocket
Sherman Mills
Patten
Mt. Katahdin
Houlton
Mars Hill
Presque Isle
Caribou
Ft. Fairfield
Van Buren
Frenchville
Fort Kent
Fort Kent Hist. Site
Allagash
Ashland
Portage
St-Pamphile
Pohénégamook
Rivière-Bleue
St-Alexandre
St-Pascal
Pocatière
Montmagny
Île aux Coudres
St-Jean-Port-Joli
Baie-St-Paul
St-Urbain
Ste-Anne-de-Beaupré
Charlesbourg
Québec
Lévis
Lauzon
Î. d'Orléans
St-Raymond
Rivière-à-Pierre
Donnacona
La Pérade
Deschaillons
Ste-Croix
Villeroy
Plessisville
Victoriaville
Thetford Mines
Black Lake
St-Gérard
Stornoway
Ste-Marie
St-Malachie
Vallée Jn.
Ste-Justine
St-Georges
La Guadeloupe
Lac-Mégantic
Jackman
Scotstown
East Angus
Sherbrooke
Cookshire
Coaticook
Asbestos
Daaquam
St-Philémon
Moosehead Lake
Chesuncook Lake
Chamberlain Lake
Greenville
Dover-Foxcroft
Bingham
The Forks
Coburn Mt.
Stratton
Sugarloaf Mt.
Oquossoc
Rangeley
Phillips
Farmington
Skowhegan
Pittsfield
Waterville
Newport
Corinth
Orono
Bangor
Brewer
Bucksport
Ellsworth
Machias
Jonesport
Milbridge
Bar Harbor
Schoodic Pt.
Acadia Nat. Park
Mt. Desert I.
Belfast
Rockland
Stonington
Vinalhaven I.
Vinalhaven
Isle au Haut
Augusta
Gardiner
Livermore Falls
Lewiston
Auburn
South Paris
Brunswick
Bath
Wiscasset
Boothbay Harbor
Port Clyde
Portland
Small Point
Saco
Biddeford
Bridgton
Bethel
Berlin
Mexico
Gorham
Errol
Colebrook
Island Pond
Lancaster
Littleton
Mt. Washington
Lafayette
Glen
Conway
Ossipee
Lincoln
Wolfeboro
Laconia
Sanbornville
Rochester
Sanford
Dover
Concord
Manchester
Exeter
Portsmouth
Kittery
Hampton
Amesbury
Derry
Newburyport
Nashua
White Mountains
Gulf of Maine
Bigelow Bight
Yarmouth
Pubnico
Barrington
Clyde River
Cape Sable
Cape Sable I.
Shelburne
Lockeport
Liverpool
Carleton
Mill Village
Bridgewater
Lunenburg
New Germany
Chester
Hubbards
Peggys Cove
Sambro
Halifax
Dartmouth
Musquodoboit
Jeddore C.
Middle Sackville
Enfield
Shubenacadie Ind. Res.
Upper Musquodoboit
Newton Mills
Sheet Harbour
Windsor
Walton
Noel
Newport
Grand Pré N.H.P.
Kentville
Middleton
Bridgetown
Annapolis Royal
Port Royal N.H.P.
Digby
Sth. Milford
Weymouth
Meteghan
Long I.
Kejimkujik Nat. Park
Chibougamau 259 km
Montréal 419 km
Montréal 261 km
Montréal 256 km
Montréal 182 km
Montréal 365 km
Barre 67 mi
Rock Island 232 mi
River Jn. 141 mi
0 20 40 60 80 100km
0 20 40 60miles

Re
Rf
Rg
Rh
Rj
Rk
19
20
21
22
23
24
U.S.A.
Canada
Newfoundland and Labrador
Island of Newfoundland
Long Range Mountains
ATLANTIC OCEAN
Cabot Strait
Lawrence
3h30 Gr.Time
-3h30 Gr.Time
-4h Gr.Time
-3h Gr.Time
Square Islands
Port Hope Simpson
St. Michaels B.
Alexis R.
Gilbert R.
Alexis Bay
Battle Harbour
St. Lewis R.
St. Lewis
Pinware R.
Table Hd.
Northeast Pt.
Belle Isle
Red Bay
Strait of Belle Isle
Cooks Harbour
C. Bauld
Raleigh
L'Anse aux Meadows N. H. P.
Griquet
St. Anthony
Blanc Sablon
St-Paul
Eddies Cove
Savage Cove
Main Brook
Ten Mile L.
St. Barbe
Groais I.
Brig Bay
St. Margaret B.
Roddickton
Englee
Canada B.
Bell I.
French Cove
St. John I.
Port au Choix
Port au Choix N.H.P.
Igornachoix B.
Hawke's Bay
Harbour Deep
Bellburns
Portland Creek Pond
Fleur de Lys
Horse Is. (St. Barbe)
Confusion Bay
C. St. John
La Scie
Parson's Pond
Gros Morne Nat.P.
Jackson Arm
Seal Cove
Notre Dame Bay
Burlington
Green B.
Westport
Sally's Cove
Baie Verte
Rattling Brook
Springdale
Long I.
Fortune Harbour
Robert's Arm
South Arm
Twillingate
New World I.
Fogo
Fogo I.
Joe Batts Arm
Wadham Is.
Exploits Is.
Village Cove
Hamilton Sound
Leading Tickles
Lewisporte
Carmanville
C. Freels
Wesleyville
Bonne B.
Norris Point
Gros Morne
806
Hampden
Squires Mem. Prov. P.
Trout River
Woody Pt.
Mt. St. Gregory
Wiltondale
Deer Lake
Cox's Cove
686
Lark Harbour
B. of Islands
Corner Brook
Pasadena
Sandy L.
Hinds L.
Grand L.
Buchans
Red Indian L.
Botwood
Notre Dame Junction
Gander Bay
Ten Mile Pond
Indian Bay
St. Brendan's
South Brook
North Twin L.
South Twin L.
Hodges Hill
Badger
227
Windsor
Bishop's Falls
Grand Falls
Exploits R.
Gander
Gander L.
Gambo
Glovertown
Burnside
Salvage
Kings Cove
Bonavista Bay
C. Bonavista
Bonavista
Catalina
Terra Nova Nat. P.
Bonavista Pen.
Millertown
Glover I.
Lewis Hills
814
Long Pt.
Port au Port Peninsula
Mainland
Petit Jardin
C. St. George
Stephenville
Stephenville Crossing
St. George's Bay
St. George's
Fischell
Barachois Pond Prov. P.
Meelpaeg L.
Victoria L.
Island Pond
Deer Pond
Middle Ridge
Port Blandfort
Clarenville
Random I.
Trinity
Monroe
Britannia
Grates Pt.
Grates Cove
Old Perlican
Southport
Heart's Content
Trinity Bay
Jubilee L.
Bay du Nord Wilderness Res.
Round Pond
Goobies
Robinsons R.
Anguille Mts.
South Branch
Cape Anguille
St. Andrew's
Cape Ray
Channel-Port-aux-Basques
La Poile
Rose Blanche
Grand Bruit
Burgeo
Ramea
Ramea I.
Penguin I.
Blue Hills of Couteau
636
Grey River
White Bear B.
La Poile B.
Mc Callum
Gaultois
Hermitage Bay
François
Pass Island
Harb. Breton
Brunette I.
St. Albans
Milltown
Pools Cove
Rencontre East
Belleoram
English Harb. West
Fortune Bay
Grand le Pierre
Terrenceville
English Harb. East
St. Bernard's
Merasheen
Long Harb.
Beach
Fairhaven
Spaniard's Bay
Carbonear
Conception Bay
C. St. Francis
Pouch Cove
Torbay
Bell I.
Signal Hill N. H. P.
St. John's
Holyrood
Bay Bulls
La Manche Valley Prov. P.
Whitbourne
Argentia
Placentia
South East Bight
Petite Forte
Placentia Bay
Colinet
Avalon Pen.
Avalon Wilderness Area
Fermeuse
St. Josephs
Branch
St. Bride's
C. St. Mary's
St. Mary's Bay
Trepassey
Trepassey Bay
Cape Race
Saint Shott's
Burin Peninsula
Marystown
Burin
Fortune
Lawn Bay
St-Pierre
Grande Miquelon
Langlade ou Petit Miquelon
St-Pierre et Miquelon (Fr.)
Î. de St-Pierre
Sable I.
Î. Brion
Grande-Entrée
Île-d'Entrée
Pointe de l'Est
St. Paul I.
C. St. Lawrence
Cape North
Aspy Bay
South Harbour
C. Breton Highlands Nat. P.
Chéticamp
Ingonish Beach
Cape Breton Island
Margaree Forks
St. Ann's Bay
Sth. Gut St. Ann's
New Waterford
Nth. Sydney
Glace Bay
Inverness
Baddeck
A.Gr.Bell N. H. P.
Sydney
Main à Dieu
Cape Breton
Mabou
Whycocomagh Ind. Res.
Louisbourg
Fortress of Louisbourg N.H.P.
Big Pond
Gabarouse
Bras d'Or L.
Chapel Island Ind. Res.
Port Hastings
St. Peters
Louisdale
Arichat
Strait of Canso
Chedabucto Bay
Canso
Larry's River
Pt. Bickerton
Kegaska
Romaine
Cap-Whittle
Olomane
St-Mary Îs.
Harrington Harbour
Î.du Petit Mécatina
C. Mécatina
Î.du Grand Mécatina
Mutton Bay
J. Monger
St-Augustin
Î. des Genévriers
Nord Ouest
Rivière St-Augustin
Lac Briconnet
Lac Fontêneau
Lac Musquaro
Lac Goyelle
Minipi L.
Kenamu R.
St. Paul R.
564
585
577
466
125
• A.Gr.Bell N.H.P. Re22
• Acadian Hist. Vill. Rc22
• Daniel Johnson Dam Ra20
• Fort Kent Hist. Site Ra22
• Fortress of Louisbourg N.H.P. Re23
• Ft. Beauséjour N.H.P. Rc23
• Ft. Edwards N.H.S. Rc23
• Ft.Amherst N.H.P. Rd22
• Grand Pré N.H.P. Rc23
• Joggins Fossil Cliffs Rc23
• Kings Landing Hist. Settlement Rb23
• L'Anse aux Meadows N.H.P. Rh20
• Marine Mus. Ra24
• Oldest Christian Mission Site Ra21
• Port au Choix N.H.P. Rg20
• Port Royal N.H.P. Rc23
• Signal Hill N.H.P. Rj22
• St. Croix I. Nat. Mon. Rb23
• Val-Jalbert Qj21

Sacramento 232 mi
32 Reno 355 mi
San Francisco 386 mi
Austin 139 mi

0 20 40 60 80 100km
0 20 40 60miles

Vancouver → 148-151
Seattle → 154
Olympic N.P. → 101

U.S.A.
Canada
• Avenue of the Giants Od25
• Balanced Rock Oh24
• Big Hole National Battlefield Oj23
• Cove Hot Springs Og23
• Doukhobor Village Og21
• Ft.Steele Heritage Town Oh21
• Ghost Town Oh24
• Golden Spike N.H.S. Oj25
• Grand Coulee Dam Of22
• Grant-Kohrs Ranch N.H.S. Oj22
• Great Falls Ok22
• Head-Smashed-In Buffalo Jump Oj21
• Hells Gate Airtram Oe21
• Hot Springs Oh23
• Ice Caves Oe23
• Nez Perce N.H.P. Og22
• Old Faithful Geysir Ok23
• Shoshone Ice Caves Oh24
• Snake River Canyon Og22
• Spokane House Og22
• Whitmann Mission N.H.S. Of22
• World's Largest Mineral Hot Sprs. Pa24
Calgary 169 km
Medicine Hat 222 km
Regina 691 km
Williston 214 mi
Miles City 280 mi
Bismarck 411 mi
Belle Fourche 261 mi
Buffalo 151 mi
Buffalo 155 mi
Casper 97 mi
Rawlins 256 mi
Rawlins 111 mi
Granby 244 mi
Ely 137 mi
Las Vegas 420 mi
Price 122 mi
Price 113 mi
Montana
Wyoming
Yellowstone N.P. → 102
Grand Teton N.P. → 103
Waterton Lakes N.P. / Glacier N.P. → 100

Pa
Pb
Regina 116 km
Pc
18
Regina 277 km
Pd
Pe
CANADA
Minnedosa 47 km
Pf
21
22
23
24
25
Havre 86 mi
Lewistown 134 mi
White Sulphur Sprs. 280 mi
Butte 220 mi
Bridger 83 mi
West Yellowstone 187 mi
Moran 157 mi
Moran 256 mi
Salt Lake City 275 mi
Vernal 244 mi
Montana
North Dakota
South Dakota
Wyoming
Nebraska
Bighorn Mountains
Bighorn Basin
Shoshone Basin
Great Divide Basin
Bull Mountain
Piney Buttes
Black Hills
Badlands
Medicine Bow Mts.
Laramie
Front Range
Sand Hills
Coteau du Missouri
Ft. Belknap Ind. Res.
Fort Peck Indian Reservation
Crow Indian Reserv.
Northern Cheyenne Ind. Res.
Standing Rock Indian Reservation
Cheyenne River Indian Reservation
Pine Ridge Ind. Res.
Rosebud Ind. Res.
Devils Tower Nat. Mon.
Mt. Rushmore Nat. Memorial
Jewel Cave Nat. Mon.
Wind Cave Nat. Park
Scotts Bluff Nat. Mon.
Chimney Rock N.H.S.
Agate Fossil Beds Nat. Mon.
Como Bluff Fossil Beds
Independence Rock S.H.S.
World's Largest Mineral Hot Sprs.
Little Bighorn Battlefield Nat. Mon.
Billings
Sheridan
Gillette
Casper
Cheyenne
Laramie
Ft. Collins
Greeley
Rapid City
Pierre
Bismarck
Mandan
Minot
Williston
Dickinson
Miles City
Glendive
Scottsbluff
North Platte
Valentine
Brandon
Moose Jaw
Rocky Mountain N.P. → 114
Denver 244 mi
Denver 102 mi
Denver 86 mi
34
Lamar 240 mi
McCook 123 mi
Garden City 251 mi
0 20 40 60 80 100km
0 20 40 60miles

Pg
Ph
19
Pj
Pk
Qa
U.S.A.
Canada
21
22
23
24
25
Thunder Bay 122 km
Escanaba 295 mi
Stevens Pt. 279 mi
Escanaba 347 mi
Green Bay 191 mi
Stevens Pt. 108 mi
Madison 182 mi
Madison 140 mi
Madison 97 mi
Chicago 177 mi
Chicago 201 mi
Clinton 41 mi
Chicago 175 mi
Indianapolis 311 mi
Peoria 79 mi
St. Louis 153 mi
• Burning Coal Mines Pd22
• Crystal Cave Pj23
• Eagle Cave Pk24
• Fort Belmont Ph24
• Fort la Reine Pf21
• Ft. Abercrombie Pg22
• Ft. Detroit Ph22
• Ft. Phil Kearny Pb23
• Ft. Randall Dam Pf24
• Geograph. Center of U.S. Pd23
• Grotto of the Redemption Ph24
• Mystery Cave Pj24
• Neligh Mills Pg24
• Petrified Wood Park Pd23
• Prairie Village Pg24
• Prehistoric Mounds Pe21
• Saratoga Hot Springs Pb25
• Sioux Ind. Mus. Pe24
• Sitting Bull's Grave Pe23
• Village of Yesteryear Pj23
• Wounded Knee Battlefield Pd24
• Writing Rock Pd21
WINNIPEG
Lake Superior
Minnesota
Wisconsin
Iowa
MINNEAPOLIS
ST. PAUL
DES MOINES
OMAHA
LINCOLN
CEDAR RAPIDS
DAVENPORT
Wichita 300 mi
Wichita 284 mi
Wichita 302 mi
Kansas City 188 mi
Kansas City 146 mi
35
Kansas City 197 mi
Kansas City 226 mi
St. Louis 276 mi
St. Louis 284 mi

Pj
International Falls 150 mi
Pk
Thunder Bay 169 mi
Qa
20
Qb
Qc
Wawa 222 km
Wawa 133 km
Lake Superior
Isle Royale National Park
Keweenaw Pen.
Apostle Islands Nat. Lakeshore
Pictured Rocks Nat. Lakeshore
Upper Peninsula
Minnesota
Wisconsin
Michigan
Lower Peninsula
Iowa
Illinois
Indiana
Missouri
Lake Michigan
Green Bay
Sleeping Bear Dunes Nat. Lakeshore
Duluth
Superior
Minneapolis
St. Paul
Eau Claire
Rochester
La Crosse
Madison
Milwaukee
Waukesha
Racine
Kenosha
Waukegan
Evanston
Skokie
Chicago
Joliet
Gary
Hammond
Elgin
Aurora
Rockford
Dubuque
Waterloo
Cedar Rapids
Iowa City
Davenport
Peoria
Springfield
Decatur
Champaign
Bloomington
St. Louis
East St. Louis
Florissant
Columbia
Terre Haute
Indianapolis
Muncie
Anderson
Bloomington
Kokomo
Lafayette
Ft. Wayne
South Bend
Kalamazoo
Grand Rapids
Lansing
Muskegon
Marquette
Escanaba
Sault Ste.Marie
Appleton
Oshkosh
Fond du Lac
Sheboygan
Manitowoc
Green Bay
Traverse City
Cincinnati
Hamilton
Louisville
Kettering
22
23
24
25
26
27
Bemidji 72 mi
Fargo 226 mi
Fargo 248 mi
Fargo 253 mi
Sioux Falls 261 mi
Mankato 157 mi
Sioux Falls 162 mi
Sheldon 168 mi
Des Moines 140 mi
Dodge 117 mi
Des Moines 166 mi
Omaha 208 mi
Princeton 101 mi
St.Joseph 128 mi
Carrollton 65 mi
Kansas City 252 mi
Wichita 460 mi
Poplar Bluff 163 mi
36
Vienna 74 mi
Nashville 332 mi
Owensboro 35 mi
Nashville 173 mi
Knoxville 262 mi
0 20 40 60 80 100km
Chicago → 122-123

Qd
Matheson 270 km
Qe
CANADA
Matheson 294 km
Arntfield 295 km
Qf
21
Louvicourt 246 km
Qg
Qh
22
CANADA
Montreal 504 km
Montreal 178 km
Montreal 243 km
23
Montreal 295 mi
Albany 134 mi
24
Albany 312 mi
Albany 133 mi
New York 178 mi
New York 254 mi
New York 194 mi
25
New York 217 mi
Philadelphia 183 mi
Philadelphia 109 mi
Philadelphia 105 mi
Portsmouth 393 mi
26
Portsmouth 248 mi
27
U.S.A.
Canada
• Blue Springs Caverns Qb26
• Bridal Cave Pj26
• Cahokia Mounds Pk26
• Crystal Cave Pj23
• Dickson Mounds Pk25
• Dutch Village Qb24
• Ft. Mackinac Qc23
• Ft. McHenry Qg26
• Ft. Sheridan Qb24
• Gettysburg N.M.P. Qg26
• Great America Qb24
• Harpers Ferry N.H.P. Qg26
• Mormon Print Shop Qc23
• Motor Speedway Qb26
• Mystery Cave Pj24
• Old Ft. Henry Qg23
• Pine Creek Gorge Qg25
• Piqua Historic Area Qc25
• Rideau Canal Qg23
• Sainte-Marie Among the Hurons Qf23
• Skyline Caverns Qf26
• Upper Canada Vill. Qh23
• Village of Yesteryear Pj23
TORONTO
Lake Ontario
Lake Erie
Lake Huron
Georgian Bay
APPALACHIAN MOUNTAINS
Allegheny Plateau
Williamson 78 mi
Knoxville 304 mi
Charlotte 285 mi
Princeton 147 mi
Covington 57 mi
37
Charlotte 470 mi
Richmond 189 mi
Richmond 105 mi
Richmond 161 mi
Toronto → 146-147
Washington D.C. → 152-153

QUÉBEC
MONTREAL
OTTAWA
TORONTO
BOSTON
Lake Ontario
Gulf of Maine
Bay of Fundy
Adirondack Mountains
Monts Notre Dame
Laurentides
Appalachian Mountains
-4h Gr.Time
-5h Gr.Time
Sudbury 125 km
Owen Sound 241 km
Boston → 118-119
Montréal → 136-137
Toronto → 146-147

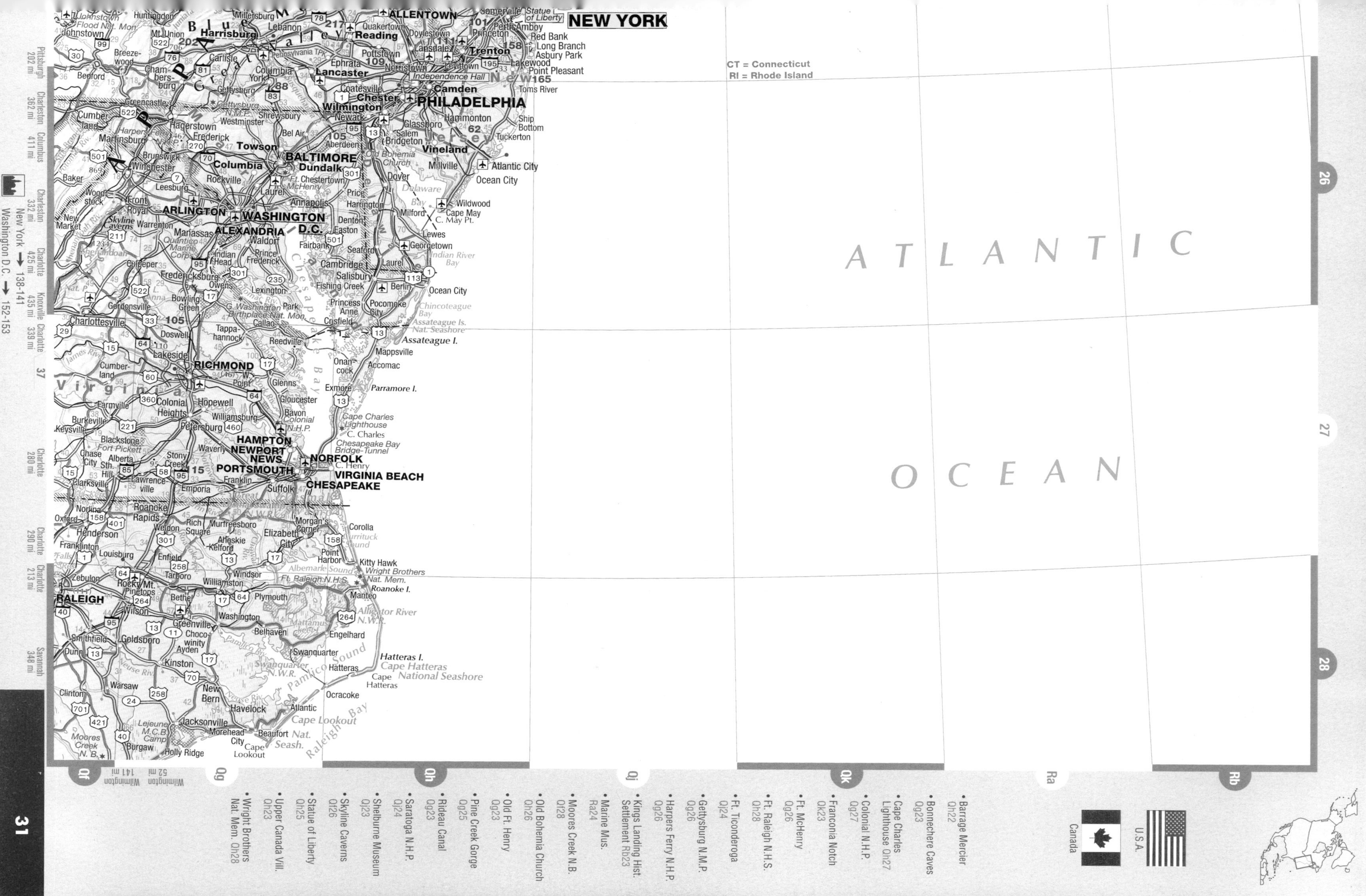
NEW YORK
ALLENTOWN
Reading
Harrisburg
Trenton
Lancaster
Camden
PHILADELPHIA
Chester
Wilmington
Vineland
Atlantic City
Ocean City
BALTIMORE
Dundalk
Towson
Columbia
ARLINGTON
WASHINGTON D.C.
ALEXANDRIA
Annapolis
Dover
Wildwood
Cape May
Lewes
Georgetown
Salisbury
Fredericksburg
Charlottesville
RICHMOND
Petersburg
HAMPTON
NEWPORT NEWS
NORFOLK
PORTSMOUTH
VIRGINIA BEACH
CHESAPEAKE
Suffolk
Kitty Hawk
Manteo
Elizabeth City
RALEIGH
Wilson
Greenville
Goldsboro
Kinston
New Bern
Jacksonville
Morehead City
Hatteras I.
Cape Hatteras National Seashore
Cape Lookout
Raleigh Bay
Chesapeake Bay
Delaware Bay
Assateague I.
Pamlico Sound
CT = Connecticut
RI = Rhode Island
ATLANTIC
OCEAN
26
27
28
Rb
Ra
Qk
Qj
Qh
Qg
Qf
U.S.A.
Canada
• Barrage Mercier Qh22
• Bonnechere Caves Qg23
• Cape Charles Lighthouse Qh27
• Colonial N.H.P. Qg27
• Franconia Notch Qk23
• Ft. McHenry Qg26
• Ft. Raleigh N.H.S. Qh28
• Ft. Ticonderoga Qj24
• Gettysburg N.M.P. Qg26
• Harpers Ferry N.H.P. Qg26
• Kings Landing Hist. Settlement Rb23
• Marine Mus. Ra24
• Moores Creek N.B. Qf28
• Old Bohemia Church Qh26
• Old Ft. Henry Qg23
• Pine Creek Gorge Qg25
• Rideau Canal Qg23
• Saratoga N.H.P. Qj24
• Shelburne Museum Qj23
• Skyline Caverns Qf26
• Statue of Liberty Qh25
• Upper Canada Vill. Qh23
• Wright Brothers Nat. Mem. Qh28
Pittsburgh 202 mi
Charleston 362 mi
Columbus 411 mi
Charleston 332 mi
Charlotte 425 mi
Knoxville 435 mi
Charlotte 339 mi
37
Charlotte 280 mi
Charlotte 290 mi
Charlotte 213 mi
Savannah 348 mi
Wilmington 52 mi
Wilmington 141 mi
New York → 138-141
Washington D.C. → 152-153

0 20 40 60 80 100km
0 20 40 60miles

El Crucero 464 km

San Francisco → 142-145
Los Angeles → 126-129
Yosemite N.P. → 104
Kings Canyon N.P., Sequoia N.P. → 105
Death Valley N.P. →
Joshua Tree N.P. →

Las Vegas → 124-125
Grand Canyon N.P. → 108-109
Zion N.P. → 110
Bryce Canyon N.P. → 111
Canyonlands N.P. → 112
Arches N.P. → 113

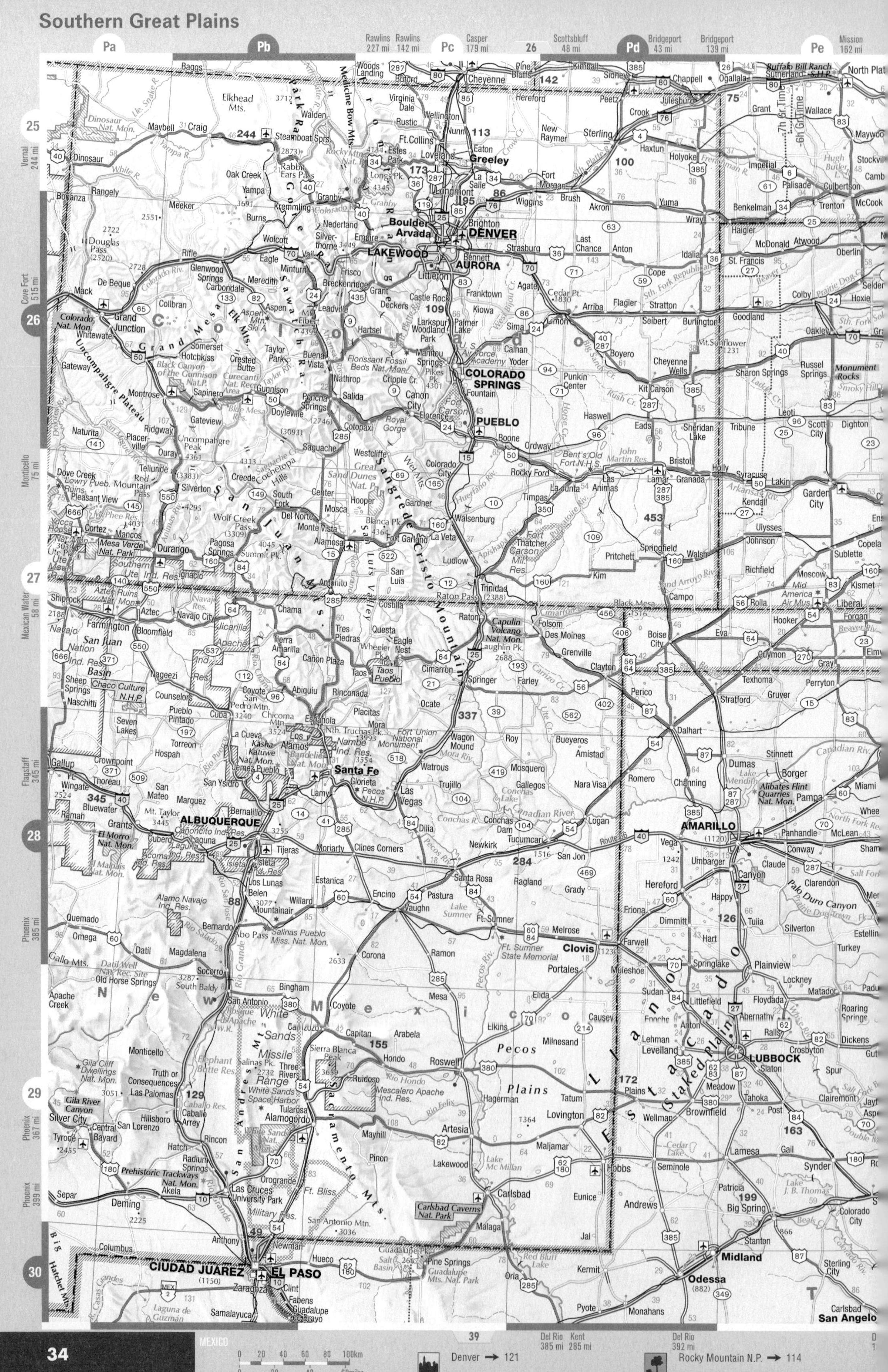

Denver → 121

Rocky Mountain N.P. → 114

U.S.A.
Mexico
• Bent's Old Fort N.H.S. Pd26
• Bridal Cave Pj26
• Buffalo Bill Ranch S.H.P. Pe25
• Colorado Nat. Mon. Pa26
• El Morro Nat. Mon. Pa28
• Florissant Fossil Beds Nat. Mon. Pc26
• Fort Griffin Pf29
• Fort Larned N.H.S. Pf26
• Fort Union National Monument Pc28
• Fort Washita Pg28
• Gila River Canyon Pa29
• Hodges Gardens Pj30
• Lowry Pueb. Ruins Pa27
• Mid America Air Mus. Pe27
• Monument Rocks Pe26
• Old Ft. Dodge Pf27
• Onyx Cave Pj27
• Pawnee Indian Village Pg26
• Pecos N.H.P. Pc28
• Pony Express Station Pg26
• Royal Gorge Pc26
• Sequoyah's Cabin Ph28
• White Sands Space Harbor Pb29

Seadalia 60 mi
Pj
Kansas City 151 mi
Pk
Kansas City 252 mi
Indianapolis 244 mi
Decatur 91 mi
Qa
Chicago 532 mi
28
Chicago 439 mi
Qb
Cincinnati 358 mi
Indianapolis 164 mi
26
27
28
29
30
31
ST. LOUIS
East St. Louis
SPRINGFIELD
Ozark Plateau
Boston Mts.
EVANSVILLE
Owensboro
LOUIS-VILLE
Paducah
Clarksville
NASHVILLE
Jackson
MEMPHIS
Nth. Little Rock
LITTLE ROCK
Pine Bluff
HUNTSVILLE
CHATTANOO
BIRMINGHAM
Gadsden
Tuscaloosa
Columbus
Tupelo
JACKSON
Meridian
MONTGOMERY
Monroe
Vicksburg
Natchez
Alexandria
Hattiesburg
BATON ROUGE
Lafayette
NEW ORLEANS
Kenner
METAIRIE
Biloxi
Pascagoula
MOBILE
Pensacola
Panama City
Dothan
Houma
Mississippi River Delta
Chandeleur Islands
Breton Sound
Isles Dernieres
Gulf of Me
Central Time -6h Gr.Time
Eastern -5h Gr.
0 20 40 60 80 100km
0 20 40 60miles

Cincinnati 51 mi
Indianapolis 304 mi
Qd
Columbus 135 mi
Columbus 160 mi
Cleveland 243 mi
Qe
Pittsburgh 228 mi
29
Qf
Washington D.C. 487 mi
Washington D.C. 70 mi
Qg
Washington D.C. 105 mi
26
Norfolk 93 mi
Norfolk 94 mi
U.S.A.
27
Norfolk 76 mi
Norfolk 155 mi
Manteo 81 mi
Havelock 19 mi
28
Atlantic 77 mi
29
30
31
West Virginia
APPALACHIAN MOUNTAINS
Blue Ridge
North Carolina
South Carolina
Georgia
Virginia
Clinch Mts.
Sea Islands
Long Bay
Onslow Bay
ATLANTIC OCEAN
LEXINGTON
Huntington
Charleston
RICHMOND
ROANOKE
LYNCHBURG
KNOXVILLE
WINSTON-SALEM
GREENSBORO
DURHAM
RALEIGH
Asheville
CHARLOTTE
Greenville
COLUMBIA
Fayetteville
Wilmington
Myrtle Beach
ATLANTA
Augusta
MACON
COLUMBUS
Albany
North Charleston
Charleston
SAVANNAH
JACKSONVILLE
Gainesville
DAYTONA BEACH
St. Augustine
Great Smoky Mts. Nat. P.
St. Petersburg 254 mi
Tampa 200 mi
Orlando 183 mi
43
Orlando 144 mi
Miami 349 mi
Great Smoky Mountains N.P. → 115
• Andersonville N.H.S. Qc29
• Appomattox Court House N.H.P. Qf27
• A. Lincoln Birthplace N.H.S. Qc27
• Brices Cross Roads N.B.S. Qa28
• Bridal Cave Pj26
• Brookgreen Gardens Qf29
• Cahokia Mounds Pk26
• Fort Fisher Qg29
• Fort Gadsden State Historical Site Qc31
• Fort Massachusetts Qa30
• Ft. Donelson N.B. Qb27
• Ft. Gaines Qa30
• Ft. Jackson Qa31
• Marineland of Florida Qe31
• Moores Creek N.B. Qf28
• Natural Arch Qc27
• Natural Bridge Qb28
• Ninety Six N.H.S. Qd28
• Shakertown Qc27
• Stones River N.B. Qb28
• Tupelo N.B. Qa28
• Tuskegee Institute N.H.S. Qc29
• Wyandotte Caves Qb26

Tijuana 119km
Og
Tecate 111 km
MEXICO
Mexicali 197 km
Oh
Mexicali 522 km
33
Oj
Phoenix 247 mi
Phoenix 119 mi
Ok
Phoenix 139 mi
Phoenix 290 mi
29
30
31
32
33
34
Cantamar
La Misión
ENSENADA
Maneadero
Santo Tomás
Colnett
Cabo Colnett
Baja
Colonia Vicente Guerrero
San Martín
San Quintín
Cabo San Quintín
El Rosario
Punta Baja
California
Campo Nuevo
Punta Canoas
Norte
Punta Blanca
San Luis
Rosarito
Tomatán
Isla Cedros
-8h Gr.Time
-7h Gr.Time
Punta Eugenia
Peninsula de Vizcaíno
Bahía Tortugas
Guerrero Negro
Sanctuario Ballenaro El Vizcaíno
Reserva de la Biósfera El Vizcaíno
Punta San Pablo
Bahía Asunción
San Roque
Sierra Pintada
Díaz Ordaz
Santa Clara
San Ignacio
Desierto de Vizcaíno
Punta Abreojos
Isla Arena
Baja
La Purísima
California
San Javier
Ej. Pancho Villa
Santo Domingo
Villa Insurgentes
Puerto Adolfo López Mateos
Ciudad Constitución
Isla Magdalena
El Refugio
El Cirnelo
San Carlos
Puerto Magdalena
Santa Rita
Isla Santa Margarita
Sur
El Conejo
El Centenario
LA PAZ
San Pedro
San Antonio
San Juan de los Planes
Los Inocentes
Todos Santos
Santiago
Sta. Rosa
Cabo San Lucas
Tropic of Cancer
PACIFIC
OCEAN
Rocas Alijos
Sierra de Juarez
Sierra de San Pedro Mártir
Lázaro Cárdenas
Ojos Negros
Guadalupe
Cerro Colorado
San Felipe
Punta Estrella
Puertecitos
Misión de S. Fernando
San Agustín
Cataviña
La Bocana
Campo Calamajue
El Crucero
Bahía de Los Angeles
Misión de San Borja
Sierra de San Borja
Bahía de Sebastián Vizcaíno
El Arco
Isla Angel de la Guarda
Punta Refugio
Canal de Ballenas
Isla Tiburón
Isla S. Lorenzo
Isla S. Esteban
Isla San Pedro Mártir
San Francisquito
Punta San Carlos
Bahía San Carlos
Santa Rosalía
Isla Tortuga
I. San Marcos
Mulegé
Punta Concepción
Punta Santa Teresa
Rosarito
Loreto
Isla El Carmen
P. N. Bahía de Loreto
Nopoló
Puerto Escondido
Isla Santa Catalina
Isla Monserat
Isla San José
Pta. Cabeza Mechuda
Bahía Coyote
Isla Espíritu Santo
Pichilingue
Isla Cerralvo
Sierra de la Giganta
Sonora
El Golfo de Santa Clara
El Chinero
Puerto Peñasco
Desierto de Altar
Golfo de California
Sonoyta
Lukeville
San Pedro
El Sahuaro
Caborca
Altar
El Desemboque
Puerto Libertad
Bahía Kino
San Pedro
HERMOSILLO
Pico de Johnson
Punta Baja
Emiliano Zapata
Cholay
Sahuaral
Guaymas
Empalme
Cabo Haro
Isla San Pedro Nolasco
Isla Lobos
Isla Siari
Huivulai
Bacobampo
Huatabampo
Etchoropo
Punta Santa Lugarda
San José
Yaqui
CIUDAD
Esperanza
Cerro Otatal
Ortiz
Villa de Sari
Mazatán
San José de Dimas
Carbó
El Oasis
Benjamin Hill
Meresichic
Santa Ana
Magdalena de Kino
Imuris
Cananea
Nogales
NOGALES
Saric
Cibuta
TUCSON
Marana
Sahuarita
Sonoita
Tubac
Sierra Vista
Benson
Tombstone
Bisbee
Pearce
Willcox
Cochise
Redington
Fronteras
Nacozari de García
Arizpe
Cumpas
Baviácora
Rayón
Ures
Mazocahui
Ajo
Why
Quijotoa
Tohono O'Odham
Indian Reservation
Sells
Microondas
Sierra de S. Antonio
Llanura Sonorense
Costa
38
0 20 40 60 80 100km
0 20 40 60miles

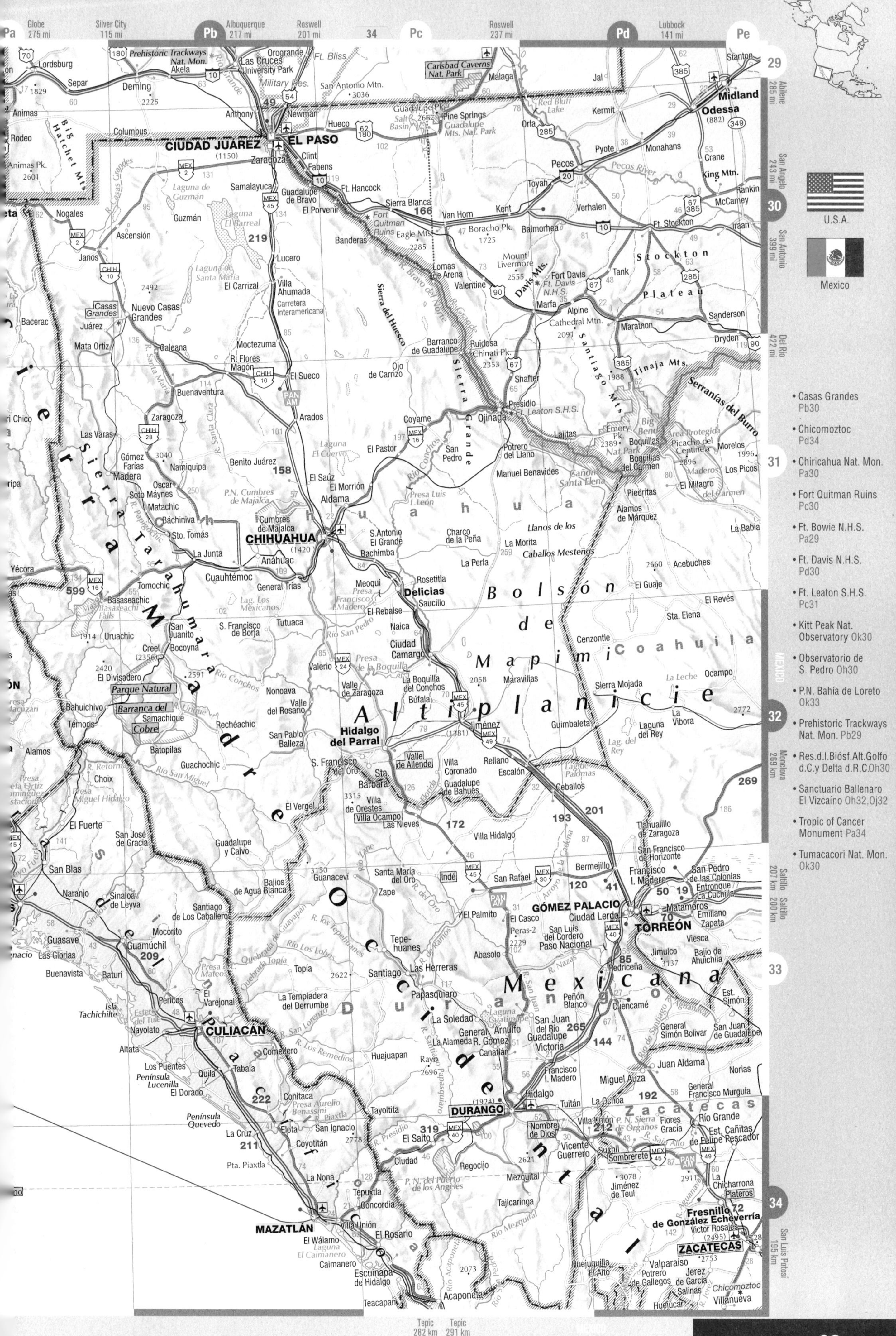

- Casas Grandes Pb30
- Chicomoztoc Pd34
- Chiricahua Nat. Mon. Pa30
- Fort Quitman Ruins Pc30
- Ft. Bowie N.H.S. Pa29
- Ft. Davis N.H.S. Pd30
- Ft. Leaton S.H.S. Pc31
- Kitt Peak Nat. Observatory Ok30
- Observatorio de S. Pedro Oh30
- P.N. Bahía de Loreto Ok33
- Prehistoric Trackways Nat. Mon. Pb29
- Res.d.l.Biósf.Alt.Golfo d.C.y Delta d.R.C.Oh30
- Sanctuario Ballenaro El Vizcaíno Oh32,Oj32
- Tropic of Cancer Monument Pa34
- Tumacacori Nat. Mon. Ok30

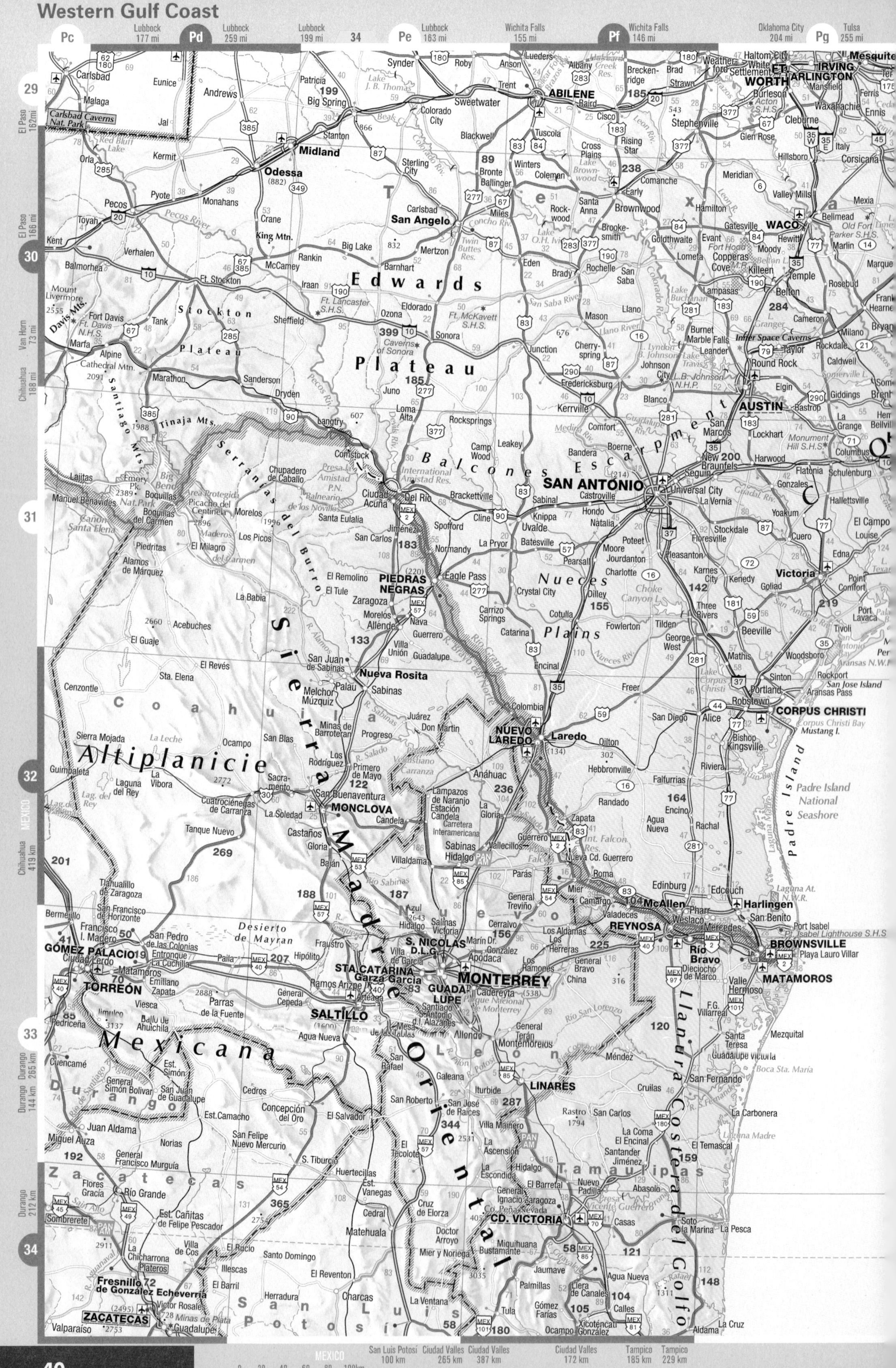
Pc
Lubbock 177 mi
Pd
Lubbock 259 mi
Lubbock 199 mi
34
Pe
Lubbock 163 mi
Wichita Falls 155 mi
Pf
Wichita Falls 146 mi
Oklahoma City 204 mi
Pg
Tulsa 255 mi
29
30
31
32
33
34
El Paso 162 mi
El Paso 166 mi
Van Horn 73 mi
Chihuahua 188 mi
Chihuahua 419 km
Durango 265 km
Durango 144 km
Durango 212 km
MEXICO
Carlsbad
Malaga
Eunice
Andrews
Jal
Carlsbad Caverns Nat. Park
Red Bluff Lake
Orla
Kermit
Odessa
Midland
Big Spring
Colorado City
Snyder
Sweetwater
Roby
Anson
Trent
ABILENE
Albany
Breckenridge
Brad
Strawn
Cisco
Baird
Stephenville
Weatherford
FT. WORTH
IRVING
ARLINGTON
Mesquite
Mansfield
Burleson
Cleburne
Waxahachie
Ennis
Glen Rose
Hillsboro
Corsicana
Italy
Ferris
Pecos
Pyote
Monahans
Crane
Toyah
Kent
Balmorhea
Verhalen
King Mtn.
McCamey
Rankin
Big Lake
Mertzon
San Angelo
Sterling City
Bronte
Ballinger
Winters
Coleman
Tuscola
Blackwell
Cross Plains
Rising Star
Comanche
Brownwood
Early
Santa Anna
Rockwood
Brookesmith
Goldthwaite
Hamilton
Meridian
Valley Mills
WACO
Bellmead
Mexia
Gatesville
Hewitt
Moody
Marlin
Lometa
Evant
Fort Hood
Copperas Cove
Killeen
Temple
Belton
Rosebud
Marquez
Lampasas
Cameron
Lake Buchanan
Burnet
Marble Falls
Inner Space Caverns
Leander
Georgetown
Taylor
Rockdale
Milano
Round Rock
Caldwell
Elgin
Giddings
AUSTIN
Bastrop
La Grange
Lockhart
Monument Hill S.H.S.
Columbus
Flatonia
Schulenburg
Hallettsville
Gonzales
Harwood
Yoakum
Cuero
El Campo
Victoria
Edna
Goliad
Port Lavaca
Tivoli
Rockport
Aransas Pass
Woodsboro
Refugio
Sinton
Portland
CORPUS CHRISTI
Corpus Christi Bay
Mustang I.
Robstown
Bishop
Kingsville
Alice
San Diego
Riviera
Falfurrias
Padre Island National Seashore
Padre Island
Laguna Madre
Ft. Stockton
Iraan
Ozona
Eldorado
Ft. Lancaster S.H.S.
Ft. McKavett S.H.S.
Sonora
Caverns of Sonora
Eden
Brady
Mason
Llano
Junction
Cherry-spring
Fredericksburg
Johnson City
L.B. Johnson N.H.P.
Kerrville
Comfort
Blanco
San Marcos
New Braunfels
Seguin
Boerne
Bandera
SAN ANTONIO
Universal City
La Vernia
Castroville
Hondo
Natalia
Sabinal
Knippa
Uvalde
Stockdale
Floresville
Poteet
Pleasanton
Jourdanton
Karnes City
Kenedy
Three Rivers
Beeville
George West
Tilden
Fowlerton
Cotulla
Dilley
Pearsall
Charlotte
Choke Canyon L.
Moore
Edwards Plateau
Stockton Plateau
Balcones Escarpment
Nueces Plains
Mount Livermore 2555
Davis Mts.
Fort Davis
Fort Davis N.H.S.
Marfa
Alpine
Cathedral Mtn.
Marathon
Tank
Sheffield
Sanderson
Dryden
Langtry
Juno
Loma Alta
Rocksprings
Camp Wood
Leakey
Comstock
Del Rio
Ciudad Acuña
Brackettville
International Amistad Res.
Presa La Amistad
Santiago Mts.
Tinaja Mts.
Lajitas
Big Bend Nat. Park
Boquillas
Manuel Benavides
Boquillas del Carmen
Cañon Santa Elena
Piedritas
El Milagro
Alamos de Marquez
Morelos
Los Picos
Santa Eulalia
Jiménez
San Carlos
Spofford
Cline
La Pryor
Batesville
Normandy
Eagle Pass
PIEDRAS NEGRAS
El Remolino
El Tule
Zaragoza
Morelos
Allende
Nava
Guerrero
Crystal City
Carrizo Springs
Catarina
Encinal
Freer
La Babia
Acebuches
El Guaje
Villa Unión
Guadalupe
San Juan de Sabinas
Nueva Rosita
Palau
Sabinas
Melchor Múzquiz
Minas de Barroterán
Juárez
Don Martín
Progreso
Columbia
NUEVO LAREDO
Laredo
Oilton
Hebbronville
Randado
Encino
Rachal
Agua Nueva
Zapata
Int. Falcon Res.
Nueva Cd. Guerrero
Roma
Edinburg
McAllen
Pharr
Weslaco
Mercedes
Harlingen
San Benito
Port Isabel
BROWNSVILLE
Playa Lauro Villar
MATAMOROS
REYNOSA
Río Bravo
Valle Hermoso
Camargo
Valadeces
Mier
Sierra del Burro
Serranías del Burro
Sierra Madre Oriental
Coahuila
Altiplanicie Mexicana
Sierra Mojada
Ocampo
San Blas
Cenzontle
Sta. Elena
El Revés
Guimbaleta
Laguna del Rey
La Vibora
Cuatrociénegas de Carranza
Sacramento
San Buenaventura
MONCLOVA
La Soledad
Castaños
Candela
Gloria
Bajan
Tanque Nuevo
Primero de Mayo
Lampazos de Naranjo
Anáhuac
Sabinas Hidalgo
Vallecillos
Villaldama
Parás
General Treviño
Cerralvo
Salinas Victoria
Hidalgo
Ciénega de Flores
Marín
Apodaca
S. NICOLAS
Los Ramones
China
General Bravo
Los Herreras
Los Aldamas
Tlahualillo de Zaragoza
Bermejillo
San Francisco de Horizonte
Francisco I. Madero
GÓMEZ PALACIO
Ciudad Lerdo
TORREÓN
Matamoros
San Pedro de las Colonias
La Cuchilla
Emiliano Zapata
Viesca
Parras de la Fuente
Desierto de Mayran
Paila
Hipólito
Frausto
STA.CATARINA
Garza García
MONTERREY
GUADALUPE
Cadereyta
Ramos Arizpe
Arteaga
General Cepeda
SALTILLO
Santiago
Allende
Agua Nueva
General Terán
Montemorelos
LINARES
Méndez
Cruilas
San Fernando
Mezquital
Guadalupe Victoria
Santa Teresa
Boca Sta. María
La Carbonera
Laguna Madre
Llanura Costera del Golfo
Tamaulipas
Nuevo León
Durango
Zacatecas
San Luis Potosí
Cuencamé
Pedriceña
General Simón Bolívar
San Juan de Guadalupe
Juan Aldama
Miguel Auza
Cedros
Concepción del Oro
El Salvador
San Rafael
Galeana
Iturbide
San Roberto
San José de Raíces
Villa Mainero
Rastro
San Carlos
La Coma
El Encinal
Santander Jiménez
El Temascal
Abasolo
Soto la Marina
La Pesca
Casas
CD. VICTORIA
Padilla
Nuevo Padilla
Hidalgo
La Escondida
General Ignacio Zaragoza
El Barretal
La Ascensión
El Tecolote
S. Tiburcio
Huertecillas
Est. Vanegas
Cruz de Elorza
Cedral
Matehuala
Doctor Arroyo
Mier y Noriega
Miquihuana
Bustamante
Jaumave
Palmillas
Llera de Canales
Gómez Farías
Tula
Ocampo
Xicoténcatl
González
Calles
Aldama
La Cruz
Flores
Gracia
Río Grande
General Francisco Murguía
Sombrerete
Est. Cañitas de Felipe Pescador
Villa de Cos
La Chicharrona
Plateros
Fresnillo de González Echeverría
ZACATECAS
Guadalupe
Valparaíso
Santo Domingo
El Reventon
Herradura
Charcas
La Ventana
El Rucio
Illescas
El Barril
San Luis Potosí 100 km
Ciudad Valles 265 km
Ciudad Valles 387 km
Ciudad Valles 172 km
Tampico 185 km
Tampico 229 km
0 20 40 60 80 100km
0 20 40 60miles

- Acton S.H.S. Pg29
- Caverns of Sonora Pe30
- Fort Massachusetts Qa30
- Fort Polk Pj30
- Ft. Davis N.H.S. Pd30
- Ft. Jackson Qa31
- Ft. Lancaster S.H.S. Pe30
- Ft. McKavett S.H.S. Pe30
- Grand I.S.P. Pk31
- Hodges Gardens Pj30
- Inner Space Caverns Pg30
- L.B. Johnson N.H.P. Pf30
- Minas de Plata Pd34
- Monument Hill S.H.S. Pg31
- Old Fort Parker S.H.S. Pg30
- Pt. Isabel Lighthouse S.H.S. Pg32

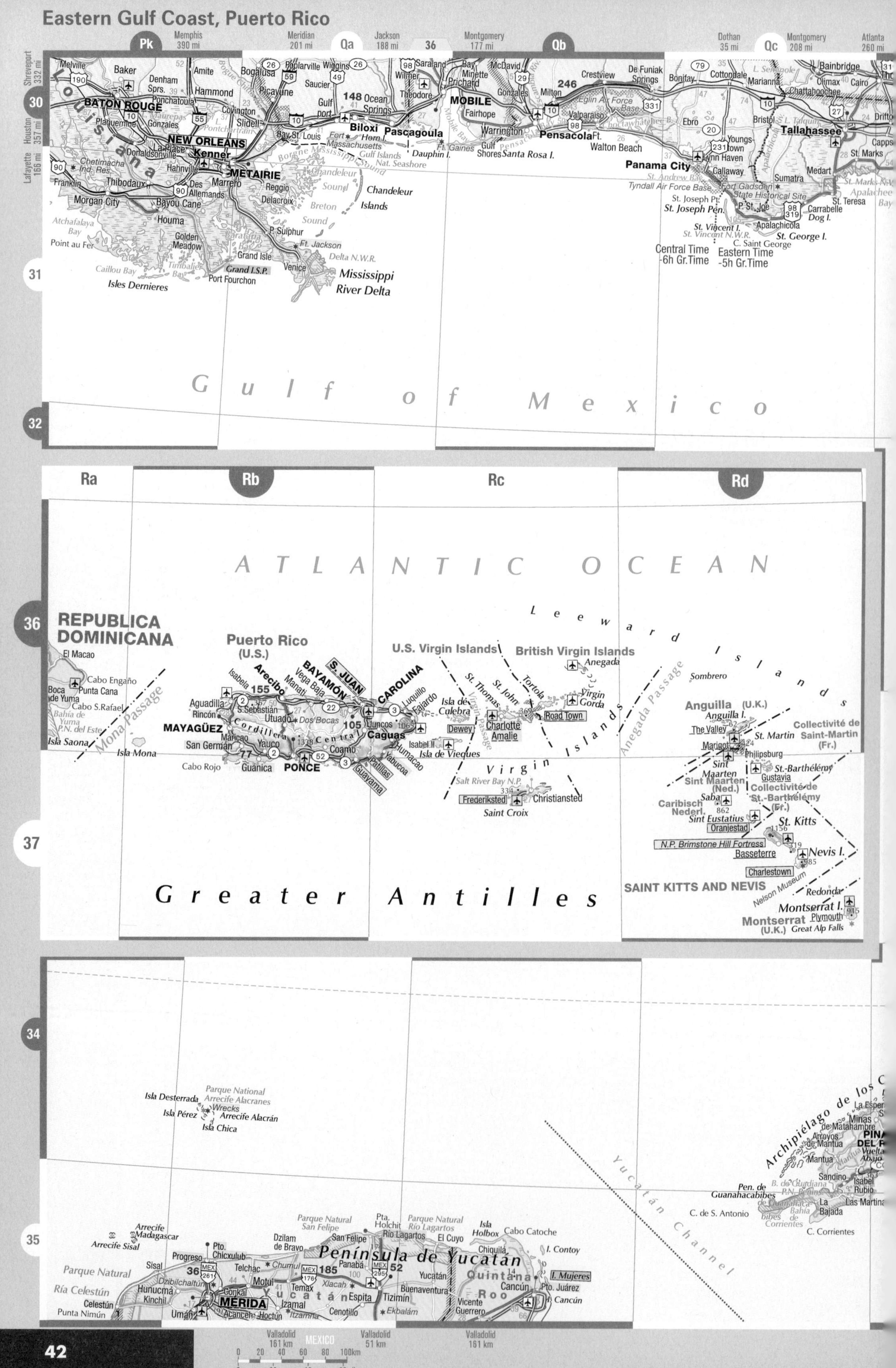

Gulf of Mexico
BATON ROUGE
NEW ORLEANS
Kenner
METAIRIE
Biloxi
Pascagoula
MOBILE
Pensacola
Panama City
Tallahassee
Mississippi River Delta
Central Time -6h Gr.Time
Eastern Time -5h Gr.Time
ATLANTIC OCEAN
REPUBLICA DOMINICANA
Puerto Rico (U.S.)
S. JUAN
BAYAMÓN
CAROLINA
MAYAGÜEZ
PONCE
Caguas
Mona Passage
U.S. Virgin Islands
British Virgin Islands
Leeward Islands
Virgin Islands
Anegada Passage
Anguilla (U.K.)
Collectivité de Saint-Martin (Fr.)
Sint Maarten (Ned.)
Collectivité de St.-Barthélemy (Fr.)
Caribisch Nederl.
SAINT KITTS AND NEVIS
Montserrat (U.K.)
Greater Antilles
Yucatán Channel
Archipiélago de los Canarreos
Península de Yucatán
MÉRIDA
Quintana Roo
Cancún
Valladolid 161 km
MEXICO
Valladolid 51 km
Valladolid 161 km
0 20 40 60 80 100km
0 20 40 60miles

- Castillo de San Marcos Nat. Mon. Qu31
- Chumul Qa35
- Congo Town Qg33
- Crystal River St. Arch.S. Qd31
- Cypress Gardens Qe32
- De Soto Nat. Mon. Qd32
- Dzibilchaltún Qa35
- Ekbalám Qa35
- Fort Gadsden State Historical Site Qc31
- Fort Jefferson Nat. Mem. Qd33
- Fort Massachusetts Qa30
- Fort Matanzas Nat. Mon. Qe31
- Ft. Caroline Nat. Mem. Qe30
- Ft. Gaines Qa30
- Ft. Jackson Qa31
- Grand I.S.P. Pk31
- Hole in the Wall Qg33
- Itzamna Qa35
- Kennedy Space Center Qe31
- Marineland of Florida Qe31
- V. Viñales Qd34
- Wrecks Qa34
- Xlacah Qa35

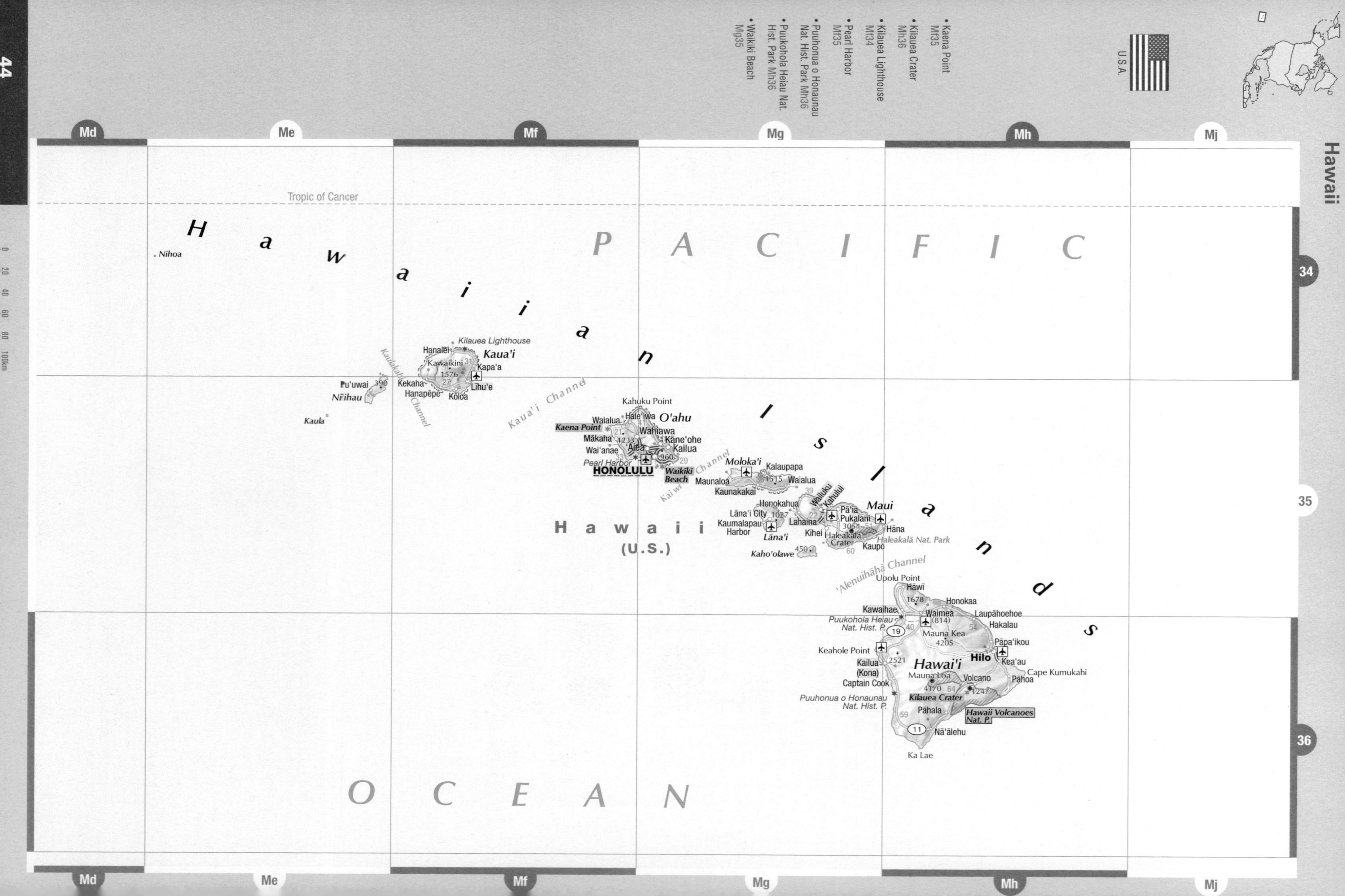

- Kaena Point Mf35
- Kilauea Crater Mh36
- Kilauea Lighthouse Mf34
- Pearl Harbor Mf35
- Puuhonua o Honaunau Nat. Hist. Park Mh36
- Puukohola Heiau Nat. Hist. Park Mh36
- Waikiki Beach Mg35

Kalifornien
1:800 000 / 1cm = 8km

Photo: Transamerica Gebäude, San Francisco, Kalifornien (DuMont Bildarchiv, Christian Heeb)

Fm
Coos Bay
77 mi
Fn
Fo
Eugene
138 mi
Fp
Oregon
95
96
97
98
Blacklock Pt.
Oregon Islands N.W.R.
Cape Blanco
Cape Blanco S.P.
Paradise Pt. S.W.
Denmark
Port Orford Cedar Forest S.W.
Sixes
Edson Butte
849
Sugarloaf Mtn.
778
Powers
877
Eden Ridge
COAST
RANGES
Garrison L.
Port Orford
Port Orford Heads S.W.
The Heads
Grassy Knob Wilderness
Barklow Mtn.
1091
1316
1204
Humbug Mtn. S.P.
Humbug Mtn.
535
927
Rocky Pk.
1242
Iron Mtn.
Marial
Prehistoric Gardens
633
Sisters Rocks
Ophir
Siskiyou
Wild Rogue Wilderness
Illahe
Brandy Pk.
5316
Sawtooth Rock
1056
Agness
Agness-Illahe Hist. Center
1533
767
Nesika Beach
Geisel Mon. S.W.
Otter Pt. S.W.
Wedderburn
Signal Buttes
1070
Gold Beach
Curry Co. Hist. Mus.
713
101
Saddle Mtn.
1339
Buena Vista Ocean S.W.
Cape Sebastian S.P.
Cape Sebastian
648
Pistol River
Pistol River S.P.
Crook Pt.
Carpenterville
Bosley Butte
1046
Samuel H. Boardman S.P.
52
Carpenterville-Brookings Forest S.W.
Loeb S.P.
Mt. Emily
892
Cape Ferrelo
Azalea S.P.
Harris S.B.
Brookings
Harbor
Chetco Valley Hist. Mus.
McVay Rock S.W.
Silver Pk.
1258
National
Collier Butte
1323
1408
Big Craggies
Kalmiopsis
Chetco R.
Forest
Wilderness
Pearsoll Pk.
5098
1419
Chetco Pk.
1420
Dutchman Butte
1191
West Fork
Rogue River
1224
Mt. Peavine
1230
Rand
Galice
Onion Mtn.
1353
Klamath Mountains
Canyon Creek Forest S.W.
Silver Butte
1211
Grayback
1226
Fortune Branch
Azalea
Cedar Springs Mtn.
1528
Cow Creek Gorge
Glendale
Stagecoach Forest S.W.
Wolf Creek
Wolf Creek Tavern S.W.
Mackin Gulch Forest S.W.
King Mtn.
1605
Round Top
1388
Leland
1072
Placer
Sunny Valley
Battle Mtn.
1214
1230
Hugo
Sexton Mtn.
1169
Elk Mtn.
1351
Wimer
Merlin
Grants Pass
Sams Valley
234
Table Rock
Josephine Co. Hist. Soc.
99
Rogue River
Gold Hill
Tolo
Valley of the Rogue S.P.
Ben Hur Lampman S.W.
Seven Oaks
Central Point
Pacific N.W. Mus. of Natural History
Wilderville
Wonder
238
Applegate River
Murphy
199
Squaw Mtn.
1433
Roundtop Mtn.
1430
Mt. Isabelle
1370
Jacksonville N.H. Landmark
Jacksonville
Selma
Dryden
Provolt
Applegate
1220
Mungers Butte
Williams
Ruch
Kirbyville Mus.
Kerby
Canyon Pk.
1494
Cave Junction
46
Tallowbox Mtn.
1531
Illinois R. S.P.
Bridgeview
Holland
1598
Grayback Mtn.
2150
Rough & Ready S.W.
O'Brien
Oregon Caves N.M.
Craggy Mtn.
1930
Rogue River
Little Grayback Mtn.
1550
Takilma
Siskiyou National Forest
Lake Pk.
2024
Copper
Gateway S.W.
Winchuck S.W.
Pelican S.B.
Smith River Rancheria
Prince I.
Smith River
Ship Ashore Mus.
High Plateau Mtn.
1065
Smith River
80
Horse Flat
Sanger Pk.
1787
1834
Thompson Ridge
Red Butte Wild.
National Forest
1672
Red Butte
2054
Condrey Mtn.
2168
Siskiyou Mountains
Patrick Creek
889
Washington Pk.
Ft. Dick
Gasquet
197
Lakes Earl and Talawa
Earl
Preston Pk.
2228
Baldy Mtn.
1751
Fort Goff
Seiad Valley
1206
96
1303
Horse Creek
Pt. St. George
Undersea World
Crescent City
Battery Pt. Lighthouse Mus.
Hiouchi
Jedediah Smith Redwoods S.P.
Gordon Mtn.
1266
Natl. Rec. Area
1606
Ship Mtn.
Happy Camp
Karok Ind. Res.
Klamath
National
Hamburg
Forest
Crescent Beach
Del Norte Coast Redwoods S.P.
Clear Creek
Bear Pk.
1750
Lake Mtn.
2104
Scott Bar
Scott Bar Mt.
1276
545
Rattlesnake Mtn.
1115
Sawtooth Mtn.
1762
Siskiyou Wilderness
Kings Castle
2257
PACIFIC
Trees of Mystery
145
Marble Mountains
Ukonom Lake
1292
Oro F
Mugginsville
Greenview
Klamath
Requa
Resighini Rancheria
Klamath Glen
Red Mtn.
1300
Dillon Mtn.
1426
Medicine Mtn.
2084
Marble Mountains Wilderness
2364
Native Daughters of the Golden West Mus.
Etna
Bear Wallow Pk.
Prairie Creek Redwoods S.P.
OCEAN
Trail Mtn.
1473
Offield Mtn.
1254
Hancock Lake
Klamath
Blue Creek Mtn.
Yurok Ind. Res.
Johnsons
Somes Bar
Chimney Rock
2095
Yellow Dog Pk.
Snowden
978
76
Holter Ridge
Lady Bird Johnson Grove
Orick
169
Orleans
Orleans Mtn.
1887
Salmon Mountains
National
N. Fk. Salmon R.
Sawyers Bar
Russian Pk.
2498
Redwood Nat. Park
Humboldt Lagoons S.P.
Burrill Pk.
1326
Forks of Salmon
2091
Harry A. Merlo S.R.A.
Big Lagoon Rancheria
1227
Weitchpec
Salmon Mtn.
2120
Black Bear
Forest
2359
Patricks Pt. S.P.
Patricks Point
Rodgers Pk.
850
Schoolhouse Pk.
942
Redwood Creek
Pine Ridge
Hoopa Valley Indian Res.
1297
Cecilville
1939
Dees Peak
2105
Packers Pk.
2386
Trinidad S.B.
Trinidad
Trinidad Head
Trinidad Rancheria
440
Hupe Mtn.
1248
802
Hoopa
Westhaven
Trinity Mtn.
1857
McKinleyville
72 mi
50
Willow Creek
145 mi
California
0 20 40 60 20km
0 4 8 12miles

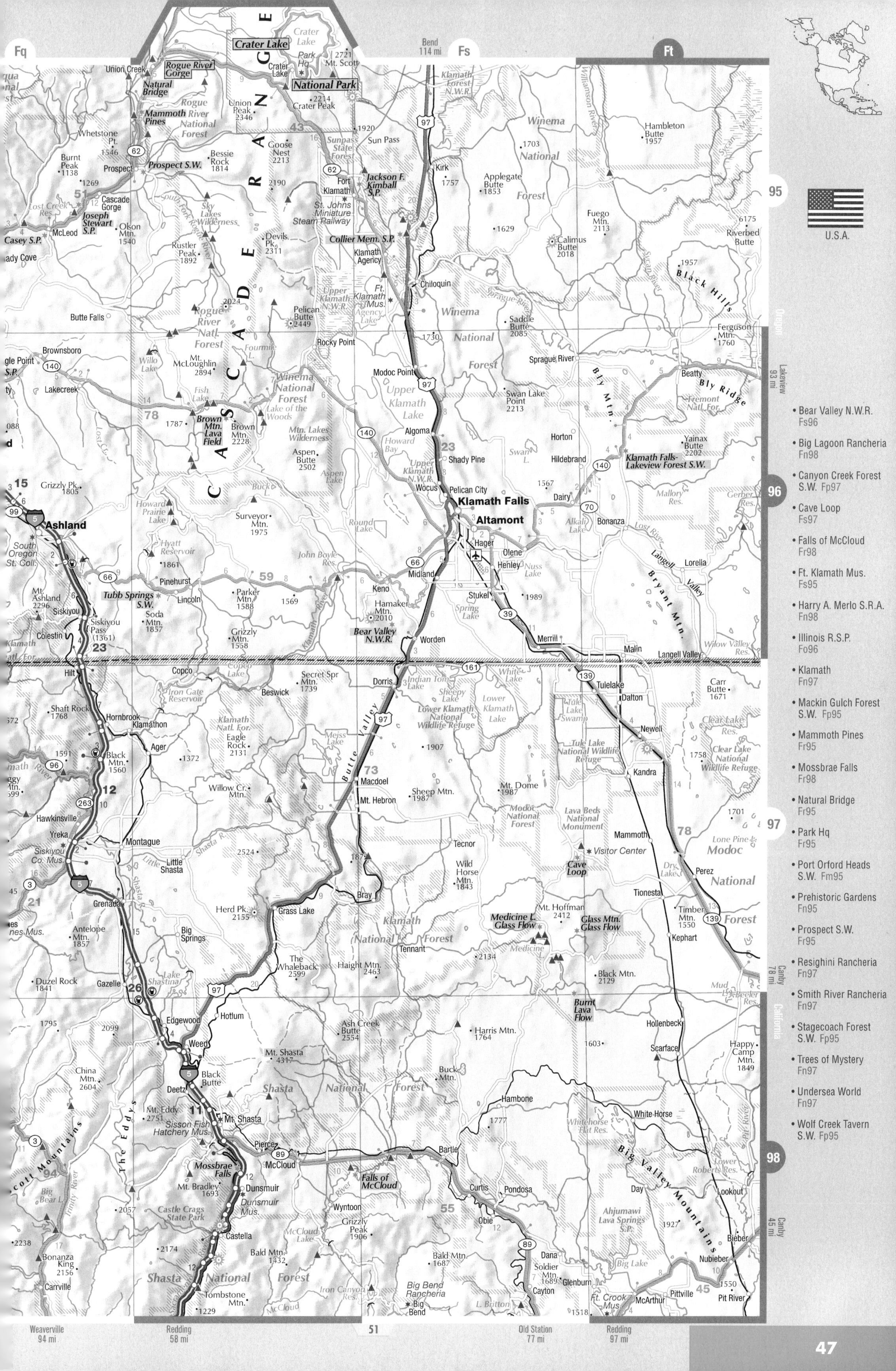

Fq
Fs
Ft
Bend
114 mi
Crater Lake
Crater Lake
Park Hq
2721 Mt. Scott
National Park
2214 Crater Peak
Rogue River Gorge
Natural Bridge
Union Creek
Rogue River National Forest
Mammoth Pines
Union Peak 2346
Whetstone Pt. 1546
Burnt Peak 1138
Prospect
Prospect S.W.
Bessie Rock 1814
Goose Nest 2213
2190
1920
Sun Pass
Sunpass State Forest
Jackson F. Kimball S.P.
Fort Klamath
St. Johns Miniature Steam Railway
Collier Mem. S.P.
Klamath Agency
Chiloquin
Ft. Klamath Mus.
Upper Klamath N.W.R.
Agency Lake
Kirk
1757
Klamath Forest N.W.R.
Winema
1703
National
Forest
Applegate Butte 1853
1629
Calimus Butte 2018
Fuego Mtn. 2113
Hambleton Butte 1957
6175
Riverbed Butte
1957
Black Hills
Ferguson Mtn. 1760
Williamson River
Sycan River
Sprague River
Cascade Gorge
Joseph Stewart S.P.
Lost Creek Res.
Olson Mtn. 1540
McLeod
Casey S.P.
Shady Cove
Rustler Peak 1892
Sky Lakes Wilderness
South Fork Rogue River
Devils Pk. 2311
2024
Rogue River Natl. Forest
Butte Falls
Pelican Butte 2449
Rocky Point
Winema National Forest
Saddle Butte 2085
Sprague River
Bly Mtn.
Beatty
Bly Ridge
Fremont Natl. For.
Brownsboro
Eagle Point
Lakecreek
Willow Lake
Mt. McLoughlin 2894
Fourmile L.
Fish Lake
Lake of the Woods
Brown Mtn. Lava Field
Brown Mtn. 2228
1787
Mtn. Lakes Wilderness
Aspen Butte 2502
Aspen Lake
Modoc Point
Upper Klamath Lake
Howard Bay
Algoma
Shady Pine
Upper Klamath N.W.R.
Wocus
Pelican City
Klamath Falls
Altamont
Swan Lake Point 2213
Swan L.
Horton
Hildebrand
1730
Yainax Butte 2202
Klamath Falls-Lakeview Forest S.W.
1567
Dairy
Alkali Lake
Bonanza
Mallory Res.
Gerber Res.
Lost River
Langell Valley
Lorella
Bryant Mtn.
Cascade Range
Grizzly Pk. 1805
Ashland
South Oregon St. Coll.
Howard Prairie Lake
Hyatt Reservoir
Buck L.
Surveyor Mtn. 1975
John Boyle Res.
Round Lake
Hager
Olene
Henley
Nuss Lake
1861
Pinehurst
Tubb Springs S.W.
Lincoln
Parker Mtn. 1588
1569
Soda Mtn. 1857
Keno
Midland
Hamaker Mtn. 2010
Bear Valley N.W.R.
Stukel
1989
Spring Lake
Mt. Ashland 2296
Siskiyou
Siskiyou Pass (1361)
Colestin
Grizzly Mtn. 1558
Klamath River
Worden
Merrill
Malin
Langell Valley
Willow Valley Res.
Hilt
Copco
Copco Lake
Iron Gate Reservoir
Beswick
Secret Spr Mtn. 1739
Dorris
Indian Tom Lake
Sheepy Lake
White Lake
Lower Klamath National Wildlife Refuge
Lower Klamath Lake
Tulelake
Dalton
Carr Butte 1671
Shaft Rock 1768
Hornbrook
Klamathon
Klamath Natl. For.
Eagle Rock 2131
Meiss Lake
Butte Valley
1907
Tule Lake Swamp
Tule Lake National Wildlife Refuge
Newell
Clear Lake Res.
Clear Lake National Wildlife Refuge
1758
Ager
1372
Black Mtn. 1560
1591
Klamath River
Macdoel
Mt. Hebron
Sheep Mtn. 1987
Mt. Dome 1987
Kandra
Willow Cr. Mtn.
Hawkinsville
Modoc National Forest
Lava Beds National Monument
1701
Yreka
Siskiyou Co. Mus.
Montague
Tecnor
Mammoth
Lone Pine
Modoc
Visitor Center
Little Shasta
2524
1872
Wild Horse Mtn. 1843
Cave Loop
Dry Lake
Perez
National
Shasta R.
Little Shasta
Grenada
Bray
Tionesta
Herd Pk. 2155
Grass Lake
Klamath
Mt. Hoffman 2412
Timber Mtn. 1550
Antelope Mtn. 1857
Medicine L. Glass Flow
Glass Mtn. Glass Flow
Forest
National
Forest
Kephart
Big Springs
Tennant
Medicine L.
2134
The Whaleback 2599
Haight Mtn. 2463
Black Mtn. 2129
Duzel Rock 1841
Gazelle
Lake Shastina
Mud L.
Beeler Res.
Burnt Lava Flow
Edgewood
Hotlum
Weed
1795
2099
Ash Creek Butte 2554
Harris Mtn. 1764
1603
Hollenbeck
Scarface
Happy Camp Mtn. 1849
China Mtn. 2604
Mt. Shasta 4317
Black Butte
Shasta
National
Forest
Buck Mtn.
Deetz
Hambone
Mt. Eddy 2751
The Eddys
Sisson Fish Hatchery Mus.
Mt. Shasta
1777
White Horse
Whitehorse Flat Res.
Big Valley Mountains
Scott Mountains
Pierce
McCloud
Bartle
Mossbrae Falls
Falls of McCloud
Lower Roberts Res.
Mt. Bradley 1693
Dunsmuir
Dunsmuir Mus.
Curtis
Pondosa
Day
Lookout
Big Bear L.
Trinity River
2057
Castle Crags State Park
Wyntoon
Obie
Ahjumawi Lava Springs S.P.
1927
2238
Castella
McCloud Lake
Grizzly Peak 1906
Bieber
Bonanza King 2156
2174
Bald Mtn. 1432
Bald Mtn. 1687
Dana
Nubieber
Carrville
Shasta
National
Forest
Soldier Mtn. 1689
Glenburn
Big Lake
Tombstone Mtn.
Iron Canyon Res.
Big Bend Rancheria
Big Bend
Cayton
L. Britton
1518
Ft. Crook Mus.
McArthur
Pittville
1550
Pit River
1229
Pit River
Weaverville 94 mi
Redding 58 mi
51
Old Station 77 mi
Redding 97 mi
Lakeview 93 mi
Canby 78 mi
Canby 45 mi
Oregon
California
95
96
97
98
U.S.A.
• Bear Valley N.W.R. Fs96
• Big Lagoon Rancheria Fn98
• Canyon Creek Forest S.W. Fp97
• Cave Loop Fs97
• Falls of McCloud Fr98
• Ft. Klamath Mus. Fs95
• Harry A. Merlo S.R.A. Fn98
• Illinois R.S.P. Fo96
• Klamath Fn97
• Mackin Gulch Forest S.W. Fp95
• Mammoth Pines Fr95
• Mossbrae Falls Fr98
• Natural Bridge Fr95
• Park Hq Fr95
• Port Orford Heads S.W. Fm95
• Prehistoric Gardens Fn95
• Prospect S.W. Fr95
• Resighini Rancheria Fn97
• Smith River Rancheria Fn97
• Stagecoach Forest S.W. Fp95
• Trees of Mystery Fn97
• Undersea World Fn97
• Wolf Creek Tavern S.W. Fp95

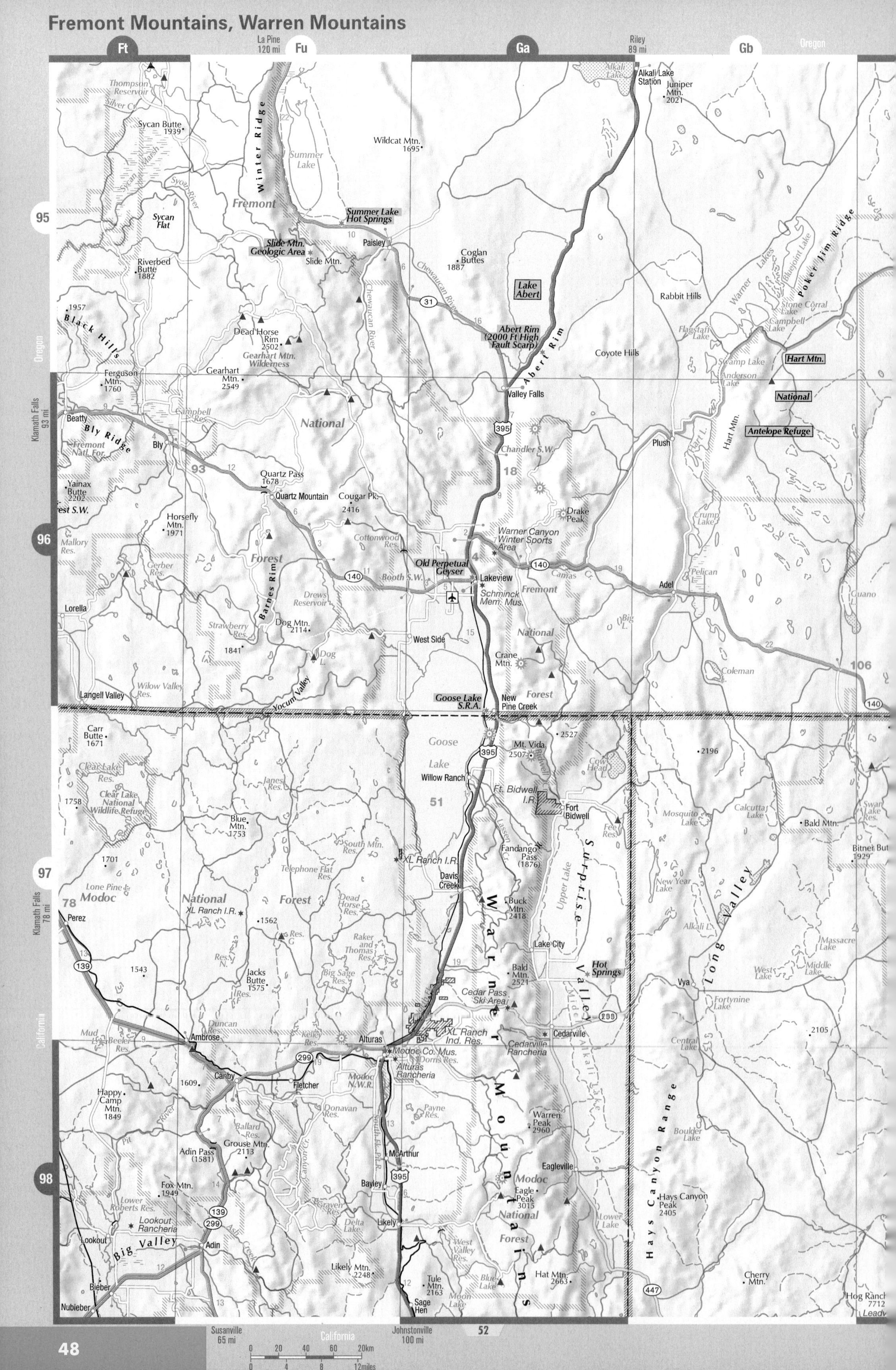
Fremont Mountains, Warren Mountains
Ft
Fu
Ga
Gb
La Pine 120 mi
Riley 89 mi
Oregon
95
96
97
98
106
Klamath Falls 93 mi
Klamath Falls 78 mi
Thompson Reservoir
Sycan Butte 1939
Winter Ridge
Summer Lake
Wildcat Mtn. 1695
Alkali Lake
Alkali Lake Station
Juniper Mtn. 2021
Sycan Flat
Fremont
Summer Lake Hot Springs
Slide Mtn. Geologic Area
Slide Mtn.
Paisley
Riverbed Butte 1882
Coglan Buttes 1887
Chewaucan River
Lake Abert
Rabbit Hills
Warner Lakes
Bluejoint Lake
Poker Jim Ridge
Stone Corral Lake
Campbell Lake
Flagstaff Lake
Black Hills
Dead Horse Rim 2502
Gearhart Mtn. Wilderness
Abert Rim (2000 Ft High Fault Scarp)
Abert Rim
Coyote Hills
Swamp Lake
Anderson Lake
Hart Mtn.
National
Antelope Refuge
Ferguson Mtn. 1760
Gearhart Mtn. 2549
Valley Falls
Beatty
Bly Ridge
Fremont Natl. For.
Bly
Campbell Res.
National
Chandler S.W.
Plush
Hart L.
Yainax Butte 2202
Quartz Pass 1678
Quartz Mountain
Cougar Pk. 2416
Drake Peak
Horsefly Mtn. 1971
Mallory Res.
Warner Canyon Winter Sports Area
Crump Lake
Cottonwood Res.
Forest
Gerber Res.
Barnes Rim
Old Perpetual Geyser
Booth S.W.
Lakeview
Schminck Mem. Mus.
Fremont
Camas Cr.
Adel
Pelican
Guano
Lorella
Drews Reservoir
Strawberry Res.
Dog Mtn. 2114
West Side
National
Big L.
Crane Mtn.
Dog L.
Coleman
Langell Valley
Wilow Valley Res.
Yocum Valley
Goose Lake S.R.A.
New Pine Creek
Forest
Carr Butte 1671
Goose Lake
Mt. Vida 2507
2527
2196
Clear Lake Res.
Clear Lake National Wildlife Refuge
Janes Res.
Willow Ranch
Cow Head L.
Ft. Bidwell I.R.
Fort Bidwell
1758
Blue Mtn. 1753
Mosquito Lake
Calcutta Lake
Swan Lake Res.
Bald Mtn.
Fee Res.
South Mtn. Res.
Fandango Pass (1876)
Surprise
XL Ranch I.R.
Bitner Butte 1929
1701
Telephone Flat Res.
Davis Creek
Upper Lake
New Year Lake
Long Valley
Lone Pine L.
Modoc
National
Forest
Dead Horse Res.
Buck Mtn. 2418
Warner
Perez
XL Ranch I.R.
1562
Res. G
Raker and Thomas Res.
Lake City
Alkali L.
Massacre Lake
Res. N.
Hot Springs
Valley
West Lake
Middle Lake
1543
Jacks Butte 1575
Big Sage Res.
Bald Mtn. 2521
Vya
Cedar Pass Ski Area
Fortynine Lake
Duncan Res.
Kelley Res.
Alturas
XL Ranch Ind. Res.
Cedarville
Mud L.
Beeler Res.
Ambrose
Modoc Co. Mus.
Dorris Res.
Cedarville Rancheria
Middle Alkali Lake
Central Lake
2105
Alturas Rancheria
Canby
1609
Fletcher
Modoc N.W.R.
Mountains
Happy Camp Mtn. 1849
Donavan Res.
Payne Res.
Warren Peak 2960
Ballard Res.
Grouse Mtn. 2113
Adin Pass (1581)
McArthur
Hays Canyon Range
Boulder Lake
Eagleville
Fox Mtn. 1949
Bayley
Modoc
Eagle Peak 3015
Hays Canyon Peak 2405
Lower Roberts Res.
Lookout Rancheria
Graven Res.
Delta Lake
Likely
National
Lower Lake
Lookout
Big Valley
Adin
Forest
West Valley Res.
Likely Mtn. 2248
Hat Mtn. 2663
Bieber
Tule Mtn. 2163
Blue Lake
Cherry Mtn.
Nubieber
Sage Hen
Moon Lake
Hog Ranch 7712
Leadv
California
Susanville 65 mi
Johnstonville 100 mi
52
0 20 40 60 20km
0 4 8 12miles

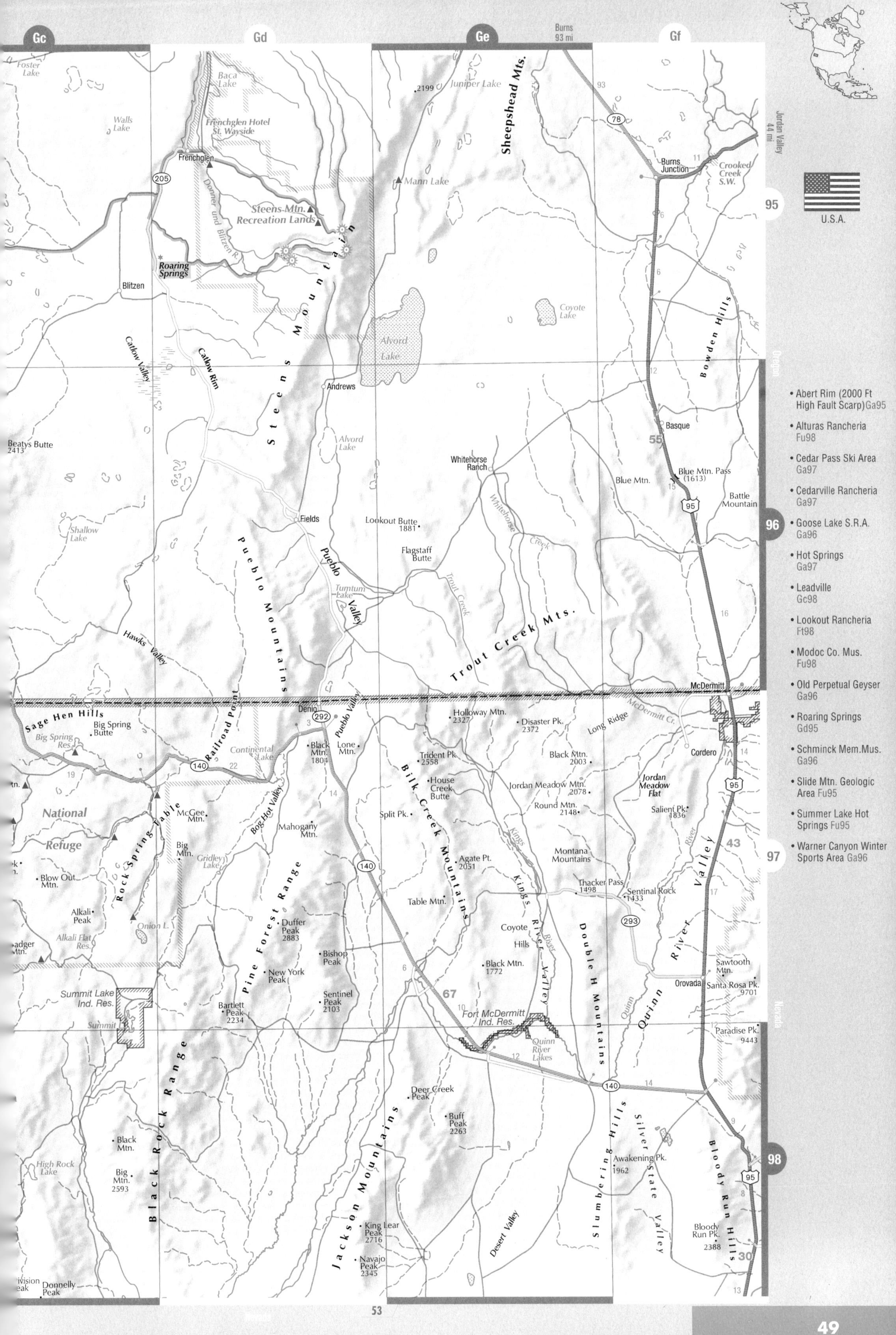

- Abert Rim (2000 Ft High Fault Scarp) Ga95
- Alturas Rancheria Fu98
- Cedar Pass Ski Area Ga97
- Cedarville Rancheria Ga97
- Goose Lake S.R.A. Ga96
- Hot Springs Ga97
- Leadville Gc98
- Lookout Rancheria Ft98
- Modoc Co. Mus. Fu98
- Old Perpetual Geyser Ga96
- Roaring Springs Gd95
- Schminck Mem.Mus. Ga96
- Slide Mtn. Geologic Area Fu95
- Summer Lake Hot Springs Fu95
- Warner Canyon Winter Sports Area Ga96

53

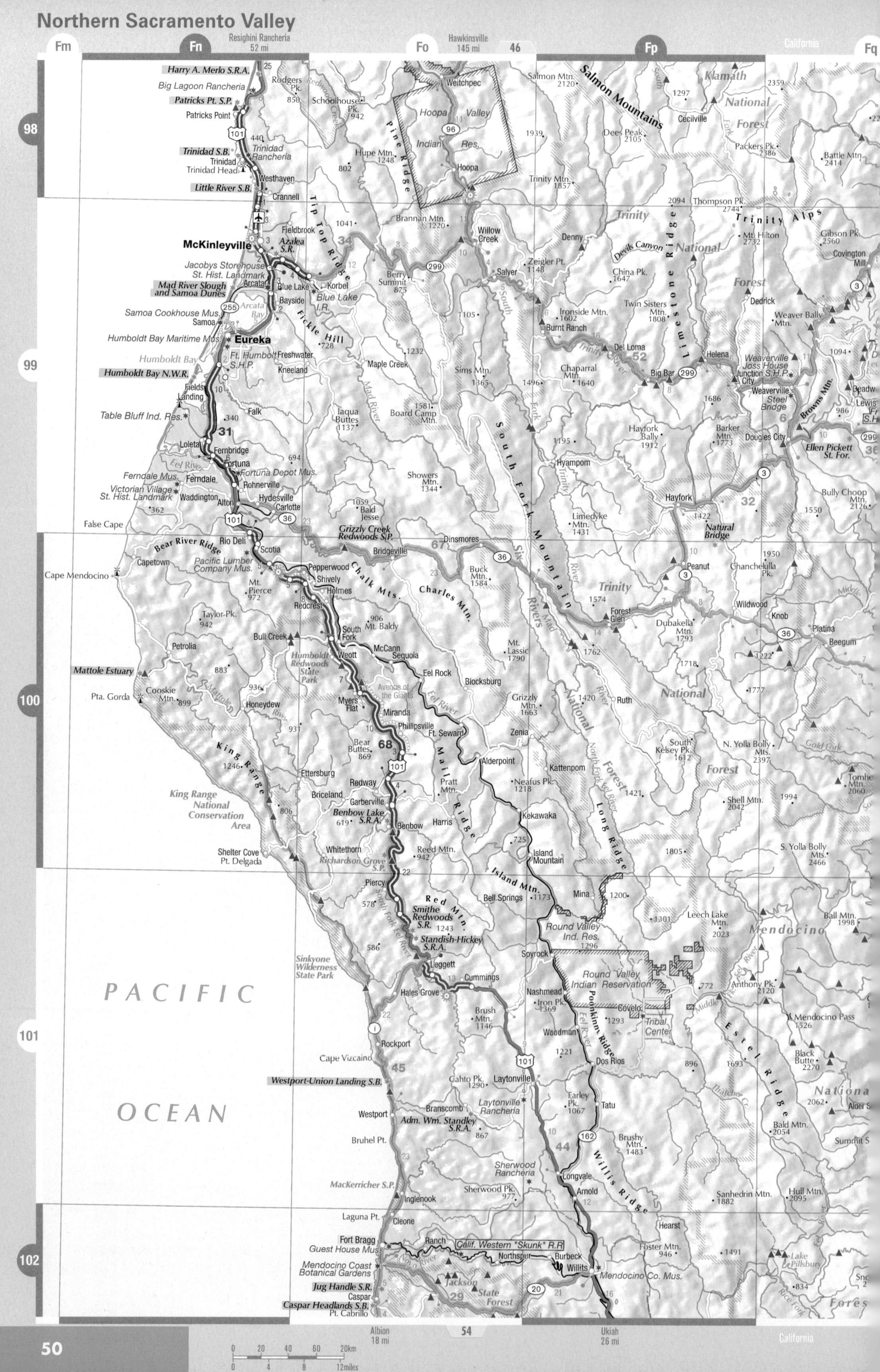
Fm
Fn
Fo
Fp
Fq
Resighini Rancheria
52 mi
Hawkinsville
145 mi
46
California
98
99
100
101
102
Harry A. Merlo S.R.A.
Big Lagoon Rancheria
Patricks Pt. S.P.
Patricks Point
Trinidad S.B.
Trinidad Rancheria
Trinidad
Trinidad Head
Westhaven
Little River S.B.
Crannell
Fieldbrook
McKinleyville
Azalea S.R.
Jacobys Storehouse St. Hist. Landmark
Mad River Slough and Samoa Dunes
Arcata
Blue Lake
Korbel
Blue Lake I.R.
Bayside
Samoa Cookhouse Mus.
Samoa
Arcata Bay
Humboldt Bay Maritime Mus.
Eureka
Humboldt Bay
Humboldt Bay N.W.R.
Ft. Humboldt S.H.P.
Freshwater
Kneeland
Fields Landing
Table Bluff Ind. Res.
Falk
Loleta
Fernbridge
Fortuna
Fortuna Depot Mus.
Eel River
Ferndale Mus.
Ferndale
Rohnerville
Victorian Village St. Hist. Landmark
Waddington
Alton
Hydesville
Carlotte
False Cape
Rio Dell
Scotia
Bear River Ridge
Capetown
Cape Mendocino
Pacific Lumber Company Mus.
Mt. Pierce
Taylor Pk.
Petrolia
Mattole Estuary
Pta. Gorda
Cooskie Mtn.
Honeydew
King Range
King Range National Conservation Area
Shelter Cove
Pt. Delgada
Rodgers Pk.
Schoolhouse Pk.
Redwood Creek
Pine Ridge
Hupe Mtn.
Tip Top Ridge
Fickle Hill
Maple Creek
Mad River
Iaqua Buttes
Board Camp Mtn.
Showers Mtn.
Bald Jesse
Grizzly Creek Redwoods S.P.
Bridgeville
Pepperwood
Shively
Holmes
Redcrest
Chalk Mts.
Charles Mtn.
Mt. Baldy
South Fork
Bull Creek
Humboldt Redwoods State Park
Weott
McCann
Sequoia
Eel Rock
Avenue of the Giants
Myers Flat
Miranda
Phillipsville
Ft. Seward
Bear Buttes
Ettersburg
Briceland
Redway
Garberville
Benbow Lake S.R.A.
Benbow
Harris
Mail Ridge
Pratt Mtn.
Whitethorn
Richardson Grove S.P.
Reed Mtn.
Piercy
Red Mtn.
Smithe Redwoods S.R.
Standish-Hickey S.R.A.
Sinkyone Wilderness State Park
Leggett
Cummings
Hales Grove
Rockport
Cape Vizcaino
Westport-Union Landing S.B.
Westport
Bruhel Pt.
MacKerricher S.P.
Inglenook
Laguna Pt.
Cleone
Fort Bragg
Guest House Mus.
Mendocino Coast Botanical Gardens
Jug Handle S.R.
Caspar
Caspar Headlands S.B.
Pt. Cabrillo
Noyo River
Ranch
Calif. Western "Skunk" R.R.
Northspur
Jackson State Forest
Burbeck
Willits
Mendocino Co. Mus.
PACIFIC
OCEAN
Weitchpec
Hoopa Valley Indian Res.
Hoopa
Brannan Mtn.
Willow Creek
Berry Summit
Salyer
South Fork
Sims Mtn.
Salmon Mtn.
Salmon Mountains
Trinity Mtn.
Denny
Zeigler Pt.
Ironside Mtn.
Burnt Ranch
Chaparral Mtn.
Del Loma
Trinity River
South Fork Mountain
Hyampom
Limedyke Mtn.
Dinsmores
Buck Mtn.
Six Rivers
Mad River
Forest Glen
Mt. Lassic
Blocksburg
Grizzly Mtn.
Zenia
Alderpoint
Neafus Pk.
Kekawaka
Island Mountain
Island Mtn.
Bell Springs
Kattenpom
Mina
National Forest
North Fork Eel River
Long Ridge
Ruth
Round Valley Ind. Res.
Spyrock
Round Valley Indian Reservation
Nashmead
Iron Pk.
Covelo
Tribal Center
Poonkinny Ridge
Eel River
Woodman
Dos Rios
Brush Mtn.
Gahto Pk.
Laytonville
Laytonville Rancheria
Branscomb
Adm. Wm. Standley S.R.A.
Farley Pk.
Tatu
Brushy Mtn.
Sherwood Rancheria
Sherwood Pk.
Longvale
Arnold
Willis Ridge
Hearst
Foster Mtn.
Klamath National Forest
Cecilville
Dees Peak
Packers Pk.
Battle Mtn.
Thompson Pk.
Trinity Alps
Mt. Hilton
Gibson Pk.
Covington Mill
Trinity National Forest
Devils Canyon
Limestone Ridge
China Pk.
Twin Sisters Mtn.
Dedrick
Weaver Bally Mtn.
Helena
Big Bar
Weaverville Joss House S.H.P.
Junction City
Weaverville
Steel Bridge
Browns Mtn.
Hayfork Bally
Barker Mtn.
Douglas City
Ellen Pickett St. For.
Hayfork
Bully Choop Mtn.
Natural Bridge
Peanut
Chanchelulla Pk.
Trinity
Wildwood
Dubakella Mtn.
Knob
Platina
Beegum
National
South Kelsey Pk.
N. Yolla Bolly Mts.
Forest
Shell Mtn.
S. Yolla Bolly Mts.
Leech Lake Mtn.
Mendocino
Ball Mtn.
Anthony Pk.
Mendocino Pass
Estel Ridge
Black Butte
Thatcher Cr.
National
Alder Spr.
Bald Mtn.
Sanhedrin Mtn.
Hull Mtn.
Lake Pillsbury
Rice Fork
Gold Fork
Tomhead Mtn.
Albion
18 mi
54
Ukiah
26 mi
0 20 40 60 20km
0 4 8 12miles

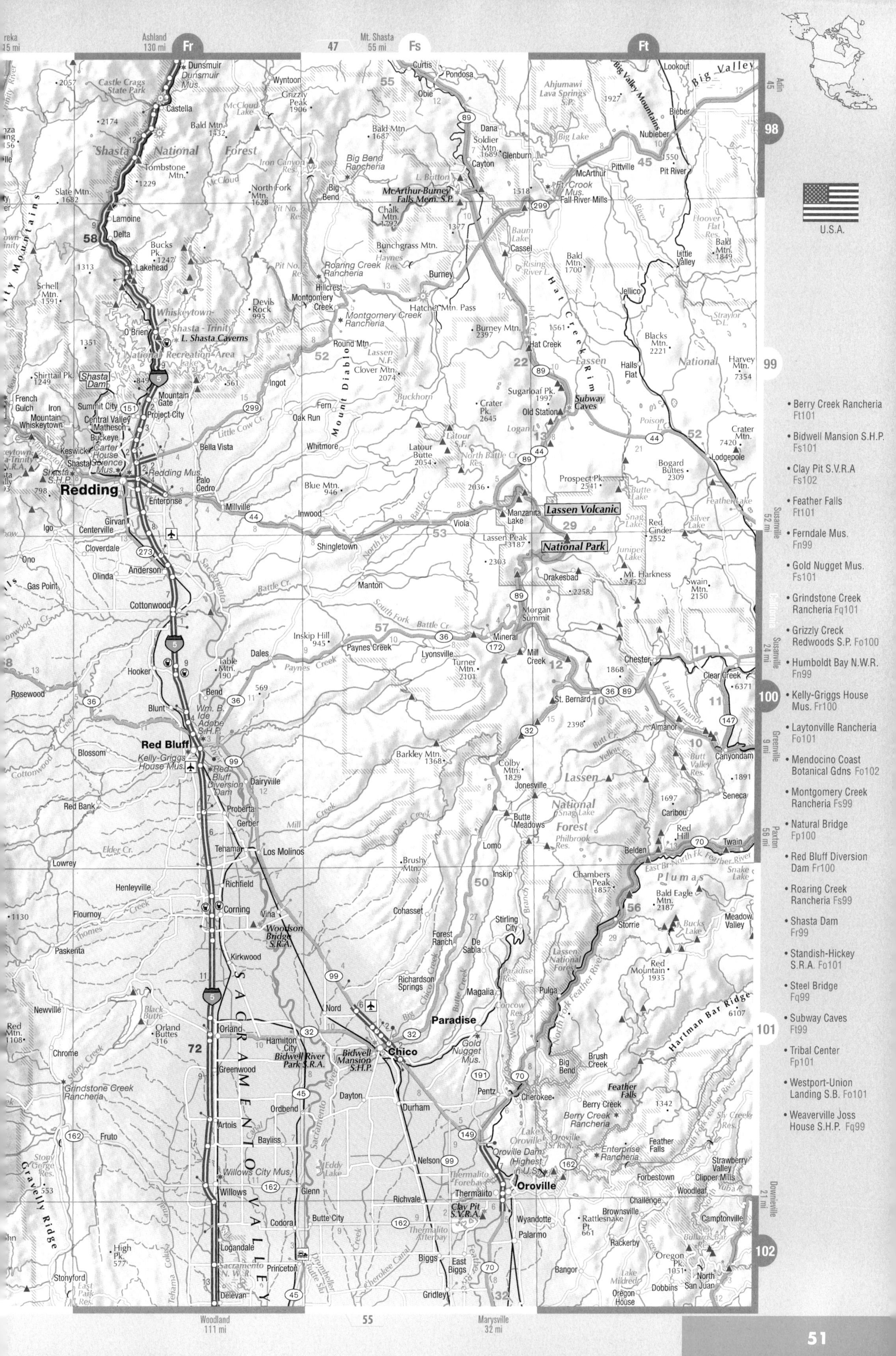
Ashland 130 mi
Fr
47
Mt. Shasta 55 mi
Fs
Ft
Dunsmuir
Dunsmuir Mus.
Castle Crags State Park
Castella
Wyntoon
Grizzly Peak 1906
McCloud Lake
Bald Mtn. 1432
Shasta National Forest
Tombstone Mtn.
Iron Canyon Res.
Slate Mtn. 1682
North Fork Mtn. 1628
Lamoine
Delta
Bucks Pk. 1247
Lakehead
Schell Mtn. 1591
Whiskeytown-Shasta-Trinity National Recreation Area
O'Brien
L. Shasta Caverns
Shasta Dam
Shirttail Pk. 1249
French Gulch
Iron Mountain
Whiskeytown
Summit City
Central Valley
Project City
Mountain Gate
Matheson
Buckeye
Keswick
Shasta
Shasta S.H.P.
Carter House Science Mus.
Redding Mus.
Redding
Enterprise
Palo Cedro
Bella Vista
Millville
Ingot
Igo
Centerville
Girvan
Cloverdale
Olinda
Anderson
Ono
Gas Point
Cottonwood
Hooker
Rosewood
Bend
Blunt
Wm. B. Ide Adobe S.H.P.
Red Bluff
Kelly-Griggs House Mus.
Red Bluff Diversion Dam
Blossom
Red Bank
Dairyville
Proberta
Gerber
Tehama
Los Molinos
Lowrey
Henleyville
Richfield
Flournoy
Corning
Vina
Woodson Bridge S.R.A.
Paskenta
Kirkwood
Newville
Orland Buttes 316
Orland
Hamilton City
Bidwell River Park S.R.A.
Bidwell Mansion S.H.P.
Chico
Chrome
Grindstone Creek Rancheria
Greenwood
Ordbend
Artois
Bayliss
Fruto
Willows City Mus.
Willows
Glenn
Codora
Butte City
Logandale
Sacramento N.W.R.
Princeton
Stonyford
Delevan
High Pk. 577
Gravelly Ridge
Sacramento Valley
Curtis
Pondosa
Obie
Bald Mtn. 1687
Big Bend Rancheria
Big Bend
McArthur-Burney Falls Mem. S.P.
L. Britton
Chalk Mtn. 1792
Bunchgrass Mtn.
Roaring Creek Rancheria
Hillcrest
Montgomery Creek
Montgomery Creek Rancheria
Hatchet Mtn. Pass
Burney
Round Mtn.
Lassen N.F.
Clover Mtn. 2074
Mount Diablo
Fern
Oak Run
Whitmore
Latour Butte 2054
Latour S.F.
Blue Mtn. 946
Inwood
Shingletown
Viola
Manton
Inskip Hill 945
Paynes Creek
Dales
Lyonsville
Turner Mtn. 2101
Mineral
Barkley Mtn. 1368
Brushy Mtn.
Cohasset
Forest Ranch
De Sabla
Richardson Springs
Magalia
Paradise
Gold Nugget Mus.
Durham
Dayton
Nelson
Thermalito
Thermalito Forebay
Clay Pit S.V.R.A.
Richvale
Thermalito Afterbay
Biggs
East Biggs
Gridley
Dana
Soldier Mtn. 1689
Cayton
Glenburn
Cassel
Baum Lake
Hat Creek
Burney Mtn. 2397
Crater Pk. 2645
Sugarloaf Pk. 1997
Old Station
Subway Caves
Manzanita Lake
Lassen Volcanic National Park
Lassen Peak 3187
Drakesbad
Morgan Summit
Mill Creek
Chester
St. Bernard
Almanor
Lake Almanor
Colby Mtn. 1829
Jonesville
Lassen National Forest
Butte Meadows
Lomo
Inskip
Stirling City
Pulga
Big Bend
Brush Creek
Cherokee
Pentz
Feather Falls
Berry Creek
Berry Creek Rancheria
Oroville
Oroville Dam (Highest in U.S.)
Enterprise Rancheria
Wyandotte
Palermo
Bangor
Rackerby
Rattlesnake Pt. 661
Brownsville
Challenge
Forbestown
Woodleaf
Clipper Mills
Strawberry Valley
Feather Falls
Oregon House
Dobbins
Oregon Pk. 1051
North San Juan
Camptonville
Ahjumawi Lava Springs S.P.
Big Valley Mountains
Lookout
Big Valley
Bieber
Nubieber
Pittville
McArthur
Ft. Crook Mus.
Fall River Mills
Pit River
Little Valley
Jellico
Hat Creek Rim
Blacks Mtn. 2221
Halls Flat
Lassen National
Harvey Mtn. 7354
Crater Mtn. 7420
Lodgepole
Bogard Buttes 2309
Prospect Pk. 2541
Red Cinder 2552
Mt. Harkness 2452
Swain Mtn. 2150
Clear Creek
Canyondam
Caribou
Belden
Twain
Chambers Peak 1857
Bald Eagle Mtn. 2187
Storrie
Meadow Valley
Red Mountain 1935
Hartman Bar Ridge
Plumas
Adin 45
Susanville 52 mi
Susanville 24 mi
Greenville 9 mi
Paxton 56 mi
Downieville 21 mi
Woodland 111 mi
55
Marysville 32 mi
98
99
100
101
102
U.S.A.
California
• Berry Creek Rancheria Ft101
• Bidwell Mansion S.H.P. Fs101
• Clay Pit S.V.R.A Fs102
• Feather Falls Ft101
• Ferndale Mus. Fn99
• Gold Nugget Mus. Fs101
• Grindstone Creek Rancheria Fq101
• Grizzly Creek Redwoods S.P. Fo100
• Humboldt Bay N.W.R. Fn99
• Kelly-Griggs House Mus. Fr100
• Laytonville Rancheria Fo101
• Mendocino Coast Botanical Gdns Fo102
• Montgomery Creek Rancheria Fs99
• Natural Bridge Fp100
• Red Bluff Diversion Dam Fr100
• Roaring Creek Rancheria Fs99
• Shasta Dam Fr99
• Standish-Hickey S.R.A. Fo101
• Steel Bridge Fq99
• Subway Caves Ft99
• Tribal Center Fp101
• Westport-Union Landing S.B. Fo101
• Weaverville Joss House S.H.P. Fq99
51

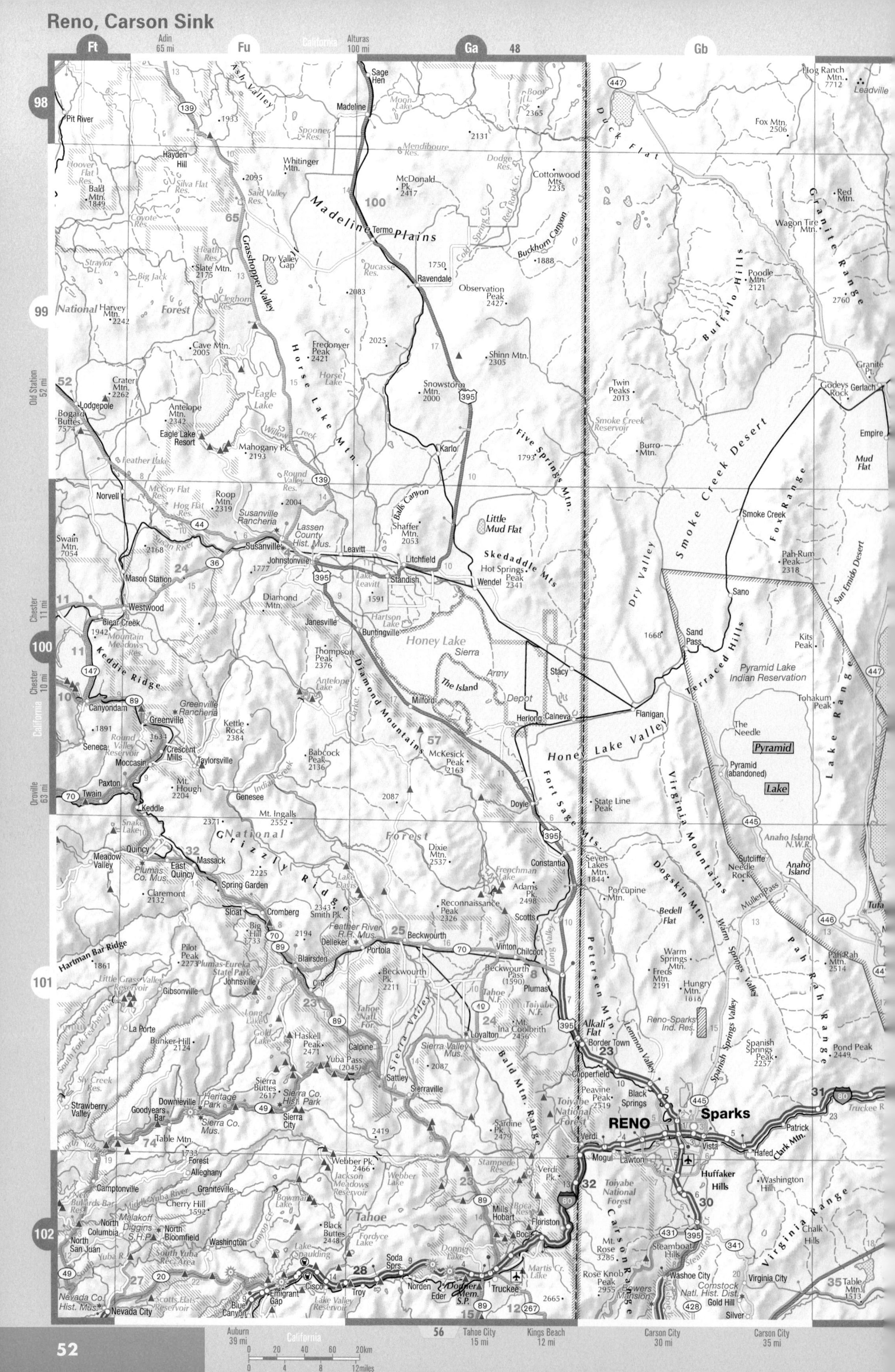

Ft
Fu
Ga
Gb
48
Adin 65 mi
California
Alturas 100 mi
98
99
100
101
102
Old Station 52 mi
Chester 11 mi
Chester 10 mi
California
Oroville 63 mi
Pit River
Hayden Hill
Hoover Flat Res.
Bald Mtn. 1849
Silva Flat Res.
Coyote Res.
Said Valley Res.
Ash Valley
Sage Hen
Madeline
Moon Lake
Spooner Res.
Whitinger Mtn.
Mendiboure Res.
McDonald Pk. 2417
Madeline Plains
Termo
Dodge Res.
Cottonwood Mts. 2235
Boot L.
Red Rock Cr.
Buckhorn Canyon
Duck Flat
Fox Mtn. 2506
Hog Ranch Mtn. 7712
Leadville
Red Mtn.
Wagon Tire Mtn.
Granite Range
Buffalo Hills
Poodle Mtn. 2121
Granite Pt.
Gerlach
Godeys Rock
Empire
Mud Flat
Smoke Creek Desert
Smoke Creek
Fox Range
Pah-Rum Peak 2318
San Emido Desert
Sano
Sand Pass
Terraced Hills
Kits Peak
Pyramid Lake Indian Reservation
Tohakum Peak
The Needle
Pyramid
Pyramid (abandoned)
Lake
Lake Range
Anaho Island N.W.R.
Anaho Island
Sutcliffe
Needle Rock
Mullen Pass
Pah Rah Range
Pah Rah Mtn. 2514
Pond Peak 2449
Tule
Heath Res.
Slate Mtn. 2175
Straylor L.
Big Jack L.
Cleghorn Res.
Grasshopper Valley
Dry Valley Gap
Ducasse Res.
Ravendale
Observation Peak 2427
National Forest
Harvey Mtn. 2242
Cave Mtn. 2005
Fredonyer Peak 2421
Horse Lake Mtn.
Horse Lake
Shinn Mtn. 2305
Twin Peaks 2013
Smoke Creek Reservoir
Burro Mtn.
Crater Mtn. 2262
Lodgepole
Bogard Buttes 7574
Antelope Mtn. 2342
Eagle Lake
Eagle Lake Resort
Willow Creek
Mahogany Pk. 2193
Snowstorm Mtn. 2000
Karlo
Five Springs Mtn.
Feather Lake
Round Valley Res.
Norvell
McCoy Flat Res.
Hog Flat Res.
Roop Mtn. 2319
Susanville Rancheria
Balls Canyon
Shaffer Mtn. 2053
Little Mud Flat
Skedaddle Mts
Hot Springs Peak 2341
Wendel
Swain Mtn. 7054
Susan River
Susanville
Lassen County Hist. Mus.
Leavitt
Litchfield
Johnstonville
Standish
Lake Leavitt
Mason Station
Westwood
Diamond Mtn.
Janesville
Buntingville
Hartson Lake
Honey Lake
Sierra Army Depot
The Island
Stacy
Dry Valley
Flanigan
Clear Creek
Mountain Meadows Res.
Keddie Ridge
Thompson Peak 2376
Antelope Lake
Diamond Mountains
Milford
Herlong
Calneva
Honey Lake Valley
Virginia Mountains
Canyondam
Greenville Rancheria
Greenville
Kettle Rock 2384
Seneca
Round Valley Reservoir
Crescent Mills
Taylorsville
Moccasin
Babcock Peak 2136
McKesick Peak 2163
Fort Sage Mts.
Doyle
State Line Peak
Paxton
Twain
Mt. Hough 2204
Genesee
Indian Creek
Mt. Ingalls 2552
Keddle
Snake Lake
Grizzly Ridge
National Forest
Dixie Mtn. 2537
Seven Lakes Mtn. 1844
Porcupine Mtn.
Dogskin Mtn.
Bedell Flat
Quincy
Meadow Valley
East Quincy
Massack
Plumas Co. Mus.
Spring Garden
Claremont 2132
Lake Davis
Smith Pk.
Frenchman Lake
Adams Pk. 2498
Constantia
Reconnaissance Peak 2326
Scotts
Sloat
Cromberg
Big Hill 1733
Feather River R.R. Mus.
Delleker
Portola
Beckwourth
Vinton
Chilcoot
Long Valley
Peterson Mtn.
Warm Springs Mtn.
Freds Mtn. 2191
Hungry Mtn. 1818
Warm Springs Valley
Hartman Bar Ridge
Pilot Peak 2273
Plumas-Eureka State Park
Blairsden
Johnsville
Clio
Beckwourth Pk. 2211
Beckwourth Pass (1590)
Plumas
Tahoe N.F.
Toiyabe N.F.
Little Grass Valley Reservoir
Gibsonville
La Porte
Long Lake
Gold Lake
Tahoe Natl. For.
Sierra Valley
Loyalton
Mt. Ina Coolbrith 2456
Alkali Flat
Lemmon Valley
Reno-Sparks Ind. Res.
Spanish Springs Valley
Spanish Springs Peak 2257
Bunker Hill 2124
Haskell Peak 2471
Calpine
Sierra Valley Mus.
Bald Mtn. Range
Border Town
South Fork Feather River
Sly Creek Res.
Yuba Pass (2045)
Sattley
Sierraville
Sierra Buttes 2617
Sierra Co. Hist. Park
Copperfield
Peavine Peak 2519
Black Springs
Strawberry Valley
Downieville
Heritage Park
Goodyears Bar
Sierra Co. Mus.
Sierra City
Toiyabe National Forest
RENO
Sparks
Verdi
Vista
Patrick
Truckee
Hafed
Clark Mtn.
Table Mtn.
Sardine Pk. 2479
Mogul
Lawton
Forest
Alleghany
Webber Pk. 2466
Jackson Meadows Reservoir
Webber Lake
Stampede Res.
Verdi Pk.
Huffaker Hills
Washington Hill
Campionville
Graniteville
Middle Yuba River
Bullards Bar Res.
Cherry Hill 1592
Bowman Lake
Toiyabe National Forest
Carson Range
Virginia Range
Malakoff Diggins S.H.P.
North Columbia
North Bloomfield
North San Juan
Washington
Tahoe
Black Buttes 2448
Fordyce Lake
Mills
Hobart
Boca Res.
Boca
Floriston
Mt. Rose 3285
Steamboat Hills
Chalk Hills
South Yuba Rec. Area
Yuba R.
Lake Spaulding
Soda Sprs.
Donner Lake
Martis Cr. Lake
Washoe City
Virginia City
Table Mtn. 1513
Nevada Co. Hist. Mus.
Nevada City
Scotts Flat Reservoir
Emigrant Gap
Cisco
Troy
Norden
Eder
Donner Mem. S.P.
Rose Knob Peak 2955
Bowers Mansion
Comstock Natl. Hist. Dist.
Gold Hill
Silver
Blue Canyon
Lake Valley Reservoir
Auburn 39 mi
California
56
Tahoe City 15 mi
Kings Beach 12 mi
Carson City 30 mi
Carson City 35 mi
0 20 40 60 20km
0 4 8 12miles

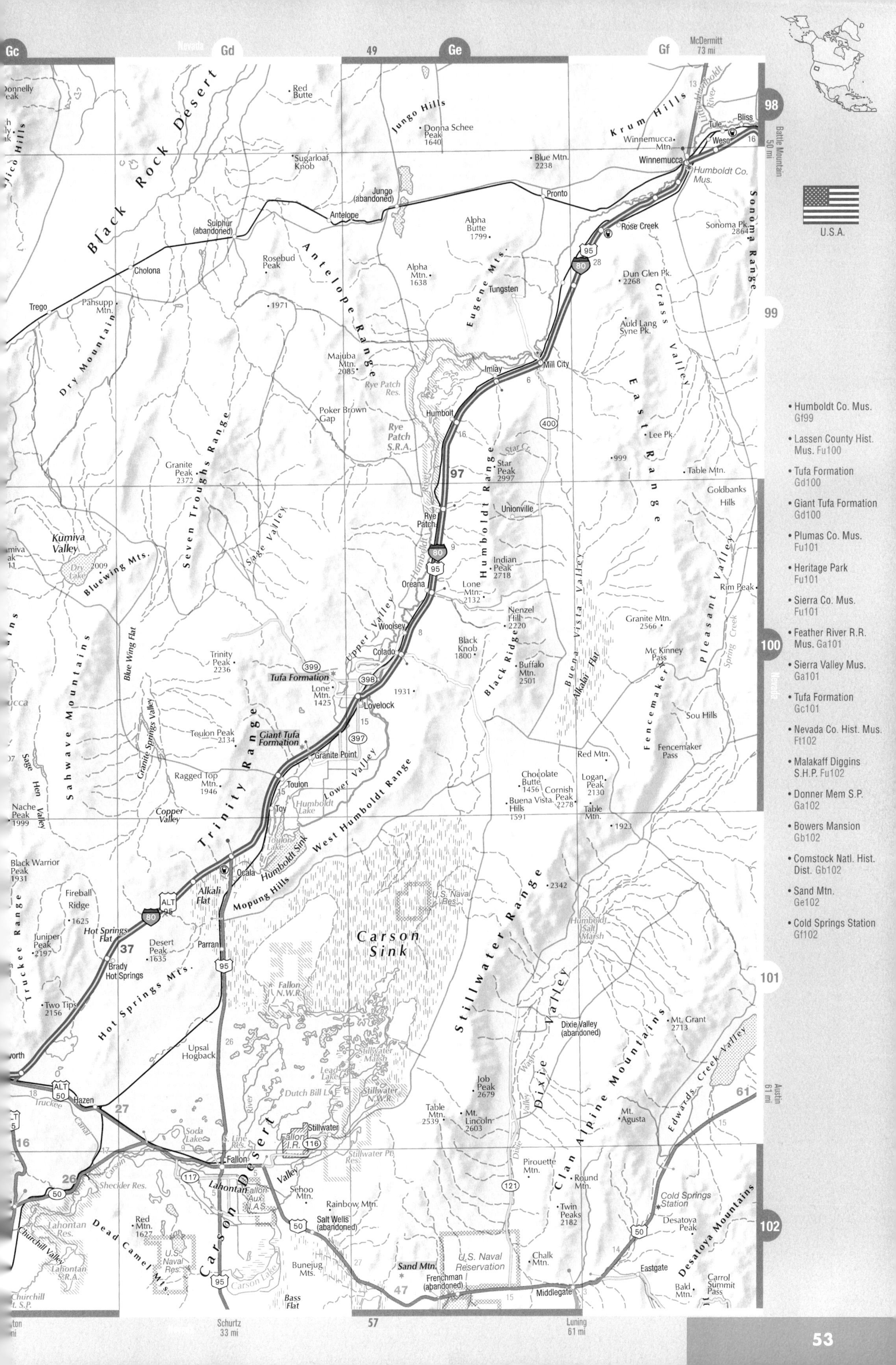

Gc
Nevada
Gd
49
Ge
Gf
McDermitt
73 mi
98
Battle Mountain
50 mi
99
100
Nevada
101
61
Austin
61 mi
102
U.S.A.
Black Rock Desert
Red Butte
Jungo Hills
Donna Schee Peak 1640
Krum Hills
Winnemucca Mtn.
Winnemucca
Tule
Bliss
Weso
Humboldt Co. Mus.
Sugarloaf Knob
Blue Mtn. 2238
Jungo (abandoned)
Pronto
Antelope
Sulphur (abandoned)
Rose Creek
Sonoma Pk. 2864
Sonoma Range
Alpha Butte 1799
Cholona
Rosebud Peak
Antelope Range
Alpha Mtn. 1638
Eugene Mts.
Tungsten
Dun Glen Pk. 2268
Grass Valley
Trego
Pahsupp Mtn.
Dry Mountain
Auld Lang Syne Pk.
Majuba Mtn. 2085
Rye Patch Res.
Imlay
Mill City
East Range
Poker Brown Gap
Humboldt
Rye Patch S.R.A.
Lee Pk.
Seven Troughs Range
Granite Peak 2372
Star Peak 2997
Humboldt Range
Table Mtn.
Goldbanks Hills
Unionville
Rye Patch
Kumiva Valley
Dry Lake
Bluewing Mts.
Sage Valley
Indian Peak 2718
Oreana
Lone Mtn. 2132
Buena Vista Valley
Pleasant Valley
Rim Peak
Nenzel Hill 2220
Granite Mtn. 2566
Upper Valley
Woolsey
Black Knob 1800
Black Ridge
Buffalo Mtn. 2501
Alkali Flat
Mc Kinney Pass
Spring Creek
Trinity Peak 2236
Colado
Tufa Formation
Lone Mtn. 1425
Lovelock
Blue Wing Flat
Sahwave Mountains
Fencemaker
Sou Hills
Toulon Peak 2134
Giant Tufa Formation
Granite Springs Valley
Granite Point
Lower Valley
Fencemaker Pass
Red Mtn.
Sage Hen Valley
Ragged Top Mtn. 1946
Toulon
Trinity Range
Humboldt Lake
West Humboldt Range
Chocolate Butte 1456
Buena Vista Hills 1591
Cornish Peak 2278
Logan Peak 2130
Table Mtn.
Nache Peak 1999
Copper Valley
Toy
Toulon Lake
Humboldt Sink
Black Warrior Peak 1931
Ocala
Alkali Flat
Mopung Hills
U.S. Naval Res.
Stillwater Range
Humboldt Salt Marsh
Fireball Ridge
Juniper Peak 2197
Hot Springs Flat
Desert Peak 1635
Parran
Carson Sink
Brady Hot Springs
Hot Springs Mts.
Fallon N.W.R.
Dixie Valley
Dixie Valley (abandoned)
Mt. Grant 2713
Truckee Range
Two Tips 2156
Upsal Hogback
Stillwater Marsh
Clan Alpine Mountains
Edwards Creek Valley
Hazen
Truckee Canal
Lead Lake
Dutch Bill L.
Stillwater N.W.R.
Job Peak 2679
Table Mtn. 2539
Mt. Lincoln 2603
Mt. Agusta
Soda Lake
S. Line Res.
Stillwater
Fallon I.R.
Stillwater Pt. Res.
Fallon
Carson
Sheckler Res.
Lahontan
Fallon Aux. N.A.S.
Valley
Pirouette Mtn.
Round Mtn.
Cold Springs Station
Lahontan Res.
Carson Desert
Sehoo Mtn.
Rainbow Mtn.
Salt Wells (abandoned)
Twin Peaks 2182
Desatoya Peak
Desatoya Mountains
Red Mtn. 1627
Dead Camel Mts.
Churchill Valley
Lahontan S.R.A.
U.S. Naval Res.
Carson Lake
Bunejug Mts.
Sand Mtn.
U.S. Naval Reservation
Frenchman (abandoned)
Chalk Mtn.
Eastgate
Middlegate
Bald Mtn.
Carrol Summit Pass
Churchill Lt. S.P.
Bass Flat
Schurtz
33 mi
57
Luning
61 mi
• Humboldt Co. Mus. Gf99
• Lassen County Hist. Mus. Fu100
• Tufa Formation Gd100
• Giant Tufa Formation Gd100
• Plumas Co. Mus. Fu101
• Heritage Park Fu101
• Sierra Co. Mus. Fu101
• Feather River R.R. Mus. Ga101
• Sierra Valley Mus. Ga101
• Tufa Formation Gc101
• Nevada Co. Hist. Mus. Ft102
• Malakaff Diggins S.H.P. Fu102
• Donner Mem S.P. Ga102
• Bowers Mansion Gb102
• Comstock Natl. Hist. Dist. Gb102
• Sand Mtn. Ge102
• Cold Springs Station Gf102

San Francisco → 142-145

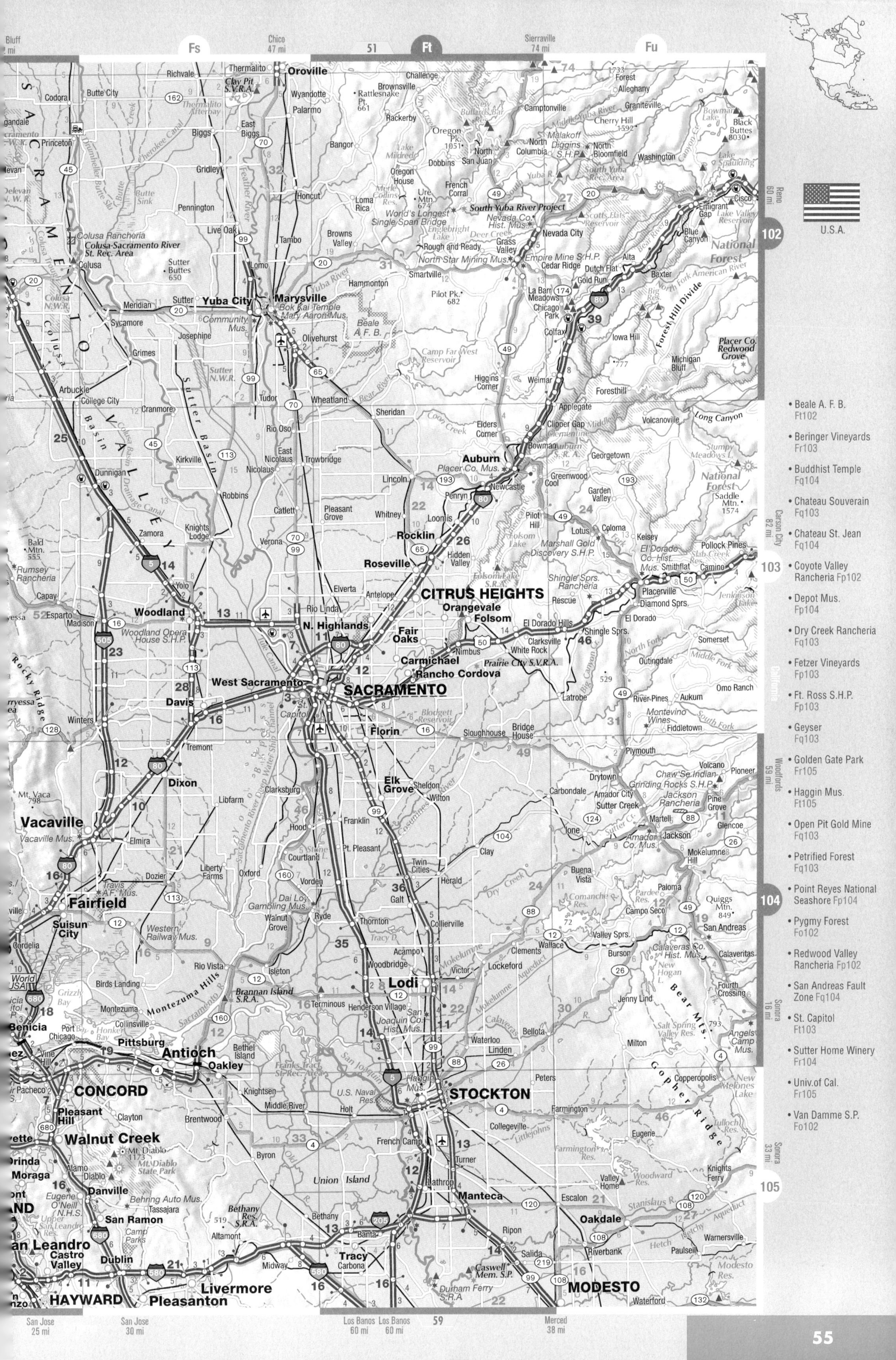
Fs
Ft
Fu
51
Chico 47 mi
Sierraville 74 mi
Reno 60 mi
Carson City 82 mi
Woodfords 59 mi
Sonora 16 mi
Sonora 33 mi
San Jose 25 mi
San Jose 30 mi
Los Banos 60 mi
Los Banos 60 mi
59
Merced 38 mi
102
103
104
105
U.S.A.
California
Oroville
Marysville
Yuba City
Auburn
Roseville
Rocklin
CITRUS HEIGHTS
Folsom
SACRAMENTO
West Sacramento
Davis
Woodland
Vacaville
Fairfield
Lodi
STOCKTON
MODESTO
Manteca
Tracy
Antioch
CONCORD
Walnut Creek
HAYWARD
Pleasanton
Livermore
Nevada City
Placerville
Elk Grove
Dixon
Oakdale
• Beale A. F. B. Ft102
• Beringer Vineyards Fr103
• Buddhist Temple Fq104
• Chateau Souverain Fq103
• Chateau St. Jean Fq104
• Coyote Valley Rancheria Fp102
• Depot Mus. Fp104
• Dry Creek Rancheria Fq103
• Fetzer Vineyards Fp103
• Ft. Ross S.H.P. Fp103
• Geyser Fq103
• Golden Gate Park Fr105
• Haggin Mus. Ft105
• Open Pit Gold Mine Fq103
• Petrified Forest Fq103
• Point Reyes National Seashore Fp104
• Pygmy Forest Fo102
• Redwood Valley Rancheria Fp102
• San Andreas Fault Zone Fq104
• St. Capitol Ft103
• Sutter Home Winery Fr104
• Univ.of Cal. Fr105
• Van Damme S.P. Fo102

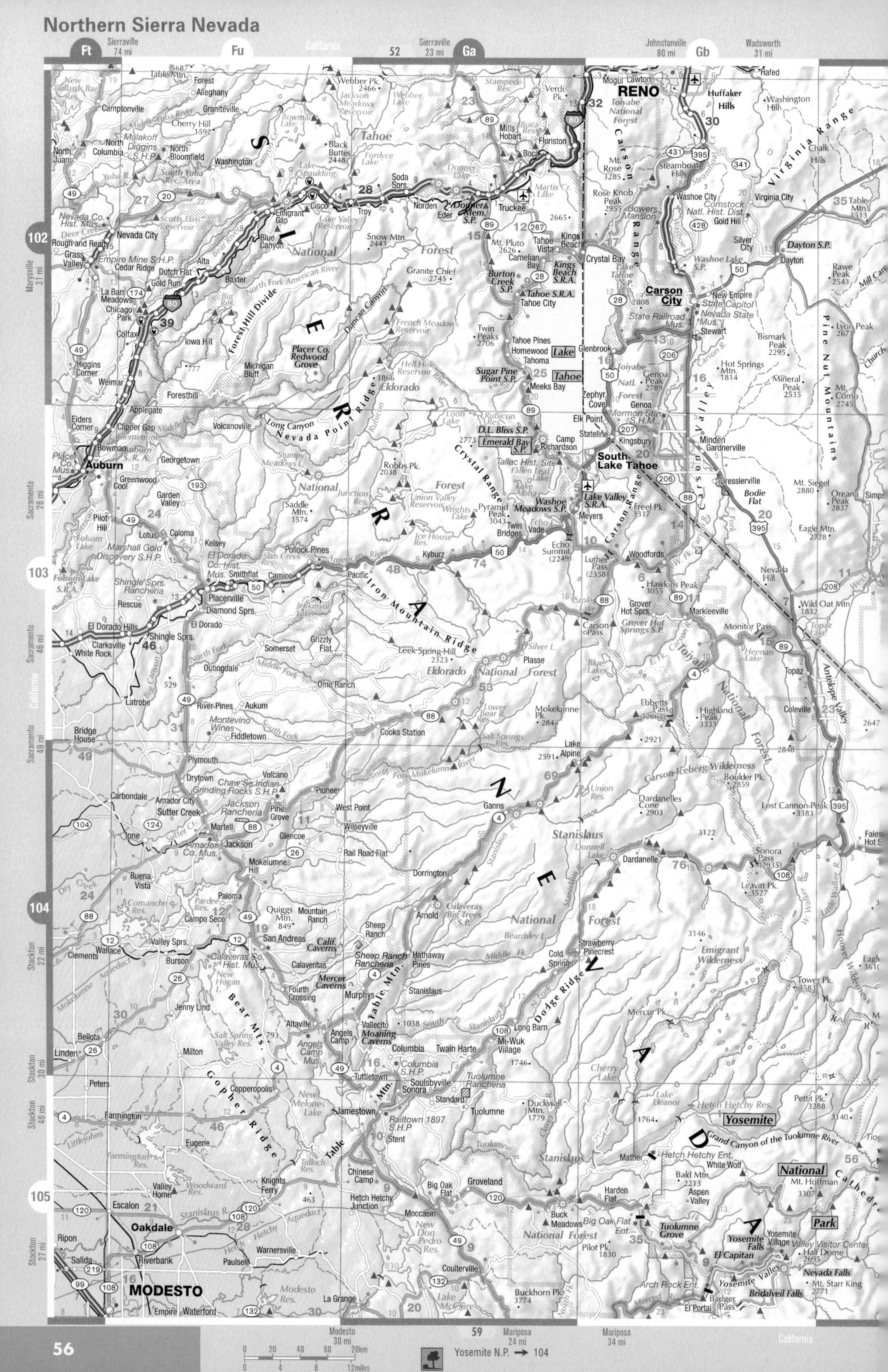
Ft
Sierraville 74 mi
Fu
California
52
Sierraville 23 mi
Ga
Johnstonville 80 mi
Gb
Wadsworth 31 mi
102
Marysville 31 mi
103
Sacramento 26 mi
Sacramento 46 mi
Sacramento 49 mi
104
Stockton 22 mi
Stockton 30 mi
Stockton 46 mi
105
Stockton 27 mi
RENO
Huffaker Hills
Washington Hill
Virginia Range
Toiyabe National Forest
Carson Range
Mt. Rose 3285
Steamboat Hills
Washoe City
Comstock Natl. Hist. Dist.
Virginia City
Gold Hill
Silver City
Dayton S.P.
Dayton
Rawe Peak 2543
Carson City
Nevada State Capitol
Nevada State Railroad Mus.
Stewart
Pine Nut Mountains
Lyon Peak 2671
Bismark Peak 2295
Hot Springs Mtn. 1814
Mineral Peak 2535
Mt. Como 2745
Genoa
Mormon Sta. S.H.M.
Minden
Gardnerville
Dresslerville
Bodie Flat
Mt. Siegel 2880
Oreana Peak 2837
Eagle Mtn. 2728
Nevada Hill
Wild Oat Mtn 1832
Monitor Pass
Topaz
Topaz Lake
Antelope Valley
Coleville
Truckee
Donner Mem. S.P.
Donner Lake
Norden
Eder
Boca
Floriston
Verdi Pk.
Mogul
Lawton
Hafed
Stampede Res.
Mills
Hobart
Kings Beach
Kings Beach S.R.A.
Crystal Bay
Tahoe Vista
Carnelian Bay
Mt. Pluto 2626
Burton Creek S.P.
Tahoe S.R.A.
Tahoe City
Twin Peaks 2706
Tahoe Pines
Homewood
Tahoma
Lake Tahoe
Sugar Pine Point S.P.
Meeks Bay
Glenbrook
Zephyr Cove
Elk Point
Stateline
Kingsbury
South Lake Tahoe
D.L. Bliss S.P.
Emerald Bay S.P.
Camp Richardson
Tallac Hist. Site
Fallen Leaf Lake
Lake Valley S.R.A.
Washoe Meadows S.P.
Meyers
Freel Pk. 3317
Echo Summit (2249)
Luther Pass (2358)
Woodfords
Hawkins Peak 3055
Grover Hot Sprs.
Grover Hot Springs S.P.
Markleeville
Carson Pass
Caples Lake
Silver L.
Plasse
Blue Lakes
Ebbetts Pass (2661)
Highland Peak 3333
Mokelumne Pk. 2844
Lake Alpine
2591
2921
Carson-Iceberg Wilderness
Boulder Pk. 2859
Lost Cannon Peak 3383
Dardanelles Cone 2903
Union Res.
Ganns
Stanislaus
Donnell Lake
Dardanelle
Sonora Pass (2935)
Leavitt Pk. 3527
Emigrant Wilderness
Tower Pk. 3583
Hoover Wilderness
Strawberry
Pinecrest
Cold Springs
Dodge Ridge
Mercur Pk.
Cherry Lake
Lake Eleanor
Hetch Hetchy Res.
Yosemite National Park
Grand Canyon of the Tuolumne River
Pettit Pk. 3288
Mather
Hetch Hetchy Ent.
White Wolf
Bald Mtn. 2213
Aspen Valley
Mt. Hoffman 3307
Tuolumne Grove
Yosemite Falls
Yosemite Village
Valley Visitor Center
Half Dome 2695
El Capitan
Nevada Falls
Mt. Starr King 2771
Bridalveil Falls
Yosemite Valley
Arch Rock Ent.
El Portal
Badger Pass
Big Oak Flat Ent.
Harden Flat
Buck Meadows
Pilot Pk. 1830
Buckhorn Pk. 3774
Groveland
Big Oak Flat
Moccasin
New Don Pedro Res.
Coulterville
Lake McClure
La Grange
Webber Pk. 2466
Jackson Meadows Reservoir
Webber Lake
Tahoe
Black Buttes 2448
Fordyce Lake
Lake Spaulding
Soda Sprs.
Cisco
Troy
Emigrant Gap
Lake Valley Reservoir
Blue Canyon
Snow Mtn. 2443
Granite Chief 2745
Tahoe National Forest
French Meadows Reservoir
Duncan Canyon
Placer Co. Redwood Grove
Hell Hole Reservoir
Eldorado
Loon Lake
Rubicon Res.
Crystal Range
Robbs Pk. 2038
Union Valley Reservoir
Wrights Lake
Pyramid Peak 3043
Twin Bridges
Ice House Res.
Kyburz
Echo
Vade
Iron Mountain Ridge
Pacific
Leek Spring Hill 2323
Eldorado National Forest
Lower Bear R. Res.
Salt Springs Res.
Cooks Station
Omo Ranch
Grizzly Flat
Somerset
Outingdale
Aukum
River Pines
Montevino Wines
Fiddletown
Table Mtn.
Forest
Alleghany
Camptonville
Graniteville
Cherry Hill 1592
North Columbia
Malakoff Diggins S.H.P.
North Bloomfield
North San Juan
Washington
South Yuba Rec. Area
Nevada Co. Hist. Mus.
Nevada City
Scotts Flats Reservoir
Rough and Ready
Grass Valley
Empire Mine S.H.P.
Cedar Ridge
Dutch Flat
Alta
Gold Run
Baxter
La Barr Meadows
Chicago Park
Colfax
Forest Hill Divide
Iowa Hill
Michigan Bluff
Higgins Corner
Weimar
Foresthill
Applegate
Elders Corner
Clipper Gap
Bowman
Auburn
Auburn S.R.A.
Placer Co. Mus.
Volcanoville
Long Canyon
Nevada Point Ridge
Stumpy Meadows L.
Georgetown
Greenwood
Cool
Garden Valley
Saddle Mtn. 1574
Junction Res.
Pilot Hill
Lotus
Coloma
Kelsey
Marshall Gold Discovery S.H.P.
Folsom Lake
Folsom Lake S.R.A.
El Dorado Co. Hist. Mus.
Smithflat
Camino
Pollock Pines
Shingle Sprs. Rancheria
Placerville
Diamond Sprs.
Rescue
El Dorado
El Dorado Hills
Clarksville
White Rock
Shingle Sprs.
Latrobe
Bridge House
Plymouth
Drytown
Volcano
Chaw'Se Indian Grinding Rocks S.H.P.
Pioneer
Carbondale
Amador City
Sutter Creek
Jackson Rancheria
Pine Grove
West Point
Wilseyville
Ione
Martell
Jackson
Amador Co. Mus.
Glencoe
Rail Road Flat
Mokelumne Hill
Dorrington
Buena Vista
Paloma
Pardee Res.
Comanche Res.
Campo Seco
Quiggs Mtn. 849
Mountain Ranch
Arnold
Calaveras Big Trees S.P.
Sheep Ranch
San Andreas
Calif. Caverns
Sheep Ranch Rancheria
Hathaway Pines
Wallace
Clements
Valley Sprs.
Burson
Calaveras Co. Hist. Mus.
Calaveritas
Mercer Caverns
Murphys
Stanislaus
Fourth Crossing
New Hogan L.
Jenny Lind
Bear Mts.
Altaville
Vallecito
Moaning Caverns
Angels Camp
Angels Camp Mus.
Columbia
Columbia S.H.P.
Twain Harte
Long Barn
Mi-Wuk Village
Bellota
Linden
Milton
Peters
Copperopolis
Gopher Ridge
Tuttletown
Soulsbyville
Sonora
Standard
Tuolumne Rancheria
Tuolumne
Duckwall Mtn. 1779
New Melones Lake
Jamestown
Railtown 1897 S.H.P
Stent
Farmington
Eugene
Littlejohns
Tulloch Res.
Chinese Camp
Knights Ferry
Valley Home
Woodward Res.
Escalon
Oakdale
Hetch Hetchy Junction
Stanislaus R.
Warnersville
Ripon
Salida
Riverbank
Paulsell
MODESTO
Empire
Waterford
Modesto Res.
Stanislaus National Forest
Beardsley L.
Modesto 30 mi
59
Mariposa 24 mi
Mariposa 34 mi
Yosemite N.P. → 104
0 20 40 60 20km
0 4 8 12miles

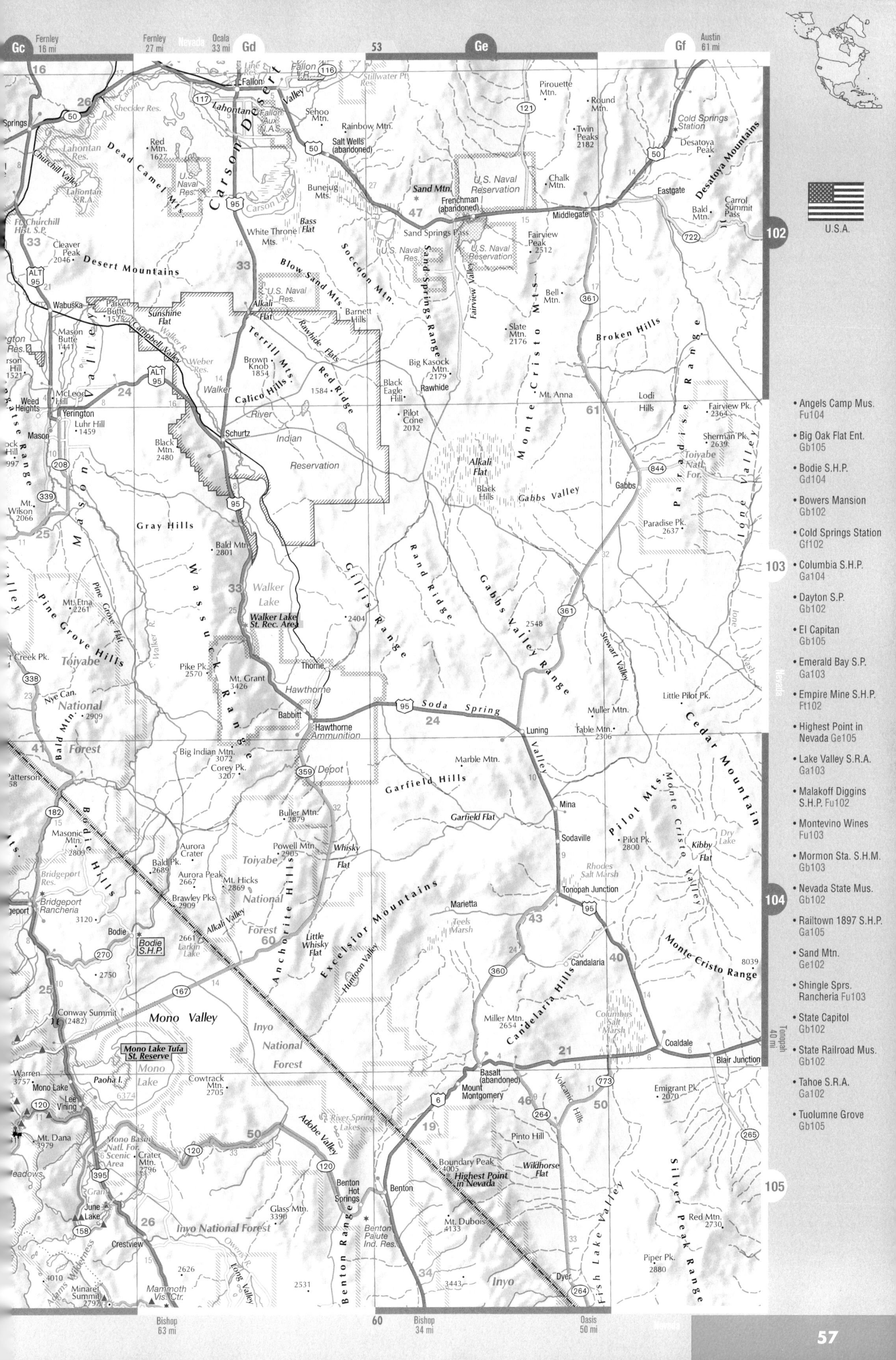

Gc
Fernley 16 mi
Fernley 27 mi
Nevada
Ocala 33 mi
Gd
53
Ge
Gf
Austin 61 mi
Carson Desert
Fallon
Lahontan
Fallon Aux. N.A.S.
Stillwater Pt. Res.
Sehoo Mtn.
Rainbow Mtn.
Salt Wells (abandoned)
Pirouette Mtn.
Round Mtn.
Twin Peaks 2182
Cold Springs Station
Desatoya Peak
Desatoya Mountains
Eastgate
Carroll Summit Pass
Bald Mtn.
Chalk Mtn.
Middlegate
U.S. Naval Reservation
Sand Mtn.
Frenchman (abandoned)
Sand Springs Pass
Fairview Peak 2512
Fairview Valley
Sand Springs Range
Bunejug Mts.
Bass Flat
Carson Lake
White Throne Mts.
Sheckler Res.
Lahontan Res.
Churchill Valley
Lahontan S.R.A.
Ft. Churchill Hist. S.P.
Dead Camel Mts.
Red Mtn. 1627
U.S. Naval Res.
Cleaver Peak 2046
Desert Mountains
Wabuska
Parker Butte 1528
Sunshine Flat
Campbell Valley
Alkali Flat
Blow Sand Mts.
Barnett Hills
Soccoon Mtn.
Bell Mtn.
Slate Mtn. 2176
Broken Hills
Monte Cristo Mts.
Mason Butte 1441
Weber Res.
Terrill Mts.
Rawhide Flats
Brown Knob 1854
Red Ridge 1584
Big Kasock Mtn. 2179
Rawhide
Black Eagle Hill
Calico Hills
Walker River
McLeod Hill
Weed Heights
Yerington
Luhr Hill 1459
Mason
Schurtz
Indian Reservation
Pilot Cone 2012
Mt. Anna
Lodi Hills
Fairview Pk. 2364
Sherman Pk. 2639
Toiyabe Natl. For.
Paradise Range
Alkali Flat
Black Hills
Gabbs Valley
Gabbs
Black Mtn. 2480
Mt. Wilson 2066
Gray Hills
Bald Mtn. 2801
Paradise Pk. 2637
Ione Valley
Rand Ridge
Gillis Range
Gabbs Valley Range
Stewart Valley
Walker Lake
Walker Lake St. Rec. Area
Pine Grove Hills
Mt. Etna 2261
Pine Grove Flat
Wassuk Range
2548
2404
Toiyabe
Pike Pk. 2570
Mt. Grant 3426
Thorne
Hawthorne
Babbitt
Hawthorne Ammunition Depot
Soda Spring Valley
Luning
Muller Mtn.
Table Mtn. 2306
Little Pilot Pk.
Cedar Mountain
Nye Can.
National Forest
Bald Mtn. 2909
Big Indian Mtn. 3072
Corey Pk. 3207
Marble Mtn.
Garfield Hills
Garfield Flat
Mina
Sodaville
Pilot Mts.
Pilot Pk. 2800
Monte Cristo Valley
Kibby Flat
Dry Lake
Rhodes Salt Marsh
Tonopah Junction
Patterson
Bodie Hills
Masonic Mtn. 2809
Buller Mtn. 2879
Aurora Crater
Powell Mtn. 2905
Whisky Flat
Bald Pk. 2689
Aurora Peak 2667
Mt. Hicks 2869
Toiyabe National Forest
Anchorite Hills
Brawley Pks. 2909
Alkali Valley
Bridgeport Res.
Bridgeport Rancheria
Bodie
Bodie S.H.P.
Larkin Lake
Little Whisky Flat
Excelsior Mountains
Huntoon Valley
Marietta
Teels Marsh
Candalaria
Candelaria Hills
Monte Cristo Range
8039
Conway Summit (2482)
Mono Valley
Inyo National Forest
Miller Mtn. 2654
Columbus Salt Marsh
Coaldale
Blair Junction
Tonopah 40 mi
Mono Lake Tufa St. Reserve
Mono Lake
Paoha I.
Warren 3757
Mono Lake
Lee Vining
Cowtrack Mtn. 2705
Basalt (abandoned)
Mount Montgomery
Volcanic Hills
Emigrant Pk. 2070
Mt. Dana 3979
Mono Basin Natl. For. Scenic Area
Crater Mtn. 2796
River Spring Lakes
Adobe Valley
Pinto Hill
Silver Peak Range
Boundary Peak 4005
Highest Point in Nevada
Wildhorse Flat
Benton Hot Springs
Benton
Benton Paiute Ind. Res.
Glass Mtn. 3390
Mt. Dubois 4133
Fish Lake Valley
Red Mtn. 2730
June Lake
Inyo National Forest
Crestview
Owens R.
Long Valley
2626
2531
Benton Range
Ansel Adams Wilderness
4010
Minaret Summit 2797
Mammoth Vis. Ctr.
3443
Inyo
Dyer
Piper Pk. 2880
Bishop 63 mi
60
Bishop 34 mi
Oasis 50 mi
102
103
104
105
U.S.A.
• Angels Camp Mus. Fu104
• Big Oak Flat Ent. Gb105
• Bodie S.H.P. Gd104
• Bowers Mansion Gb102
• Cold Springs Station Gf102
• Columbia S.H.P. Ga104
• Dayton S.P. Gb102
• El Capitan Gb105
• Emerald Bay S.P. Ga103
• Empire Mine S.H.P. Ft102
• Highest Point in Nevada Ge105
• Lake Valley S.R.A. Ga103
• Malakoff Diggins S.H.P. Fu102
• Montevino Wines Fu103
• Mormon Sta. S.H.M. Gb103
• Nevada State Mus. Gb102
• Railtown 1897 S.H.P. Ga105
• Sand Mtn. Ge102
• Shingle Sprs. Rancheria Fu103
• State Capitol Gb102
• State Railroad Mus. Gb102
• Tahoe S.R.A. Ga102
• Tuolumne Grove Gb105
57

0 20 40 60 20km
0 4 8 12miles

San Francisco → 142-145

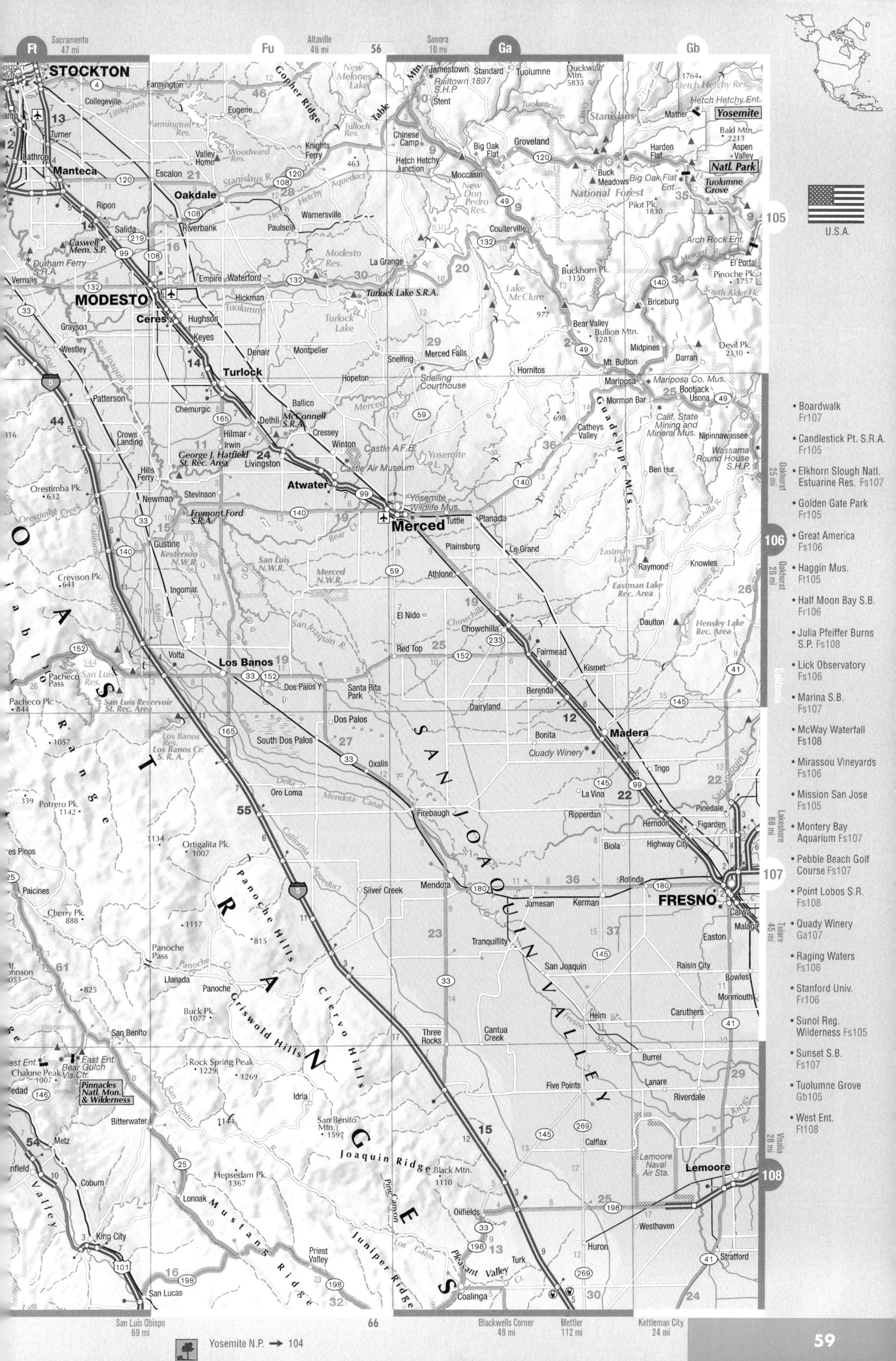
Ft
Sacramento 47 mi
Fu
Altaville 46 mi
56
Sonora 10 mi
Ga
Gb
STOCKTON
Farmington
Collegeville
Littlejohns
Eugene
Farmington Res.
Gopher Ridge
New Melones Lake
Tulloch Res.
Table Mtn.
Jamestown
Railtown 1897 S.H.P.
Stent
Standard
Tuolumne
Duckwall Mtn. 5835
Hetch Hetchy Res.
Hetch Hetchy Ent.
Mather
Yosemite
Bald Mtn. 2213
Aspen Valley
Natl. Park
Tuolumne Grove
Stanislaus
National Forest
Harden Flat
Big Oak Flat Ent.
Buck Meadows
Pilot Pk. 1830
Groveland
Big Oak Flat
Chinese Camp
Hetch Hetchy Junction
Moccasin
New Don Pedro Res.
Coulterville
Knights Ferry
Turner
Lathrop
Manteca
Escalon
Valley Home
Woodward Res.
Stanislaus R.
Oakdale
Ripon
Riverbank
Warnersville
Paulsell
Salida
Caswell Mem. S.P.
Durham Ferry S.R.A.
Vernalis
Modesto Res.
La Grange
Empire
Waterford
Hickman
Tuolumne
Turlock Lake S.R.A.
MODESTO
Ceres
Hughson
Turlock Lake
Grayson
Westley
Keyes
Denair
Montpelier
Delta Mendota Canal
San Joaquin R.
Turlock
Snelling
Merced Falls
Lake McClure
Bear Valley
Bullion Mtn. 1281
Buckhorn Pk. 1150
Briceburg
Arch Rock Ent.
El Portal
Pinoche Pk. 1757
South Alder Fk.
Midpines
Devil Pk. 2130
Darrah
Mt. Bullion
Hornitos
Mariposa
Mariposa Co. Mus.
Bootjack
Usona
Mormon Bar
Calif. State Mining and Mineral Mus.
Nipinnawassee
Wassama Round House S.H.P.
Ben Hur
Catheys Valley
Guadalupe Mts.
Hopeton
Snelling Courthouse
Patterson
Ballico
Chemurgic
Delhi
McConnell S.R.A.
Cressey
Winton
Castle A.F.B.
Castle Air Museum
Yosemite L.
Crows Landing
Hilmar
Irwin
George J. Hatfield St. Rec. Area
Livingston
Atwater
Hills Ferry
Orestimba Pk. 632
Orestimba Creek
Newman
Stevinson
Fremont Ford S.R.A.
Yosemite Wildlife Mus.
Merced
Tuttle
Planada
Gustine
Kesterson N.W.R.
San Luis N.W.R.
Merced N.W.R.
Plainsburg
Le Grand
Eastman Lake
Raymond
Knowles
Eastman Lake Rec. Area
Crevison Pk. 641
Ingomar
Athlone
El Nido
Chowchilla
Daulton
Hensley Lake Rec. Area
Volta
Los Banos
Red Top
Fairmead
Kismet
Pacheco Pass
San Luis Res.
San Luis Reservoir St. Rec. Area
Pacheco Pk. 844
Dos Palos Y
Santa Rita Park
Berenda
Dairyland
Dos Palos
South Dos Palos
Los Banos Res.
Los Banos Cr. S. R. A.
Bonita
Madera
Quady Winery
Oxalis
Trigo
Oro Loma
Mendota Canal
La Vina
Firebaugh
Ripperdan
Pinedale
Herndon
Figarden
Potrero Pk. 1142
Ortigalita Pk. 1007
Biola
Highway City
Tres Pinos
Paicines
Panoche Hills
Silver Creek
Mendota
Rolinda
FRESNO
Jamesan
Kerman
Calwa
Malaga
Cherry Pk. 888
Easton
Tranquillity
San Joaquin
Raisin City
Bowles
Panoche Pass
Llanada
Panoche
Monmouth
Caruthers
Helm
Fresno Slough
Buck Pk. 1077
Griswold Hills
Ciervo Hills
Three Rocks
Cantua Creek
Burrel
San Benito
East Ent.
Bear Gulch Vis. Ctr.
Chalone Peak 1007
Pinnacles Natl. Mon. & Wilderness
Rock Spring Peak 1229
Lanare
Riverdale
Five Points
Idria
Bitterwater
San Benito Mtn. 1597
Calflax
Lemoore Naval Air Sta.
Lemoore
Metz
Joaquin Ridge
Black Mtn. 1110
Hepsedam Pk. 1367
Coburn
Lonoak
Mustang Ridge
Pine Canyon
Oilfields
Westhaven
Huron
King City
Priest Valley
Juniper Ridge
Los Gatos
Pleasant Valley
Turk
Stratford
San Lucas
Coalinga
DIABLO RANGE
COAST RANGES
SAN JOAQUIN VALLEY
Salinas Valley
U.S.A.
105
106
107
108
Oakhurst 25 mi
Oakhurst 28 mi
California
Lakeshore 68 mi
Tulare 45 mi
Visalia 28 mi
• Boardwalk Fr107
• Candlestick Pt. S.R.A. Fr105
• Elkhorn Slough Natl. Estuarine Res. Fs107
• Golden Gate Park Fr105
• Great America Fs106
• Haggin Mus. Ft105
• Half Moon Bay S.B. Fr106
• Julia Pfeiffer Burns S.P. Fs108
• Lick Observatory Fs106
• Marina S.B. Fs107
• McWay Waterfall Fs108
• Mirassou Vineyards Fs106
• Mission San Jose Fs105
• Montery Bay Aquarium Fs107
• Pebble Beach Golf Course Fs107
• Point Lobos S.R. Fs108
• Quady Winery Ga107
• Raging Waters Fs106
• Stanford Univ. Fr106
• Sunol Reg. Wilderness Fs105
• Sunset S.B. Fs107
• Tuolumne Grove Gb105
• West Ent. Ft108
San Luis Obispo 69 mi
66
Blackwells Corner 49 mi
Mettler 112 mi
Kettleman City 24 mi
Yosemite N.P. → 104
59

Bakersfield 62 mi
67
Bakersfield 71 mi
California
0 20 40 60 20km
0 4 8 12miles
Yosemite N.P. → 104
Kings Canyon N.P., Sequoia N.P. → 105

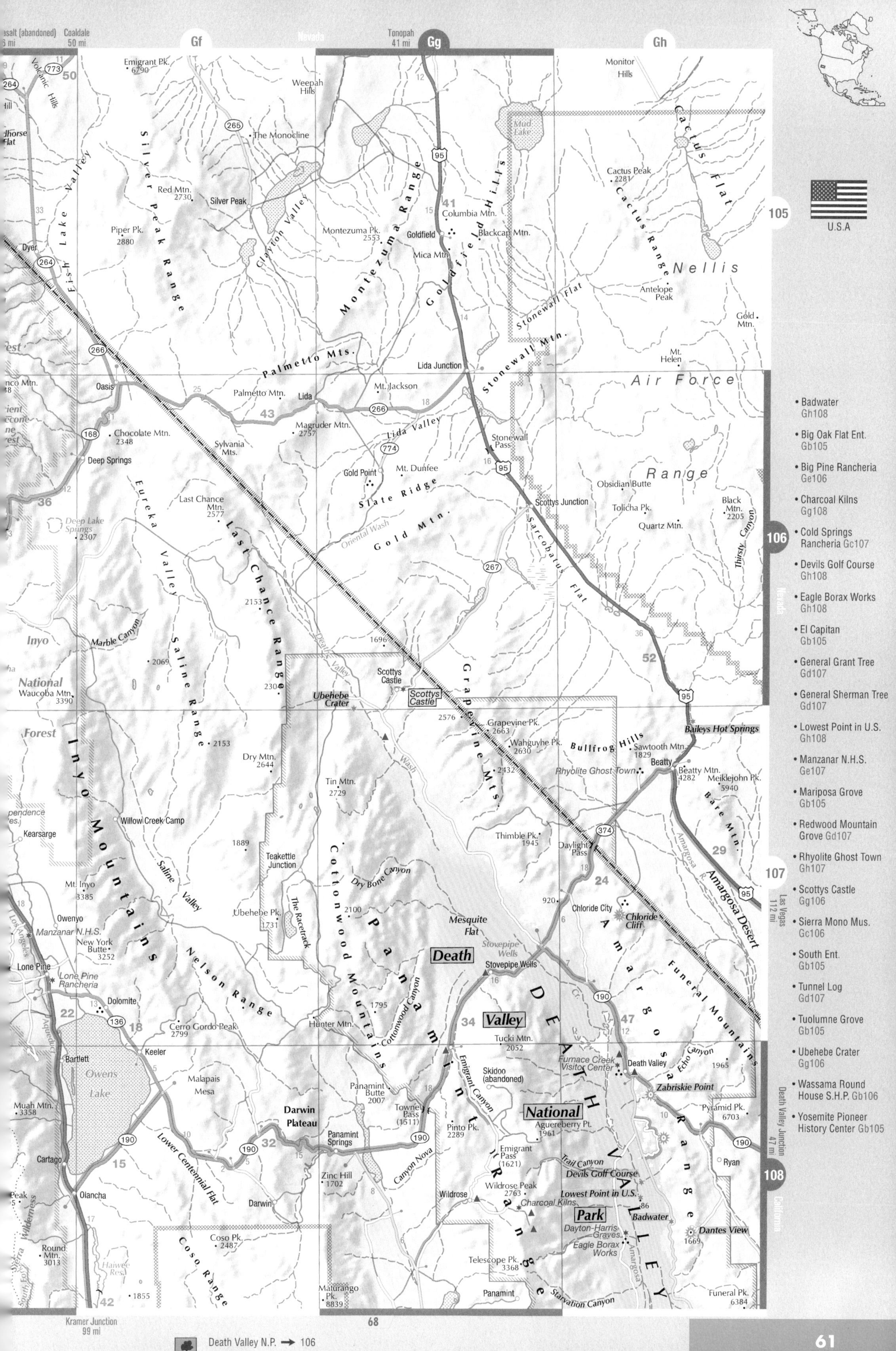
Coaldale
50 mi
Gf
Nevada
Tonopah
41 mi
Gg
Gh
Emigrant Pk.
6790
Weepah Hills
Monitor Hills
Volcanic Hills
Silver Peak Range
The Monocline
Mud Lake
Cactus Flat
Red Mtn.
2730
Silver Peak
Clayton Valley
Montezuma Range
Goldfield Hills
Cactus Peak
2281
Cactus Range
Piper Pk.
2880
Montezuma Pk.
2553
Columbia Mtn.
Goldfield
Blackcap Mtn.
Mica Mtn.
Dyer
Fish Lake Valley
Nellis
Antelope Peak
Stonewall Flat
Gold Mtn.
Palmetto Mts.
Stonewall Mtn.
Mt. Helen
Lida Junction
Air Force
Oasis
Palmetto Mtn.
Lida
Mt. Jackson
Magruder Mtn.
2757
Lida Valley
Chocolate Mtn.
2348
Deep Springs
Sylvania Mts.
Stonewall Pass
Range
Gold Point
Mt. Dunfee
Slate Ridge
Obsidian Butte
Scottys Junction
Tolicha Pk.
Black Mtn.
2205
Last Chance Mtn.
2577
Eureka Valley
Deep Lake Springs
2307
Gold Mtn.
Quartz Mtn.
Thirsty Canyon
Oriental Wash
Last Chance Range
Sarcobatus Flat
Marble Canyon
Inyo
National
Forest
Waucoba Mtn.
3390
Saline Range
Scottys Castle
Ubehebe Crater
Grapevine Mts.
Grapevine Pk.
2663
Wahguyhe Pk.
2630
Bullfrog Hills
Sawtooth Mtn.
1829
Baileys Hot Springs
Beatty
Rhyolite Ghost Town
Beatty Mtn.
4282
Meiklejohn Pk.
5940
Bare Mtn.
Dry Mtn.
2644
Tin Mtn.
2729
Inyo Mountains
Willow Creek Camp
Kearsarge
Thimble Pk.
1945
Daylight Pass
Teakettle Junction
Cottonwood Mountains
Dry Bone Canyon
Amargosa Desert
Mt. Inyo
3385
Saline Valley
Ubehebe Pk.
1731
The Racetrack
Chloride City
Chloride Cliff
Mesquite Flat
Owenyo
Manzanar N.H.S.
New York Butte
3252
Panamint Range
Death
Stovepipe Wells
Lone Pine
Lone Pine Rancheria
Nelson Range
Amargosa Range
Funeral Mountains
Dolomite
Cottonwood Canyon
Valley
Death Valley
Cerro Gordo Peak
2799
Hunter Mtn.
Tucki Mtn.
2052
Keeler
Owens Lake
Bartlett
Malapais Mesa
Emigrant Canyon
Skidoo (abandoned)
Furnace Creek Visitor Center
Echo Canyon
Zabriskie Point
Muah Mtn.
3358
Darwin Plateau
Panamint Butte
2007
Towne Pass
(1511)
National
Aguereberry Pt.
1961
Pyramid Pk.
6703
Lower Centennial Flat
Panamint Springs
Pinto Pk.
2289
Cartago
Canyon Nova
Emigrant Pass
(1621)
Trail Canyon
Devils Golf Course
Ryan
Zinc Hill
1702
Olancha
Darwin
Wildrose
Wildrose Peak
2763
Charcoal Kilns
Lowest Point in U.S.
Park
Badwater
Dayton-Harris Graves
Eagle Borax Works
Dantes View
Coso Pk.
2487
Coso Range
Round Mtn.
3013
Haiwee Res.
South Fork
Sierra Wilderness
Telescope Pk.
3368
Maturango Pk.
8839
Panamint
Starvation Canyon
Funeral Pk.
6384
Kramer Junction
99 mi
Las Vegas
112 mi
Death Valley Junction
47 mi
California
U.S.A
105
106
107
108
• Badwater Gh108
• Big Oak Flat Ent. Gb105
• Big Pine Rancheria Ge106
• Charcoal Kilns Gg108
• Cold Springs Rancheria Gc107
• Devils Golf Course Gh108
• Eagle Borax Works Gh108
• El Capitan Gb105
• General Grant Tree Gd107
• General Sherman Tree Gd107
• Lowest Point in U.S. Gh108
• Manzanar N.H.S. Ge107
• Mariposa Grove Gb105
• Redwood Mountain Grove Gd107
• Rhyolite Ghost Town Gh107
• Scottys Castle Gg106
• Sierra Mono Mus. Gc106
• South Ent. Gb105
• Tunnel Log Gd107
• Tuolumne Grove Gb105
• Ubehebe Crater Gg106
• Wassama Round House S.H.P. Gb106
• Yosemite Pioneer History Center Gb105
68
Death Valley N.P. → 106
61

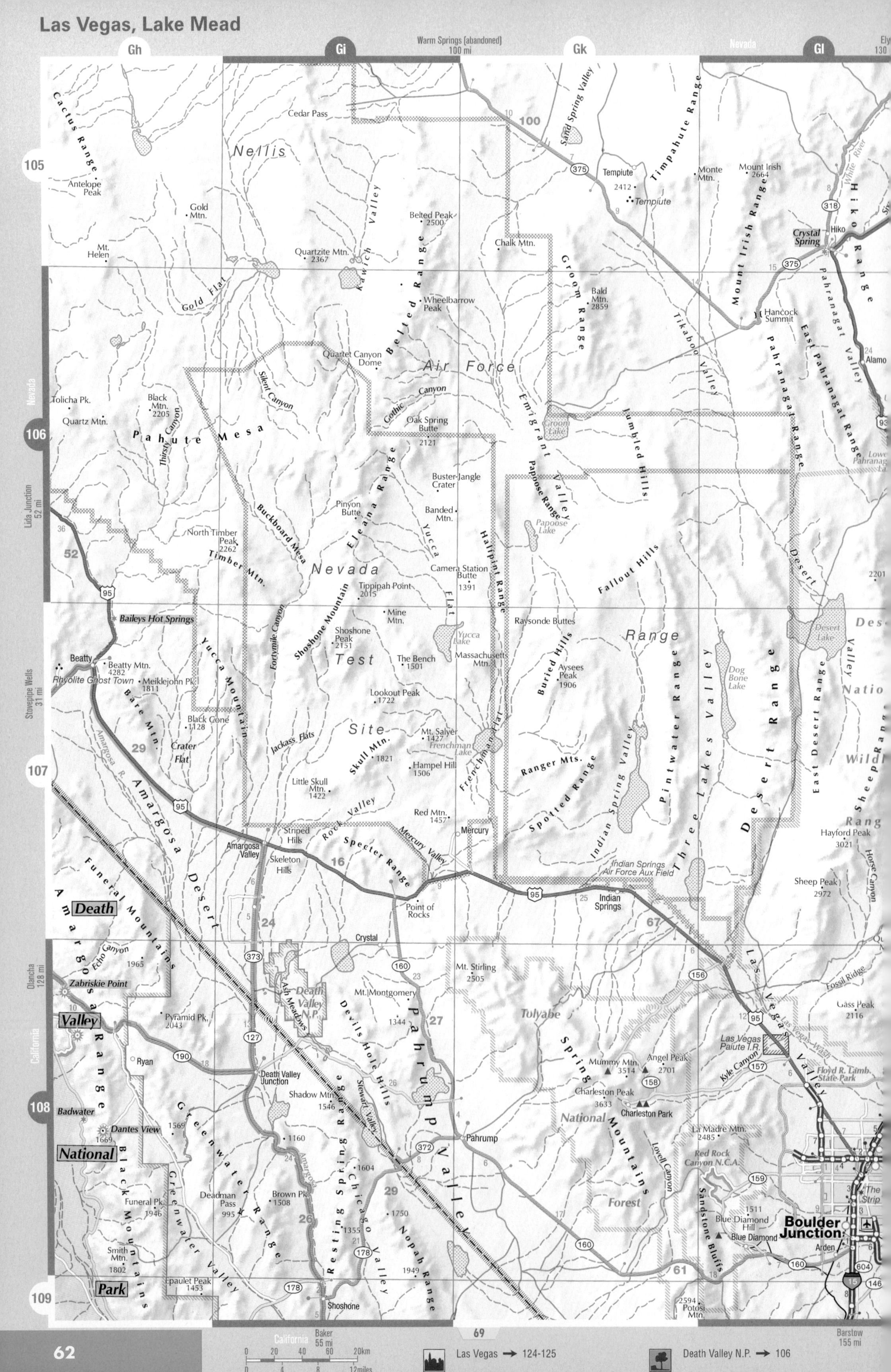
Gh
Gi
Warm Springs (abandoned)
100 mi
Gk
Nevada
Gl
Ely
130
105
106
107
108
109
Nevada
California
Lida Junction
52 mi
Stovepipe Wells
31 mi
Olancha
128 mi
Cactus Range
Antelope Peak
Gold Mtn.
Mt. Helen
Cedar Pass
Nellis
Kawich Valley
Belted Peak
2500
Quartzite Mtn.
2367
Gold Flat
Belted Range
Wheelbarrow Peak
Quartet Canyon Dome
Air Force
Gothic Canyon
Oak Spring Butte
2121
Silent Canyon
Tolicha Pk.
Quartz Mtn.
Black Mtn.
2205
Thirsty Canyon
Pahute Mesa
Buckboard Mesa
Eleana Range
Pinyon Butte
Buster-Jangle Crater
Banded Mtn.
Yucca Flat
North Timber Peak
2262
Timber Mtn.
Nevada
Tippipah Point
2015
Camera Station Butte
1391
Halfpint Range
Shoshone Mountain
Fortymile Canyon
Mine Mtn.
Shoshone Peak
2151
Test
The Bench
1501
Yucca Lake
Massachusetts Mtn.
Baileys Hot Springs
Beatty
Beatty Mtn.
4282
Rhyolite Ghost Town
Meiklejohn Pk.
1811
Yucca Mountain
Bare Mtn.
Black Cone
1128
Crater Flat
Lookout Peak
1722
Site
Jackass Flats
Skull Mtn.
1821
Mt. Salyer
1427
Frenchman Lake
Frenchman Flat
Hampel Hill
1506
Little Skull Mtn.
1422
Rock Valley
Red Mtn.
1457
Mercury
Mercury Valley
Striped Hills
Amargosa Valley
Skeleton Hills
Specter Range
Point of Rocks
Amargosa R.
Amargosa Desert
Funeral Mountains
Amargosa Range
Death Valley
National Park
Echo Canyon
1965
Zabriskie Point
Pyramid Pk.
2043
Ryan
Death Valley Junction
Ash Meadows
Death Valley N.P.
Crystal
Mt. Montgomery
1344
Devils Hole Hills
Pahrump Valley
Mt. Stirling
2505
Shadow Mtn.
1546
Stewart Valley
Pahrump
Badwater
Dantes View
1669
1569
Greenwater Range
Greenwater Valley
1160
Resting Spring Range
Chicago Valley
1604
Amargosa
Black Mountains
Funeral Pk.
1946
Deadman Pass
995
Brown Pk.
1508
1355
1750
Nopah Range
1949
Smith Mtn.
1802
Epaulet Peak
1453
Shoshone
Sand Spring Valley
Tempiute
2412
Timpahute Range
Monte Mtn.
Mount Irish
2664
Mount Irish Range
White River
Hiko Range
Crystal Spring
Hiko
Chalk Mtn.
Groom Range
Bald Mtn.
2859
Tikaboo Valley
Hancock Summit
Pahranagat Valley
East Pahranagat Range
Pahranagat Range
Alamo
Groom Lake
Emigrant Valley
Papoose Range
Papoose Lake
Jumbled Hills
Lower Pahranagat
Desert
Fallout Hills
2201
Raysonde Buttes
Range
Desert Lake
Desert Valley
Buried Hills
Aysees Peak
1906
Dog Bone Lake
Three Lakes Valley
Pintwater Range
Desert Range
East Desert Range
Desert National Wildlife Range
Sheep Range
Ranger Mts.
Spotted Range
Indian Spring Valley
Indian Springs Air Force Aux Field
Indian Springs
Hayford Peak
3021
Sheep Peak
2972
Horse Canyon
Fossil Ridge
Gass Peak
2116
Las Vegas Valley
Las Vegas Wash
Las Vegas Paiute I.R.
Toiyabe
Spring Mountains
National Forest
Mummy Mtn.
3514
Angel Peak
2701
Kyle Canyon
Floyd R. Lamb State Park
Charleston Peak
3633
Charleston Park
La Madre Mtn.
2485
Red Rock Canyon N.C.A.
Lovell Canyon
Sandstone Bluffs
Blue Diamond Hill
1511
Blue Diamond
Boulder Junction
Arden
The Strip
2594
Potosi Mtn.
375
318
95
52
373
160
127
190
372
178
156
157
158
159
604
146
15
16
24
26
27
29
61
67
100

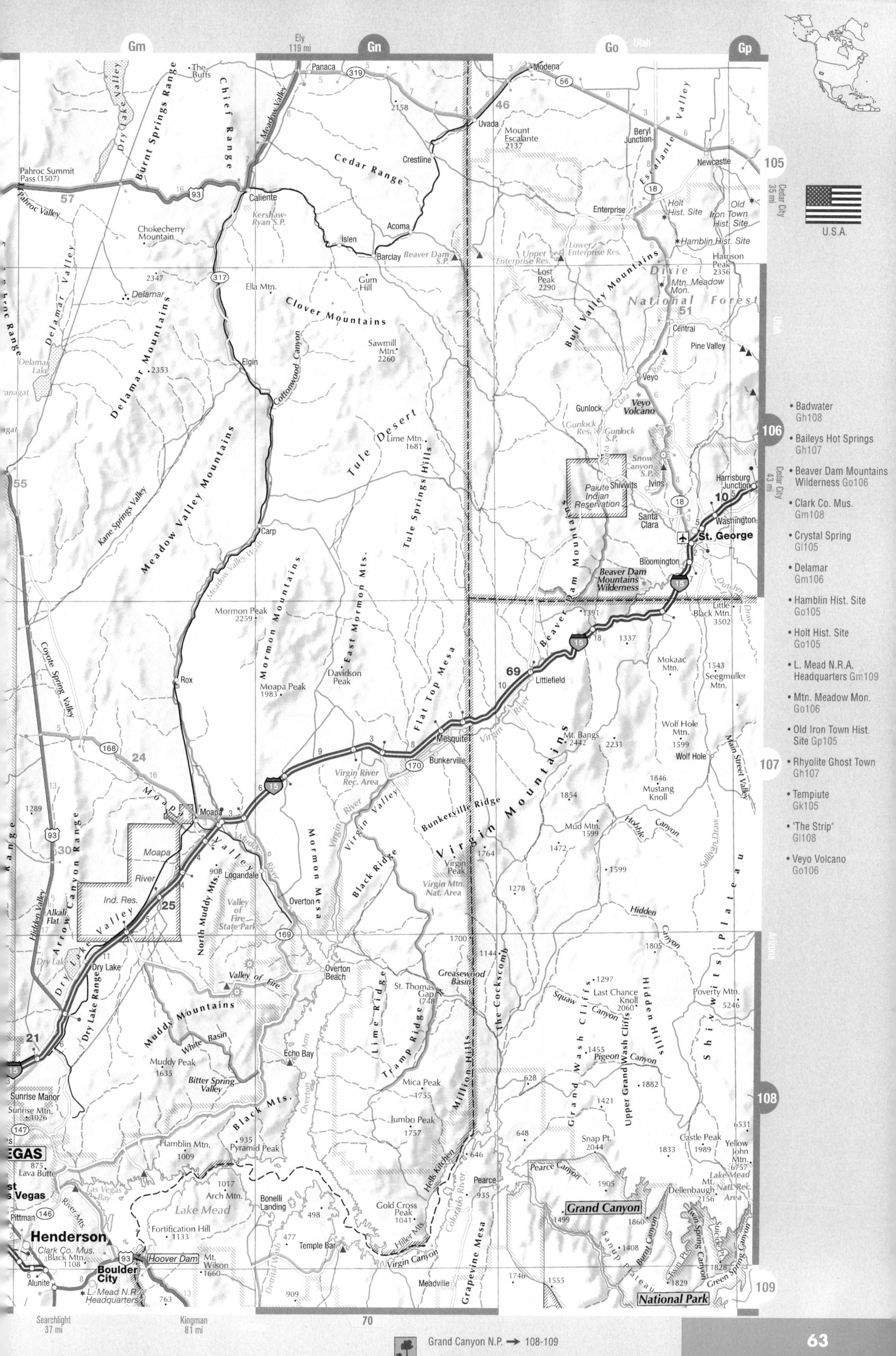

- Badwater Gh108
- Baileys Hot Springs Gh107
- Beaver Dam Mountains Wilderness Go106
- Clark Co. Mus. Gm108
- Crystal Spring Gl105
- Delamar Gm106
- Hamblin Hist. Site Go105
- Holt Hist. Site Go105
- L. Mead N.R.A. Headquarters Gm109
- Mtn. Meadow Mon. Go106
- Old Iron Town Hist. Site Gp105
- Rhyolite Ghost Town Gh107
- Tempiute Gk105
- "The Strip" Gl108
- Veyo Volcano Go106

Grand Canyon N.P. → 108-109

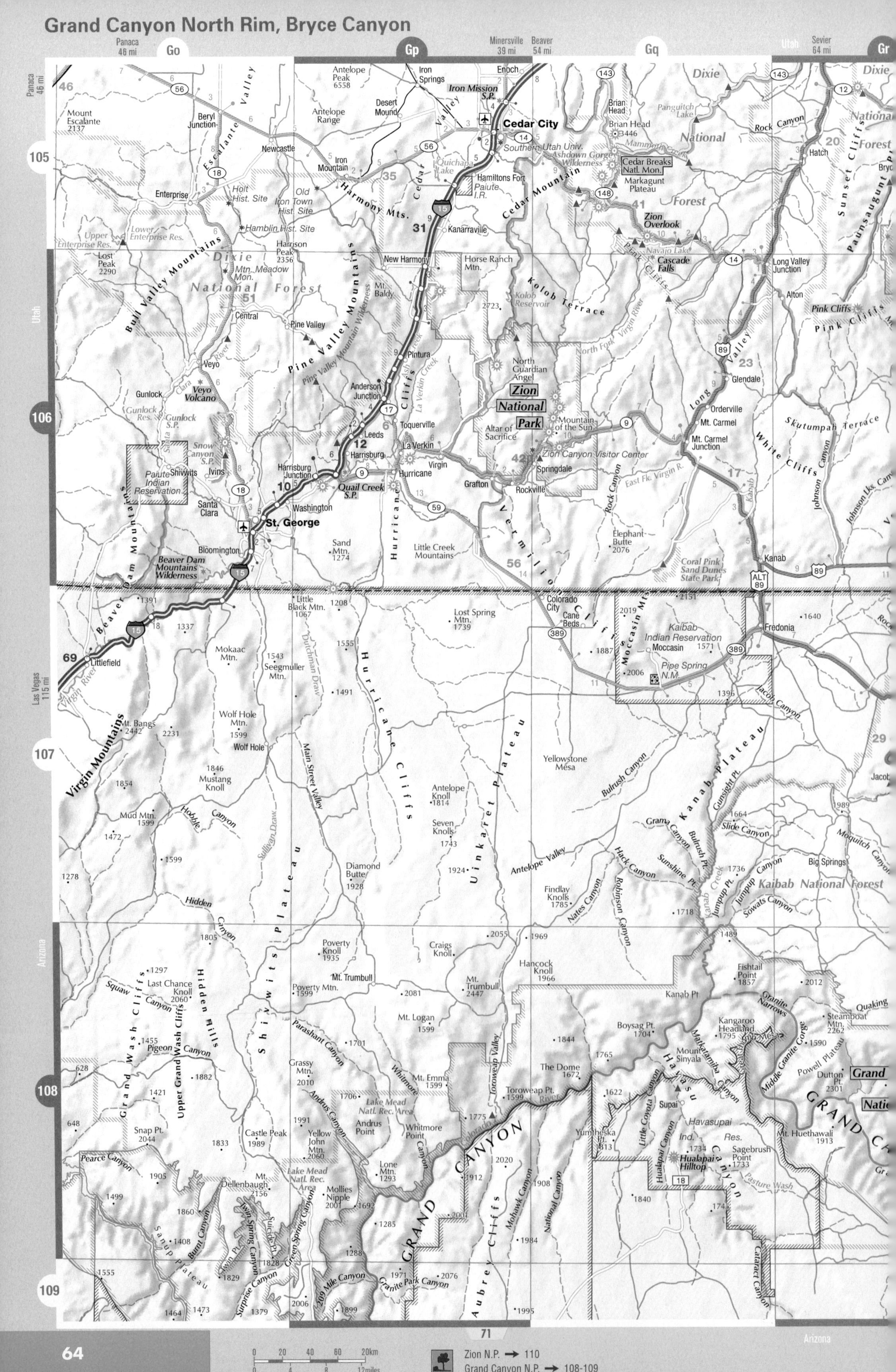

0 20 40 60 20km
0 4 8 12miles

Zion N.P. → 110
Grand Canyon N.P. → 108-109

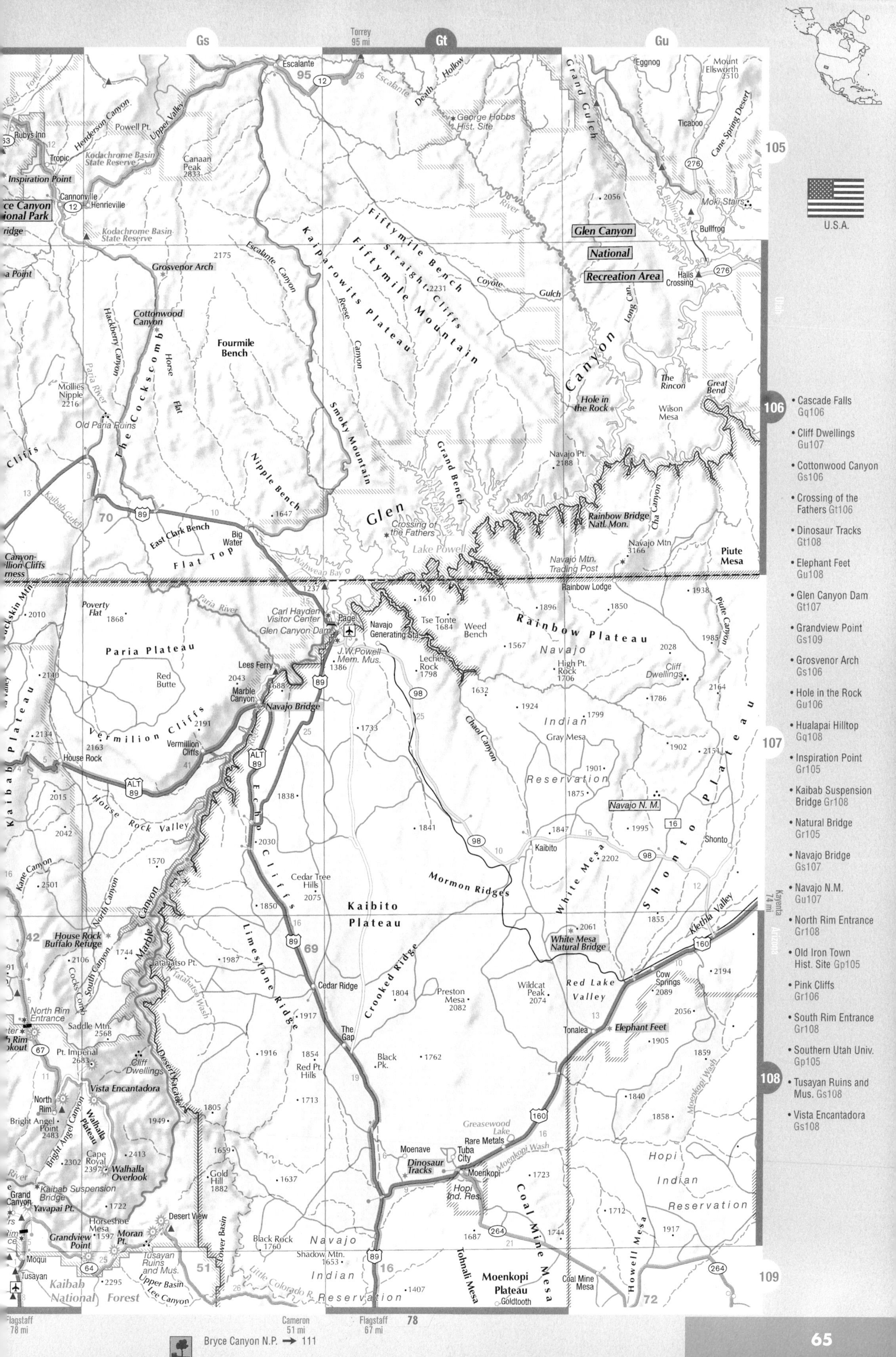

Gs
Torrey 95 mi
Gt
Gu
105
U.S.A.
Utah
106
107
108
109
Arizona
Kayenta 74 mi
Escalante
Death Hollow
George Hobbs Hist. Site
Eggnog
Mount Ellsworth 2510
Grand Gulch
Ticaboo
Cane Spring Desert
Rubys Inn
Tropic
Henderson Canyon
Powell Pt.
Upper Valley
Kodachrome Basin State Reserve
Canaan Peak 2833
Inspiration Point
Cannonville
Henrieville
Bryce Canyon National Park
Moki Stairs
Bullfrog
Glen Canyon National Recreation Area
Halls Crossing
Grosvenor Arch
Escalante Canyon
Fiftymile Bench
Straight Cliffs
Fiftymile Mountain
Kaiparowits Plateau
Coyote Gulch
Long Can.
Cottonwood Canyon
Hackberry Canyon
The Cockscomb
Horse Flat
Fourmile Bench
Reese Canyon
Canyon
Paria River
Mollies Nipple 2216
Old Paria Ruins
The Rincon
Great Bend
Hole in the Rock
Wilson Mesa
Smoky Mountain
Nipple Bench
Grand Bench
Navajo Pt. 2188
Cliffs
Kaibab Gulch
East Clark Bench
Big Water
Flat Top
Glen
Crossing of the Fathers
Lake Powell
Wahweap Bay
Rainbow Bridge Natl. Mon.
Cha Canyon
Navajo Mtn. 3166
Navajo Mtn. Trading Post
Piute Mesa
Rainbow Lodge
Poverty Flat
Carl Hayden Visitor Center
Glen Canyon Dam
Page
Navajo Generating Sta.
Tse Tonte 1684
Weed Bench
Rainbow Plateau
Navajo
Piute Canyon
Paria Plateau
Red Butte
Lees Ferry
Marble Canyon
Navajo Bridge
J.W. Powell Mem. Mus.
Lechee Rock 1798
High Pt. Rock 1706
Cliff Dwellings
Vermilion Cliffs
House Rock
Chaol Canyon
Indian
Gray Mesa
Reservation
Navajo N. M.
Kaibab Plateau
House Rock Valley
Echo Cliffs
Kaibito
White Mesa
Shonto
Shonto Plateau
Kane Canyon
North Canyon
Cedar Tree Hills
Mormon Ridges
Kaibito Plateau
Limestone Ridge
Klethla Valley
House Rock Buffalo Refuge
Marble Canyon
South Canyon
Cocks Comb
Tatahatso Pt.
Tatahatso Wash
White Mesa Natural Bridge
Cedar Ridge
Crooked Ridge
Preston Mesa 2082
Wildcat Peak 2074
Red Lake Valley
Cow Springs
North Rim Entrance
Saddle Mtn. 2568
Pt. Imperial 2683
Cliff Dwellings
The Gap
Black Pk.
Red Pt. Hills
Tonalea
Elephant Feet
Vista Encantadora
Desert Facade
North Rim
Bright Angel Point 2483
Bright Angel Canyon
Walhalla Plateau
Cape Royal 2397
Walhalla Overlook
Greasewood Lake
Rare Metals
Moenave
Tuba City
Dinosaur Tracks
Moenkopi
Moenkopi Wash
Hopi Ind. Res.
Hopi Indian Reservation
Gold Hill 1882
Kaibab Suspension Bridge
Grand Canyon
Yavapai Pt.
Horseshoe Mesa
Desert View
Grandview Point
Moran Pt.
Lower Basin
Black Rock 1760
Navajo
Shadow Mtn. 1653
Indian Reservation
Tohnali Mesa
Coal Mine Mesa
Howell Mesa
Moqui
Tusayan
Tusayan Ruins and Mus.
Upper Basin
Lee Canyon
Kaibab National Forest
Little Colorado R.
Moenkopi Plateau
Goldtooth
Coal Mine Mesa
Flagstaff 78 mi
Cameron 51 mi
Flagstaff 67 mi
78
Bryce Canyon N.P. → 111
• Cascade Falls Gq106
• Cliff Dwellings Gu107
• Cottonwood Canyon Gs106
• Crossing of the Fathers Gt106
• Dinosaur Tracks Gt108
• Elephant Feet Gu108
• Glen Canyon Dam Gt107
• Grandview Point Gs109
• Grosvenor Arch Gs106
• Hole in the Rock Gu106
• Hualapai Hilltop Gq108
• Inspiration Point Gr105
• Kaibab Suspension Bridge Gr108
• Natural Bridge Gr105
• Navajo Bridge Gs107
• Navajo N.M. Gu107
• North Rim Entrance Gr108
• Old Iron Town Hist. Site Gp105
• Pink Cliffs Gr106
• South Rim Entrance Gr108
• Southern Utah Univ. Gp105
• Tusayan Ruins and Mus. Gs108
• Vista Encantadora Gs108

Monterey 100 mi
Fs
Salinas 54 mi
Ft
59
San Jose 111 mi
Fu
Oilfields 9 mi
Ga
Hayward 186 mi
108
109
110
111
112
72
PACIFIC
OCEAN
Santa Lucia Range
Julia Pfeiffer Burns S.P.
McWay Waterfall
Lopez Point
Lucia
Cape San Martin
Gorda
Ragged Point
Pt. Piedras Blancas
San Simeon Point
San Simeon
Wm. Randolph Hearst Mem. S.B.
San Simeon S.B.
Hearst San Simeon S.H.M.
Cambria
Harmony
Point Estero
Cayucos
Cayucos S.B.
Morro Strand S.B.
Estero Bay
Morro Rock
Morro Bay
Baywood Park
Los Osos
Montana de Oro S.P.
Point Buchon
Irish Hills
Avila Beach
Point San Luis
San Luis Obispo Bay
Grover City
Pismo S.B.
Pismo Dunes S.V.R.A.
Guadalupe
Point Sal
Point Sal S.B.
Purisima Point
Vandenburg Air Force Base
Surf
Space Shuttle Launch Complex
Honda
Point Arguello
Jalama
Point Conception
King City
San Lucas
San Ardo
Jolon
Lockwood
Bradley
Lake San Antonio Rec. Area
Lake Nacimiento Rec. Area
Camp Roberts Military Res.
San Miguel
Mission San Miguel Arcangel
Paso Robles
Templeton
Atascadero
Santa Margarita
San Luis Obispo
Mission San Luis Obispo de Tolosa
Pismo Beach
Arroyo Grande
Oceano
Nipomo
Santa Maria
Orcutt
Lompoc
Buellton
Solvang
Gaviota
Coalinga
Parkfield
Shandon
Cholame
Cholame Hills
Creston
Lopez Lake R.A.
Huasna
Los Padres National Forest
La Panza Range
Solomon Hills
Purisima Hills
La Purisima Mission S.H.P.
Los Alamos
Gaviota S.P.
Refugio
66

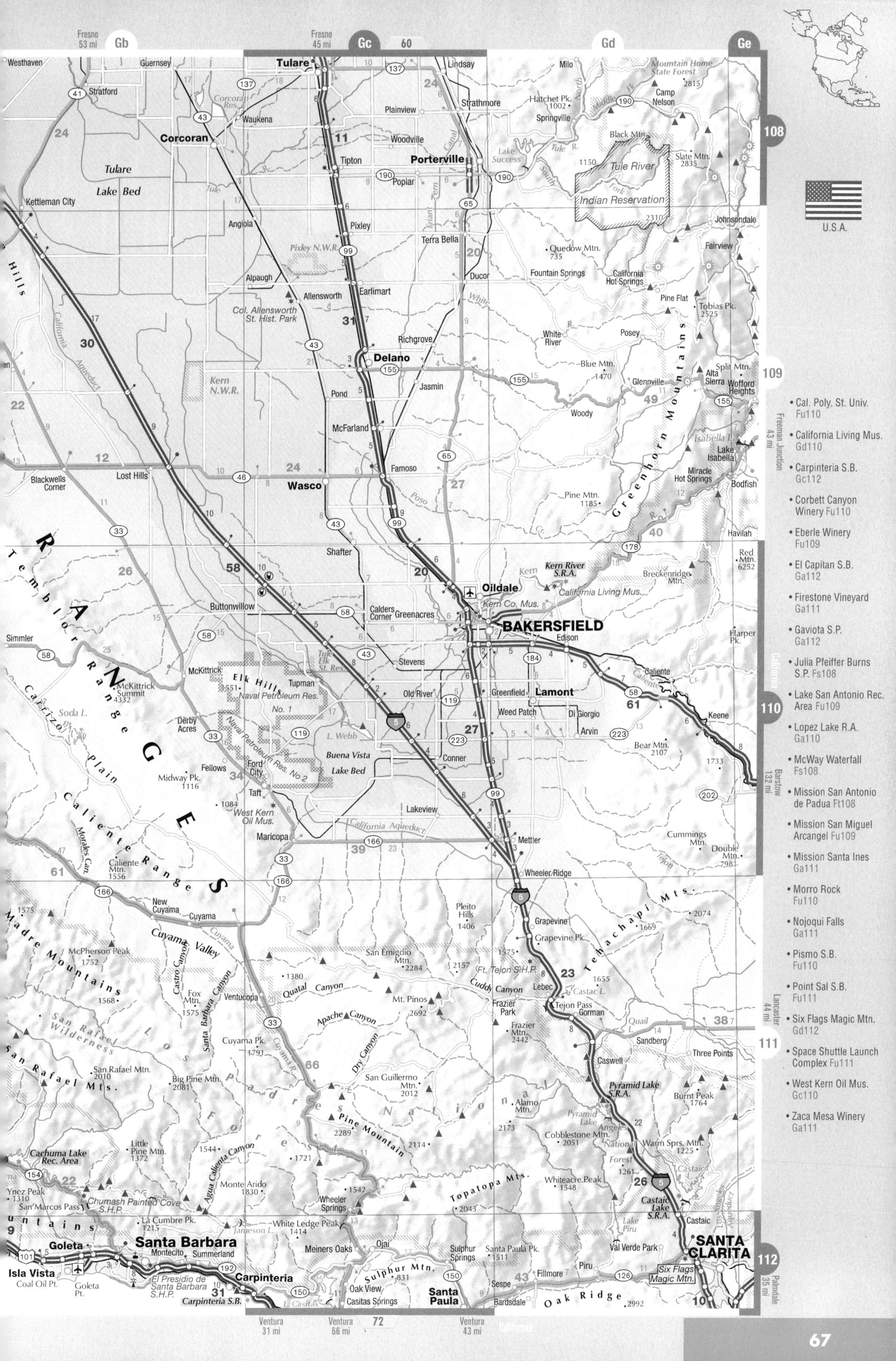

Fresno 53 mi
Gb
Fresno 45 mi
Gc
60
Gd
Ge
108
109
110
111
112
U.S.A.
Freeman Junction 43 mi
Barstow 132 mi
Lancaster 44 mi
Palmdale 35 mi
California
Ventura 31 mi
Ventura 66 mi
72
Ventura 43 mi
Westhaven
Stratford
Guernsey
Corcoran
Waukena
Tulare
Tulare Lake Bed
Kettleman City
Angiola
Alpaugh
Lindsay
Strathmore
Plainview
Woodville
Tipton
Porterville
Popiar
Pixley
Pixley N.W.R.
Terra Bella
Ducor
Earlimart
Allensworth
Col. Allensworth St. Hist. Park
Richgrove
Delano
Jasmin
Pond
McFarland
Kern N.W.R.
Famoso
Wasco
Lost Hills
Blackwells Corner
Shafter
Buttonwillow
Calders Corner
Greenacres
Oildale
Kern Co. Mus.
BAKERSFIELD
Edison
Stevens
Tule Elk St. Res.
McKittrick
McKittrick Summit 4332
Elk Hills Naval Petroleum Res. No. 1
Naval Petroleum Res. No 2
Tupman
Old River
Greenfield
Lamont
Weed Patch
Di Giorgio
Arvin
Derby Acres
L. Webb
Buena Vista Lake Bed
Conner
Fellows
Midway Pk. 1116
Ford City
Taft
West Kern Oil Mus.
Lakeview
California Aqueduct
Maricopa
Mettler
Wheeler Ridge
Simmler
Soda L.
Carrizo Plain
Temblor Range
RANGES
Caliente Range
Caliente Mtn. 1556
Morales Can.
New Cuyama
Cuyama
Cuyama Valley
Sierra Madre Mountains
McPherson Peak 1752
Castro Canyon
Fox Mtn. 1575
Ventucopa
Santa Barbara Canyon
Quatal Canyon
San Rafael Wilderness
San Rafael Mts.
San Rafael Mtn. 2010
Big Pine Mtn. 2081
Cuyama Pk. 1791
Los Padres National Forest
Apache Canyon
Dry Canyon
San Emigdio Mtn. 2284
Mt. Pinos 2692
San Guillermo Mtn. 2012
Pine Mountain
Pleito Hills 1406
Ft. Tejon S.H.P.
Cuddy Canyon
Frazier Park
Frazier Mtn. 2442
Lebec
Castac L.
Tejon Pass
Gorman
Grapevine
Grapevine Pk.
Tehachapi Mts.
Quail L.
Sandberg
Three Points
Caswell
Pyramid Lake S.R.A.
Burnt Peak 1764
Alamo Mtn.
Cobblestone Mtn. 2051
Angeles National Forest
Warm Sprs. Mtn. 1225
Whiteacre Peak 1548
Topatopa Mts.
Castaic Lake S.R.A.
Castaic
Lake Piru
Val Verde Park
SANTA CLARITA
Six Flags Magic Mtn.
Piru
Fillmore
Sespe
Bardsdale
Oak Ridge 2992
Santa Paula Pk. 1511
Sulphur Springs
Santa Paula
Sulphur Mtn.
Ojai
Oak View
Casitas Springs
Meiners Oaks
Wheeler Springs
White Ledge Peak 1414
Monte Arido 1830
Agua Caliente Canyon
Little Pine Mtn. 1372
Cachuma Lake Rec. Area
Ynez Peak 1310
San Marcos Pass
Chumash Painted Cove S.H.P.
La Cumbre Pk. 1213
Santa Ynez Mountains
Goleta
Santa Barbara
Montecito
Summerland
Isla Vista
Coal Oil Pt.
Goleta Pt.
El Presidio de Santa Barbara S.H.P.
Carpinteria
Carpinteria S.B.
Milo
Mountain Home State Forest 2815
Camp Nelson
Hatchet Pk. 1002
Springville
Lake Success
Tule R.
Black Mtn.
Tule River Indian Reservation
Slate Mtn. 2835
Johnsondale
Quedow Mtn. 735
Fountain Springs
California Hot Springs
Fairview
Pine Flat
Tobias Pk. 2525
White River
Posey
Blue Mtn. 1470
Glennville
Woody
Split Mtn.
Alta Sierra
Wofford Heights
Greenhorn Mountains
Isabella L.
Lake Isabella
Miracle Hot Springs
Bodfish
Pine Mtn. 1185
Havilah
Kern River S.R.A.
California Living Mus.
Breckenridge Mtn.
Red Mtn. 6252
Harper Pk.
Caliente
Keene
Bear Mtn. 2107
Cummings Mtn.
Double Mtn. 7981
Tejon
• Cal. Poly. St. Univ. Fu110
• California Living Mus. Gd110
• Carpinteria S.B. Gc112
• Corbett Canyon Winery Fu110
• Eberle Winery Fu109
• El Capitan S.B. Ga112
• Firestone Vineyard Ga111
• Gaviota S.P. Ga112
• Julia Pfeiffer Burns S.P. Fs108
• Lake San Antonio Rec. Area Fu109
• Lopez Lake R.A. Ga110
• McWay Waterfall Fs108
• Mission San Antonio de Padua Ft108
• Mission San Miguel Arcangel Fu109
• Mission Santa Ines Ga111
• Morro Rock Fu110
• Nojoqui Falls Ga111
• Pismo S.B. Fu110
• Point Sal S.B. Fu111
• Six Flags Magic Mtn. Gd112
• Space Shuttle Launch Complex Fu111
• West Kern Oil Mus. Gc110
• Zaca Mesa Winery Ga111

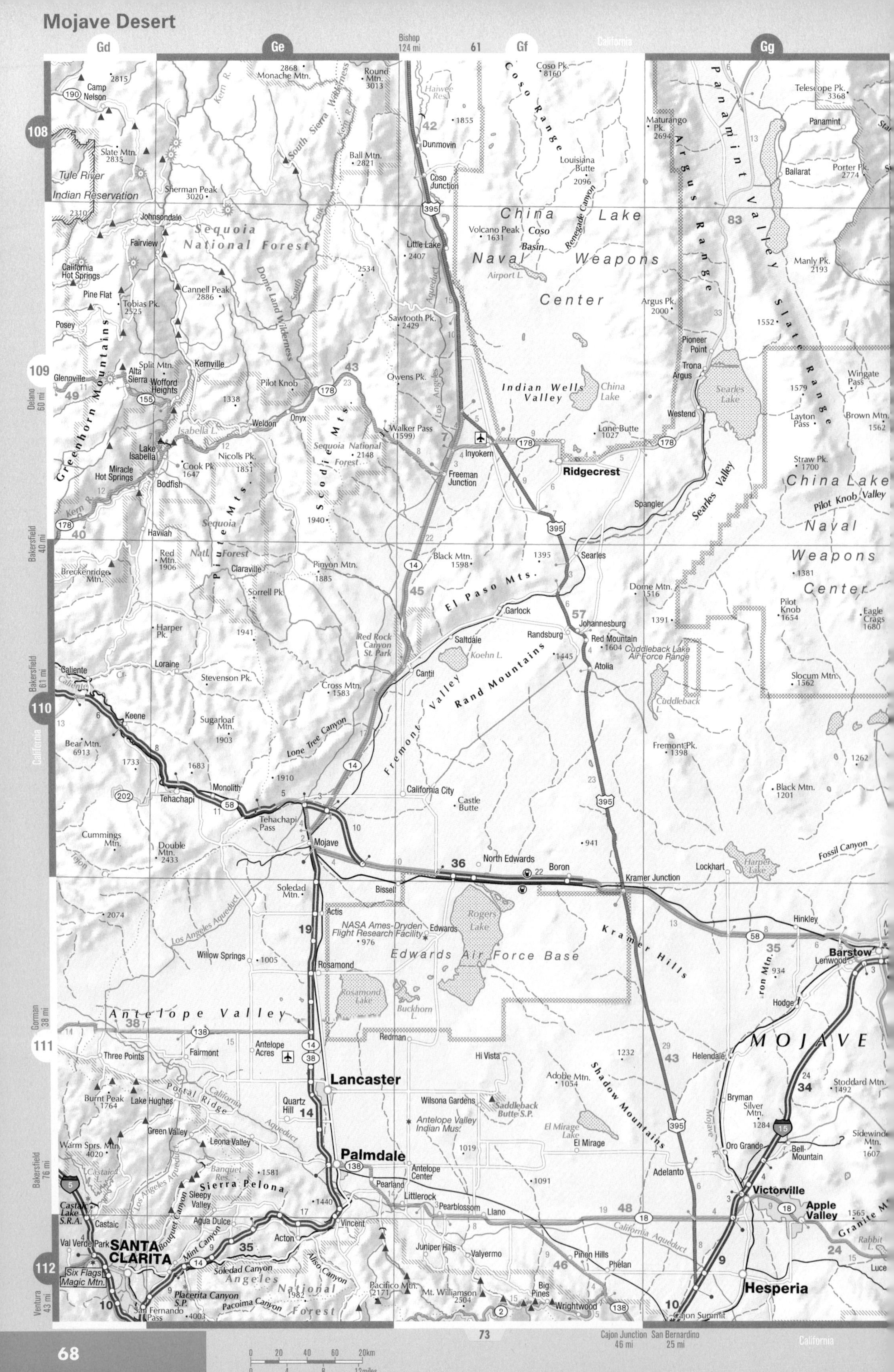
Gd
Ge
Gf
Gg
Bishop 124 mi
61
California
108
109
110
111
112
Delano 60 mi
Bakersfield 40 mi
Bakersfield 61 mi
California
Gorman 38 mi
Bakersfield 76 mi
Ventura 43 mi
73
Cajon Junction 46 mi
San Bernardino 25 mi
California
Camp Nelson
2815
Slate Mtn. 2835
Tule River Indian Reservation
Sherman Peak 3020
2868 Monache Mtn.
Round Mtn. 3013
South Sierra Wilderness
Kern R.
Ball Mtn. 2821
Haiwee Res.
1855
Dunmovin
Coso Junction
Coso Pk. 8160
Coso Range
Louisiana Butte 2096
Renegade Canyon
Maturango Pk. 2694
Argus Range
Panamint Valley
Telescope Pk. 3368
Panamint
Ballarat
Porter Pk. 2774
Slate Range
Manly Pk. 2193
2310
Johnsondale
Sequoia National Forest
Fairview
California Hot Springs
Dome Land Wilderness
2534
Cannell Peak 2886
Pine Flat
Tobias Pk. 2525
Posey
Greenhorn Mountains
Glennville
Alta Sierra
Split Mtn.
Wofford Heights
Kernville
Pilot Knob
1338
Isabella L.
Lake Isabella
Weldon
Onyx
Scodie Mts.
Sequoia National Forest
2148
Walker Pass (1599)
Owens Pk.
Sawtooth Pk. 2429
Little Lake 2407
Aqueduct
Los Angeles
China Lake Naval Weapons Center
Volcano Peak 1631
Coso Basin
Airport L.
Argus Pk. 2000
1552
Pioneer Point
Trona
Argus
Searles Lake
Westend
Wingate Pass
1579
Layton Pass
Brown Mtn. 1562
Indian Wells Valley
China Lake
Lone Butte 1027
Inyokern
Ridgecrest
Freeman Junction
Straw Pk. 1700
China Lake
Pilot Knob Valley
Naval Weapons Center
Searles Valley
Spangler
Miracle Hot Springs
Cook Pk. 1647
Nicolls Pk. 1851
Bodfish
Piute Mts.
Kern R.
Havilah
1940
Red Mtn. 1906
Breckenridge Mtn.
Claraville
Pinyon Mtn. 1885
Black Mtn. 1598
1395
Searles
El Paso Mts.
Sorrell Pk.
Garlock
Johannesburg
Dome Mtn. 1516
1381
Pilot Knob 1654
Eagle Crags 1680
Harper Pk.
1941
Red Rock Canyon St. Park
Saltdale
Randsburg
Red Mountain 1604
Cuddleback Lake Air Force Range
1391
Koehn L.
1445
Atolia
Loraine
Caliente
Stevenson Pk.
Cantil
Rand Mountains
Cuddleback L.
Slocum Mtn. 1562
Keene
Cross Mtn. 1583
Fremont Valley
Bear Mtn. 6913
Sugarloaf Mtn. 1903
Lone Tree Canyon
Fremont Pk. 1398
1262
1733
1683
1910
Black Mtn. 1201
Monolith
Tehachapi
California City
Castle Butte
Tehachapi Pass
Mojave
Cummings Mtn.
Double Mtn. 2433
941
Fossil Canyon
Tejon Cr.
North Edwards
Boron
Lockhart
Harper Lake
Kramer Junction
Soledad Mtn.
Bissell
2074
Actis
Rogers Lake
Hinkley
Los Angeles Aqueduct
NASA Ames-Dryden Flight Research Facility 976
Edwards
Kramer Hills
Barstow
Lenwood
934
Willow Springs 1005
Rosamond
Edwards Air Force Base
Rosamond Lake
Buckhorn L.
Hodge
Antelope Valley
Redman
MOJAVE
Three Points
Fairmont
Antelope Acres
Hi Vista
1232
Helendale
Adobe Mtn. 1054
Shadow Mountains
Stoddard Mtn. 1492
Burnt Peak 1764
Lake Hughes
Portal Ridge
California Aqueduct
Lancaster
Quartz Hill
Wilsona Gardens
Saddleback Butte S.P.
Antelope Valley Indian Mus.
El Mirage Lake
El Mirage
Bryman
Silver Mtn. 1284
Mojave R.
Green Valley
Leona Valley
Warm Sprs. Mtn. 4020
1019
Oro Grande
Bell Mountain
Sidewinder Mtn. 1607
Castaic L.
Banquet Res.
1581
Palmdale
Antelope Center
1091
Adelanto
Sierra Pelona
Sleepy Valley
Pearland
Victorville
Apple Valley
1565
Granite Mts.
Castaic Lake S.R.A.
Castaic
1440
Littlerock
Pearblossom
Llano
Agua Dulce
Vincent
Val Verde Park
SANTA CLARITA
Bouquet Canyon
Mint Canyon
Acton
Juniper Hills
Valyermo
Pinon Hills
Phelan
Rabbit L.
Luce
Six Flags Magic Mtn.
Soledad Canyon
Angeles National Forest
Aliso Canyon
Pacifico Mtn. 2171
Mt. Williamson 2504
Big Pines
Wrightwood
Hesperia
Placerita Canyon S.P.
Pacoima Canyon
1982
San Fernando Pass
4003
Cajon Summit
0 20 40 60 20km
0 4 8 12miles

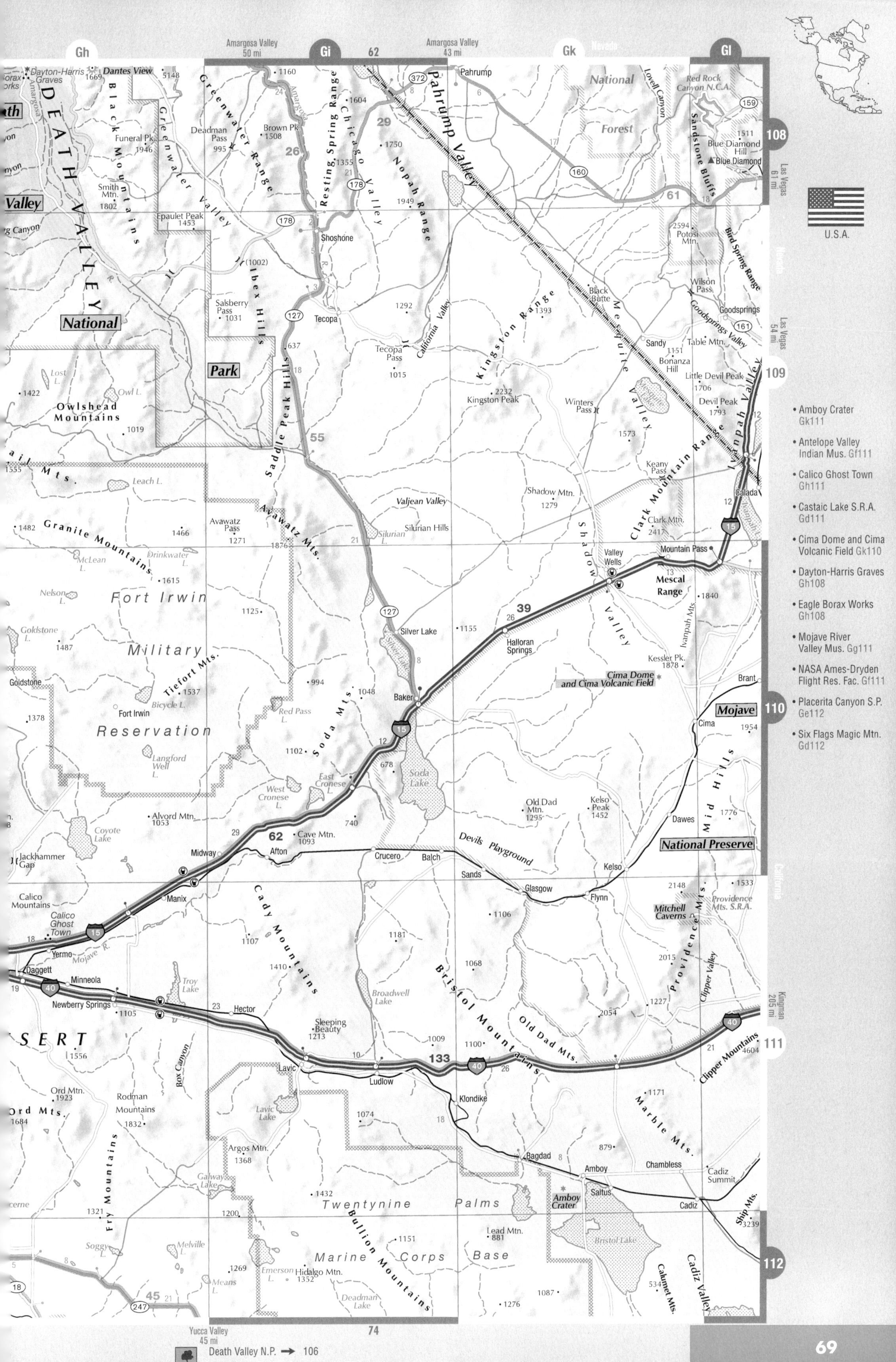

- Amboy Crater Gk111
- Antelope Valley Indian Mus. Gf111
- Calico Ghost Town Gh111
- Castaic Lake S.R.A. Gd111
- Cima Dome and Cima Volcanic Field Gk110
- Dayton-Harris Graves Gh108
- Eagle Borax Works Gh108
- Mojave River Valley Mus. Gg111
- NASA Ames-Dryden Flight Res. Fac. Gf111
- Placerita Canyon S.P. Ge112
- Six Flags Magic Mtn. Gd112

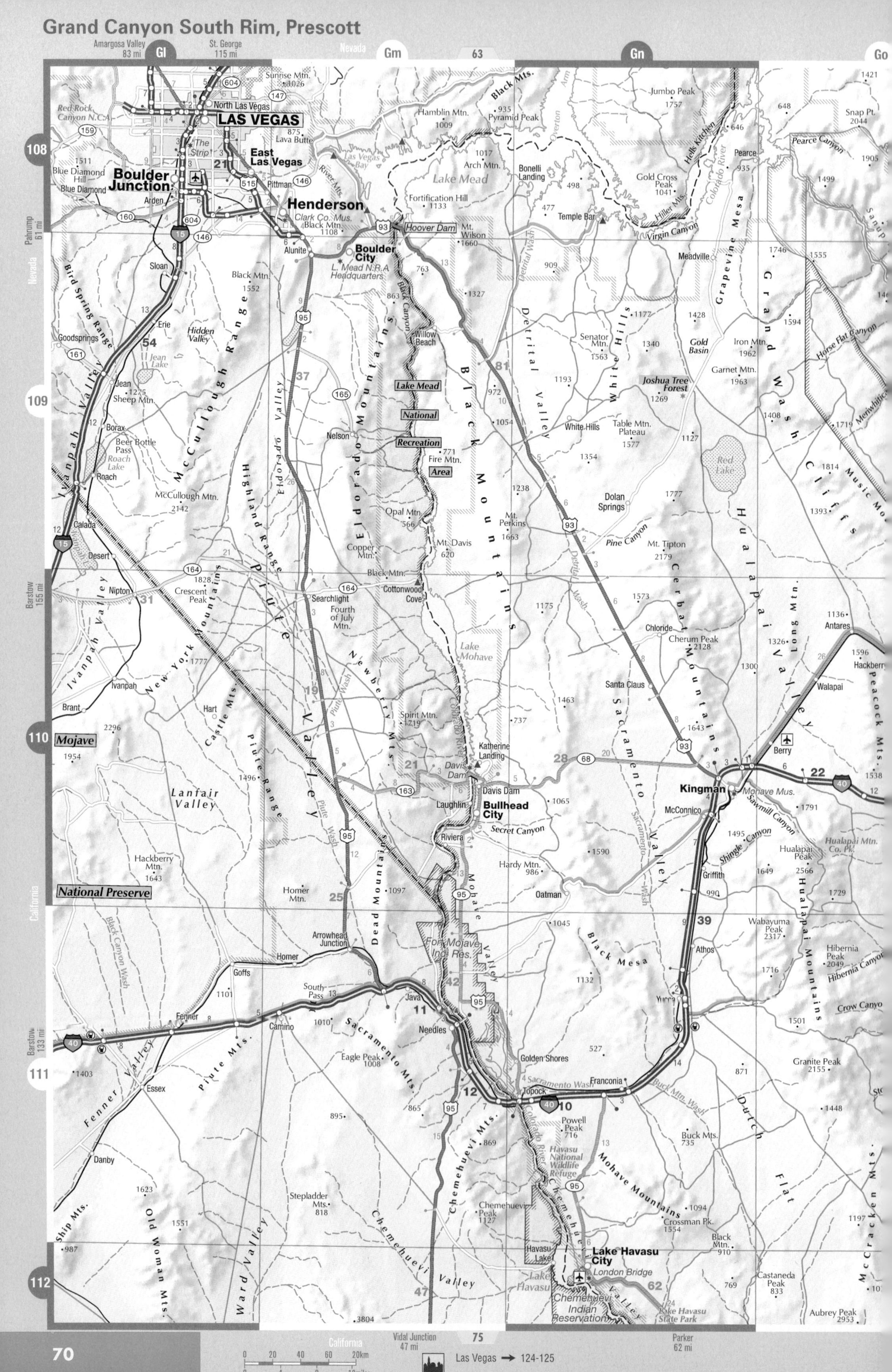

Las Vegas → 124-125

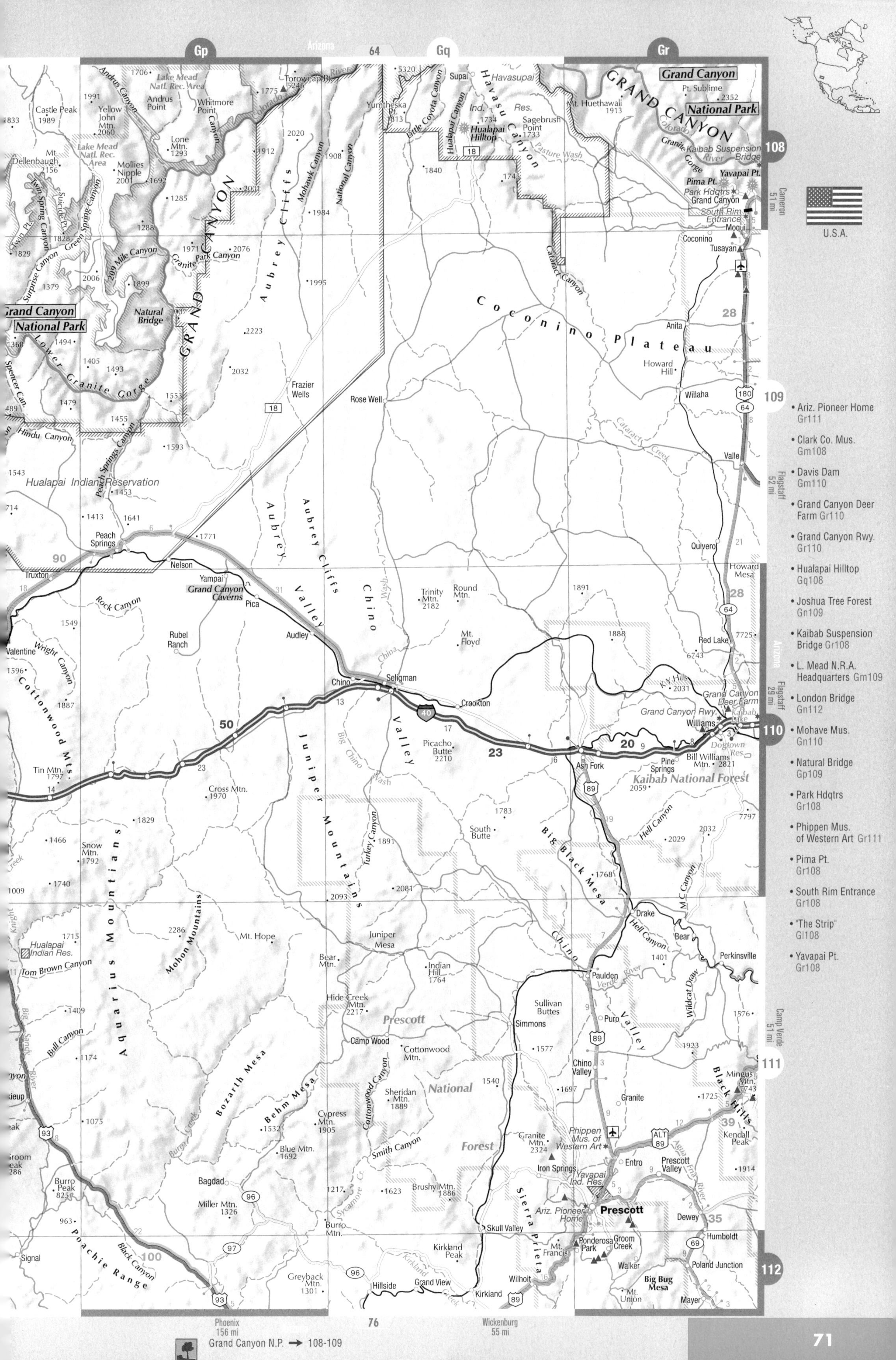

Gp
Arizona
64
Gq
Gr
Grand Canyon
National Park
GRAND CANYON
Pt. Sublime
Mt. Huethawali
Havasupai
Supai
Hualapai Hilltop
Havasu Canyon
Sagebrush Point
Kaibab Suspension Bridge
Yavapai Pt.
Pima Pt.
Park Hdqtrs
Grand Canyon
South Rim Entrance
Moqui
Coconino
Tusayan
108
Cameron 51 mi
U.S.A.
Lake Mead Natl. Rec. Area
Andrus Canyon
Andrus Point
Whitmore Point
Toroweap Pt.
Castle Peak
Yellow John Mtn.
Mt. Dellenbaugh
Mollies Nipple
Lone Mtn.
Twin Spring Canyon
Suicide Pt.
Green Spring Canyon
209 Mile Canyon
Granite Park Canyon
Surprise Canyon
Natural Bridge
Lower Granite Gorge
Spencer Can.
Hindu Canyon
Peach Springs Canyon
Aubrey Cliffs
Mohawk Canyon
National Canyon
Yumtheska Pt.
Little Coyota Canyon
Hualapai Canyon
Cataract Canyon
Coconino Plateau
Anita
Howard Hill
Frazier Wells
Rose Well
Willaha
109
Cataract Creek
Valle
Flagstaff 52 mi
Quivero
Howard Mesa
Hualapai Indian Reservation
Peach Springs
Truxton
Nelson
Yampai
Grand Canyon Caverns
Pica
Rock Canyon
Rubel Ranch
Audley
Chino Valley
Trinity Mtn.
Round Mtn.
Mt. Floyd
Red Lake
K.Y. Hills
Grand Canyon Deer Farm
Grand Canyon Rwy.
Williams
Flagstaff 29 mi
110
Valentine
Wright Canyon
Cottonwood Mts.
Chino
Seligman
Crookton
Picacho Butte
Junipe Mountains
Big Chino Wash
Ash Fork
Pine Springs
Bill Williams Mtn.
Dogtown
Kaibab National Forest
Tin Mtn.
Cross Mtn.
Snow Mtn.
Aquarius Mountains
South Butte
Big Black Mesa
Hell Canyon
Turkey Canyon
MC Canyon
Drake
Bear
Perkinsville
Hualapai Indian Res.
Tom Brown Canyon
Mohon Mountains
Mt. Hope
Juniper Mesa
Bear Mtn.
Indian Hill
Paulden
Verde River
Wildcat Draw
Hide Creek Mtn.
Prescott
Camp Wood
Cottonwood Mtn.
Sullivan Buttes
Simmons
Puro
Verde Valley
Camp Verde 51 mi
111
Bull Canyon
Big Sandy River
Bozarth Mesa
Behm Mesa
Cottonwood Canyon
Sheridan Mtn.
National Forest
Chino Valley
Granite
Mingus Mtn.
Black Hills
Cypress Mtn.
Blue Mtn.
Smith Canyon
Granite Mtn.
Phippen Mus. of Western Art
Kendall Peak
Groom Peak
Burro Peak
Bagdad
Miller Mtn.
Brushy Mtn.
Iron Springs
Yavapai Ind. Res.
Entro
Prescott Valley
Agua Fria River
Sierra Prieta
Ariz. Pioneer Home
Prescott
Dewey
Humboldt
Burro Creek
Sycamore Cr.
Burro Mtn.
Skull Valley
Ponderosa Park
Groom Creek
Mt. Francis
Poland Junction
112
Signal
Poachie Range
Black Canyon
Kirkland Peak
Greyback Mtn.
Hillside
Grand View
Kirkland Creek
Kirkland
Wilhoit
Walker
Big Bug Mesa
Mt. Union
Mayer
Phoenix 156 mi
76
Wickenburg 55 mi
Grand Canyon N.P. → 108-109
• Ariz. Pioneer Home Gr111
• Clark Co. Mus. Gm108
• Davis Dam Gm110
• Grand Canyon Deer Farm Gr110
• Grand Canyon Rwy. Gr110
• Hualapai Hilltop Gq108
• Joshua Tree Forest Gn109
• Kaibab Suspension Bridge Gr108
• L. Mead N.R.A. Headquarters Gm109
• London Bridge Gn112
• Mohave Mus. Gn110
• Natural Bridge Gp109
• Park Hdqtrs Gr108
• Phippen Mus. of Western Art Gr111
• Pima Pt. Gr108
• South Rim Entrance Gr108
• "The Strip" Gl108
• Yavapai Pt. Gr108

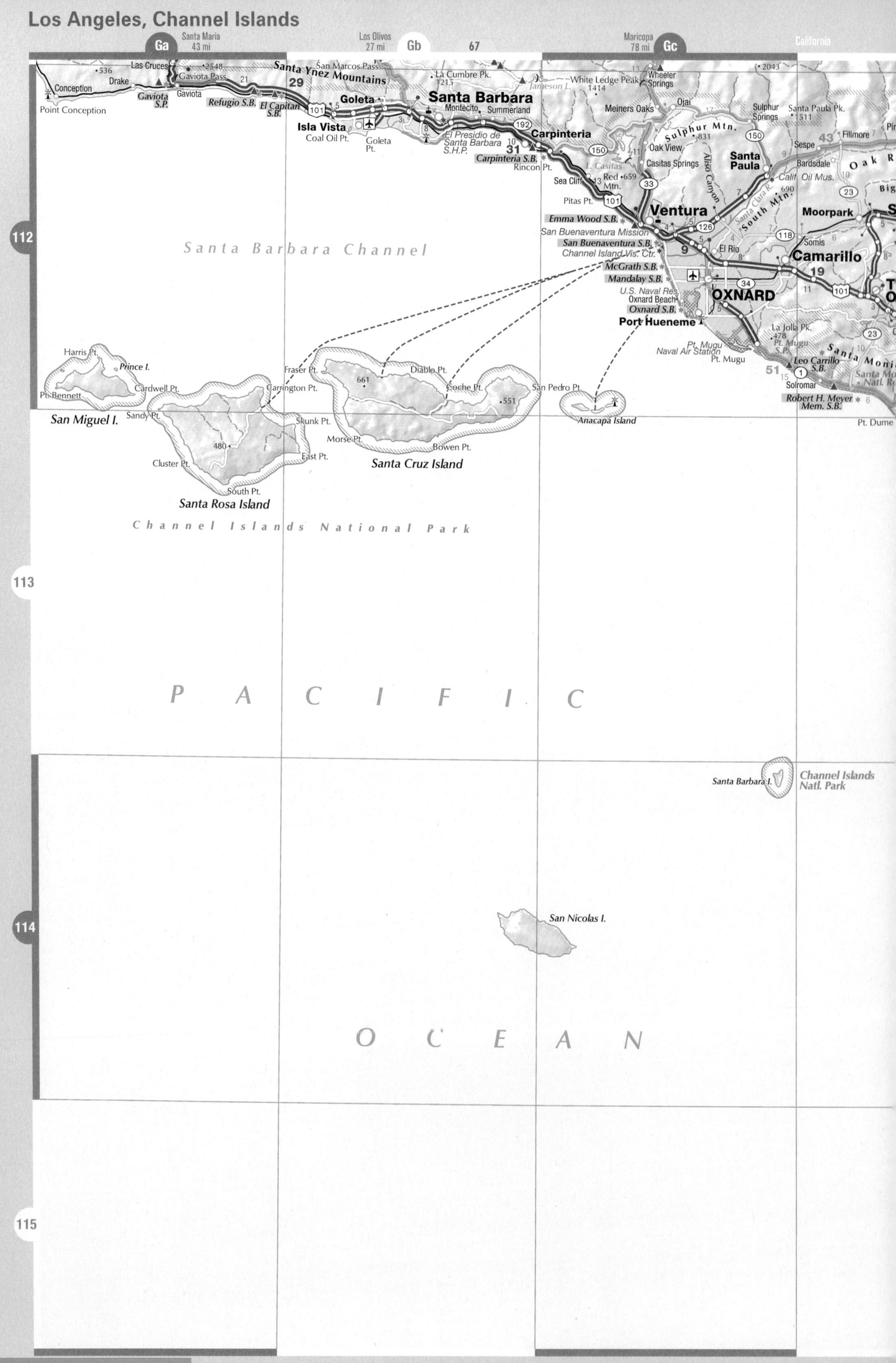
Santa Maria 43 mi
Ga
Los Olivos 27 mi
Gb
67
Maricopa 78 mi
Gc
California
112
113
114
115
Conception
Point Conception
Drake
Las Cruces
Gaviota Pass
Gaviota
Gaviota S.P.
Refugio S.B.
El Capitan S.B.
Santa Ynez Mountains
San Marcos Pass
La Cumbre Pk.
Goleta
Isla Vista
Coal Oil Pt.
Goleta Pt.
Santa Barbara
Montecito
Summerland
El Presidio de Santa Barbara S.H.P.
Carpinteria
Carpinteria S.B.
Rincon Pt.
Jameson L.
White Ledge Peak
Wheeler Springs
Meiners Oaks
Ojai
Sulphur Mtn.
Oak View
Casitas Springs
L. Casitas
Aliso Canyon
Sea Cliff
Red Mtn.
Pitas Pt.
Emma Wood S.B.
San Buenaventura Mission
San Buenaventura S.B.
Channel Island Vis. Ctr.
McGrath S.B.
Mandalay S.B.
U.S. Naval Res.
Oxnard Beach
Oxnard S.B.
Port Hueneme
Ventura
OXNARD
El Rio
Sulphur Springs
Santa Paula Pk.
Santa Paula
Fillmore
Sespe
Bardsdale
Calif. Oil Mus.
Oak R
South Mtn.
Moorpark
Somis
Camarillo
La Jolla Pk.
Pt. Mugu S.P.
Pt. Mugu Naval Air Station
Pt. Mugu
Leo Carrillo S.B.
Solromar
Robert H. Meyer Mem. S.B.
Santa Monica
Pt. Dume
Santa Barbara Channel
Harris Pt.
Prince I.
Cardwell Pt.
Pt. Bennett
San Miguel I.
Sandy Pt.
Carrington Pt.
Skunk Pt.
East Pt.
Cluster Pt.
South Pt.
Santa Rosa Island
Fraser Pt.
Diablo Pt.
Coche Pt.
Morse Pt.
Bowen Pt.
Santa Cruz Island
San Pedro Pt.
Anacapa Island
Channel Islands National Park
PACIFIC
Santa Barbara I.
Channel Islands Natl. Park
San Nicolas I.
OCEAN
0 20 40 60 20km
0 4 8 12miles

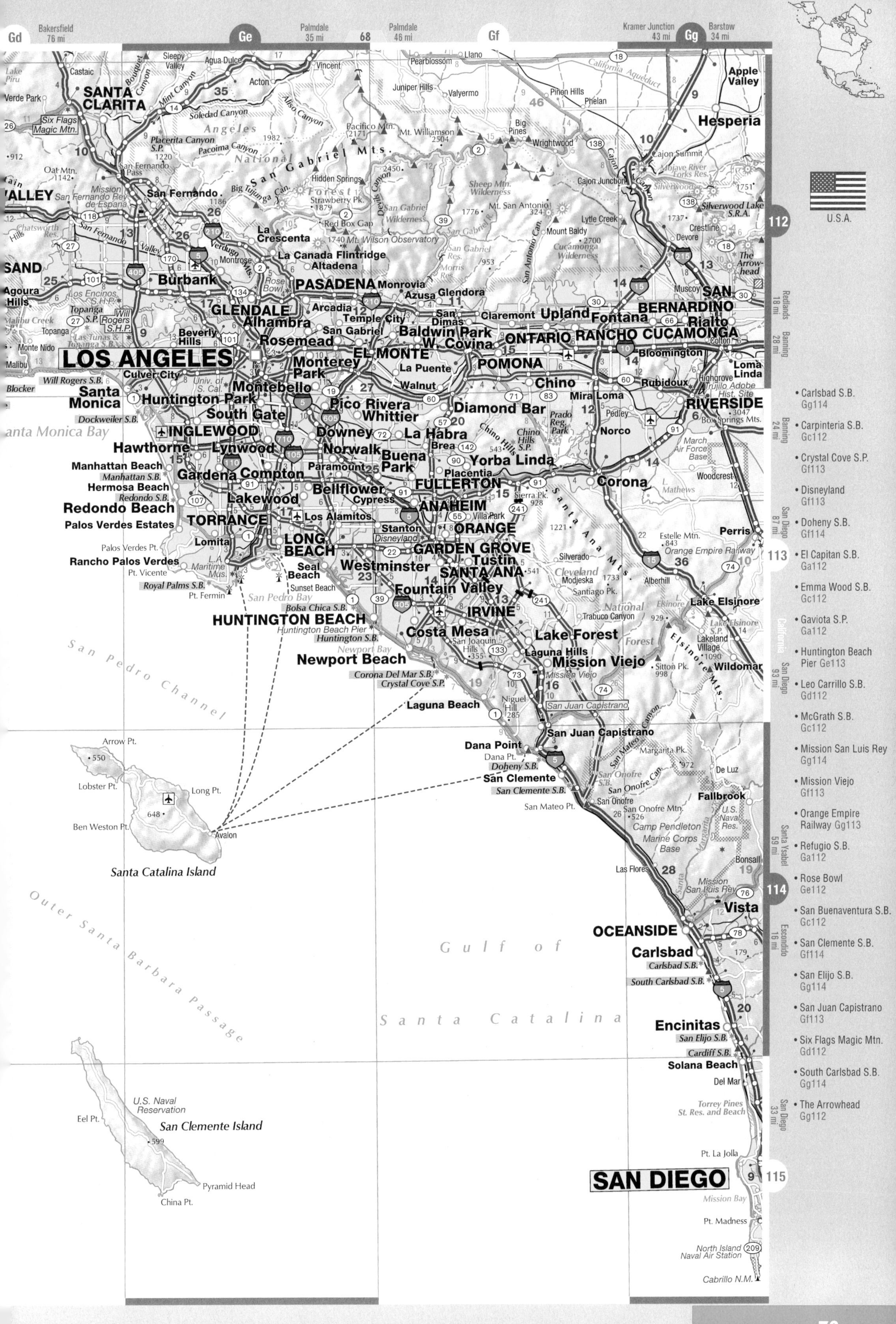

Gd
Bakersfield 76 mi
Ge
Palmdale 35 mi
68
Palmdale 46 mi
Gf
Kramer Junction 43 mi
Gg
Barstow 34 mi
112
113
114
115
U.S.A.
Redlands 18 mi
Banning 28 mi
Banning 24 mi
San Diego 87 mi
California
San Diego 93 mi
Santa Ysabel 59 mi
Escondido 16 mi
San Diego 33 mi
SANTA CLARITA
Castaic
Verde Park
Six Flags Magic Mtn.
Sleepy Valley
Agua Dulce
Acton
Vincent
Pearblossom
Llano
Juniper Hills
Valyermo
Pinon Hills
Phelan
Apple Valley
Hesperia
Cajon Summit
Cajon Junction
Wrightwood
Big Pines
Pacifico Mtn.
Mt. Williamson
San Gabriel Mts.
Angeles National Forest
San Fernando
San Fernando Pass
Mission San Fernando Rey de Espana
Oat Mtn.
VALLEY
Hidden Springs
Strawberry Pk.
Red Box Gap
Sheep Mtn. Wilderness
Mt. San Antonio
Mount Baldy
Lytle Creek
Cucamonga Wilderness
Silverwood Lake
Silverwood Lake S.R.A.
Crestline
Devore
The Arrowhead
La Crescenta
Mt. Wilson Observatory
La Canada Flintridge
Altadena
Burbank
Montrose
Rose Bowl
PASADENA
Monrovia
Azusa
Glendora
Agoura Hills
Los Encinos S.H.P.
Topanga S.P.
Will Rogers S.H.P.
Topanga
Malibu Creek
Monte Nido
Malibu
GLENDALE
Alhambra
Arcadia
Temple City
San Gabriel
San Dimas
Claremont
Upland
Fontana
SAN BERNARDINO
Rialto
Muscoy
Beverly Hills
Rosemead
EL MONTE
Baldwin Park
W. Covina
ONTARIO
RANCHO CUCAMONGA
Colton
Bloomington
Loma Linda
LOS ANGELES
Culver City
Univ. of S. Cal.
Will Rogers S.B.
Monterey Park
La Puente
POMONA
Chino
Walnut
Rubidoux
Highgrove
Trujillo Adobe Hist. Site
Blocker
Santa Monica
Montebello
Huntington Park
South Gate
Pico Rivera
Whittier
Diamond Bar
Mira Loma
Pedley
RIVERSIDE
Box Springs Mts.
Dockweiler S.B.
Santa Monica Bay
INGLEWOOD
Hawthorne
Lynwood
Downey
La Habra
Brea
Chino Hills S.P.
Prado Reg. Park
Norco
March Air Force Base
Manhattan Beach
Manhattan S.B.
Hermosa Beach
Redondo S.B.
Redondo Beach
Palos Verdes Estates
Gardena
Compton
Norwalk
Paramount
Buena Park
Yorba Linda
Placentia
FULLERTON
Corona
Woodcrest
L. Mathews
TORRANCE
Lakewood
Bellflower
Cypress
ANAHEIM
Villa Park
Sierra Pk.
Lomita
Los Alamitos
Stanton
Disneyland
ORANGE
Santa Ana Mts.
Perris
Estelle Mtn.
Orange Empire Railway
Palos Verdes Pt.
Rancho Palos Verdes
Pt. Vicente
Royal Palms S.B.
Pt. Fermin
L.A. Maritime Mus.
LONG BEACH
GARDEN GROVE
Tustin
Westminster
Seal Beach
Sunset Beach
SANTA ANA
Silverado
Cleveland National Forest
Modjeska
Santiago Pk.
Alberhill
San Pedro Bay
Bolsa Chica S.B.
Fountain Valley
IRVINE
Trabuco Canyon
Lake Elsinore
Lake Elsinore S.P.
Lakeland Village
Wildomar
HUNTINGTON BEACH
Huntington Beach Pier
Huntington S.B.
Costa Mesa
San Joaquin Hills
Lake Forest
Laguna Hills
Mission Viejo
Sitton Pk.
Elsinore Mts.
Newport Bay
Newport Beach
Corona Del Mar S.B.
Crystal Cove S.P.
Laguna Beach
Niguel Hill
San Juan Capistrano
San Pedro Channel
Dana Point
Dana Pt.
Doheny S.B.
San Clemente
San Clemente S.B.
San Mateo Pt.
Margarita Pk.
De Luz
Fallbrook
San Onofre
San Onofre S.B.
San Onofre Mtn.
Camp Pendleton Marine Corps Base
U.S. Naval Res.
Bonsall
Las Flores
Mission San Luis Rey
Vista
OCEANSIDE
Carlsbad
Carlsbad S.B.
South Carlsbad S.B.
Encinitas
San Elijo S.B.
Cardiff S.B.
Solana Beach
Del Mar
Torrey Pines St. Res. and Beach
Pt. La Jolla
SAN DIEGO
Mission Bay
Pt. Madness
North Island Naval Air Station
Cabrillo N.M.
Arrow Pt.
Lobster Pt.
Long Pt.
Ben Weston Pt.
Avalon
Santa Catalina Island
Outer Santa Barbara Passage
Gulf of Santa Catalina
U.S. Naval Reservation
Eel Pt.
San Clemente Island
Pyramid Head
China Pt.
• Carlsbad S.B. Gg114
• Carpinteria S.B. Gc112
• Crystal Cove S.P. Gf113
• Disneyland Gf113
• Doheny S.B. Gf114
• El Capitan S.B. Ga112
• Emma Wood S.B. Gc112
• Gaviota S.P. Ga112
• Huntington Beach Pier Ge113
• Leo Carrillo S.B. Gd112
• McGrath S.B. Gc112
• Mission San Luis Rey Gg114
• Mission Viejo Gf113
• Orange Empire Railway Gg113
• Refugio S.B. Ga112
• Rose Bowl Ge112
• San Buenaventura S.B. Gc112
• San Clemente S.B. Gf114
• San Elijo S.B. Gg114
• San Juan Capistrano Gf113
• Six Flags Magic Mtn. Gd112
• South Carlsbad S.B. Gg114
• The Arrowhead Gg112

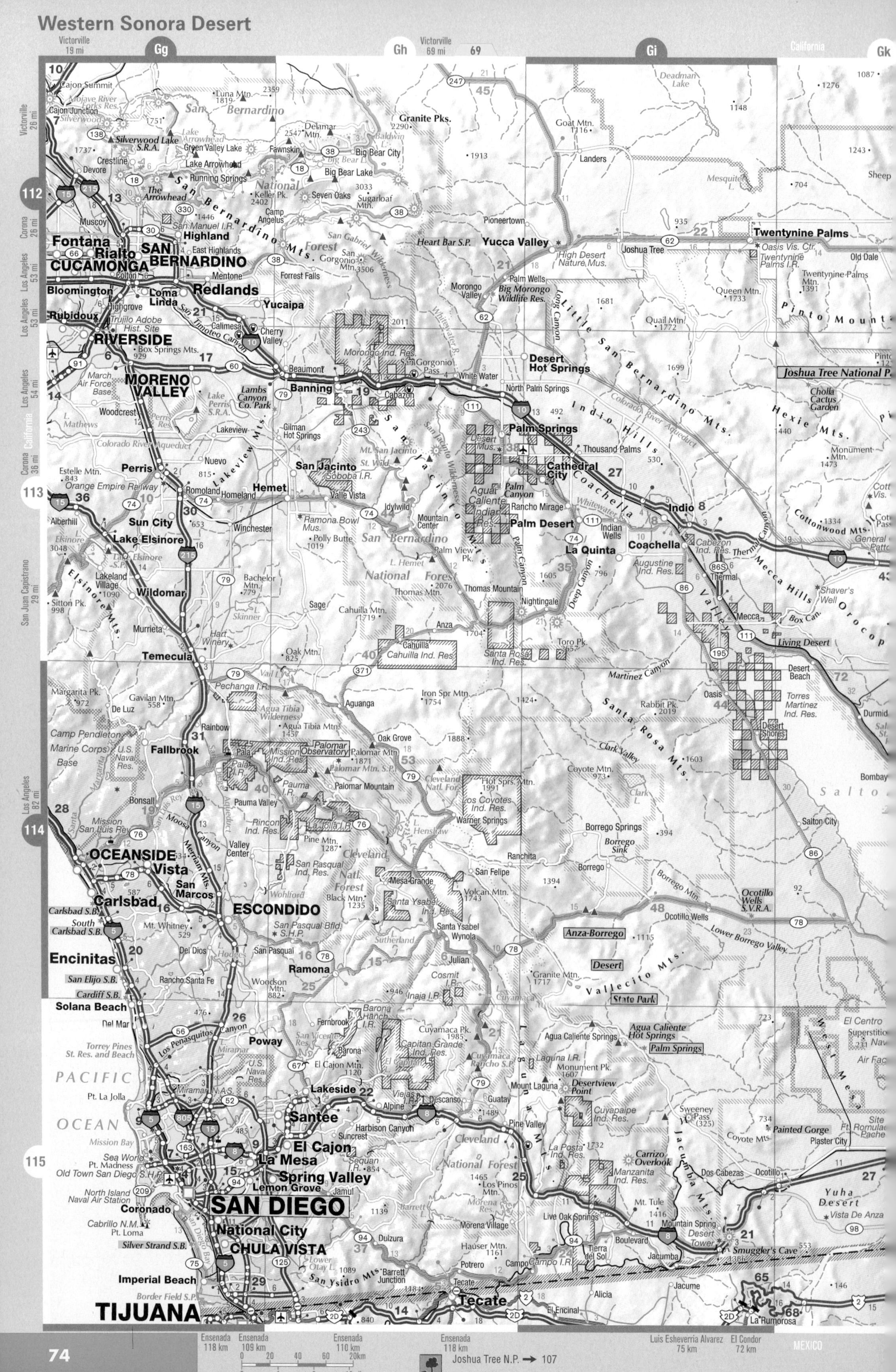
Victorville 19 mi
Gg
Gh
Victorville 69 mi
69
Gi
California
Gk
112
113
114
115
Cajon Summit
Cajon Junction
San Bernardino
Silverwood Lake S.R.A.
Crestline
Devore
Lake Arrowhead
Green Valley Lake
Running Springs
Fawnskin
Big Bear City
Big Bear Lake
Granite Pks.
Landers
Goat Mtn.
Deadman Lake
Mesquite L.
The Arrowhead
San Bernardino Mts.
National Forest
Seven Oaks
Sugarloaf Mtn.
Keller Pk.
Camp Angelus
San Gorgonio Mtn.
Heart Bar S.P.
Yucca Valley
Pioneertown
Joshua Tree
Twentynine Palms
Oasis Vis. Ctr.
Twentynine Palms I.R.
Old Dale
Twentynine Palms Mtn.
Queen Mtn.
High Desert Nature Mus.
Fontana
Rialto
San Bernardino
Cucamonga
Highland
East Highlands
San Manuel I.R.
Mentone
Forrest Falls
Bloomington
Colton
Loma Linda
Redlands
Yucaipa
Muscoy
Rubidoux
Highgrove
Trujillo Adobe Hist. Site
Calimesa
Cherry Valley
Riverside
Box Springs Mts.
Palm Wells
Morongo Valley
Big Morongo Wildlife Res.
Little San Bernardino Mts.
Quail Mtn.
Pinto Mount
Morongo Ind. Res.
San Gorgonio Pass
Beaumont
Banning
Cabazon
White Water
Desert Hot Springs
North Palm Springs
Joshua Tree National P
Moreno Valley
March Air Force Base
Lambs Canyon Co. Park
Lake Perris S.R.A.
Woodcrest
L. Mathews
Colorado River Aqueduct
Lakeview
Gilman Hot Springs
San Jacinto Mts.
Palm Springs
Thousand Palms
Indio Hills
Cholla Cactus Garden
Hexie Mts.
Monument Mtn.
Perris
Nuevo
Estelle Mtn.
Orange Empire Railway
Romoland
Homeland
Hemet
San Jacinto
Soboba I.R.
Valle Vista
Mt. San Jacinto St. Wild.
Desert Mus.
Cathedral City
Agua Caliente Indian Res.
Palm Canyon
Rancho Mirage
Palm Desert
Indio
Coachella
La Quinta
Indian Wells
Cottonwood Mts.
Alberhill
Sun City
Lake Elsinore
Winchester
Ramona Bowl Mus.
Polly Butte
Idyllwild
Mountain Center
San Bernardino National Forest
Palm View Pk.
L. Hemet
Cabezon Ind. Res.
Thermal
Augustine Ind. Res.
Mecca Hills
Shaver's Well
Lakeland Village
Wildomar
Bachelor Mtn.
Elsinore Mts.
Sitton Pk.
Murrieta
Hart Winery
L. Skinner
Sage
Cahuilla Mtn.
Thomas Mtn.
Thomas Mountain
Nightingale
Deep Canyon
Mecca
Box Can.
Living Desert
Temecula
Oak Mtn.
Anza
Cahuilla Ind. Res.
Santa Rosa Ind. Res.
Toro Pk.
Martinez Canyon
Desert Beach
Margarita Pk.
De Luz
Gavilan Mtn.
Pechanga I.R.
Vail L.
Agua Tibia Wilderness
Agua Tibia Mtn.
Aguanga
Iron Spr Mtn.
Rabbit Pk.
Santa Rosa Mts.
Oasis
Torres Martinez Ind. Res.
Desert Shores
Camp Pendleton
U.S. Marine Corps Base
Naval Res.
Rainbow
Fallbrook
Pala
Mission Ind. Res.
Palomar Observatory
Palomar Mtn.
Palomar Mtn. S.P.
Oak Grove
Palomar Mountain
Cleveland Natl. For.
Hot Sprs. Mtn.
Los Coyotes Ind. Res.
Warner Springs
Clark Valley
Coyote Mtn.
Clark L.
Salton
Bombay
Salton City
Bonsall
Mission San Luis Rey
Moosa Canyon
Pauma Valley
Pauma I.R.
Rincon Ind. Res.
La Jolla I.R.
L. Henshaw
Borrego Springs
Borrego Sink
Oceanside
Vista
San Marcos
Valley Center
Pine Mtn.
Merriam Mts.
San Pasqual Ind. Res.
Cleveland Natl. Forest
Ranchita
San Felipe
Borrego
Borrego Mtn.
Carlsbad
Carlsbad S.B.
South Carlsbad S.B.
Escondido
Mt. Whitney
Lake Wohlford
Black Mtn.
Mesa Grande
Santa Ysabel Ind. Res.
Volcan Mtn.
Santa Ysabel
Wynola
Ocotillo Wells S.V.R.A.
Ocotillo Wells
Lower Borrego Valley
Anza-Borrego Desert State Park
Encinitas
Del Dios
L. Hodges
San Pasqual
San Pasqual Bfld. S.H.P.
Ramona
L. Sutherland
Julian
Granite Mtn.
Vallecito Mts.
San Elijo S.B.
Cardiff S.B.
Rancho Santa Fe
Woodson Mtn.
Cosmit I.R.
Inaja I.R.
Cuyamaca
Solana Beach
Del Mar
Torrey Pines St. Res. and Beach
Los Penasquitos Canyon
Poway
Fernbrook
Barona Ranch I.R.
San Vicente Res.
Barona
Cuyamaca Pk.
Capitan Grande Ind. Res.
Cuyamaca Rancho S.P.
Laguna Mts.
Agua Caliente Springs
Agua Caliente Hot Springs
Palm Springs
Laguna I.R.
Monument Pk.
El Centro
Superstition
Air Fac
West Mesa
Pacific Ocean
Miramar
U.S. Naval Res.
Miramar N.A.S.
El Cajon Mtn.
Lakeside
Alpine
Viejas I.R.
Descanso
Guatay
Mount Laguna
Desertview Point
Pt. La Jolla
Santee
Harbison Canyon
Suncrest
Pine Valley
Cuyapaipe Ind. Res.
Sweeney Pass
Jacumba Mts.
Painted Gorge
Coyote Mts.
Plaster City
Ft. Romulac Pache Site
Mission Bay
Sea World
Pt. Madness
Old Town San Diego S.H.P.
El Cajon
La Mesa
Sequan I.R.
Spring Valley
Lemon Grove
Jamul
Cleveland National Forest
La Posta Ind. Res.
Carrizo Overlook
Manzanita Ind. Res.
Dos Cabezas
Ocotillo
Yuha Desert
Vista De Anza
North Island Naval Air Station
Coronado
San Diego
Los Pinos Mtn.
Barrett L.
Morena Res.
Mt. Tule
Live Oak Springs
Mountain Spring
Desert Tower
Cabrillo N.M.
Pt. Loma
Silver Strand S.B.
National City
Chula Vista
Dulzura
Morena Village
Hauser Mtn.
Boulevard
Tierra del Sol
Jacumba
Smuggler's Cave
Imperial Beach
Lower Otay L.
San Ysidro Mts.
Barrett Junction
Potrero
Campo
Campo I.R.
Tecate
Alicia
Jacume
Border Field S.P.
Tijuana
El Encinal
La Rumorosa
Ensenada 118 km
Ensenada 109 km
Ensenada 110 km
Ensenada 118 km
Luis Esheverria Alvarez 75 km
El Condor 72 km
MEXICO
Joshua Tree N.P. → 107

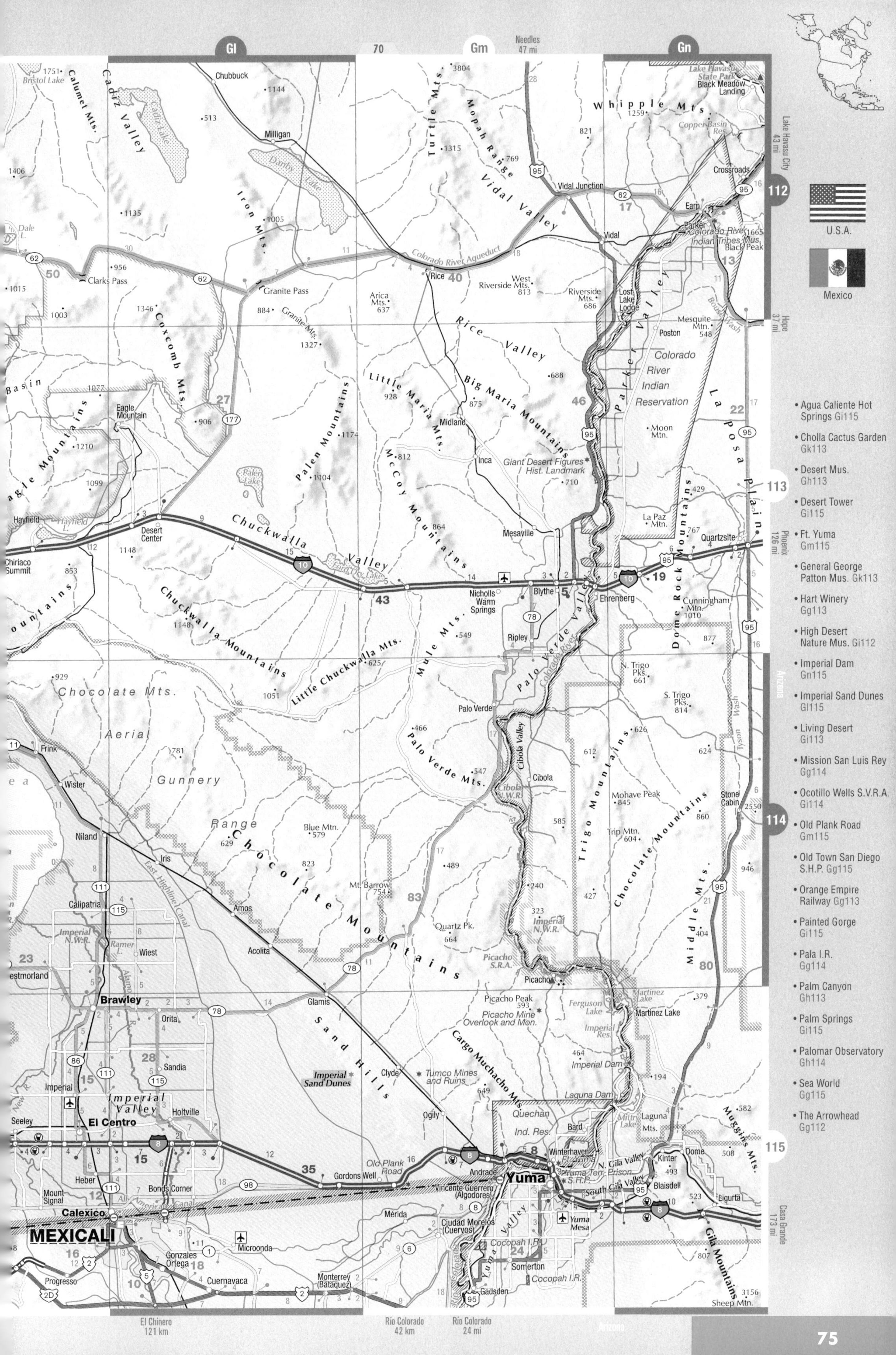

Gl
70
Gm
Needles 47 mi
Gn
Lake Havasu City 43 mi
112
U.S.A.
Mexico
Hope 37 mi
113
Phoenix 126 mi
114
Arizona
115
Casa Grande 173 mi
El Chinero 121 km
Río Colorado 42 km
Río Colorado 24 mi
• Agua Caliente Hot Springs Gi115
• Cholla Cactus Garden Gk113
• Desert Mus. Gh113
• Desert Tower Gi115
• Ft. Yuma Gm115
• General George Patton Mus. Gk113
• Hart Winery Gg113
• High Desert Nature Mus. Gi112
• Imperial Dam Gn115
• Imperial Sand Dunes Gi115
• Living Desert Gi113
• Mission San Luis Rey Gg114
• Ocotillo Wells S.V.R.A. Gi114
• Old Plank Road Gm115
• Old Town San Diego S.H.P. Gg115
• Orange Empire Railway Gg113
• Painted Gorge Gi115
• Pala I.R. Gg114
• Palm Canyon Gh113
• Palm Springs Gi115
• Palomar Observatory Gh114
• Sea World Gg115
• The Arrowhead Gg112
Bristol Lake
Calumet Mts.
Cadiz Valley
Cadiz Lake
Chubbuck
Milligan
Danby Lake
Iron Mts.
Turtle Mts.
Mopah Range
Vidal Valley
Vidal Junction
Vidal
Whipple Mts.
Lake Havasu State Park
Black Meadow Landing
Copper Basin Res.
Crossroads
Earp
Parker
Colorado River Indian Tribes Mus.
Black Peak
Clarks Pass
Granite Pass
Colorado River Aqueduct
Rice
Arica Mts.
West Riverside Mts.
Riverside Mts.
Lost Lake Lodge
Coxcomb Mts.
Granite Mts.
Rice Valley
Mesquite Mtn.
Poston
Colorado River Indian Reservation
Parker Valley
La Posa Plain
Basin
Eagle Mountain
Eagle Mountains
Palen Mountains
Little Maria Mts.
Big Maria Mountains
Midland
Inca
Giant Desert Figures Hist. Landmark
Moon Mtn.
Palen Lake
McCoy Mountains
Hayfield
Hayfield L.
Desert Center
Chuckwalla Valley
Ford Dry Lake
Mesaville
La Paz Mtn.
Dome Rock Mountains
Quartzsite
Chiriaco Summit
Blythe
Ehrenberg
Nicholls Warm Springs
Cunningham Mtn.
Chuckwalla Mountains
Mule Mts.
Ripley
Palo Verde Valley
Colorado River
Little Chuckwalla Mts.
N. Trigo Pks.
S. Trigo Pks.
Chocolate Mts.
Palo Verde
Aerial
Gunnery
Range
Frink
Wister
Palo Verde Mts.
Cibola Valley
Cibola
Cibola N.W.R.
Trigo Mountains
Mohave Peak
Stone Cabin
Trip Mtn.
Chocolate Mountains
Niland
Blue Mtn.
Tyson Wash
Iris
East Highline Canal
Mt. Barrow
Middle Mts.
Calipatria
Amos
Imperial N.W.R.
Ramer L.
Quartz Pk.
Wiest
Acolita
Picacho S.R.A.
Westmorland
Brawley
Glamis
Picacho
Picacho Peak
Picacho Mine Overlook and Mon.
Ferguson Lake
Martinez Lake
Orita
Sand Hills
Imperial Res.
Sandia
Imperial Dam
Imperial
Imperial Sand Dunes
Clyde
Tumco Mines and Ruins
Cargo Muchacho Mts.
Imperial Valley
Holtville
Seeley
El Centro
Ogilby
Quechan Ind. Res.
Laguna Dam
Laguna Mts.
Mittry Lake
Muggins Mts.
Bard
Winterhaven
Ft. Yuma
Yuma Terr. Prison S.H.P.
N. Gila Valley
Kinter
Dome
Gordons Well
Old Plank Road
Andrade
Yuma
South Gila Valley
Blaisdell
Heber
Bonds Corner
Vicente Guerrero (Algodores)
Ligurta
Mount Signal
All American Canal
Calexico
Mérida
Ciudad Morelos (Cuervos)
Yuma Valley
Yuma Mesa
MEXICALI
Microonda
Cocopah I.R.
Gila Mountains
Gonzales Ortega
Somerton
Progresso
Cuernavaca
Monterrey (Bataquez)
Gadsden
Río Colorado
Sheep Mtn.

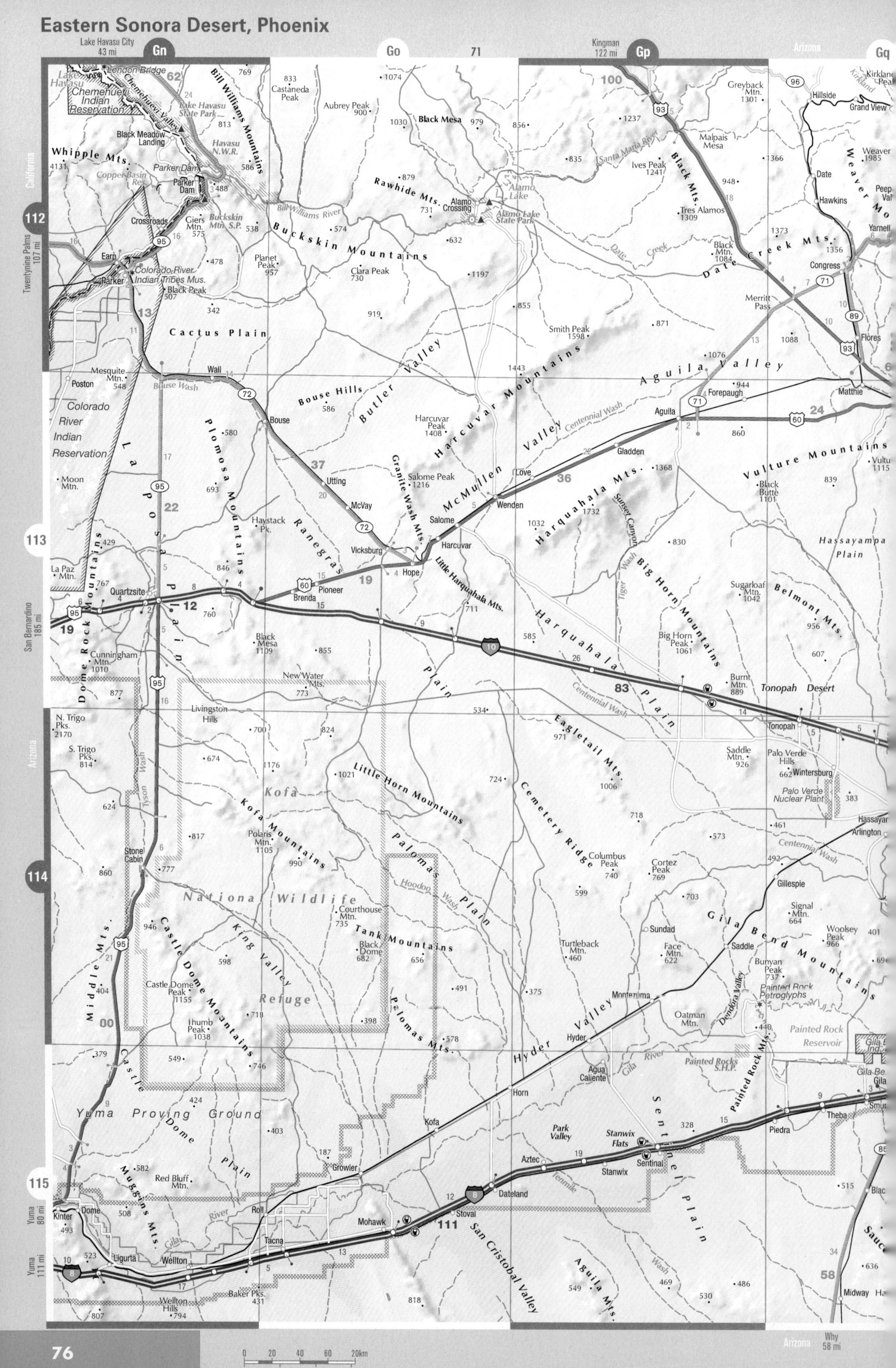

Lake Havasu City 43 mi
Gn
Go
71
Kingman 122 mi
Gp
Arizona
Gq
California
112
Twentynine Palms 107 mi
113
San Bernardino 185 mi
Arizona
114
115
Yuma 80 mi
Yuma 111 mi
London Bridge
Lake Havasu
Chemehuevi Indian Reservation
Chemehuevi Valley
Lake Havasu State Park
Bill Williams Mountains
Black Meadow Landing
Havasu N.W.R.
Whipple Mts.
4131
Copper Basin Res.
Parker Dam
Parker Dam
488
Crossroads
Giers Mtn. 575
Buckskin Mtn. S.P.
538
Earp
Parker
Colorado River Indian Tribes Mus.
Black Peak 507
478
342
Cactus Plain
Mesquite Mtn. 548
Poston
Wall
Bouse Wash
Colorado River Indian Reservation
La Posa Plain
Plomosa Mountains
Moon Mtn.
693
La Paz Mtn.
429
767
Quartzsite
Dome Rock Mountains
760
846
Cunningham Mtn. 1010
877
N. Trigo Pks. 2170
S. Trigo Pks. 814
Tyson Wash
624
Stone Cabin
777
860
Middle Mts.
946
404
379
Castle Dome Plain
Yuma Proving Ground
Muggins Mts.
582
Red Bluff Mtn.
Dome
508
Kinter
493
Ligurta
Wellton
Wellton Hills 794
807
833 Castaneda Peak
Aubrey Peak 900
1074
1030
Black Mesa
979
Bill Williams River
Rawhide Mts.
879
Alamo Crossing
731
Alamo Lake
Alamo Lake State Park
574
632
Buckskin Mountains
Planet Peak 957
Clara Peak 730
1197
919
Bouse Hills 586
Butler Valley
Bouse
580
Utting
McVay
Vicksburg
Haystack Pk.
Ranegras
Granite Wash Mts.
Salome Peak 1216
Salome
Harcuvar
Hope
Pioneer
Brenda
Little Harquahala Mts.
711
Black Mesa 1109
855
New Water Mts. 773
Livingston Hills
700
824
674
1176
1021
Kofa
Kofa Mountains
Polaris Mtn. 1105
990
817
Little Horn Mountains
National Wildlife Refuge
King Valley
Castle Dome Mountains
Castle Dome Peak 1155
Thumb Peak 1038
598
710
549
746
424
403
Courthouse Mtn. 735
Black Dome 682
Tank Mountains
656
Palomas Plain
Hoodoo Wash
Palomas Mts.
491
398
578
187
Growler
Kofa
Roll
Mohawk
Tacna
Baker Pks. 431
818
Stoval
San Cristobal Valley
Dateland
Gila River
856
835
1237
100
Greyback Mtn. 1301
Santa Maria River
Ives Peak 1241
Black Mts.
Malpais Mesa
1366
948
Tres Alamos 1309
Black Mtn. 1084
Date Creek
Date Creek Mts.
1373
1356
855
Smith Peak 1598
871
Merritt Pass
1088
Harcuvar Mountains
Harcuvar Peak 1408
1443
1076
Aguila Valley
944
Forepaugh
Aguila
Centennial Wash
Gladden
McMullen Valley
Love
Wenden
Harquahala Mts.
1368
1732
Sunset Canyon
1032
830
Tiger Wash
Big Horn Mountains
Big Horn Peak 1061
Harquahala Plain
585
Burnt Mtn. 889
Tonopah Desert
534
Eagletail Mts.
971
1006
724
Cemetery Ridge
718
Columbus Peak 740
599
Cortez Peak 769
703
573
Sundad
Turtleback Mtn. 460
Face Mtn. 622
375
Montezuma
Hyder Valley
Hyder
Agua Caliente
Oatman Mtn.
Horn
Park Valley
Stanwix Flats
Sentinal
Sentinel Plain
328
Aztec
Stanwix
Tenmile Wash
469
Aguila Mts.
549
530
486
Painted Rocks S.H.P.
Painted Rock Mts.
Hillside
Kirkland Peak
Kirkland
Grand View
Weaver Mountains
Weaver 1985
Date
Hawkins
Peeples Valley
Yarnell
Congress
Flores
Matthie
860
Vulture Mountains
Vulture 1115
Black Butte 1101
839
Hassayampa Plain
Sugarloaf Mtn. 1042
Belmont Mts.
956
607
Tonopah
Saddle Mtn. 926
Palo Verde Hills
662 Wintersburg
Palo Verde Nuclear Plant
383
461
Hassayampa
Arlington
Centennial Wash
492
Gillespie
Signal Mtn. 664
Woolsey Peak 966
401
Gila Bend Mountains
Saddle
Bunyan Peak 737
Painted Rock Petroglyphs
Dendora Valley
440
Painted Rock Reservoir
Gila Bend Ind. Res.
Gila Bend
Theba
Smurr
Piedra
515
636
Midway
Sauceda
Black
58
Arizona
Why 58 mi
0 20 40 60 20km
0 4 8 12miles

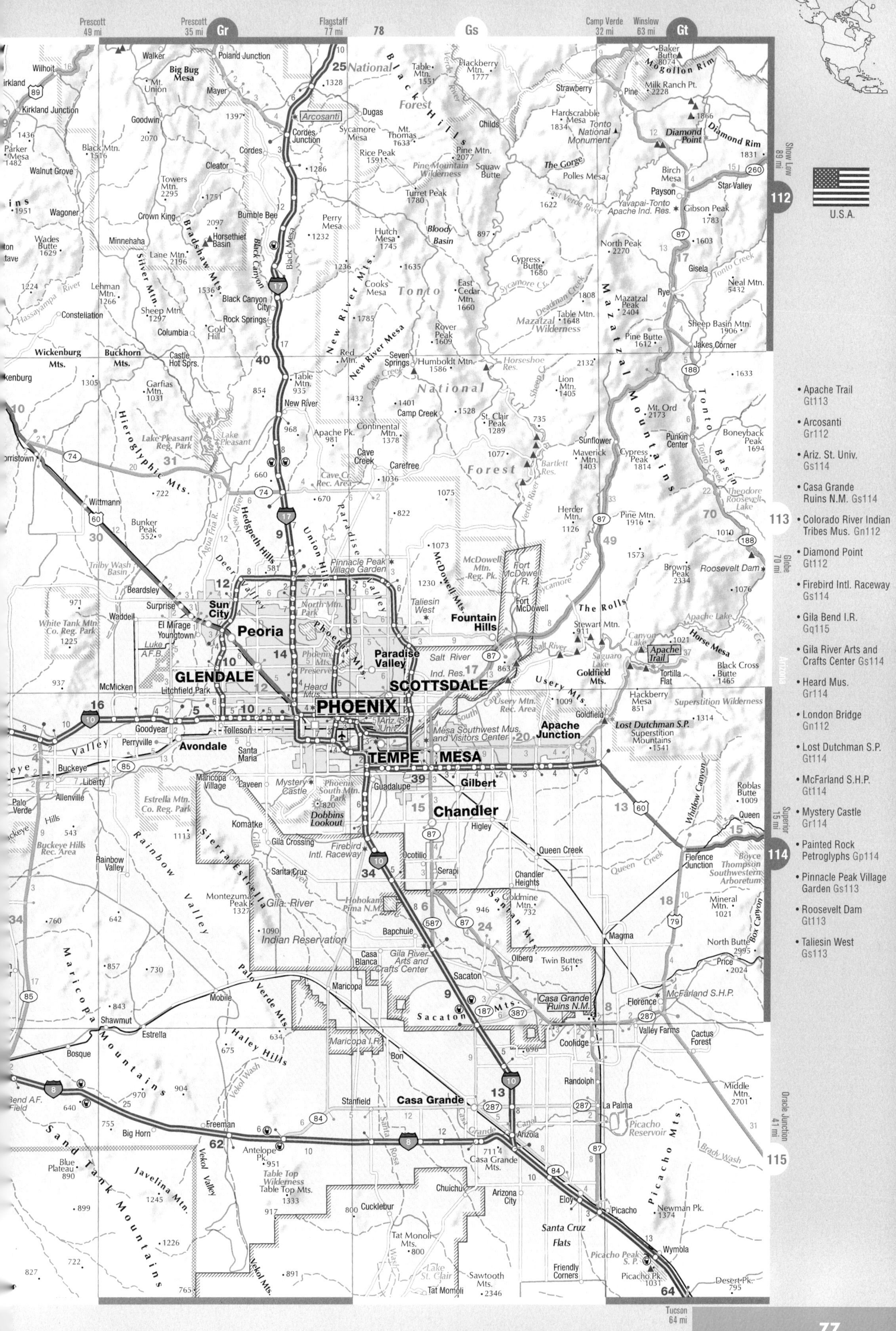
Prescott 49 mi
Prescott 35 mi
Gr
Flagstaff 77 mi
78
Gs
Camp Verde 32 mi
Winslow 63 mi
Gt
U.S.A.
Show Low 89 mi
112
113
Globe 70 mi
Arizona
114
Superior 15 mi
Oracle Junction 41 mi
115
Tucson 64 mi
• Apache Trail Gt113
• Arcosanti Gr112
• Ariz. St. Univ. Gs114
• Casa Grande Ruins N.M. Gs114
• Colorado River Indian Tribes Mus. Gn112
• Diamond Point Gt112
• Firebird Intl. Raceway Gs114
• Gila Bend I.R. Gq115
• Gila River Arts and Crafts Center Gs114
• Heard Mus. Gr114
• London Bridge Gn112
• Lost Dutchman S.P. Gt114
• McFarland S.H.P. Gt114
• Mystery Castle Gr114
• Painted Rock Petroglyphs Gp114
• Pinnacle Peak Village Garden Gs113
• Roosevelt Dam Gt113
• Taliesin West Gs113
PHOENIX
GLENDALE
SCOTTSDALE
TEMPE
MESA
Peoria
Chandler
Gilbert
Sun City
Paradise Valley
Fountain Hills
Apache Junction
Avondale
Goodyear
Casa Grande
Wickenburg Mts.
Bradshaw Mts.
Mazatzal Mountains
Tonto National Forest
Sierra Estrella
Maricopa Mountains
Sand Tank Mountains
Gila River Indian Reservation
Salt River Ind. Res.
Mogollon Rim
Payson
Florence
Coolidge
Eloy
Picacho
Arizona City
Maricopa
Buckeye
Cave Creek
Carefree
New River
Black Canyon City
Cordes Junction
Arcosanti
Pine
Strawberry
Roosevelt Dam
Superstition Wilderness
Lost Dutchman S.P.
Casa Grande Ruins N.M.
McFarland S.H.P.
Picacho Peak S.P.

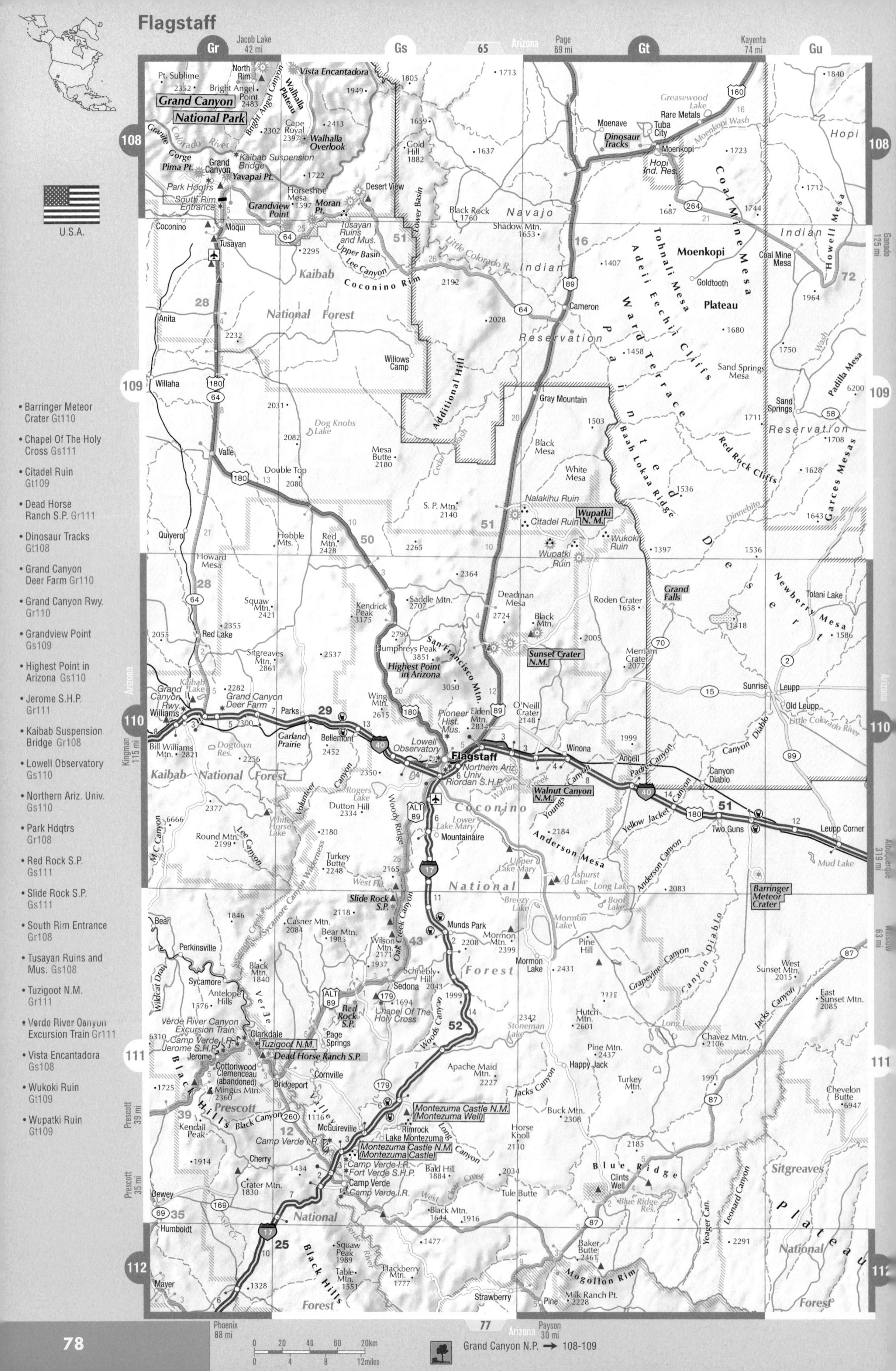
U.S.A.
• Barringer Meteor Crater Gt110
• Chapel Of The Holy Cross Gs111
• Citadel Ruin Gt109
• Dead Horse Ranch S.P. Gr111
• Dinosaur Tracks Gt108
• Grand Canyon Deer Farm Gr110
• Grand Canyon Rwy. Gr110
• Grandview Point Gs109
• Highest Point in Arizona Gs110
• Jerome S.H.P. Gr111
• Kaibab Suspension Bridge Gr108
• Lowell Observatory Gs110
• Northern Ariz. Univ. Gs110
• Park Hdqtrs Gr108
• Red Rock S.P. Gs111
• Slide Rock S.P. Gs111
• South Rim Entrance Gr108
• Tusayan Ruins and Mus. Gs108
• Tuzigoot N.M. Gr111
• Verde River Canyon Excursion Train Gr111
• Vista Encantadora Gs108
• Wukoki Ruin Gt109
• Wupatki Ruin Gt109
Gr
Jacob Lake 42 mi
Gs
65
Arizona
Page 69 mi
Gt
Kayenta 74 mi
Gu
108
109
110
111
112
Grand Canyon National Park
Vista Encantadora
Walhalla Overlook
Kaibab Suspension Bridge
Yavapai Pt.
Park Hdqtrs
South Rim Entrance
Grandview Point
Moran Pt.
Desert View
Tusayan Ruins and Mus.
Tusayan
Kaibab National Forest
Coconino Rim
Navajo Indian Reservation
Moenkopi Plateau
Tuba City
Dinosaur Tracks
Moenkopi
Hopi Ind. Res.
Coal Mine Mesa
Cameron
Gray Mountain
Painted Desert
Hopi Indian Reservation
Wupatki N.M.
Citadel Ruin
Wukoki Ruin
Wupatki Ruin
Nalakihu Ruin
Grand Falls
Sunset Crater N.M.
Humphreys Peak 3851
Highest Point in Arizona
San Francisco Mtn.
Williams
Grand Canyon Rwy.
Grand Canyon Deer Farm
Parks
Bellemont
Flagstaff
Lowell Observatory
Northern Ariz. Univ.
Riordan S.H.P.
Pioneer Hist. Mus.
Walnut Canyon N.M.
Winona
Leupp
Two Guns
Leupp Corner
Barringer Meteor Crater
Coconino National Forest
Anderson Mesa
Mormon Lake
Munds Park
Slide Rock S.P.
Sedona
Chapel Of The Holy Cross
Red Rock S.P.
Cottonwood
Clarkdale
Tuzigoot N.M.
Jerome
Jerome S.H.P.
Dead Horse Ranch S.P.
Verde River Canyon Excursion Train
Montezuma Castle N.M. (Montezuma Well)
Montezuma Castle N.M. (Montezuma Castle)
Camp Verde
Fort Verde S.H.P.
Prescott National Forest
Black Hills
Mogollon Rim
Sitgreaves National Forest
Blue Ridge
Strawberry
Pine
Kingman 115 mi
Prescott 39 mi
Prescott 35 mi
Albuquerque 319 mi
Ganado 125 mi
Phoenix 88 mi
77
Arizona
Payson 30 mi
Grand Canyon N.P. → 108-109

Florida

1:800 000 / 1cm = 8km

Photo: Florida, Miami, South Beach, Strand, Rettungsschwimmerhütte (Gerald Haenel/laif)

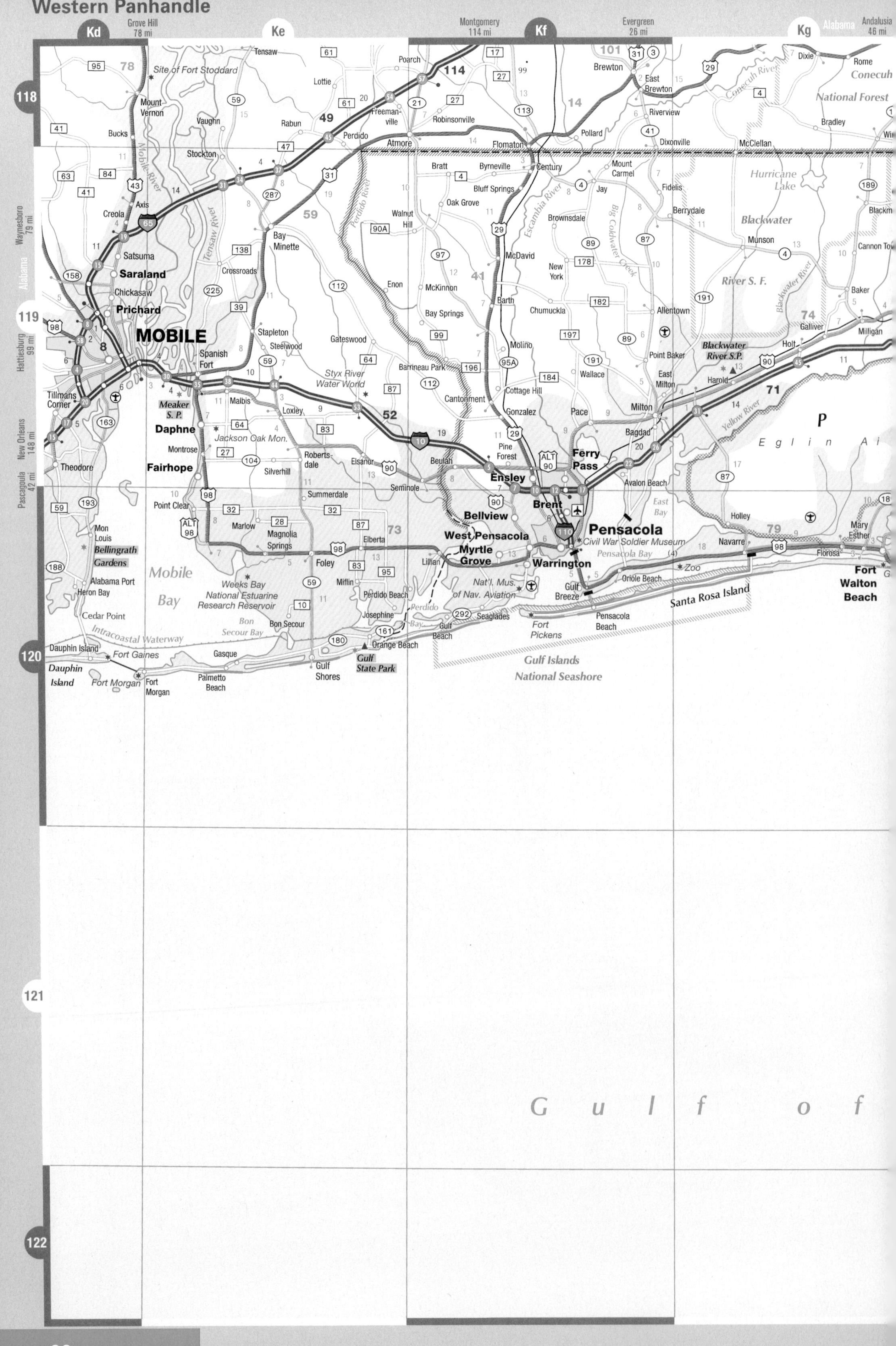
MOBILE
Pensacola
Mobile Bay
Gulf Islands National Seashore
Santa Rosa Island
Gulf of

- Bellingrath Gardens Kd120
- Blackwater River S.P. Kg119
- Civil War Soldier Museum Kf120
- Dead Lakes S.P. Ki120
- Eden State Gardens Kh120
- Falling Waters S.R.A Ki119
- F. Gannon Rocky Bay S.P. Kh120
- Florala State Park Kh118
- Florida Caverns State Park Kk119
- Fort Gaines Kd120
- Fort Morgan Kd120
- Fort Pickens Kf120
- Gulf State Park Ke120
- Gulfarium Kg120
- Henderson Beach S.R.A. Kh120
- Jackson Oak Mon. Ke119
- Meaker S.P. Ke119
- Nat'l. Mus. of Nav. Aviation Kf120
- Ponce de Leon Springs S.R.A. Ki119
- Site of Fort Stoddard Ke118
- Styx River Water World Ke119
- Topsail Hill S.P. Kh120
- Zoo Kg120

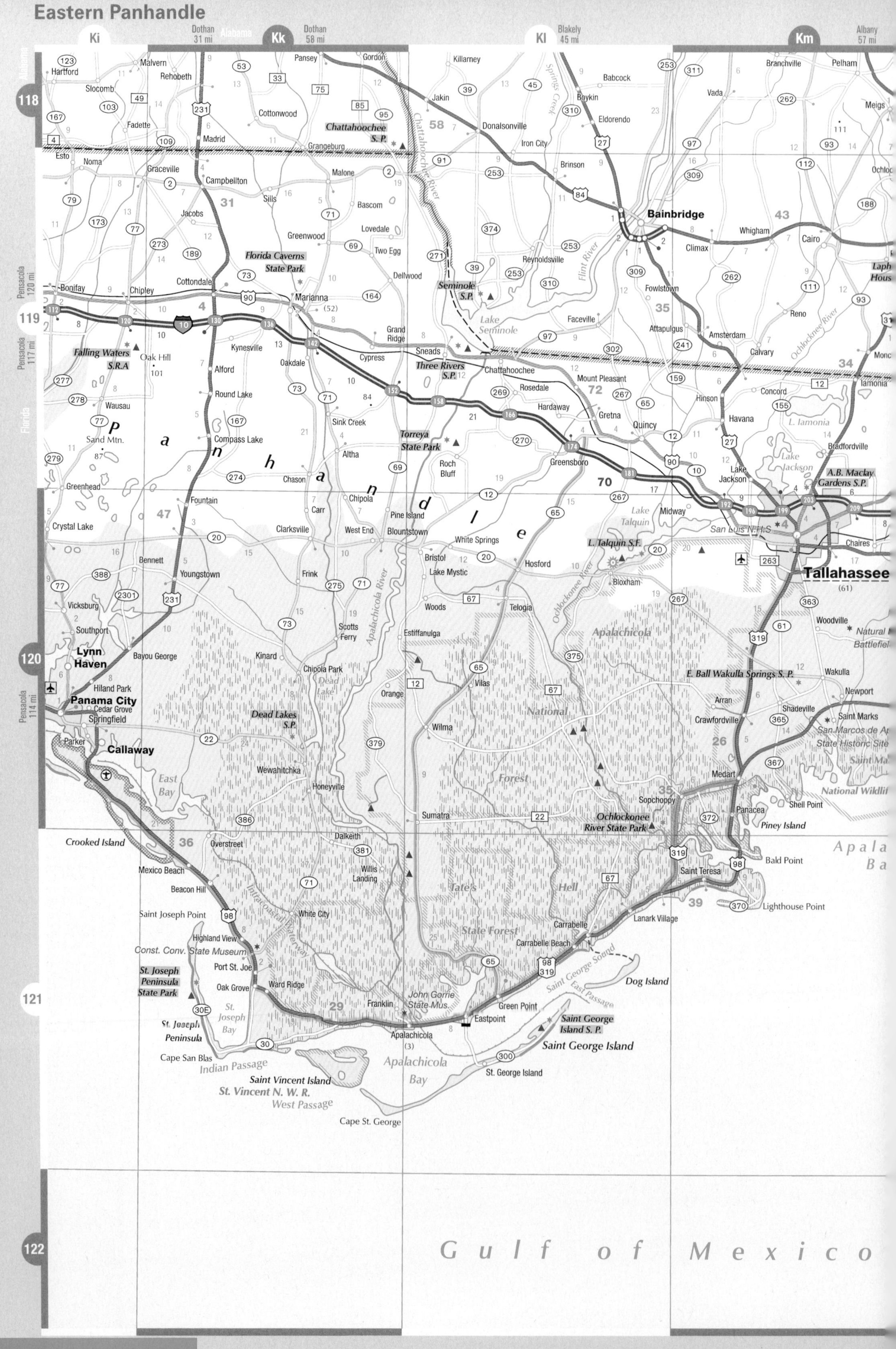
Dothan 31 mi
Dothan 58 mi
Blakely 45 mi
Albany 57 mi
Pensacola 120 mi
Pensacola 117 mi
Pensacola 114 mi
Alabama
Florida
Hartford
Malvern
Rehobeth
Slocomb
Fadette
Madrid
Esto
Noma
Graceville
Campbellton
Jacobs
Cottondale
Bonifay
Chipley
Marianna
Kynesville
Oakdale
Alford
Round Lake
Compass Lake
Wausau
Sand Mtn.
Falling Waters S.R.A
Oak Hill
Greenhead
Crystal Lake
Fountain
Chason
Altha
Carr
Clarksville
Bennett
Youngstown
Vicksburg
Southport
Lynn Haven
Bayou George
Hiland Park
Panama City
Cedar Grove
Springfield
Parker
Callaway
East Bay
Crooked Island
Mexico Beach
Beacon Hill
Saint Joseph Point
Highland View
Const. Conv. State Museum
Port St. Joe
St. Joseph Peninsula State Park
Oak Grove
St. Joseph Bay
Cape San Blas
Indian Passage
Saint Vincent Island
St. Vincent N. W. R.
West Passage
Cape St. George
Pansey
Gordon
Cottonwood
Grangeburg
Chattahoochee S. P.
Malone
Sills
Bascom
Greenwood
Lovedale
Two Egg
Dellwood
Florida Caverns State Park
Grand Ridge
Sneads
Cypress
Three Rivers S.P.
Sink Creek
Torreya State Park
Roch Bluff
Chipola
Pine Island
West End
Blountstown
Frink
Scotts Ferry
Kinard
Chipola Park
Dead Lake
Dead Lakes S.P.
Wewahitchka
Honeyville
Overstreet
Dalkeith
Willis Landing
White City
Intracoastal Waterway
Ward Ridge
Franklin
John Gorrie State Mus.
Apalachicola
Apalachicola Bay
Eastpoint
Green Point
St. George Island
Saint George Island
Saint George Island S. P.
East Passage
Saint George Sound
Dog Island
Carrabelle
Carrabelle Beach
Lanark Village
Apalachicola River
Chattahoochee River
Estiffanulga
Orange
Wilma
Sumatra
Tate's Hell State Forest
Killarney
Jakin
Donalsonville
Iron City
Spring Creek
Seminole S.P.
Lake Seminole
Reynoldsville
Chattahoochee
Rosedale
Hardaway
Greensboro
White Springs
Bristol
Lake Mystic
Woods
Telogia
Hosford
Vilas
Babcock
Boykin
Eldorendo
Brinson
Bainbridge
Flint River
Faceville
Attapulgus
Mount Pleasant
Gretna
Quincy
Fowlstown
Climax
Whigham
Cairo
Amsterdam
Calvary
Reno
Ochlocknee River
Hinson
Havana
Concord
Midway
Lake Talquin
L. Talquin S.F.
Bloxham
Ochlockonee River
Apalachicola National Forest
Ochlockonee River State Park
Sopchoppy
Saint Teresa
Lighthouse Point
Bald Point
Panacea
Piney Island
Shell Point
Medart
Crawfordville
Arran
E. Ball Wakulla Springs S. P.
Wakulla
Newport
Shadeville
Saint Marks
San Marcos de Apalache State Historic Site
National Wildlife
Woodville
Natural Bridge Battlefield
Tallahassee
San Luis N.H.S.
Lake Jackson
A.B. Maclay Gardens S.P.
Bradfordville
L. Iamonia
Iamonia
Chaires
Lake Jackson
Branchville
Pelham
Vada
Meigs
Ochlocknee
Panhandle
Apalachee Bay
Gulf of Mexico

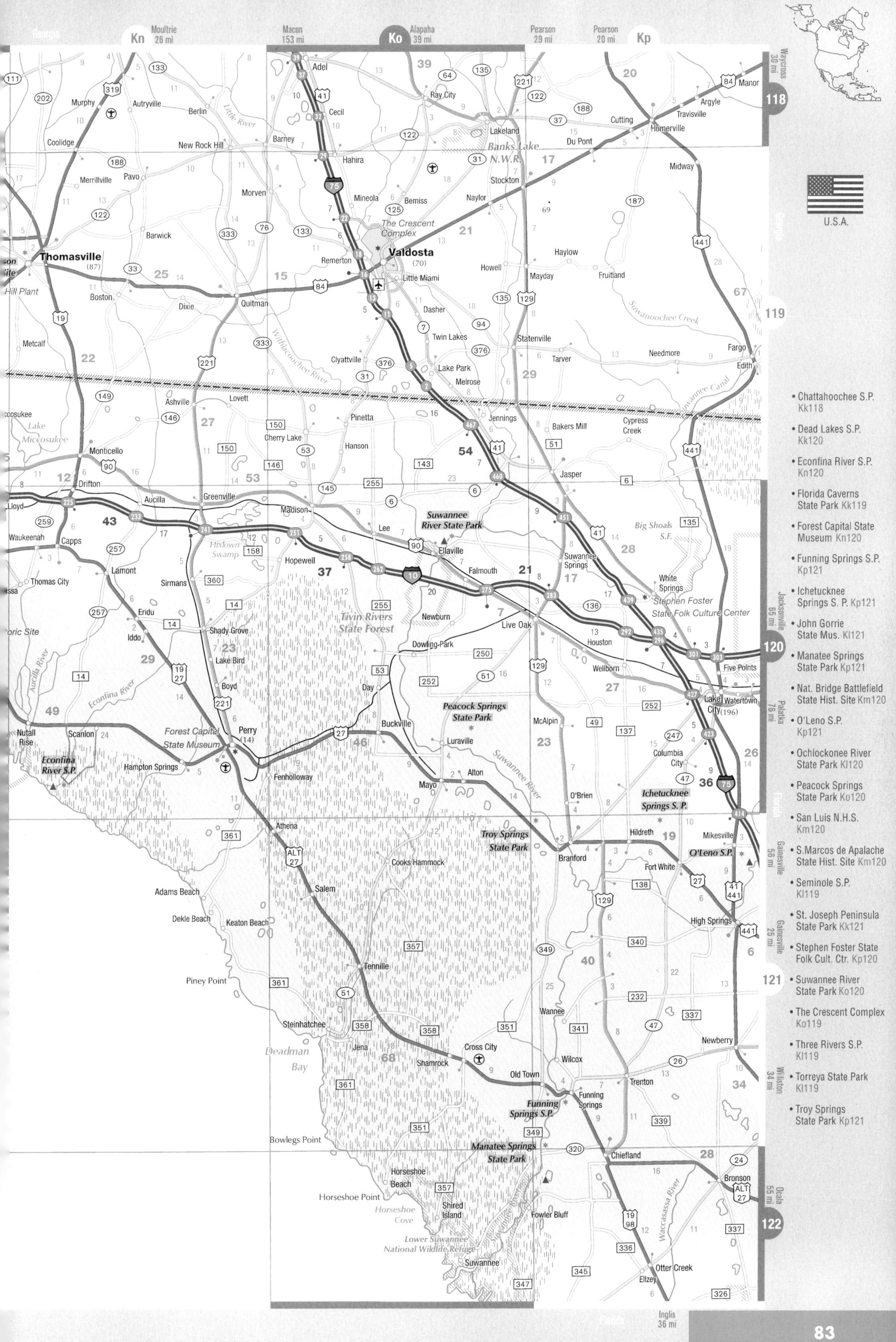

Georgia
Kn
Moultrie 26 mi
Macon 153 mi
Ko
Alapaha 39 mi
Pearson 29 mi
Pearson 20 mi
Kp
Waycross 30 mi
118
119
120
121
122
Jacksonville 65 mi
Palatka 76 mi
Gainesville 56 mi
Gainesville 25 mi
Williston 34 mi
Ocala 55 mi
Inglis 36 mi
Florida
U.S.A.
Murphy
Autryville
Berlin
Little River
Coolidge
New Rock Hill
Barney
Adel
Cecil
Hahira
Ray City
Lakeland
Banks Lake N.W.R.
Du Pont
Cutting
Homerville
Argyle
Travisville
Manor
Midway
Merrillville
Pavo
Morven
Mineola
Bemiss
Stockton
Naylor
Barwick
The Crescent Complex
Valdosta
Remerton
Little Miami
Howell
Haylow
Mayday
Fruitland
Thomasville
Hill Plant
Boston
Dixie
Quitman
Dasher
Twin Lakes
Suwanoochee Creek
Statenville
Tarver
Needmore
Fargo
Edith
Metcalf
Clyattville
Withlacoochee River
Lake Park
Melrose
Suwannee Canal
Ashville
Lovett
Pinetta
Jennings
Bakers Mill
Cypress Creek
Lake Miccosukee
Cherry Lake
Hanson
Monticello
Drifton
Jasper
Aucilla
Greenville
Madison
Lee
Suwannee River State Park
Ellaville
Big Shoals S.F.
Lloyd
Waukeenah
Capps
Hixtown Swamp
Hopewell
Falmouth
Suwannee Springs
White Springs
Stephen Foster State Folk Culture Center
Lamont
Sirmans
Thomas City
Twin Rivers State Forest
Newburn
Live Oak
Eridu
Shady Grove
Iddo
Houston
Lake Bird
Dowling Park
Wellborn
Five Points
Lake City
Watertown
Aucilla River
Boyd
Econfina River
Day
Peacock Springs State Park
McAlpin
Nutall Rise
Scanlon
Forest Capital State Museum
Perry
Buckville
Luraville
Columbia City
Econfina River S.P.
Hampton Springs
Fenholloway
Suwannee River
Mayo
Alton
O'Brien
Ichetucknee Springs S.P.
Athena
Troy Springs State Park
Hildreth
Mikesville
Branford
O'Leno S.P.
Fort White
Cooks Hammock
Adams Beach
Salem
Dekle Beach
Keaton Beach
High Springs
Piney Point
Tennille
Wannee
Steinhatchee
Jena
Deadman Bay
Shamrock
Cross City
Newberry
Wilcox
Old Town
Trenton
Funning Springs S.P.
Funning Springs
Bowlegs Point
Manatee Springs State Park
Chiefland
Bronson
Horseshoe Beach
Horseshoe Point
Horseshoe Cove
Shired Island
Fowler Bluff
Waccasassa River
Lower Suwannee National Wildlife Refuge
Suwannee
Otter Creek
Ellzey
• Chattahoochee S.P. Kk118
• Dead Lakes S.P. Kk120
• Econfina River S.P. Kn120
• Florida Caverns State Park Kk119
• Forest Capital State Museum Kn120
• Funning Springs S.P. Kp121
• Ichetucknee Springs S. P. Kp121
• John Gorrie State Mus. Kl121
• Manatee Springs State Park Kp121
• Nat. Bridge Battlefield State Hist. Site Km120
• O'Leno S.P. Kp121
• Ochlockonee River State Park Kl120
• Peacock Springs State Park Ko120
• San Luis N.H.S. Km120
• S.Marcos de Apalache State Hist. Site Km120
• Seminole S.P. Kl119
• St. Joseph Peninsula State Park Kk121
• Stephen Foster State Folk Cult. Ctr. Kp120
• Suwannee River State Park Ko120
• The Crescent Complex Ko119
• Three Rivers S.P. Kl119
• Torreya State Park Kl119
• Troy Springs State Park Kp121
83

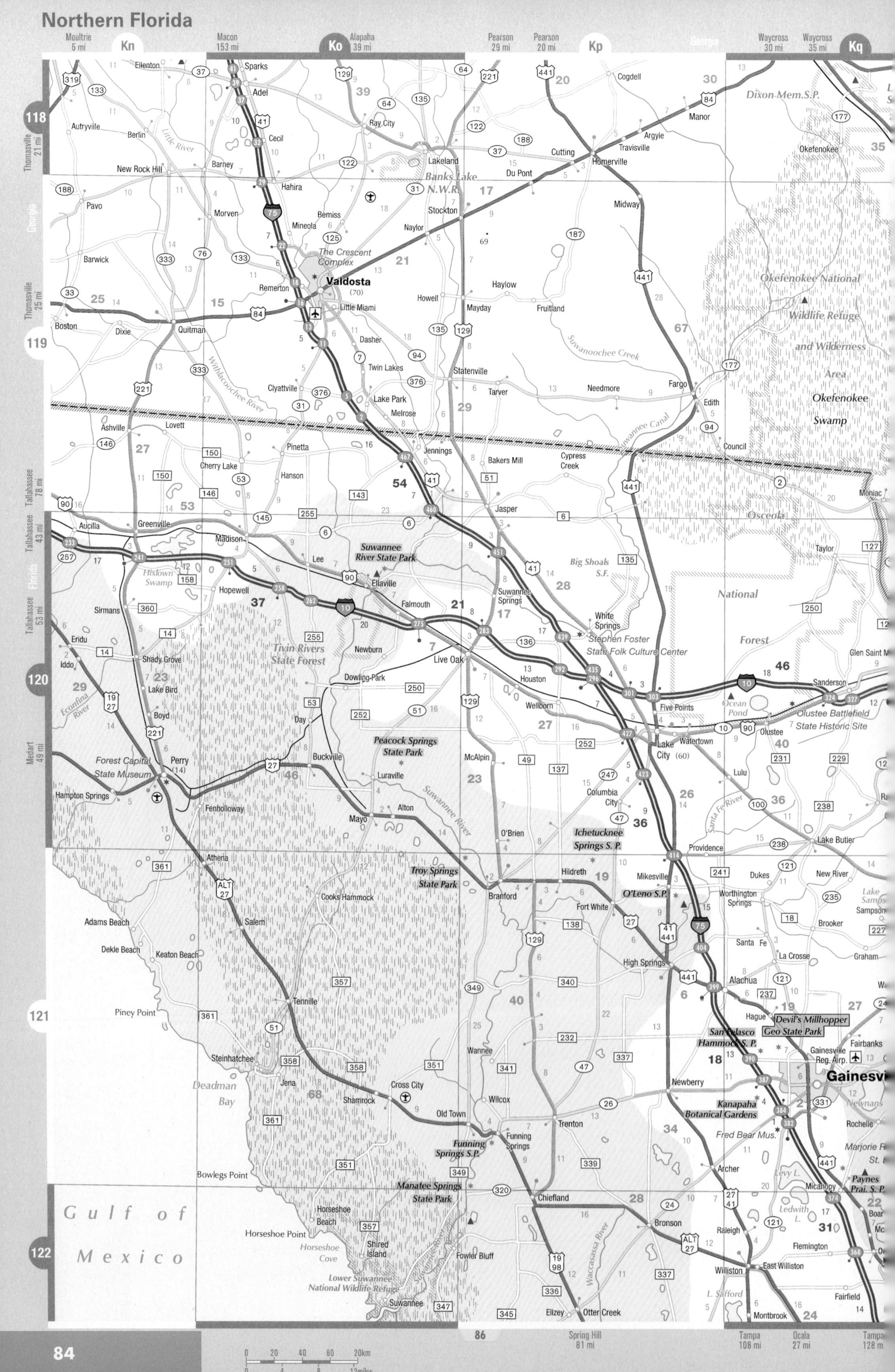
Moultrie 5 mi
Kn
Macon 153 mi
Ko
Alapaha 39 mi
Pearson 29 mi
Pearson 20 mi
Kp
Georgia
Waycross 30 mi
Waycross 35 mi
Kq
118
Thomasville 21 mi
Georgia
Thomasville 25 mi
119
Tallahassee 78 mi
Tallahassee 43 mi
Florida
Tallahassee 53 mi
120
Medart 49 mi
121
122
Ellenton
Sparks
Adel
Cecil
Autryville
Berlin
Little River
Barney
New Rock Hill
Hahira
Ray City
Lakeland
Banks Lake N.W.R.
Du Pont
Cutting
Homerville
Travisville
Argyle
Manor
Cogdell
Dixon Mem. S.P.
Okefenokee
Pavo
Morven
Mineola
Bemiss
Naylor
Stockton
Midway
Barwick
The Crescent Complex
Valdosta
(70)
Remerton
Little Miami
Howell
Mayday
Haylow
Fruitland
Boston
Dixie
Quitman
Dasher
Withlacoochee River
Twin Lakes
Statenville
Suwanoochee Creek
Okefenokee National Wildlife Refuge and Wilderness Area
Okefenokee Swamp
Clyattville
Lake Park
Melrose
Tarver
Needmore
Fargo
Edith
Ashville
Lovett
Jennings
Suwannee Canal
Council
Pinetta
Cherry Lake
Hanson
Bakers Mill
Cypress Creek
Moniac
Jasper
Osceola
Aucilla
Greenville
Madison
Lee
Suwannee River State Park
Ellaville
Big Shoals S.F.
Taylor
Hixtown Swamp
Hopewell
Falmouth
Suwannee Springs
National Forest
Sirmans
White Springs
Stephen Foster State Folk Culture Center
Eridu
Iddo
Shady Grove
Twin Rivers State Forest
Newburn
Live Oak
Houston
Glen Saint Mary
Lake Bird
Dowling Park
Wellborn
Five Points
Sanderson
Ocean Pond
Olustee Battlefield State Historic Site
Econfina River
Boyd
Day
Olustee
Peacock Springs State Park
Lake City
(60)
Watertown
Forest Capital State Museum
Perry
(14)
Buckville
McAlpin
Luraville
Columbia City
Lulu
Hampton Springs
Fenholloway
Mayo
Alton
Suwannee River
Santa Fe River
O'Brien
Ichetucknee Springs S. P.
Providence
Lake Butler
Athena
Troy Springs State Park
Hildreth
Mikesville
Branford
Dukes
New River
O'Leno S.P.
Worthington Springs
Lake Sampson
Cooks Hammock
Fort White
Brooker
Adams Beach
Salem
Santa Fe
Dekle Beach
Keaton Beach
High Springs
La Crosse
Graham
Alachua
Tennille
Piney Point
Hague
Devil's Millhopper Geo State Park
San Felasco Hammock S. P.
Fairbanks
Gainesville Reg. Airp.
Steinhatchee
Wannee
Gainesville
Deadman Bay
Jena
Cross City
Newberry
Shamrock
Wilcox
Kanapaha Botanical Gardens
Newnans
Rochelle
Old Town
Trenton
Fred Bear Mus.
Funning Springs
Funning Springs S.P.
Marjorie
Archer
Levy L.
Bowlegs Point
Manatee Springs State Park
Chiefland
Micanopy
Paynes Prai. S. P.
Gulf of Mexico
Horseshoe Beach
Horseshoe Point
Bronson
Ledwith L.
Raleigh
Flemington
Horseshoe Cove
Shired Island
Fowler Bluff
Waccasassa River
Lower Suwannee National Wildlife Refuge
Williston
East Williston
Suwannee
L. Stafford
Fairfield
Ellzey
Otter Creek
Montbrook
86
Spring Hill 81 mi
Tampa 108 mi
Ocala 27 mi
Tampa 128 m
0 20 40 60 20km
0 4 8 12miles

- Alligator Farm Ks121
- Anastasia State Park Ks121
- Forest Capital State Museum Kn120
- Fort Caroline National Memorial Ks120
- Fort Clinch Ks119
- Fort Clinch State Park Ks119
- Fred Bear Mus. Kq121
- Guana River State Park Ks120
- Jekyll Island Historic District Ks118
- Kanapaha Botanical Gardens Kq121
- Lightner Museum Ks121
- Manatee Springs State Park Kp121
- Marineland of Florida Ks121
- Old Town Ks118
- Oldest Store Mus. Ks121
- Peacock Springs State Park Ko120
- Ravine State Gardens Kr121
- Stephen Foster State Folk Cult. Ctr. Kp120
- Suwannee River State Park Ko120
- Tomoka S.P. Ks122
- Troy Springs State Park Kp121
- Washington Oaks State Gardens Ks121
- Zoo Kr120

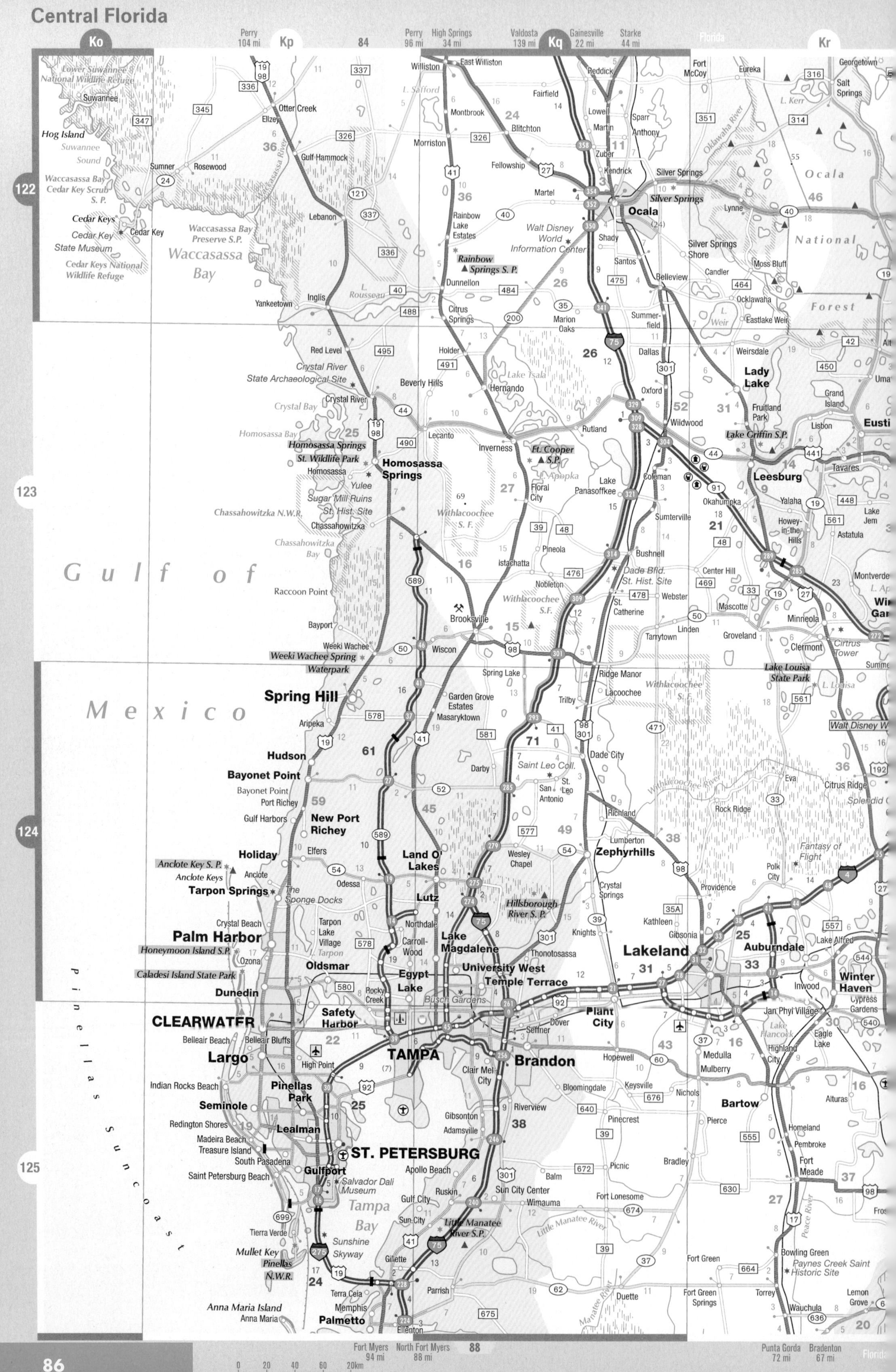
Ko
Kp
84
Kq
Kr
Perry 104 mi
Perry 96 mi
High Springs 34 mi
Valdosta 139 mi
Gainesville 22 mi
Starke 44 mi
Lower Suwannee National Wildlife Refuge
Suwannee
Hog Island
Suwannee Sound
Waccasassa Bay
Cedar Key Scrub S. P.
Cedar Keys
Cedar Key State Museum
Cedar Key
Cedar Keys National Wildlife Refuge
Waccasassa Bay Preserve S.P.
Waccasassa Bay
Sumner
Rosewood
Otter Creek
Ellzey
Gulf Hammock
Lebanon
Yankeetown
Inglis
L. Rousseau
Williston
East Williston
L. Stafford
Montbrook
Morriston
Blitchton
Fellowship
Fairfield
Reddick
Lowell
Martin
Sparr
Anthony
Zuber
Kendrick
Martel
Ocala
Silver Springs
Shady
Santos
Belleview
Summerfield
Dallas
Oxford
Wildwood
Rainbow Lake Estates
Rainbow Springs S. P.
Walt Disney World Information Center
Dunnellon
Citrus Springs
Marion Oaks
Holder
Beverly Hills
Hernando
Lake Tsala
Inverness
Lecanto
Rutland
Ft. Cooper S.P.
L. Apopka
Floral City
Lake Panasoffkee
Coleman
Sumterville
Okahumpka
Bushnell
Fort McCoy
Eureka
Georgetown
Salt Springs
L. Kerr
Oklawaha River
Ocala National Forest
Lynne
Silver Springs Shore
Candler
Moss Bluff
Ocklawaha
Eastlake Weir
L. Weir
Weirsdale
Lady Lake
Fruitland Park
Lake Griffin S.P.
Grand Island
Lisbon
Eustis
Umatilla
Leesburg
Tavares
Yalaha
Howey-in-the-Hills
Lake Jem
Astatula
Center Hill
Mascotte
Groveland
Minneola
Clermont
Montverde
Cirtrus Tower
Lake Louisa State Park
L. Louisa
Walt Disney World
Red Level
Crystal River State Archaeological Site
Crystal River
Crystal Bay
Homosassa Bay
Homosassa Springs St. Wildlife Park
Homosassa
Homosassa Springs
Yulee Sugar Mill Ruins St. Hist. Site
Chassahowitzka N.W.R.
Chassahowitzka
Chassahowitzka Bay
Withlacoochee S. F.
Istachatta
Pineola
Nobleton
Dade Bfld. St. Hist. Site
Webster
St. Catherine
Linden
Tarrytown
Gulf of Mexico
Raccoon Point
Bayport
Brooksville
Weeki Wachee
Weeki Wachee Spring Waterpark
Wiscon
Spring Lake
Ridge Manor
Lacoochee
Tribly
Spring Hill
Aripeka
Garden Grove Estates
Masaryktown
Hudson
Bayonet Point
Port Richey
Gulf Harbors
New Port Richey
Elfers
Holiday
Anclote Key S. P.
Anclote Keys
Anclote
Tarpon Springs
The Sponge Docks
Odessa
Darby
Saint Leo Coll.
St. Leo
San Antonio
Dade City
Richland
Wesley Chapel
Zephyrhills
Lumberton
Crystal Springs
Hillsborough River S. P.
Eva
Citrus Ridge
Rock Ridge
Fantasy of Flight
Polk City
Providence
Kathleen
Gibsonia
Knights
Land O' Lakes
Lutz
Crystal Beach
Palm Harbor
Honeymoon Island S.P.
Ozona
Caladesi Island State Park
Tarpon Lake Village
L. Tarpon
Northdale
Carrollwood
Lake Magdalene
Thonotosassa
Oldsmar
Egypt Lake
University West
Temple Terrace
Dunedin
Rocky Creek
Busch Gardens
CLEARWATER
Safety Harbor
Plant City
Dover
Seffner
Lakeland
Auburndale
Lake Alfred
Inwood
Winter Haven
Jan Phyl Village
Cypress Gardens
Eagle Lake
Lake Hancock
Highland City
Belleair Beach
Belleair Bluffs
Largo
High Point
TAMPA
Brandon
Clair Mel City
Hopewell
Medulla
Mulberry
Bartow
Alturas
Indian Rocks Beach
Pinellas Park
Seminole
Bloomingdale
Keysville
Nichols
Riverview
Pinecrest
Pierce
Redington Shores
Lealman
Gibsonton
Adamsville
Homeland
Pembroke
Madeira Beach
Treasure Island
South Pasadena
ST. PETERSBURG
Gulfport
Saint Petersburg Beach
Apollo Beach
Balm
Picnic
Bradley
Fort Meade
Salvador Dali Museum
Tampa Bay
Ruskin
Sun City Center
Wimauma
Fort Lonesome
Gulf City
Sun City
Little Manatee River S.P.
Little Manatee River
Tierra Verde
Sunshine Skyway
Mullet Key
Pinellas N.W.R.
Gillette
Fort Green
Bowling Green
Paynes Creek Saint Historic Site
Peace River
Terra Ceia
Memphis
Palmetto
Ellenton
Parrish
Duette
Manatee River
Fort Green Springs
Torrey
Wauchula
Lemon Grove
Anna Maria Island
Anna Maria
Pinellas Suncoast
Fort Myers 94 mi
North Fort Myers 88 mi
88
Punta Gorda 72 mi
Bradenton 67 mi
Florida
0 20 40 60 20km
0 4 8 12miles

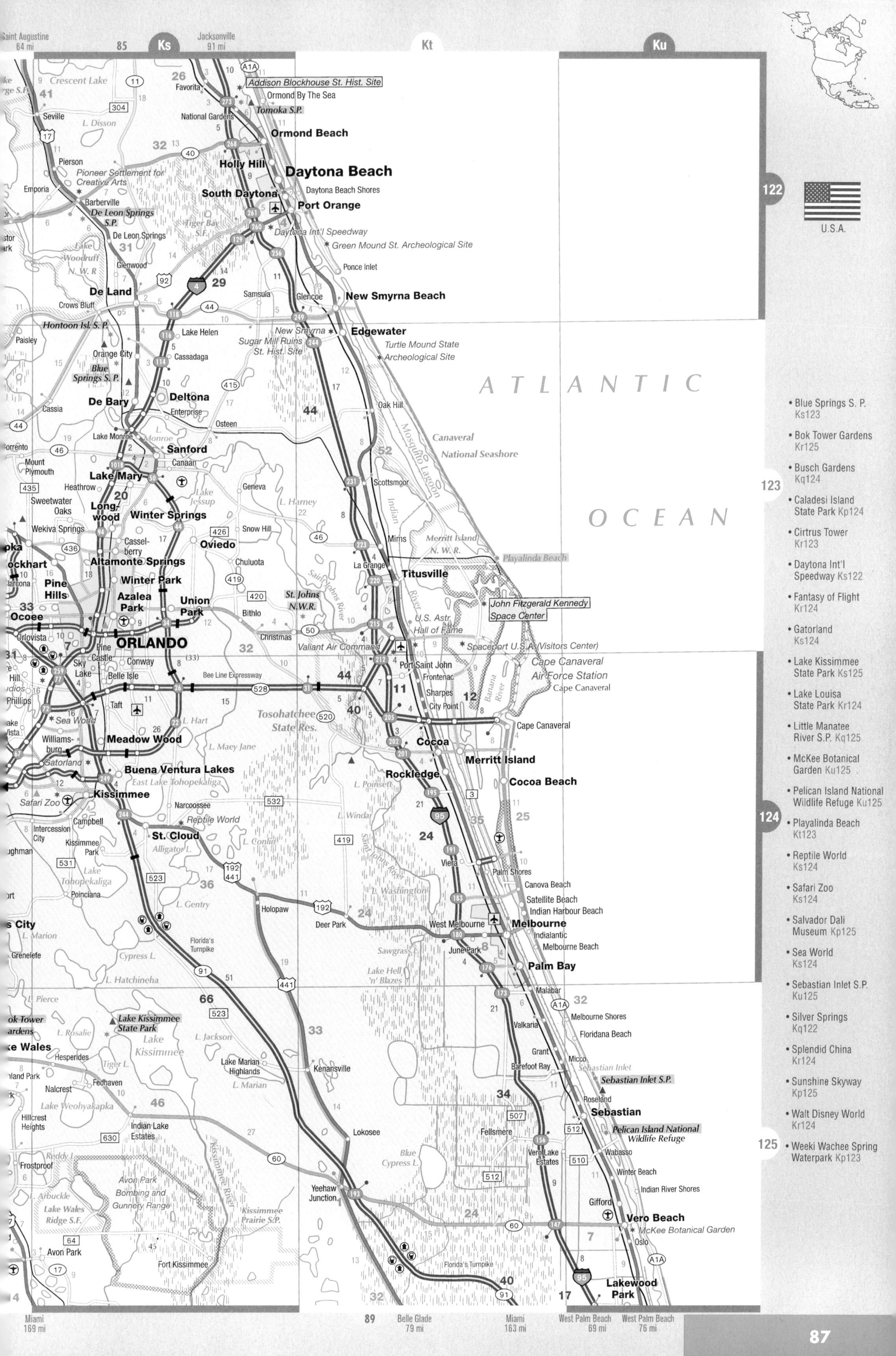

• Blue Springs S. P. Ks123
• Bok Tower Gardens Kr125
• Busch Gardens Kq124
• Caladesi Island State Park Kp124
• Cirtrus Tower Kr123
• Daytona Int'l Speedway Ks122
• Fantasy of Flight Kr124
• Gatorland Ks124
• Lake Kissimmee State Park Ks125
• Lake Louisa State Park Kr124
• Little Manatee River S.P. Kq125
• McKee Botanical Garden Ku125
• Pelican Island National Wildlife Refuge Ku125
• Playalinda Beach Kt123
• Reptile World Ks124
• Safari Zoo Ks124
• Salvador Dali Museum Kp125
• Sea World Ks124
• Sebastian Inlet S.P. Ku125
• Silver Springs Kq122
• Splendid China Kr124
• Sunshine Skyway Kp125
• Walt Disney World Kr124
• Weeki Wachee Spring Waterpark Kp123

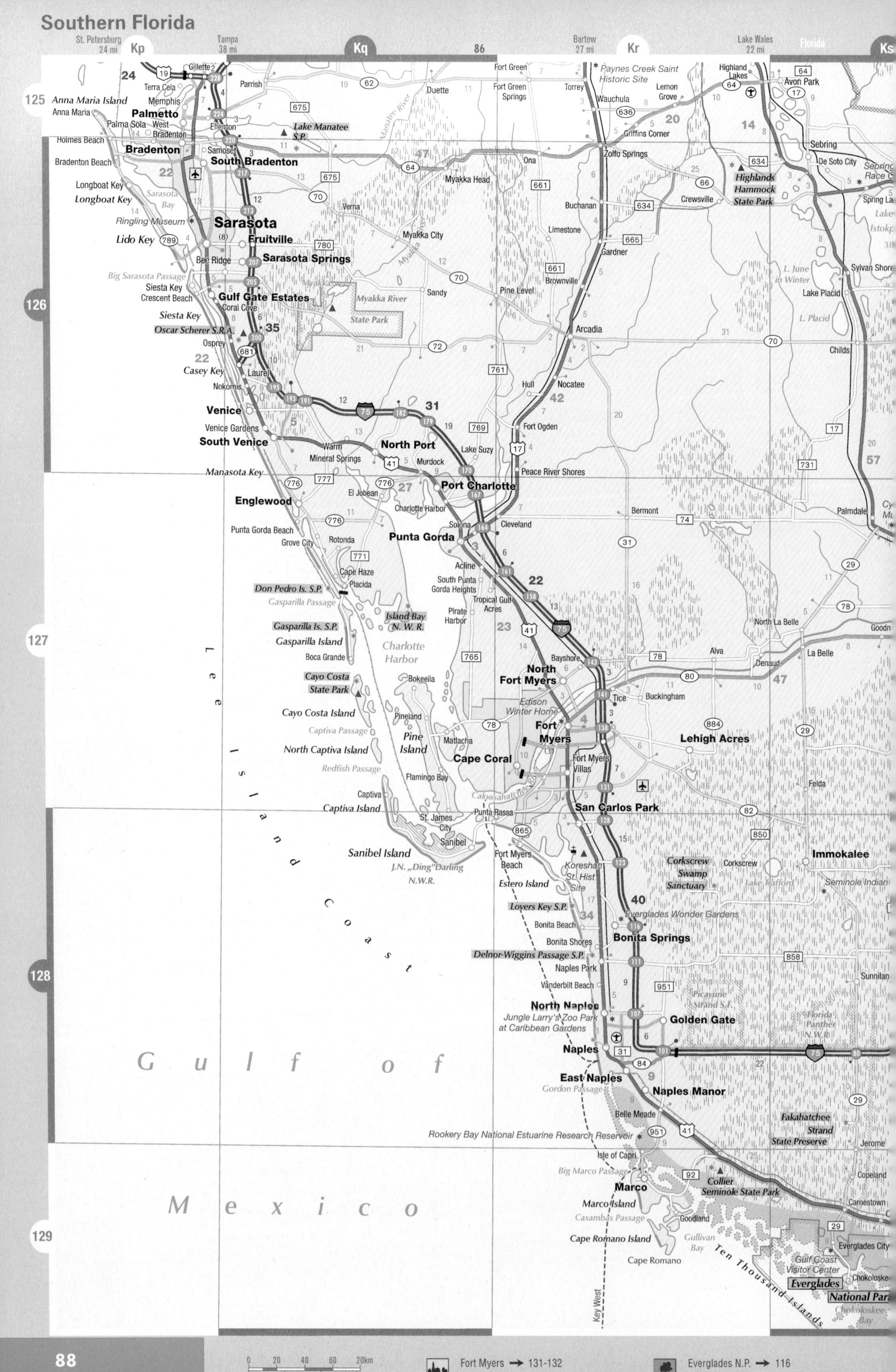

0 20 40 60 20km
0 4 8 12miles

Fort Myers → 131-132
Everglades N.P. → 116

- Burt Reynolds Ranch Ku127
- Cayo Costa State Park Kq127
- Collier Seminole State Park Kr129
- Corkscrew Swamp Sanctuary Kr128
- Cypress Knee Museum Ks127
- Edison Winter Home Kr127
- Everglades Wonder Gardens Kr128
- Fakahatchee Strand State Preserve Ks128
- Florida Oceanographic Coastal Center Ku126
- Gatorama Ks127
- Highlands Hammock State Park Kr126
- Hugh Taylor Birch S.P. Ku128
- Island Bay N. W. R. Kq127
- Lake Manatee S.P. Kq126
- Lion Country Ku127
- Lovers Key S.P. Kr128
- Manatee Center Ku126
- Miccosukee Cultural Center Kt129
- Ringling Museum Kp126
- Seminole Indian Casino Ks128
- The Devil's Garden Ks127
- Tree Snail Hammock Kt129

Fort Lauderdale → 130
Miami → 133-134

Kp
Kq
Fort Myers 34 mi
Kr
Fort Myers 44 mi
88
128
129
130
131
132
Vanderbilt Beach
Fort Myers
North Naples
Jungle Larry's Zoo Park at Caribbean Gardens
Golden Gate
Picayune Strand S.F.
Naples
East Naples
Gordon Passage
Naples Manor
Belle Meade
Rookery Bay National Estuarine Research Reservoir
Isle of Capri
Big Marco Passage
Marco
Collier Seminole State Park
Marco Island
Caxambas Passage
Goodland
Cape Romano Island
Gullivan Bay
Cape Romano
Ten Thousand
Gulf of Mexico
Content Key
Great White Heron N.W.R
Johnston Key
Sugarloaf Key
Mud Keys
Snipe Keys
Cudjoe
Cudjoe Key
Key West N.W.R
Dry Tortugas National Park
Loggerhead Key
Fort Jefferson National Memorial
Dry Tortugas
Florida Keys National Marine Sanctuary
Marquesas Keys
Key West
Stock Island
El Chico
Aquarium
Boca Chica Key
Intracoastal W
Key West
Playa del Carmen, Cozumel

Ks
Florida
Kt
89
South Bay 41 mi
Deerfield Beach 55 mi
Ku
West Palm Beach 46 mi
Sunniland
Big Cypress Seminole Indian Reservation
76
Alligator Alley (Everglades Parkway)
Big Cypress
National
Preserve
Jerome
Copeland
Carnestown
Ochopee
Everglades City
Chokoloskee
Chokoloskee Bay
Tamiami Canal
Oasis Visitor Center
Monroe Station
Tree Snail Hammock
Miccosukee Indian Reservation
Miccosukee Cultural Center
Shark Valley Visitor Center
Observation Tower
South New River Canal
Chevelier Bay
Alligator Bay
Big Lostmans Bay
First Bay
Key Mc Laughlin
Highland Point
Everglades
National Park
Pa-hay-okee Overlook
Ernest F. Coe Visitor Center
Anhinga Trail
Gumbo Limbo Trail
Mahogany Hammock
Shark Point
Ponce de Leon Bay
Shark River Island
Whitewater Bay
Northwest Cape
Cape Sable
Middle Cape
East Cape
West Lake Trail
Mangrove Swamp
Flamingo Visitor Center
Flamingo
Oyster Keys
Madiera Bay
Joe Bay
Florida Bay
North Lauderdale
Tamarac
Lauderdale Lakes
Sunrise
Lauderhill
Lauderdale by the Sea
Oakland Park
Hugh Taylor Birch S.P.
Wilton Manors
Melrose Park
Plantation
FORT LAUDERDALE
Weston
Davie
John U. Lloyd Beach S.P.
PEMBROKE PINES
Cooper City
Dania Beach
HOLLYWOOD
Miramar
Carol City
Norland
Aventura
Hallandale Beach
Miami Lakes
Ojus
Sunny Isles Beach
North Miami
HIALEAH
Opa Locka
Surfside
Miami Shores
Miami Springs
Brownsville
North Bay Village
Miami Beach
Sweetwater
MIAMI
Westchester
West Miami
Coral Gables
South Miami
Westwood Lakes
Parrot Jungle
Bill Baggs Cape Florida S.R.A.
Key Biscayne
Key Biscayne
Kendall
Richmond Heights
Perrine
Monkey Jungle
Cutler Ridge
Princeton
Goulds
Biscayne National Park
Naranja
Leisure City
Homestead
Florida City
Sands Key
Biscayne Bay
Dante Fascell Visitor Center
Elliott Key
Islandia
Intracoastal Waterway
Old Rhodes Key
John Pennekamp
Key Largo
Coral Reef
State Park
Barnes Sound
Key Largo
Key Largo National Marine Sanctuary
Sunset Point
Plantation Key
Tavernier
Plantation
McKee's Museum
Theater of The Sea
Upper Matecumbe Key
Islamorada
Lignumvitae Key State Botanical Site
Indian Key State Historic Site
Lower Matecumbe Key
Florida Keys National Marine Sanctuary
Great White Heron N.W.R
Long Key
Layton
Long Key State Park
Dolphin Research Center
Duck Key
Vaca Key
No Name Key
Marathon
Key Colony Beach
Big Pine Key
Seven Mile Bridge
Institute of Marine Science
Bahia Honda State Park
Big Pine Key
Florida Keys
Straits of Florida
Fort Lauderdale
ATLANTIC OCEAN
128
129
130
131
132
U.S.A.
• Anhinga Trail Kt130
• Aquarium Kr131
• Bahia Honda State Park Ks131
• Bill Baggs Cape Florida S.R.A. Ku129
• Collier Seminole State Park Kr129
• Dolphin Research Center Kt131
• Fakahatchee Strand State Preserve Ks128
• Gumbo Limbo Trail Kt130
• Hugh Taylor Birch S.P. Ku128
• Indian Key State Historic Site Kt131
• Institute of Marine Science Ks131
• Lignumvitae Key State Botanical Site Kt131
• Long Key State Park Kt131
• Mahogany Hammock Kt130
• McKee's Museum Kt131
• Miccosukee Cultural Center Kt129
• Monkey Jungle Ku129
• Pa-hay-okee Overlook Kt130
• Parrot Jungle Ku129
• Seven Mile Bridge Ks131
• Theater of The Sea Kt131
• Tree Snail Hammock Kt129
• West Lake Trail Kt130

Fort Lauderdale → 130
Miami → 133-134
Everglades N.P. → 116

Notes

National Parks

- Arches
- Bryce Canyon
- Canyonlands
- Death Valley
- Denali
- Everglades
- Grand Canyon
- Grand Teton
- Great Smoky Mountains
- Jasper / Banff / Kootenay / Yoho
- Joshua Tree
- Kings Canyon, Sequoia
- Olympic
- Rocky Mountain
- Waterton Lakes / Glacier
- Yellowstone
- Yosemite
- Zion

Photo: Utah, Colorado Plateau, Arches National Park (Reiner Harscher/laif)

U.S.A.

www.nps.gov

NP = National Park NPRES = National Preserves NHP = National Historical Park NRES = National Reserve NRA = National Recreation Area

Page/ Search Grid	Name	Type	Area in mi²	Address	City	ZIP	Phone (+1...)	Visitor Center	Camping	Back-packing	Hiking	Skiing	Fishing	Boating	Swimming	Hotel/ Lodge
Alaska																
11 Na14	Denali	NP	9492	P.O. Box 9	Denali	AK 99755	(907) 683-2294	●	●	●	●	●				
10 Mh12	Gates of the Artic	NP	13238	P.O. Box 30	Bettles	AK 99726	(907) 692-5494	●	●	●	●	●	●	●		
14 Ng16	Glacier Bay	NP	5130	P.O. Box 140	Gustavus	AK 99826-0140	(907) 697-2230	●	●		●		●	●		
12 Mh16	Katmai	NP	7383	P.O. Box 7	King Salmon	AK 99613	(907) 246-3305	●		●	●		●	●		
13 Mk16	Kenai Fjords	NP	1094	P.O. Box 1727	Seward	AK 99664	(907) 422-0500	●			●	●	●	●		
10 Mf12	Kobuk Valley	NP	2609	P.O. Box 1029	Kotzebue	AK 99752	(907) 442-3890	●			●	●	●	●		
12 Mj15	Lake Clark	NP	6293	240 West 5th Avenue, Suite 236	Anchorage	AK 99501	(907) 644-3626	●	●	●	●	●	●	●		
13 Nd15	Wrangell-St. Elias	NP	20	P.O. Box 439	Copper Center	AK 99573	(907) 822-5234	●	●	●	●	●	●	●		
12 Mg17	Aniakchak	NPRES	214	P.O. Box 245	King Salmon	AK 99613	(907) 246-3305				●		●			
10 Mc12	Bering Land Bridge	NPRES	4.2	PO Box 220	Nome	AK 99762	(907) 443-2522				●	●	●	●		
10 Mf11	Noatak	NPRES	10265	P.O. Box 1029	Kotzebue	AK 99752	(907) 442-3890				●		●	●		
11 Nd13	Yukon-Charley Rivers	NPRES	3946	P.O. Box 167	Eagle	AK 99738	(907) 547-2233	●			●	●	●	●		
154 B4	Klondike Gold Rush	NHP	20	P.O. Box 517	Skagway	AK 99840	(907) 983-9200	●	●		●	●	●	●		
14 Nh17	Sitka	NHP	0.17	103 Monastery Street	Sitka	AK 99835	(907) 747-0110	●			●		●			
Pacific States																
32 Oe29	Channel Islands	NP	390	1901 Spinnaker Drive	Ventura	CA 93001	(805) 658-5730	●	●	●	●		●	●	●	
24 Od24	Crater Lake	NP	286	P.O. Box 7	Crater Lake	OR 97604	(541) 594-3000	●			●	●	●			
32 Og27	Death Valley	NP	5262	P.O. Box 579	Death Valley	CA 92328	(760) 786-3200	●	●	●	●				●	
33 Oh29	Joshua Tree	NP	1234	74485 National Park Drive	Twentynine Palms	CA 92277	(760) 367-5500	●	●	●	●					
32 Of27	Kings Canyon	NP	1353	47050 Generals Highway	Three Rivers	CA 93271-9700	(559) 565-3341	●	●	●	●	●	●			
24 Oe25	Lassen Volcanic	NP	166	P.O. Box 100	Mineral	CA 96063-0100	(530) 595-4480	●	●	●	●	●	●	●		
24 Od22	Mount Rainier	NP	368	55210 238th Ave. East	Ashford	WA 98304	(360) 569-2211	●	●		●	●	●			
16 Oe21	North Cascades	NP	790	810 State Route 20	Sedro-Woolley	WA 98284	(360) 854-7200	●	●	●	●		●	●		
24 Od22	Olympic	NP	1442	600 East Park Avenue	Port Angeles	WA 98362	(360) 565-3130	●	●	●	●	●	●	●	●	●
24 Oc25	Redwood	NP	206	1111 Second Street	Crescent City	CA 95531	(707) 464-6101	●	●	●	●					
32 Of27	Sequoia & Kings Canyon	NP	1353	47050 Generals Highway	Three Rivers	CA 93271-9700	(559) 565-3341	●	●	●	●	●	●			
32 Of27	Yosemite	NP	1190	P.O. Box 577	Yosemite National Park	CA 95389	(209) 372-0200	●	●	●	●	●	●	●	●	
33 Oh28	Mojave	NPRES	2398	2701 Barstow Road	Barstow	CA 92311	(760) 252-6100				●					
142 B1	Golden Gate	NRA	117	Fort Mason, Building 201	San Francisco	CA 94123-1307	(415) 561-4700	●	●		●		●	●	●	
24 Oe21	Lake Chelan	NRA	97	810 State Route 20	Sedro-Woolley	WA 98284	(360) 854-7200	●	●	●	●	●	●	●		●
18 Pd22	Lake Roosevelt	NRA	157	1008 Crest Drive	Coulee Dam	WA 99116	(509) 633-9441	●	●		●		●	●	●	
24 Oe21	Ross Lake	NRA	184	810 State Route 20	Sedro-Woolley	WA 98284	(360) 854-7200		●	●	●	●	●	●		●
-	Santa Monica Mountains	NRA	241	401 West Hillcrest Drive	Thousand Oaks	CA 91360	(805) 370-2301	●	●		●		●	●	●	
-	Whiskeytown-Shasta-Trinity	NRA	318	14412 Kennedy Memorial Drive	Whiskeytown	CA 96095-0188	(530) 246-1225	●	●	●	●		●	●	●	
18 Pe21	Lewis and Clark	NHP	5	92343 Fort Clatsop Road	Astoria	OR 97103-9197	(503) 861-2471 ext. 214	●	●							
-	Rosie The Riveter	NHP	0.23	P.O. Box 336, Station A	Richmond	CA 94804	(510) 232-5050	●						●		
145 E1	San Francisco Maritime	NHP	0.08	Fort Mason Center, Building E	San Francisco	CA 94123	(415) 447-5000	●								
16 Od21	San Juan Island	NHP		P.O. Box 429	Friday Harbor	WA 98250	(360) 378-2240	●			●		●	●		
Southwest States																
39 Pd31	Big Bend	NP	1252	P.O. Box 129	Big Bend National Park	TX 79834	(432) 477-2251	●	●	●	●		●	●		
34 Pc29	Carlsbad Caverns	NP	73	3225 National Parks Highway	Carlsbad	NM 88220	(575) 785-2232	●			●					
33 Oj27	Grand Canyon	NP	1902	P.O. Box 129	Grand Canyon	AZ 86023	(928) 638-7888	●	●	●	●	●	●	●		●
34 Pc30	Guadalupe Mountains	NP	135	400 Pine Canyon Road	Salt Flat	TX 79847	(915) 828-3251	●	●	●	●					
36 Pk29	Petrified Forest	NP	342	P.O. Box 2217	Petrified Forest	AZ 86028	(928) 524-6228	●	●	●	●	●				
33 Ok29	Saguaro	NP	137	3693 South Old Spanish Trail	Tucson	AZ 85730	(520) 733-5153	●			●					
-	Big Thicket	NPRES	166	6044 FM 420	Kountze	TX 77625	(409) 951-6700	●			●		●	●	●	
-	Valles Caldera	NPRES	147	18161 Highway 4	Jemez Springs	NM 87025	(505) 661-3333				●					
40 Pe31	Amistad	NRA	104	4121 Veterans Blvd.	Del Rio	TX 78840	(830) 775-7491	●	●		●		●	●	●	
-	Chickasaw	NRA	15	1008 West Second Street	Sulphur	OK 73086	(580) 622-3161	●	●		●		●	●	●	
-	Glen Canyon	NRA	1960	P.O. Box 1507	Page	AZ 86040	(928) 608-6200	●	●		●		●	●	●	
17 Pa18	Lake Meredith	NRA	73	P.O. Box 1460	Fritch	TX 79036	(806) 857-3151		●		●		●	●	●	
33 Pb27	Chaco Culture	NHP	53	P. O. Box 220	Nageezi	NM 87037	(505) 786-7014	●	●		●					
40 Pf30	Lyndon B. Johnson	NHP	2.3	P.O. Box 329	Johnson City	TX 78636	(830) 868-7128 ext. 244	●			●		●			
34 Pc28	Pecos	NHP	10	P.O. Box 418	Pecos	NM 87552	(505) 757-7200	●								
-	San Antonio Missions	NHP	1.16	2202 Roosevelt Avenue	San Antonio	TX 78210	(210) 932-1001	●			●					
33 Ok30	Tumacácori	NHP	0.58	P. O. Box 8067	Tumacácori	AZ 85640	(520) 398-2341	●			●					
Rocky Mountain States																
33 Pa26	Arches	NP	120	P.O. Box 907	Moab	UT 84532-0907	(435) 719-2299	●	●	●	●					
33 Pa26	Black Canyon of the Gunnison	NP	48	102 Elk Creek	Gunnison	CO 814230	(970) 641-2337	●	●		●	●	●			
33 Oj27	Bryce Canyon	NP	56	P.O. Box 170001	Bryce Canyon	UT 84717-0001	(435) 834-5322	●	●	●	●	●				
33 Ok26	Canyonlands	NP	527	2282 SW Resource Blvd	Moab	UT 84532	(435) 719-2313	●	●	●	●			●		
33 Ok26	Capitol Reef	NP	378	HC 70 Box 15	Torrey	UT 84775	(435) 425-3791 ext. 111	●	●	●	●		●			
17 Og20	Glacier	NP	1583	P.O. Box 128	West Glacier	MT 59936	(406) 888-7800	●	●	●	●	●	●	●		
25 Ok24	Grand Teton	NP	485	P.O. Drawer 170	Moose	WY 83012	(307) 739-3300	●	●	●	●	●	●	●	●	

33 Oh26	Great Basin	NP	120	100 Great Basin National Park	Baker	NV 89311	(775) 234-7331
34 Pb26	Great Sand Dunes	NP	132	11999 Highway 150	Mosca	CO 81146	(719) 378-6399
33 Pa27	Mesa Verde	NP	81	P.O. Box 8	Mesa Verde	CO 81330	(970) 529-4465
26 Pb25	Rocky Mountain	NP	416	1000 Highway 36	Estes Park	CO 80517	(970) 586-1206
25 Ok23	Yellowstone	NP	3470	P.O. Box 168	Yellowstone Nat. Park	WY 82190-0168	(307) 344-7381
33 Oj27	Zion	NP	224	Zion National Park	Springdale	UT 84767	(435) 772-3256
25 Oj24	Craters of the Moon	NPRES	1117	P.O. Box 29	Arco	ID 83213	(208) 527-1300
-	City of the Rocks	NRES	22	P.O. Box 169	Almo	ID 83312	(208) 824-5901
25 Pa23	Bighorn Canyon	NRA	149	P.O. Box 7458	Fort Smith	MT 59035	(406) 666-2412
33 Pb26	Curecanti	NRA	162	102 Elk Creek	Gunnison	CO 81230	(970) 641-2337
33 Oh27	Lake Mead	NRA	2337	601 Nevada Way	Boulder City	NV 89005	(702) 293-8906
24 Og22	Nez Perce	NHP	3.5	P.O. Box 1000	Lapwai	ID 83540	(208) 843-7001

Mid West States

26 Pd24	Badlands	NP	379	25216 Ben Reifel Road	Interior	SD 57750	(605) 433-5361
29 Qe25	Cuyahoga Valley	NP	51	15610 Vaughn Road	Brecksville	OH 44141	(800) 257-9477
20 Qa21	Isle Royale	NP	842	800 East Lakeshore Drive	Houghton	MI 49931-1869	(906) 482-0984
18 Pd22	Theodore Roosevelt	NP	110	P.O. Box 7	Medora	ND 58645	(701) 623-4730 ext. 3417
19 Pj21	Voyageurs	NP	341	360 Highway 11 East	International Falls	MN 56649	(218) 283-6600
26 Pc24	Wind Cave	NP	44	26611 U.S. Highway 385	Hot Springs	SD 57747	(605) 745-4600
-	Tallgrass Prairie	NPRES	62	P.O. Box 585	Cottonwood Falls	KS 66845	(620) 273-8494
-	Mississippi	NRA	84	111 East Kellogg Blvd., Suite 105	Saint Paul	MN 55101	(651) 290-4160
-	Dayton Aviation Heritage	NHP	0.14	16 South Williams Street	Dayton	OH 45402	(937) 225-7705
28 Qb26	George Rogers Clark	NHP	0.04	401 S. 2nd St.	Vincennes	IN 47591	(812) 882-1776 ext. 110
-	Hopewell Culture	NHP	1.9	16062 State Route 104	Chillicothe	Ohio 45601	(740) 774-1126
-	Keewenaw	NHP	3.1	25970 Red Jacket Road	Calumet	MI 49913-2948	(906) 337-3168

Southern States

43 Qe33	Biscayne	NP	270	9700 SW 328 Street	Homestead	FL 33033	(305) 230-7275
37 Qe29	Congaree	NP	34	100 National Park Road	Hopkins	SC 29061	(803) 776-4396 ext. 0
43 Qd33	Dry Tortugas	NP	101	P.O. Box 6208	Key West	FL 33041	(305) 242-7700
43 Qe33	Everglades	NP	2357	40001 State Road 9336	Homestead	FL 33034-6733	(305) 242-7700
37 Qd28	Great Smoky Mountains	NP	815	107 Park Headquarters Road	Gatlinburg	TN 37738	(865) 436-1200
35 Pj28	Hot Springs	NP	9	101 Reserve Street	Hot Springs	AR 71901	(501) 624-2701
36 Qb27	Mammoth Cave	NP	83	1 Mammoth Cave Parkway	Mammoth Cave	KY 42259	(270) 758-2180
-	Big Cypress	NPRES	1156	33100 Tamiami Trail East	Ochopee	Fl 34141	(239) 695-1201
-	Jean Lafitte	NPRES	31	419 Decatur Street	New Orleans	LA 70130	(504) 589-3882
20 Qb20	Little River	NPRES	21	4322 Little River Trail NE, Suite 100	Fort Payne	AL 35967	(256) 845-9605
37 Qc27	Big South Fork	NRA	196	4564 Leatherwood Road	Oneida	TN 37841	(423) 286-7275
-	Chattahoochee River	NRA	14	1978 Island Ford Pkwy	Sandy Springs	GA 30350	(678) 538-1200
36 Qc27	Abraham Lincoln Birthplace	NHP	0.58	2995 Lincoln Farm Road	Hodgenville	KY 42748	(270) 358-3137
-	Cane River Creole	NHP	0.32	400 Rapides Drive	Natchitoches	LA 71457	(318) 356-8441
31 Qh27	Chesapeake and Ohio Canal	NHP	31	1850 Dual Highway, Suite 100	Hagerstown	MD 21740-6620	(301) 739-4200
37 Qe30	Cumberland Gap	NHP	32	91 Bartlett Park Road	Middlesboro	KY 40965	(606) 248-2817
36 Pk30	Natchez	NHP	0.17	1 Melrose Montebello Parkway	Natchez	MS 39120	(601) 446-5790
36 Pk30	New Orleans Jazz	NHP	0.008	419 Decatur Street	New Orleans	LA 70130	(504) 589-4841

Mid Atlantic States

-	New York Harbor	NP	42	26 Wall Street	New York	NY 10005	(212) 668-5180
29 Qf26	Shenandoah	NP	311	3655 US Highway 211 East	Luray	VA 22835	(540) 999-3500
-	Wolf Trap	NP	0.20	1551 Trap Road	Vienna	VA 22182	(703) 255-1800
-	New Jersey Pinelands	NRES	1819	15 Springfield Rd	New Lisbon	NJ 08064	(609) 894-7300
-	Delaware Water Gap	NRA	107	Delaware Water Gap NRA	Bushkill	PA 18324-9999	(570) 426-2452
-	Gateway	NRA	42	210 New York Avenue	Staten Island	NY 10305	(718) 354-4606
-	Gauley River	NRA	18	P. O. Box 246	Glen Jean	WV 25846	(304) 465-0508
37 Qf27	Appomatox Court House	NHP	1.5	P.O. Box 218, Hwy 24	Appomattox	VA 24522	(434) 352-8987 ext. 26
-	Cedar Creek & Belle Groove	NHP	5.8	P.O. Box 700	Middletown	VA 22645	(540) 869-3051
28 Qc23	Colonial	NHP	15	P.O. Box 210	Yorktown	VA 23690	(757) 898-2410
29 Qg26	Harpers Ferry	NHP	358	P.O. Box 65	Harpers Ferry	WV 25425	(304) 535-6029
30 Qh25	Independence	NHP	0.08	143 S. Third Street	Philadelphia	PA 19106	(800) 537-7676
-	Morristown	NHP	2.7	30 Washington Place	Morristown	NJ 07960-4299	(973) 543-4030
30 Qj24	Saratoga	NHP	5.29	648 Route 32	Stillwater	NY 12170	(518) 664-9821 ext. 224
-	Thomas Edison	NHP	0.03	211 Main Street	West Orange	NJ 07052-5612	(973) 736-0550 ext. 11
-	Valley Forge	NHP	5.4	1400 North Outer Line Drive	King of Prussia	PA 19406	(610) 783-1099
29 Qg24	Women's Right	NHP	0.01	136 Fall Street	Seneca Falls	NY 13148	(315) 568-0024

New England States

22 Ra23	Acadia	NP	74	Eagle Lake Road	Bar Harbor	ME 04609-0177	(207) 288-3338
30 Qk24	Boston Harbor Islands	NRA	2.3	408 Atlantic Avenue, Suite 228	Boston	MA 02110	(617) 223-8666
30 Qk24	Adams	NHP	0.04	135 Adams Street	Quincy	MA 02169	(617) 770-1175
30 Qk24	Boston	NHP	0.07	Charlestown Navy Yard	Boston	MA 02129	(617) 242-5642
30 Qk24	Lowell	NHP	0.22	67 Kirk Street	Lowell	MA 01852	(978) 970-5000
-	Marsh-Billings-Rockefeller	NHP	1	54 Elm Street	Woodstock	VT 05091	(802) 457-3368 ext. 22
-	Minute Man	NHP	1.5	174 Liberty St.	Concord	MA 01742	(978) 369-6993
30 Qk25	New Bedford Whaling	NHP	0.05	33 William Street	New Bedford	MA 02740	(508) 996-4095

Page/ Search Grid	Name	Type	Area in mi²	Address	City	ZIP	Phone	Visitor Center	Camping	Back-packing	Hiking	Skiing	Fishing	Boating	Swimming	Hotel/ Lodge
Hawaii																
44 Mg35	Haleakalā	NP	46	P.O. Box 369	Makawao, Maui	HI 96768	(808) 572-4400	✓	✓		✓				✓	
44 Mh36	Hawaii Volcanoes	NP	505	P.O. Box 52	Hawai'i National Park	HI 96718-0052	(808) 985-6000	✓	✓		✓					
44 Mg35	Kalaupapa	NHP	17	P.O. Box 2222	Kalaupapa	HI 96742	(808) 567-6802	✓								
-	Kaloko-Honokahau	NHP	1.9	73-4786 Kanalani St., #14	Kailua-Kona	HI 96740	(808) 326-9057				✓		✓	✓	✓	
44 Mh36	Pu'uhonua o Honaunau	NHP	0.8	P.O. Box 129	Honaunau	HI 96726	(808) 328-2326	✓			✓		✓		✓	
Insular Areas (Caribbean)																
-	Virgin Islands	NP	20	1300 Cruz Bay Creek	St. John	VI 00830	(340) 776-6201 ext. 238	✓		✓	✓		✓	✓	✓	
42 Rc37	Salt River Bay	NHP	1.5	2100 Church St #100	Christiansted, St. Croix	VI 00820	(340) 773-1460				✓			✓	✓	
Insular Areas (Pacific)																
-	American Samoa	NP	14		Pago Pago	AS 96799	(684) 633-7082	✓					✓		✓	
-	War in the Pacific	NHP	3.2	135 Murray Boulevard	Hagåtña	Guam 96910	(671) 333-4050	✓			✓		✓	✓	✓	

Canada

www.pc.gc.ca
NP = National Park NPRES = National Preserves NHP = National Historical Park NRES = National Reserve NRA = National Recreation Area

Page/ Search Grid	Name	Type	Area in mi²	Address	City	ZIP	Phone (+1...)	Visitor Center	Camping	Back-packing	Hiking	Skiing	Fishing	Boating	Swimming	Hotel/ Lodge
Northern Canada																
-	Aulavik	NP	4710	P.O. Box 29	Sachs Harbour	NT, X0E0Z0	867-690-3904		✓		✓		✓	✓		
-	Auyuittuq	NP	7915	P.O. Box 353	Pangnirtung	NU, X0A 0R0	867-473-2500	✓	✓		✓	✓		✓		✓
11 Nf11	Ivvavik	NP	3926	P.O. Box 1840	Inuvik	NWT, X0E 0T0	867-777-8800		✓		✓		✓	✓		
13 Ne15	Kluane	NP	8500	P.O. Box 5495	Haines Junction	YT, Y0B 1L0	867-634-7207	✓	✓		✓	✓	✓	✓		
15 Oc15	Nahanni	NP	1840	10002 100 Street	Fort Simpson	NT, X0E 0N0	867-695-7750		✓		✓		✓	✓		
-	Quttinirpaaq	NP	14585	P.O. Box 278	Iqaluit	NU, X0A 0H0	867-975-4673	✓	✓		✓	✓	✓			
-	Sirmillik	NP	8571	P.O. Box 300	Pond Inlet	NU, X0A 0S0	867-899-8092	✓	✓		✓	✓		✓	✓	
-	Tuktut Nogait	NP	6309	P.O. Box 91	Paulatuk	NT, X0E 1N0	867-580-3233		✓		✓		✓	✓		
-	Ukkusiksalik	NP	7722	P.O. Box 220	Repulse Bay	NU, X0C 0H0	867-462-4500		✓	✓	✓					
11 Ne11	Vuntut	NP	1699	P.O. Box 19	Old Crow	YT, Y0B 1N0	867-667-3910	✓					✓	✓		
15 Oj16	Wood Buffalo	NP	17298	P.O. Box 750	Fort Smith	NT, X0E 0P0	867-872-7960	✓	✓		✓	✓	✓	✓		
Western Canada																
17 Og20	Banff	NP	2564	224 Banff Avenue	Banff	AB, T1L 1K2	403-762-1550	✓	✓		✓	✓	✓	✓	✓	✓
17 Oj19	Elk Islands	NP	75	Site 4, R.R.#1	Fort Saskatchewan	AB, T8L 2N7	780-922-5790		✓		✓	✓				
17 Og20	Glacier	NP	521	P.O. Box 350	Revelstoke	BC, V0E 2S0	250-837-7500		✓		✓	✓	✓	✓		
18 Pb21	Grasslands	NP	350	P.O. Box 150	Val Marie	SK, S0N 2T0	877-345-2257	✓	✓		✓					
16 Od21	Gulf Islands	NP	12.7	2220 Harbour Road	Sidney	BC, V8L 2P6	250-654-4000		✓		✓			✓		
-	Gwaii Haanas	NP	568	P.O. Box 37	Queen Charlotte	BC, V0T 1S0	250-559-8818	✓	✓		✓		✓	✓		
16 Of19	Jasper	NP	4200	P.O. Box 10	Jasper	AB, T0E 1E0	780-852-6176	✓	✓	✓	✓	✓	✓	✓	✓	✓
17 Oh20	Kootenay	NP	543	P.O. Box 220	Radium Hot Springs	BC, V0A 1M0	250-347-9505	✓	✓		✓	✓	✓	✓	✓	
16 Of20	Mount Revelstoke	NP	100	P.O. Box 350	Revelstoke	BC, V0E 2S0	250-837-7500		✓		✓	✓	✓			
16 Oc21	Pacific Rim	NP	193	2185 Ocean Terrace Rd.	Ucluelet	BC, V0R 3A0	250-726-3500	✓	✓		✓		✓	✓		
18 Pb18	Prince Albert	NP	1496	P.O. Box 100	Waskesiu Lake	SK, S0J 2Y0	306-663-4522	✓	✓		✓			✓	✓	
18 Pe20	Riding Mountain	NP	1148		Wasagaming	MB, R0J 2H0	204-848-7275	✓	✓		✓	✓	✓	✓	✓	
-	Wapusk	NP	4431	P.O. Box 127	Churchill	MB, R0B 0E0	204-675-8863	✓			✓					
17 Oh21	Waterton Lakes	NP	203	P.O. Box 200	Waterton Park	AB, T0K 2M0	403-859-5133	✓	✓	✓	✓	✓	✓	✓	✓	
17 Og20	Yoho	NP	507	Trans-Canada Highway	Field	BC, V0A 1G0	250-343-6783	✓	✓	✓	✓	✓	✓	✓		
Ontario																
29 Qe23	Bruce Peninsula	NP	104	P.O. Box 189	Tobermory	ON, N0H 2R0	519-596-2233		✓		✓		✓		✓	
29 Qe23	Georgian Bay Islands	NP	4.6	901 Wye Valley Rd.	Midland	ON, L4R 4K6	705-526-9804		✓		✓		✓	✓		
29 Qd25	Point Pelee	NP	6	1118 Point Pelee Drive	Leamington	ON, N8H 3V4	519-322-2365	✓			✓			✓		
20 Qb21	Pukaskwa	NP	725	P.O. Box 212	Heron Bay	ON, P0T 1R0	807-229-0801	✓	✓	✓	✓	✓	✓	✓		
29 Qh23	St.Lawrence Islands	NP	3.5	2 County Road 5, RR 3	Mallorytown	ON, K0E 1R0	613-923-5261		✓		✓			✓		
Québec																
22 Rc21	Forillon	NP	93	122 Gaspé Boulevard	Gaspé	QC, G4X 1A9	418-368-5505		✓		✓	✓	✓	✓		
30 Qj22	La Mauricie	NP	210	P.O. Box 160	Shawinigan	QC, G9N 6T9	819-538-3232	✓	✓		✓	✓	✓		✓	✓
22 Rd20	Minigan Archipelago	NP	58	1340 de la Digue Street	Havre-Saint-Pierre	QC, G0G 1P0	418-538-3285	✓	✓		✓			✓		
Atlantic Canada																
23 Re22	Cape Breton Highlands	NP	367		Ingonish Beach	NS, B0C 1L0	902-224-2306	✓	✓		✓	✓	✓		✓	
22 Rc23	Fundy	NP	80	P.O. Box 1001	Alma	NB, E4H 1B4	506-887-6000	✓	✓	✓	✓	✓		✓	✓	
23 Rg21	Gros Morne	NP	697	P.O. Box 130	Rocky Harbour	NL, A0K 4N0	709-458-2417	✓	✓		✓	✓	✓	✓	✓	
22 Rc23	Kejmkujik	NP	147	P.O. Box 236	Maitland Bridge	NS, B0T 1B0	902-682-2772	✓	✓		✓	✓	✓		✓	
22 Rc22	Kouchibouguac	NP	92	186, Route 117	Kouchibouguac Nat. Park	NB, E4X 2P1	506-876-2443	✓	✓	✓	✓			✓	✓	
22 Rd22	Prince Edward Island	NP	8.5	2 Palmers Lane	Charlottetown	PE, C1A 5V8	902-672-6350	✓	✓		✓		✓	✓	✓	
23 Rj21	Terra Nova	NP	154	General Delivery	Glovertown	NL, A0G 2L0	709-533-2801		✓	✓	✓	✓		✓		
-	Torngat Mountains	NP	3745	P.O. Box 471	Nain	NL, A0P 1L0	709-922-1290		✓		✓			✓		

ARCTIC OCEAN
Queen Elizabeth Islands
Ellesmere Island
Qaanaaq Thule
Grønland (DANMARK)
Parry Islands
Baffin Bay
Baffin Island
Nuuk Godthåb
AK (U.S.A.)
Anchorage
Victoria Island
NU
Iqaluit
YK
Whitehorse
NT
Yellowknife
Mackenzie R.
Back R.
Juneau
Alexander Archipelago
Hudson Bay
NL
Queen Charlotte Islands
BC
AB
MB
Edmonton
SK
Vancouver Island
Lake Winnipeg
QC
Vancouver
Calgary
CANADA
ON
NB
WA
Seattle
Regina
Winnipeg
Québec
Missouri Riv.
ND
Montreal
ME
MT
Bismarck
Ottawa
VT
Salem
OR
MN
NH
Boston
Boise
Toronto
MA
WI
NY
CT
RI
ID
SD
WY
Pierre
Saint Paul
MI
Detroit
New York
PA
NJ
Cheyenne
NE
IA
Chicago
MD
NV
Salt Lake City
UT
OH
DE
San Francisco
Lincoln
WV
Washington D.C.
Denver
IL
IN
Ohio R.
CO
MO
KS
VA
Las Vegas
KY
UNITED STATES
NC
CA
Raleigh
Los Angeles
TN
Nashville
OK
Columbia
Santa Fe
Little Rock
AZ
Oklahoma City
SC
AR
Atlanta
Phoenix
NM
MS
GA
Dallas
AL
ATLANTIC OCEAN
Jackson
TX
Mississippi R.
LA
Tallahassee
Houston
New Orleans
FL
Fort Lauderdale
BAHAMAS
Miami
Fort Myers
Nassau
Everglades
PACIFIC OCEAN
Monterrey
Gulf of Mexico
La Habana
MÉXICO
CUBA
Guadalajara
Mérida
JAMAICA
Mexico
Belmopan
BELIZE
GUATEMALA
HONDURAS

Denali National Park

U.S.A.

US State: Alaska
Founded: 1917 as Mount McKinley National Park; expanded in 1980 to Denali National Park
Area: 9,492 mi²

High alpine mountain ranges, glaciers, tundra: Alaska out of a picture book! The second biggest national park in the US north of the Alaska Range covers 9,266 mi² and is home to grizzlies, wolves, reindeers and moose. The double peaks of majestic Mt. McKinley soar to the southwest. Denali is Native American for "the high one" or "the highest one." The best time to visit is between May and September, however, ice and snow can also be found all summer long in the high alpine region.

DENALI PARK ROAD

1 Denali Visitor Center by Riley Creek at the park entrance is the first contact point. Denali Park Road, branching off from State Rd. 3, is the only road in the park. Only the first 15 miles to **2 Savage River** are publicly accessible; then you have to get on one of the park's shuttle buses. For those who want to explore the park road on their own, a mountain bike is a good alternative. The park road extends around 100 miles through high alpine countryside along the Alaska Range. Along the way, you also pass **3 Polychrome Overlook**. Rarely has a lookout point been so aptly named when the sun, landscape and mountain panorama come together for a symphony of colors. Before reaching **4 Eielson Visitor Center** in the interior of the park, Stony Hill Overlook serves up another magnificent view of the mountains.

BUS TOURS

You are spoiled for choice with various bus tours through the park. Along with the different shuttle buses, public buses also access the park, and there are several guided themed bus tours. Learn about the history and geology of the park with the Natural History Tour, wildlife spotting with the Tundra Wilderness Tour, or explore the entire length of Park Road with the Kantishna Experience Tour, including the Kantishna Area–from **5 Wonder Lake** accompanied by a park ranger.

CONTACT INFORMATION

Denali National Park & Preserve | P.O. Box 9 | Denali Park | Alaska 99755 | Tel. 907 683-2294 | www.nps.gov/dena

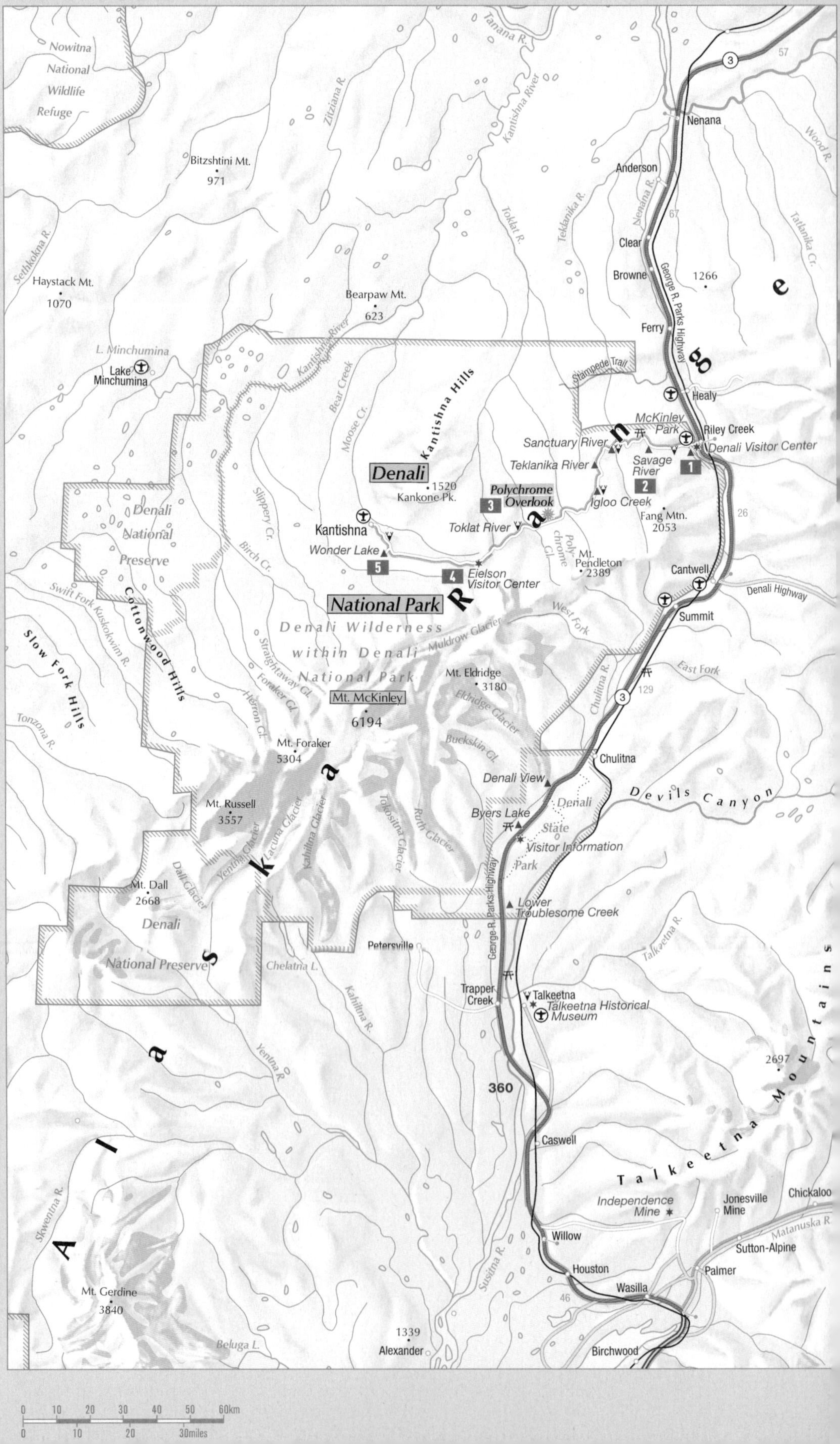

Jasper National Park, Banff National Park, Kootenay National Park, Yoho National Park

Canada

Canadian Provinces: Alberta (Banff, Jasper), British Columbia (Kootenay, Yoho)
Founded: Banff 1885, Jasper 1907, Kootenay 1920, Yoho 1886
Area: Banff 2,564 mi², Jasper 4,200 mi², Kootenay 543 mi², Yoho 507 mi²

Four national parks, two Canadian provinces and one legendary mountain range, the Rocky Mountains are all linked by the Icefields Parkway, also known as Highway 93. However, something else connects the four parks: In 1984 they were declared UNESCO World Heritage Sites.

KOOTENAY NATIONAL PARK

Arriving from the south, the **1 Visitor Center** in Radium Hot Springs marks the beginning of Kootenay National Park. The springs for which the spa town is named make it a popular health resort. The famous Rockwall Trail traversing the park also goes past the colorful **2 Paint Pots** ponds.

YOHO NATIONAL PARK

Yoho National Park adjoins to the north and the main **3 Visitor's Center** is located in the village of Field. Yoho Valley Road leads into the park. The mighty 833 ft. high **4 Takakaw Falls**, the third largest Falls in Canada, are reached through a narrow valley.

BANFF NATIONAL PARK

Kicking Horse Pass leads into Canada's oldest national park. After a few miles, you reach Lake Louise the **5 Visitor Center**. Lake Louise und **6 Banff** to the south-east are good starting points for hiking in the mountains in summer and a popular ski resort in the winter.

ICEFIELDS PARKWAY

The "dream road of the rockies" spans around 143 miles from Lake Louise to Jasper.

JASPER NATIONAL PARK

Jasper National Park is reached on the **7 Sunwapta Pass**. Shortly afterwards, you pass both **8 Sunwapta Falls**. However, the **9 Athabasca Falls** that follow are more spectacular. Although "only" 75 feet high, the sheer force of the water funneling through a small gap is amazing. The wonderful journey through the Rockies ends with the thermal baths in **10 Miette Hot Springs**, as relaxing as it began, in Radium Hot Springs.

CONTACT INFORMATION

Parks Canada National Office | 25-7-N Eddy Street | Gatineau | Quebec | Tel. 888-773-8888 | www.pc.gc.ca

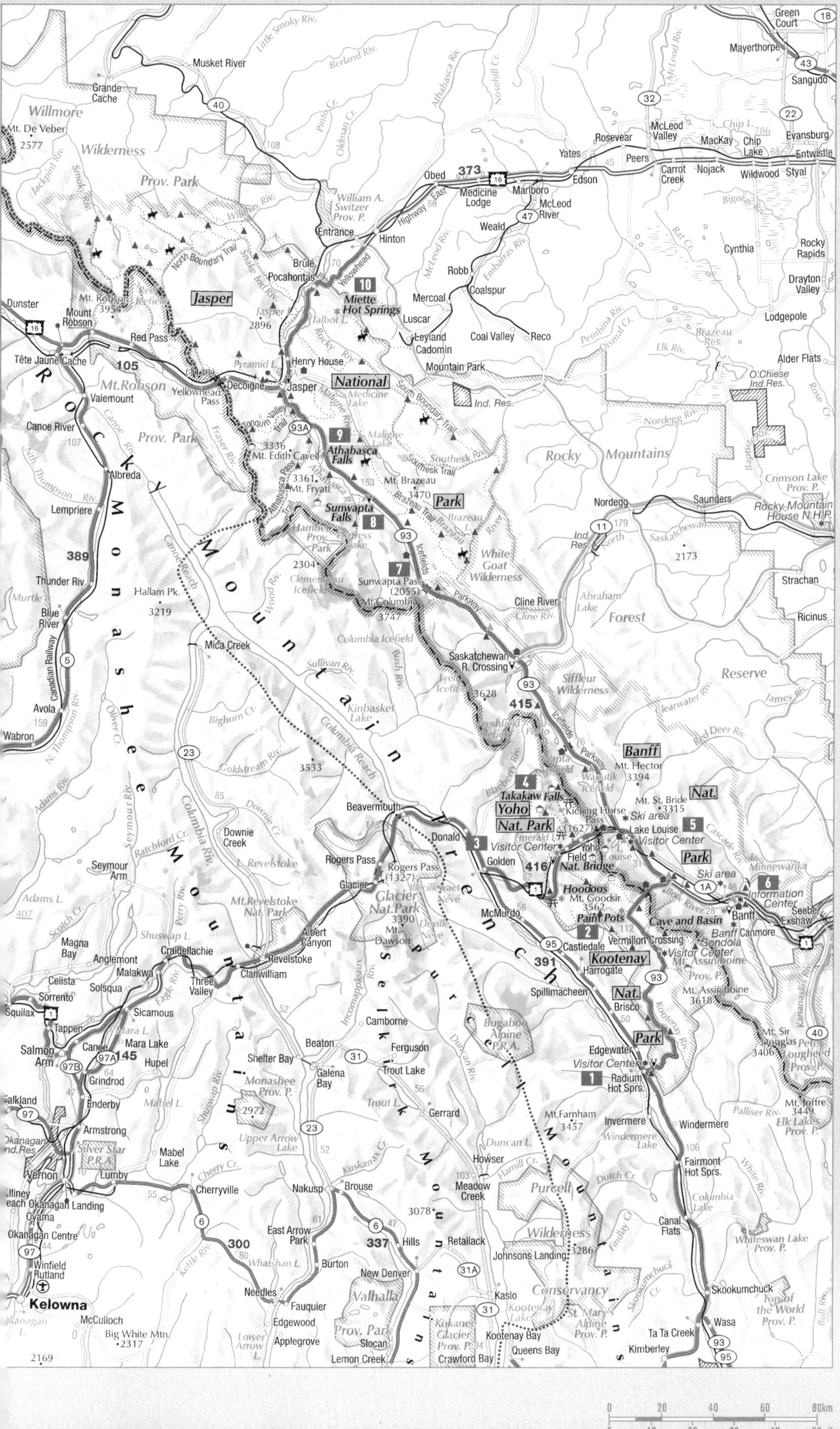

Waterton Lakes National Park, Glacier National Park

U.S.A.

Canada

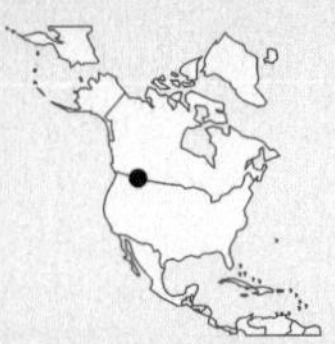

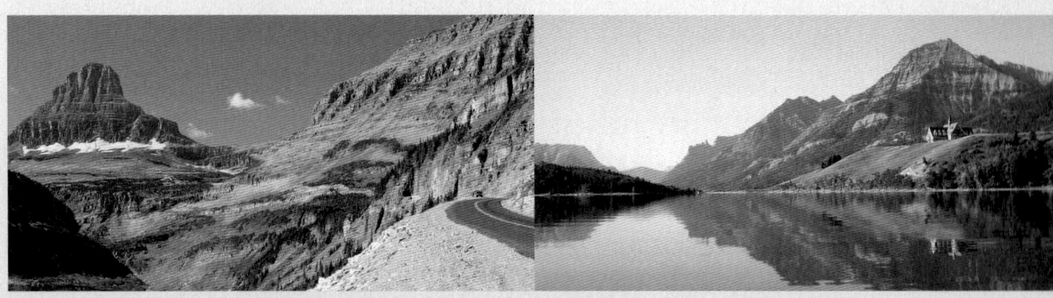

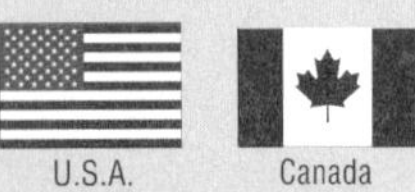

US State: Montana
Canadian Province: Alberta
Founded: 1895 (Waterton), 1910 (Glacier), 1932 (Peace Park)
Area: 1,787 mi²

The park has over 200 clear lakes, 50 glaciers, 70 mammal species and 260 species of bird. Over 700 miles of hiking trails take you deep into this world of mountains, valleys, snow and ice. Since 1932, Waterton National Park in Canadian Alberta and Northwestern Montana's Glacier National Park together have been called the International Peace Park. **1 Mt. Cleveland** (elevation 10,465 ft.) or "Crown of the Continent" is the highest elevation of this magnificent high mountain landscape. The U-shaped valleys of the parks were formed in the last ice age and the fauna here include black and grizzly bears, red deer, pumas and coyotes. The separately run parks are accessible all year round; however, many roads are closed in winter.

GOING TO THE SUN ROAD

The prettiest park road is the "Going to the Sun Road." The 50-mile-long road traverses the Glacier National Park of **2 St. Mary** at the eastern edge over **3 Logan Pass** (elevation 6,646 ft.) past the **4 West Glacier**. The view of **5 St. Mary Lake** and the surrounding mountain tops is the most photographed scenery in the park. The length between Logan Pass and McDonald Valley, where the road winds into hairpin curves is a technical feat of some magnitude.

MANY GLACIER

US Highway 89 takes you north from St. Mary. In Babb it branches off to **6 Many Glacier**, where you can see mountain goats and black bears. Many Glacier Hotel, built in 1914, is on the shores of Swiftcurrent Lake from where you can hike to Grinnell Glacier and its famous Iceberg Lake with its shimmering aquamarine waters.

WATERTON NATIONAL PARK

Chief Mountain International Hwy. takes you to Canadian Waterton National Park (MT 17/Hwy. 6) and also traverses a Blackfoot Indian Reservation. The Canadian part is considerably smaller. A good starting point to access the mountain region is the main town of **7 Waterton**.

CONTACT INFORMATION

Glacier National Park | PO Box 128 | West Glacier | Montana 59936 | Tel. 406 888-7800 | www.nps.gov/glac

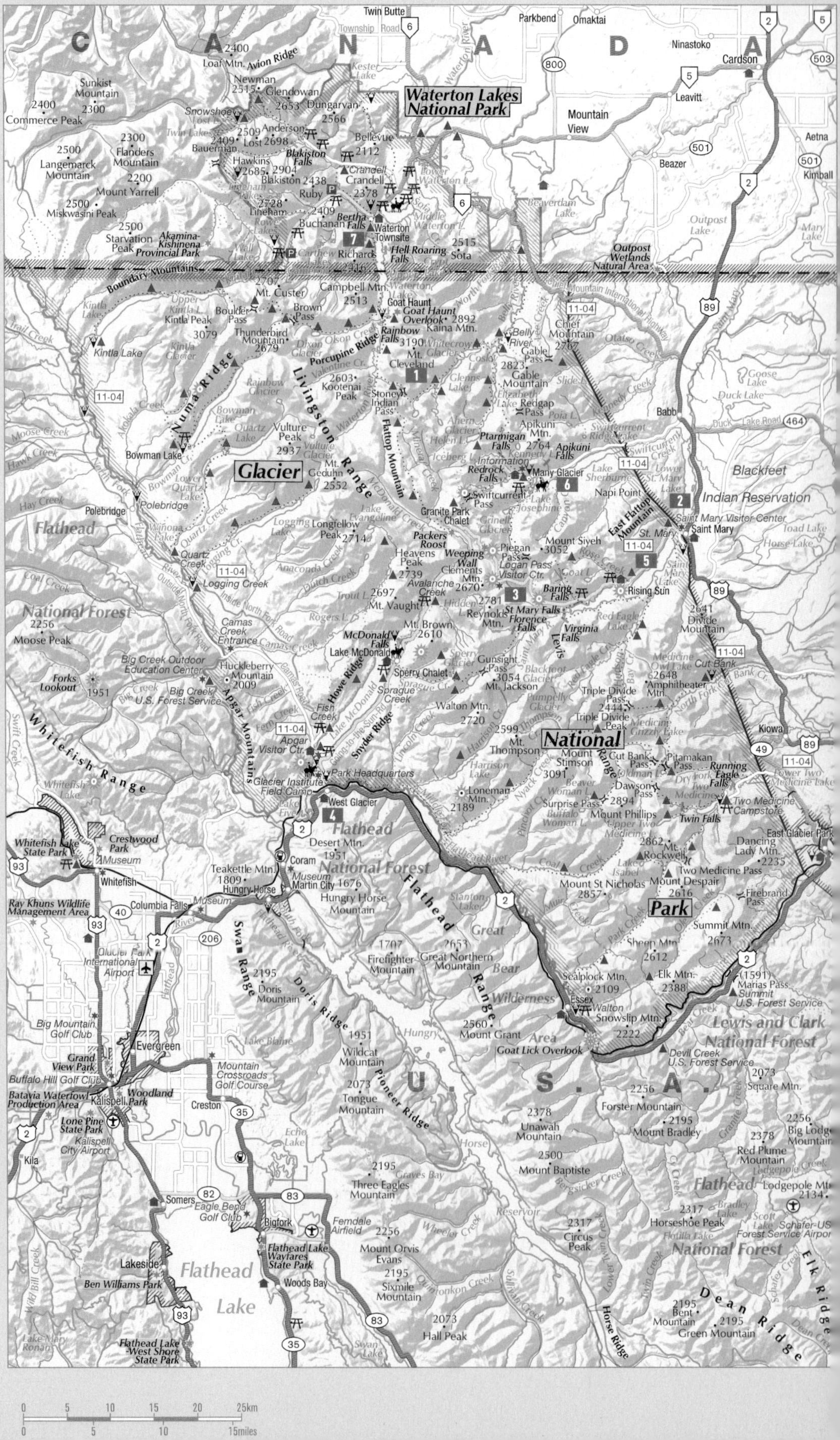

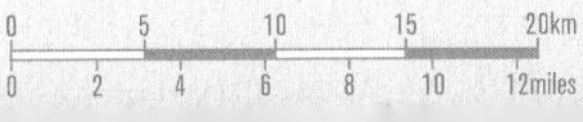

U.S.A.

US State: Washington
Founded: 1938
Area: 1,442 mi^2

The national park west of Seattle is famous for its unreal, mist-shrouded mountains. Framed by the Pacific and the Juan de Fuca trail, the Olympic Peninsula houses the biggest and most beautiful rain forest in the US. Isolated from the rest of the continent, unique flora and fauna can grow here.

OLYMPIC PENINSULA DRIVE (HWY. 101)

Some of the scenic route takes you along the Olympic Peninsula coastline, passes through fern-covered rain forests, to remote sandy beaches and up to alpine meadows. A good starting point is the **1 National Park Visitor Center** in Port Angeles. Highlights along the way include the photogenic **2 Lake Crescent** and **3 Marymere Falls. 4 Sol Duc Hot Springs** to the west invites you to bathe in its springs. Another scenic road leads from Port Angeles to the **5 Hurricane Ridge Visitor Center** (elevation 5,200 ft.), where you have a breathtaking view of the glacier-covered mountains, all the way to Vancouver Island in Canada.

HOH RAIN FOREST

The most beautiful rain forest of the national park covers the hillside of the valleys extending to the Pacific along the Quinault, Queets and Hoh rivers. Over 16 ft. of precipitation each year makes for a lush, green vegetation, in which Douglas firs reaching 300 ft., Sitka spruce and western hemlock thrive, canopying a floor blanketed with thick moss and fern. The **6 Hoh Rain Forest Visitor Center** provides information on the rain forest and trails that begin here.

OLYMPIC WILDERNESS

Lonely sandy beaches strewn with driftwood, as well as cliffs, rock arches and steep rocks rising out of the sea shape the coastline. The **7 Hole in the Wall** and Split Rock at Mora are famous. In the south, the scenic drive stretches from **8 Ruby Beach** to **9 Queets**, where you can see bald eagles and seals; as well as gray whales passing by.

CONTACT INFORMATION

Olympic National Park | 600 East Park Avenue | Port Angeles | WA 98362 | Tel. 360 565-3130 | www.nps.gov/olym

U.S.A.

US State: Wyoming
Founded: 1872
Area: 3,470 mi²

With steam and bubbles everywhere, Yellowstone National Park with its many geysers, is itself an enormous volcano. The last big eruption was around 640,000 years ago, which was when the gigantic caldera was formed, measuring 135 mi². The variety of plant species ranges from desert-like vegetation to subalpine meadows and forests. In addition to bison, you can also see moose, black bears and grizzlies here.

GRAND LOOP ROAD

The "main artery" through the wilderness is the 142-mile Grand Loop Road. It passes through the best-known sights in the shape of a large figure eight. A good starting point is the **1 Albright Visitor Center** in Mammoth Hot Springs, where thermal springs have created up to 200-ft.-tall splendid terraces from travertine pools in different colors, due to bacterial activity.

GEYSER BASINS

2 Norris Geyser Basin and the Norris Museum is the first geyser area in the loop. Further southwest is the **3 Lower Geyser Basin** where the Fountain Paint Pot bubbles with red mud. Most impressive is the immense crater of the Excelsior Geyser in the **4 Midway Geyser Basin**. Most of the gushing action is in the small **5 Upper Geyser Basin**. Experience the eruptions of the famous **6 Old Faithfull** during a two-hour tour on boardwalks.

YELLOWSTONE RIVER

There is another Visitor Center at **7 Fishing Bridge**. The Yellowstone River flows from Yellowstone Lake and is rich in fish. Walking along the river, you discover areas of geothermal activity, such as the **8 Mud Volcano** and **9 Sulphur Caldron**. From the easily accessible **10 Upper Falls**, the river plunges 109 ft. A few hundred feet further, it thunders at the **11 Lower Falls**, with an earsplitting roar, into a gorge from a height of 308 ft. At the northern edge of the national park is the small tourist center, Tower Roosevelt at 6,200 ft. Noteworthy are the 130 ft. high **12 Tower Fall** and the **13 Petrified Tree**.

CONTACT INFORMATION

Yellowstone National Park | P.O. Box 168 | WY 82190-0168 | Tel. 307 344-7381 | www.nps.gov/yell

0 5 10 15 20 25km
0 5 10 15miles

U.S.A.

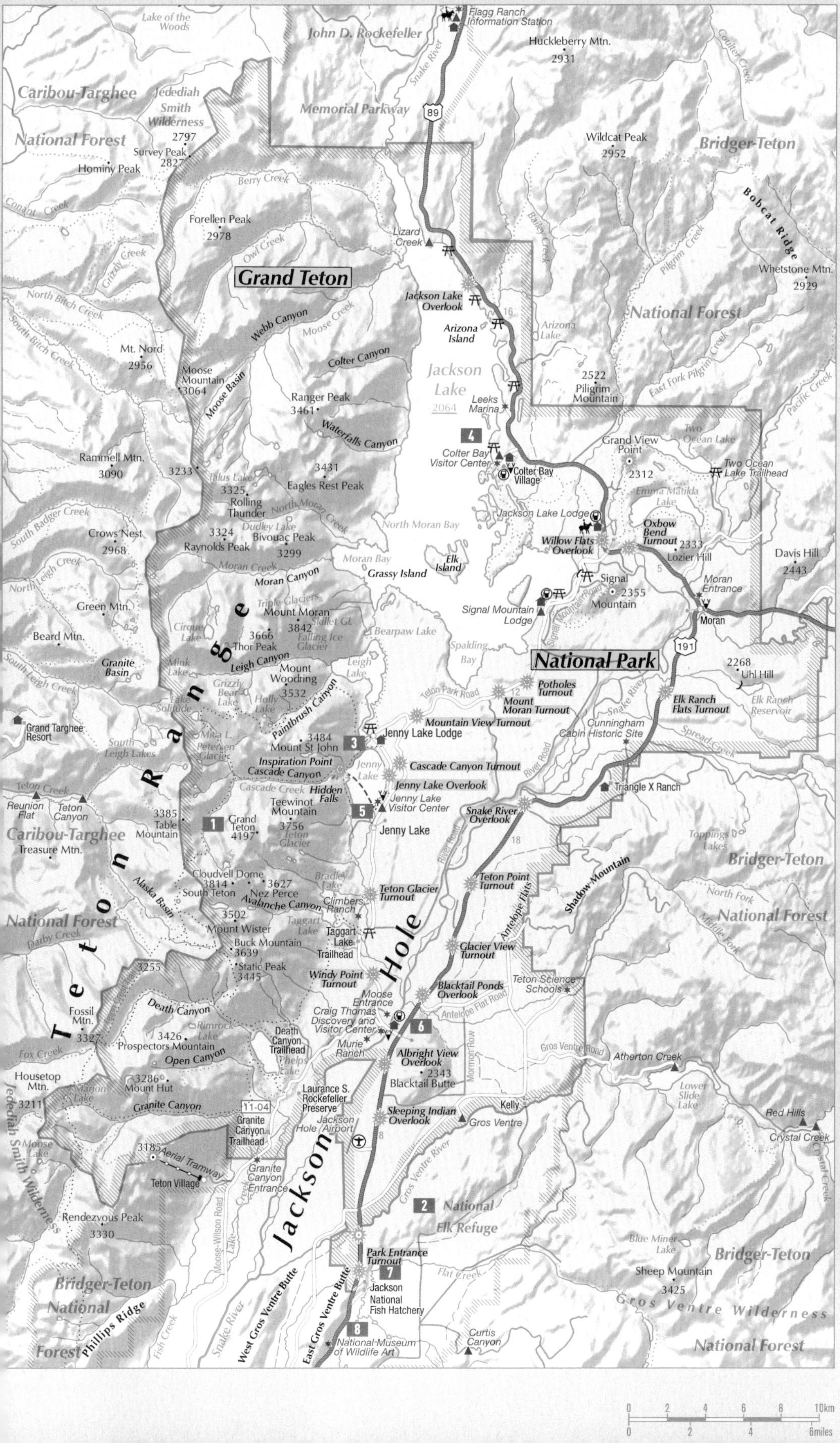

US State: Wyoming
Founded: 1929
Area: 485 mi²

This magnificent natural preserve is directly south of Yellowstone National Park. Grand Teton National Park, the heart of which is the 40-mile-long and 14-mile-wide Teton Range, rises like a wall over Jackson Hole valley at a height of almost 6,500 ft.; its serrated peaks make it one of the most popular photographic subjects in the West.

FAUNA AND FLORA

The tallest mountain is the towering 13,770 ft. **1 Grand Teton**; twelve other peaks are higher than 11,800 ft. The park protects a landscape of extraordinary beauty. Over 100 alpine lakes and ponds await just a few feet from the Teton Range and backcountry. Hiking, fishing and canoeing on the Snake River, which threads through Jackson Hole, are some of the favorite activities. Jackson Hole valley is home to moose, elk and mule deer. The park borders the **2 National Elk Refuge** to the south, where the biggest herd of elk in the US hibernates.

ROCKEFELLER PARKWAY AND TETON PARK ROAD

The park offers magnificent scenic routes because of the exemplary road infrastructure. Spectacular panoramas can be enjoyed from Rockefeller Parkway along the eastern bank of Jackson Lake, as well as on Teton Park Road and the Teton Range in the south. However, it's when you take to your feet that you'll really discover the park. More than 200 miles of hiking trails of all lengths and levels of difficulty lead to amazing views and tranquil settings. The easier trails include the path from the east bank of Jenny Lake to **3 Inspiration Point**. You can obtain information about the trails, fauna and flora in the **4 Colter Bay Visitor Center** on Jackson Lake, the **5 Jenny Lake Visitor Center** and the **6 Craig Thomas Discovery and Visitor Center** in Moose, which is open all year round.

JACKSON

The little Wild West town of **7 Jackson** at the south of the park is the supply center for the region. Ranchers and tourists shop in the stores around the lively Town Square. The exceptional **8 National Museum of Wildlife Art**, which deals creatively with the subject of wilderness, is also worth a visit.

CONTACT INFORMATION

Grand Teton National Park | P.O. Drawer 170 | Moose | WY 83012 | Tel. 307 739-3300 | www.nps.gov/grte

Yosemite National Park

U.S.A.

US State: California
Founded: 1890
Area: 1,189 mi²

Yosemite is full of superlatives: Three of the ten highest waterfalls in the world and the biggest granite rock on earth can be found here. There is also a wide variety of fauna and flora, like sequoias, incense cedars, southern live oaks, bay trees, and azaleas; with mule deer, racoons and black bears cavorting among them.

YOSEMITE VALLEY

The Merced River runs through the 8-mile-long, 2-mile-wide valley, which is the heart of the park–a beautiful green oasis surrounded by up to 3,300 ft. of towering rocks. **1 El Capitan** (elevation 7,570 ft.) to the west forms the cornerstone of the valley landscape. In the east, the **2 Half Dome** (elevation 8,840 ft.), a monolith shaped like a vertical ball cut in half, is the most impressive cliff of all, and completes the valley. **3 Yosemite Village** with the main visitor center is in the middle. Bus shuttle service is provided from here to the west end of the valley. The often photographed **4 Yosemite Falls** drops over three levels from a height of 2,425 ft. Also lovely is **5 Bridalveil Falls**, whose spray in the valley basin creates a glistening veil. The H41 takes you to the southwest part of the park and leads to **6 Glacier Point**, the most spectacular lookout point over the valley and the peaks of the Sierra Nevada behind it.

7 MARIPOSA GROVE

Three kilometers before the south entrance of the park, you find around 500 giant sequoias, one of three species of redwood, measuring over 200 ft high, with a circumference of up to 50 ft.

TIOGA ROAD

The narrow serpentine road out of the valley works its way up to the High Sierra with its glacial lakes, high alpine meadows and granite domes, ground smooth in the last ice age. It leads to magnificent lookout points, from where you can look out on a landscape of rocks and the gorgeous ice-cold **8 Tenaya Lake**. The highest point of the stretch is reached on the **9 Tioga Pass**. At 9,900 ft. you leave the park and drive the narrow winding roads to Nevada.

CONTACT INFORMATION

Yosemite National Park | PO Box 577 | CA 95389 | Tel. 209 372-0200 | www.nps.gov/yose

U.S.A.

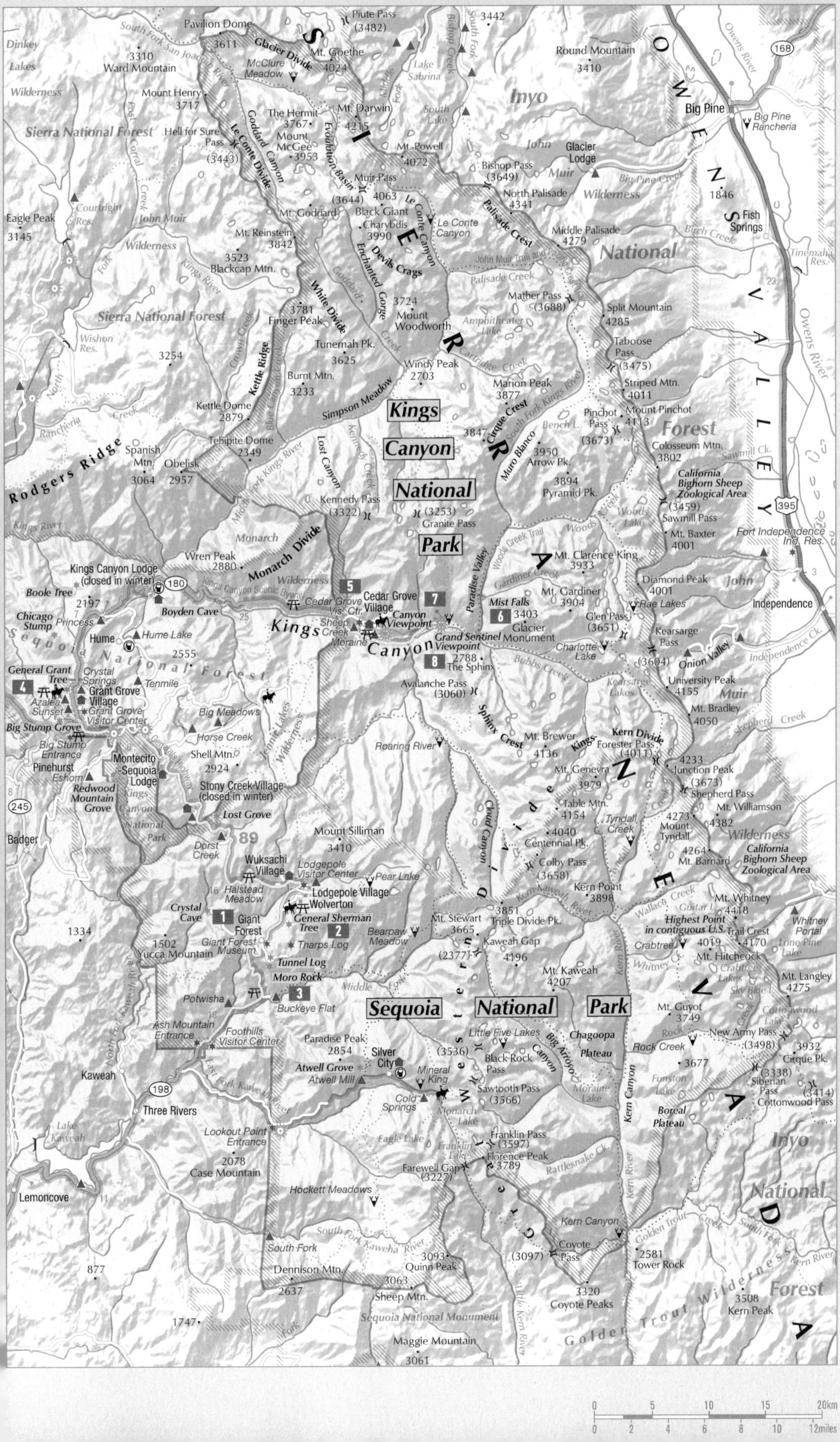

US State: California
Founded: 1890 (Sequoia), 1940 (Kings Canyon)
Area: 1,353 mi²

Visitors feel small and insignificant when walking between the giant redwoods of the Sequoia & Kings Canyon National Park on the west side of the Sierra Nevada. Botanists call the 300 ft. giant tress "Sequoia gigantea" as they have diameters of up to 40 ft. The 3,500 year old trees are among the oldest plants on earth. Size applies not just to the trees, here. Mt. Whitney (elevation 14,500 ft.) and its companions are the highest mountains in the US outside of Alaska.

SEQUOIA NATIONAL PARK

The **1 Giant Forest** to the west is the most accessible part of the park. The real star among the around 8,000 giant redwoods is the **2 "General Sherman Tree"** measuring 275 ft. with a base diameter of almost 32 ft. and an estimated age of 2,800 years. At its foot begins the 2-mile-long Congress Trail, a quiet circular path leading to other giants such as "The President" and "Chief Sequoia." South of the Giant Forest is the 6,725 ft. granite peak of **3 Moro Rock** – a steep stairway with 400 steps – leading up to wonderful views of the mountains of the Sierra Nevada.

SEQUOIA NATIONAL FOREST

Adjoining Sequoia National Park to the northwest is the beautiful Grant Grove forest, home to the immense redwoods. With a height of almost 270 ft., the **4 General Grant Tree** is the third largest redwood in the world.

KINGS CANYON NATIONAL PARK

Kings Canyon after which the park is named, is one of the deepest canyons on earth with a depth of up to 8,000 ft. Cut in the gray granite by receding glaciers and the Kings River, the natural spectacle to the northeast of **5 Cedar Grove Visitor Center** offers magnificent hiking trails, like the picturesque Zumwalt Meadow and photogenic **6 Mist Falls**. **7 Canyon Viewpoint** and **8 Grand Sentinel Viewpoint** also have wonderful views.

CONTACT INFORMATION

Sequoia and Kings Canyon National Parks | 47050 Generals Highway | Three Rivers | CA 93271-9700 | Tel. 559 565-3341 | *www.nps.gov/seki*

Death Valley National Park

U.S.A.

US State: California
Founded: 1994
Area: 5,262 mi²

Framed by high peaks like the 11,050 ft. high Telescope Peak and filled with salt lakes, the variety of desert life is nowhere more evident than in Death Valley. Enormous craters, remnants of old volcanoes and striking canyons shimmer in all colors due to the metal and mineral deposits, and contain a bizarre richness of forms.

NATIONAL MONUMENT

Death Valley received its name in 1849 when prospectors on the way to California got lost here and almost died of thirst. In the 1930s, this surreal landscape became a tourist attraction and in 1933 was declared a national monument. A well-built road network leads to the most beautiful sites in the park. Visitor centers can be found in **1 Furnace Creek**, **2 Scotty's Castle** and **3 Beatty**.

HOT AND LOW

Windows closed, air conditioner on: The "Valley of Death" is not only a spectacular desert region, but also the hottest place on earth, where temperatures can reach over 120°F in the summer. The national park is a 143-mile-long rift valley surrounded by mountain ranges with heights of up to 10,000 ft. An area of 580 mi² is below sea level, with the lowest elevation in **4 Badwater** at -280 ft., which is also the lowest elevation in the western hemisphere. Death Valley is anything but dead. Despite less than 2 inches of precipitation per year, 970 tree and plant species thrive here, as well as 13 species of cactus.

SCENIC TOURS

The park offers many scenic highlights. Artist's Palette Drive is a 9-mile, one-way road through the splendid reddish, pink and yellow rocky landscape. **5 Zabriskie Point** east of Furnace Creek offers amazing views of the wave formations of the rigid rocks. The most spectacular view of the valley is probably from **6 Dantes View**. Southwest of Beatty, **7 Titus Canyon Road** offers fascinating insights and views.

CONTACT INFORMATION

Death Valley National Park Visitor Center | Furnace Creek | Tel. 760-786-32 00 | www.nps.gov/deva

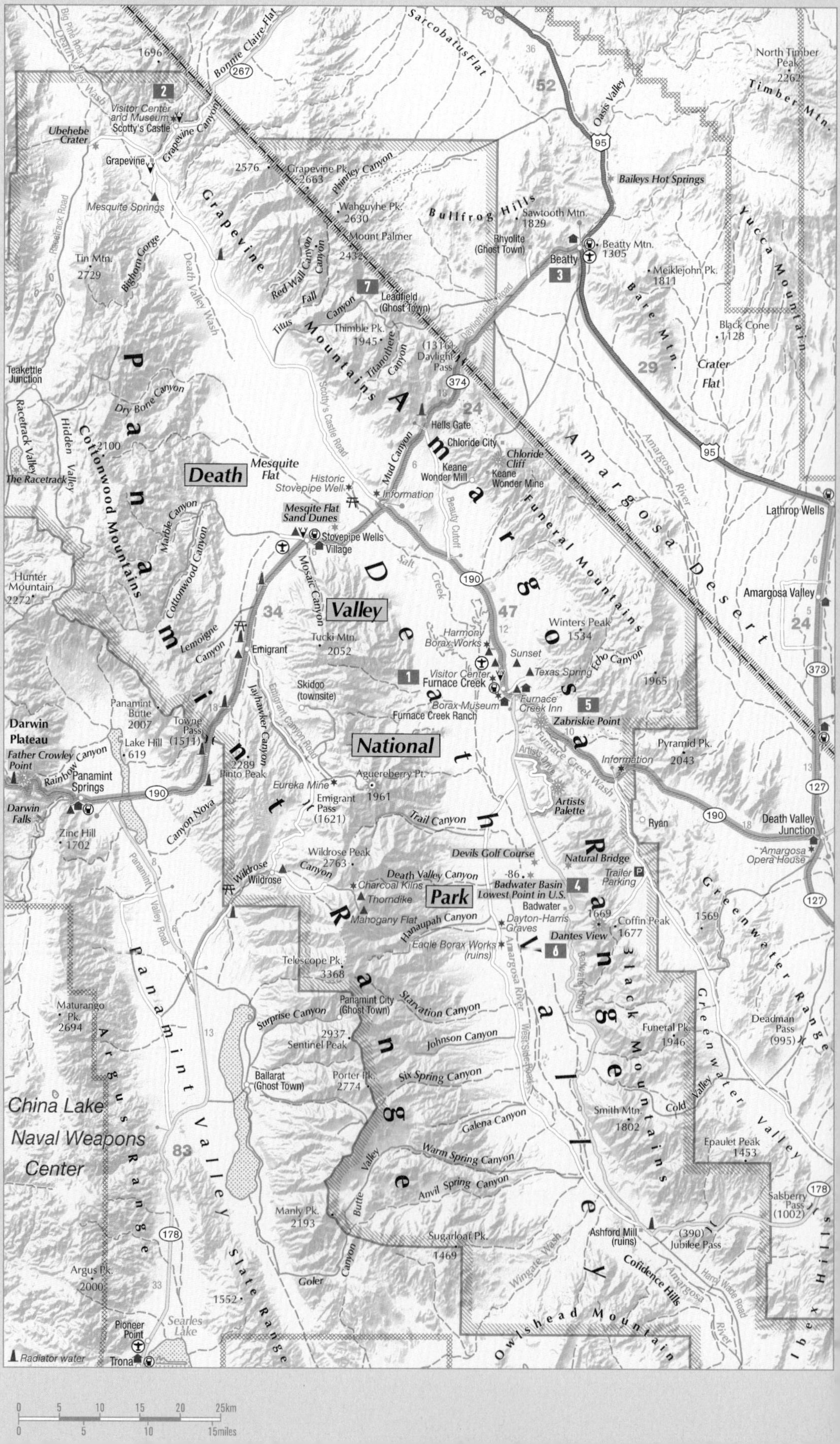

U.S.A.

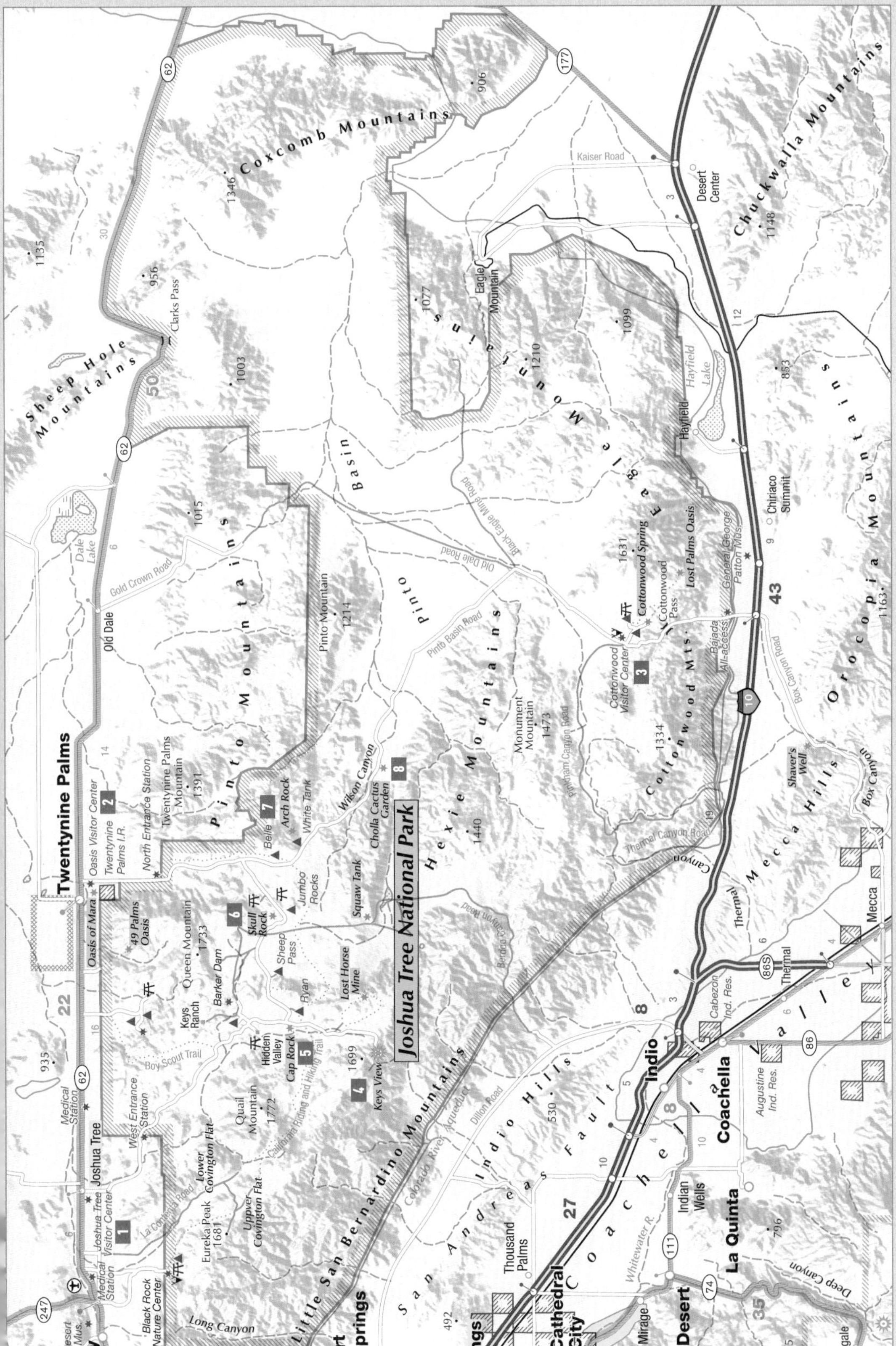

US State: California
Founded: 1994
Area: 1,234 mi²

The first white settlers passing through the area were Mormons. The outstretched arms of the yucca tree reminded them of the praying prophet Joshua, after which the magnificent Joshua Tree National Park, not far from Palm Springs, is named. The tree is typical of the 5,000-to-10,000-ft.-high Mojave Desert, which is strewn with round fragments of rock and defines the upper higher area of the national park.

DESERT FAUNA

The most well-known feature of the park are the Joshua Trees, but palm groves, sand dunes and cactus gardens are also found here. Creosote bushes dominate the lower areas; "Jumping Cholla" cactus and fragrant juniper bushes thrive alongside. Situated between the Mojave Desert to the north (elevation up to 3,300 ft.) and the Colorado Desert to the southeast, Joshua Tree National Park combines characteristics of both desert regions.

VISITOR CENTERS

The northern entrances by Joshua Tree and Twentynine Palms are reached via the Twentynine Palms Highway (Hwy. 62). The south entrance in Cottonwood Springs, 24 miles east of Indio, is directly accessible via the 1-10. The **1 Joshua Tree Visitor Center** and the **2 Oasis Visitor Center** in the north provide good information on the history and geology of the national park. In the south is the **3 Cottonwood Visitor Center.**

GEOLOGY TOUR ROAD

The park can be explored via several routes. In the northwestern part, you cross the Queen and Lost Horse Valley. The most beautiful view of the Coachella Valley can be seen from **4 Keys View** on the 5,183 ft. high top of the Little San Bernardino Mountains. The lookout point is accessed via a cul-de-sac. Back on **5 Cap Rock** going east, you pass **6 Skull Rock**, where the spectacular Geology Tour Road branches off before veering south to **7 Arch Rock** and past **8 Cholla Cactus Garden** on mostly dirt roads, on the way to Cottonwood Pass and the south exit.

CONTACT INFORMATION

Joshua Tree National Park | 74485 National Park Drive | Twentynine Palms | CA 92277 | Tel. 760 367-5500 | www.nps.gov/jotr

Grand Canyon National Park

U.S.A.

US State: Arizona
Founded: 1919
Area: 1,902 mi²

"The grandest of God's earthly places," said John Muir, father of the American environmental movement, about the Grand Canyon. This formidable canyon landscape, with all its breathtaking vastness and depth, shapes and colors, carved by the Colorado River, is one of the most spectacular natural wonders of the world. The walls of the south rim drop around 5,300 ft. into the river, and the north rim is even higher at around 6,000 ft. The Colorado has carved a length of 277 miles through the Kaibab Plateau, leaving a 4-to-18-mile-wide gorge.

SOUTH RIM

The starting point for exploring the South Rim, as the southern ridge of the Grand Canyon is called, is the 1 **Visitor Center** in Grand Canyon Village. From here, Rim Drive takes you along the canyon rim to magnificent lookout points. Going east, you pass 2 **Tusayan Ruins**, one of over 2,000 prehistoric Native American settlements in the canyon. 3 **Navajo Point** and its Indian Watchtower, built in 1932 and designed after Native American lookout towers, offers an unforgettable view of the Painted Desert to the east. The West Rim Drive also leads to spectacular lookout points and sites like 4 **Hopi Point** are very popular, especially before sunset.

NORTH RIM

The more remote North Rim of the Grand Canyon is less accessible to tourists; however it, too, offers impressive views. The starting point is the historic Grand Canyon Lodge, with trails leading east and west. 5 **Bright Angel Point** at the end of AZ 67 should not be missed. The lookout point is located high over the gorge of Bright Angel Creek and stages awesome views of the Grand Canyon's neighboring and off-shoot canyons. A few minutes by car north of Grand Canyon Lodge is a cul-de-sac to the 6 **Point Imperial**, which overlooks the highest point in the national park (9,393 ft.) and 7 **Cape Royal**, which is reached via the 8 **Walhalla Plateau**.

CONTACT INFORMATION

Grand Canyon National Park | P.O. Box 129 | Grand Canyon | AZ 86023 | Tel. 928 638-7888 | www.nps.gov/grca

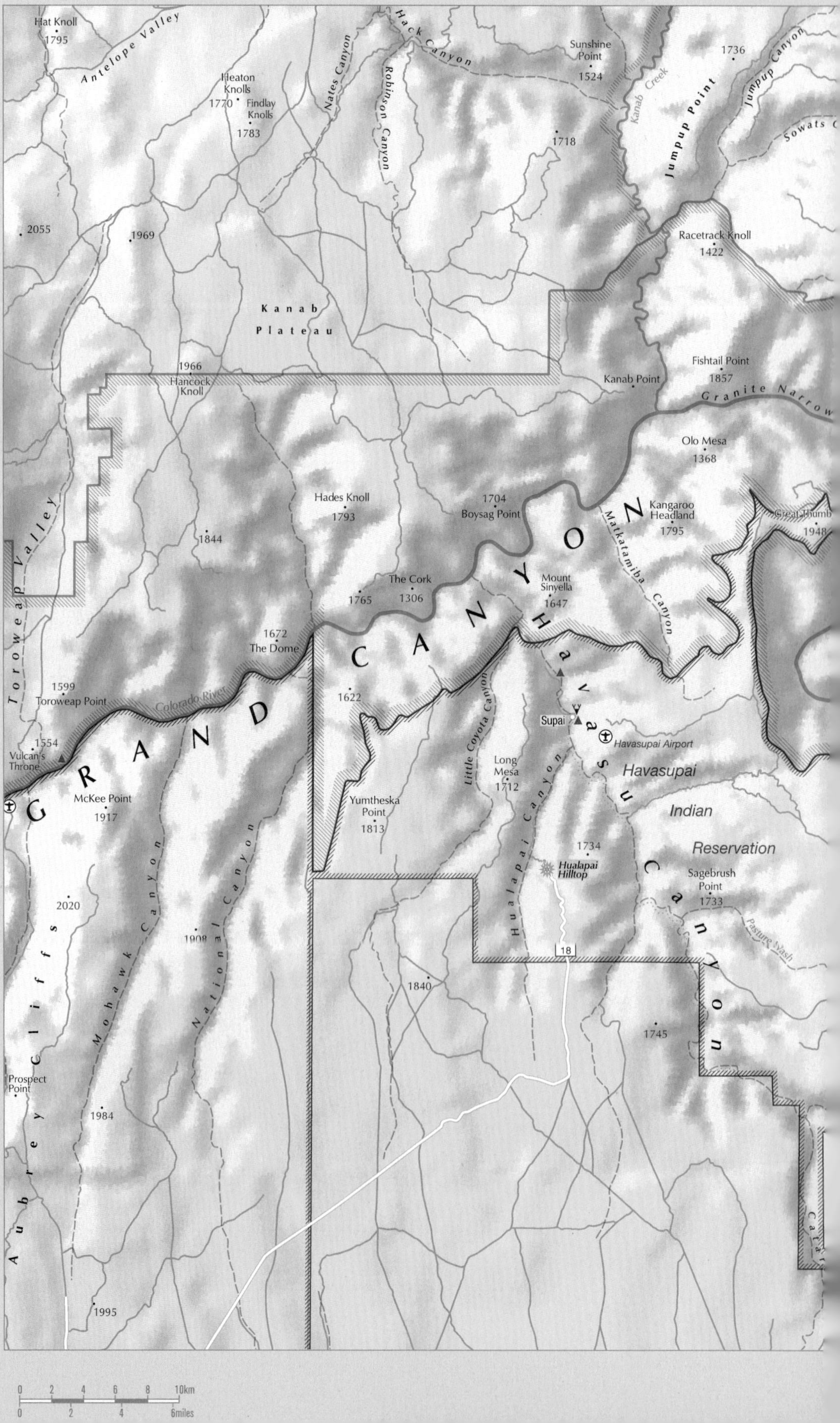

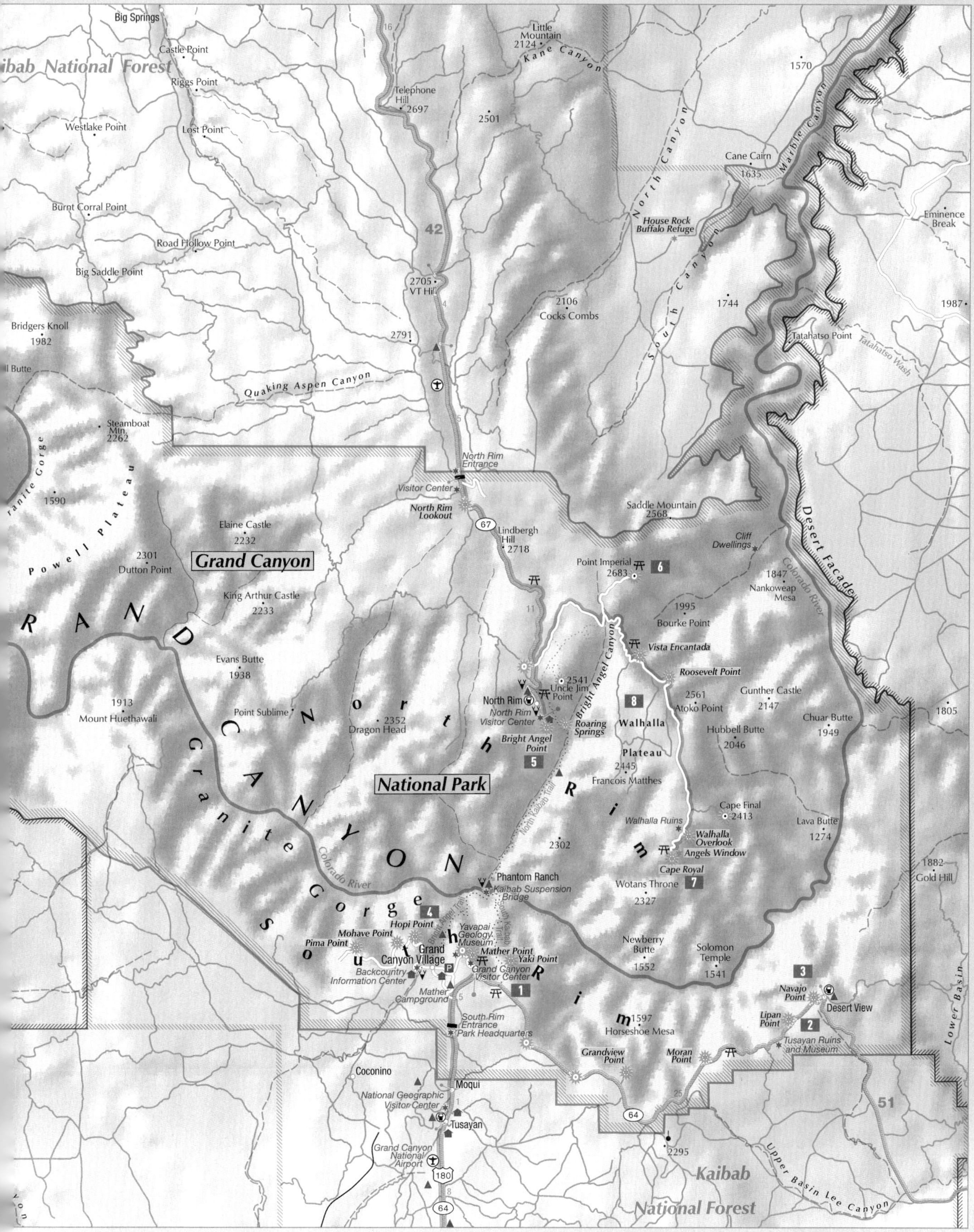

Big Springs
Castle Point
Kaibab National Forest
Riggs Point
Westlake Point
Lost Point
Telephone Hill 2697
Little Mountain 2124
Kane Canyon
2501
1570
North Canyon
Cane Cairn 1635
Marble Canyon
Burnt Corral Point
Road Hollow Point
Big Saddle Point
42
House Rock Buffalo Refuge
Eminence Break
South Canyon
2705 VT Hill
2106 Cocks Combs
1744
1987
Bridgers Knoll 1982
2791
Tatahatso Point
Tatahatso Wash
Quaking Aspen Canyon
Steamboat Mtn. 2262
Granite Gorge
Powell Plateau
1590
North Rim Entrance
Visitor Center
North Rim Lookout
Saddle Mountain 2568
Cliff Dwellings
Desert Facade
Elaine Castle 2232
67
Lindbergh Hill 2718
2301 Dutton Point
Grand Canyon
Point Imperial 2683
6
1847 Nankoweap Mesa
Colorado River
King Arthur Castle 2233
1995 Bourke Point
Vista Encantada
Evans Butte 1938
Roosevelt Point
2541 Uncle Jim Point
Bright Angel Canyon
2561 Atoko Point
Gunther Castle 2147
1913 Mount Huethawali
Point Sublime
North Rim
North Rim Visitor Center
8
Walhalla Plateau
1805
2352 Dragon Head
Roaring Springs
Bright Angel Point
5
Hubbell Butte 2046
Chuar Butte 1949
2445 Francois Matthes
National Park
North Kaibab Trail
Cape Final 2413
Lava Butte 1274
Walhalla Ruins
Walhalla Overlook
Angels Window
2302
Cape Royal
7
Wotans Throne 2327
1882 Gold Hill
Phantom Ranch
Kaibab Suspension Bridge
GRAND CANYON
North Rim
South Rim
Granite Gorge
4
Hopi Point
Mohave Point
Pima Point
Yavapai Geology Museum
Grand Canyon Village
Mather Point
Yaki Point
Grand Canyon Visitor Center
Backcountry Information Center
Mather Campground
1
Newberry Butte 1552
Solomon Temple 1541
3
Navajo Point
Desert View
Lipan Point
2
1597 Horseshoe Mesa
Lower Basin
South Rim Entrance
Park Headquarters
Tusayan Ruins and Museum
Grandview Point
Moran Point
Coconino
Moqui
51
National Geographic Visitor Center
Tusayan
64
2295
Grand Canyon National Airport
180
Kaibab National Forest
Upper Basin
Lee Canyon

Zion National Park

U.S.A.

US State: Utah
Founded: 1919
Area: 224 mi²

This is a place where you learn what reverence is about: Colossal red to orange glowing monoliths up to 3,000 ft. falling vertically into the valley basin and narrow canyons full of wild flowers make this national park the highlight of a trip through the South West.

VIRGIN RIVER

The scenery is millions of years old: The Virgin River, a tributary of the Colorado, dug itself into the mighty plateau consisting of many horizontal layers of shale, limestone and sandstone deposits to create this gorgeous landscape of deep gorges, steep rock tables and domes with peculiar pinnacles that shimmer from white to orange to red. Several Native American cultures have left their traces in Zion Canyon. Despite the rock desert, the flora watered by the Virgin River is a succulent green. Mountain goats live in the outlying Kolob section.

KOLOB CANYONS

The park has two sections, the popular Zion Canyon and the less visited Kolob Canyons in the north-west corner of the park. A main starting point in the north is the **1 Kolob Canyons Visitor Center**. **2 Kolob Canyons View** Point is reached via Lee's Pass. All other destinations are accessible only via trails.

ZION CANYON SCENIC DRIVE

Not far from the south entrance is **3 Zion Canyon Visitor Center's** first starting point. The 7-mile Zion Canyon Scenic Drive begins after Zion Mount Carmel Highway branches off. There are superb views between the mighty mountains and the splendid **4 Court of the Patriachs**. Past Zion Lodge the road continues further up to the **5 Temple of Sinawava** (6,014 ft.). The 11-mile Zion Mount Carmel Highway branches right to the east where Pine Creek merges with the Virgin River. Near the east entrance, soaring up to the right, **6 Checkerboard Mesa's** erosion formations are reminiscent of a checkerboard.

CONTACT INFORMATION

Zion National Park | Springdale | Utah 84767 | Park Headquarters | Tel. 435 772-3256 | www.nps.gov/zion

0 2 4 6 8km
0 1 2 3 4 5miles

U.S.A.

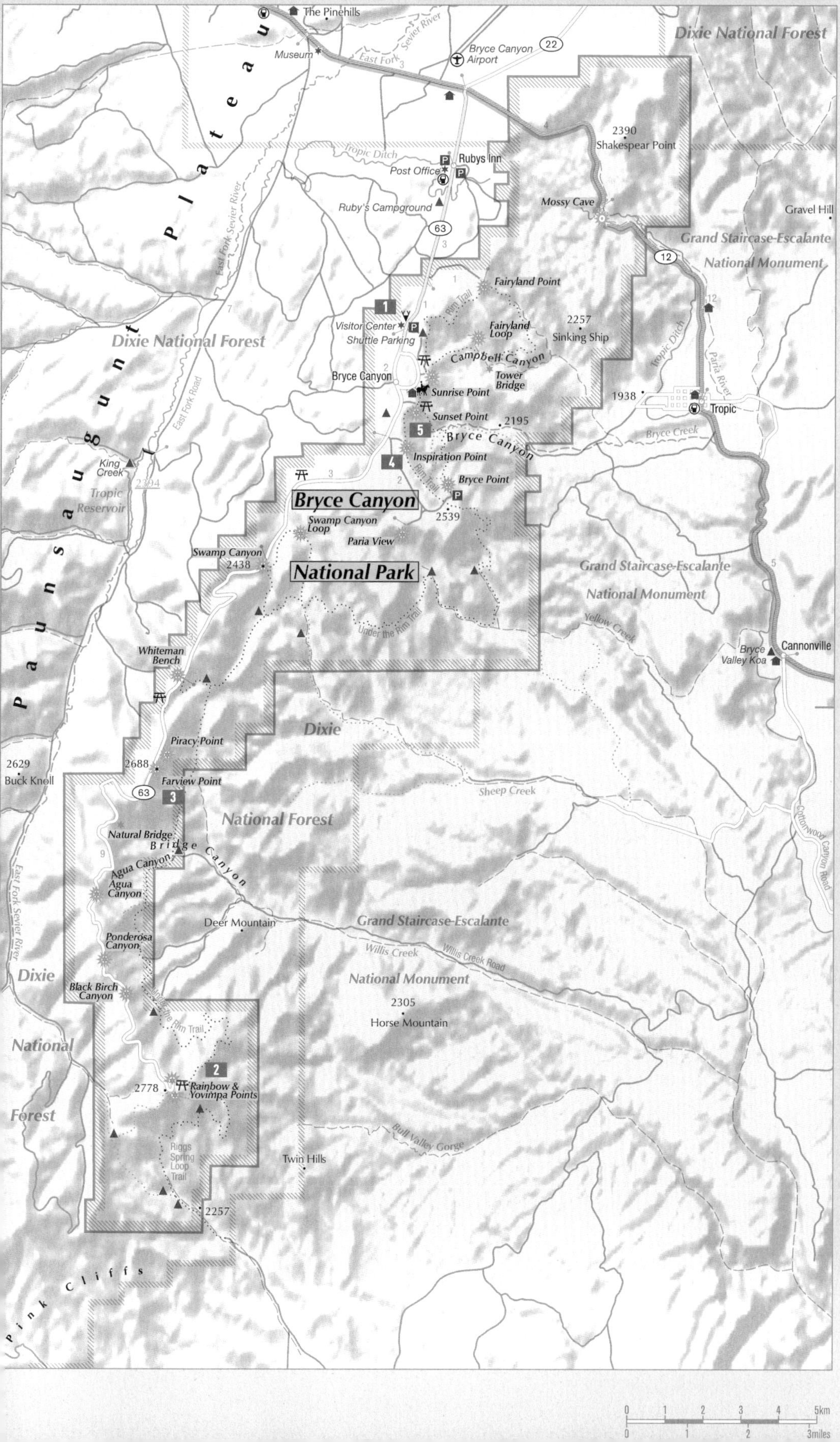

US State: Utah
Founded: 1928
Area: 60 mi^2

This is a magical world of colorful rock columns, cliffs and rock castles. The first ranchers, however, were sometimes less than enthusiastic about the amazing natural spectacle. A certain Ebenezer Bryce supposedly growled, "helluva of a place to lose a cow," as he set out once again in search of one of his cows in the rock labyrinth. Today's tourists gladly confirm this and enthusiastically take out their cameras.

SLOTS AND HOODOOS

The narrowest gorges, called "slot canyons," a plethora of daunting slender minarets; or "hoodoos," pinnacles, walls, arches, and windows–the army of bizarre shapes of red sandstone at the edge of the Paunsaugunt Plateau are among Mother Nature's more wonderful extravagances. Wind, weather and water, the architects of erosion, have created a mighty amphitheater, filled with colors from salmon to glowing red, filigree rock formations, and rows of minarets. At sunset, the enchanting play of colors on this fantastic scenery is not to be missed.

PANORAMA TRAIL

This park of a mere 60 mi^2 is very accessible. The scenic route branching off from UT-12 to the canyon follows the plateau's edge from the **1 visitor's center** at the entrance for 19 miles to **2 Rainbow & Yovimpa Point**, where you have the best views of the park. Whoever starts their sightseeing here, comes to a total of 14 lookout points on the way back, including **3 Farview Point** and **4 Inspiration Point**, and is right on time for the sunset at Bryce Canyon's **5 Sunset Point**, which lives up to its name.

TRAILS AND CANYON RIDES

Anyone who wants to experience this magnificence up close should make sure to wear hiking boots. A dozen lovely trails lead, usually near the lookout points, from the edge down to the rock amphitheater. However, you should be well prepared since at heights of 7,800 to 9,000 ft., the evenings can be quite cold. Also wonderful are the guided horse and mule tours (www.canyonrides.com).

CONTACT INFORMATION

Bryce Canyon National Park | PO Box 640201 | Bryce, UT 84764-0201 | Tel. 435 834-5322 | www.nps.gov/brca

Canyonlands National Park

U.S.A.

US State: Utah
Founded: 1964
Area: 527 mi²

This is a landscape of immense canyons whose wide ribbon-like patterns cut through a desert of rock and unforgettable views of endless vast plateaus. Utah's biggest national park is a wild, not easily conquered beauty. Roads only touch its edges. To gain access to the interior, you need a four-wheel drive vehicle or a raft, for the Colorado River.

COLORADO AND GREEN RIVER

This landscape of rocks, stones and boulders in Southern Utah is formed by the Colorado and Green Rivers. In the course of around 150 million years a 40-mile-wide basin 2,000 ft. deep has been created, with surreal rock formations, river loops called "goosenecks" and narrow gorges. Prehistoric rock drawings, like in Horseshoe Canyon, show that humans lived here as early as 3,000 years ago.

THREE SECTIONS, ONE PARK

The most accessible of the three sections of the park is the **1 Island In The Sky** district in the north. An asphalt road leads to the **2 Grand View Point Overlook**. The **3 Needles district**, named for its red sandstone minarets in the southwest corner, can be explored only on difficult dirt roads. The **4 Maze District**, also difficult to access, is a true labyrinth of gorges and rock overhangs. The adjacent **5 Dead Horse Point State Park** in the north-east offers more unforgettable views of the Canyon-lands. There are no direct roads connecting the individual parts of the Canyonlands. Those with little time should limit themselves to one of the three main regions. There are visitor centers in Island In The Sky and the Needles and a ranger station in the less accessible Maze district.

CAPITOL REEF NATIONAL PARK

Around 62 miles west of Canyonland National Park is Capitol Reef National Park, the quiet star of Utah National Park. A 24-mile scenic road leads to Grand Wash, a narrow gorge that floods in torrents in bad weather.

CONTACT INFORMATION

Canyonlands National Park | 2282 SW Resource Blvd. | Moab | Utah 84532 | Tel. 435/719-2313 | www.nps.gov/cany

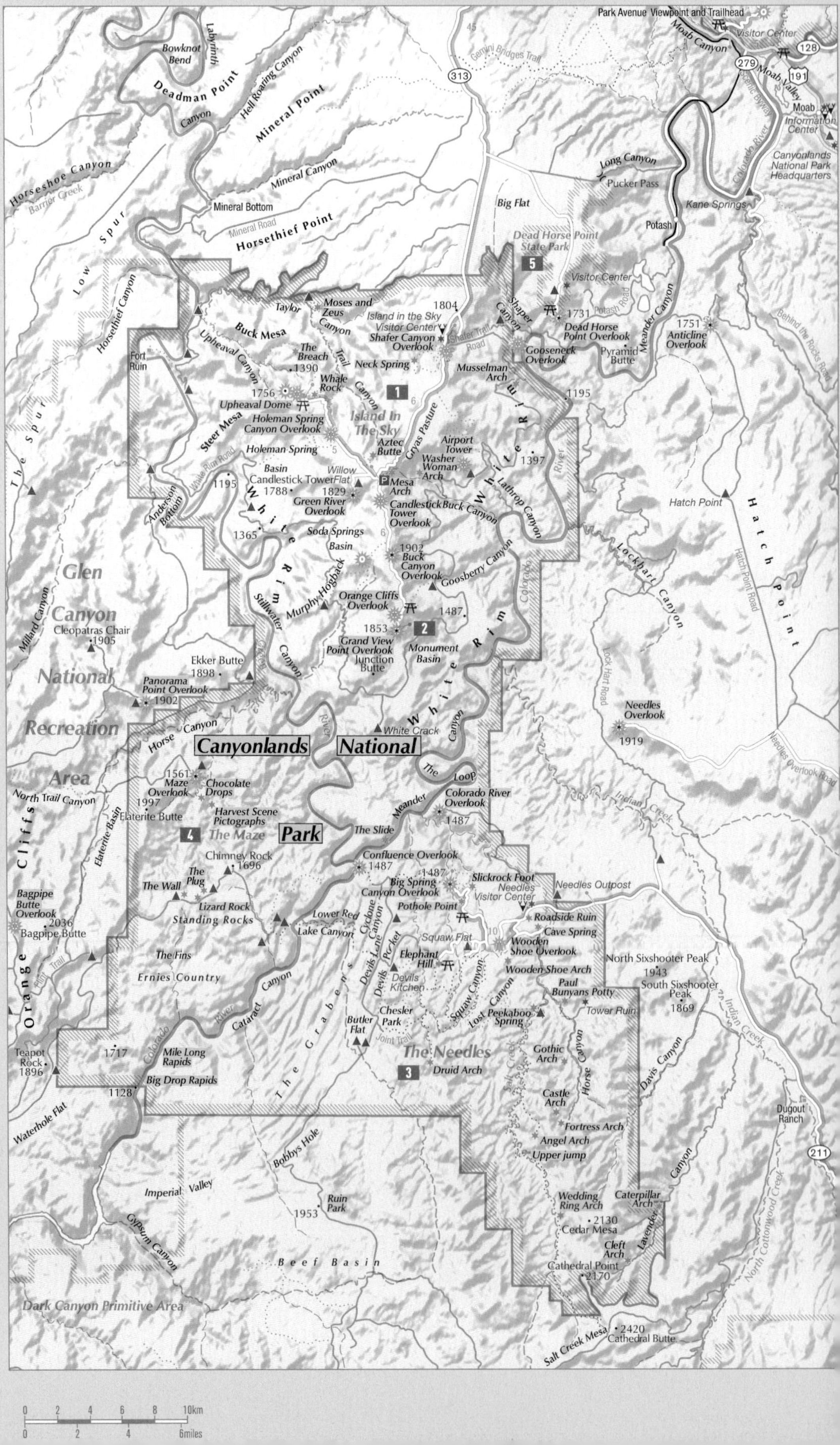

U.S.A.

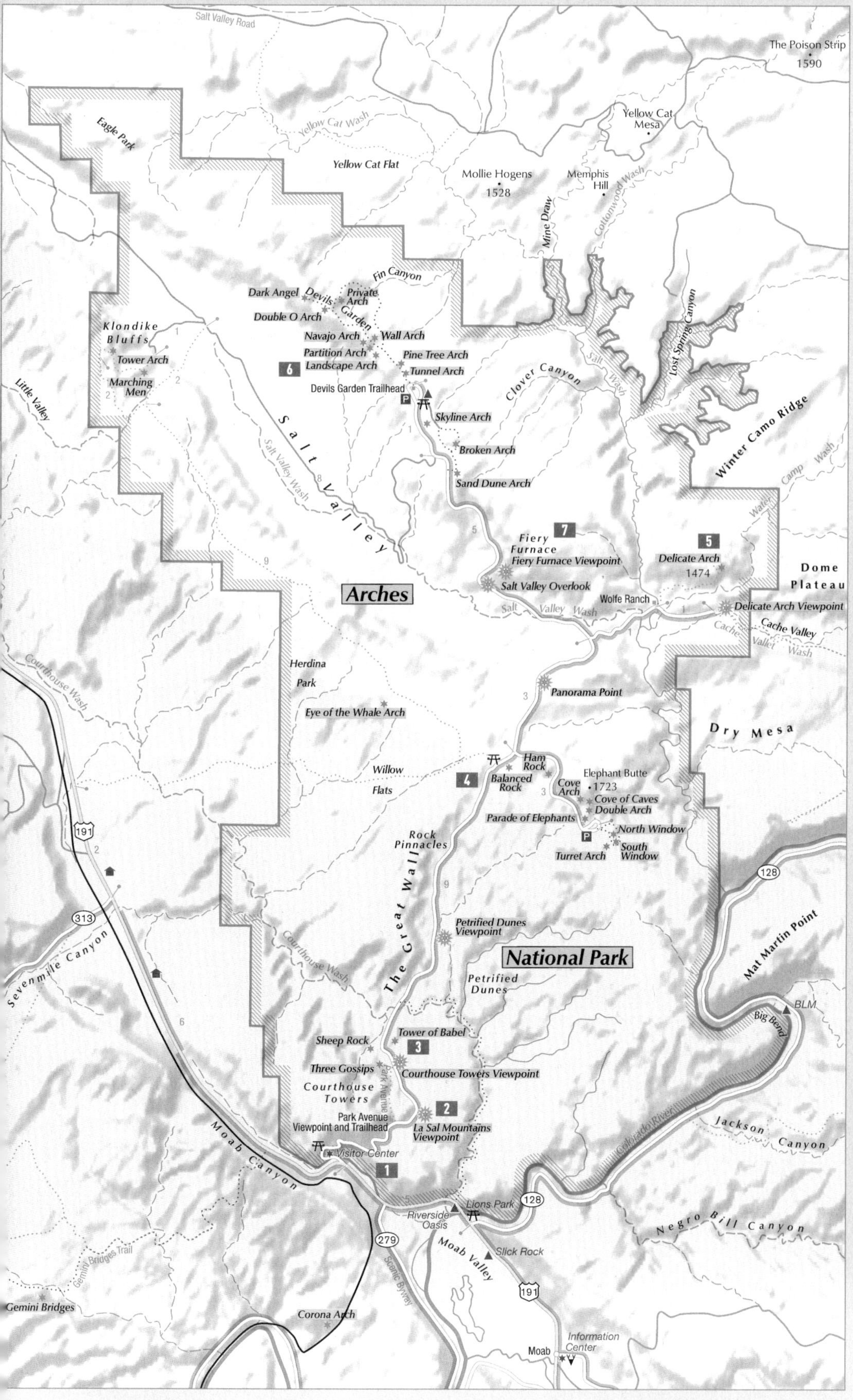

Salt Valley Road
The Poison Strip
1590
Eagle Park
Yellow Cat Wash
Yellow Cat Mesa
Yellow Cat Flat
Mollie Hogens
1528
Memphis Hill
Cottonwood Wash
Mine Draw
Fin Canyon
Dark Angel
Devils Garden
Private Arch
Double O Arch
Navajo Arch
Wall Arch
Partition Arch
Landscape Arch
Pine Tree Arch
Tunnel Arch
Klondike Bluffs
Tower Arch
Marching Men
Little Valley
Devils Garden Trailhead
Skyline Arch
Clover Canyon
Salt Wash
Lost Spring Canyon
Winter Camo Ridge
Broken Arch
Salt Valley
Salt Valley Wash
Sand Dune Arch
Camp Wash
Water
Fiery Furnace
Fiery Furnace Viewpoint
Delicate Arch
1474
Salt Valley Overlook
Dome Plateau
Arches
Wolfe Ranch
Salt Valley Wash
Delicate Arch Viewpoint
Cache Valley
Cache Valley Wash
Courthouse Wash
Herdina Park
Panorama Point
Eye of the Whale Arch
Dry Mesa
Willow Flats
Ham Rock
Balanced Rock
Elephant Butte
1723
Cove Arch
Cove of Caves
Double Arch
Parade of Elephants
North Window
South Window
Turret Arch
Rock Pinnacles
The Great Wall
Sevenmile Canyon
Petrified Dunes Viewpoint
National Park
Petrified Dunes
Mat Martin Point
BLM
Big Bend
Sheep Rock
Tower of Babel
Three Gossips
Courthouse Towers Viewpoint
Courthouse Towers
Park Avenue
Park Avenue Viewpoint and Trailhead
La Sal Mountains Viewpoint
Jackson Canyon
Colorado River
Visitor Center
Moab Canyon
Lions Park
Riverside Oasis
Negro Bill Canyon
Moab Valley
Slick Rock
Gemini Bridges Trail
Gemini Bridges
Scenic Byway
Corona Arch
Information Center
Moab
0 1 2 3 4 5km
0 1 2 3miles

US State: Utah
Founded: 1929
Area: 120 mi^2

Here you'll find rost-colored sandstone towers and arches as far as the eye can see. Some may be familiar to moviegoers. Thelma and Louise drove over the cliff and Indiana Jones hunted down villains here. While Hollywood images fade, however, the spectacular rocky desert is unforgettable. Supposedly there are people who have counted the towers and arches. They came up with 2,000–the biggest over 330 feet long and 100 feet high; the smallest only a few hands' breadth in diameter. There is an exact definition for when the term "stone arch," for which the national park is named, applies: The opening should have a minimum diameter of three feet. A 25-mile scenic drive leads to the park's most beautiful sites.

SCENIC DRIVE

The scenic road begins in Moab Canyon at the **1 visitor's center** and lead first to **2 La Sal Mountains overlook**. The almost 13,100-ft.-high mountain range to the east is covered in snow until midsummer. Later you'll pass tower-like rock formations such as the **3 Tower of Babel** and **4 Balanced Rock**, a 3,500 ton rock sitting on a 130 ft. base. Then the arches begin: **5 Delicate Arch**, which takes 20 minutes to reach on foot, is the most beautiful; **6 Landscape Arch** is reached on a 2-mile loop, With a length of 300 ft., makes it the largest rock arch in the world, next to "Kolob Arch" in Zion National Park.

TRAILS AND TOURS

The vegetation in this high desert (elevation of 3,900 to 5,200 feet) is very sensitive. That is why there are only few designated trails, which you should must never step away from. Therefore, it is worth having one of the ranger-guided tours in the Arches. These also include the rock maze, **7 Fiery Furnace**, from which it is not easy to find your way out alone. A good way to discover the park is by mountain bike. There are trails for all experience levels. Those who do not bring their own can rent one from the many outfitters in Moab, where guided tours are also offered.

CONTACT INFORMATION

Arches National Park | PO Box 907 | Moab | UT 84532 | Tel. 435 719-2299 | www.nps.gov/arch

Rocky Mountain National Park

U.S.A.

US State: Colorado
Founded: 1915
Area: 414 mi²

Variety is the magic word here. Snow covered four-thousanders, ice cold mountain lakes, rich green valleys and foamy whitewaters: In this alpine wilderness 2.5 hours drive north of Denver, the Rocky Mountains do everything to live up to their cliché. Over 3 million visitors come every year to see beavers, coyotes, elks and bears in their natural habitat and to conquer the mountains on lonely trails.

TRAIL RIDGE ROAD

Around 80 miles of road crisscross the park, including the 50-mile-long Trail Ridge Road leading from east to west. Full of winding curves and dramatic overlooks–one of the loveliest being at 1 **Medicine Bow Curve** near the Alpine Visitor Center–it reaches 3 **Hidden Valley** after passing the 2 **highest point** at 12,183 ft.; and just before 4 **Deer Mountain**, it splits into a north-south direction. The 5 **Fall River Visitor Center** is on the northern route; the 6 **Beaver Meadows Visitor Center** is reached via the southern route before leaving the park in the direction of 7 **Estes Park**.

BEAR LAKE

At the Bear Lake Road junction, the 8 **Moraine Park Visitor Center** provides information on the most popular sections of the park. Numerous trails start from the end at 9 **Bear Lake** into the mountains. Much-used short trails, like Emerald Lake Trail, lead to beautiful overlooks, and one of the most-used trails starts at Glacier Gorge Junction, and goes to 10 **Alberta** and 11 **Timberline Falls**.

GRAND LAKE AND WILD BASIN

The southwest of the national park is accessible via several trails starting from the 12 **Kawuneeche Visitor Center**. Favorite destinations here are 13 **Cascade** and 14 **Adams Falls**. The Wild Basin Entrance Station in the southeast leads into the wilderness in the direction of 15 **Boulder Grand Pass**. 16 **Ouzel Falls** and **Calypso CascadesCalypso Cascades** count among the main attractions here.

CONTACT INFORMATION

Rocky Mountain National Park | 1000 Highway 36 | Estes Park | Colorado 80517 | Tel. 970 586-1206 | www.nps.gov/romo

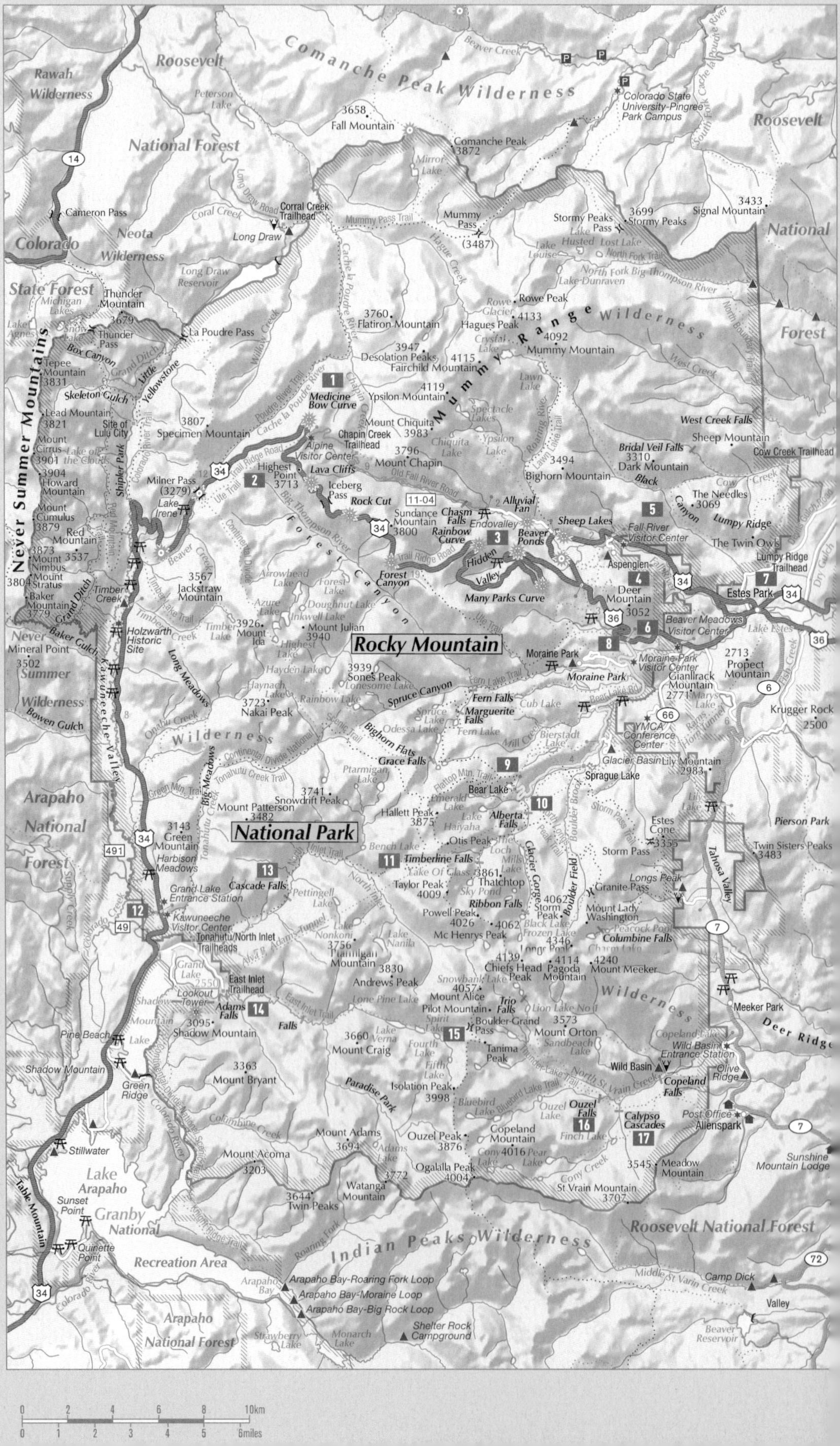

U.S.A.

US State: North Carolina and Tennessee
Founded: 1934
Area: 416 mi²

No, there is no smoke in the "Smokies." The blue mist for which the park is known is created when the evaporating moisture mixes with the natural oils of the abundant vegetation, which includes over 125 tree and 1,500 plant species. Its proximity to urban centers in the east makes Great Smoky Mountains National Park one of the most popular in the US, with over 10 million visitors per year.

TWO STATES

The park has an area of around 772 mi² and lies exactly between Tennessee and North Carolina. Geologically, the Smokies belong to the Appalachians that extend from Georgia to Canada. The park is open all year round, but at heights of between 900 and 6,500 ft. snow-covered roads may be closed in winter. **1 Townsend**, **2 Sugarlands** near Gatlinburg (Tennessee) and **3 Ocanaluftee** (North Carolina) near Cherokee have visitor centers and information is available at the **4 Cades Cove Visitor Center**.

HIGHWAY 441

Highway 441 from Pigeon Forge (TN) to Cherokee (NC) cuts the park in half. Numerous trails of all levels of difficulty start from the road. Clingmans Dome Road, which is closed in winter, leads to the 6,640 ft. **5 Clingmans Dome**, the highest mountain and favorite hiking destination of the Smokies. East of the road is the equally popular **6 Mt. Le Conte** at over 6,500 ft. The view of the fog and clouds in the valleys from **7 Newfound Gap** directly on Hwy. 441 to the ridgeline of the mountain range is magnificent, especially after it rains.

TRAILS

The extraordinary diversity of vegetation make this natural wonder the main attraction of the park. The best way to explore the Smokies is on foot: Mountain magnolias, wild azaleas, orchids, and mountain laurel are best enjoyed along the hiking trail. Over 800 miles of hiking trails crisscross the park, including the Appalachian Trail, the most famous long-distance trail in the US.

CONTACT INFORMATION

Great Smoky Mountains National Park | 107 Park Headquarters Road | Gatlinburg | TN 37738 | Tel. 865 436-1200 | www.nps.gov/grsm

U.S.A.

US State: Florida
Founded: 1947
Area: 2,357 mi²

Water, reeds, tree islands of mahogany and gumbo limbo trees here and there as far as the eye can see. The Everglades are the biggest subtropical wetlands in North America. As is often the case, the prettier and more fitting name "Pa-hay-okee," meaning "River of Grass," comes from the Native Americans. It refers to the swamps, which are actually a very flat slow moving 50-mile-wide river. The animal world is also as diverse as the flora: Alligators and the endangered American crocodile live here, wildcats hunt for deer and dolphins splash about in the mangrove forests.

ON FL 9336 TO FLAMINGO

The **1 Ernest F. Coe Visitor Center** at the park entrance has educational displays to prepare the visitor for the trip. Next is the Royal Palm Visitor Center, where the 0.5 mile long **2 Anhinga Trail** begins, a boardwalk from where alligators, turtles, otters and the Anhinga, the bird with the snakelike black neck, can be seen. The **3 Pa hay-okee Overlook Trail**, 13 miles west, ends on an overlook platform over the "River of Grass".

TAMIAMI TRAIL

US 41, better known as the "Tamiami Trail" continues along the northern edge of the park. The first stop is **4 Shark Valley Visitor Center**. A circular path from here leads a little bit into a seemingly endless fresh water marsh. The view from the **5 Observation Tower** alone is worth the side trip. The **6 Big Cypress National Preserve Visitor** halfway between Miami and Naples provides information on the ecological background. Route 29 crosses on the west border of the park. The **7 Fakahatchee Strand State Preserve** is to the north, where the dissolving limestone has left long troughs or "strands" that have turned into unbelievably photogenic cypress swamps.

TEN THOUSAND ISLANDS

Everglades City, the "Gateway to the Ten Thousand Islands" is to the south. The Gulf **8 Coast Visitor Center** offers boot tours through the mangrove labyrinth in the west called Ten Thousand Islands.

CONTACT INFORMATION

40001 State Road 9336 | Homestead | FL 33034-6733 | Tel. 305 242-7700 | www.nps.gov/ever

1:20 000 / 1cm = 200m

Boston
Calgary
Chicago
Denver
Fort Lauderdale
Fort Myers*
Las Vegas*
Los Angeles*
Miami*
Miami Beach
Montreal
New York*
San Francisco*
Seatle
Toronto
Vancouver*
Washington D.C.

* 1:100 000 / 1cm = 1km + 1:20 000 / 1cm = 200m

Photo: Miami, Biscayne Bay, Boot (Marcel Malherbe/laif)

North Cambrige
North Cambrige
Malden
Belmont
Brighton
Weston Crossing
Watertown
Brookline
Roxbury Crossing
Harvard University
Massachusetts Institute of Technology
Charles River Basin
Back Bay Fens
EAST CAMBRIDGE
LONGWOOD
BACK BAY
0 200 400 600 800m
0 0.25 0.5miles

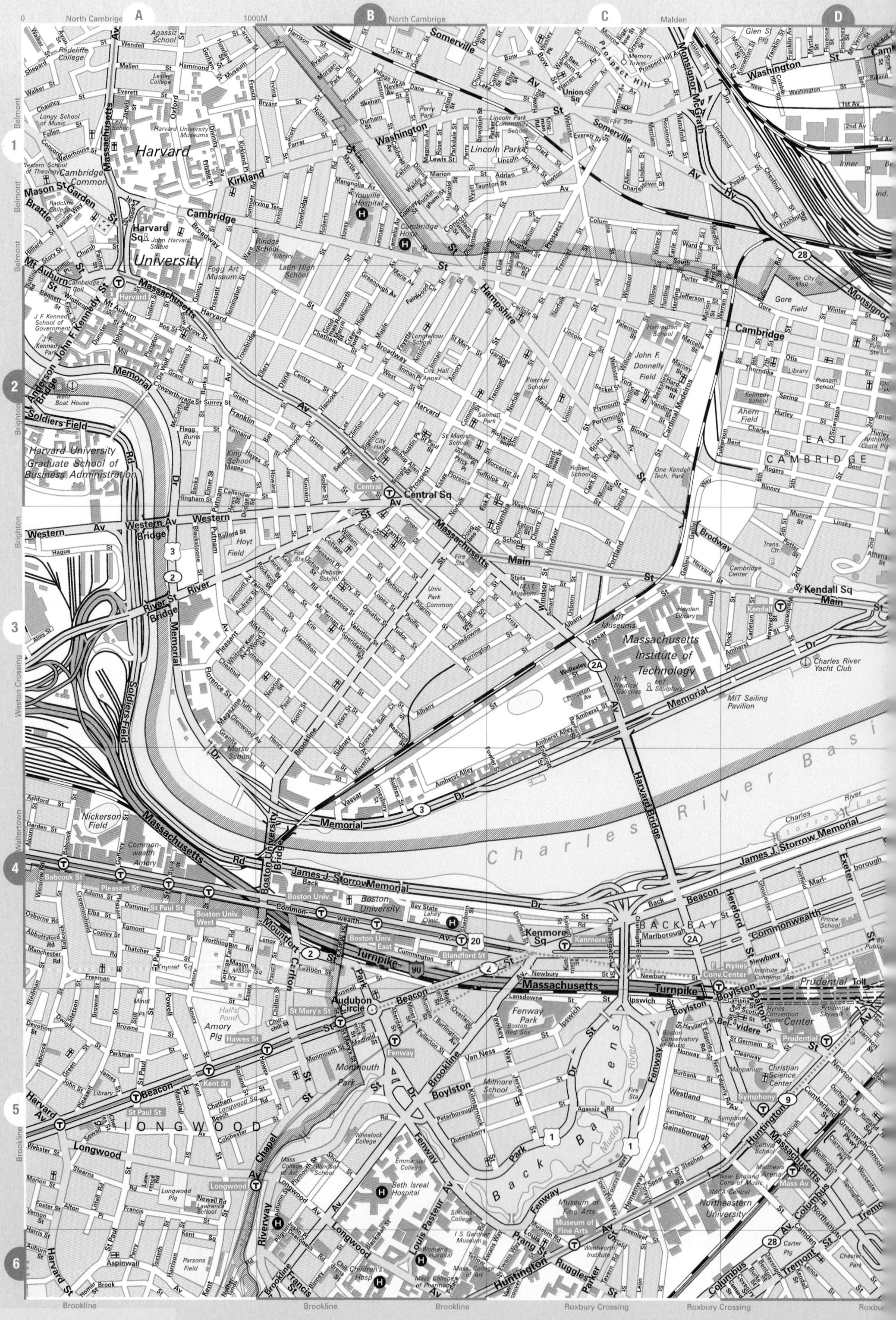

- Boston Convention and Exhibition Center G5
- Boston Tea Party Ship and Museum F4-G4
- Boston University B2
- Bunker Hill Monument F1
- Cambridgeside Gallerie D2-E2
- Fenway Park C5
- Fogg Art Museum A1
- Harvard University A2
- Hayden Planetarium E2
- John Harvard Statue A1
- Lincoln Park B1-C1
- M.I.T. Museum C3
- Massachusetts Inst. of Technology C3
- Museum of Fine Art C5
- Museum of Science E2
- National Historical Park F2-G2
- Northeastern University C5-D5
- Public Garden E4
- State House E3-F3
- Washington Monument E4

Calgary

Mountain Standard Time

Canada

- Calgary Public Library B1
- Calgary Tower B2
- City Hall B1
- Devonian Gardens B2
- Epcor Center B2
- Fort Calgary B1
- Glenbow Museum B2
- Lougheed House C3
- Olympic Plaza B2
- Prince's Island Park A2-3
- Shaw Millenium Park B4
- Theatre Calgary B2

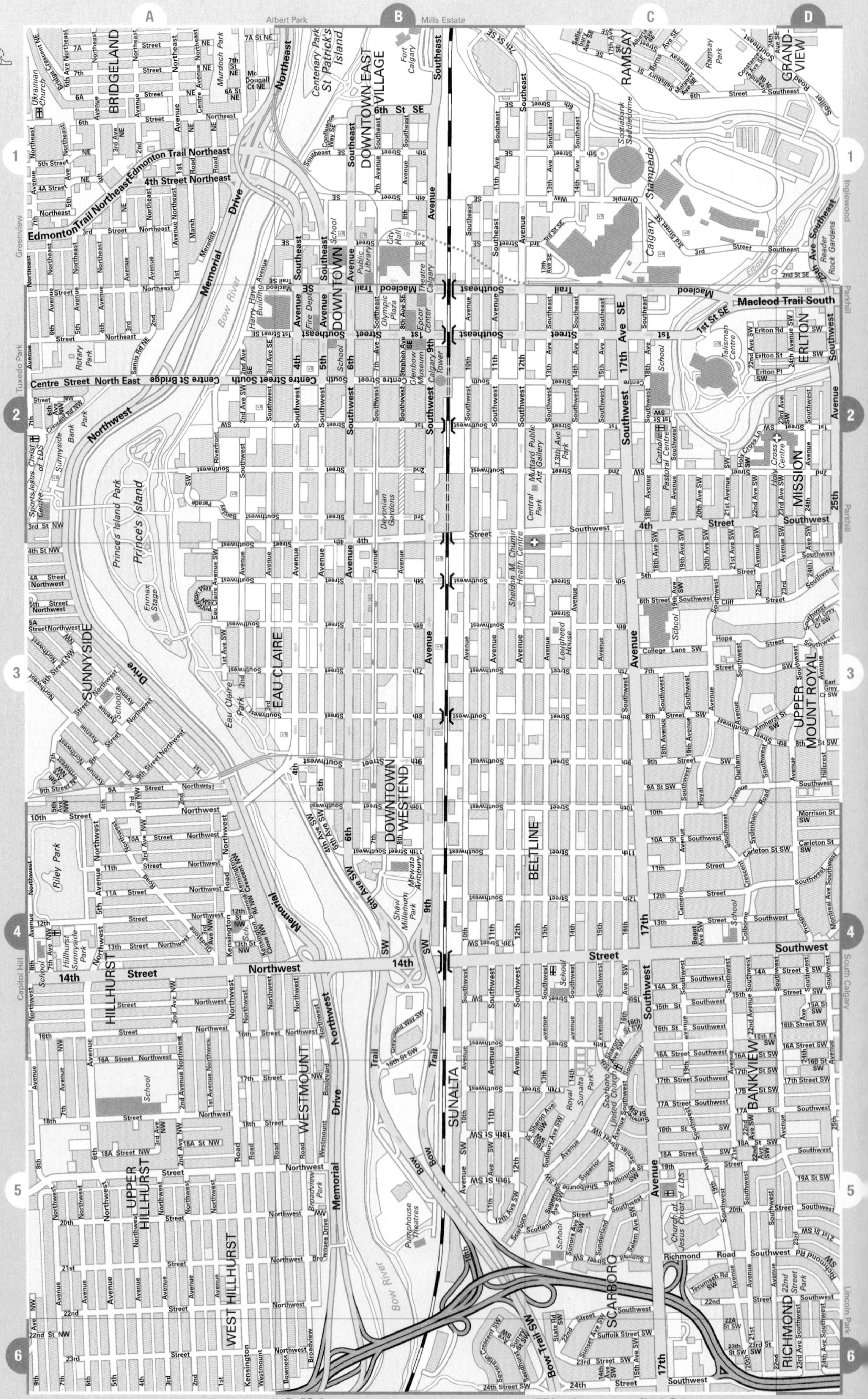

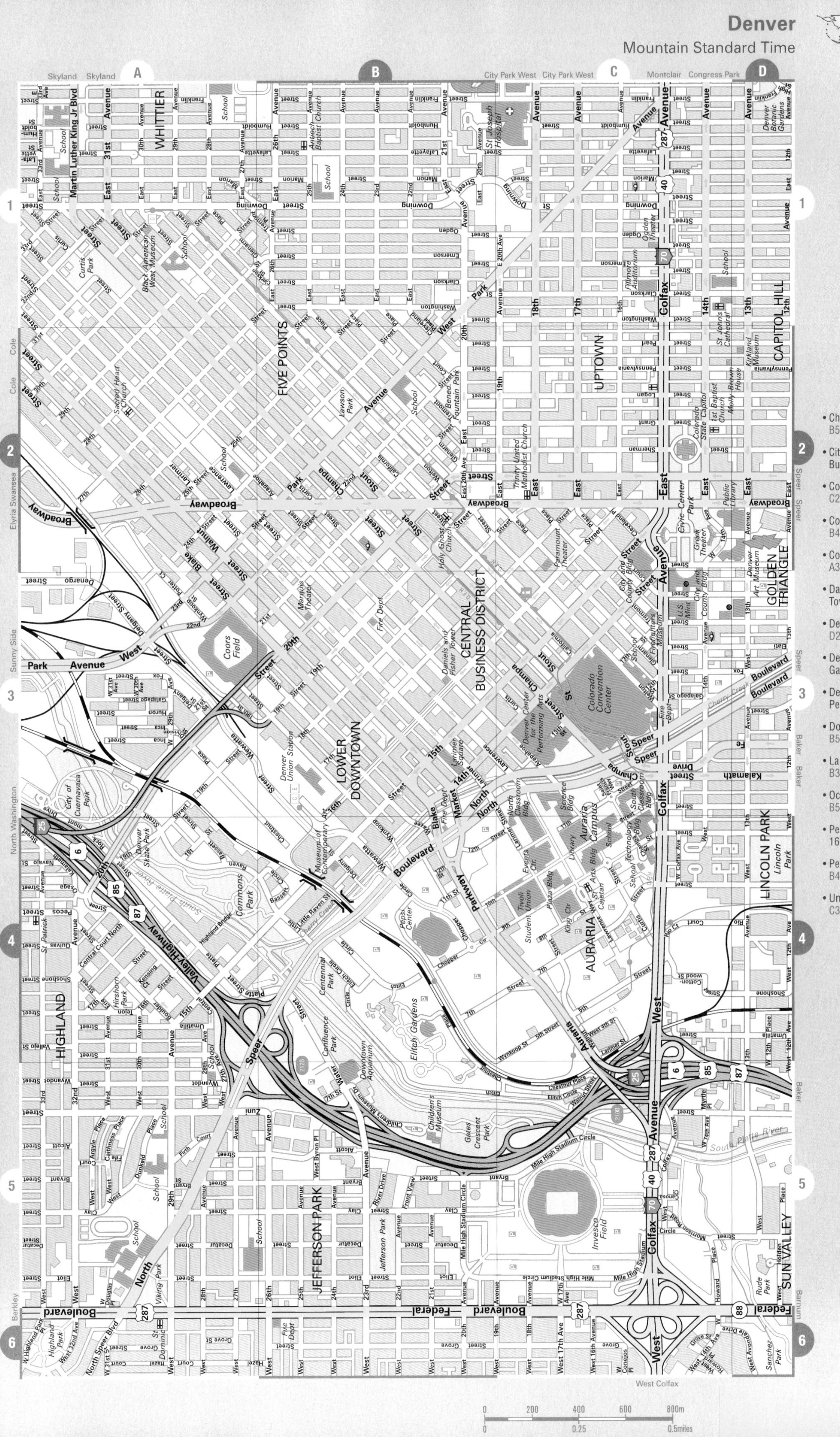

- Children's Museum B5
- City and County Building C2-3
- Colrado State Capitel C2
- Confluence Park B4
- Coors Field A3
- Daniels and Fisher Tower B3
- Denver Art Museum D2
- Denver Botanic Gardens D1
- Denver Center for the Performing Arts C3
- Downtown Aquarium B5
- Larimer Square B3
- Ocean Journey B5
- Pedestrian Mall 16th Street B3
- Pepsi Center B4
- United States Mint C3

Lake Michigan
North Ave Beach
Gold Coast
Oak St Beach
Ohio St Beach
Navy Pier
Water Filtration Plant
Outer Harbor
Chicago River
North Branch Canal
Goose Island
Old Town
Near North
Loop
N Lake Shore Drive
Magnificent Mile

West Town · Bucktown · West Town · West Town · West Town · West Town · Near West Side · Near

0 200 400 600 800m
0 0.25 0.5miles

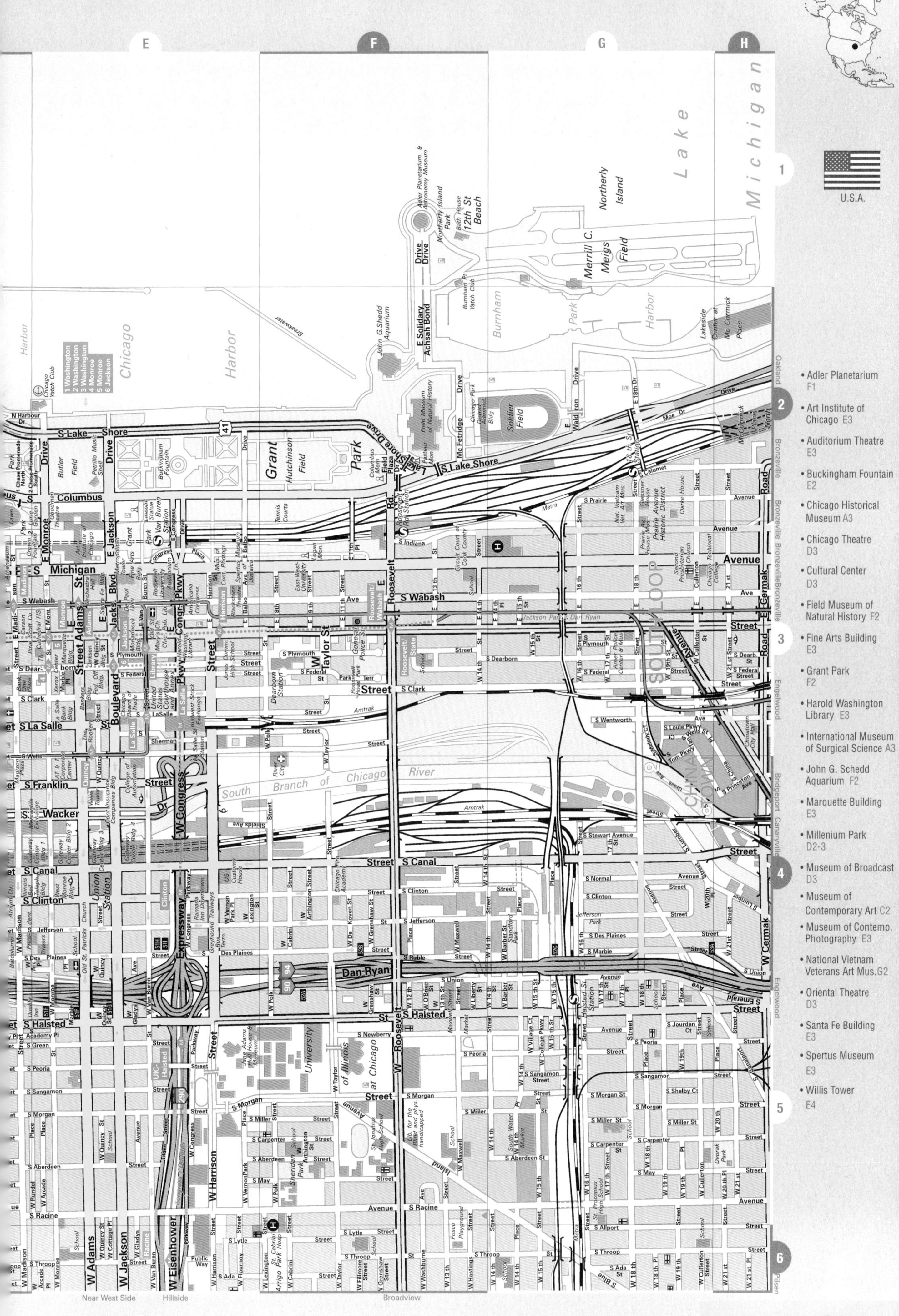

U.S.A.

- Adler Planetarium F1
- Art Institute of Chicago E3
- Auditorium Theatre E3
- Buckingham Fountain E2
- Chicago Historical Museum A3
- Chicago Theatre D3
- Cultural Center D3
- Field Museum of Natural History F2
- Fine Arts Building E3
- Grant Park F2
- Harold Washington Library E3
- International Museum of Surgical Science A3
- John G. Schedd Aquarium F2
- Marquette Building E3
- Millenium Park D2-3
- Museum of Broadcast D3
- Museum of Contemporary Art C2
- Museum of Contemp. Photography E3
- National Vietnam Veterans Art Mus. G2
- Oriental Theatre D3
- Santa Fe Building E3
- Spertus Museum E3
- Willis Tower E4

U.S.A.

- Bellagio B4
- Ceasar's Palace B3
- Circus Circus B3
- Fremont Street Experience C2
- Luxor B4
- Mandala Bay B4
- MGM Grand B4
- Nevada State Museum B2
- New York - New York B4
- Paris Las Vegas B4
- Stratosphere Tower B3
- The Mirage B3
- The Venetian B3
- Wynn Las Vegas B3

0 1 2 3 4km
0 0.5 1 1.5 2 2.5miles

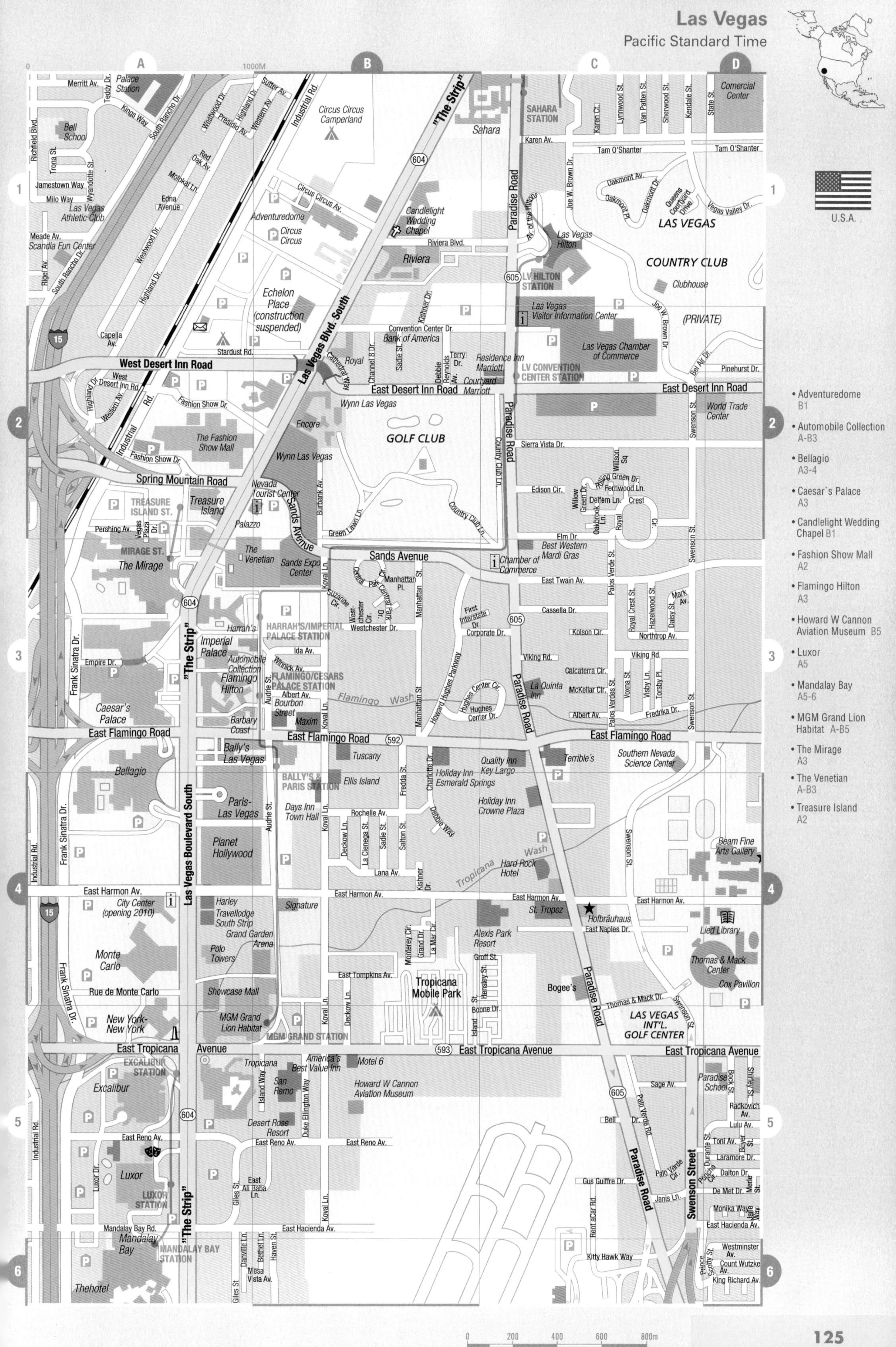
A
B
C
D
1
2
3
4
5
6
0
1000M
U.S.A.
LAS VEGAS
COUNTRY CLUB
(PRIVATE)
GOLF CLUB
"The Strip"
Las Vegas Blvd. South
Las Vegas Boulevard South
Paradise Road
Swenson Street
West Desert Inn Road
East Desert Inn Road
Spring Mountain Road
Sands Avenue
East Flamingo Road
East Harmon Av.
East Tropicana Avenue
Circus Circus Campерland
Sahara
SAHARA STATION
Comercial Center
Adventuredome
Circus Circus
Candlelight Wedding Chapel
Riviera
Las Vegas Hilton
LV HILTON STATION
Clubhouse
Echelon Place (construction suspended)
Las Vegas Visitor Information Center
Las Vegas Chamber of Commerce
LV CONVENTION CENTER STATION
Bank of America
Royal
Residence Inn Marriott
Courtyard Marriott
Wynn Las Vegas
Encore
World Trade Center
The Fashion Show Mall
Nevada Tourist Center
TREASURE ISLAND ST.
Treasure Island
Palazzo
The Venetian
Sands Expo Center
MIRAGE ST.
The Mirage
Chamber of Commerce
Best Western Mardi Gras
Harrah's
HARRAH'S/IMPERIAL PALACE STATION
Imperial Palace
Automobile Collection
Flamingo Hilton
FLAMINGO/CESARS PALACE STATION
Bourbon Street
Maxim
Barbary Coast
Caesar's Palace
La Quinta Inn
Flamingo Wash
Bellagio
Bally's Las Vegas
BALLY'S & PARIS STATION
Paris-Las Vegas
Tuscany
Ellis Island
Holiday Inn Esmerald Springs
Quality Inn Key Largo
Holiday Inn Crowne Plaza
Terrible's
Southern Nevada Science Center
Planet Hollywood
Days Inn Town Hall
Tropicana Wash
Hard Rock Hotel
Beam Fine Arts Gallery
City Center (opening 2010)
Harley
Travellodge South Strip
Grand Garden Arena
Polo Towers
Signature
Alexis Park Resort
St. Tropez
Hofbräuhaus
Lied Library
Monte Carlo
Thomas & Mack Center
Cox Pavilion
Showcase Mall
Tropicana Mobile Park
Bogee's
New York-New York
MGM Grand Lion Habitat
MGM GRAND STATION
LAS VEGAS INT'L. GOLF CENTER
EXCALIBUR STATION
Excalibur
Tropicana
San Remo
America's Best Value Inn
Motel 6
Howard W Cannon Aviation Museum
Desert Rose Resort
Paradise School
Luxor
LUXOR STATION
Mandalay Bay
MANDALAY BAY STATION
Thehotel
0 200 400 600 800m
0 0.25 0.5miles
• Adventuredome B1
• Automobile Collection A-B3
• Bellagio A3-4
• Caesar`s Palace A3
• Candlelight Wedding Chapel B1
• Fashion Show Mall A2
• Flamingo Hilton A3
• Howard W Cannon Aviation Museum B5
• Luxor A5
• Mandalay Bay A5-6
• MGM Grand Lion Habitat A-B5
• The Mirage A3
• The Venetian A-B3
• Treasure Island A2

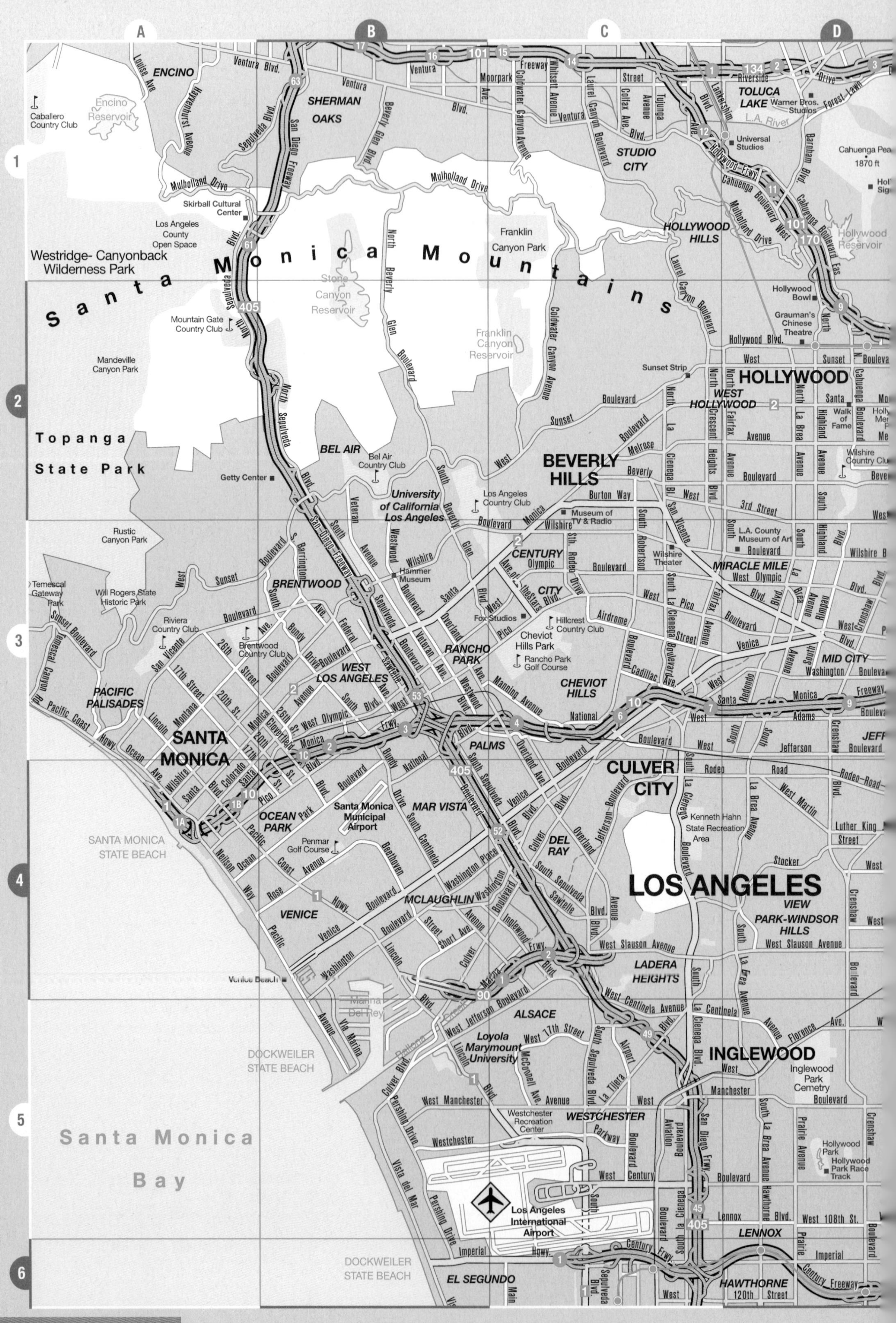
Santa Monica Mountains
Santa Monica Bay
ENCINO
SHERMAN OAKS
STUDIO CITY
TOLUCA LAKE
HOLLYWOOD HILLS
HOLLYWOOD
WEST HOLLYWOOD
BEVERLY HILLS
BEL AIR
BRENTWOOD
University of California Los Angeles
CENTURY CITY
MIRACLE MILE
MID CITY
RANCHO PARK
CHEVIOT HILLS
WEST LOS ANGELES
PACIFIC PALISADES
SANTA MONICA
OCEAN PARK
MAR VISTA
PALMS
CULVER CITY
DEL RAY
VENICE
MCLAUGHLIN
LOS ANGELES
VIEW PARK-WINDSOR HILLS
LADERA HEIGHTS
ALSACE
INGLEWOOD
WESTCHESTER
LENNOX
HAWTHORNE
EL SEGUNDO
Topanga State Park
Westridge- Canyonback Wilderness Park
Mandeville Canyon Park
Rustic Canyon Park
Will Rogers State Historic Park
Getty Center
Skirball Cultural Center
Los Angeles International Airport
Loyola Marymount University
Santa Monica Municipal Airport
Universal Studios
Warner Bros. Studios
Hollywood Bowl
Grauman's Chinese Theatre
L.A. County Museum of Art
Hammer Museum
Fox Studios
Kenneth Hahn State Recreation Area
Marina Del Rey
SANTA MONICA STATE BEACH
DOCKWEILER STATE BEACH
Venice Beach
Hollywood Park Racetrack
Inglewood Park Cemetery
0 1 2 3 4km
0 0.5 1 1.5 2 2.5miles

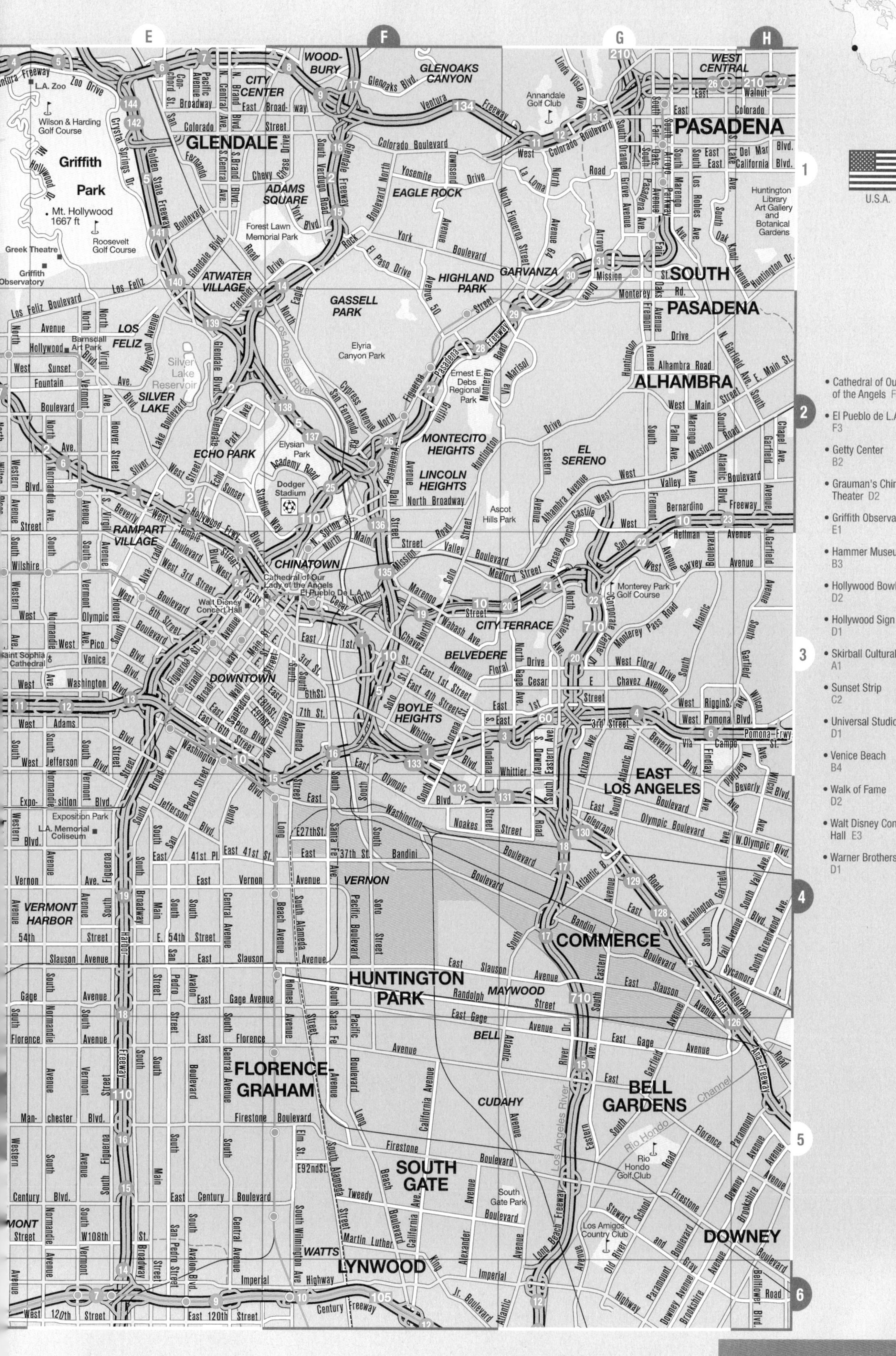

U.S.A.

- Cathedral of Our Lady of the Angels F3
- El Pueblo de L.A. F3
- Getty Center B2
- Grauman's Chinese Theater D2
- Griffith Observatory E1
- Hammer Museum B3
- Hollywood Bowl D2
- Hollywood Sign D1
- Skirball Cultural Center A1
- Sunset Strip C2
- Universal Studios D1
- Venice Beach B4
- Walk of Fame D2
- Walt Disney Concert Hall E3
- Warner Brothers Studio D1

Los Angeles

Pacific Standard Time

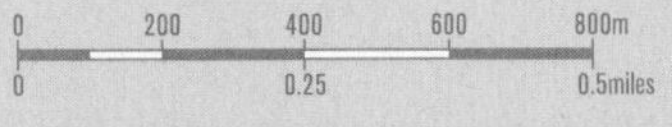

0 200 400 600 800m

0 0.25 0.5miles

U.S.A.

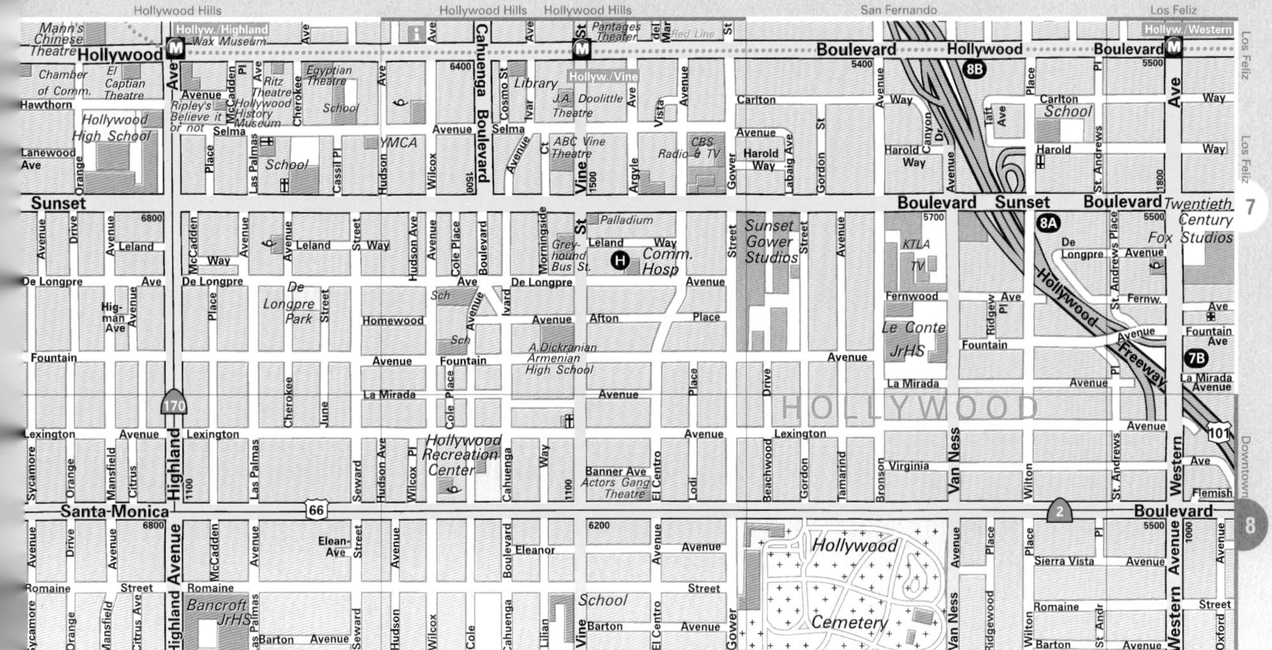

- Angels Flight D3
- Cathedral of Our Lady of the Angels D2
- Central Library C3
- City Hall D-E3
- D. Chandler Pavilion D2-3
- Dodger Stadium E1
- Fargo Tower D3
- Geffen Contemporary at MOCA E3-4
- Grand Central Market D3
- Hollywood History Museum J7
- Japanese American Museum E3
- L. A. Children Museum E3
- Little Tokyo E3-4
- Mann`s Chinese Theatre J7
- Museum of Contemp. Art D3
- Museum of Neon Art E4
- Pershing Square D3
- Ripley`s Believe it or not J7
- Union Station E3
- Walt Disney Concert Hall D3
- Wax Museum J7
- World Trade Center C-D3

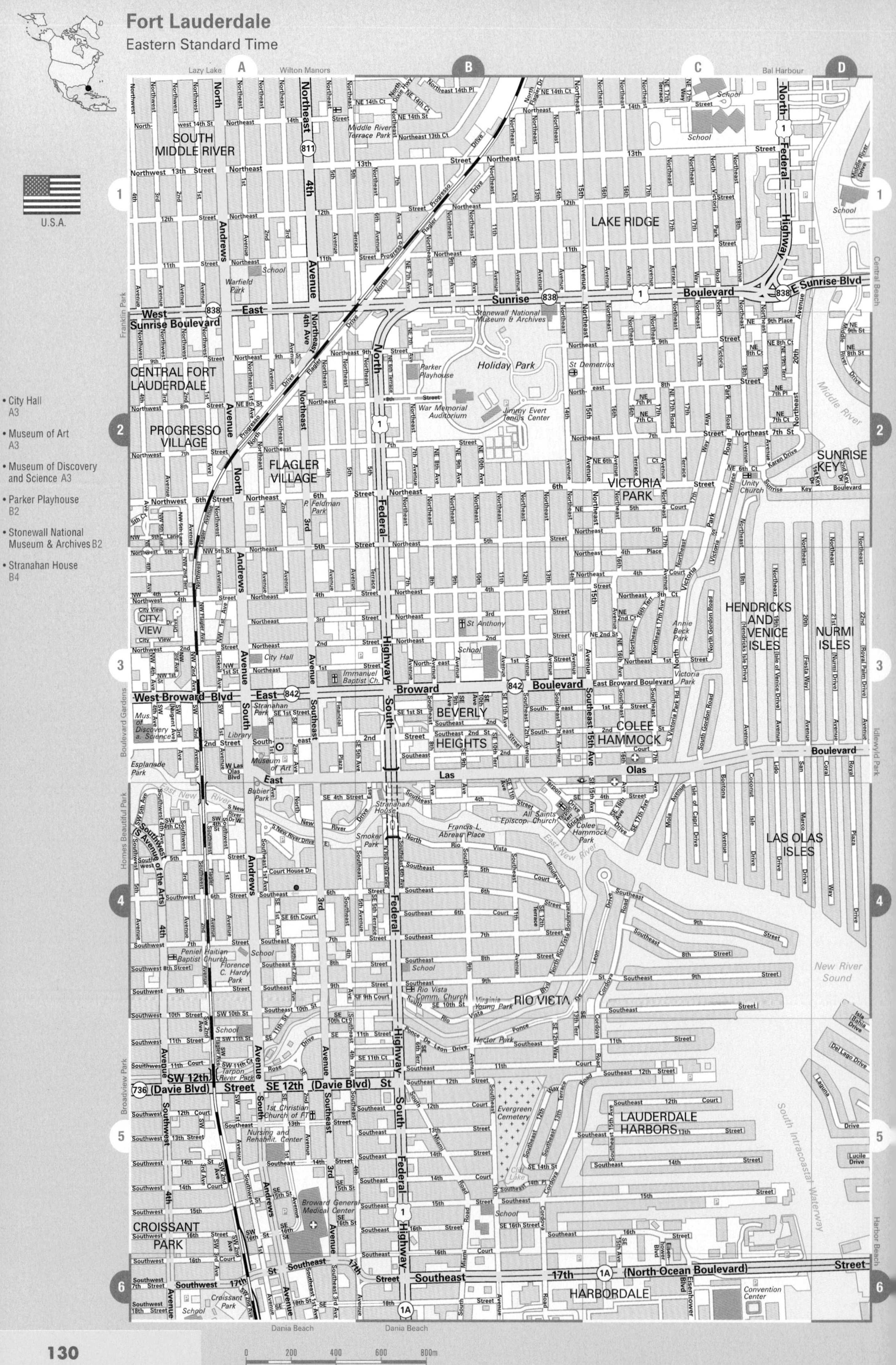

Fort Lauderdale
Eastern Standard Time
U.S.A.
• City Hall A3
• Museum of Art A3
• Museum of Discovery and Science A3
• Parker Playhouse B2
• Stonewall National Museum & Archives B2
• Stranahan House B4
Lazy Lake
Wilton Manors
Bal Harbour
Franklin Park
Boulevard Gardens
Homes Beautiful Park
Broadview Park
Central Beach
Idlewyld Park
Harbor Beach
Dania Beach
SOUTH MIDDLE RIVER
LAKE RIDGE
CENTRAL FORT LAUDERDALE
PROGRESSO VILLAGE
FLAGLER VILLAGE
VICTORIA PARK
SUNRISE KEY
CITY VIEW
HENDRICKS AND VENICE ISLES
NURMI ISLES
BEVERLY HEIGHTS
COLEE HAMMOCK
LAS OLAS ISLES
RIO VISTA
LAUDERDALE HARBORS
CROISSANT PARK
HARBORDALE
Holiday Park
New River Sound
South Intracoastal Waterway
0 200 400 600 800m
0 0.25 0.5miles

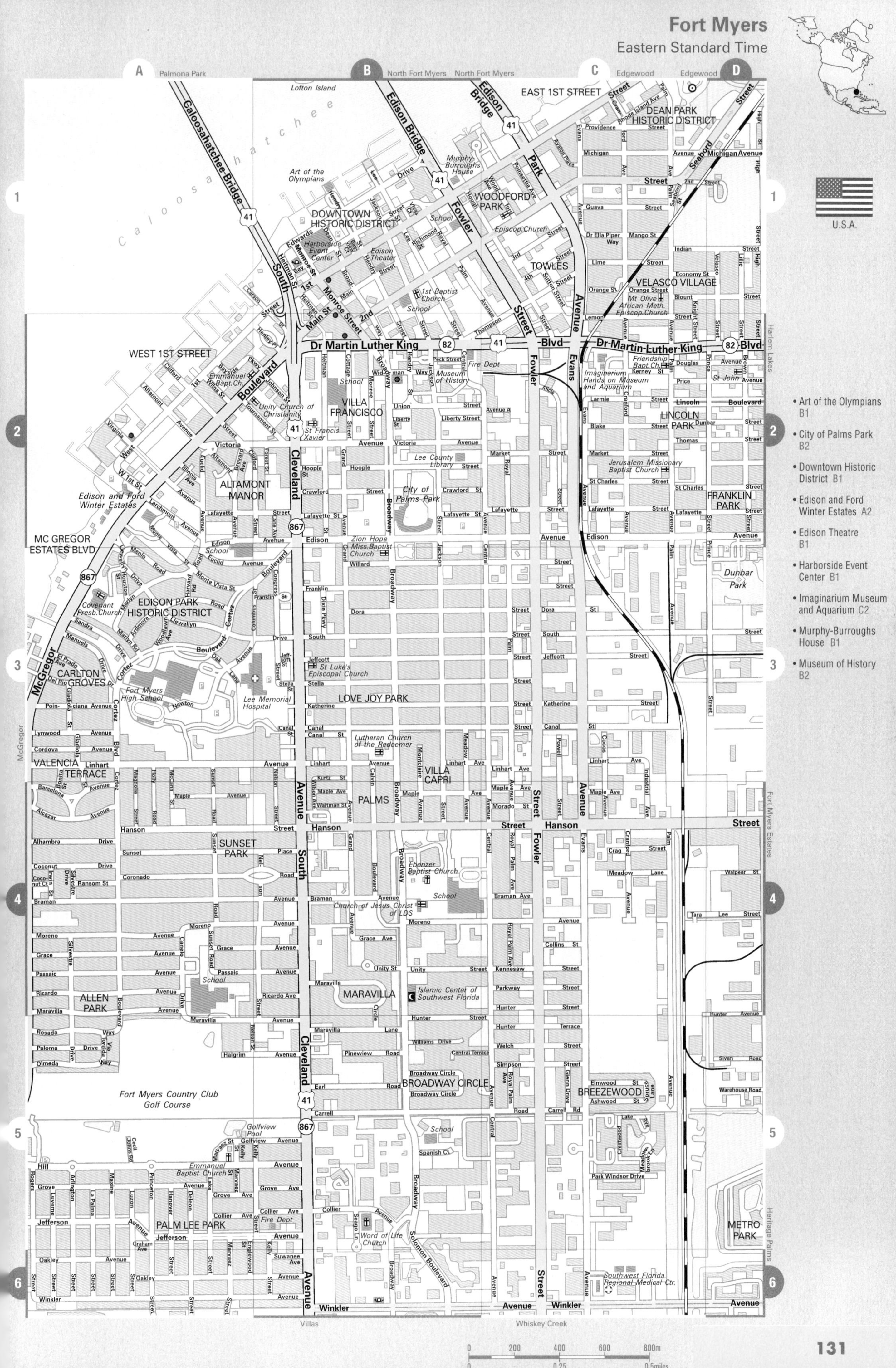
Fort Myers
Eastern Standard Time
U.S.A.
A
B
C
D
1
2
3
4
5
6
Palmona Park
North Fort Myers
Edgewood
Harlem Lakes
Fort Myers Estates
Heritage Palms
Villas
Whiskey Creek
McGregor
Caloosahatchee
Caloosahatchee Bridge
Edison Bridge
Lofton Island
Art of the Olympians
DOWNTOWN HISTORIC DISTRICT
Harborside Event Center
Edison Theater
Murphy-Burroughs House
WOODFORD PARK
Episcop.Church
TOWLES
EAST 1ST STREET
DEAN PARK HISTORIC DISTRICT
VELASCO VILLAGE
Mt Olive African Meth. Episcop.Church
1st Baptist Church
WEST 1ST STREET
Dr Martin Luther King Blvd
Museum of History
Fire Dept
Imaginarium Hands on Museum and Aquarium
Friendship Bapt.Ch.
St John
VILLA FRANCISCO
St Francis Xavier
Unity Church of Christianity
Emmanuel Bapt.Ch.
LINCOLN PARK
FRANKLIN PARK
Jerusalem Missionary Baptist Church
ALTAMONT MANOR
Lee County Library
City of Palms Park
Edison and Ford Winter Estates
MC GREGOR ESTATES BLVD
Zion Hope Miss.Baptist Church
Edison School
Covenant Presb.Church
EDISON PARK HISTORIC DISTRICT
Dunbar Park
CARLTON GROVES
Fort Myers High School
Lee Memorial Hospital
St Luke's Episcopal Church
LOVE JOY PARK
Lutheran Church of the Redeemer
VALENCIA TERRACE
VILLA CAPRI
PALMS
SUNSET PARK
Ebenezer Baptist Church
Church of Jesus Christ of LDS
ALLEN PARK
MARAVILLA
Islamic Center of Southwest Florida
BROADWAY CIRCLE
BREEZEWOOD
Fort Myers Country Club Golf Course
Golfview Pool
Emmanuel Baptist Church
PALM LEE PARK
Fire Dept
Word of Life Church
METRO PARK
Southwest Florida Regional Medical Ctr.
Cleveland Avenue
South Cleveland Avenue
McGregor Boulevard
Fowler Street
Evans Avenue
Hanson Street
Winkler Avenue
Broadway
Solomon Boulevard
0 200 400 600 800m
0 0.25 0.5miles
• Art of the Olympians B1
• City of Palms Park B2
• Downtown Historic District B1
• Edison and Ford Winter Estates A2
• Edison Theatre B1
• Harborside Event Center B1
• Imaginarium Museum and Aquarium C2
• Murphy-Burroughs House B1
• Museum of History B2

Fort Myers

U.S.A.

- Art of the Olympians A3
- City of Palms Park B3
- Downtown Historic District B3
- Edison and Ford Winter Estates A3
- Edison Mall B4
- Harborside Event Center A3
- Imaginarium Museum and Aquarium B3
- Museum of History B3

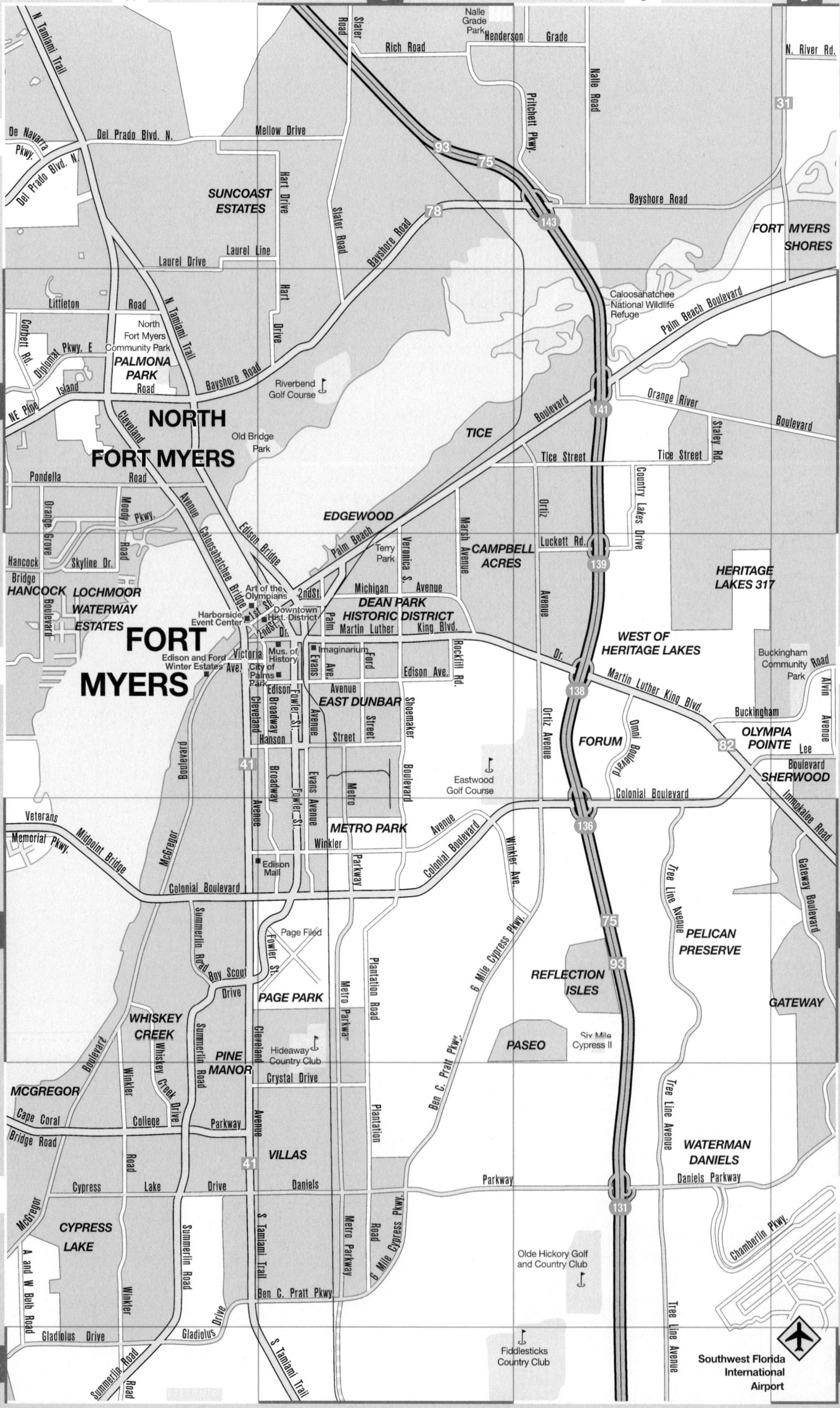

0 1 2 3 4km
0 0.5 1 1.5 2 2.5miles

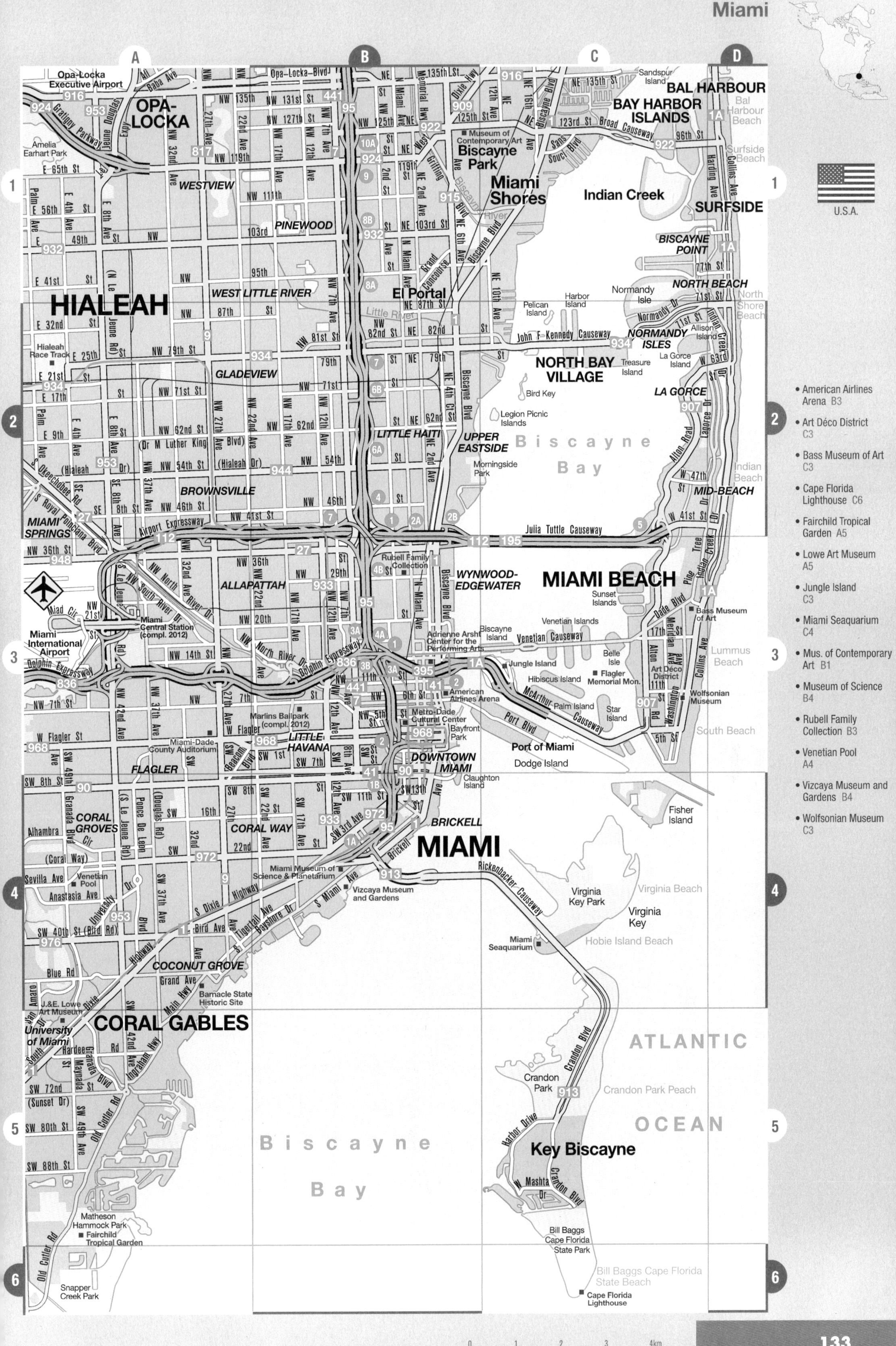
U.S.A.
A
B
C
D
1
2
3
4
5
6
Opa-Locka Executive Airport
OPA-LOCKA
Amelia Earhart Park
WESTVIEW
PINEWOOD
HIALEAH
Hialeah Race Track
WEST LITTLE RIVER
GLADEVIEW
El Portal
Little River
Museum of Contemporary Art
Biscayne Park
Miami Shores
Sandspur Island
BAL HARBOUR
Bal Harbour Beach
BAY HARBOR ISLANDS
Indian Creek
SURFSIDE
Surfside Beach
BISCAYNE POINT
NORTH BEACH
North Shore Beach
Normandy Isle
NORMANDY ISLES
Allison Island
Pelican Island
Harbor Island
John F Kennedy Causeway
NORTH BAY VILLAGE
Treasure Island
La Gorce Island
LA GORCE
Bird Key
Legion Picnic Islands
LITTLE HAITI
UPPER EASTSIDE
Biscayne Bay
Morningside Park
Indian Beach
MID-BEACH
BROWNSVILLE
MIAMI SPRINGS
Julia Tuttle Causeway
Airport Expressway
ALLAPATTAH
Rubell Family Collection
WYNWOOD-EDGEWATER
MIAMI BEACH
Sunset Islands
Venetian Islands
Bass Museum of Art
Miami International Airport
Miami Central Station (compl. 2012)
Adrienne Arsht Center for the Performing Arts
Biscayne Island
Venetian Causeway
Belle Isle
Lummus Beach
Jungle Island
Flagler Memorial Mon.
Hibiscus Island
Art Déco District
American Airlines Arena
Palm Island
Star Island
Wolfsonian Museum
McArthur Causeway
Metro-Dade Cultural Center
Bayfront Park
Marlins Ballpark (compl. 2012)
Miami-Dade County Auditorium
LITTLE HAVANA
Port Blvd
Port of Miami
Dodge Island
South Beach
FLAGLER
DOWNTOWN MIAMI
Claughton Island
Fisher Island
CORAL GROVES
CORAL WAY
BRICKELL
MIAMI
Rickenbacker Causeway
Venetian Pool
Miami Museum of Science & Planetarium
Vizcaya Museum and Gardens
Virginia Key Park
Virginia Beach
Virginia Key
Miami Seaquarium
Hobie Island Beach
COCONUT GROVE
Barnacle State Historic Site
J.&E. Lowe Art Museum
University of Miami
CORAL GABLES
ATLANTIC OCEAN
Crandon Park
Crandon Park Peach
Crandon Blvd
Harbor Drive
Key Biscayne
Matheson Hammock Park
Fairchild Tropical Garden
Bill Baggs Cape Florida State Park
Bill Baggs Cape Florida State Beach
Cape Florida Lighthouse
Snapper Creek Park
0 1 2 3 4km
0 0.5 1 1.5 2 2.5miles
• American Airlines Arena B3
• Art Déco District C3
• Bass Museum of Art C3
• Cape Florida Lighthouse C6
• Fairchild Tropical Garden A5
• Lowe Art Museum A5
• Jungle Island C3
• Miami Seaquarium C4
• Mus. of Contemporary Art B1
• Museum of Science B4
• Rubell Family Collection B3
• Venetian Pool A4
• Vizcaya Museum and Gardens B4
• Wolfsonian Museum C3

Miami

Eastern Standard Time

U.S.A.

- Bayfront Park C5
- Challenger Memorial C5
- Federal Building B-C5
- Flagler State Building B4
- Freedom Tower C4
- Gusman Center C5
- Historic Museum of South Florida C2
- Metro-Dade Cultural Center B5
- Miami Art Museum B5
- Miami Herald Building C3
- Omni Internacional Mall C3
- Teatro Marti A5
- Warner House B5

0 200 400 600 800m
0 0.25 0.5miles

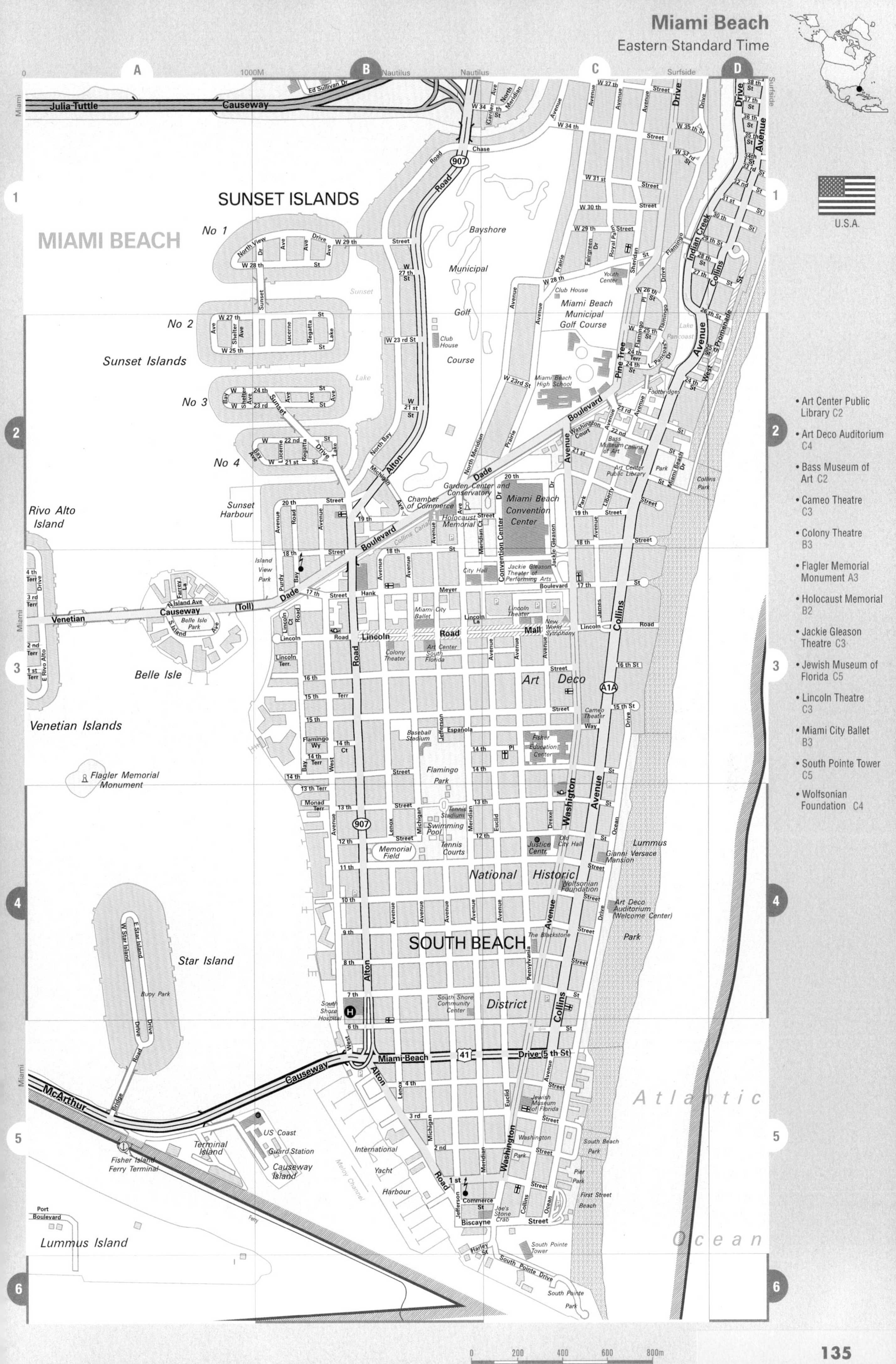
Miami Beach
Eastern Standard Time
U.S.A.
A
B
C
D
1
2
3
4
5
6
0
1000M
Nautilus
Surfside
Miami
MIAMI BEACH
SUNSET ISLANDS
No 1
No 2
No 3
No 4
Sunset Islands
Sunset Harbour
Rivo Alto Island
Belle Isle
Venetian Islands
Venetian Causeway
Flagler Memorial Monument
Star Island
Buoy Park
Julia Tuttle Causeway
McArthur Causeway
Miami Beach Drive (5 th St)
Terminal Island
US Coast Guard Station
Causeway Island
Fisher Island Ferry Terminal
International Yacht Harbour
Lummus Island
Port Boulevard
Bayshore Municipal Golf Course
Miami Beach Municipal Golf Course
Club House
Youth Center
Miami Beach High School
Garden Center and Conservatory
Chamber of Commerce
Holocaust Memorial
Miami Beach Convention Center
City Hall
Jackie Gleason Theater of Performing Arts
Lincoln Theater
Miami City Ballet
Colony Theater
Art Center South Florida
New World Symphony
Lincoln Road Mall
Bass Museum of Art
Art Center Public Library
Collins Park
Art Deco
National Historic District
SOUTH BEACH
Cameo Theater
Fisher Education Center
Flamingo Park
Tennis Stadium
Swimming Pool
Tennis Courts
Memorial Field
Baseball Stadium
Justice Centr.
Old City Hall
Gianni Versace Mansion
Wolfsonian Foundation
Art Deco Auditorium (Welcome Center)
Lummus Park
The Blackstone
South Shore Community Center
South Shore Hospital
Jewish Museum of Florida
Washington Park
South Beach Park
First Street Beach
Joe's Stone Crab
South Pointe Tower
South Pointe Park
South Pointe Drive
Atlantic Ocean
Collins Avenue
Washington Avenue
Alton Road
Dade Boulevard
Indian Creek Drive
Lake Pancoast
Collins Canal
Footbridges
907
41
A1A
0 200 400 600 800m
0 0.25 0.5miles
• Art Center Public Library C2
• Art Deco Auditorium C4
• Bass Museum of Art C2
• Cameo Theatre C3
• Colony Theatre B3
• Flagler Memorial Monument A3
• Holocaust Memorial B2
• Jackie Gleason Theatre C3
• Jewish Museum of Florida C5
• Lincoln Theatre C3
• Miami City Ballet B3
• South Pointe Tower C5
• Wolfsonian Foundation C4

Montréal

Eastern Standard Time

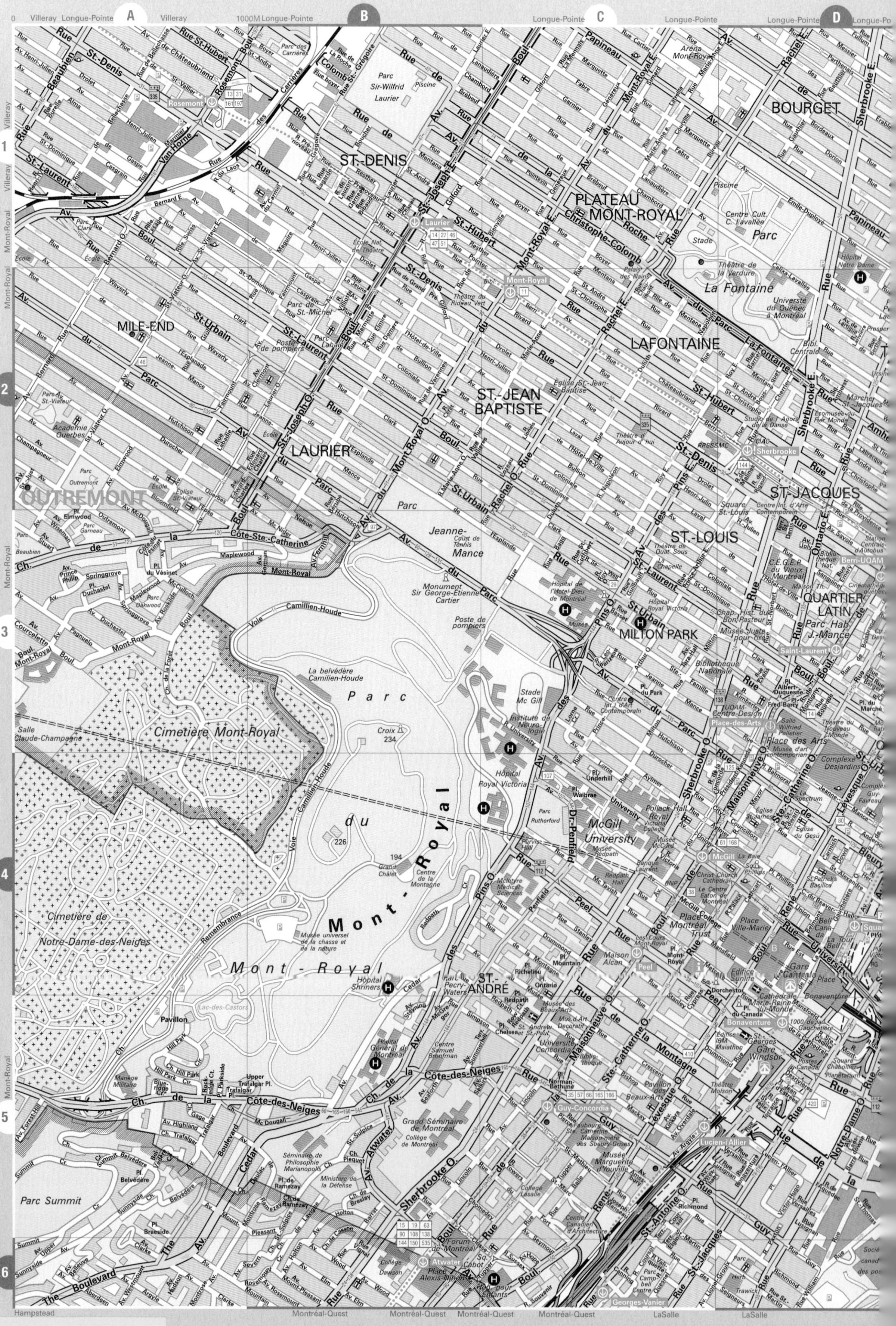

A
B
C
D
1
2
3
4
5
6
Villeray
Longue-Pointe
Mont-Royal
Hampstead
Montréal-Quest
LaSalle
ST.-DENIS
BOURGET
PLATEAU MONT-ROYAL
LA FONTAINE
LAFONTAINE
MILE-END
ST.-JEAN BAPTISTE
LAURIER
OUTREMONT
ST.-JACQUES
ST.-LOUIS
QUARTIER LATIN
MILTON PARK
ST.-ANDRÉ
Parc Sir-Wilfrid Laurier
Parc Jeanne-Mance
Parc du Mont-Royal
Mont-Royal
Cimetière Mont-Royal
Cimetière de Notre-Dame-des-Neiges
Parc Summit
McGill University
Rosemont
Laurier
Mont-Royal
Sherbrooke
Berri-UQAM
Saint-Laurent
Place-des-Arts
McGill
Peel
Bonaventure
Guy-Concordia
Lucien-l'Allier
Atwater
Georges-Vanier
Croix 234
Lac-des-Castors
Pavillon
Hôpital Royal Victoria
Hôpital Général de Montréal
Gare Windsor
Complexe Desjardins

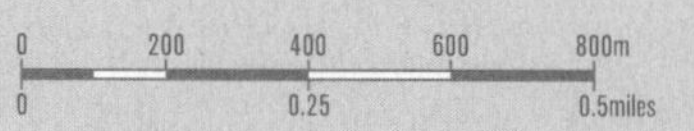

0
200
400
600
800m
0
0.25
0.5miles

- Aquarium de Montreal F2
- Basilique Notre Dame E4
- Casino de Montreal G4
- Cathédrale M.-Reine-du-Monde D5
- Centaur Théatre E4
- Centre Canadien d`Architecture C5
- Centre des sciences E4
- Chateau Ramezay E3
- Écomusée du Fier Monde D2
- Hotel de Ville E3
- La Biosphére G3
- Musée d`art contemporain D3-4
- Musée des Beaux-Arts C5
- Musée D.-M.-Stewart F2
- Musée McCord C4
- Musée Redpath C4
- Park du Mont-Royal B3-5
- Planétarium D5
- Pointe-Calliére E4
- St. Patrick`s Basilica D4

A
B
C
D
1
2
3
4
5
6
Clifton
Wood-Ridge
Ridgefield Park
Leonia
Fort Lee
Edgewater
Upper Montclair
Rutherford
Ridgefield
Carlstadt
Teterboro Airport
Little Ferry
Moonachie
South Hackensack
Fairview
Cliffside Park
NUTLEY
Lyndhurst
NORTH BERGEN
North Arlington
WEST NEW YORK
Guttenberg
Secaucus
BELLEVILLE
Weehawken
UNION CITY
KEARNY
MANHATTAN
MIDTOWN
Harrison
HOBOKEN
NEWARK
JERSEY CITY
Newark Liberty International Airport
PORT NEWARK
ELIZABETH
PORT ELIZABETH
BAYONNE
Upper Bay
Hudson River
East River
Hackensack River
Passaic River
Newark Bay
Kill Van Kull
The Narrows
Bay Ridge Channel
Statue of Liberty
Ellis Island
Governors Island
Liberty Island
St. George Ferry Terminal
MARINERS HARBOR
ST. GEORGE
BROOKLYN
Prospect Park
Green-Wood Cemetry
NEW JERSEY
NEW YORK
0 1 2 3 4km
0 0.5 1 1.5 2 2.5miles

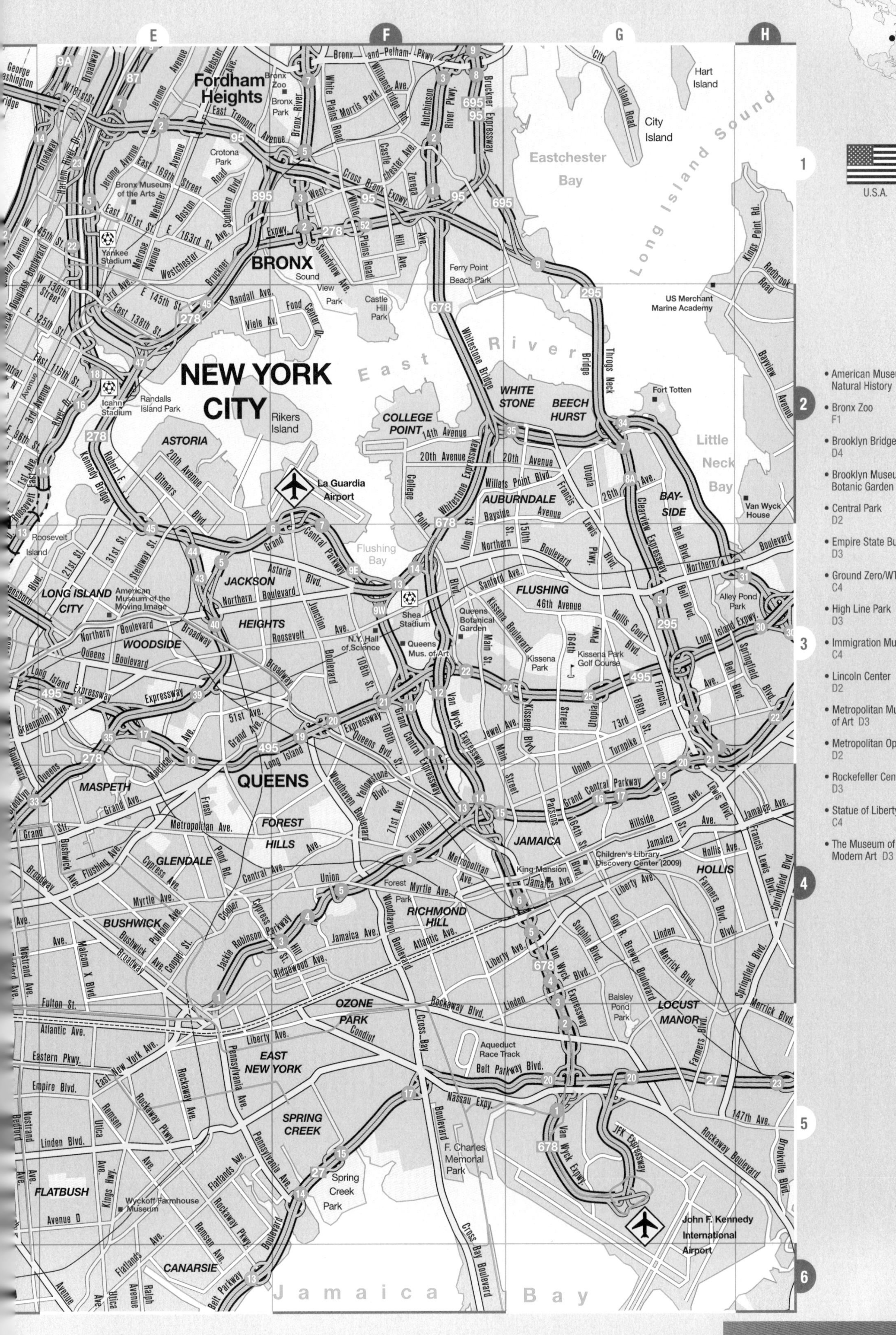

U.S.A.

- American Museum of Natural History D2
- Bronx Zoo F1
- Brooklyn Bridge D4
- Brooklyn Museum and Botanic Garden D5
- Central Park D2
- Empire State Building D3
- Ground Zero/WTC Site C4
- High Line Park D3
- Immigration Museum C4
- Lincoln Center D2
- Metropolitan Museum of Art D3
- Metropolitan Opera D2
- Rockefeller Center D3
- Statue of Liberty C4
- The Museum of Modern Art D3

New York (Lower Manhattan)
Eastern Standard Time
U.S.A.
• Battery Park A5
• Brooklyn Bridge B-C5
• Castle Clinton A5
• Chinatown B-C4
• Financial District A5
• Greenwich Village B-C2
• Guggenheim Mus. Soho B3
• Holocaust Memorial A5
• Little Italy B-C3
• Madison Square Park C1
• Museum of Am. Indians A5
• Museum of Holography B3
• Museum of Jewish Heritage A5
• New Museum of Contem. Art C3
• Soho B3
• South Str. Seaport Museum B5
• Tenement Museum C4
• Tribeca A3
• Trinity Church A5
• Wall Street A-B5
• Washington Square Park B2
• Woolworth Building A4
• World Trade Center Memorial A5
A
B
C
D
1
2
3
4
5
6
CHELSEA
GRAMERCY
LOWER GREENWICH
WEST VILLAGE
SIDE
SOHO
EAST VILLAGE
LITTLE ITALY
TRIBECA
CHINA TOWN
LOWER EAST SIDE
CIVIC CENTER
BATTERY PARK CITY (U.C.)
LOWER MANHATTAN
FINANCIAL DISTRICT
SOUTH ST SEAPORT HISTORIC DISTRICT
NEW JERSEY
NEW YORK
HUDSON CO
NEW YORK CO
KINGS CO
Holland Tunnel (Toll)
Brooklyn Battery Tunnel (Toll)
Brooklyn Bridge
Manhattan Bridge (2 Levels)
Pier 17 Pavilion
42
Staten Island Ferry Terminal
Downtown Manhattan Heliport
1 Edgar Street
2 Marketfield Street
3 Hanover Street
4 Coenties Alley Slip
5 Moore Street
6 Gouverneur Lane
7 Vine Street
8 Mc Kenny Street
9 Elizabeth Place
10 Howard Alley
Brooklyn
Carrol Gardens
Boerum Hill
Murray Hill
East Village
Clinton
0
200
400
600
800m
0.25
0.5miles
140

New York (Central Manhattan)

Eastern Standard Time

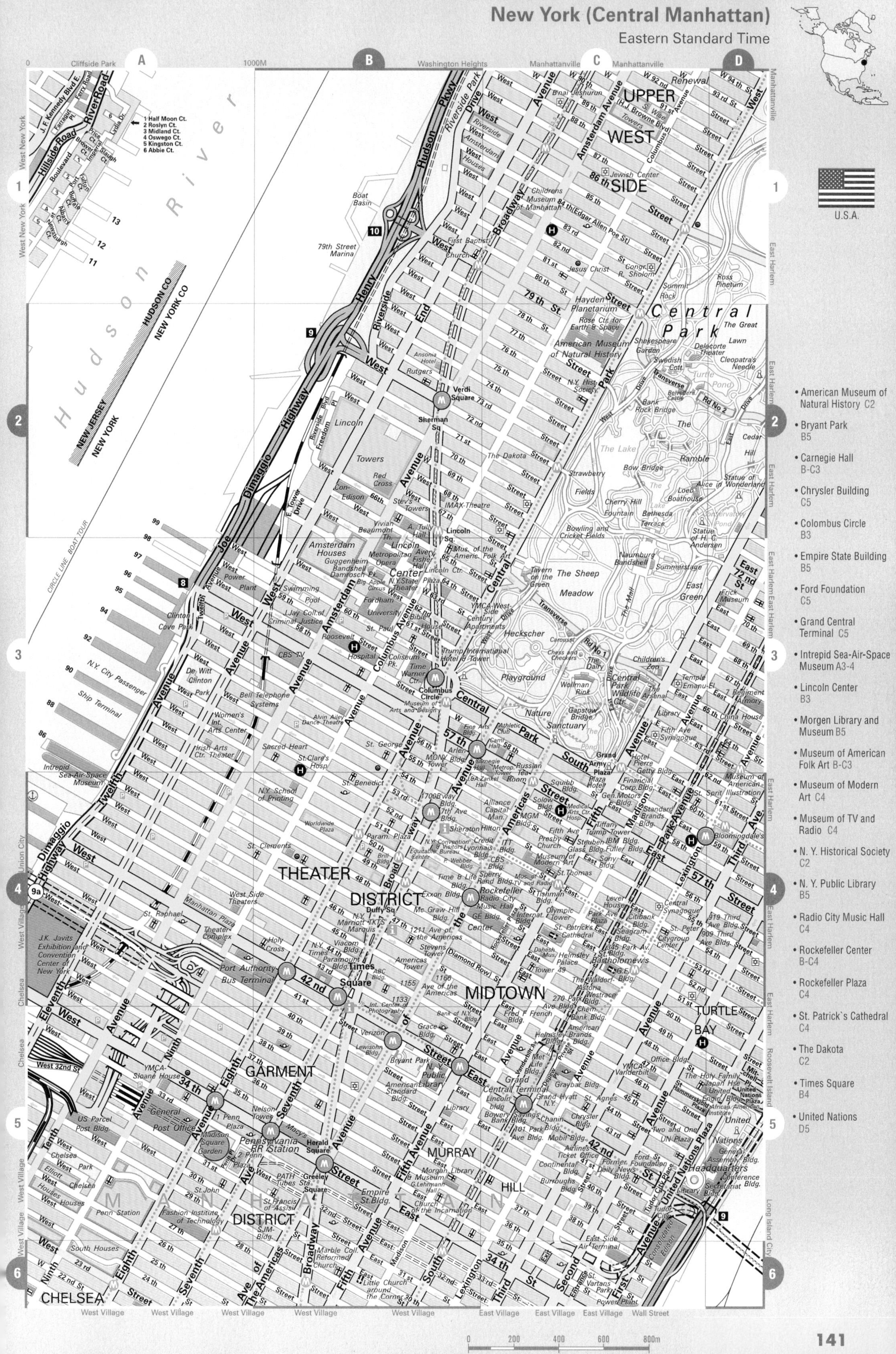

- American Museum of Natural History C2
- Bryant Park B5
- Carnegie Hall B-C3
- Chrysler Building C5
- Colombus Circle B3
- Empire State Building B5
- Ford Foundation C5
- Grand Central Terminal C5
- Intrepid Sea-Air-Space Museum A3-4
- Lincoln Center B3
- Morgen Library and Museum B5
- Museum of American Folk Art B-C3
- Museum of Modern Art C4
- Museum of TV and Radio C4
- N. Y. Historical Society C2
- N. Y. Public Library B5
- Radio City Music Hall C4
- Rockefeller Center B-C4
- Rockefeller Plaza C4
- St. Patrick`s Cathedral C4
- The Dakota C2
- Times Square B4
- United Nations D5

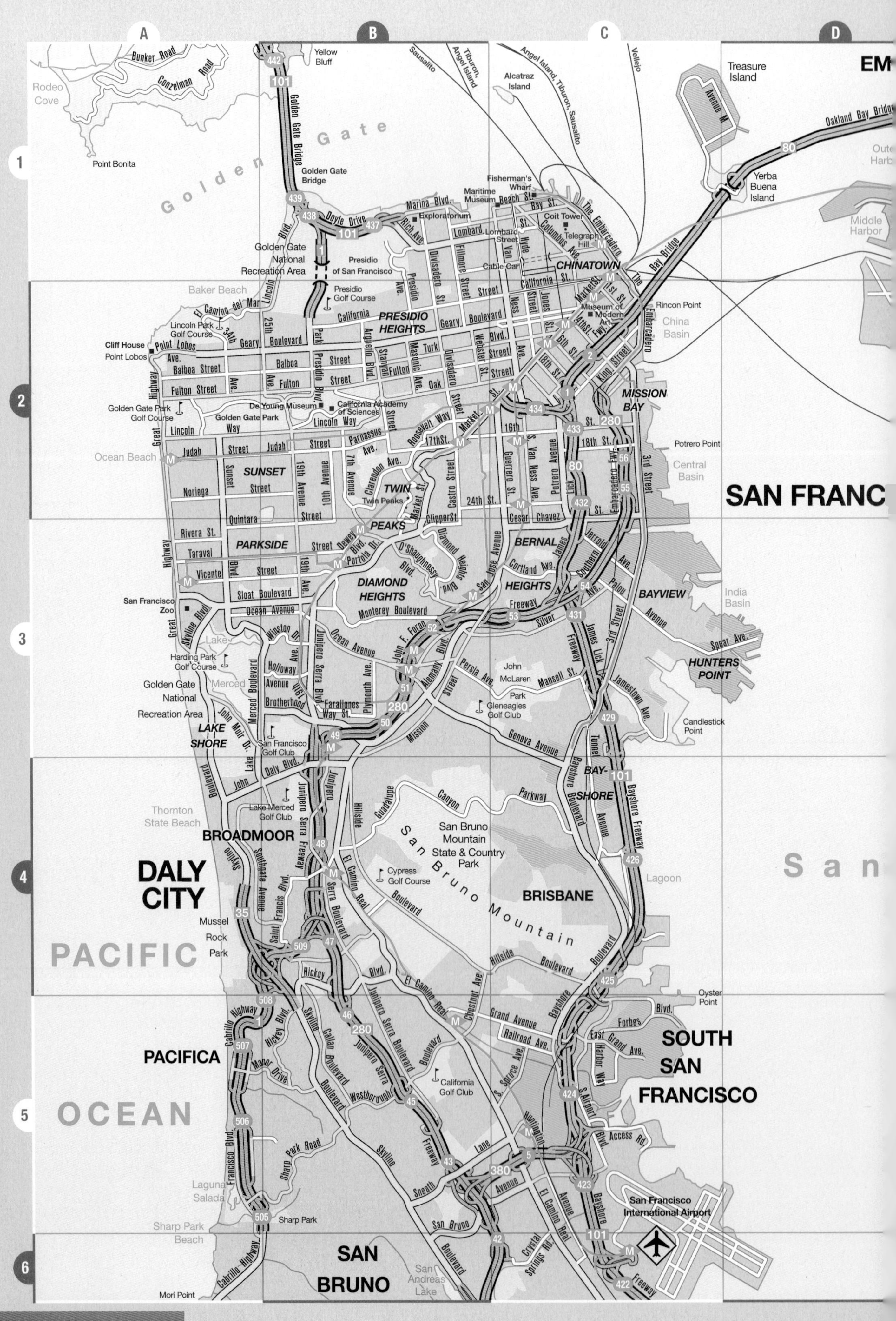

Golden Gate
Golden Gate Bridge
Presidio of San Francisco
Golden Gate National Recreation Area
Alcatraz Island
Fisherman's Wharf
Treasure Island
Yerba Buena Island
CHINATOWN
PRESIDIO HEIGHTS
MISSION BAY
SUNSET
TWIN PEAKS
PARKSIDE
DIAMOND HEIGHTS
BERNAL HEIGHTS
BAYVIEW
HUNTERS POINT
LAKE SHORE
BAY SHORE
BROADMOOR
DALY CITY
San Bruno Mountain State & Country Park
BRISBANE
PACIFIC OCEAN
PACIFICA
SOUTH SAN FRANCISCO
San Francisco International Airport
SAN BRUNO
SAN FRANC

E
F
G
H
1
2
3
4
5
6
PIEDMONT
MORAGA
OAKLAND
ALAMEDA
SAN LEANDRO
Redwood Regional Park
Upper San Leandro Reservoir
Lake Merritt
Jack London Square
Government Island
Robert Crown Mem. State Beach
Leona Heights Park
Leona Regional Open Space
Knowland State Arboretum and Park
Lake Chabot Municipal Golf Course
Lake Chabot
San Leandro Bay
Chuck Corica Golf Complex
Bay Farm Island
Western Aerospace Museum
Oakland International Airport
Metropolitan Golf Links
Oyster Bay Regional Shoreline
Mulford Landing
Monarch Bay Golf Club
Roberts Landing
Hayward Executive Airport
Hayward Landing
Johnson Landing
San Mateo - Hayward Bridge
Francisco
Bay
U.S.A.
• Alcatraz Island C1
• California Academy of Sciences B2
• Cliff House A2
• Coit Tower C1
• De Young Museum B2
• Exploratorium B1
• Fisherman's Wharf C1
• Golden Gate Bridge B1
• Golden Gate Park A2
• Lombard Street C1
• Maritime Museum C1
• Museum of Modern Art C2
• Presidio B1
• Twin Peaks B2

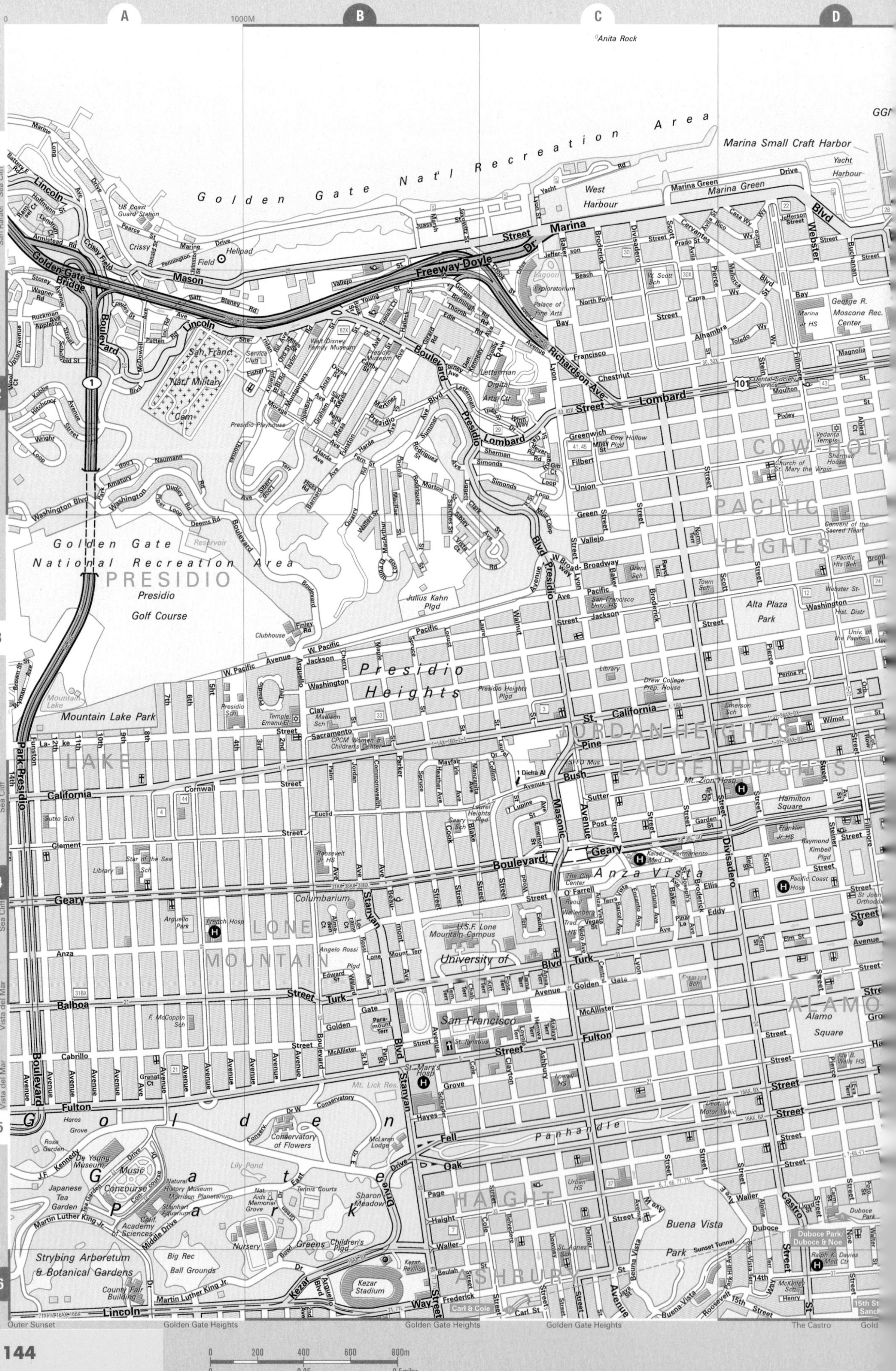
A
B
C
D
0
1000M
1
2
3
4
5
6
Anita Rock
Golden Gate Nat'l Recreation Area
Marina Small Craft Harbor
Yacht Harbour
West Harbour
Marina Green
Crissy Field
Hellpad
US Coast Guard Station
Golden Gate Bridge
Mason
Freeway-Doyle Dr.
Marina
Lincoln
Boulevard
Richardson Ave
Lombard
Chestnut
Francisco
Bay
North Point
Beach
Lagoon
Exploratorium
Palace of Fine Arts
San Franc. Nat'l Military Cem
Walt Disney Family Museum
Presidio Museum
Presidio Playhouse
Letterman Digital Arts Ctr
Presidio Blvd
Golden Gate National Recreation Area
PRESIDIO
Presidio Golf Course
Reservoir
Julius Kahn Plgd
Mountain Lake Park
Mountain Lake
Park-Presidio
Presidio Heights
Presidio Heights Plgd
Temple Emanu-El
CPCM Women & Children's Center
JORDAN HEIGHTS
LAUREL HEIGHTS
LAKE
COW HOLLOW
PACIFIC HEIGHTS
Alta Plaza Park
Lafayette
George R. Moscone Rec. Center
Marina Jr HS
Dental-Society Service
Cow Hollow Plgd
Church of St. Mary the Virgin
Convent of the Sacred Heart
Pacific Hts Sch
Webster St-Hist. Distr
Univ. of the Pacific
San Francisco Univ. HS
Drew College Prep. House
Library
Emerson Sch
Town Sch
Grant Sch
Mt. Zion Hosp
Hamilton Square
Franklin Jr HS
Raymond Kimbell Plgd
Pacific Coast Hosp
St John Orthodox
SFFD Mus
Laurel Heights Plgd
Geary Sch
Masonic Avenue
Geary Boulevard
Kaiser - Permanente Med Ctr
The City Center
Anza Vista
Divisadero
California
Clement
Geary
Anza
Balboa
Cabrillo
Fulton
Sutro Sch
Star of the Sea Sch
Roosevelt Jr HS
Arguello Park
French Hosp
LONE MOUNTAIN
Columbarium
Angelo Rossi Plgd
Edward Plgd
U.S.F. Lone Mountain Campus
University of San Francisco
St. Ignatius
F. McCoppin Sch
Turk
Golden Gate
McAllister
Stanyan Blvd
St. Mary's Hosp
Lowell HS
Mt. Lick Res.
Dept of Motor Vehic
Panhandle
ALAMO
Alamo Square
Ida B. Wells HS
Golden Gate Park
Conservatory
Conservatory of Flowers
McLaren Lodge
Lily Pond
De Young Museum
Music Concourse
Natural History Museum
Morrison Planetarium
Steinhart Aquarium
Calif. Academy Sciences
Japanese Tea Garden
Rose Garden
Heros Grove
J.F. Kennedy Drive
Martin Luther King Jr.
Middle Drive
Nat. Aids Memorial Grove
Tennis Courts
Sharon Meadow
Children's Plgd
Nursery
Strybing Arboretum & Botanical Gardens
Big Rec Ball Grounds
County Fair Building
Kezar Stadium
Kezar Pavilion
Kezar Dr.
Lincoln Way
Urban HS
HAIGHT ASHBURY
Haight
Page
Waller
Frederick
Oak
Fell
Hayes
Grove
Buena Vista Park
Sunset Tunnel
Duboce
Duboce Park / Duboce & Noe
Ralph K. Davies Med Ctr
McKinley Sch
Castro
14th
15th Street
Carl & Cole
Carl St
Outer Sunset
Golden Gate Heights
The Castro
Sea Cliff
San Rafael
Vista del Mar
0 200 400 600 800m
0 0.25 0.5miles

U.S.A.
• Aquatic Park E1
• Asian Art Museum F4
• Cable Car Museum F3
• California Academy of Science A5
• Coit Tower G2
• Colombus Tower G2
• De Young Museum A5
• Exploratorium C2
• Fischerman´s Wharf E-F1
• Fort Mason Center D1
• Golden Gate Park A-B5
• Morrison Planetarium A5
• Museum of City of San Francisco E1
• Museum of Modern Art G3-4
• Museum of World Records F1
• Natural History Museum A5
• National Maritime Museum E1
• Pacific Heritage Museum G3
• Palace of Fine Arts C2
• Presidio A3
• San Francisco Art Institute E-F2
• Steinhart Aquarium A5
• The Cannery E1

0 200 400 600 800m

0 0.25 0.5miles

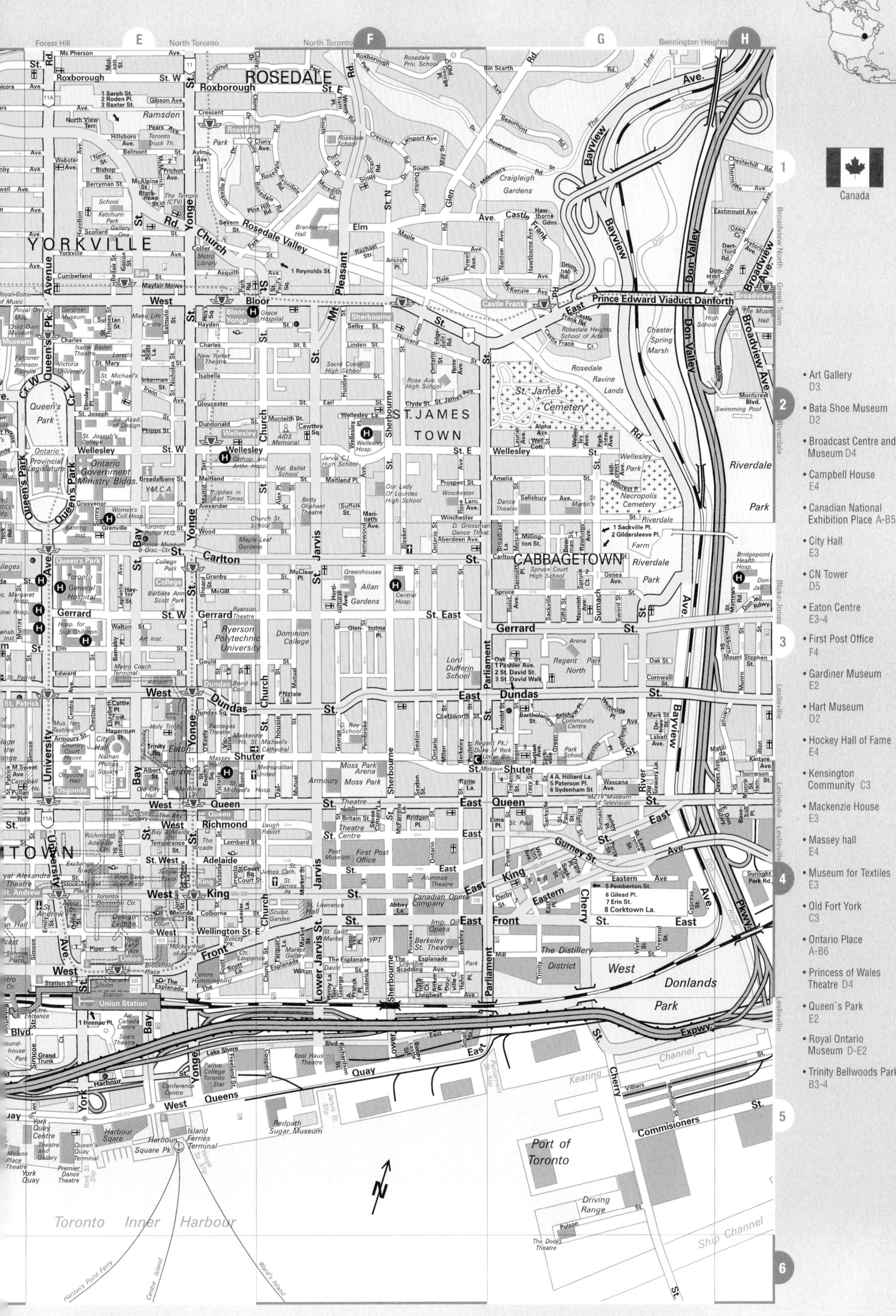
Canada
• Art Gallery D3
• Bata Shoe Museum D2
• Broadcast Centre and Museum D4
• Campbell House E4
• Canadian National Exhibition Place A-B5
• City Hall E3
• CN Tower D5
• Eaton Centre E3-4
• First Post Office F4
• Gardiner Museum E2
• Hart Museum D2
• Hockey Hall of Fame E4
• Kensington Community C3
• Mackenzie House E3
• Massey hall E4
• Museum for Textiles E3
• Old Fort York C3
• Ontario Place A-B6
• Princess of Wales Theatre D4
• Queen`s Park E2
• Royal Ontario Museum D-E2
• Trinity Bellwoods Park B3-4
ROSEDALE
YORKVILLE
ST. JAMES TOWN
CABBAGETOWN
Forest Hill
North Toronto
Bennington Heights
Craigleigh Gardens
Queen's Park
Allan Gardens
Riverdale Park
Donlands Park
Port of Toronto
Union Station
Toronto Inner Harbour
Ship Channel
Prince Edward Viaduct Danforth
Don Valley
St. James Cemetery
Necropolis Cemetery
Regent Park North
The Distillery District
Ryerson Polytechnic University
Toronto General Hospital
Ontario Government Ministry Bldgs.
Ontario Provincial Legislature

A
B
C
D
1
2
3
4
5
6
Cypress Provincial Park
Bowen Island
Gambier Island
Nanaimo
HORSESHOE BAY
Whytecliff Park
GLENEAGLES
Marine Drive
Trans-Canada
EAGLE HARBOUR
CYPRESS PARK
SANDY COVE
Lighthouse Park
Eagle Lake
Cypress Creek
Cypress Bowl Road
Highway
WEST BAY
Chippendale Road
DUNDARAVE
WEST VANCOUVER
PARK ROYAL
Ambleside Park
Capilano Lake
Grouse Mountain 1231
BRITISH PROPERTIES
Capilano Golf and Country Club
Capilano Suspension Bridge
FOREST HILLS
CAPILANO HIGHLANDS
Montroyal
Marine Drive
NORGATE
NORTH VANCOUVER
KEITH-LYNN
Lions Gate Bridge
Stanley Park
Vancouver Aquarium
Burrard Inlet
Vancouver Harbour
Lost Lagoon
COAL HARBOUR
Canada Place
GASTOWN
Strait of
Georgia
VANCOUVER
WEST END
DOWNTOWN
English Bay
Maritime Museum
Mus. of Vancouver
KITS POINT
Art Gallery
Vancouver Lookout
Police Mus.
Dr.S.Yat-Sen Classical Chinese Garden
Science World
Granville I.
FAIRVIEW
Jericho Park
UBC Museum of Anthropology
UNIVERSITY HILL
WEST POINT GREY
KITSILANO
POINT GREY
Pacific Spirit Regional Park
UBC Endowment Lands Ecological Reserve
DUNBAR
SLAUGHNESSY
Van Dusen Botanical Gardens
Queen Elizabeth Park
RILEY PARK
GRANDVIEW WOODLAND
KENSINGTON COTTAGE
John Hendry Park
KERRISDALE
Eaglequest at Musqueam Golf Club
McCleery Golf Course
OAKRIDGE
SUNSET
Langara Golf Course
MARPOLE
Sea Island
Mitchell Island
Vancouver International Airport
Grant MacConachie Way
Miller Road
BURKEVILLE
Russ Baker Way
Arthur Laing Bridge
Oak Street Bridge
Bridgeport
Cambie
Alderbridge
Number 4 Way
Lansdowne Rd.
Garden City Lands
River Road
THOMPSON
Westminster
BRIGHOUSE
RICHMOND
LULU ISLAND
Terra Nova Rural Park
Quilchena Golf & Country Club
Granville Avenue
0 1 2 3 4km
0 0.5 1 1.5 2 2.5miles

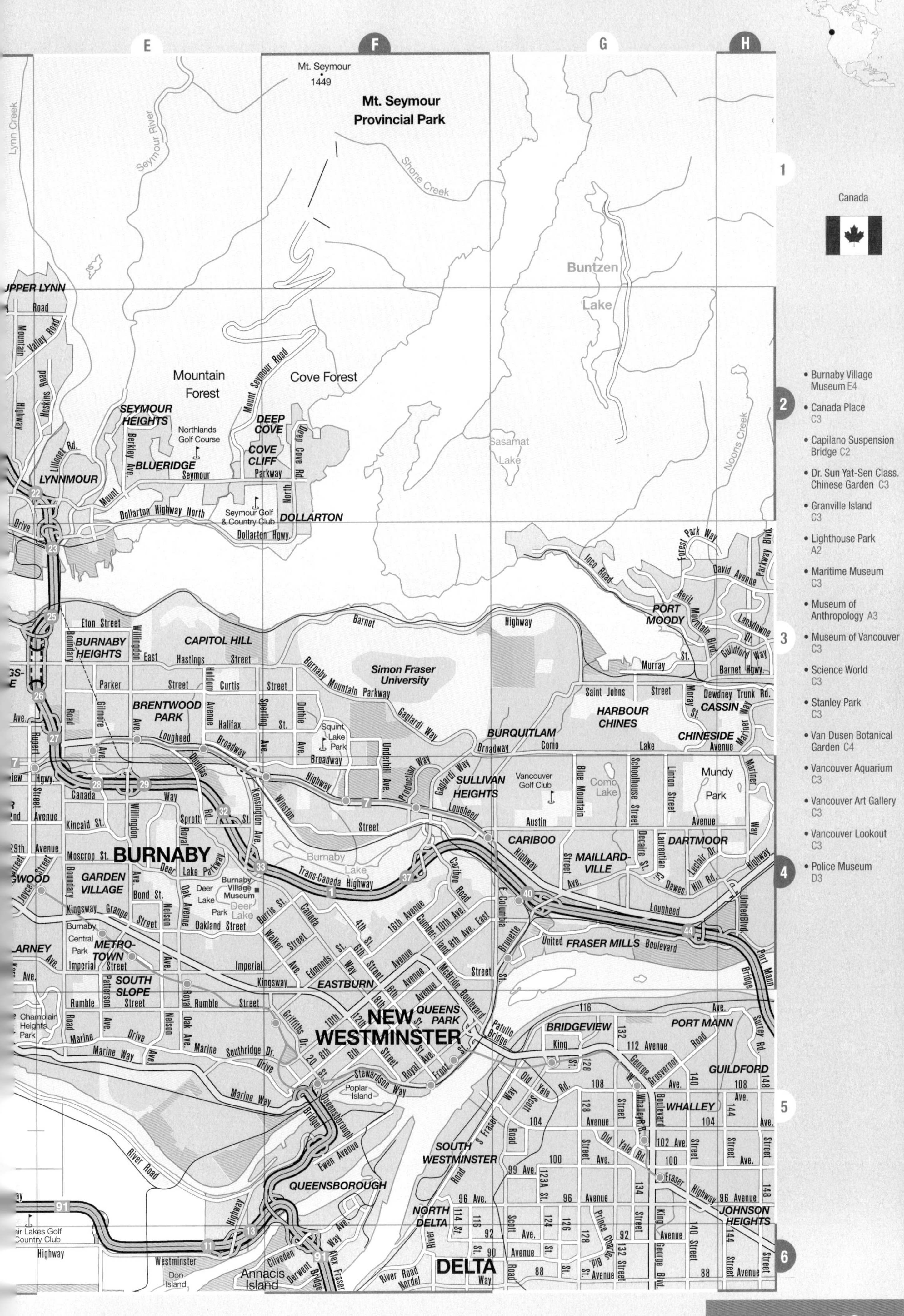

Canada

- Burnaby Village Museum E4
- Canada Place C3
- Capilano Suspension Bridge C2
- Dr. Sun Yat-Sen Class. Chinese Garden C3
- Granville Island C3
- Lighthouse Park A2
- Maritime Museum C3
- Museum of Anthropology A3
- Museum of Vancouver C3
- Science World C3
- Stanley Park C3
- Van Dusen Botanical Garden C4
- Vancouver Aquarium C3
- Vancouver Art Gallery C3
- Vancouver Lookout C3
- Police Museum D3

Vancouver

Pacific Standard Time

Stanley Park

West End

Downtown

Yaletown

Fairview

Granville Island

English Bay

Coal Harbour

Deadman's Island

1 Roundhouse Mews
2 Aquarius Mews
3 Boathouse Mews
4 Cooper's Mews

0 200 400 600 800m
0 0.25 0.5miles

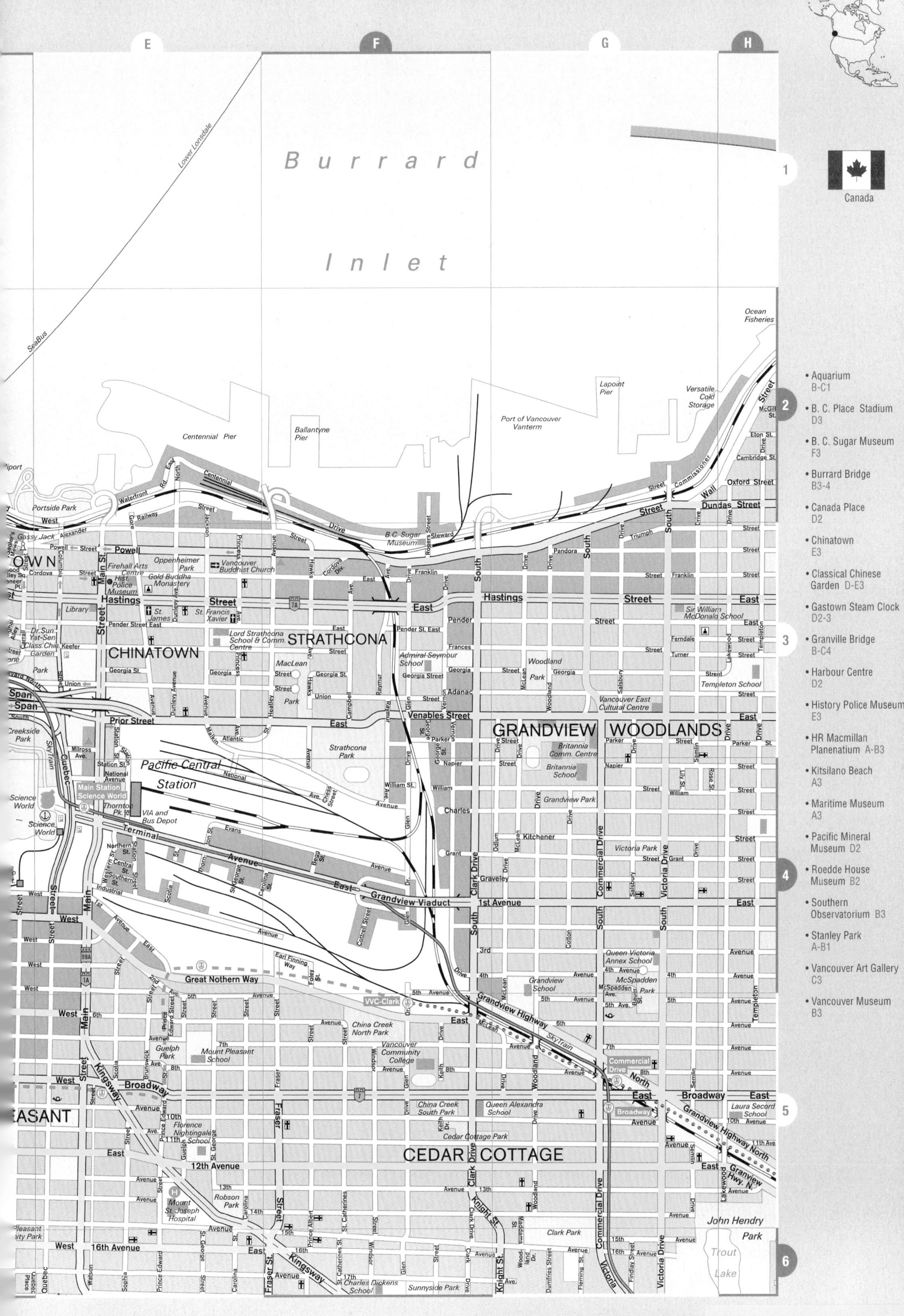
E
F
G
H
1
2
3
4
5
6
Canada
Burrard Inlet
Lower Lonsdale
SeaBus
Ocean Fisheries
Lapoint Pier
Versatile Cold Storage
Port of Vancouver Vanterm
Ballantyne Pier
Centennial Pier
Portside Park
B.C. Sugar Museum
CHINATOWN
STRATHCONA
GRANDVIEW WOODLANDS
CEDAR COTTAGE
Pacific Central Station
VIA and Bus Depot
Main Station Science World
Science World
Strathcona Park
MacLean Park
Lord Strathcona School & Comm. Centre
Admiral Seymour School
Oppenheimer Park
Vancouver Buddhist Church
Firehall Arts Centre
Hist. Police Museum
Gold Buddha Monastery
Library
Dr.Sun Yat-Sen Class.Chin. Garden
Sir William McDonald School
Templeton School
Vancouver East Cultural Centre
Britannia Comm. Centre
Britannia School
Grandview Park
Woodland Park
Victoria Park
Queen Victoria Annex School
McSpadden Park
Grandview School
China Creek North Park
Vancouver Community College
China Creek South Park
Queen Alexandra School
Cedar Cottage Park
Laura Secord School
John Hendry Park
Trout Lake
Clark Park
Sunnyside Park
Charles Dickens School
Robson Park
Mount St. Joseph Hospital
Florence Nightingale School
Mount Pleasant School
Guelph Park
Great Northern Way
Grandview Viaduct
Grandview Highway
Hastings Street
Broadway
Kingsway
Commercial Drive
Clark Drive
Victoria Drive
Main Street
VVC-Clark
Commercial Drive
Broadway
• Aquarium B-C1
• B. C. Place Stadium D3
• B. C. Sugar Museum F3
• Burrard Bridge B3-4
• Canada Place D2
• Chinatown E3
• Classical Chinese Garden D-E3
• Gastown Steam Clock D2-3
• Granville Bridge B-C4
• Harbour Centre D2
• History Police Museum E3
• HR Macmillan Planenatium A-B3
• Kitsilano Beach A3
• Maritime Museum A3
• Pacific Mineral Museum D2
• Roedde House Museum B2
• Southern Observatorium B3
• Stanley Park A-B1
• Vancouver Art Gallery C3
• Vancouver Museum B3

Washington D.C.

Eastern Standard Time

Edgewood · Ivy City · Carver/Langston · Stanton Park · Fort Totten · Pleasant Plains · Crestwood · Mt. Pleasant · Adams Morgan · Woodley Park · Lanier Heights · Georgetown · Rosslyn

A · B · C · D · 1 · 2 · 3 · 4 · 5 · 6

DOBBINS ADDITION · LE DROIT PARK · ECKINGTON · BLOOMINGDALE · NORTH WEST · DOWNTOWN · FEDERAL TRIANGLE · The Mall · The White House · The Ellipse · Union Station · U.S. Capitol · Washington Monument · Constitution Gardens · West Potomac Park · Lincoln Memorial · John F. Kennedy Center · Watergate Complex · George Washington University · State Department · Howard University Hospital · Shaw-Howard Univ. · Mt.Vernon Sq./7th St.-Convention Center · Gallery Place-Chinatown · Judiciary Square · Metro Center · McPherson Sq. · Farragut North · Farragut West · Dupont Circle · Foggy Bottom - GWVU · U St/African-Amer Civ. War Mem./Cardozo · Logan Circle · Thomas Circle · Scott Circle · Washington Circle · Sheridan Circle · Oak Hill Cemetery · Rock Creek · Georgetown Channel · Theodore Roosevelt Memorial Bridge · Whitehurst Freeway

0 200 400 600 800m

0 0.25 0.5miles

U.S.A.

- Constitution Hall D4
- Hirshhorn Mus. a. Nat. Sculpture Garden D2-3
- Jefferson Memorial E4
- J. F. Kennedy Center for the Perf. Arts C5
- Library of Congress D1
- Lincoln Memorial D4
- National Gallery of Arts D2
- National Museum of the American Indian D2
- National Museum of Women in the Arts C3
- Pentagon F5-6
- Smithsonian Nat. Air and Space Museum D2
- Supreme Court D1
- The Mall D3
- The White House C4
- United States Capitol D1
- U. S. Holocaust Memorial Museum D3
- Washington Monument D4

Seattle

Pacific Standard Time

U.S.A.

- Asian Art Museum D1
- Children's Museum A2
- Experience Music and Science Fiction Mus. A2
- Klondike Gold Rush Nat. Historical Park B4
- Municipal Tower B4
- Pacific Science Center A2
- Pioneer Square B4
- Seattle Aquarium A3-4
- Seattle Art Museum B3-4
- Seattle University C3
- Seattle Waterfall Garden Park B4
- Space Needle A2
- Volunteer Park CD1

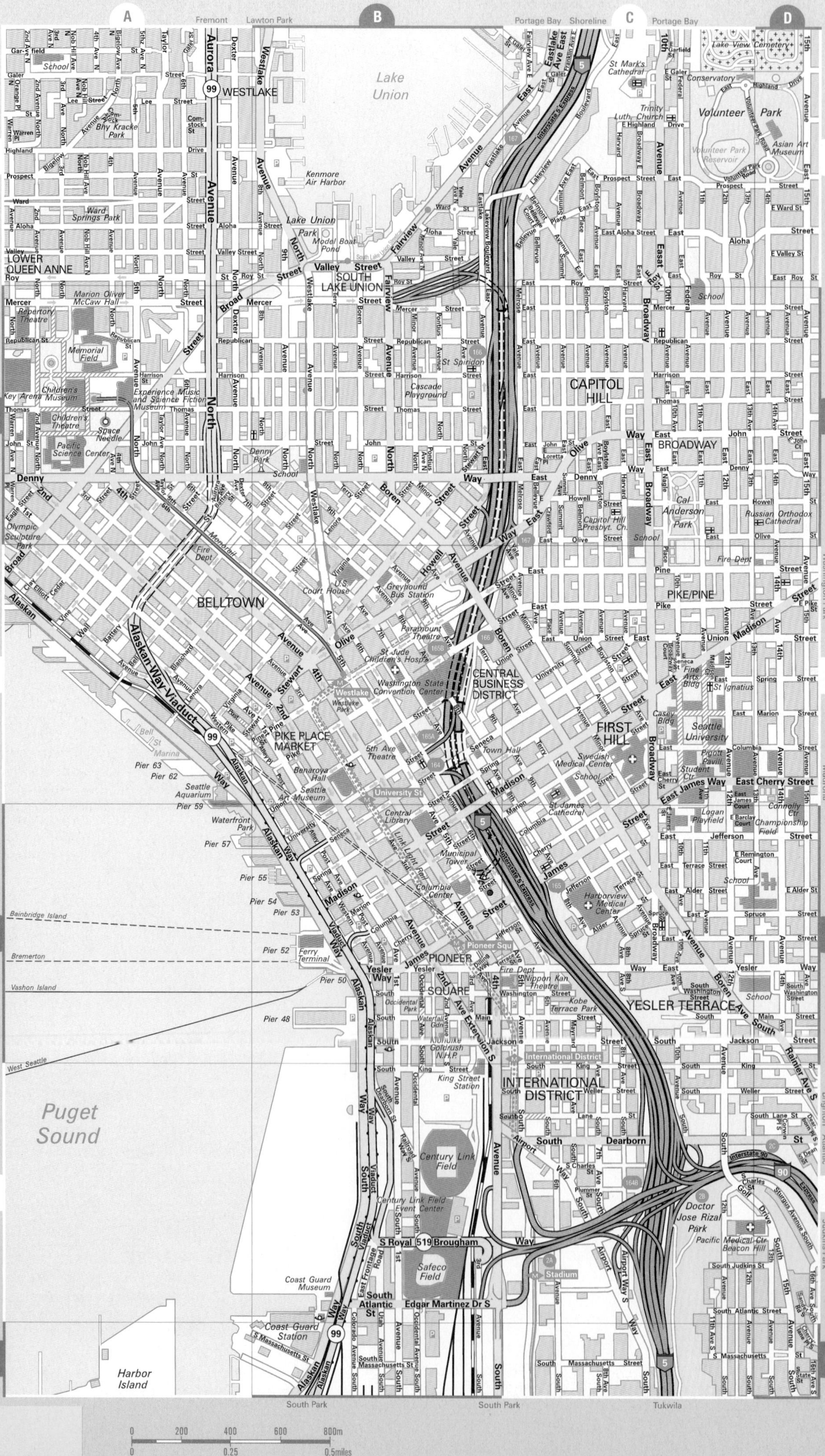

Index of names | Index des noms | Namenverzeichnis | Namenregister
Elenco dei nomi | Índice de nombres | Navnefortegnelse | Namnsförteckning
Skorowidz nazw | Rejstřík jmen | Névjegyzék | Указатель населённых пунктов

①	②	③	④	⑤	⑥
Abbeville		USA	(AL)	**36**	**Qc30**
Acadia National Park	☆	USA	(ME)	**22**	**Ra23**

	①	②	③	④	⑤	⑥
GB	Name	Place of interest	Nation	Administrative unit	Page number	Grid search reference
F	Nom	Curiosité	Nation	Circonscription administrative	Numéro de page	Coordonnées
D	Name	Sehenswürdigkeit	Nation	Verwaltungseinheit	Seitenzahl	Suchfeld
NL	Naam	Bezienswaardigheid	Natie	Administratieve eenheid	Paginanummer	Zoekveld-gegevens
I	Nome	Curiosità	Nazione	Circondario amministrativo	Numero di pagina	Riquadro nel quale si trova il nome
E	Nombre	Curiosidad	Nación	Unidad administrativa	Número de página	Coordenadas de la casilla de localización
DK	Navn	Seværdighed	Folkeslag	Administrativ enhed	Sidetal	Kvadratangivelse
S	Namn	Sevärdhet	Nationalitet	Förvaltningsområde	Sidnummer	Kartrutangivelse
PL	Nazwa	Interesujący obiekt	Naród	Jednostka administracyjna	Numer strony	Współrzędne skorowidzowe
CZ	Název	Pozoruhodnost	Národ	Administrační jednotka	Číslo strany	Údaje hledacího čtverce
H	Név	Látványosság	Nemzet	Közigazgatási egység	Oldalszám	Keresőadat
RUS	Имя населённого пункта	Достопримечательность	Национальность	Федеративное государство, провинция	Число страниц	Указатель индексного поля

③

	BG	BS	CDN	F	GB	MEX	USA
GB	Bahamas	Cuba	Canada	France	United Kingdom	Mexico	United States
F	Bahamas	Cuba	Canada	France	Royaume-Uni	Mexique	États-Unis
D	Bahamas	Kuba	Kanada	Frankreich	Royaume-Uni	Mexiko	Vereinigte Staaten
NL	Bahama's	Cuba	Canada	Frankrijk	Verenigd Koninkrijk	Mexico	Verenigde Staten
I	Bahamas	Cuba	Canada	Francia	Regno Unito	Messico	Stati Uniti
E	Bahamas	Cuba	Canadá	Francia	Reino Unido	México	Estados Unidos
DK	Bahamas	Cuba	Canada	Frankrig	Storbritannien	México	Amerikas Forenede Stater
S	Bahamas	Kuba	Kanada	Frankrike	Storbritannien	Mexiko	Förenta staterna
PL	Bahamy	Kuba	Kanada	Francja	Wielka Brytania	Meksyk	Stany Zjednoczone
CZ	Bahamy	Kuba	Kanada	Francie	Spojené království	Mexiko	Spojené státy americké
H	Bahama-szigetek	Kuba	Kanada	Franciaország	Nagy-Britannia	Mexikó	Amerikai Egyesült Államok
RUS	Багамы	Куба	Канада	Франция	Великобритания	Мексика	Соединённые Штаты Америки

1

1 de Mayo (MEX) (COA) 40 Pe32
18 de Marzo (MEX) (TAM) 40 Pg33

A

Abasolo (MEX) (DGO) 39 Pc33
Abasolo (MEX) (TAM) 40 Pf33
Abbeville (USA) (AL) 36 Qc30
Abbeville (USA) (GA) 37 Qd30
Abbeville (USA) (LA) 36 Pj31
Abbeville (USA) (SC) 37 Qd28
Abbey (CDN) (SAS) 17 Pa20
Abbotsford (CDN) (BC) 16 Od21
Abbotsford (USA) (WI) 27 Pk23
Abercrombie (USA) (ND) 27 Pg22
Aberdeen (CDN) (SAS) 18 Pb19
Aberdeen (USA) (MD) 29 Qg26
Aberdeen (USA) (MS) 36 Qa29
Aberdeen (USA) (OH) 29 Qd26
Aberdeen (USA) (SD) 26 Pf23
Aberdeen (USA) (WA) 24 Od22
Abernathy (USA) (TX) 34 Pe29
Abernethy (CDN) (SAS) 18 Pd20
Abilene (USA) (KS) 35 Pg26
Abilene (USA) (TX) 35 Pf29
Abingdon (USA) (VA) 37 Qd27
Abiquiu (USA) (NM) 34 Pb27
Abrams (USA) (WI) 28 Qa23
Absaroka-Beartooth Wilderness ☆ (USA) (MT) 25 Ok23
Acadia National Park ☆ (USA) (ME) 22 Ra23
Acadian Historic Village ☆ (CDN) (NB) 22 Rc22
Acadia Valley (CDN) (ALB) 17 Ok20
Acadie Siding (CDN) (NB) 22 Rc22
Acancéh (MEX) (YUC) 42 Qa35
Acaponeta (MEX) (NAY) 39 Pc34
Accomac (USA) (VA) 31 Qh27
Acebuches (MEX) (COA) 39 Pd31
Ackerly (USA) (TX) 34 Pe29
Ackerman (USA) (MS) 36 Qa29
Acme (USA) (LA) 36 Pk30
Acme (USA) (WA) 16 Od21
Acoma (USA) (NM) 33 Pb28
Actinolite (CDN) (ONT) 29 Qg23
Acton (USA) (MT) 25 Pa23
Acton State Historic Site ☆ (USA) (TX) 35 Pg29
Acuña, Ciudad (MEX) (COA) 40 Pe31
Ada (USA) (MN) 19 Pg22
Ada (USA) (OK) 35 Pg28
Adams (USA) (MN) 27 Pj24
Adams (USA) (ND) 19 Pf21
Adams (USA) (NE) 27 Pg25
Adams (USA) (NY) 29 Qh24
Adams Lake (CDN) (BC) 16 Of20
Addis (USA) (LA) 36 Pk30
Addison (USA) (NY) 29 Qg24
Adel (USA) (GA) 37 Qd30
Aden (CDN) (ALB) 17 Ok21
Adin (USA) (CA) 24 Oe25
Adirondack Park ☆ (USA) (NY) 29 Qh23
Admiral (CDN) (SAS) 18 Pb21
Adrian (USA) (MI) 28 Qc25
Adrian (USA) (MN) 27 Ph24
Advance (USA) (MO) 36 Qa27
Aetna (CDN) (ALB) 17 Oj21
Afton (USA) (IA) 27 Ph25
Afton (USA) (OK) 35 Ph27
Agar (USA) (SD) 26 Pe23
Agassiz (CDN) (BC) 16 Oe21
Agassiz National Wildlife Refuge ☆ (USA) (MN) 19 Pg21
Agassiz Provincial Forest ☆ (CDN) (MAN) 19 Pg20
Agate (USA) (CO) 34 Pd26
Agate Fossil Beds National Monument ☆ (USA) (NE) 26 Pd24
Agawa Canyon ☆ (CDN) (ONT) 20 Qc22
Agness (USA) (OR) 24 Oc24
Aguada de Pasajeros (C) (CF) 43 Qe34
Agua Flores (MEX) (BCN) 33 Oh30
Agua Nueva (MEX) (COA) 40 Pe33
Agua Nueva (MEX) (TAM) 40 Pf34
Agua Nueva (USA) (TX) 40 Pf32
Agua Prieta (MEX) (SON) 33 Pa30
Aguas Claras (C) (PR) 43 Qd34
Aguila (USA) (AZ) 33 Oj29
Ahmic Harbour (CDN) (ONT) 29 Qf23
Ahome (MEX) (SIN) 39 Pa33
Ahoskie (USA) (NC) 31 Qg27
Ahousat (CDN) (BC) 16 Ob21
Ahumada, Villa (MEX) (CHA) 39 Pb30
Aiea (USA) (HI) 11 Mg35
Aiken (USA) (SC) 37 Qe29
Ainsworth (USA) (NE) 26 Pf24
Aiquebelle Provincial Park ☆ (CDN) (QUE) 21 Qf21
Airdrie (CDN) (ALB) 17 Oh20
Airway Heights (USA) (WA) 17 Og22
Airways (CDN) (ALB) 17 Ok19
Aishihik (CDN) (YT) 11 Ng15
Aitkin (USA) (MN) 19 Pj22
Ajax (USA) (TX) 35 Pj30
Ajo (USA) (AZ) 33 Oj29
Akela (USA) (NM) 34 Pb29
Akeley (USA) (MN) 19 Ph22
Akeonik (USA) (AK) 10 Me10
Akhiok (USA) (AK) 12 Mh17
Akiachak (USA) (AK) 12 Me15
Aklavik (CDN) (NWT) 11 Nh11
Akron (USA) (CO) 34 Pd25
Akron (USA) (IA) 27 Pg24
Akron (USA) (NY) 29 Qf24
Akron (USA) (OH) 29 Qe25
Akulurak (USA) (AK) 10 Mc14
Alabama (USA) (NY) 29 Qf24
Alabama Port (USA) (AL) 36 Qa30
Alabaster (USA) (AL) 36 Qb29
Alachua (USA) (FL) 37 Qd31
Aladdin (USA) (WY) 26 Pc23
Alaganik (USA) (AK) 13 Nc15
Alakanuk (USA) (AK) 10 Mc14
Alaktak (USA) (AK) 10 Mh10
Alameda (CDN) (SAS) 18 Pd21
Alameda, La (MEX) (DGO) 39 Pc33
Alamo (USA) (ND) 18 Pd21
Alamo (USA) (NV) 33 Oh27
Alamo, El (MEX) (BCN) 32 Og30
Alamogordo (USA) (NM) 34 Pc29
Alamos (MEX) (SON) 39 Pa32
Alamos, Los (USA) (NM) 34 Pb28
Alamosa (USA) (CO) 34 Pc27
Alamos de Márquez (MEX) (COA) 39 Pd31
Alapaha (USA) (GA) 37 Qd30
Alba (USA) (TX) 35 Ph29
Alban (CDN) (ONT) 29 Qe22
Albanel (CDN) (QUE) 21 Qj21
Albany (USA) (GA) 36 Qc30
Albany (USA) (MN) 27 Ph23
Albany (USA) (MO) 27 Ph25
Albany (USA) (NY) 30 Qj24
Albany (USA) (OR) 24 Od23
Albany (USA) (TX) 35 Pf29
Albemarle (USA) (NC) 37 Qe28
Alberni (CDN) (BC) 16 Oc21
Alberni, Port (CDN) (BC) 16 Oc21
Alberta (USA) (VA) 31 Qg27
Albert Lea (USA) (MN) 27 Pj24
Alberto Oviedo Mata (MEX) (BCN) 33 Oh29
Albertville (USA) (AL) 36 Qb28
Albia (USA) (IA) 27 Pj25
Albion (USA) (IL) 28 Qa26
Albion (USA) (MI) 28 Qc24
Albion (USA) (NE) 27 Pg25
Albion (USA) (NY) 29 Qf24
Albion, Port (CDN) (BC) 16 Oc21
Alborn (USA) (MN) 19 Pj22
Albright (CDN) (ALB) 15 Of18
Albuquerque (USA) (NM) 33 Pb28
Alcona (CDN) (ONT) 19 Pk20
Alcova (USA) (WY) 26 Pb24
Alcurve (CDN) (ALB) 17 Ok19
Aldama (MEX) (CHA) 39 Pc31
Aldama (MEX) (TAM) 40 Pf34
Aldamas, Los (MEX) (NL) 40 Pf32
Alder Creek (USA) (NY) 29 Qh24
Alder Flats (CDN) (ALB) 17 Oh19
Aledo (USA) (IL) 27 Pk25
Aleknagik (USA) (AK) 12 Mf16
Alert Bay (CDN) (BC) 16 Ob20
Alexander (CDN) (MAN) 18 Pe21
Alexander (USA) (AK) 13 Mk15
Alexander (USA) (ND) 18 Pd22
Alexander, Port (USA) (AK) 14 Nh17
Alexander City (USA) (AL) 36 Qc29
Alexander Graham Bell National Historic Park ☆ (CDN) (NS) 23 Re22
Alexandria (CDN) (ONT) 30 Qh23
Alexandria (USA) (LA) 36 Pj30
Alexandria (USA) (MN) 27 Ph23
Alexandria (USA) (VA) 29 Qg26
Alexandria Bay (USA) (NY) 29 Qh23
Alexis (USA) (IL) 27 Pk25
Alexis Creek (CDN) (BC) 16 Od19
Alford (USA) (FL) 36 Qc30
Alfred (CDN) (ONT) 29 Qh23
Alger (USA) (MI) 28 Qc23
Algona (USA) (IA) 27 Ph24
Algonac (CDN) (ONT) 29 Qd24
Algonquin Park (CDN) (ONT) 29 Qf23
Algonquin Provincial Park ☆ (CDN) (ONT) 29 Qf23
Alibates Flint Quarries National Monument ☆ (USA) (TX) 34 Pe28
Alicante (MEX) (COA) 39 Pd32
Alice (USA) (ND) 19 Pg22
Alice (USA) (TX) 40 Pf32
Alice, Port (CDN) (BC) 16 Ob20
Alice Arm (CDN) (BC) 14 Oa18
Alice Town (BS) 43 Qf33
Aliceville (USA) (AL) 36 Qa29
Alida (CDN) (SAS) 18 Pe21
Alingly (CDN) (SAS) 18 Pc19
Allagash (USA) (ME) 22 Ra22
Allakaket (USA) (AK) 10 Mj12
Allan Water (CDN) (ONT) 19 Pk20
Allardville (CDN) (NB) 22 Rc22
Allegan (USA) (MI) 28 Qc24
Allegany, Port (USA) (PA) 29 Qf25
Allegany State Park ☆ (USA) (NY) 29 Qf25
Allemands, Des (USA) (LA) 36 Pk31
Allen, Port (USA) (LA) 36 Pk30
Allendale (USA) (IL) 28 Qb26
Allendale (USA) (SC) 37 Qe29
Allende (MEX) (COA) 40 Pe31
Allende (MEX) (NL) 40 Pe33
Allende, Valle de (MEX) (CHA) 39 Pc32
Allentown (USA) (FL) 36 Qb30
Allentown (USA) (PA) 29 Qh25
Allenwood (USA) (PA) 29 Qg25
Alliance (CDN) (ALB) 17 Oj19
Alliance (USA) (NE) 26 Pd24
Alliance (USA) (OH) 29 Qe25
Alligator River National Wildlife Refuge ☆ (USA) (NC) 31 Qh28
Allison (USA) (AR) 36 Pj28
Allison (USA) (IA) 27 Pj24
Allyn (USA) (WA) 16 Od22
Alma (CDN) (NB) 22 Rc23
Alma (USA) (GA) 37 Qd30
Alma (USA) (MI) 28 Qc24
Alma (USA) (NE) 35 Pf25
Alma (USA) (WI) 27 Pk23
Almont (USA) (ND) 18 Pe22
Almonte (CDN) (ONT) 29 Qg23
Alpena (USA) (MI) 29 Qd23
Alpha (USA) (IL) 27 Pk25
Alpine (USA) (AZ) 33 Pa29
Alpine (USA) (MT) 25 Pa23
Alpine (USA) (TX) 39 Pd30
Alpine Junction (USA) (WY) 25 Ok24
Alpine Lakes Wilderness ☆ (USA) (WA) 16 Oe22
Alsask (CDN) (SAS) 17 Pa20
Alsatia (USA) (LA) 36 Pk29
Alsen (USA) (ND) 19 Pf21
Alsike (CDN) (ALB) 17 Oh19
Alta (USA) (UT) 25 Ok25
Altamont (CDN) (MAN) 19 Pf21
Altamont (USA) (UT) 25 Ok25
Altamonte Springs (USA) (FL) 43 Qe31
Altar (MEX) (SON) 38 Ok30
Altata (MEX) (SIN) 39 Pb33
Alta Vista (USA) (KS) 35 Pg26
Altavista (USA) (VA) 37 Qf27
Altha (USA) (FL) 36 Qc30
Altheimer (USA) (AR) 36 Pk28
Alto (USA) (TX) 35 Ph30
Alto Golfo de California y Delta del Río Colorado, Reserva de la Biósfera ☆ (MEX) (SON) 33 Oh30
Alton (USA) (IL) 28 Pk26
Alton (USA) (MO) 36 Pk27
Alton (USA) (NH) 22 Qk24
Alton (USA) (NY) 29 Qg24
Altona (CDN) (BC) 15 Oe17
Altona (CDN) (MAN) 19 Pg21
Altoona (USA) (PA) 29 Qf25
Altoona (USA) (WI) 27 Pk23
Alturas (USA) (CA) 24 Oe25
Altus (USA) (OK) 35 Pf28
Alva (USA) (OK) 35 Pf27
Alvarado (USA) (TX) 35 Pg29
Alvin (USA) (TX) 41 Ph31
Alvinston (CDN) (ONT) 29 Qe24
Alvwood (USA) (MN) 19 Ph22
Aly (USA) (AR) 35 Pj28
Alzada (USA) (MT) 26 Pc23
Amana (USA) (IA) 27 Pk25
Amancio (C) (LT) 43 Qg35
Amanda Park (USA) (WA) 16 Od22
Amaranth (CDN) (MAN) 19 Pf20
Amargosa Valley (USA) (NV) 32 Og27
Amarillo (USA) (TX) 34 Pe28
Amberley (CDN) (ONT) 29 Qe23
Ambler (USA) (AK) 10 Mg12
Amboy (USA) (CA) 33 Oh28
Amboy (USA) (IL) 28 Qa25
Ambrose (USA) (ND) 18 Pd21
Amelia C.H. (USA) (VA) 31 Qg27
Amenia (USA) (NY) 30 Qj25
American Falls (USA) (ID) 25 Oj24
American Fork (USA) (UT) 25 Ok25
Americus (USA) (GA) 36 Qc29
Amery (USA) (WI) 27 Pj23
Ames (USA) (IA) 27 Pj24
Amesbury (USA) (MA) 22 Qk24
Amesdale (CDN) (ONT) 19 Pj20
Amherst (CDN) (NS) 22 Rc23
Amherst (USA) (MA) 30 Qj24
Amherst (USA) (VA) 37 Qf27
Amherstburg (CDN) (ONT) 29 Qd24
Amidon (USA) (ND) 26 Pd22
Amistad (USA) (NM) 34 Pd28
Amite (USA) (LA) 36 Pk30
Amity (USA) (AR) 35 Pj28
Amory (USA) (MS) 36 Qa29
Amos (CDN) (QUE) 21 Qf21
Amqui (CDN) (QUE) 22 Rb21
Amsterdam (CDN) (SAS) 18 Pd20
Amsterdam (USA) (NY) 30 Qh24
Anacoco (USA) (LA) 35 Pj30
Anaconda (USA) (MT) 25 Oj22
Anaconda-Pintler Wilderness ☆ (USA) (MT) 25 Oj22
Anacortes (USA) (WA) 16 Od21
Anaheim (USA) (CA) 32 Og29
Anahim Lake (CDN) (BC) 16 Oc19
Anáhuac (MEX) (CHA) 39 Pb31
Anáhuac (MEX) (NL) 40 Pe32
Anaktuk (USA) (AK) 10 Mf10
Anaktuvuk Pass (USA) (AK) 10 Mk11
Anama Bay = Dauphin River (CDN) (MAN) 19 Pf20
Anamoose (USA) (ND) 18 Pe22
Anamosa (USA) (IA) 27 Pk24
Anchorage (USA) (AK) 13 Na15
Andalusia (USA) (AL) 36 Qb30
Andalusia (USA) (IL) 27 Pk25
Anderson (USA) (IN) 28 Qc25
Anderson (USA) (MO) 35 Ph27
Anderson (USA) (SC) 37 Qd28
Andover (USA) (NY) 29 Qg24
Andover (USA) (OH) 29 Qe25
Andover (USA) (SD) 27 Pg23
Andover, Perth- (CDN) (NB) 22 Rb22
Andréville = Saint-André (CDN) (QUE) 22 Ra22
Andrew (CDN) (ALB) 17 Oj19
Andrew, Port (USA) (WI) 27 Pk24
Andrews (USA) (TX) 34 Pd29
Andros Town (BS) 43 Qg33
Angeles, Bahía de los (MEX) (BCN) 38 Oj31
Angeles, Los (USA) (CA) 32 Of28
Angeles, Port (USA) (WA) 16 Od21
Angels Camp (USA) (CA) 32 Oe26
Angle Inlet (CDN) (MAN) 19 Ph21
Angle Inlet (USA) (MN) 19 Ph21
Angleton (USA) (TX) 41 Ph31
Angliers (CDN) (QUE) 21 Qf22
Angola (USA) (IN) 28 Qc25
Angoon (USA) (AK) 14 Nh17
Aniak (USA) (AK) 12 Mf15
Aniakchak National Monument and Preserve ☆ (USA) (AK) 12 Mg17
Animas (USA) (NM) 33 Pa30
Ankeny (USA) (IA) 27 Pj25
Anna (USA) (IL) 36 Qa27
Anna (USA) (MS) 36 Pk30
Annapolis (USA) (MD) 29 Qg26
Annapolis (USA) (MO) 36 Pk27
Annapolis Royal (CDN) (NS) 22 Rc23
Ann Arbor (USA) (MI) 29 Qd24
Anniston (USA) (AL) 36 Qc29
Anola (CDN) (MAN) 19 Pg21
Anselmo (USA) (NE) 26 Pf25
Ansley (USA) (NE) 26 Pf25
Anson (USA) (TX) 35 Pf29
Antelope (CDN) (SAS) 18 Pa20
Anthony (USA) (KS) 35 Pf27
Anthony (USA) (NM) 34 Pb30
Anticosti, Parc d' ☆ (CDN) (QUE) 22 Rd21
Antigo (USA) (WI) 28 Qa23
Antigonish (CDN) (NS) 22 Rd23
Antimony (USA) (UT) 33 Oj26
Antler (CDN) (SAS) 18 Pe21
Antlers (USA) (OK) 35 Ph28
Anton (USA) (CO) 34 Pd26
Anton (USA) (TX) 34 Pd29
Antonito (USA) (CO) 34 Pb27
Anuajito, El (MEX) (SIN) 39 Pa33
Anvik (USA) (AK) 10 Me14
Anyox (CDN) (BC) 14 Oa18
Anza-Borrego Desert State Park ☆ (USA) (CA) 32 Og29
Anzac (CDN) (ALB) 17 Ok17
Apache (USA) (AZ) 33 Pa30
Apache (USA) (OK) 35 Pf28
Apache Creek (USA) (NM) 33 Pa29
Apache Junction (USA) (AZ) 33 Ok29
Apalachicola (USA) (FL) 36 Qc31
Apódaca (MEX) (NL) 40 Pe33
Apopka (USA) (FL) 43 Qe31
Apostle Islands National Lakeshore ☆ (USA) (WI) 19 Pk22
Appam (USA) (ND) 18 Pd21
Applegrove (CDN) (BC) 16 Of21
Appleton (USA) (MN) 27 Pg23
Appleton (USA) (WI) 28 Qa23
Appleton City (USA) (MO) 35 Ph26
Appomattox (USA) (VA) 37 Qf27
Appomattox Court House National Historic Park ☆ (USA) (VA) 37 Qf27
Apsley (CDN) (ONT) 29 Qf23
Aquadeo Beach (CDN) (SAS) 17 Pa19
Arab (USA) (AL) 36 Qb28
Arabela (USA) (NM) 34 Pc29
Arados (MEX) (CHA) 39 Pb31
Aragon (USA) (NM) 33 Pa29
Aransas National Wildlife Refuge ☆ (USA) (TX) 40 Pg31
Aransas Pass (USA) (TX) 40 Pg32
Arapahoe (USA) (NE) 26 Pf25
Arborg (CDN) (MAN) 19 Pg20
Arcade (USA) (NY) 29 Qf24
Arcadia (USA) (FL) 43 Qe32
Arcadia (USA) (LA) 35 Pj29
Arcadia (USA) (WI) 27 Pk23
Arcata (USA) (CA) 24 Oc25
Archdale (USA) (NC) 37 Qf28
Archer (USA) (FL) 37 Qd31
Archerwill (CDN) (SAS) 18 Pd19
Arches National Park ☆ (USA) (UT) 33 Pa26
Archie (USA) (LA) 36 Pk30
Archipel-de-Mingan, Réserve de Parc Nacional de L' ☆ (CDN) (QUE) 22 Rd20
Arco (USA) (ID) 25 Oj24
Arco, El (MEX) (BCN) 38 Oj31
Arcola (CDN) (SAS) 18 Pd21
Arctic National Wildlife Refuge ☆ (USA) (AK) 11 Nc11
Arctic Red River = Tsiigehtchic (CDN) (NWT) 11 Nj12
Arctic Village (USA) (AK) 11 Nc11
Arden (USA) (WA) 17 Og21
Ardmore (CDN) (ALB) 17 Ok18
Ardmore (USA) (OK) 35 Pg28
Ardmore (USA) (SD) 26 Pd24
Area Protegida Cañon Santa Elena ☆ (MEX) (CHA) 39 Pd31
Area Protegida Maderas del Carmen ☆ (MEX) (COA) 39 Pd31
Arecibo (USA) (PR) 42 Rb36
Argentia (CDN) (NFL) 23 Rj22
Argo (USA) (LA) 36 Pk30
Argonne (USA) (WI) 28 Qa23
Argyle (CDN) (MAN) 19 Pg20
Arichat (CDN) (NS) 23 Re23
Arivaca (USA) (AZ) 33 Ok30
Arizona (CDN) (MAN) 19 Pf21
Arizpe (MEX) (SON) 38 Ok30
Arkadelphia (USA) (AR) 35 Pj28
Arkansas City (USA) (KS) 35 Pg27
Arlee (USA) (MT) 25 Oh22
Arlington (USA) (GA) 36 Qc30
Arlington (USA) (KS) 35 Pf27
Arlington (USA) (OR) 24 Oe23
Arlington (USA) (SD) 27 Pg23
Arlington (USA) (TX) 35 Pg29
Arlington (USA) (VA) 29 Qg26
Arlington (USA) (WA) 16 Od21
Arma (USA) (KS) 35 Ph27
Arminto (USA) (WY) 25 Pb24
Armit (CDN) (SAS) 18 Pe19
Armley (CDN) (SAS) 18 Pc19
Armour (USA) (SD) 26 Pf24
Armstrong (CDN) (BC) 16 Of20
Armstrong (CDN) (ONT) 20 Qa20
Armstrong (CDN) (QUE) 22 Qk23
Arnaud (CDN) (MAN) 19 Pg21
Arnauldville (USA) (LA) 36 Pk30
Arneson (CDN) (ALB) 17 Ok20
Arnett (USA) (OK) 35 Pf27
Arnold (USA) (MI) 28 Qb22
Arnold (USA) (MO) 28 Pk26
Arnold (USA) (NE) 26 Pe25
Arnprior (CDN) (ONT) 29 Qg23
Arntfield (CDN) (QUE) 21 Qf21
Aroland (CDN) (ONT) 20 Qb20
Arrandale (CDN) (BC) 14 Oa18
Arras (CDN) (BC) 15 Oe18
Arrey (USA) (NM) 34 Pb29
Arriba (USA) (CO) 34 Pd26
Arrowhead Lodge (USA) (WY) 25 Pb23
Arrow River (CDN) (MAN) 18 Pe20
Arroyo Grande (USA) (CA) 32 Oe28
Arroyos de Mantua (C) (PR) 42 Qc34
Arteaga (MEX) (COA) 40 Pe33
Artemisa (C) (LH) 43 Qd34
Artesia (USA) (NM) 34 Pc29
Artesian (USA) (SD) 27 Pg23
Arthur (CDN) (ONT) 29 Qe24
Arthur (USA) (ND) 19 Pg22
Arthur (USA) (NE) 26 Pe25
Arthur, Port (USA) (TX) 41 Pj31
Arthurette (CDN) (NB) 22 Rb22
Artland (CDN) (SAS) 17 Pa19
Arvada (USA) (CO) 34 Pc26
Arvada (USA) (WY) 26 Pb23
Arvilla (USA) (ND) 19 Pg22
Arwin (USA) (CA) 32 Of28
Asbestos (CDN) (QUE) 22 Qk23
Asbury Park (USA) (NY) 30 Qh25
Ascensión (MEX) (CHA) 33 Pb30
Ascensión, La (MEX) (NL) 40 Pf33
Ashburn (USA) (GA) 37 Qd30
Ashdown (USA) (AR) 35 Ph29
Asheboro (USA) (NC) 37 Qf28
Asher (USA) (OK) 35 Pg28
Ashern (CDN) (MAN) 19 Pf20
Asheville (USA) (NC) 37 Qd28
Ash Flat (USA) (AR) 36 Pk27
Ash Fork (USA) (AZ) 33 Oj28
Ashkum (USA) (IL) 28 Qb25
Ashland (USA) (IL) 28 Pk26
Ashland (USA) (KS) 35 Pf27
Ashland (USA) (KY) 29 Qd26
Ashland (USA) (LA) 35 Pj29
Ashland (USA) (ME) 22 Ra22
Ashland (USA) (MO) 28 Pj26
Ashland (USA) (NE) 27 Pg25
Ashland (USA) (OH) 29 Qd25
Ashland (USA) (OR) 24 Od24
Ashland (USA) (VA) 31 Qg27
Ashland (USA) (WI) 19 Pk22
Ashland City (USA) (TN) 36 Qb27
Ashley (USA) (IL) 28 Qa26
Ashley (USA) (ND) 26 Pf22
Ashmont (CDN) (ALB) 17 Ok18
Ashtabula (USA) (OH) 29 Qe25
Ashton (USA) (ID) 25 Ok23
Ashuapmushuan, Réserve Faunique d' ☆ (CDN) (QUE) 21 Qj21
Ashville (CDN) (MAN) 18 Pe20
Ashville (USA) (PA) 29 Qf25
Aspen (USA) (CO) 34 Pb26
Aspen Grove (CDN) (BC) 16 Oe21
Aspen Mountain Ski Area ☆ (USA) (CO) 34 Pb26
Aspermont (USA) (TX) 34 Pe29
Assateague Islands National Seashore ☆ (USA) (VA) 31 Qh26
Assiniboia (CDN) (SAS) 18 Pc21
Assiniboine, Fort (CDN) (ALB) 15 Oh18
Assinica, Parc National d' ☆ (CDN) (QUE) 21 Qh20
Astoria (USA) (OR) 24 Od22
Astor Park (USA) (FL) 37 Qe31
Atanik (USA) (AK) 10 Mf10
Atascadero (USA) (CA) 32 Oe28
Atchison (USA) (KS) 35 Ph26
Athabasca (CDN) (ALB) 17 Oj18
Athapap (CDN) (MAN) 18 Pe18
Athens (CDN) (ONT) 29 Qh23
Athens (USA) (AL) 36 Qb28
Athens (USA) (GA) 37 Qd29
Athens (USA) (LA) 35 Pj29
Athens (USA) (OH) 29 Qd26
Athens (USA) (TN) 36 Qc28
Athens (USA) (TX) 35 Ph29
Athol (USA) (ID) 17 Og22
Atikaki Provincial Wilderness Park ☆ (CDN) (MAN) 19 Ph20
Atikameg (CDN) (ALB) 15 Oh18
Atikameg Lake (CDN) (MAN) 18 Pe1[illegible]
Atikokan (CDN) (ONT) 19 Pk2[illegible]
Atkinson (USA) (NC) 31 Qf2[illegible]
Atkinson (USA) (NE) 26 Pf2[illegible]
Atlanta (USA) (GA) 36 Qc2[illegible]
Atlanta (USA) (LA) 35 Pj3[illegible]
Atlanta (USA) (MI) 28 Qc2[illegible]
Atlanta (USA) (NE) 26 Pf2[illegible]
Atlanta (USA) (TX) 35 Ph2[illegible]
Atlantic (USA) (IA) 27 Ph2[illegible]
Atlantic (USA) (ME) 22 Ra2[illegible]
Atlantic (USA) (NC) 31 Qg2[illegible]
Atlantic Beach (USA) (FL) 37 Qe3[illegible]
Atlantic City (USA) (NJ) 31 Qh2[illegible]
Atlee (CDN) (ALB) 17 Ok2[illegible]
Atlin (CDN) (BC) 14 Nj1[illegible]
Atlin Provincial Park ☆ (CDN) (BC) 14 Nj1[illegible]
Atmore (CDN) (ALB) 17 Oj1[illegible]
Atmore (USA) (AL) 36 Qb3[illegible]
Atoka (USA) (OK) 35 Pg2[illegible]
Atomic City (USA) (ID) 25 Oj2[illegible]
Atotonilco de los Martinez (MEX) (ZAC) 39 Pd3[illegible]
Atqasuk (USA) (AK) 10 Mg[illegible]
Attachie (CDN) (BC) 15 Oe[illegible]
Attalla (USA) (AL) 36 Qb2[illegible]
Attawapiskat (CDN) (ONT) 20 Qd[illegible]
Attica (USA) (IN) 28 Qb2[illegible]
Attica (USA) (KS) 35 Pf2[illegible]
Attica (USA) (NY) 29 Qf2[illegible]
Attica (USA) (OH) 29 Qd2[illegible]
Atwater (USA) (CA) 32 Oe2[illegible]
Atwood (USA) (CO) 26 Pd2[illegible]
Atwood (USA) (IL) 28 Qa2[illegible]
Atwood (USA) (KS) 34 Pe[illegible]
Aubigny (CDN) (MAN) 19 Pg[illegible]
Auburn (USA) (AL) 36 Qc[illegible]
Auburn (USA) (CA) 32 Oe[illegible]
Auburn (USA) (IA) 27 Ph[illegible]
Auburn (USA) (IN) 28 Qc[illegible]
Auburn (USA) (ME) 22 Qk[illegible]
Auburn (USA) (NE) 27 Ph[illegible]
Auburn (USA) (NY) 29 Qg[illegible]
Auburn (USA) (WA) 16 Od[illegible]
Auden (CDN) (ONT) 20 Qb[illegible]
Augusta (USA) (GA) 37 Qe[illegible]
Augusta (USA) (IL) 27 Pk[illegible]
Augusta (USA) (KS) 35 Pg[illegible]
Augusta (USA) (ME) 22 Ra[illegible]
Augusta (USA) (MT) 17 Oj[illegible]
Augusta (USA) (OH) 28 Qc[illegible]
Augusta (USA) (WI) 27 Pk[illegible]
Aulio Day (USA) (AK) 11 N[illegible]
Aulander (USA) (NC) 31 Qg[illegible]
Ault (USA) (CO) 26 Pc[illegible]
Aura (USA) (MI) 28 Qa[illegible]
Aurora (CDN) (ONT) 29 Q[illegible]
Aurora (USA) (AK) 10 Mc[illegible]
Aurora (USA) (CO) 34 Pc[illegible]
Aurora (USA) (IL) 28 Qa[illegible]
Aurora (USA) (ME) 22 Ra[illegible]
Aurora (USA) (MO) 35 P[illegible]
Aurora (USA) (NE) 27 Pg[illegible]
Aurora (USA) (NY) 29 Qg[illegible]
Auroraville (USA) (WI) 28 Qa[illegible]
Austin (CDN) (MAN) 19 P[illegible]
Austin (USA) (MN) 27 P[illegible]
Austin (USA) (NV) 32 Og[illegible]
Austin (USA) (TX) 40 Pg[illegible]
Austin, Port (USA) (MI) 29 Qd[illegible]
Autec (U.S. Navy research center) ☆ (BS) 43 Qg[illegible]
Ava (USA) (MO) 35 P[illegible]
Avalon (USA) (CA) 32 O[illegible]
Avalon (USA) (TX) 35 P[illegible]
Avalon Wilderness Area ☆ (CDN) (NFL) 23 R[illegible]
Avenal (USA) (CA) 32 O[illegible]
Avenue of the Giants ☆ (USA) (CA) 24 O[illegible]
Avery (USA) (ID) 17 O[illegible]
Avola (CDN) (BC) 16 O[illegible]
Avon (USA) (MT) 25 O[illegible]
Avondale (USA) (AZ) 33 O[illegible]
Avonlea (CDN) (SAS) 18 P[illegible]
Avon Park (USA) (FL) 43 Q[illegible]
Axtell (USA) (NE) 26 P[illegible]
Ayden (USA) (NC) 31 Q[illegible]
Azle (USA) (TX) 35 P[illegible]

c (USA) (AZ) 33 Oj29
c (USA) (NM) 33 Pb27
c Ruins National Monument ☆ (USA) (NM) 33 Pb27
ell (USA) (WA) 16 Of22

B

(USA) (MT) 17 Oj21
itt (USA) (MN) 19 Pk22
a, La (MEX) (COA) 39 Pd31
anora (MEX) (SON) 39 Pa31
arac (MEX) (SON) 39 Pa30
imba (MEX) (CHA) 39 Pc31
iniva (MEX) (CHA) 39 Pb31
bampo (MEX) (SON) 39 Pa32
Axe (USA) (MI) 29 Qd24
eck (CDN) (NS) 23 Re22
er (CDN) (NFL) 23 Rg21
ands National Park ☆ (USA) (SD) 26 Pd24
skin Lake (CDN) (ONT) 19 Pk19
lad (USA) (AZ) 33 Oj28
s (USA) (WY) 25 Pb25
ey (USA) (MN) 19 Ph22
t (CDN) (MAN) 19 Pf21
a de Loreto, Parque Nacional ☆ (MEX) 38 Ok33
a de los Angeles (MEX) (BCN) 38 Oj31
a Honda (C) (PR) 43 Qd34
a Kino (MEX) (SON) 38 Ok31
a Tortugas (MEX) (BCS) 38 Oh32
ichivo (MEX) (CHA) 39 Pa32
La (CDN) (QUE) 22 Qk21
à-la-Loutre = Otter (CDN) (QUE) 22 Rd21
Comeau (CDN) (QUE) 22 Ra21
des-Sables (CDN) (QUE) 22 Rb21
du-Poste = Mistassini (CDN) (QUE) 21 Qj20
Johan-Beetz (CDN) (QUE) 22 Rd20
Sainte-Claire (CDN) (QUE) 22 Rc21
Saint-Paul (CDN) (QUE) 22 Qk22
bridge (USA) (GA) 36 Qc30
bridge Island (USA) (WA) 16 Od22
ville (USA) (MT) 18 Pc21
(USA) (TX) 35 Pf29
il (USA) (WY) 25 Pb24
mar (MEX) (BCN) 32 Og29
n (MEX) (COA) 40 Pe32
de Ahuichila (MEX) (COA) 39 Pd33
s de Agua Blanca (MEX) (CHA) 39 Pb33
r (USA) (CA) 32 Og28
r (USA) (LA) 36 Pk30
r (USA) (MT) 26 Pc22
r (USA) (WV) 29 Qf26
r City (USA) (OR) 24 Og23
rsfield (USA) (CA) 32 Of28
rsfield (USA) (TX) 39 Pd30
(CDN) (ONT) 29 Qf23
arres (CDN) (SAS) 18 Pd20
oms Corners (USA) (NY) 29 Qf24
Knob (USA) (AR) 36 Pk28
onnel (CDN) (BC) 15 Oe17
ur (CDN) (MAN) 19 Pf21
win (USA) (FL) 37 Qe30
win (USA) (IA) 27 Pk24
win (USA) (MI) 28 Qc24
win (USA) (WI) 27 Pj23
winsville (USA) (NY) 29 Qg24
winton (CDN) (SAS) 17 Pa19
ur (CDN) (BC) 17 Og21
ur (USA) (ND) 18 Pe22
onie (CDN) (SAS) 18 Pc20
lger (USA) (TX) 35 Pf30
(USA) (PA) 29 Qh25
orhea (USA) (TX) 39 Pd30
eario de los Novillos, Parque Nacional ☆ (MEX) (COA) 40 Pe31
(USA) (ND) 18 Pe21
more (USA) (MD) 29 Qg26
berg (USA) (SC) 37 Qe29
ield (CDN) (BC) 16 Oc21
o (C) (CG) 43 Qg35
o (C) (SS) 43 Qf35
roft (CDN) (ONT) 29 Qg23
roft (USA) (ID) 25 Ok24
elier National Monument ☆ (USA) (NM) 34 Pb28
era (USA) (TX) 40 Pf31
eras (MEX) (CHA) 39 Pc30
on (USA) (OR) 24 Oc24
(CDN) (ALB) 17 Oh20
National Park ☆ (CDN) (ALB) 17 Og20
or (USA) (IA) 27 Pj24
or (USA) (ME) 22 Ra23
s (USA) (TX) 35 Pf30
ing (USA) (CA) 32 Og29
ockburn (CDN) (ONT) 29 Qg23
s, Los (USA) (CA) 32 Oe27
oo (USA) (WI) 28 Qa24
chois (CDN) (QUE) 22 Rc21
ga (USA) (MI) 20 Qa22
hof (USA) (AK) 14 Nh17
erville (USA) (FL) 37 Qe31
stown (USA) (KY) 36 Qc27
Harbor (USA) (ME) 22 Ra23
g (USA) (MO) 27 Pj25
erville (CDN) (BC) 16 Oe19
way (CDN) (ONT) 29 Qf23
aby River (CDN) (NB) 22 Rc22
esville (USA) (MN) 19 Pg22
hart (USA) (TX) 40 Pe30
stable (USA) (MA) 30 Qk25
um (USA) (WY) 26 Pb24
well (CDN) (ALB) 17 Oj21
well (USA) (SC) 37 Qe29
hs (CDN) (ALB) 17 Oj21
nca del Cobre, Parque Natural ☆ (MEX) (CHA) 39 Pa32
nco de Guadalupe (MEX) (CHA) 39 Pc30
ute (CDN) (QUE) 21 Qg21
(USA) (VT) 30 Qj23
, Port (USA) (LA) 36 Pk30
tal, El (MEX) (TAM) 40 Pf33
tt (USA) (MN) 27 Ph23
ead (CDN) (ALB) 17 Oh18
e (CDN) (ONT) 29 Qf23
ere (CDN) (BC) 16 Oe20
, El (MEX) (SLP) 40 Pd34
es, Los (MEX) (BCS) 39 Pa34

Barrington (CDN) (NS) 22 Rc24
Barron (USA) (WI) 27 Pk23
Barrow (USA) (AK) 10 Mg10
Barrows (CDN) (MAN) 18 Pe19
Barry's Bay (CDN) (ONT) 29 Qg23
Barryville (CDN) (NB) 22 Rc22
Barstow (USA) (CA) 32 Og28
Barstow (USA) (TX) 34 Pd30
Barthel (CDN) (SAS) 17 Pa19
Bartlesville (USA) (OK) 35 Ph27
Bartlett (USA) (MT) 17 Oj21
Bartlett (USA) (NE) 26 Pf25
Bartlett (USA) (TN) 36 Qa28
Barton (USA) (ND) 18 Pe21
Bartow (USA) (FL) 43 Qe32
Bartow (USA) (WV) 29 Qf26
Barwick (CDN) (ONT) 19 Pj21
Basalt (USA) (CO) 33 Pb26
Basaseachic (MEX) (CHA) 39 Pa31
Bashaw (CDN) (ALB) 17 Oj19
Basile (USA) (LA) 36 Pj30
Basin (USA) (WY) 25 Pa23
Bassano (CDN) (ALB) 17 Oj20
Bassett (USA) (NE) 26 Pf24
Bassfield (USA) (MS) 36 Qa30
Bastrop (USA) (LA) 36 Pk29
Bastrop (USA) (TX) 40 Pg30
Batabanó (C) (LH) 43 Qd34
Batavia (USA) (NY) 29 Qf24
Batchawana (CDN) (ONT) 20 Qc22
Batchawana Bay (CDN) (ONT) 20 Qc22
Batchelor (USA) (LA) 36 Pk30
Bateman (CDN) (SAS) 18 Pb21
Batesburg (USA) (SC) 37 Qe29
Batesville (USA) (AR) 35 Pj28
Batesville (USA) (MS) 36 Qa28
Batesville (USA) (TX) 40 Pf31
Bath (CDN) (ONT) 29 Qg23
Bath (USA) (ME) 22 Ra24
Bath (USA) (NY) 29 Qg24
Bathurst (CDN) (NB) 22 Rc22
Bathurst Mines (CDN) (NB) 22 Rc22
Baton Rouge (USA) (LA) 36 Pk30
Batopilas (MEX) (CHA) 39 Pb32
Battleboro (USA) (NC) 31 Qg27
Battle Creek (USA) (MI) 28 Qc24
Battleford (CDN) (SAS) 17 Pa19
Battle Harbour (CDN) (NFL) 23 Rh19
Battle Lake (USA) (MN) 27 Ph22
Battle Mountain (USA) (NV) 24 Og25
Battleview (USA) (ND) 18 Pd21
Baturi (MEX) (SIN) 39 Pa33
Baudette (USA) (MN) 19 Ph21
Bauta (C) (LH) 43 Qd34
Bauxite (USA) (AR) 35 Pj28
Baviácora (MEX) (SON) 38 Ok31
Bavon (USA) (VA) 31 Qg27
Baxley (USA) (GA) 37 Qd30
Baxter (USA) (FL) 37 Qd30
Baxter (USA) (MS) 36 Qa29
Baxterville (USA) (MS) 36 Qa30
Bayamón (USA) (PR) 42 Rb36
Bayard (USA) (NE) 26 Pd25
Bayard (USA) (NM) 33 Pa29
Bay Bulls (CDN) (NFL) 23 Rj22
Bay City (USA) (MI) 29 Qd24
Bay City (USA) (TX) 41 Ph31
Bay du Nord Wilderness Reserve ☆ (CDN) (NFL) 23 Rh21
Bayfield (USA) (CO) 33 Pb27
Bayfield (USA) (WI) 19 Pk22
Bay Mills Indian Reservation ☆ (USA) (MI) 28 Qc22
Bay Minette (USA) (AL) 36 Qb30
Baynes Lake (CDN) (BC) 17 Oh21
Bayonet Point (USA) (FL) 43 Qd31
Bayou Cane (USA) (LA) 36 Pk31
Bayou La Batre (USA) (AL) 36 Qa30
Bayou Sauvage National Wildlife Refuge ☆ (USA) (LA) 36 Qa30
Bayou Sorrel (USA) (LA) 36 Pk30
Bay Port (USA) (MI) 29 Qd24
Bay Saint Louis (USA) (MS) 36 Qa30
Bay Shore (USA) (NY) 30 Qj25
Bay Springs (USA) (MS) 36 Qa30
Baysville (CDN) (ONT) 29 Qf23
Baytown (USA) (TX) 41 Ph31
Bay Tree (CDN) (ALB) 15 Of18
Bayview (USA) (ID) 17 Og22
Beach (USA) (ND) 18 Pd22
Beachburg (CDN) (ONT) 29 Qg23
Beacon (USA) (NY) 30 Qj25
Beadle (CDN) (SAS) 17 Pa20
Bealeton (USA) (VA) 29 Qg26
Bear Canyon (CDN) (ALB) 15 Of17
Bear Cove (CDN) (BC) 16 Ob20
Bear Creek Springs (USA) (AR) 35 Pj27
Bearden (USA) (AR) 35 Pj29
Beardmore (CDN) (ONT) 20 Qb21
Beardstown (USA) (IL) 28 Pk25
Bear Flat (CDN) (BC) 15 Oe17
Bear Lake (CDN) (BC) 14 Ob17
Beatrice (USA) (NE) 35 Pg25
Beatton River (CDN) (BC) 15 Oe17
Beatty (CDN) (SAS) 18 Pc19
Beatty (USA) (NV) 32 Og27
Beattyville (CDN) (QUE) 21 Qg21
Beauceville (CDN) (QUE) 22 Qk22
Beaufield (CDN) (SAS) 17 Pa20
Beaufort (USA) (NC) 31 Qg28
Beaufort (USA) (SC) 37 Qe29
Beaumont (USA) (MS) 36 Qa30
Beaumont (USA) (TX) 41 Ph30
Beaupré (CDN) (QUE) 22 Qk22
Beauséjour (CDN) (MAN) 19 Pg20
Beauséjour National Historical Park, Fort ☆ (CDN) (NB) 22 Rc23
Beauval (CDN) (SAS) 17 Pb18
Beauvallon (CDN) (ALB) 17 Ok19
Beaver (USA) (AK) 11 Nb12
Beaver (USA) (UT) 33 Oj26
Beaver Brook Station (CDN) (NB) 22 Rc22
Beaverdam (CDN) (ALB) 17 Ok18
Beaver Dam (USA) (WI) 28 Qa24
Beaverdell (CDN) (BC) 16 Of21
Beaver Falls (USA) (PA) 29 Qe25
Beaverlodge (CDN) (ALB) 15 Of18
Beaver Mines (CDN) (ALB) 17 Oh21
Beavermouth (CDN) (BC) 17 Og20
Beaver Springs (USA) (PA) 29 Qg25

Beaverton (CDN) (ONT) 29 Qf23
Beazer (CDN) (ALB) 17 Oj21
Bécancour (CDN) (QUE) 21 Qj22
Beckley (USA) (WV) 37 Qe27
Beckton (USA) (WY) 25 Pb23
Bedford (CDN) (QUE) 30 Qj23
Bedford (USA) (IA) 27 Ph25
Bedford (USA) (IN) 28 Qb26
Bedford (USA) (PA) 29 Qf26
Bedford (USA) (VA) 37 Qf27
Bednesti (CDN) (BC) 16 Od19
Bee (USA) (NE) 27 Pg25
Beebe (USA) (AR) 36 Pk28
Beecher (USA) (IL) 28 Qb25
Beechey Point (USA) (AK) 11 Na10
Beechy (CDN) (SAS) 18 Pb20
Beeler (USA) (KS) 34 Pe26
Beeville (USA) (TX) 40 Pg31
Beggs (USA) (OK) 35 Pg28
Behan (CDN) (ALB) 17 Ok18
Beiseker (CDN) (ALB) 17 Oj20
Bejucal (C) (LH) 43 Qd34
Bel Air (USA) (MD) 29 Qg26
Belden (USA) (CA) 32 Oe25
Belden (USA) (ND) 18 Pd21
Belen (USA) (NM) 34 Pb28
Belfair (USA) (WA) 16 Od22
Belfast (USA) (AR) 35 Pj28
Belfast (USA) (ME) 22 Ra23
Belfield (USA) (ND) 18 Pd22
Belgrade (USA) (ME) 22 Ra23
Belgrade (USA) (MN) 27 Ph23
Belgrade (USA) (MT) 25 Ok23
Belhaven (USA) (NC) 31 Qg28
Bell (USA) (FL) 37 Qd31
Bella Bella (CDN) (BC) 16 Oa19
Bella Coola (CDN) (BC) 16 Ob19
Bellaire (USA) (OH) 29 Qe25
Bellburns (CDN) (NFL) 23 Rg20
Belle (USA) (MO) 28 Pk26
Belle, La (USA) (FL) 43 Qe32
Bellefontaine (USA) (OH) 29 Qd25
Bellefonte (USA) (PA) 29 Qg25
Belle Fourche (USA) (SD) 26 Pd23
Belle Glade (USA) (FL) 43 Qe32
Belleoram (CDN) (NFL) 23 Rh22
Belle Plaine (USA) (KS) 35 Pg27
Belleterre (CDN) (QUE) 21 Qf22
Belleview (CDN) (MAN) 18 Pe21
Belleville (CDN) (NS) 22 Rc24
Belleville (CDN) (ONT) 29 Qg23
Belleville (USA) (IL) 28 Qa26
Belleville (USA) (KS) 35 Pg26
Belleville (USA) (TX) 40 Pg31
Bellevue (CDN) (ALB) 17 Oh21
Bellevue (USA) (IA) 27 Pk24
Bellevue (USA) (NE) 27 Ph25
Bellevue (USA) (WA) 16 Od22
Bellingham (USA) (WA) 16 Od21
Bellis (CDN) (ALB) 17 Oj18
Bell Island Hot Springs (USA) (AK) 14 Nk18
Bellmead (USA) (TX) 35 Pg30
Bellows Falls (USA) (VT) 30 Qj24
Bellvue (USA) (CO) 26 Pc25
Belmond (USA) (IA) 27 Pj24
Belmont (CDN) (MAN) 19 Pf21
Belmont (USA) (NY) 29 Qf24
Beloit (USA) (KS) 35 Pf26
Beloit (USA) (WI) 28 Qa24
Belpre (USA) (KS) 35 Pf27
Belt (USA) (MT) 17 Ok22
Belton (USA) (SC) 37 Qd28
Belton (USA) (TX) 40 Pg30
Belvidere (USA) (IL) 28 Qa24
Belzoni (USA) (MS) 36 Pk29
Bemersyde (CDN) (SAS) 18 Pd21
Bemidji (USA) (MN) 19 Ph22
Bena (USA) (MN) 19 Ph22
Bend (USA) (OR) 24 Oe23
Benge (USA) (WA) 24 Of22
Bengough (CDN) (SAS) 18 Pc21
Benito (CDN) (MAN) 18 Pe20
Benito Juárez (MEX) (CHA) 39 Pb31
Benito Juárez (MEX) (DGO) 39 Pd33
Benjamin (USA) (TX) 35 Pf29
Benjamin Hill (MEX) (SON) 38 Ok30
Benkelman (USA) (NE) 34 Pe25
Benndale (USA) (MS) 36 Qa30
Bennett (CDN) (YT) 14 Nh16
Bennett (USA) (CO) 34 Pc26
Bennettsville (USA) (SC) 37 Qf28
Bennington (USA) (VT) 30 Qj24
Benny (CDN) (ONT) 20 Qe22
Benoit (USA) (WI) 19 Pk22
Benson (CDN) (SAS) 18 Pd21
Benson (USA) (AZ) 33 Ok30
Benson (USA) (MN) 27 Ph23
Bentley (CDN) (ALB) 17 Oh19
Benton (USA) (AL) 36 Qb29
Benton (USA) (AR) 35 Pj28
Benton (USA) (CA) 32 Of27
Benton (USA) (LA) 35 Pj29
Benton Harbor (USA) (MI) 28 Qb24
Bentonia (USA) (MS) 36 Pk29
Bentonsport (USA) (IA) 27 Pk25
Bentonville (USA) (AR) 35 Ph27
Bentonville (USA) (NC) 31 Qf28
Ben Wheeler (USA) (TX) 35 Ph29
Beowawe (USA) (NV) 24 Og25
Beque, De (USA) (CO) 33 Pa26
Berea (USA) (KY) 36 Qc27
Berenda (USA) (CA) 32 Oe27
Berens River (CDN) (MAN) 19 Pg19
Beresford (USA) (SD) 27 Pg24
Bergland (CDN) (ONT) 19 Ph21
Bergland (USA) (MI) 20 Qa22
Bering Land Bridge Nature Reserve ☆ (USA) (AK) 10 Mc12
Berino (USA) (NM) 34 Pb29
Berkeley (USA) (CA) 32 Od27
Berlin (USA) (NH) 22 Qk23
Berlin (USA) (NJ) 31 Qh26
Berlin (USA) (PA) 29 Qf26
Bermejillo (MEX) (DGO) 39 Pd33
Bernalillo (USA) (NM) 34 Pb28
Bernardo (USA) (NM) 34 Pb28
Berne (USA) (WA) 16 Oe22
Bernice (USA) (LA) 35 Pj29

Berry, De (USA) (TX) 35 Ph29
Berrydale (USA) (FL) 36 Qb30
Berryville (USA) (AR) 35 Pj27
Berthierville (CDN) (QUE) 30 Qj22
Berthold (USA) (ND) 18 Pe21
Bertram (CDN) (ONT) 20 Qc21
Bertrand (CDN) (NB) 22 Rc22
Bertrandville (USA) (LA) 36 Qa31
Bertwell (CDN) (SAS) 18 Pd19
Berwick (CDN) (NB) 22 Rc23
Berwick (USA) (PA) 29 Qg25
Beryl Junction (USA) (UT) 33 Oj27
Bessemer (USA) (AL) 36 Qb29
Bessemer (USA) (MI) 20 Pk22
Bethany (USA) (MO) 27 Ph25
Bethel (USA) (AK) 12 Me15
Bethel (USA) (ME) 22 Qk23
Bethel (USA) (NC) 31 Qg28
Bethel (USA) (VT) 30 Qj24
Bethlehem (USA) (PA) 30 Qh25
Bettles (USA) (AK) 10 Mk12
Beulah (USA) (ND) 18 Pe22
Beulaville (USA) (NC) 31 Qg28
Beverley (CDN) (SAS) 18 Pb20
Beverly (USA) (FL) 36 Qc31
Beverly (USA) (WA) 24 Of22
Beverly Beach (USA) (MD) 29 Qg26
Bewdley (CDN) (ONT) 29 Qf23
Bezanson (CDN) (ALB) 15 Of18
Biddeford (USA) (ME) 22 Qk24
Biddle (USA) (MT) 26 Pc23
Bienfait (CDN) (SAS) 18 Pd21
Bienville (USA) (LA) 35 Pj29
Big Arm (USA) (MT) 17 Oh22
Big Bar (USA) (CA) 24 Od25
Big Bay (USA) (MI) 20 Qb22
Big Bear Lake (USA) (CA) 32 Og28
Big Beaver (CDN) (SAS) 18 Pc21
Big Beaver House (CDN) (ONT) 19 Qa19
Big Bend National Park ☆ (USA) (TX) 39 Pd31
Big Boggy ☆ N.W.R. (USA) (LA) 41 Ph31
Big Creek (USA) (ID) 25 Oh23
Big Creek Provincial Park ☆ (CDN) (BC) 16 Od20
Big Falls (USA) (MN) 19 Pj21
Big Field (USA) (AZ) 33 Oj30
Bigfork (USA) (MT) 17 Oh21
Biggar (CDN) (SAS) 18 Pb19
Biggs (USA) (OR) 24 Oe23
Bighorn (USA) (MT) 25 Pb22
Big Horn (USA) (WY) 25 Pb23
Bighorn Canyon National Recreation Area ☆ (USA) (MT) 25 Pa23
Big Lake (USA) (TX) 40 Pe30
Big Lake Ranch (CDN) (BC) 16 Oe19
Big Pine (USA) (CA) 32 Of27
Big Pine Key (USA) (FL) 43 Qe33
Big Piney (USA) (WY) 25 Ok24
Big Pond (CDN) (NS) 23 Re23
Big Rapids (USA) (MI) 28 Qc24
Big River (CDN) (SAS) 18 Pb19
Big Sandy (USA) (MT) 17 Ok21
Big Sandy (USA) (TX) 35 Ph29
Big Sky (USA) (MT) 25 Ok23
Big Spring (USA) (TX) 34 Pe29
Big Stone (CDN) (ALB) 17 Ok20
Big Sur (USA) (CA) 32 Oe27
Big Timber (USA) (MT) 25 Pa23
Big Trout Lake (CDN) (ONT) 19 Qa19
Billings (USA) (MT) 25 Pa23
Billsburg (USA) (SD) 26 Pe23
Biloxi (USA) (MS) 36 Qa30
Binger (USA) (OK) 35 Pf28
Bingham (USA) (ME) 22 Ra23
Bingham (USA) (NM) 34 Pb29
Binghamton (USA) (NY) 29 Qh24
Binscarth (CDN) (MAN) 18 Pe20
Biosphere II ☆ (USA) (AZ) 33 Ok29
Birch Bay (CDN) (MAN) 19 Pf20
Birch Creek (USA) (AK) 11 Nc12
Birchdale (USA) (MN) 19 Ph21
Birches (USA) (AK) 10 Mj13
Birch Harbor (USA) (ME) 22 Ra23
Birch Hills (CDN) (SAS) 18 Pc19
Birch River (CDN) (MAN) 18 Pe19
Birchwood (USA) (WI) 27 Pk23
Birdseye (USA) (IN) 28 Qb26
Birmingham (USA) (AL) 36 Qb29
Birtle (CDN) (SAS) 18 Pe20
Bisbee (USA) (AZ) 33 Pa30
Biscayne National Park ☆ (USA) (FL) 43 Qe33
Bishop (USA) (CA) 32 Of27
Bishop (USA) (TX) 40 Pg32
Bishop's Falls (CDN) (NFL) 23 Rh21
Bishopville (USA) (SC) 37 Qe28
Bismarck (USA) (AR) 35 Pj28
Bismarck (USA) (ND) 18 Pe22
Bison (USA) (SD) 26 Pd23
Biwabik (USA) (MN) 19 Pj22
Bixby (USA) (MN) 36 Pk27
Black (USA) (AK) 10 Mc14
Black Canyon of the Gunnison National Park ☆ (USA) (CO) 33 Pa26
Black Creek (USA) (WI) 28 Qa23
Black Diamond (CDN) (ALB) 17 Oh20
Blackfoot (CDN) (ALB) 17 Ok19
Blackfoot (USA) (ID) 25 Oj24
Blackfoot (USA) (MT) 17 Oj21
Black Hawk (CDN) (ONT) 19 Pj21
Blackie (CDN) (ALB) 17 Oj20
Black Island ☆ (CDN) (MAN) 19 Pg20
Black Lake (CDN) (QUE) 22 Qk22
Black River Falls (USA) (WI) 27 Pk23
Black Rock (USA) (AR) 36 Pk27
Blacksburg (USA) (VA) 37 Qe27
Blacks Harbour (CDN) (NB) 22 Rb23
Blackstone (USA) (VA) 31 Qg27
Blackville (CDN) (NB) 22 Rc22
Blackwell (USA) (TX) 34 Pe29
Blackwells Corner (USA) (CA) 32 Of28
Blaine (USA) (KS) 35 Pg26
Blaine (USA) (MN) 27 Pj23
Blaine (USA) (WA) 16 Od21
Blaine Lake (CDN) (SAS) 18 Pb19
Blair (USA) (NE) 27 Pg25
Blair (USA) (WI) 27 Pk23
Blairmore (CDN) (ALB) 17 Oh21
Blairsden (USA) (CA) 32 Oe26
Blairsville (USA) (GA) 37 Qd28

Blairsville (USA) (PA) 29 Qf25
Blakely (USA) (GA) 36 Qc30
Blanchard (USA) (ID) 17 Og21
Blanchard (USA) (ND) 19 Pg22
Blanchard Springs Caverns ☆ (USA) (AR) 35 Pj27
Blanco (USA) (NM) 33 Pb27
Blanco (USA) (TX) 40 Pf30
Blanc-Sablon (CDN) (QUE) 23 Rg20
Blandfort, Port (CDN) (NFL) 23 Rh21
Blanding (USA) (IL) 27 Pk24
Blanding (USA) (UT) 33 Pa27
Blanket (USA) (TX) 35 Pf30
Blenheim (CDN) (ONT) 29 Qd24
Bleue, Rivière- (CDN) (QUE) 22 Ra22
Blewett (USA) (WA) 16 Oe22
Blind Channel (CDN) (BC) 16 Oc20
Blind River (CDN) (ONT) 29 Qd22
Bliss Landing (CDN) (BC) 16 Oc20
Blissville (CDN) (NB) 22 Rb23
Blitchton (USA) (GA) 37 Qe29
Block Island (USA) (RI) 30 Qk25
Bloomer (USA) (WI) 27 Pk23
Bloomfield (USA) (IA) 27 Pj25
Bloomfield (USA) (IN) 28 Qb26
Bloomfield (USA) (MT) 18 Pc22
Bloomfield (USA) (NM) 33 Pb27
Blooming Grove (USA) (TX) 35 Pg29
Blooming Prairie (USA) (MN) 27 Pj24
Bloomington (USA) (IL) 28 Qa25
Bloomington (USA) (IN) 28 Qb26
Bloomington (USA) (MN) 27 Pj23
Bloomington (USA) (WI) 27 Pk24
Bloomsburg (USA) (PA) 29 Qg25
Bloomsdale (USA) (MO) 28 Pk26
Blountstown (USA) (FL) 36 Qc30
Blubber Bay (CDN) (BC) 16 Oc21
Blueberry Mountain (CDN) (ALB) 15 Of18
Bluecreek (USA) (WA) 17 Og21
Blue Earth (USA) (MN) 27 Ph24
Bluefield (USA) (WV) 37 Qe27
Blue Hill (USA) (ME) 22 Ra23
Blue Hill (USA) (NE) 26 Pf25
Blue Lick Springs (USA) (KY) 28 Qc26
Blue Mountain Lake (USA) (NY) 30 Qh24
Blue Ridge (USA) (GA) 36 Qc28
Blue River (CDN) (BC) 16 Of19
Blueslide (USA) (WA) 17 Og21
Bluewater (USA) (NM) 33 Pa28
Bluff (USA) (AK) 10 Md13
Bluff (USA) (UT) 33 Pa27
Bluff Dale (USA) (TX) 35 Pf29
Blum (USA) (TX) 35 Pg29
Blunt (USA) (SD) 26 Pf23
Bly (USA) (OR) 24 Oe24
Blythe (USA) (CA) 33 Oh29
Blytheville (USA) (AR) 36 Qa28
Boardman (USA) (OR) 24 Of23
Boat Basin (CDN) (BC) 16 Ob21
Bobcaygeon (CDN) (ONT) 29 Qf23
Bocana, La (MEX) (BCN) 32 Og30
Bocana, La (MEX) (BCN) 38 Oh31
Boca Raton (USA) (FL) 43 Qe32
Bochart (CDN) (QUE) 21 Qj21
Bocoyna (MEX) (CHA) 39 Pb32
Bodie Ghost Town ☆ (USA) (CA) 32 Of26
Bodmin (CDN) (SAS) 18 Pb19
Bodo (CDN) (ALB) 17 Ok19
Boerne (USA) (TX) 40 Pf31
Bogalusa (USA) (LA) 36 Qa30
Bogata (USA) (TX) 35 Ph29
Bogue Chitto (USA) (MS) 36 Pk30
Bohemia (USA) (LA) 36 Qa31
Boiestown (CDN) (NB) 22 Rb22
Boise (USA) (ID) 24 Og24
Boise City (USA) (OK) 34 Pd27
Boissevain (CDN) (MAN) 18 Pe21
Bolger (CDN) (QUE) 21 Qg21
Bolivar (USA) (MO) 35 Pj27
Bolivar (USA) (NY) 29 Qf24
Bolivar (USA) (TN) 36 Qa28
Bolivar, Port (USA) (TX) 41 Ph31
Bolivia (C) (CA) 43 Qf34
Bolsa, La (MEX) (SON) 33 Oh29
Bolton (USA) (NC) 37 Qf28
Bonanza (CDN) (ALB) 15 Of18
Bonanza (USA) (ID) 25 Oh23
Bonanza (USA) (UT) 25 Pa25
Bonaventure (CDN) (QUE) 22 Rc21
Bonavista (CDN) (NFL) 23 Rj21
Bonavista, Cape ☆ (CDN) (NFL) 23 Rj21
Bonavista Peninsula ☆ (CDN) (NFL) 23 Rj21
Bondurant (USA) (WY) 25 Ok24
Bonfield (CDN) (ONT) 29 Qf22
Bonham (USA) (TX) 35 Pg29
Bonifay (USA) (FL) 36 Qc30
Bonnechere Caves ☆ (CDN) (ONT) 29 Qg23
Bonners Ferry (USA) (ID) 17 Og21
Bonneville (USA) (WY) 25 Pa24
Bonnyville (CDN) (ALB) 17 Ok18
Bon Wier (USA) (TX) 41 Pj30
Boone (USA) (CO) 34 Pc26
Boone (USA) (IA) 27 Pj24
Boone (USA) (NC) 37 Qe27
Booneville (USA) (AR) 35 Pj28
Booneville (USA) (KY) 37 Qd27
Booneville (USA) (MS) 36 Qa28
Boonsboro (USA) (MD) 29 Qg26
Boonville (USA) (IN) 28 Qb26
Boonville (USA) (MO) 28 Pj26
Boonville (USA) (NY) 29 Qh24
Boothbay Harbor (USA) (ME) 22 Ra24
Boquilla del Conchos, La (MEX) (CHA) 39 Pc32
Boquillas (USA) (TX) 39 Pd31
Boquillas del Carmen (MEX) (COA) 39 Pd31
Borden (CDN) (PEI) 22 Rd22
Border (USA) (WY) 25 Ok24
Border City Lodge (USA) (AK) 11 Ne14
Borger (USA) (TX) 34 Pe28
Borgia, De (USA) (MT) 17 Oh22
Boron (USA) (CA) 32 Og28
Borradaile (CDN) (ALB) 17 Ok19
Borups Corners (CDN) (ONT) 19 Pj21
Boscobel (USA) (WI) 27 Pk24
Bosler (USA) (WY) 26 Pc25
Bosque del Apache National Wildlife Refuge ☆ (USA) (NM) 34 Pb29
Bossier City (USA) (LA) 35 Pj29
Boston (USA) (GA) 37 Qd30

Boston USA (MA) 30 Qk24
Boston Bar CDN (BC) 16 Oe21
Boswell CDN (BC) 17 Og21
Boswell USA (OK) 35 Ph28
Bothell USA (WA) 16 Od22
Bottineau USA (ND) 18 Pe21
Botwood CDN (NFL) 23 Rh21
Boulder USA (CO) 34 Pc25
Boulder USA (MT) 25 Oj22
Boulder USA (WY) 25 Pa24
Boulder City USA (NV) 33 Oh28
Boundary CDN (BC) 14 Nk17
Boundary USA (WA) 17 Og21
Bountiful USA (UT) 25 Ok25
Bovill USA (ID) 24 Og22
Bowbells USA (ND) 18 Pd21
Bowdle USA (SD) 26 Pf23
Bowdon USA (ND) 19 Pf22
Bowell CDN (ALB) 17 Ok20
Bowen USA (IL) 27 Pk25
Bowen Island CDN (BC) 16 Od21
Bowie USA (AZ) 33 Pa29
Bowie USA (MD) 29 Qg26
Bowie USA (TX) 35 Pg29
Bow Island CDN (ALB) 17 Ok21
Bowling Green USA (KY) 36 Qb27
Bowling Green USA (MO) 28 Pk26
Bowling Green USA (OH) 29 Qd25
Bowling Green USA (VA) 29 Qg26
Bowman USA (ND) 26 Pd22
Bowmans Corner USA (MT) 17 Oj22
Bowmanville CDN (ONT) 29 Qf24
Bowron Lake Provincial Park ☆ CDN (BC) 16 Oe19
Bowser CDN (BC) 16 Oc21
Boyce USA (LA) 36 Pj30
Boyd CDN (MAN) 19 Pg18
Boyd USA (MT) 25 Pa23
Boyds USA (WA) 16 Of21
Boyero USA (CO) 34 Pd26
Boykins USA (VA) 31 Qg27
Boyle CDN (ALB) 17 Oj18
Boylston CDN (NS) 23 Re23
Boyne CDN (ALB) 17 Ok18
Boy River USA (MN) 19 Ph22
Bozeman USA (MT) 25 Ok23
Bracebridge CDN (ONT) 29 Qf23
Bracken CDN (SAS) 18 Pa21
Brackendale CDN (BC) 16 Od21
Brackettville USA (TX) 40 Pe31
Brad USA (TX) 35 Pf29
Braddyville USA (IA) 27 Ph25
Bradenton USA (FL) 43 Qd32
Bradford USA (IL) 28 Qa25
Bradford USA (PA) 29 Qf25
Bradley USA (CA) 32 Oe28
Bradleyville USA (MO) 35 Pj27
Bradshaw USA (NE) 27 Pg25
Bradshaw USA (TX) 35 Pf29
Bradwardine CDN (MAN) 18 Pe20
Bradwell CDN (SAS) 18 Pb20
Brady USA (MT) 17 Ok21
Brady USA (TX) 40 Pf30
Bragg, Fort USA (CA) 32 Od26
Bragg Creek CDN (ALB) 17 Oh20
Braham USA (MN) 27 Pj23
Brainard CDN (ALB) 15 Of18
Brainerd USA (MN) 27 Ph22
Brampton CDN (ONT) 29 Qf24
Branch CDN (NFL) 23 Rj22
Branchville USA (SC) 37 Qe29
Brandenburg USA (KY) 36 Qb27
Brandon CDN (MAN) 19 Pf21
Brandon USA (FL) 43 Qd32
Brandon USA (MS) 36 Qa29
Brandon USA (SD) 27 Pg24
Brandywine USA (MD) 29 Qg26
Branford USA (FL) 37 Qd31
Branson USA (MO) 35 Pj27
Brantford CDN (ONT) 29 Qe24
Brantley USA (AL) 36 Qb30
Brasil C (CG) 43 Qg35
Brattleboro USA (VT) 30 Qj24
Brawley USA (CA) 33 Oh29
Breaux Bridge USA (LA) 36 Pk30
Brechin CDN (ONT) 29 Qf23
Breckenridge USA (CO) 34 Pb26
Breckenridge USA (MN) 27 Pg22
Breckenridge USA (TX) 35 Pf29
Breezewood USA (PA) 29 Qf25
Brelen USA (ND) 26 Pe22
Bremen USA (GA) 36 Qc29
Bremen USA (ND) 19 Pf22
Bremerton USA (WA) 16 Od22
Brenham USA (TX) 40 Pg30
Brenton Lake N.W.R. ☆ USA (MT) 17 Ok22
Bresaylor CDN (SAS) 17 Pa19
Brevard USA (NC) 37 Qd28
Brewer USA (ME) 22 Ra23
Brewster USA (WA) 16 Of21
Brewton USA (AL) 36 Qb30
Breynat CDN (ALB) 17 Oj18
Bridal Cave USA ☆ (MO) 28 Pj26
Bridesville CDN (BC) 16 Of21
Bridge Lake CDN (BC) 16 Oe20
Bridgenorth CDN (ONT) 29 Qf23
Bridgeport USA (AL) 36 Qc28
Bridgeport USA (CA) 32 Of26
Bridgeport USA (CT) 30 Qj25
Bridgeport USA (NE) 26 Pd25
Bridgeport USA (WA) 16 Of21
Bridger USA (MT) 25 Pa23
Bridgeton USA (NJ) 29 Qh26
Bridgetown CDN (NS) 22 Rc23
Bridgeville USA (CA) 24 Od25
Bridgewater CDN (NS) 22 Rc23
Bridgewater USA (NY) 29 Qh24
Bridgewater USA (VA) 29 Qf26
Bridgton USA (ME) 22 Qk23
Brig Bay CDN (NFL) 23 Rg20
Briggsdale USA (CO) 26 Pc25
Brigham City USA (UT) 25 Oj25
Brighton CDN (ONT) 29 Qg23
Brighton USA (AL) 36 Qb29
Brighton USA (CO) 34 Pc26
Brighton USA (IA) 27 Pk25
Brightsand River Provincial Park ☆ CDN (ONT) 19 Pk21
Brimley USA (MI) 20 Qc22
Brinkley USA (AR) 36 Pk28
Brinkleyville USA (NC) 31 Qg27
Brinnon USA (WA) 16 Od22
Brisbane CDN (ONT) 29 Qe24
Bristol CDN (NB) 22 Rb22
Bristol USA (CO) 34 Pd26
Bristol USA (FL) 36 Qc30
Bristol USA (TN) 37 Qd27
Britannia CDN (NFL) 23 Rj21
Britannia Beach CDN (BC) 16 Od21
Britton USA (SD) 27 Pg23
Broadacres CDN (SAS) 17 Pa19
Broadus USA (MT) 26 Pc23
Broadview CDN (SAS) 18 Pd20
Broadview USA (MT) 25 Pa22
Broadway USA (VA) 29 Qf26
Brock CDN (SAS) 17 Pa20
Brocket CDN (ALB) 17 Oj21
Brocket USA (ND) 19 Pf21
Brockport USA (NY) 29 Qg24
Brockton USA (MA) 30 Qk24
Brockton USA (MT) 18 Pc21
Brockville CDN (ONT) 29 Qh23
Brockway USA (MT) 18 Pc22
Brockway USA (PA) 29 Qf25
Brogan USA (OR) 24 Og23
Broken Arrow USA (OK) 35 Ph27
Broken Bow USA (NE) 26 Pf25
Broken Bow USA (OK) 35 Ph28
Brokenburg USA (VA) 29 Qg26
Bronson USA (FL) 37 Qd31
Bronson USA (TX) 35 Pj30
Bronte USA (TX) 34 Pe30
Brookesmith USA (TX) 35 Pf30
Brookfield USA (MO) 35 Pj26
Brookhaven USA (MS) 36 Pk30
Brookings USA (OR) 24 Oc24
Brookings USA (SD) 27 Pg23
Brooklyn USA (IA) 27 Pj25
Brooklyn USA (MS) 36 Qa30
Brookneal USA (VA) 37 Qf27
Brooks CDN (ALB) 17 Ok20
Brooksby CDN (SAS) 18 Pc19
Brookston USA (MN) 19 Pj22
Brooksville USA (FL) 43 Qd31
Brookville USA (IN) 28 Qc26
Brookville USA (PA) 29 Qf25
Broomhill CDN (MAN) 18 Pe21
Brown CDN (MAN) 19 Pf21
Browne USA (AK) 11 Na13
Brownfield CDN (ALB) 17 Ok19
Brownfield USA (TX) 34 Pd29
Browning USA (MT) 17 Oj21
Browns USA (AL) 36 Qb29
Browns Valley USA (MN) 27 Pg23
Brownsville USA (TN) 36 Qa28
Brownsville USA (TX) 40 Pg33
Brownwood USA (TX) 35 Pf30
Broxton USA (GA) 37 Qd30
Bruce USA (WI) 27 Pk23
Bruce Crossing USA (MI) 20 Qa22
Bruce Peninsula National Park ☆ CDN (ONT) 29 Qe23
Bruceton USA (TN) 36 Qa27
Brudenell CDN (ONT) 29 Qg23
Brule USA (WI) 19 Pk22
Bruneau USA (ID) 25 Oh24
Bruning USA (NE) 27 Pg25
Brunkild CDN (MAN) 19 Pg21
Bruno USA (MN) 27 Pj22
Brunswick USA (GA) 37 Qe30
Brunswick USA (MD) 29 Qg26
Brunswick USA (ME) 22 Ra24
Brunswick USA (MN) 27 Pj23
Brusett USA (MT) 18 Pb22
Brush USA (CO) 26 Pd25
Bryan USA (OH) 28 Qc25
Bryan USA (TX) 40 Pg30
Bryant CDN (SAS) 18 Pd21
Bryant USA (SD) 27 Pg23
Bryce Canyon National Park ☆ USA (UT) 33 Oj27
Bryson City USA (NC) 37 Qd28
Buchanan USA (ND) 19 Pf22
Buchans CDN (NFL) 23 Rg21
Buckeye USA (AZ) 33 Oj29
Buckhannon USA (WV) 29 Qe26
Buckhorn USA (NM) 33 Pa29
Buckingham CDN (QUE) 29 Qh23
Buckland USA (AK) 10 Me13
Buckley Bay CDN (BC) 16 Oc21
Bucklin USA (KS) 35 Pf27
Buck Ridge CDN (BC) 16 Od19
Bucksport USA (ME) 22 Ra23
Buck Valley USA (PA) 29 Qf26
Buctouche CDN (NB) 22 Rc22
Bucyrus USA (OH) 29 Qd25
Bude USA (MS) 36 Pk30
Buena USA (WA) 24 Oe22
Buenaventura C (HO) 43 Qg35
Buenaventura MEX (CHA) 39 Pb31
Buenaventura MEX (YUC) 42 Qb35
Buenavista MEX (SIN) 39 Pa33
Buenavista MEX (ZAC) 39 Pd34
Buena Vista USA (CO) 34 Pb26
Buena Vista USA (GA) 36 Qc29
Buena Vista USA (VA) 37 Qf27
Buenos Aires N.W.R. ☆ USA (AZ) 33 Ok30
Bueyeros USA (NM) 34 Pd28
Búfadora, La MEX (BCN) 32 Og30
Búfala MEX (CHA) 39 Pc32
Buffalo CDN (ALB) 17 Ok20
Buffalo CDN (SAS) 18 Pc21
Buffalo USA (IA) 27 Pk25
Buffalo USA (MN) 27 Pj23
Buffalo USA (MO) 35 Pj27
Buffalo USA (ND) 19 Pg22
Buffalo USA (NY) 29 Qf24
Buffalo USA (OK) 35 Pf27
Buffalo USA (SD) 26 Pd23
Buffalo USA (TX) 35 Pg30
Buffalo USA (WV) 29 Qe26
Buffalo USA (WY) 26 Pb23
Buffalo City USA (AR) 35 Pj27
Buffalo Narrows CDN (SAS) 17 Pa18
Buffalo National River ☆ USA (AR) 35 Pj28
Buford USA (CO) 25 Pb26
Buford USA (GA) 36 Qc28
Buford USA (ND) 18 Pd22
Buford USA (WY) 26 Pc25
Bugaboo Alpine Provincial Recreation Area ☆ CDN (BC) 17 Og20
Buick CDN (BC) 15 Oe17
Bullard USA (TX) 35 Ph29
Bullhead City USA (AZ) 33 Oh28
Bullock USA (NC) 31 Qf27
Bullock's Harbour BS 43 Qg33
Bulwark CDN (ALB) 17 Ok19
Bunker USA (MO) 36 Pk27
Bunker Hill USA (AK) 10 Mc13
Bunkie USA (LA) 36 Pj30
Bunnell USA (FL) 37 Qe31
Buras USA (LA) 36 Qa31
Burbank USA (CA) 32 Of28
Burbank USA (WA) 24 Of22
Burgaw USA (NC) 31 Qg28
Burgdorf USA (ID) 25 Oh23
Burgdorf Hot Springs ☆ USA (ID) 25 Oh23
Burgeo CDN (NFL) 23 Rg22
Burgess USA (VA) 31 Qg27
Burien USA (WA) 16 Od22
Burin CDN (NFL) 23 Rh22
Burkburnett USA (TX) 35 Pf28
Burke USA (SD) 26 Pf24
Burkesville USA (KY) 36 Qc27
Burkett USA (TX) 35 Pf29
Burkeville USA (VA) 31 Qf27
Burk's Falls CDN (ONT) 29 Qf23
Burleson USA (TX) 35 Pg29
Burley USA (ID) 25 Oj24
Burlingame USA (KS) 35 Ph26
Burlington CDN (NFL) 23 Rg21
Burlington CDN (ONT) 29 Qf24
Burlington USA (CO) 34 Pd26
Burlington USA (IA) 27 Pk25
Burlington USA (KS) 35 Ph26
Burlington USA (NC) 37 Qf27
Burlington USA (VT) 30 Qj23
Burlington USA (WA) 16 Od21
Burlington Junction USA (MO) 27 Ph25
Burmis CDN (ALB) 17 Oh21
Burnaby CDN (BC) 16 Od21
Burnet USA (TX) 40 Pf30
Burney USA (CA) 24 Oe25
Burns USA (CO) 34 Pb26
Burns USA (OR) 24 Of24
Burns USA (WY) 26 Pc25
Burnside CDN (NFL) 23 Rj21
Burns Junction USA (OR) 24 Og24
Burns Lake CDN (BC) 16 Oc18
Burnt Ranch USA (CA) 24 Od25
Burr Ferry USA (LA) 41 Pj30
Burrton USA (KS) 35 Pg26
Burstall CDN (SAS) 17 Pa20
Burton CDN (BC) 17 Og21
Burwell USA (NE) 26 Pf25
Burwell, Port CDN (ONT) 29 Qe24
Busby CDN (ALB) 17 Oj19
Busby USA (MT) 25 Pb23
Bush USA (LA) 36 Qa30
Bushnell USA (IL) 27 Pk25
Bushnell USA (NE) 26 Pd25
Bustamante MEX (TAM) 40 Pf34
Butedale CDN (BC) 16 Oa19
Butler USA (AL) 36 Qa29
Butler USA (GA) 36 Qc29
Butler USA (MO) 35 Ph26
Butler USA (PA) 29 Qf25
Butler USA (TX) 35 Ph30
Butte USA (MT) 25 Oj22
Butte USA (ND) 18 Pe22
Butte USA (NE) 26 Pf24
Butterpot Provincial Park ☆ CDN (NFL) 23 Rj22
Bylas USA (AZ) 33 Ok29
Bynum USA (MT) 17 Oj22

C

Cabaiguán C (SS) 43 Qf34
Caballo USA (NM) 34 Pb29
Caballo, El MEX (COA) 39 Pd32
Cabañas C (LH) 43 Qd34
Cabano CDN (QUE) 22 Ra22
Cabeza Prieta National Wildlife Refuge ☆ USA (AZ) 33 Oj29
Cable USA (WI) 20 Pk22
Cabool USA (MO) 35 Pj27
Cabo Pulmo MEX (BCS) 39 Pa34
Caborca MEX (SON) 38 Oj30
Cabo San Lucas ☆ MEX (BCS) 39 Pa34
Cabot USA (AR) 35 Pj28
Cabrillo National Monument ☆ USA (CA) 32 Og29
Cabullona MEX (SON) 33 Pa30
Cache USA (OK) 35 Pf28
Cache Creek CDN (BC) 16 Oe20
Cactus Lake CDN (SAS) 17 Pa19
Caddo USA (TX) 35 Pf29
Cadereyta MEX (NL) 40 Pf33
Cadillac CDN (SAS) 18 Pb21
Cadillac USA (MI) 28 Qc23
Cadiz USA (KY) 36 Qb27
Cadiz USA (OH) 29 Qe25
Cadogan CDN (ALB) 17 Ok19
Cadomin CDN (ALB) 17 Og19
Cadott USA (WI) 27 Pk23
Cadotte Lake CDN (ALB) 15 Og17
Cahkwaktolik USA (AK) 12 Md15
Caibarién C (VC) 43 Qf34
Caimanero MEX (SIN) 39 Pb34
Cairo USA (GA) 36 Qc30
Cairo USA (NE) 26 Pf25
Cajon USA (CA) 32 Og28
Cajon, El USA (CA) 32 Og29
Calabazar de Sagua C (VC) 43 Qf34
Calabogie CDN (ONT) 29 Qg23
Calais USA (ME) 22 Rb23
Calamus USA (IA) 27 Pk25
Caldwell USA (ID) 24 Og24
Caldwell USA (KS) 35 Pg27
Caldwell USA (OH) 29 Qe26
Caldwell USA (TX) 40 Pg30
Caledonia CDN (ONT) 29 Qf24
Caledonia USA (MN) 27 Pk24
Calexico USA (CA) 33 Oh29
Calgary CDN (ALB) 17 Oh20
Calhan USA (CO) 34 Pc26
Calhoun USA (GA) 36 Qc28
Calhoun USA (LA) 35 Pj29
Calhoun City USA (MS) 36 Qa29
Calhoun Falls USA (SC) 37 Qd28
Caliente USA (CA) 32 Of28
Caliente USA (NV) 33 Oh27
California USA (MO) 28 Pj26
Calion USA (AR) 36 Pj29
Calipatria USA (CA) 33 Oh29
Caliper Lake CDN (ONT) 19 Pj21
Calistoga USA (CA) 32 Od26
Callahan USA (CA) 24 Od25
Callahan USA (FL) 37 Qe30
Callander CDN (ONT) 29 Qf22
Callao USA (VA) 29 Qg27
Callaway USA (FL) 36 Qc30
Callaway USA (MN) 19 Ph22
Calles MEX (TAM) 40 Pf34
Calling Lake CDN (ALB) 17 Oj18
Calmar CDN (ALB) 17 Oj19
Calmar USA (IA) 27 Pk24
Calstock CDN (ONT) 20 Qc21
Calvin USA (OK) 35 Pg28
Camacho, Estacia MEX (DGO) 40 Pd33
Camagüey C (CG) 43 Qg35
Camargo MEX (TAM) 40 Pf32
Camargo, Ciudad MEX (CHA) 39 Pc32
Camas USA (MT) 17 Oh22
Campbellford CDN (ONT) 29 Qg23
Cambridge CDN (ONT) 29 Qe24
Cambridge USA (ID) 24 Og23
Cambridge USA (MA) 30 Qk24
Cambridge USA (MD) 29 Qg26
Cambridge USA (MN) 27 Pj23
Cambridge USA (NE) 26 Pe25
Cambridge USA (OH) 29 Qe25
Camden USA (AL) 36 Qb30
Camden USA (AR) 35 Pj29
Camden USA (ME) 22 Ra23
Camden USA (NJ) 31 Qh26
Camden USA (NY) 29 Qh24
Camden USA (SC) 37 Qe28
Camdenton USA (MO) 28 Pj26
Cameron USA (AZ) 33 Ok28
Cameron USA (LA) 41 Pj31
Cameron USA (MO) 35 Ph26
Cameron USA (TX) 40 Pg30
Cameron Prairie N.W.R. ☆ USA (LA) 41 Pj31
Camilla USA (GA) 36 Qc30
Campbell River CDN (BC) 16 Oc20
Campbell's Bay CDN (QUE) 29 Qg23
Campbellsville USA (KY) 36 Qc27
Campbellton CDN (NB) 22 Rb22
Camp Crook USA (SD) 26 Pd23
Camperville CDN (MAN) 18 Pe20
Campo USA (CO) 34 Pd27
Campo, El USA (TX) 40 Pg31
Campo Calamajue MEX (BCN) 38 Oh31
Campo Nuevo MEX (BCN) 38 Oh31
Camp Point USA (IL) 28 Pk25
Campti USA (LA) 35 Pj30
Camp Verde USA (UT) 33 Ok28
Camp Wood USA (TX) 40 Pf31
Camrose CDN (ALB) 17 Oj19
Canaan USA (NH) 30 Qj25
Canadian USA (TX) 34 Pe28
Canal Flats CDN (BC) 17 Oh20
Canandaigua USA (NY) 29 Qg24
Cananea MEX (SON) 38 Ok30
Cañas, Playa las C (PR) 43 Qd34
Canatlán MEX (DGO) 39 Pc33
Canaveral, Cape USA (FL) 43 Qe31
Canby USA (CA) 24 Oe25
Canby USA (MN) 27 Pg23
Cancún MEX (QR) 42 Qb35
Candela MEX (COA) 40 Pe32
Candela, Estación MEX (NL) 40 Pe32
Cándido González C (CG) 43 Qf35
Candle USA (AK) 10 Me13
Candle Lake CDN (SAS) 18 Pc19
Cando CDN (SAS) 17 Pa19
Cando USA (ND) 19 Pf21
Canelo USA (AZ) 33 Ok30
Canim Lake CDN (BC) 16 Oe20
Canisteo USA (NY) 29 Qg24
Canmore CDN (ALB) 17 Oh20
Cannon Ball USA (ND) 26 Pe22
Cannon Falls USA (MN) 27 Pj23
Cannonville USA (UT) 33 Oj27
Canoe Narrows CDN (SAS) 17 Pa18
Canon City USA (CO) 34 Pc26
Cañon Plaza USA (NM) 34 Pb27
Cañon Santa Elena, Area Protegida ☆ MEX (CHA) 39 Pd31
Canopus CDN (SAS) 18 Pb21
Canora CDN (SAS) 18 Pd20
Canso CDN (NS) 23 Re23
Cantabro, El MEX (COA) 39 Pd33
Cantamar MEX (BCN) 32 Og29
Canti USA (CA) 32 Og28
Canton USA (GA) 36 Qc28
Canton USA (MO) 27 Pk25
Canton USA (MS) 36 Pk29
Canton USA (NY) 29 Qh23
Canton USA (OH) 29 Qe25
Canton USA (PA) 29 Qg25
Canton USA (SD) 27 Pg24
Canton USA (TX) 35 Ph29
Cantwell USA (AK) 11 Na14
Canutillo USA (TX) 34 Pb30
Canyon CDN (ONT) 19 Pj21
Canyon CDN (ONT) 20 Qc22
Canyon USA (TX) 34 Pe28
Canyon Creek CDN (ALB) 15 Oh18
Canyon Creek USA (MT) 25 Oj22
Canyon de Chelly National Monument ☆ USA (AZ) 33 Pa27
Canyon Ferry USA (MT) 25 Ok22
Canyonlands National Park ☆ USA (UT) 33 Ok26
Canyons of the Ancients National Monument ☆ USA (CO) 33 Pa27
Cap-aux-Meules CDN (QUE) 23 Re22
Cap-de-la-Madeleine CDN (QUE) 21 Qj22
Cap-des-Rosiers CDN (QUE) 22 Rc21
Cape Anguille CDN (NFL) 23 Rf22
Cape Breton Highlands National Park ☆ CDN (NS) 23 Re22
Cape Canaveral USA (FL) 43 Qe31
Cape Cod National Seashore ☆ USA (MA) 30 Ra24
Cape Conavista ☆ CDN (NFL) 23 Rj21
Cape Coral USA (FL) 43 Qe32
Cape Elizabeth USA (ME) 22 Qk24
Cape Girardeau USA (MO) 36 Qa27
Cape Hatteras National Seashore ☆ USA (NC) 31 Qh28
Cape Krusenstern National Monument ☆ USA (AK) 10 Mc12
Cape Lookout National Seashore ☆ USA (MS) 31 Qg28
Cape May USA (NJ) 31 Qh26
Cape Pole USA (AK) 14 Nj17
Cape Race CDN (NFL) 23 Rj22
Cape Tormentine CDN (NB) 22 Rd22
Cape Vincent USA (NY) 29 Qg23
Capitan USA (NM) 34 Pc29
Capitol USA (MT) 26 Pc23
Capitol Reef National Park ☆ USA (UT) 33 Ok26
Capps USA (FL) 37 Qd30
Capreol CDN (ONT) 20 Qe22
Capron USA (VA) 31 Qg27
Cap-Seize CDN (QUE) 22 Rb21
Captain Cook USA (HI) 44 Mh36
Capulin Mountain National Monument ☆ USA (NM) 34 Pd27
Caramat CDN (ONT) 20 Qb2
Caraquet CDN (NB) 22 Rc22
Carberry CDN (MAN) 19 Pf2
Carbó MEX (SON) 38 Ok3
Carbon USA (TX) 35 Pf2
Carbonado USA (WA) 24 Od2
Carbondale USA (CO) 33 Pb2
Carbondale USA (IL) 36 Qa2
Carbondale USA (PA) 29 Qh2
Carbonear CDN (NFL) 23 Rj2
Carbonera, La MEX (TAM) 40 Pg3
Carcross CDN (YT) 14 Nh1
Cárdenas C (MZ) 43 Qe3
Cardinal CDN (MAN) 19 Pf2
Cardston CDN (ALB) 17 Oj2
Carefree USA (IN) 28 Qb2
Carey USA (ID) 25 Oj2
Caribou USA (ME) 22 Rb2
Caribou Depot CDN (NB) 22 Rb2
Carievale CDN (SAS) 18 Pe2
Carleton CDN (NS) 22 Rc2
Carleton Place CDN (ONT) 29 Qg2
Carlin USA (NV) 24 Og2
Carlin Gold Mine USA (NV) 24 Og2
Carlinville USA (IL) 28 Qa2
Carlisle USA (PA) 29 Qg2
Carlisle USA (SC) 37 Qe2
Carlowrie CDN (MAN) 19 Pg2
Carlsbad USA (CA) 32 Og2
Carlsbad USA (NM) 34 Pc2
Carlsbad USA (TX) 34 Pe3
Carlsbad Caverns National Park ☆ USA (NY) 34 Pc2
Carlton USA (WA) 16 Oe2
Carlyle CDN (SAS) 18 Pd
Carlyle USA (IL) 28 Qa
Carlyle USA (MT) 18 Pc
Carlyle Lake CDN (SAS) 18 Pd
Carmacks CDN (YT) 14 Ng
Carman CDN (MAN) 19 Pf
Carmangay CDN (ALB) 17 Oj
Carmanville CDN (NFL) 23 Rh
Carmi CDN (BC) 16 O
Carmi USA (IL) 28 Qa
Carmichael USA (MS) 36 Qa
Carnarvon CDN (ONT) 29 Qf
Carnduff CDN (SAS) 18 Pe
Carnegie USA (PA) 29 Qe
Carol City USA (FL) 43 Qe
Carolina USA (PR) 42 Rc
Carolina Sandhills National Wildlife Refuge ☆ USA (SC) 37 Qe
Caroline CDN (ALB) 17 Oh
Carolside CDN (ALB) 17 Ok
Caron Brook CDN (NB) 22 Ra
Carpenter USA (WY) 26 Pc
Carpinteria USA (CA) 32 O
Carpio USA (ND) 18 Pe
Carr USA (CO) 26 Pc
Carrabelle USA (FL) 36 Q
Carriere USA (MS) 36 Q
Carrillo MEX (CHA) 39 P
Carrington USA (ND) 19 P
Carrizal, El MEX (CHA) 39 P
Carrizo Plain National Monument ☆ USA (CA) 32 O
Carrizo Springs USA (TX) 40 P
Carrizozo USA (NM) 34 P
Carroll CDN (MAN) 18 P
Carroll USA (IA) 27 P
Carrollton USA (GA) 36 Q
Carrollton USA (KY) 28 Q
Carrollton USA (MO) 35 P
Carruthers CDN (SAS) 17 P
Carseland CDN (ALB) 17 C
Carson City USA (NV) 32 C
Carstairs CDN (ALB) 17 O
Cartago USA (CA) 32 C
Carter USA (MT) 17 C
Cartersville USA (GA) 36 C
Cartersville USA (IA) 27
Carthage USA (AR) 35
Carthage USA (IL) 27 F
Carthage USA (MO) 35 F
Carthage USA (MS) 36 C
Carthage USA (NY) 29 C
Carthage USA (TX) 35 F
Cartier CDN (ONT) 20 C
Cartier, Port- CDN (QUE) 22 F
Cartwright CDN (MAN) 19
Caruthersville USA (MO) 36 C
Carvel CDN (ALB) 17 C
Carway CDN (ALB) 17
Casadepaga USA (AK) 10 M
Casa Grande USA (AZ) 33 C
Casa Piedra USA (TX) 39
Casas MEX (TAM) 40
Casas Adobes USA (AZ) 33
Cascade CDN (BC) 16
Cascade USA (IA) 27
Cascade USA (MT) 17

Cascade-Siskiyou National Monument (USA) (OR) 24 Od24
Cascajal (C) (VC) 43 Qe34
Casco, El (MEX) (DGO) 39 Pc33
Cascorro (C) (CG) 43 Qg35
Cashton (USA) (WI) 27 Pk24
Casper (USA) (WY) 26 Pb24
Cassatot ☆ (USA) (AR) 35 Ph28
Cass City (USA) (MI) 29 Qd24
Casselman (CDN) (ONT) 29 Qh23
Casselton (USA) (ND) 19 Pg22
Cassiar (CDN) (BC) 14 Oa16
Cassidy (CDN) (BC) 16 Od21
Cass Lake (USA) (MN) 19 Ph22
Cassville (USA) (WI) 27 Pk24
Castaic (USA) (CA) 32 Of28
Castaños (MEX) (COA) 40 Pe32
Castella (USA) (CA) 24 Od25
Castillo de San Marcos National Monument ☆ (USA) (FL) 37 Qe31
Castlegar (CDN) (BC) 17 Og21
Castle Rock (USA) (CO) 34 Pc26
Castle Rock (USA) (SD) 26 Pd23
Castor (CDN) (ALB) 17 Ok19
Castor (USA) (LA) 35 Pj29
Castroville (USA) (TX) 40 Pf31
Casummit Lake (CDN) (ONT) 19 Pj20
Caswell (USA) (AK) 11 Na15
Catahoula National Wildlife Refuge ☆ (USA) (LA) 36 Pj30
Catalina (CDN) (NFL) 23 Rj21
Cataract (USA) (WI) 27 Pk23
Catarina (USA) (TX) 40 Pf31
Cataviña (MEX) (BCN) 38 Oh31
Catawba (USA) (WI) 27 Pk23
Cater (CDN) (SAS) 17 Pa19
Cathay (USA) (ND) 19 Pf22
Cathedral Provincial Park ☆ (CDN) (BC) 16 Oe21
Cathlamet (USA) (WA) 24 Od22
Cat Lake (CDN) (ONT) 19 Pk20
Catskill (USA) (NY) 30 Qj24
Causapscal (CDN) (QUE) 22 Rb21
Causey (USA) (NM) 34 Pd29
Cavalier (USA) (ND) 19 Pg21
Cave City (USA) (AR) 36 Pk28
Cavell (CDN) (SAS) 17 Pa19
Cavendish (CDN) (ALB) 17 Ok20
Cayajabos (C) (LH) 43 Qd34
Cayce (USA) (SC) 37 Qe29
Cayo Coco ☆ (C) (CA) 43 Qf34
Cayo Guillermo (C) (CA) 43 Qf34
Cayo Largo (C) (JU) 43 Qe35
Cayo Ramona (C) (MZ) 43 Qe34
Cayuga (USA) (TX) 35 Ph30
Ceballos (MEX) (DGO) 39 Pc32
Cecil Lake (CDN) (BC) 15 Oe17
Cedar (CDN) (BC) 16 Od21
Cedar Bluff (USA) (IA) 27 Pk25
Cedar City (USA) (UT) 33 Oj27
Cedaredge (USA) (CO) 33 Pb26
Cedar Falls (USA) (IA) 27 Pj24
Cedar Hill (USA) (MO) 28 Pk26
Cedar Hill (USA) (TX) 35 Pg29
Cedar Key (USA) (FL) 37 Qd31
Cedar Point (CDN) (ONT) 29 Qe23
Cedar Rapids (USA) (IA) 27 Pk25
Cedartown (USA) (GA) 36 Qc28
Cedarvale (CDN) (BC) 14 Oa18
Cedarville (USA) (CA) 24 Oe25
…doux (CDN) (SAS) 18 Pd21
…dral (MEX) (SLP) 40 Pe34
…dros (MEX) (DGO) 40 Pe33
…dros (MEX) (SON) 39 Pa32
…ina (USA) (OH) 28 Qc25
…ina (USA) (TN) 36 Qc27
…notillo (MEX) (YUC) 42 Qa35
…ntenario, El (MEX) (BCS) 38 Ok33
…nter (USA) (CO) 34 Pb27
…nter (USA) (TX) 35 Ph30
…nter, Le (USA) (MN) 27 Pj23
…nter Ossipee (USA) (NH) 22 Qk24
…nterville (USA) (IA) 27 Pj25
…nterville (USA) (NC) 31 Qf27
…nterville (USA) (TN) 36 Qb28
…nterville (USA) (WI) 27 Pk23
…ntra Butte (CDN) (SAS) 18 Pb20
…ntral (USA) (NM) 33 Pa29
…ntral City (USA) (IA) 27 Pk24
…ntral City (USA) (KY) 36 Qb27
…ntral City (USA) (NE) 26 Pf25
…ntralia (USA) (IL) 28 Qa26
…ntralia (USA) (MO) 28 Pj26
…tralia (USA) (WA) 24 Od22
…tral Patricia (CDN) (ONT) 19 Pk20
…tral Point (USA) (OR) 24 Od24
…tral Saanich (CDN) (BC) 16 Od21
…tral Valley (USA) (CA) 24 Od25
…treville (CDN) (NB) 22 Rb22
…treville (USA) (AL) 36 Qb29
…treville (USA) (MD) 29 Qg26
…reville (USA) (MS) 36 Pk30
…tro, El (USA) (CA) 33 Oh29
…zontle (MEX) (COA) 39 Pd32
…al (CDN) (ALB) 17 Ok20
…esco (USA) (NE) 27 Pg25
…alvo (MEX) (NL) 40 Pf32
…o Gamo (MEX) (SON) 33 Oj30
…on (CDN) (SAS) 18 Pc21
…co Culture National Historic Park ☆ (USA) (NM) 33 Pb27
…dron (USA) (NE) 26 Pd24
…aktolik (USA) (AK) 10 Md15
…k River (CDN) (ONT) 29 Qg22
…kyitsik (USA) (AK) 11 Nd12
…is (USA) (ID) 25 Oh23
…mette (USA) (LA) 36 Qa31
…na (USA) (NM) 34 Pb27
…bas (C) (CA) 43 Qf34
…berlain (CDN) (SAS) 18 Pc20
…berlain (USA) (SD) 26 Pf24
…bersburg (USA) (PA) 29 Qg26
…bord (CDN) (QUE) 21 Qj21
…pagne (CDN) (NWT) 14 Ng15
…paign (USA) (IL) 28 Qa25
…pion (USA) (MI) 20 Qb22
…daler (USA) (AK) 11 Na12
…dler (CDN) (QUE) 22 Rc21
…dler (USA) (TX) 35 Ph29

Channel Islands National Park ☆ (USA) (CA) 32 Oe29
Channel-Port-aux-Basques (CDN) (NFL) 23 Rf22
Channing (USA) (TX) 34 Pd28
Chanute (USA) (KS) 35 Ph27
Chapais (CDN) (QUE) 21 Qh21
Chapel Hill (USA) (NC) 37 Qf28
Chapleau (CDN) (ONT) 20 Qd22
Chapleau Crown Game Preserve ☆ (CDN) (ONT) 20 Qc21
Chaplin (CDN) (SAS) 18 Pb20
Chapmanville (USA) (WV) 37 Qd27
Chappell (USA) (NE) 26 Pd25
Chaptico (USA) (MD) 29 Qg26
Charcas (MEX) (SLP) 40 Pe34
Charco de la Aguja (MEX) (CHA) 39 Pc31
Charco de la Peña (MEX) (CHA) 39 Pc31
Chard (CDN) (ALB) 17 Ok18
Chariton (USA) (IA) 27 Pj25
Charles (CDN) (MAN) 18 Pe18
Charlesbourg (CDN) (QUE) 22 Qk22
Charles City (USA) (IA) 27 Pj24
Charles City (USA) (VA) 31 Qg27
Charles M. Russell National Wildlife Refuge ☆ (USA) (MT) 18 Pa22
Charleston (USA) (IL) 28 Qa26
Charleston (USA) (MO) 36 Qa27
Charleston (USA) (SC) 37 Qf29
Charleston (USA) (WV) 29 Qe26
Charlestown (USA) (IN) 28 Qc26
Charles Town (USA) (WV) 29 Qg26
Charlevoix (USA) (MI) 28 Qc23
Charlie Lake (CDN) (BC) 15 Oe17
Charliste (USA) (AR) 36 Pk28
Charlotte (USA) (MI) 28 Qc24
Charlotte (USA) (NC) 37 Qe28
Charlotte (USA) (TX) 40 Pf31
Charlotte Amalie (USA) (VI) 42 Rc36
Charlotte, Port (USA) (FL) 43 Qd32
Charlotte Court House (USA) (VA) 31 Qf27
Charlottesville (USA) (VA) 29 Qf27
Charlottetown (CDN) (PEI) 22 Rd22
Charlson (USA) (ND) 18 Pd21
Charlton (CDN) (ONT) 21 Qf22
Chase City (USA) (VA) 31 Qf27
Châteauguay (CDN) (QUE) 30 Qj23
Château-Richer (CDN) (QUE) 22 Qk22
Chater (CDN) (MAN) 19 Pf21
Chatfield (USA) (MN) 27 Pj24
Chatham (CDN) (NB) 22 Rc22
Chatham (CDN) (ONT) 29 Qd24
Chatham (USA) (AK) 14 Nh17
Chatham (USA) (LA) 36 Pj29
Chatham (USA) (MI) 20 Qb22
Chatham (USA) (VA) 37 Qf27
Chatsworth (CDN) (ONT) 29 Qe23
Chatsworth (USA) (GA) 36 Qc28
Chattahoochee (USA) (FL) 36 Qc30
Chattanooga (USA) (TN) 36 Qc28
Chattaroy (USA) (WA) 17 Og22
Chauvin (USA) (LA) 36 Pk31
Chebogue Point (CDN) (NS) 22 Rb24
Cheboygan (USA) (MI) 28 Qc23
Checotah (USA) (OK) 35 Ph28
Cheektowaga (USA) (NY) 29 Qf24
Chefornak (USA) (AK) 12 Mc15
Chehalis (USA) (WA) 24 Od22
Chelan (CDN) (SAS) 18 Pd19
Chelan (USA) (WA) 16 Oe22
Chelmsford (CDN) (ONT) 20 Qe22
Chemainus (CDN) (BC) 16 Od21
Chemong (CDN) (SAS) 18 Pd19
Chemult (USA) (OR) 24 Oe24
Chena Hot Springs (USA) (AK) 11 Nb13
Chénéville (CDN) (QUE) 29 Qh23
Cheney (USA) (WA) 17 Og22
Chenik (USA) (AK) 12 Mh16
Chenoa (USA) (IL) 28 Qa25
Cheraw (USA) (SC) 37 Qf28
Cherhill (CDN) (ALB) 17 Oh19
Cherokee (USA) (IA) 27 Ph24
Cherokee Sound (BS) 43 Qg32
Cherry Creek (USA) (SD) 26 Pe23
Cherryfield (USA) (ME) 22 Rb23
Cherry Grove (CDN) (ALB) 17 Ok18
Cherry Hill (USA) (VA) 31 Qg27
Cherryspring (USA) (TX) 40 Pf30
Cherryville (CDN) (BC) 16 Of20
Cherryville (USA) (MO) 36 Pk27
Chesapeake (USA) (VA) 31 Qg27
Chesapeake Bay Bridge Tunnel ☆ (USA) (VA) 31 Qh27
Chesapeake Beach (USA) (MD) 29 Qg26
Chester (CDN) (NS) 22 Rc23
Chester (USA) (IA) 27 Pj24
Chester (USA) (IL) 36 Qa27
Chester (USA) (MT) 17 Ok21
Chester (USA) (PA) 31 Qh26
Chester (USA) (SC) 37 Qe28
Chester (USA) (VA) 31 Qg27
Chestertown (USA) (MD) 29 Qg26
Chesterville (CDN) (ONT) 29 Qh23
Chetek (USA) (WI) 27 Pk23
Chéticamp (CDN) (NS) 23 Re22
Chetwynd (CDN) (BC) 15 Oe18
Chevak (USA) (AK) 10 Mc15
Chewelah (USA) (WA) 17 Og21
Cheyenne (USA) (OK) 35 Pf28
Cheyenne (USA) (WY) 26 Pc25
Cheyenne Wells (USA) (CO) 34 Pd26
Chibougamau (CDN) (QUE) 21 Qh21
Chibougamau, Parc provincial ☆ (CDN) (QUE) 21 Qj21
Chicago (USA) (IL) 28 Qb25
Chicago Heights (USA) (IL) 28 Qb25
Chic-Chocs, Réserve Faunique des ☆ (CDN) (QUE) 22 Rc21
Chichagof (USA) (AK) 14 Ng17
Chicharrona, La (MEX) (ZAC) 39 Pd34
Chickaloon (USA) (AK) 13 Na15
Chickasaw (USA) (AL) 36 Qa30
Chickasha (USA) (OK) 35 Pg28
Chicken (USA) (AK) 11 Ne13
Chico (USA) (CA) 32 Oe26
Chicomoztoc ☆ (MEX) (ZAC) 39 Pd34
Chicopee (USA) (MA) 30 Qj24
Chicot State Park ☆ (USA) (LA) 36 Pj30
Chicotte, Rivière- (CDN) (QUE) 22 Rd21
Chicoutimi (CDN) (QUE) 22 Qk21
Chidester (USA) (AR) 35 Pj29
Chiefland (USA) (FL) 37 Qd31

Chief Menominee Monument ☆ (USA) (IN) 28 Qb25
Chiftak (USA) (AK) 12 Md15
Chignik (USA) (AK) 12 Mf17
Chihuahua (MEX) (CHA) 39 Pb31
Chilcoot (USA) (CA) 32 Oe26
Childersburg (USA) (AL) 36 Qb29
Childress (USA) (TX) 34 Pe28
Chilesburg (USA) (VA) 29 Qg26
Chilkat (USA) (AK) 13 Nc15
Chilkat Bald Eagle Preserve ☆ (USA) (AK) 14 Ng16
Chilkoot, Port (USA) (AK) 14 Nh16
Chillicothe (USA) (IL) 28 Qa25
Chillicothe (USA) (MO) 35 Pj26
Chillicothe (USA) (OH) 29 Qd26
Chilliwack (CDN) (BC) 16 Oe21
Chiloquin (USA) (OR) 24 Oe24
Chilton (USA) (WI) 28 Qa23
China (MEX) (NL) 40 Pf33
Chinero, El (MEX) (BCN) 33 Oh30
Chinle (USA) (AZ) 33 Pa27
Chino (USA) (CA) 32 Og29
Chinook (CDN) (ALB) 17 Oh20
Chinook (USA) (MT) 17 Pa21
Chinook Valley (CDN) (ALB) 15 Og17
Chino Valley (USA) (AZ) 33 Oj28
Chipley (USA) (FL) 36 Qc30
Chipman (CDN) (ALB) 17 Oj19
Chipman (CDN) (NB) 22 Rc22
Chippewa Falls (USA) (WI) 27 Pk23
Chiquilá (MEX) (QR) 42 Qb35
Chisana (USA) (AK) 11 Ne14
Chisasibi (CDN) (QUE) 21 Qf19
Chisholm (USA) (MN) 19 Pj22
Chitek (CDN) (SAS) 18 Pb19
Chitina (USA) (AK) 13 Nc15
Chivicahua National Monument ☆ (USA) (AZ) 33 Pa30
Choate (CDN) (BC) 16 Oe21
Chocowinity (USA) (NC) 31 Qg28
Choice (USA) (MN) 27 Pk24
Choiseland (CDN) (SAS) 18 Pc19
Choix (MEX) (SIN) 39 Pa32
Choix, Port (CDN) (NFL) 23 Rg20
Cholame (USA) (CA) 32 Oe28
Cholay (MEX) (SON) 38 Ok31
Choteau (USA) (MT) 17 Oj22
Chouteau (USA) (OK) 35 Ph27
Chowchilla (USA) (CA) 32 Oe27
Chrisman (USA) (IL) 28 Qb26
Christiansburg (USA) (VA) 37 Qe27
Christina Lake (CDN) (BC) 16 Of21
Chub Cay (BS) 43 Qg33
Chugiak (USA) (AK) 13 Na15
Chugwater (USA) (WY) 26 Pc25
Chula Vista (USA) (CA) 32 Og29
Chulitna = Hurricane (USA) (AK) 11 Na14
Chumul ☆ (MEX) (YUC) 42 Qa35
Chupadero de Caballo (MEX) (COA) 40 Pe31
Church (USA) (VA) 31 Qg27
Churchbridge (CDN) (SAS) 18 Pe20
Church Point (USA) (LA) 36 Pj30
Churchs Ferry (USA) (ND) 19 Pf21
Churchville (USA) (VA) 29 Qf26
Churubusco (USA) (IN) 28 Qc25
Chute Lake (CDN) (BC) 16 Of21
Chutine Landing (CDN) (BC) 14 Nk17
Cibola National Wildlife Refuge ☆ (USA) (CA) 33 Oh29
Ciego de Ávila (C) (CA) 43 Qf35
Cienfuegos (C) (CF) 43 Qe34
Cifuentes (C) (VC) 43 Qe34
Cigarette Springs Cave ☆ (USA) (UT) 33 Pa27
Cimarron (USA) (CO) 33 Pb26
Cimarron (USA) (KS) 34 Pe27
Cimarron (USA) (NM) 34 Pc27
Cincinnati (USA) (OH) 28 Qc26
Cinco, El (MEX) (DGO) 39 Pd33
Circle (USA) (AK) 11 Nc13
Circle (USA) (MT) 18 Pc22
Circleville (USA) (OH) 29 Qd26
Ciruelo, El (MEX) (BCS) 38 Ok33
Cisco (USA) (TX) 35 Pf29
Cisco (USA) (UT) 33 Pa26
Citra (USA) (FL) 37 Qd31
Citronelle (USA) (AL) 36 Qa30
Citrus Heights (USA) (CA) 32 Oe26
Ciudad (MEX) (DGO) 39 Pc34
Ciudad Acuña (MEX) (COA) 40 Pe31
Ciudad Camargo (MEX) (CHA) 39 Pc32
Ciudad Constitución (MEX) (BCS) 38 Ok33
Ciudad Juárez (MEX) (CHA) 33 Pb30
Ciudad Lerdo (MEX) (DGO) 39 Pd33
Ciudad Obregón (MEX) (SON) 39 Pa32
Ciudad Victoria (MEX) (TAM) 40 Pf34
Clagstone (USA) (ID) 17 Og21
Claire, Le (USA) (IA) 27 Pk25
Claire City (USA) (SD) 27 Pg23
Clairemont (USA) (TX) 34 Pe29
Clairmont (CDN) (ALB) 15 Of18
Clallam Bay (USA) (WA) 16 Oc21
Clam Lake (USA) (WI) 20 Pk22
Clandonald (CDN) (ALB) 17 Ok19
Clanton (USA) (AL) 36 Qb29
Clara City (USA) (MN) 27 Ph23
Clare (USA) (MI) 28 Qc24
Claremont (USA) (NH) 30 Qj24
Claremore (USA) (OK) 35 Ph27
Clarence (USA) (LA) 35 Pj30
Clarence (USA) (MO) 28 Pj26
Clarendon (USA) (TX) 34 Pe28
Clarenville (CDN) (NFL) 23 Rh21
Claresholm (CDN) (ALB) 17 Oj20
Clarinda (USA) (IA) 27 Ph25
Clarion (USA) (IA) 27 Pj24
Clarion (USA) (PA) 29 Qf25
Clark (USA) (SD) 27 Pg23
Clarkdale (USA) (AZ) 33 Oj28
Clarkdon (CDN) (ONT) 19 Pk21
Clarke City (CDN) (QUE) 22 Rb20
Clarkfield (USA) (MN) 27 Ph23
Clark Fork (USA) (ID) 17 Og21
Clarkleigh (CDN) (MAN) 19 Pf20
Clarks (USA) (NE) 27 Pg25
Clarksburg (USA) (WV) 29 Qe26
Clarksdale (USA) (MS) 36 Pk28
Clark's Harbour (CDN) (NS) 22 Rc24
Clarks Point (USA) (AK) 12 Mf16
Clarks Summit (USA) (PA) 29 Qh25
Clarkston (USA) (WA) 24 Og22
Clarksville (USA) (AR) 35 Pj28

Clarksville (USA) (FL) 36 Qc30
Clarksville (USA) (TN) 36 Qb27
Clarksville (USA) (TX) 35 Ph29
Clarksville (USA) (VA) 31 Qf27
Clarkville (USA) (CO) 26 Pd25
Claude (USA) (TX) 34 Pe28
Claxton (USA) (GA) 37 Qe29
Claybank (CDN) (SAS) 18 Pc20
Clay Center (USA) (KS) 35 Pg26
Clay Center (USA) (NE) 26 Pf25
Clay City (USA) (KY) 37 Qd27
Claydon (CDN) (SAS) 18 Pa21
Clayhurst (CDN) (BC) 15 Oe17
Claysville (USA) (KY) 28 Qc26
Clayton (USA) (AL) 36 Qc30
Clayton (USA) (GA) 37 Qd28
Clayton (USA) (LA) 36 Pk30
Clayton (USA) (MO) 28 Pk26
Clayton (USA) (NM) 34 Pd27
Clayton (USA) (NY) 29 Qg23
Clayton (USA) (OK) 35 Ph28
Clayton (USA) (TX) 35 Ph29
Clearbrook (USA) (MN) 19 Ph22
Cleardale (CDN) (ALB) 15 Of17
Clearfield (USA) (PA) 29 Qf25
Clearfield (USA) (SD) 26 Pe24
Clearfield (USA) (UT) 25 Oj25
Clear Hills (CDN) (ALB) 15 Og17
Clear Lake (USA) (IA) 27 Pj24
Clear Lake (USA) (SD) 27 Pg23
Clear Lake (USA) (WI) 27 Pj23
Clear Prairie (CDN) (ALB) 15 Of17
Clearwater (CDN) (BC) 16 Oe20
Clearwater (USA) (FL) 43 Qd32
Clearwater (USA) (MT) 25 Oj22
Clearwater Provincial Park ☆ (CDN) (MAN) 18 Pe18
Cleburne (USA) (TX) 35 Pg29
Cle Elum (USA) (WA) 24 Oe22
Clementson (USA) (MN) 19 Ph21
Clemson (USA) (SC) 37 Qd28
Clendenin (USA) (WV) 29 Qe26
Clermont (CDN) (QUE) 22 Qk22
Clermont (USA) (FL) 43 Qe31
Cleveland (USA) (AR) 35 Pj28
Cleveland (USA) (GA) 37 Qd28
Cleveland (USA) (MS) 36 Pk29
Cleveland (USA) (MT) 17 Pa21
Cleveland (USA) (ND) 19 Pf22
Cleveland (USA) (OH) 29 Qe25
Cleveland (USA) (TN) 36 Qc28
Cleveland (USA) (TX) 41 Ph30
Cleveland Heights (USA) (OH) 29 Qe25
Clewiston (USA) (FL) 43 Qe32
Cliff (USA) (NM) 33 Pa29
Clifton (USA) (KS) 35 Pg26
Clifton (USA) (LA) 36 Pk30
Clifton (USA) (TX) 35 Pg30
Clifton Forge (USA) (VA) 37 Qf27
Climax (CDN) (SAS) 18 Pa21
Climax (USA) (GA) 36 Qc30
Climax (USA) (MN) 19 Pg22
Cline (USA) (TX) 40 Pe31
Clines Corners (USA) (NM) 34 Pc28
Clint (USA) (TX) 34 Pb30
Clinton (CDN) (BC) 16 Oe20
Clinton (CDN) (ONT) 29 Qe24
Clinton (USA) (AR) 35 Pj28
Clinton (USA) (IA) 28 Pk25
Clinton (USA) (IL) 28 Qa25
Clinton (USA) (IN) 28 Qb26
Clinton (USA) (KY) 36 Qa27
Clinton (USA) (LA) 36 Pk30
Clinton (USA) (MI) 29 Qd24
Clinton (USA) (MO) 35 Pj26
Clinton (USA) (MS) 36 Pk29
Clinton (USA) (NC) 31 Qf28
Clinton (USA) (OK) 35 Pf28
Clinton (USA) (SC) 37 Qe28
Clinton, Port (USA) (OH) 29 Qd25
Clintonville (USA) (WI) 28 Qa23
Clio (USA) (AL) 36 Qc30
Clo-oose (CDN) (BC) 16 Oc21
Cloquet (USA) (MN) 19 Pj22
Cloridorme (CDN) (QUE) 22 Rc21
Cloverdale (USA) (CA) 32 Od26
Cloverdale (USA) (MN) 27 Pj22
Cloverton (USA) (MN) 27 Pj22
Clovis (USA) (CA) 32 Of27
Clovis (USA) (NM) 34 Pd28
Cloyne (CDN) (ONT) 29 Qg23
Club Mayanabo (C) (CG) 43 Qg35
Clyde (CDN) (ALB) 17 Oj18
Clyde (USA) (ND) 19 Pf21
Clyde (USA) (NY) 29 Qg24
Clyde, Port (USA) (ME) 22 Ra24
Clyde Park (USA) (MT) 25 Ok23
Clyde River (CDN) (NS) 22 Rc24
Coachella (USA) (CA) 32 Og29
Coahoma (USA) (TX) 34 Pe29
Coahuila, Estación (MEX) (BCN) 33 Oh29
Coal Creek (CDN) (BC) 17 Oh21
Coal Creek (USA) (AK) 11 Nd13
Coaldale (CDN) (ALB) 17 Oj21
Coaldale (USA) (NV) 32 Og26
Coalhurst (CDN) (ALB) 17 Oj21
Coalinga (USA) (CA) 32 Oe27
Coalmont (CDN) (BC) 16 Oe21
Coalridge (USA) (MT) 18 Pc21
Coal River (CDN) (BC) 14 Ob16
Coalspur (CDN) (ALB) 17 Og19
Coalville (USA) (UT) 25 Ok25
Coatesville (USA) (PA) 29 Qh26
Coaticook (CDN) (QUE) 22 Qk23
Cobalt (CDN) (ONT) 21 Qf22
Cobden (CDN) (ONT) 29 Qg23
Cobleskill (USA) (NY) 30 Qh24
Coboconk (CDN) (ONT) 29 Qf23
Cobourg (CDN) (ONT) 29 Qf24
Cochagne (CDN) (NB) 22 Rc22
Cochenour (CDN) (ONT) 19 Pj20
Cochin (CDN) (SAS) 17 Pa19
Cochise (USA) (AZ) 33 Pa29
Cochran (USA) (GA) 37 Qd29
Cochrane (CDN) (ALB) 17 Oh20
Cochrane (CDN) (ONT) 20 Qe21
Coco, Cayo ☆ (C) (CA) 43 Qf34
Cocoa (USA) (FL) 43 Qe31
Cocolalla (USA) (ID) 17 Og21

Cody (USA) (NE) 26 Pe24
Cody (USA) (WY) 25 Pa23
Coeur d'Alene (USA) (ID) 17 Og22
Coffee Creek (CDN) (YT) 11 Nf14
Coffeeville (USA) (AL) 36 Qa30
Coffeyville (USA) (KS) 35 Ph27
Cohagen (USA) (MT) 18 Pb22
Cohoes (USA) (NY) 30 Qj24
Cokeville (USA) (WY) 25 Ok24
Colbert (USA) (WA) 17 Og22
Colborne (CDN) (ONT) 29 Qg23
Colborne, Port (CDN) (ONT) 29 Qf24
Colby (USA) (KS) 34 Pe26
Colchester (USA) (VT) 30 Qj23
Cold Bay (USA) (AK) 12 Md18
Coldwater (USA) (MI) 28 Qc25
Cole Bay (CDN) (SAS) 17 Pa18
Colebrook (USA) (NH) 22 Qk23
Cole Camp (USA) (MO) 35 Pj26
Coleman (CDN) (ALB) 17 Oh21
Coleman (USA) (TX) 35 Pf30
Coleraine (USA) (MN) 19 Pj22
Coles Island (CDN) (NB) 22 Rc23
Coleville (CDN) (SAS) 17 Pa20
Colfax (USA) (CA) 32 Oe26
Colfax (USA) (IA) 27 Pj25
Colfax (USA) (LA) 36 Pj30
Colfax (USA) (WA) 24 Og22
Colfax (USA) (WI) 27 Pk23
Colgate (CDN) (SAS) 18 Pd21
Colinet (CDN) (NFL) 23 Rj22
Coliseo (C) (MZ) 43 Qe34
Collbran (USA) (CO) 33 Pb26
College Park (USA) (GA) 36 Qc29
College Place (USA) (WA) 24 Of22
College Station (USA) (TX) 40 Pg30
Collierville (USA) (TN) 36 Qa28
Collingwood (CDN) (ONT) 29 Qe23
Collins (CDN) (ONT) 20 Qa20
Collins (USA) (AR) 36 Pk29
Collins (USA) (IA) 27 Pj25
Collins (USA) (MO) 35 Pj27
Collins (USA) (MS) 36 Qa30
Collins (USA) (MT) 17 Ok22
Collinsville (USA) (AL) 36 Qc28
Collinsville (USA) (IL) 28 Qa26
Collinsville (USA) (OK) 35 Pg27
Colnett (MEX) (BCN) 38 Og30
Coloma (USA) (WI) 28 Qa23
Colombia (C) (LT) 43 Qg35
Colombia (MEX) (NL) 40 Pf32
Colombier (CDN) (QUE) 22 Ra21
Colome (USA) (SD) 26 Pf24
Colón (C) (MZ) 43 Qe34
Colonial Beach (USA) (MD) 29 Qg26
Colonial Heights (USA) (VA) 31 Qg27
Colonial Michilimackinac ☆ (USA) (MI) 28 Qc23
Colonia Vicente Guerrero (MEX) (BCN) 38 Oh30
Colony (USA) (WY) 26 Pc23
Colorado (C) (CA) 43 Qf35
Colorado City (USA) (CO) 34 Pc27
Colorado City (USA) (TX) 34 Pe29
Colorado Springs (USA) (CO) 34 Pc26
Colquitt (USA) (GA) 36 Qc30
Coltons Point (USA) (MD) 29 Qg26
Columbia (USA) (KY) 36 Qc27
Columbia (USA) (LA) 35 Pj29
Columbia (USA) (MD) 29 Qg26
Columbia (USA) (MO) 28 Pj26
Columbia (USA) (MS) 36 Qa30
Columbia (USA) (PA) 29 Qg25
Columbia (USA) (SC) 37 Qe29
Columbia (USA) (TN) 36 Qb28
Columbia Beach (USA) (WA) 16 Od22
Columbia City (USA) (FL) 37 Qd30
Columbia Falls (USA) (ME) 22 Rb23
Columbia Falls (USA) (MT) 17 Oh21
Columbine (USA) (CO) 26 Pb25
Columbus (USA) (GA) 36 Qc29
Columbus (USA) (IN) 28 Qc26
Columbus (USA) (KS) 35 Ph27
Columbus (USA) (MS) 36 Qa29
Columbus (USA) (ND) 18 Pd21
Columbus (USA) (NE) 27 Pg25
Columbus (USA) (NM) 34 Pb30
Columbus (USA) (OH) 29 Qd26
Columbus (USA) (TX) 40 Pg31
Columbus (USA) (WI) 28 Qa24
Columbus Junction (USA) (IA) 27 Pk25
Colville (USA) (WA) 17 Og21
Coma, La (MEX) (TAM) 40 Pf33
Comanche (USA) (TX) 35 Pf30
Combermere (CDN) (ONT) 29 Qg23
Comedero (MEX) (SIN) 39 Pb33
Comer (USA) (GA) 37 Qd28
Comfort (USA) (TX) 40 Pf31
Commerce (USA) (TX) 35 Ph29
Comox (CDN) (BC) 16 Oc21
Compadre, El (MEX) (BCN) 32 Og29
Compass Lake (USA) (FL) 36 Qc30
Compeer (CDN) (ALB) 17 Ok20
Comstock (USA) (TX) 40 Pe31
Concepción del Oro (MEX) (DGO) 40 Pe33
Conchas Dam (USA) (NM) 34 Pc28
Conconully (USA) (WA) 16 Of21
Concord (USA) (CA) 32 Oe27
Concord (USA) (KY) 29 Qd26
Concord (USA) (NC) 37 Qe28
Concord (USA) (NH) 22 Qk24
Concordia (MEX) (SIN) 39 Pb34
Concordia (USA) (KS) 35 Pg26
Concordia (USA) (MO) 35 Pj26
Conde (USA) (SD) 26 Pf23
Condon (USA) (OR) 24 Oe23
Conejo, El (MEX) (BCS) 38 Ok33
Congaree National Park ☆ (USA) (SC) 37 Qe29
Congress (CDN) (SAS) 18 Pc21
Congress (USA) (AZ) 33 Oj28
Coniston (CDN) (ONT) 20 Qe22
Conitaca (MEX) (SIN) 39 Pb33
Conkal (MEX) (YUC) 42 Qa35
Conklin (CDN) (ALB) 17 Ok18
Conmee (CDN) (ONT) 20 Qa21
Conn (USA) (MS) 36 Pk30
Conneaut (USA) (OH) 29 Qe25
Connell (USA) (WA) 24 Of22
Connellsville (USA) (PA) 29 Qf25
Connersville (USA) (IN) 28 Qc26

Connors (CDN) (NB) 22 Ra22
Connorsville (USA) (WI) 27 Pj23
Conover (USA) (MI) 27 Qa22
Conrad (USA) (MT) 17 Ok21
Conroe (USA) (TX) 41 Ph30
Consolación del Sur (C) (PR) 43 Qd34
Consort (CDN) (ALB) 17 Ok20
Constitución, Ciudad (MEX) (BCS) 38 Ok33
Constitución de 1857, Parque Nacional ☆ (MEX) (BCN) 32 Og29
Consul (CDN) (SAS) 17 Pa21
Contact (USA) (NV) 25 Oh25
Continental (USA) (AZ) 33 Ok30
Converse (USA) (LA) 35 Pj30
Conway (USA) (AR) 35 Pj28
Conway (USA) (NH) 22 Qk24
Conway (USA) (SC) 37 Qf29
Conway (USA) (TX) 34 Pe28
Cook (USA) (MN) 19 Pj22
Cookeville (USA) (TN) 36 Qc27
Cooking Lake (CDN) (ALB) 17 Oj19
Cooksburg (USA) (NY) 30 Qh24
Cooks Harbour (CDN) (NFL) 23 Rh20
Cookshire (CDN) (QUE) 22 Qk23
Coolidge (USA) (TX) 35 Pg30
Coolin (USA) (ID) 17 Og21
Coon Rapids (USA) (MN) 27 Pj23
Cooper (USA) (ME) 22 Rb23
Cooper (USA) (NM) 34 Pd29
Cooper (USA) (TX) 35 Ph29
Coopers Mills (USA) (ME) 22 Ra23
Cooper's Town (BS) 43 Qg32
Cooperstown (USA) (ND) 19 Pf22
Coos Bay (USA) (OR) 24 Oc24
Copas (USA) (MN) 27 Pj23
Cope (USA) (CO) 34 Pd26
Copeland (USA) (ID) 17 Og21
Copeland (USA) (KS) 34 Pe27
Copperas Cove (USA) (TX) 40 Pg30
Copper Harbor (USA) (WI) 20 Qb22
Coquitlam (CDN) (BC) 16 Od21
Coral Heights (BS) 43 Qg33
Corberrie (CDN) (NS) 22 Rc23
Corbin (USA) (KY) 36 Qc27
Corcoran (USA) (CA) 32 Of27
Cordele (USA) (GA) 37 Qd30
Cordell (USA) (OK) 35 Pf28
Cordova (USA) (AK) 13 Nc15
Corey, La (CDN) (ALB) 17 Ok18
Corinna (USA) (ME) 22 Ra23
Corinne (CDN) (SAS) 18 Pc20
Corinth (USA) (KY) 28 Qc26
Corinth (USA) (ME) 22 Ra23
Corinth (USA) (MS) 36 Qa28
Cormorant (CDN) (MAN) 18 Pe18
Cormorant Provincial Forest ☆ (CDN) (MAN) 18 Pe18
Cornell (USA) (WI) 27 Pk23
Corner Brook (CDN) (NFL) 23 Rg21
Corning (USA) (AR) 36 Pk27
Corning (USA) (CA) 32 Od26
Corning (USA) (IA) 27 Ph25
Corning (USA) (KS) 35 Pg26
Corning (USA) (NY) 29 Qg24
Cornudas (USA) (TX) 34 Pc30
Cornwall (BS) 43 Qg33
Cornwall (CDN) (ONT) 30 Qh23
Corolla (USA) (NC) 31 Qh27
Corona (USA) (NM) 34 Pc28
Coronach (CDN) (SAS) 18 Pc21
Coronado, Villa (MEX) (CHA) 39 Pc32
Coronado National Monument ☆ (USA) (AZ) 33 Ok30
Coronation (CDN) (ALB) 17 Ok19
Coronation Island Wilderness ☆ (USA) (AK) 14 Nh18
Corpus Christi (USA) (TX) 40 Pg32
Corry (USA) (PA) 29 Qf25
Corsicana (USA) (TX) 35 Pg29
Cortaro (USA) (AZ) 33 Ok29
Cortez (USA) (CO) 33 Pa27
Cortez Gold Mine (USA) (NV) 24 Og25
Cortland (USA) (NE) 27 Pg25
Cortland (USA) (NY) 29 Qg24
Corvallis (USA) (OR) 24 Od23
Corwin (USA) (AK) 10 Mc11
Corydon (USA) (IA) 27 Pj25
Corydon (USA) (IN) 28 Qb26
Cos, Villa de (MEX) (ZAC) 40 Pd34
Coshocton (USA) (OH) 29 Qe25
Costilla (USA) (NM) 34 Pc27
Cotopaxi (USA) (CO) 34 Pc26
Cotorro (C) (H) 43 Qd34
Cottage Grove (USA) (MN) 27 Pj23
Cottage Grove (USA) (OR) 24 Od24
Cotter (USA) (AR) 35 Pj27
Cotton (USA) (MN) 19 Pj22
Cottondale (USA) (FL) 36 Qc30
Cottonport (USA) (LA) 36 Pj30
Cotton Valley (USA) (LA) 35 Pj29
Cottonwood (CDN) (BC) 16 Od19
Cottonwood (USA) (AZ) 33 Oj28
Cottonwood (USA) (CA) 24 Od25
Cottonwood (USA) (ID) 24 Og22
Cotulla (USA) (TX) 40 Pf31
Coudersport (USA) (PA) 29 Qg25
Coulee (USA) (ND) 18 Pe21
Coulee City (USA) (WA) 16 Of22
Coulee Dam (USA) (WA) 16 Of22
Coulterville (USA) (IL) 28 Qa26
Council (USA) (AK) 10 Md13
Council (USA) (ID) 24 Og23
Council Bluffs (USA) (IA) 27 Ph25
Council Grove (USA) (KS) 35 Pg26
Counselors (USA) (NM) 33 Pb27
Coupeville (USA) (WA) 16 Od21
Court (CDN) (SAS) 17 Pa20
Courtenay (CDN) (BC) 16 Oc21
Courtenay (USA) (ND) 19 Pf22
Courtright (CDN) (ONT) 29 Qd24
Coushatta (USA) (LA) 35 Pj29
Coutts (CDN) (ALB) 17 Ok21
Cove Fort (USA) (UT) 33 Oj26
Covered Wells (USA) (AZ) 33 Oj29
Covington (USA) (GA) 37 Qd29
Covington (USA) (LA) 36 Pk30
Covington (USA) (MI) 20 Qa22
Covington (USA) (OH) 28 Qc25
Covington (USA) (TN) 36 Qa28
Covington (USA) (VA) 37 Qe27
Cowan (CDN) (MAN) 18 Pe19
Cowansville (CDN) (QUE) 30 Qj23
Cowdrey (USA) (CO) 26 Pb25
Cowley (CDN) (ALB) 17 Oh21
Cowlic (USA) (AZ) 33 Oj30
Cox's Cove (CDN) (NFL) 23 Rf21
Coyame (MEX) (CHA) 39 Pc31
Coyote (USA) (NM) 33 Pa27
Coyote (USA) (NM) 34 Pc29
Coyote, El (MEX) (BCN) 32 Og30
Coyotitán (MEX) (SIN) 39 Pb34
Cozad (USA) (NE) 26 Pf25
Craig (USA) (AK) 14 Nj18
Craig (USA) (CO) 25 Pb25
Craigend (CDN) (ALB) 17 Ok18
Craigmore (CDN) (NS) 23 Re23
Craigsville (USA) (WV) 29 Qe26
Craik (CDN) (SAS) 18 Pc20
Cranberry Junction (CDN) (BC) 14 Oa18
Cranberry Portage (CDN) (MAN) 18 Pe18
Cranbrook (CDN) (BC) 17 Oh21
Crandall (CDN) (MAN) 18 Pe20
Crane (USA) (MO) 35 Pj27
Crane (USA) (OR) 24 Of24
Crane (USA) (TX) 39 Pd30
Crane Lake (USA) (MN) 19 Pj21
Crane Valley (CDN) (SAS) 18 Pc21
Cranfills Gap (USA) (TX) 35 Pg30
Cranford (CDN) (ALB) 17 Oj21
Cranston (USA) (RI) 30 Qk25
Crater Lake National Park ☆ (USA) (OR) 24 Od24
Crater of Diamonds State Park ☆ (USA) (AR) 35 Pj28
Craters of the Moon National Monument ☆ (USA) (ID) 25 Oj24
Craven (CDN) (SAS) 18 Pc20
Crawford (USA) (CO) 33 Pb26
Crawford (USA) (GA) 37 Qd29
Crawford (USA) (NE) 26 Pd24
Crawford (USA) (TX) 35 Pg30
Crawfordsville (USA) (IN) 28 Qb25
Creede (USA) (CO) 33 Pb27
Creedmoor (USA) (NC) 31 Qf27
Creel (MEX) (CHA) 39 Pb32
Creelman (CDN) (SAS) 18 Pd21
Cremona (CDN) (ALB) 17 Oh20
Creola (USA) (AL) 36 Qa30
Cresbard (USA) (SD) 26 Pf23
Crescent (USA) (OR) 24 Oe24
Crescent, La (USA) (MN) 27 Pk24
Crescent City (USA) (CA) 24 Oc25
Crescent City (USA) (FL) 37 Qe31
Crescent Junction (USA) (UT) 33 Pa26
Crescent Lake National Wildlife Refuge ☆ (USA) (NE) 26 Pd25
Crescent Valley (USA) (NV) 24 Og25
Cresco (USA) (IA) 27 Pj24
Cresson (USA) (TX) 35 Pg29
Crested Butte (USA) (CO) 34 Pb26
Creston (CDN) (BC) 17 Og21
Creston (USA) (IA) 27 Ph25
Creston (USA) (MT) 17 Oh21
Creston (USA) (WY) 25 Pb25
Crestview (USA) (FL) 36 Qb30
Crete (USA) (NE) 27 Pg25
Crewe (USA) (VA) 31 Qf27
Crichton (CDN) (SAS) 18 Pb21
Crilly (CDN) (ONT) 19 Pj21
Cripple (USA) (AK) 10 Mg14
Cripple Creek (USA) (CO) 34 Pc26
Crisfield (USA) (MD) 29 Qh27
Crockett (USA) (TX) 35 Ph30
Crofton (USA) (NE) 27 Pg24
Cromer (CDN) (MAN) 18 Pe21
Cromwell (CDN) (MAN) 19 Pg20
Cromwell (USA) (MN) 19 Pj22
Crook (USA) (CO) 26 Pd25
Crooked Creek (USA) (AK) 10 Mf15
Crooked River (CDN) (SAS) 18 Pd19
Crookston (USA) (MN) 19 Pg22
Crosby (CDN) (ONT) 29 Qg23
Crosby (USA) (MS) 36 Pk30
Crosby (USA) (ND) 18 Pd21
Crosbyton (USA) (TX) 34 Pe29
Cross City (USA) (FL) 37 Qd31
Crosse, La (USA) (WI) 27 Pk24
Crossett (USA) (AR) 36 Pk29
Crossfield (CDN) (ALB) 17 Oh20
Cross Lake (CDN) (MAN) 19 Pg18
Cross Lake (USA) (MN) 19 Ph22
Cross Plains (USA) (TX) 35 Pf29
Cross Roads (USA) (TX) 35 Ph29
Crossville (USA) (TN) 36 Qc28
Crow Agency (USA) (MT) 25 Pb23
Crowell (USA) (TX) 35 Pf29
Crow Lake (CDN) (ONT) 19 Pj21
Crowley (USA) (LA) 36 Pj30
Crown Point (USA) (IN) 28 Qb25
Crownpoint (USA) (NM) 33 Pa28
Crows (USA) (AR) 35 Pj28
Crucero, El (MEX) (BCN) 38 Oh31
Cruces (C) (CF) 43 Qe34
Cruces, Las (USA) (NM) 34 Pb29
Cruillas (MEX) (TAM) 40 Pf33
Cruz, La (MEX) (SIN) 39 Pb34
Cruz, La (MEX) (TAM) 40 Pg34
Cruz de Elorza (MEX) (NL) 40 Pe34
Crystal Cave ☆ (USA) (WI) 27 Pj23
Crystal City (CDN) (MAN) 19 Pf21
Crystal City (USA) (TX) 40 Pf31
Crystal Falls (USA) (MI) 28 Qa22
Crystal Lake (USA) (FL) 36 Qc30
Crystal Lake Cave ☆ (USA) (IA) 27 Pk24
Crystal River State Archaeological Site ☆ (USA) (FL) 37 Qd31
Crystal Springs (CDN) (SAS) 18 Pc19
Crystal Springs (USA) (MS) 36 Pk30
Cuatro Caminos (C) (CG) 43 Qg35
Cuatrocienegas de Carranza (MEX) (COA) 40 Pd32
Cuauhtémoc (MEX) (CHA) 39 Pb31
Cuba (USA) (AL) 36 Qa29
Cuba (USA) (MO) 28 Pk26
Cuba (USA) (NM) 34 Pb27
Cuba City (USA) (WI) 27 Pk24
Cubero (USA) (NM) 34 Pb28
Cubitas (C) (LT) 43 Qg35
Cuckoo (USA) (VA) 29 Qg27
Cuencamé (MEX) (DGO) 39 Pd33
Cuero (USA) (TX) 40 Pg31
Cuesta, La (MEX) (COA) 39 Pd31
Cueva, La (USA) (NM) 34 Pb28
Culbertson (USA) (MT) 18 Pc21
Culbertson (USA) (NE) 34 Pe25
Culiacán Rosales (MEX) (SIN) 39 Pb33
Cullmann (USA) (AL) 36 Qb28
Culpeper (USA) (VA) 29 Qf26
Cumanayagua (C) (CF) 43 Qe34
Cumberland (CDN) (BC) 16 Oc21
Cumberland (USA) (IA) 27 Ph25
Cumberland (USA) (KY) 37 Qd27
Cumberland (USA) (MD) 29 Qf26
Cumberland (USA) (VA) 31 Qf27
Cumberland (USA) (WI) 27 Pj23
Cumberland House (CDN) (SAS) 18 Pd19
Cumberland Island National Seashore ☆ (USA) (GA) 37 Qe30
Cumbres de Majalca (MEX) (CHA) 39 Pb31
Cumbres de Majalca, Parque Nacional ☆ (MEX) (CHA) 39 Pb31
Cumbres de Monterrey, Parque Nacional ☆ (MEX) (NL) 40 Pe33
Cumpas (MEX) (SON) 39 Pa30
Curecanti National Recreation Area ☆ (USA) (CO) 33 Pb26
Curlew (USA) (WA) 16 Of21
Curran (CDN) (ONT) 29 Qh23
Currant (USA) (NV) 33 Oh26
Currie (USA) (NV) 25 Oh25
Curtis (USA) (NE) 26 Pe25
Cushing (USA) (OK) 35 Pg28
Cushing (USA) (TX) 35 Ph30
Cushing (USA) (WI) 27 Pj23
Cusick (USA) (WA) 17 Og21
Cusseta (USA) (GA) 36 Qc29
Custavo Sotelo (MEX) (SON) 33 Oj30
Custer (USA) (MT) 25 Pb22
Custer (USA) (SD) 26 Pd24
Custer State Park ☆ (USA) (SD) 26 Pd24
Cut Bank (USA) (MT) 17 Oj21
Cuthbert (USA) (GA) 36 Qc30
Cutknife (CDN) (SAS) 17 Pa19
Cutler (USA) (ME) 22 Rb23
Cuyahoya Valley National Recreation Area ☆ (USA) (OH) 29 Qe25
Cuyo, El (MEX) (YUC) 42 Qb35
Cynthiana (USA) (KY) 28 Qc26
Cypress (USA) (LA) 35 Pj30
Cypress Gardens (USA) (FL) 43 Qe32
Cypress Hills Interprovincial Park ☆ (CDN) (ALB) 17 Ok21
Cypress River (CDN) (MAN) 19 Pf21
Czar (CDN) (ALB) 17 Ok19

D

Daaquam (CDN) (QUE) 22 Qk22
Dacre (CDN) (ONT) 29 Qg23
Dade City (USA) (FL) 43 Qd31
Dafoe (CDN) (SAS) 18 Pc20
Dafter (USA) (MI) 28 Qc22
Daggett (USA) (CA) 32 Og28
Dagmar (USA) (MT) 18 Pc21
Dahinda (CDN) (SAS) 18 Pc21
Daingerfield (USA) (TX) 35 Ph29
Dairyland (USA) (WI) 27 Pj22
Daisy, Soddy- (USA) (TN) 36 Qc28
Dakota (USA) (MN) 27 Pk24
Dakota City (USA) (NE) 27 Pg24
Dalark (USA) (AR) 35 Pj29
Dalbo (USA) (MN) 27 Pj23
Dale (USA) (IN) 28 Qb26
Dale (USA) (OR) 24 Of23
Dalhart (USA) (TX) 34 Pd27
Dalhousie (CDN) (NB) 22 Rb21
Dallas (CDN) (MAN) 19 Pg20
Dallas (USA) (OR) 24 Od23
Dallas (USA) (TX) 35 Pg29
Dallas City (USA) (IL) 27 Pk25
Dalles, The (USA) (OR) 24 Oe23
Dalny (CDN) (MAN) 18 Pe21
Dalton (USA) (GA) 36 Qc28
Dalton (USA) (NE) 26 Pd25
Dalton Gardens (USA) (ID) 17 Og22
Daly City (USA) (CA) 32 Od27
Dalzell (CDN) (SAS) 18 Pd20
Damariscotta (USA) (ME) 22 Ra23
Damascus (USA) (AR) 35 Pj28
Danbury (USA) (CT) 30 Qj25
Danbury (USA) (WI) 27 Pj22
Danforth (USA) (ME) 22 Rb23
Daniel (USA) (WY) 25 Ok24
Dansville (USA) (NY) 29 Qg24
Danville (CDN) (QUE) 22 Qj23
Danville (USA) (AR) 35 Pj28
Danville (USA) (IL) 28 Qb25
Danville (USA) (IN) 28 Qb26
Danville (USA) (KY) 36 Qc27
Danville (USA) (PA) 29 Qg25
Danville (USA) (VA) 37 Qf27
Danville (USA) (WA) 16 Of21
D'Arcy (CDN) (SAS) 17 Pa20
Dardanelle (USA) (AR) 35 Pj28
Darien Center (USA) (NY) 29 Qf24
Darlingford (CDN) (MAN) 19 Pf21
Darlington (USA) (FL) 36 Qb30
Darlington (USA) (SC) 37 Qf28
Darlington (USA) (WI) 28 Pk24
Darrington (USA) (WA) 16 Oe21
Dartmouth (CDN) (NS) 22 Rd23
Darvills (USA) (VA) 31 Qg27
Dashwood (CDN) (BC) 16 Oc21
Dassel (USA) (MN) 27 Ph23
Datil (USA) (NM) 33 Pb28
Datil Well National Recreation Site ☆ (USA) (NM) 33 Pb28
Dauphin (CDN) (MAN) 18 Pe20
Dauphin Island (USA) (AL) 36 Qa30
Dauphin River (CDN) (MAN) 19 Pf20
Davenport (USA) (IA) 27 Pk25
Davenport (USA) (ND) 19 Pg22
Davenport (USA) (WA) 16 Of22
David City (USA) (NE) 27 Pg25
Davidson (CDN) (SAS) 18 Pc20
Davidson (USA) (OK) 35 Pf28
Davis (USA) (CA) 32 Oe26
Davis Dam (USA) (AZ) 33 Oh28
Davison (USA) (MI) 29 Qd24
Dawn (USA) (VA) 31 Qg27
Dawson (CDN) (YT) 11 Nf13
Dawson (USA) (GA) 36 Qc30
Dawson (USA) (ND) 19 Pf22
Dawson Creek (CDN) (BC) 15 Oe18
Dawson Springs (USA) (KY) 36 Qb27
Dayaniguas, Playa (C) (PR) 43 Qd34
Daysland (CDN) (ALB) 17 Oj19
Dayton (USA) (MT) 17 Oh22
Dayton (USA) (NV) 32 Of26
Dayton (USA) (OH) 28 Qc26
Dayton (USA) (TN) 36 Qc28
Dayton (USA) (TX) 41 Ph30
Dayton (USA) (WA) 24 Og22
Dayton (USA) (WY) 25 Pb23
Daytona Beach (USA) (FL) 37 Qe31
Dazey (USA) (ND) 19 Pf22
Deadwood (CDN) (ALB) 15 Og17
Dearborn (USA) (MI) 29 Qd24
Deary (USA) (ID) 24 Og22
Dease Lake (CDN) (BC) 14 Nk16
Death Valley Junction (USA) (CA) 32 Og27
Death Valley National Park ☆ (USA) (CA) 32 Og27
Deaver (USA) (WY) 25 Pa23
Debden (CDN) (SAS) 18 Pb19
De Berry (USA) (TX) 35 Ph29
Debolt (CDN) (ALB) 15 Og18
De Borgia (USA) (MT) 17 Oh22
Decatur (USA) (AL) 36 Qb28
Decatur (USA) (GA) 36 Qc29
Decatur (USA) (IL) 28 Qa26
Decatur (USA) (IN) 28 Qc25
Decatur (USA) (MS) 36 Qa29
Decatur (USA) (NE) 27 Pg25
Decatur (USA) (TX) 35 Pg29
Decker (USA) (MT) 26 Pb23
Deckers (USA) (CO) 34 Pc26
Decorah (USA) (IA) 27 Pk24
Deep Creek (USA) (WA) 17 Og22
Deep River (CDN) (ONT) 29 Qg22
Deepwater (USA) (MO) 35 Pj26
Deer (USA) (AR) 35 Pj28
Deerfield Beach (USA) (FL) 43 Qe32
Deering (USA) (AK) 10 Md12
Deering (USA) (ND) 18 Pe21
Deer Isle (USA) (ME) 22 Ra23
Deer Lake (CDN) (NFL) 23 Rg21
Deer Lake (CDN) (ONT) 19 Ph19
Deer Lodge (USA) (MT) 25 Oj22
Deer Park (CDN) (BC) 16 Of21
Deer Park (USA) (LA) 36 Pk30
Deer Park (USA) (MI) 20 Qc22
Deer Park (USA) (WA) 17 Og22
Deer River (USA) (MN) 19 Pj22
Deerton (USA) (MI) 20 Qb22
Deerwood (USA) (MN) 27 Pj22
Deeth (USA) (NV) 25 Oh25
Defiance (USA) (OH) 28 Qc25
De Funiak Springs (USA) (FL) 36 Qb30
Dégelis (CDN) (QUE) 22 Ra22
De Kalb (USA) (IL) 28 Qa25
De Kalb (USA) (TX) 35 Ph29
Delacroix (USA) (LA) 36 Qa31
Delaney (USA) (WA) 24 Og22
Delano (USA) (CA) 32 Of28
Delavan (USA) (WI) 28 Qa24
Delaware (USA) (AR) 35 Pj28
Delaware (USA) (OH) 29 Qd25
Del Bonita (CDN) (ALB) 17 Oj21
Delburne (CDN) (ALB) 17 Oj19
Delcampre (USA) (LA) 36 Pk31
Deleau (CDN) (MAN) 18 Pe21
De Leon (USA) (TX) 35 Pf29
Delhi (USA) (LA) 36 Pk29
Delhi (USA) (NY) 30 Qh24
Delicias (MEX) (CHA) 39 Pc31
Delisle (CDN) (SAS) 18 Pb20
Dell (USA) (MT) 25 Oj23
Dell City (USA) (TX) 34 Pc30
Delle (USA) (UT) 25 Oj25
Dell Rapids (USA) (SD) 27 Pg24
Delmas (CDN) (SAS) 17 Pa19
Del Norte (USA) (CO) 34 Pb27
Deloraine (CDN) (MAN) 18 Pe21
Delphi (USA) (IN) 28 Qb25
Delray Beach (USA) (FL) 43 Qe32
Del Rio (USA) (TX) 40 Pe31
Delta (CDN) (BC) 16 Od21
Delta (CDN) (MAN) 19 Pf20
Delta (USA) (CO) 33 Pa26
Delta (USA) (UT) 33 Oj26
Delta Junction (USA) (AK) 11 Nc13
Delta National Wildlife Refuge ☆ (USA) (LA) 00 Qa01
Deltona (USA) (FL) 37 Qe31
Demers Centre (CDN) (QUE) 29 Qg23
Deming (USA) (NM) 34 Pb29
Deming (USA) (WA) 16 Od21
Demopolis (USA) (AL) 36 Qb29
Demotte (USA) (IN) 28 Qb25
Denali National Park (USA) (AK) 11 Na14
Denali National Park and Preserve ☆ (USA) (AK) 10 Mk14
Denbigh (CDN) (ONT) 29 Qg23
Denham Springs (USA) (LA) 36 Pk30
Denholm (CDN) (SAS) 18 Pb19
Denio Junction (USA) (NV) 24 Of25
Denison (USA) (IA) 27 Ph24
Denison (USA) (TX) 35 Pg29
Denman (USA) (NE) 26 Pf25
Denman Island (CDN) (BC) 16 Oc21
Denmark (USA) (SC) 37 Qe29
Dennysville (USA) (ME) 22 Rb23
Denton (USA) (MD) 29 Qh26
Denton (USA) (MT) 17 Pa22
Denton (USA) (TX) 35 Pg29
Dentons Corner (USA) (VA) 31 Qf27
Denver (USA) (CO) 34 Pc26
Denver (USA) (IA) 27 Pj24
Denzil (CDN) (SAS) 17 Pa19
Departure Bay (CDN) (BC) 16 Od21
Depew (USA) (NY) 29 Qf24
Depew (USA) (OK) 35 Pg28
Deposit (USA) (NY) 29 Qh24
Depot d'Aigle (CDN) (QUE) 29 Qg22
De Queen (USA) (AR) 35 Ph28
Dermott (USA) (AR) 36 Pk29
Deroche (CDN) (BC) 16 Od21
Derramadero (C) (CA) 43 Qf35
Derry (USA) (NH) 22 Qk24
Derwent (CDN) (ALB) 17 Ok19
Des Allemands (USA) (LA) 36 Pk31
Des Arc (USA) (AR) 36 Pk28
Desbarats (CDN) (ONT) 29 Qd22
Descanso (USA) (CA) 32 Og29
Descanso, El (MEX) (BCN) 32 Og29
Deschaillons (CDN) (QUE) 21 Qj22
Desemboque, El (MEX) (SON) 38 Oj30
Desert Center (USA) (CA) 33 Oh29
Desert Hot Springs (USA) (CA) 32 Og29
Desert National Wildlife Range ☆ (USA) (NV) 33 Oh27
Des Lacs (USA) (ND) 18 Pe21
De Smet (USA) (SD) 27 Pg23
Des Moines (USA) (IA) 27 Pj25
Des Moines (USA) (NM) 34 Pd27
Des Moines (USA) (WA) 16 Od22
Desoronto (CDN) (ONT) 29 Qg23
De Soto (USA) (MO) 28 Pk26
De Soto (USA) (WI) 27 Pk24
De Soto National Monument ☆ (USA) (FL) 43 Qd32
Des Plaines (USA) (IL) 28 Qb2
Des Roches (CDN) (QUE) 22 Qk2
Destin (USA) (FL) 36 Qb30
Destruction Bay (CDN) (YT) 14 Nf1
De Tour Village (USA) (MI) 29 Qd2
Detroit (USA) (MI) 29 Qd2
Detroit Lakes (USA) (MN) 19 Ph2
Devils Lake (USA) (ND) 19 Pf2
Devils Postpile National Monument ☆ (USA) (CA) 32 Of2
Devlin (CDN) (ONT) 19 Pj2
Devon (USA) (MT) 17 Ok2
Dewatto (USA) (WA) 16 Od2
Dewberry (CDN) (ALB) 17 Ok1
Dewdney (CDN) (BC) 16 Od2
De Witt (USA) (AR) 36 Pk2
De Witt (USA) (IA) 27 Pk2
Dexter (USA) (ME) 22 Ra2
Dexter (USA) (MO) 36 Qa2
Dexter (USA) (MS) 36 Qa
Dezadeash (CDN) (NWT) 14 Ng
Díaz Ordaz (MEX) (BCS) 38 Oj
Diboll (USA) (TX) 41 Ph
Dickens (USA) (TX) 34 Pe
Dickeyville (USA) (WI) 27 Pk
Dickinson (USA) (ND) 18 Pd
Dickinson (USA) (TX) 41 Ph
Dickson (USA) (AK) 10 Mc
Dickson (USA) (TN) 36 Qb
Dieciocho de Marzo (MEX) (TAM) 40 Pg
Dierks (USA) (AR) 35 Ph
Digby (CDN) (NS) 22 Rc
Dighton (USA) (KS) 34 Pe
Dilia (USA) (NM) 34 Pc
Dilke (CDN) (SAS) 18 Pc
Dilkon (USA) (AZ) 33 Ok
Dilley (USA) (TX) 40 Pf
Dillingham (USA) (AK) 12 M
Dillon (CDN) (SAS) 17 Pa
Dillon (USA) (MT) 25 O
Dillon (USA) (SC) 37 Q
Dillsburg (USA) (PA) 29 Qg
Dimmitt (USA) (TX) 34 Pd
Dinorwic (CDN) (ONT) 19 P
Dinosaur (USA) (CO) 25 Pa
Dinosaur National Monument ☆ (USA) (CO) 25 Pa
Dinosaur Provincial Park ☆ (CDN) (ALB) 17 Ok
Dinsmore (CDN) (SAS) 18 Pb
Dinuba (USA) (CA) 32 O
Disautel (USA) (WA) 16 O
Discovery Bay (USA) (WA) 16 Oc
Dishkakat (USA) (AK) 10 Mg
Disraeli (CDN) (QUE) 22 Qk
Divide (CDN) (SAS) 17 Pa
Divide (USA) (MT) 25 O
Divisadero, El (MEX) (SON) 39 Pb
Divisaderos (MEX) (SON) 39 Pa
Dixfield (USA) (ME) 22 Q
Dixmont (USA) (ME) 22 Ra
Dixon (USA) (IL) 28 Q
Dixon (USA) (MO) 28 P
Dixon (USA) (MT) 17 O
Dixon (USA) (WY) 25 P
Dixonville (CDN) (ALB) 15 O
Doaktown (CDN) (NB) 22 R
Doctor, El (MEX) (SON) 33 O
Doctor Arroyo (MEX) (NL) 40 P
Doctor González (MEX) (NL) 40 P
Dodge (USA) (ND) 18 P
Dodge Center (USA) (MN) 27
Dodge City (USA) (KS) 34
Dodgeville (USA) (WI) 28 P
Dodsland (CDN) (SAS) 17 P
Dodson (USA) (LA) 36
Dodson (USA) (MT) 18 P
Dog Creek (CDN) (BC) 16 C
Doland (USA) (SD) 26
Dolbeau (CDN) (QUE) 21
Dolores (USA) (CO) 33
Doloroso (USA) (MS) 36
Domain (CDN) (MAN) 19
Dominion City (CDN) (MAN) 19
Domremy (CDN) (SAS) 18
Doña Ana (USA) (NM) 34
Donald Landing (CDN) (BC) 16
Donaldson (USA) (AR) 35
Donaldson (USA) (MN) 19
Donaldsonville (USA) (LA) 36
Donie (USA) (TX) 35
Doniphan (USA) (MO) 36
Don Martin (MEX) (COA) 40
Donnacona (CDN) (QUE) 22
Donnelly (CDN) (ALB) 15
Donnybrook (USA) (ND) 18
Dorado, El (MEX) (SIN) 39
Dorado, El (USA) (AR) 35
Dorado, El (USA) (KS) 35
Dorado Springs, El (USA) (MO) 35
Dora Lake (USA) (MN) 19
Doré, La (CDN) (QUE) 21
Doré Lake (CDN) (SAS) 18
Dorintosh (CDN) (SAS) 17
Dorion (CDN) (ONT) 20
Dorion (CDN) (QUE) 30

orothy (CDN) (ALB) 17 Oj20
orrance (USA) (KS) 35 Pf26
orreen (CDN) (BC) 14 Oa18
orset (CDN) (ONT) 29 Qf23
os Bocas ☆ (USA) (PR) 42 Rb36
os Cabezas (USA) (AZ) 33 Pa29
osquet (CDN) (QUE) 22 Qk22
oswell (USA) (VA) 31 Qg27
ot (CDN) (BC) 16 Oe20
othan (USA) (AL) 36 Qc30
ouglas (CDN) (MAN) 19 Pf21
ouglas (USA) (AK) 14 Nh16
ouglas (USA) (AZ) 33 Pa30
ouglas (USA) (GA) 37 Qd30
ouglas (USA) (WA) 16 Oe22
ouglas (USA) (WY) 26 Pc24
ouglas City (USA) (CA) 24 Od25
ouglass (USA) (KS) 35 Pg27
ouglass (USA) (TX) 35 Ph30
ove Creek (USA) (CO) 33 Pa27
over (USA) (AR) 35 Pj28
over (USA) (DE) 31 Qh26
over (USA) (NH) 22 Qk24
over (USA) (TN) 36 Qb27
over-Foxcroft (USA) (ME) 22 Ra23
owagiac (USA) (MI) 28 Qb25
owne (CDN) (SAS) 17 Pa20
owney (USA) (ID) 25 Oj24
owns (USA) (KS) 35 Pf26
oyle (USA) (CA) 32 Oe25
oylestown (USA) (PA) 30 Qh25
oyleville (USA) (CO) 34 Pb26
oyon (USA) (ND) 19 Pf21
ragoon (USA) (AZ) 33 Ok29
ake (USA) (MO) 28 Pk26
ake (USA) (ND) 18 Pe22
ayton (USA) (ND) 19 Pg21
ayton Valley (CDN) (ALB) 17 Oh19
esden (USA) (OH) 29 Qd25
ifton (USA) (FL) 37 Qd30
iftpile (CDN) (ALB) 15 Oh18
iftwood (CDN) (BC) 14 Ob18
iftwood (USA) (PA) 29 Qf25
iggs (USA) (ID) 25 Ok24
inkwater (CDN) (SAS) 18 Pc20
uid (CDN) (SAS) 17 Pa20
umheller (CDN) (ALB) 17 Oj20
ummond (USA) (MI) 29 Qd22
ummond (USA) (MT) 25 Oj22
ummond (USA) (WI) 19 Pk22
ummondville (CDN) (QUE) 30 Qj23
y Creek (USA) (LA) 36 Pj30
yden (CDN) (ONT) 19 Pj21
yden (USA) (NY) 29 Qg24
yden (USA) (TX) 39 Pd30
y Prong (USA) (LA) 36 Pj30
y Tortugas National Park ☆ (USA) (FL) 43 Qd33
ubach (USA) (LA) 35 Pj29
ublin (USA) (GA) 37 Qd29
ublin (USA) (TX) 35 Pf29
ubois (USA) (ID) 25 Oj23
u Bois (USA) (PA) 29 Qf25
ubois (USA) (WY) 25 Pa24
uque (USA) (IA) 27 Pk24
hénier, Réserve provincial du ☆ (CDN) (QUE) 22 Ra21
hesne (USA) (UT) 25 Ok25
kabush (USA) (WA) 16 Od22
k Lake (CDN) (SAS) 18 Pb19
k Mountain Provincial Forest ☆ (CDN) (MAN) 18 Pe20
k Mountain Provincial Park ☆ (CDN) (MAN) 18 Pe20
ald (CDN) (MAN) 19 Pg21
way (USA) (UT) 25 Oj25
amel (CDN) (QUE) 29 Qh22
e (USA) (OK) 35 Pf28
th (USA) (MN) 19 Pj22
as (USA) (AR) 36 Pk29
as (USA) (TX) 34 Pe28
fries (USA) (VA) 29 Qg26
mer (CDN) (SAS) 18 Pc21
can (CDN) (BC) 16 Od21
can (USA) (AZ) 33 Pa29
can (USA) (OK) 35 Pg28
dalk (USA) (MD) 29 Qg26
dee (USA) (TX) 35 Pf29
edin (USA) (FL) 43 Qd31
ère, Réserve Faunique de ☆ (CDN) (QUE) 22 Rb21
irk (USA) (NY) 29 Qf24
ap (USA) (IA) 27 Ph25
ap (USA) (TN) 36 Qc28
more (CDN) (ALB) 17 Ok21
more (USA) (PA) 29 Qh25
(USA) (NC) 31 Qf28
(USA) (TX) 34 Pe29
ellon (USA) (FL) 37 Qd31
ing (USA) (NE) 26 Pe25
ville (CDN) (ONT) 29 Qf24
aven (USA) (NY) 30 Qh24
ea (CDN) (MAN) 19 Pf21
eith (USA) (ND) 18 Pe21
egan (CDN) (ALB) 15 Of18
rquet (CDN) (QUE) 21 Qf21
yer (USA) (MT) 17 Oj21
esne (USA) (AZ) 33 Ok30
boin (USA) (IL) 28 Qa26
La (MEX) (SON) 39 Pa31
d (USA) (WI) 27 Pk23
go (USA) (CO) 33 Pb27
go = Victoria de Durango (MEX) (DGO) 39 Pc33
t (USA) (MS) 36 Qa29
t (USA) (OK) 35 Pg29
m (CDN) (ONT) 29 Qe23
m (USA) (KS) 35 Pg26
m (USA) (NC) 37 Qf28
re (USA) (PA) 29 Qg25
John (USA) (NV) 25 Pa25
(USA) (MT) 17 Ok22
w (USA) (MO) 28 Pk26
(USA) (WA) 16 Oe22
nay (CDN) (ALB) 17 Ok19
(CDN) (ONT) 29 Qf23
(USA) (IL) 28 Qa25
(USA) (NM) 33 Pb29
burg (USA) (TN) 36 Qa27
ville (USA) (IA) 27 Pk24
Dysart (USA) (IA) 27 Pj24
Dzibilchaltún ☆ (MEX) (YUC) 42 Qa35
Dzilam de Bravo (MEX) (YUC) 42 Qa35

E

Eads (USA) (CO) 34 Pd26
Eagle (USA) (AK) 11 Ne13
Eagle (USA) (CO) 33 Pb26
Eagle (USA) (NE) 27 Pg25
Eagle Bend (USA) (MN) 27 Ph22
Eagle Butte (USA) (SD) 26 Pe23
Eagle Cape Wilderness Area ☆ (USA) (OR) 24 Og23
Eagle Cave ☆ (USA) (WI) 27 Pk24
Eagle Harbor (USA) (MI) 20 Qa22
Eagle Lake (USA) (ME) 22 Ra22
Eagle Lake (USA) (TX) 40 Pg31
Eagle Nest (USA) (NM) 34 Pc27
Eagle Pass (USA) (TX) 40 Pe31
Eagle Picher Mine (USA) (NV) 24 Of25
Eagle Plains (CDN) (YT) 11 Ng12
Eagle Point (USA) (OR) 24 Od24
Eagle River (CDN) (ONT) 19 Pj21
Eagle River (USA) (WI) 28 Qa23
Eaglesham (CDN) (ALB) 15 Og18
Eagleville (USA) (MO) 27 Pj25
Ear Falls (CDN) (ONT) 19 Pj20
Earls Cove (CDN) (BC) 16 Od21
Earlton (CDN) (ONT) 21 Qf22
Early (USA) (IA) 27 Ph24
Early (USA) (TX) 35 Pf30
Easley (USA) (SC) 37 Qd28
East Angus (CDN) (QUE) 22 Qk23
East Arrow Park (CDN) (BC) 17 Og20
East Aurora (USA) (NY) 29 Qf24
East Bethel (USA) (MN) 27 Pj23
East Brady (USA) (PA) 29 Qf25
Eastend (CDN) (SAS) 18 Pa21
East Fairview (USA) (ND) 18 Pd22
East Glacier Park (USA) (MT) 17 Oj21
East Grand Forks (USA) (MN) 19 Pg22
East Holden (USA) (ME) 22 Ra23
Eastland (USA) (TX) 35 Pf29
East Lansing (USA) (MI) 28 Qc24
East Liverpool (USA) (OH) 29 Qe25
Eastmain (CDN) (QUE) 21 Qf19
Eastman (USA) (GA) 37 Qd29
East Millinocket (USA) (ME) 22 Ra23
East Missoula (USA) (MT) 25 Oj22
Easton (USA) (MD) 29 Qg26
Easton (USA) (PA) 30 Qh25
East Palatka (USA) (FL) 37 Qe31
East Pine (CDN) (BC) 15 Oe18
Eastpoint (USA) (FL) 36 Qc31
East Poplar (CDN) (SAS) 18 Pc21
Eastport (USA) (ME) 22 Rb23
East Saint Louis (USA) (IL) 28 Pk26
East Waterboro (USA) (ME) 22 Qk24
East Wenatchee (USA) (WA) 16 Oe22
Eaton (USA) (CO) 26 Pc25
Eaton (USA) (OH) 28 Qc26
Eatonia (CDN) (SAS) 17 Pa20
Eatonton (USA) (GA) 37 Qd29
Eatonville (USA) (WA) 24 Od22
Eau Claire (USA) (WI) 27 Pk23
Ebenezer (CDN) (SAS) 18 Pd20
Ebensburg (USA) (PA) 29 Qf25
Ebro (USA) (FL) 36 Qc30
Echo Bay (CDN) (ONT) 20 Qc22
Eckermann (USA) (MI) 28 Qc22
Eckville (CDN) (ALB) 17 Oh19
Ecoole (CDN) (BC) 16 Oc21
Edam (CDN) (SAS) 17 Pa19
Edcouch (USA) (TX) 40 Pg32
Eddies Cove (CDN) (NFL) 23 Rg20
Eddington (USA) (ME) 22 Ra23
Eddystone (CDN) (MAN) 19 Pf20
Eddyville (USA) (IA) 27 Pj25
Eddyville (USA) (NE) 26 Pf25
Eden (USA) (NC) 37 Qf27
Eden (USA) (TX) 40 Pf30
Edenwold (CDN) (SAS) 18 Pc20
Eder (USA) (MT) 17 Ok22
Edgar (USA) (WI) 27 Qa23
Edgartown (USA) (MA) 30 Qk25
Edgeley (USA) (ND) 26 Pf22
Edgemont (USA) (SD) 26 Pd24
Edgerton (CDN) (ALB) 17 Ok19
Edgerton (USA) (MN) 27 Pg24
Edgertown (USA) (VA) 31 Qg27
Edgewater (CDN) (BC) 17 Og20
Edgewater (USA) (FL) 37 Qe31
Edgewood (CDN) (BC) 16 Of21
Edgewood (USA) (MD) 29 Qg26
Edgewood (USA) (TX) 35 Ph29
Edina (USA) (MO) 27 Pj25
Edinburg (USA) (ND) 19 Pg21
Edinburg (USA) (TX) 40 Pf32
Edmond (USA) (OK) 35 Pg28
Edmonds (USA) (WA) 16 Od22
Edmonton (CDN) (ALB) 17 Oj19
Edmore (USA) (ND) 19 Pf21
Edmundston (CDN) (NB) 22 Ra22
Edna (USA) (TX) 40 Pg31
Edrans (CDN) (MAN) 19 Pf20
Edson (CDN) (ALB) 17 Og19
Edwall (USA) (WA) 17 Og22
Edwards (USA) (CA) 32 Og28
Edwards (USA) (MS) 36 Pk29
Edwin (CDN) (MAN) 19 Pf21
Edzo (CDN) (NWT) 15 Oh14
Eek (USA) (AK) 12 Md15
Effie (USA) (LA) 36 Pj30
Effie (USA) (MN) 19 Pj22
Effingham (USA) (IL) 28 Qa26
Eganville (CDN) (ONT) 29 Qg23
Egeland (USA) (ND) 19 Pf21
Egmont (CDN) (BC) 16 Od21
Egnar (USA) (CO) 33 Pa27
Eholt (CDN) (BC) 16 Of21
Eielson (USA) (AK) 11 Nb13
Ejido Alianza para la Producion (MEX) (BCN) 33 Oh30
Ejido Chapultulpec (MEX) (BCN) 32 Og30
Ejido El Provenir (MEX) (BCN) 32 Og29
Ejido Eréndira (MEX) (BCN) 32 Og30
Ejido Héroes de la Independencia (MEX) (BCN) 33 Oh30
Ejido Pancho Villa (MEX) (BCS) 38 Oj33
Ejido Uruapan (MEX) (BCN) 32 Og30
Ekalaka (USA) (MT) 26 Pc23
Ekbalám ☆ (MEX) (YUC) 42 Qa35
El Alamo (MEX) (BCN) 32 Og30
El Anuajito (MEX) (SIN) 39 Pa33
El Arco (MEX) (BCN) 38 Oj31
El Barreal (MEX) (CHA) 39 Pb30
El Barretal (MEX) (TAM) 40 Pf33
El Barril (MEX) (SLP) 40 Pd34
Elbe (USA) (WA) 24 Od22
Elberta (USA) (UT) 33 Ok26
Elberton (USA) (GA) 37 Qd28
Elbow (CDN) (SAS) 18 Pb20
Elbow Lake (USA) (MN) 27 Ph23
El Caballo (MEX) (COA) 39 Pd32
El Cajon (USA) (CA) 32 Og29
El Campo (USA) (TX) 40 Pg31
El Cantabro (MEX) (COA) 39 Pd33
El Carrizal (MEX) (CHA) 39 Pb30
El Centenario (MEX) (BCS) 38 Ok33
El Centro (USA) (CA) 33 Oh29
El Chinero (MEX) (BCN) 33 Oh30
El Cinco (MEX) (DGO) 39 Pd33
El Ciruelo (MEX) (BCS) 38 Ok33
El Compadre (MEX) (BCN) 32 Og29
El Conejo (MEX) (BCS) 38 Ok33
El Corojal (C) (MZ) 43 Qe34
El Coyote (MEX) (BCN) 32 Og30
El Crucero (MEX) (BCN) 38 Oh31
El Cuyo (MEX) (YUC) 42 Qb35
El Descanso (MEX) (BCN) 32 Og29
El Desemboque (MEX) (SON) 38 Oj30
El Divisadero (MEX) (SON) 39 Pb32
El Doctor (MEX) (SON) 33 Oh30
Eldon (USA) (IA) 27 Pj25
Eldon (USA) (MO) 28 Pj26
Eldora (USA) (IA) 27 Pj24
El Dorado (USA) (AR) 35 Pj29
Eldorado (USA) (IL) 36 Qa27
El Dorado (USA) (KS) 35 Pg27
Eldorado (USA) (OK) 35 Pf28
Eldorado (USA) (TX) 40 Pe30
El Dorado Springs (USA) (MO) 35 Ph27
Eldred (USA) (PA) 29 Qf25
Eldridge (USA) (IA) 27 Pk25
Electric Mills (USA) (MS) 36 Qa29
El Encinal (MEX) (TAM) 40 Pf33
Elephant Point (USA) (AK) 10 Me12
Eleva (USA) (WI) 27 Pk23
El Faro (MEX) (BCN) 33 Oh29
Elfin Cove (USA) (AK) 14 Ng16
Elfrida (USA) (AZ) 33 Pa30
Elfros (CDN) (SAS) 18 Pd20
Elgin (CDN) (MAN) 19 Pf21
Elgin (CDN) (ONT) 29 Qg23
Elgin (USA) (IL) 28 Qa24
Elgin (USA) (ND) 26 Pe22
Elgin (USA) (NV) 33 Oh27
Elgin (USA) (TN) 36 Qc27
Elgin (USA) (TX) 40 Pg30
El Golfo de Santa Clara (MEX) (SON) 33 Oh30
El Guaje (MEX) (COA) 39 Pd31
Elida (USA) (NM) 34 Pd29
Elie (CDN) (MAN) 19 Pg21
Elim (USA) (AK) 10 Md13
Elizabeth (USA) (NJ) 30 Qh25
Elizabeth City (USA) (NC) 31 Qg27
Elizabethton (USA) (TN) 37 Qd27
Elizabethtown (USA) (KY) 36 Qc27
Elizabethtown (USA) (NC) 37 Qf28
Elizabethville (USA) (PA) 29 Qg25
Elk (USA) (WA) 17 Og21
Elkader (USA) (IA) 27 Pk24
Elk City (USA) (ID) 25 Oh23
Elk City (USA) (OK) 35 Pf28
Elk Creek (USA) (CA) 32 Od26
Elkford (CDN) (BC) 17 Oh20
Elk Grove (USA) (CA) 32 Oe26
Elkhart (USA) (IN) 28 Qb25
Elkhart (USA) (TX) 35 Ph30
Elkhorn (CDN) (MAN) 18 Pe21
Elkhorn (USA) (WI) 28 Qa24
Elkin (USA) (NC) 37 Qe27
Elkins (USA) (NM) 34 Pc29
Elkins (USA) (WV) 29 Qf26
Elk Island National Park ☆ (CDN) (ALB) 17 Oj19
Elk Lake (CDN) (ONT) 20 Qe22
Elko (CDN) (BC) 17 Oh21
Elko (USA) (NV) 25 Oh25
Elk Point (CDN) (ALB) 17 Ok19
Elk Point (USA) (SD) 27 Pg24
Elk River (USA) (ID) 24 Og22
Elk River (USA) (MN) 27 Pj23
Elk Springs (USA) (CO) 25 Pa25
Elkton (USA) (MD) 29 Qh26
Elkton (USA) (VA) 29 Qf26
Elkwater (CDN) (ALB) 17 Ok21
Ellendale (USA) (ND) 26 Pf22
Ellensburg (USA) (WA) 24 Oe22
Ellicott City (USA) (MD) 29 Qg26
Ellicottville (USA) (NY) 29 Qf24
Elliot Lake (CDN) (ONT) 29 Qd22
Elliott (USA) (MD) 29 Qh26
Ellis (USA) (ID) 25 Oh23
Ellisforde (USA) (WA) 16 Of21
Ellisville (USA) (MS) 36 Qa30
Ellsworth (USA) (KS) 35 Pf26
Ellsworth (USA) (ME) 22 Ra23
Ellsworth (USA) (NE) 26 Pd24
Ellsworth (USA) (WI) 27 Pj23
Elma (CDN) (MAN) 19 Ph21
Elma (USA) (IA) 27 Pj24
Elma (USA) (WA) 24 Od22
El Magueyal (MEX) (COA) 39 Pd32
El Malpais National Monument ☆ (USA) (AZ) 33 Pa28
El Mayor (MEX) (BCN) 33 Oh29
Elm Creek (CDN) (MAN) 19 Pg21
Elm Creek (USA) (NE) 26 Pf25
Elmer City (USA) (WA) 16 Of21
El Mezquite (MEX) (ZAC) 39 Pd34
El Milagro (MEX) (COA) 39 Pd31
Elmira (CDN) (PEI) 22 Rd22
Elmira (USA) (ID) 17 Og21
Elmira (USA) (NY) 29 Qg24
Elmo (USA) (KS) 35 Pg26
Elmore (CDN) (SAS) 18 Pe21
El Morrión (MEX) (CHA) 39 Pc31
El Morro National Monument ☆ (USA) (NM) 33 Pa28
Elmwood (USA) (MI) 20 Qa22
Elmwood (USA) (OK) 34 Pe27
Elmwood (USA) (WI) 27 Pj23
Elmworth (CDN) (ALB) 15 Of18
El Oasis (MEX) (SON) 38 Ok31
El Oro (MEX) (COA) 39 Pd32
El Oso (MEX) (COA) 39 Pd32
Elota (MEX) (SIN) 39 Pb34
Eloy (USA) (AZ) 33 Ok29
El Palmito (MEX) (DGO) 39 Pc33
El Papalote (MEX) (COA) 39 Pd32
El Paso (USA) (TX) 34 Pb30
El Paso Gap (USA) (NM) 34 Pc29
El Pastor (MEX) (CHA) 39 Pc31
Elphinstone (CDN) (MAN) 18 Pe20
El Portal (USA) (CA) 32 Of27
El Porvenir (MEX) (CHA) 39 Pc30
El Rebalse (MEX) (CHA) 39 Pc31
El Refugio (MEX) (BCS) 38 Ok33
El Refugio de Abreojo (MEX) (ZAC) 39 Pd34
El Remolino (MEX) (COA) 40 Pe31
El Reno (USA) (OK) 35 Pg28
El Reventon (MEX) (SLP) 40 Pe34
El Revés (MEX) (COA) 39 Pd32
El Rosario (MEX) (BCN) 38 Oh30
El Rosario (MEX) (SIN) 39 Pc34
Elrose (CDN) (SAS) 18 Pa20
Elroy (USA) (WI) 27 Pk24
El Rucio (MEX) (ZAC) 40 Pd34
El Sahuaro (MEX) (SON) 38 Oj30
El Salvador (MEX) (ZAC) 40 Pe33
El Santo (C) (VC) 43 Qf34
El Sasabe (MEX) (SON) 33 Ok30
El Saúz (MEX) (CHA) 39 Pb31
El Sauzal (MEX) (BCN) 32 Og30
Elsberry (USA) (MO) 28 Pk26
Elstow (CDN) (SAS) 18 Pb19
El Sueco (MEX) (CHA) 39 Pb31
El Tecolote (MEX) (NL) 40 Pe33
El Temascal (MEX) (TAM) 40 Pf33
El Testerazo (MEX) (BCN) 32 Og29
Elton (USA) (LA) 36 Pj30
El Tren (MEX) (SON) 33 Oj30
El Trópico (C) (H) 43 Qe34
El Tule (MEX) (COA) 40 Pe31
El Varejonal (MEX) (SIN) 39 Pb33
El Vergel (MEX) (CHA) 39 Pb32
El Vizcaíno, Reserva de la Biósfera ☆ (MEX) (BCS) 38 Oh32
El Wálamo (MEX) (SIN) 39 Pb34
Elwood (USA) (IN) 28 Qc25
Elwood (USA) (NE) 26 Pf25
Ely (USA) (MN) 19 Pk22
Ely (USA) (NV) 33 Oh26
Elyria (USA) (OH) 29 Qd25
Emblem (USA) (WY) 25 Pa23
Embrun (CDN) (ONT) 29 Qh23
Emerald (USA) (NE) 27 Pg25
Emerson (CDN) (MAN) 19 Pg21
Emerson (USA) (AR) 35 Pj29
Emigrant Gap (USA) (CA) 32 Oe26
Emiliano Zapata (MEX) (COA) 39 Pd33
Emiliano Zapata (MEX) (SON) 38 Ok31
Eminence (USA) (KY) 28 Qc26
Emmetsburg (USA) (IA) 27 Ph24
Emmitsburg (USA) (MD) 29 Qg26
Emmonak (USA) (AK) 10 Mc14
Emo (CDN) (ONT) 19 Pj21
Empalme (MEX) (SON) 38 Ok32
Empire (USA) (CO) 34 Pc26
Empire (USA) (MI) 28 Qb23
Emporia (USA) (KS) 35 Pg26
Emporia (USA) (VA) 31 Qg27
Emporium (USA) (PA) 29 Qf25
Empress (CDN) (ALB) 17 Ok20
Encinal (USA) (TX) 40 Pf31
Encinal, El (MEX) (TAM) 40 Pf33
Encinitas (USA) (CA) 32 Og29
Encino (USA) (NM) 34 Pc28
Encino (USA) (TX) 40 Pf32
Endako (CDN) (BC) 16 Oc18
Endeavor (CDN) (SAS) 18 Pd19
Enderby (CDN) (BC) 16 Of20
Endiang (CDN) (ALB) 17 Oj20
Endicott (USA) (NY) 29 Qg24
Enfield (CDN) (NS) 22 Rd23
Enfield (USA) (CT) 30 Qj25
Enfield (USA) (NC) 31 Qg27
Engadine (USA) (MI) 28 Qc22
Engelhard (USA) (NC) 31 Qh28
Engelmine (USA) (CA) 24 Oe25
Engineer (CDN) (BC) 14 Nh16
England (USA) (AR) 36 Pk28
Englee (CDN) (NFL) 23 Rg20
Englehart (CDN) (ONT) 21 Qf22
English Harbour East (CDN) (NFL) 23 Rh22
English Harbour West (CDN) (NFL) 23 Rh22
English River (CDN) (ONT) 19 Pk21
Enid (USA) (OK) 35 Pg27
Enilda (CDN) (ALB) 15 Og18
Ennis (USA) (MT) 25 Oj23
Ennis (USA) (TX) 35 Pg29
Enniskillen (CDN) (ONT) 29 Qf23
Enochs (USA) (TX) 34 Pd29
Ensenada (MEX) (BCN) 32 Og30
Ensign (USA) (KS) 34 Pe27
Ensley (USA) (FL) 36 Qb30
Enterprise (CDN) (NWT) 15 Og15
Enterprise (USA) (AL) 36 Qc30
Enterprise (USA) (MS) 36 Qa29
Enterprise (USA) (OR) 24 Og23
Entiat (USA) (WA) 16 Oe22
Entrance (CDN) (ALB) 17 Og19
Entriken (USA) (PA) 29 Qf25
Entronque La Cuchilla (MEX) (COA) 39 Pd33
Entwistle (CDN) (ALB) 17 Oh19
Enumclaw (USA) (WA) 24 Oe22
Ephraim (USA) (UT) 33 Ok26
Ephrata (USA) (PA) 29 Qg25
Ephrata (USA) (WA) 16 Of22
Epping (USA) (ND) 18 Pd21
Epping (USA) (NH) 22 Qk24
Epps (USA) (LA) 36 Pk29
Eric (CDN) (QUE) 22 Rc20
Erick (USA) (OK) 35 Pf28
Erickson (CDN) (MAN) 19 Pf20
Erie (USA) (PA) 29 Qe24
Eriksdale (CDN) (MAN) 19 Pf20
Erin (USA) (TN) 36 Qb27
Ermita de los Correa (MEX) (ZAC) 39 Pd34
Ernul (USA) (NC) 31 Qg28
Errington (CDN) (BC) 16 Oc21
Errol (USA) (NH) 22 Qk23
Erskine (USA) (MN) 19 Ph22
Ervay (USA) (WY) 25 Pb24
Escalante (USA) (UT) 33 Ok27
Escalón (MEX) (CHA) 39 Pc32
Escanaba (USA) (MI) 28 Qb23
Escondida, La (MEX) (NL) 40 Pf33
Escondido (USA) (CA) 32 Og29
Escoumins, Les (CDN) (QUE) 22 Ra21
Escuinapa de Hidalgo (MEX) (SIN) 39 Pc34
Escuminac (CDN) (NB) 22 Rc22
Esmeralda (C) (CG) 43 Qf35
Esmond (USA) (ND) 19 Pf21
Espanola (CDN) (ONT) 29 Qe22
Espanola (USA) (NM) 34 Pb28
Espenberg (USA) (AK) 10 Md12
Esperanza (MEX) (SON) 39 Pa32
Espita (MEX) (YUC) 42 Qa35
Esquimalt (CDN) (BC) 16 Od21
Essex (USA) (CA) 33 Oh28
Essex (USA) (IA) 27 Ph25
Essex (USA) (MD) 29 Qg26
Essex (USA) (MT) 17 Oj21
Essex Junction (USA) (VT) 30 Qj23
Estacada (USA) (OR) 24 Od23
Estacia Camacho (MEX) (DGO) 40 Pd33
Estación Candela (MEX) (NL) 40 Pe32
Estación Coahuila (MEX) (BCN) 33 Oh29
Estacione Don (MEX) (SON) 39 Pa32
Estación Simón (MEX) (DGO) 39 Pd33
Estación Vanegas (MEX) (SLP) 40 Pe34
Estado Cañitas de Felipe Pescador (MEX) (ZAC) 39 Pd34
Estado Ojuelos (MEX) (ZAC) 39 Pd34
Estanica (USA) (NM) 34 Pb28
Estelline (USA) (TX) 34 Pe28
Ester (USA) (AK) 11 Nb13
Esterhazy (CDN) (SAS) 18 Pd20
Estero (USA) (FL) 43 Qe32
Esterwood (USA) (LA) 36 Pj30
Estes Park (USA) (CO) 26 Pc25
Estevan (CDN) (SAS) 18 Pd21
Esther (CDN) (ALB) 17 Ok20
Esther (USA) (LA) 36 Pj31
Estherville (USA) (IA) 27 Ph24
Estill (USA) (SC) 37 Qe29
Estlin (CDN) (SAS) 18 Pc20
Esto (USA) (LA) 35 Pj30
Eston (CDN) (SAS) 17 Pa20
Estuary (CDN) (SAS) 17 Pa20
Etchojoa (MEX) (SON) 39 Pa32
Etchoropo (MEX) (SON) 39 Pa32
Ethelbert (CDN) (MAN) 18 Pe20
Ethridge (USA) (MT) 17 Oj21
Etoile (USA) (TX) 35 Ph30
Eton (CDN) (ONT) 20 Qc22
Etowah (USA) (TN) 36 Qc28
Ettington (CDN) (SAS) 18 Pb21
Etzikom (CDN) (ALB) 17 Ok21
Euclid (USA) (MN) 19 Pg22
Euclid (USA) (OH) 29 Qe25
Eudora (USA) (AR) 36 Pk29
Eufaula (USA) (AL) 36 Qc30
Eufaula (USA) (OK) 35 Ph28
Eugene (USA) (OR) 24 Od23
Euless (USA) (TX) 35 Pg29
Eulogy (USA) (TX) 35 Pg29
Eunice (USA) (LA) 36 Pj30
Eunice (USA) (NM) 34 Pd29
Eupora (USA) (MS) 36 Qa29
Eureka (USA) (CA) 24 Oc25
Eureka (USA) (CO) 33 Pb27
Eureka (USA) (KS) 35 Pg27
Eureka (USA) (MT) 17 Oh21
Eureka (USA) (NV) 33 Oh26
Eureka (USA) (SD) 26 Pf23
Eureka (USA) (UT) 33 Oj26
Eureka River (CDN) (ALB) 15 Of17
Eureka Springs (USA) (AR) 35 Pj27
Eustis (USA) (FL) 43 Qe31
Eutaw (USA) (AL) 36 Qb29
Eva (USA) (LA) 36 Pk30
Eva (USA) (OK) 34 Pe27
Evandale (CDN) (NB) 22 Rb23
Evans (USA) (CO) 26 Pc25
Evans (USA) (WA) 17 Og21
Evanston (USA) (IL) 28 Qb24
Evanston (USA) (WY) 25 Ok25
Evansville (CDN) (ONT) 29 Qd23
Evansville (USA) (IN) 36 Qb27
Evant (USA) (TX) 35 Pf30
Eveleth (USA) (MN) 19 Pj22
Evelyn (CDN) (BC) 14 Ob18
Everett (CDN) (NB) 22 Rb22
Everett (USA) (GA) 37 Qe30
Everett (USA) (WA) 16 Od22
Everglades City (USA) (FL) 43 Qe33
Everglades National Park ☆ (USA) (FL) 43 Qe33
Evergreen (USA) (AL) 36 Qb30
Evergreen (USA) (MN) 19 Ph22
Evesham (CDN) (SAS) 17 Pa19
Ewan (USA) (WA) 24 Og22
Ewart (CDN) (MAN) 18 Pe21
Ewell (USA) (MD) 29 Qg27
Ewing (USA) (MO) 28 Pk26
Ewing (USA) (NE) 26 Pf24
Excello (USA) (MO) 28 Pj26
Excelsior Springs (USA) (MO) 35 Ph26
Exeter (CDN) (ONT) 29 Qe24
Exeter (USA) (CA) 32 Of27
Exeter (USA) (NH) 22 Qk24
Exira (USA) (IA) 27 Ph25
Exmore (USA) (VA) 31 Qh27
Exstew (CDN) (BC) 16 Oa18
Exuma Cays Land and Sea Park ☆ (BS) 43 Qg33
Eyebrow (CDN) (SAS) 18 Pb20
Eyota (USA) (MN) 27 Pj24
Eyre (CDN) (SAS) 17 Pa20

F

Fabens USA (TX) 34 Pb30
Fabyan CDN (ALB) 17 Ok19
Fairbank USA (MD) 29 Qg26
Fairbanks USA (AK) 11 Nb13
Fairbanks USA (MN) 19 Pk22
Fairbury USA (NE) 35 Pg25
Fairchild USA (WI) 27 Pk23
Fairfax USA (MO) 27 Ph25
Fairfax USA (SC) 37 Qe29
Fairfax USA (SD) 26 Pf24
Fairfax USA (VA) 29 Qg26
Fairfield USA (AL) 36 Qb29
Fairfield USA (CA) 32 Od26
Fairfield USA (IA) 27 Pk25
Fairfield USA (ID) 25 Oh24
Fairfield USA (IL) 28 Qa26
Fairfield USA (ME) 22 Ra23
Fairfield USA (MT) 17 Ok22
Fairfield USA (TX) 35 Pg30
Fairfield USA (UT) 25 Oj25
Fair Harbour CDN (BC) 16 Ob20
Fairhaven CDN (NFL) 23 Rj22
Fairholme CDN (SAS) 17 Pa19
Fairhope USA (AL) 36 Qb30
Fairlight CDN (SAS) 18 Pe21
Fairmont USA (MN) 27 Ph24
Fairmont USA (NE) 27 Pg25
Fairmont USA (WV) 29 Qe26
Fairmont Hot Springs CDN (BC) 17 Oh20
Fairmount CDN (SAS) 17 Pa20
Fair Oaks USA (AR) 36 Pk28
Fair Play USA (MO) 35 Pj27
Fairport USA (MI) 28 Qb23
Fairview CDN (ALB) 15 Of17
Fairview USA (KS) 35 Ph26
Fairview USA (MI) 28 Qc23
Fairview USA (MT) 18 Pc22
Fairview USA (OK) 35 Pf27
Fairview USA (TX) 34 Pe29
Fairy USA (TX) 35 Pg30
Faith USA (SD) 26 Pd23
Falcon Lake CDN (MAN) 19 Ph21
Falfurrias USA (TX) 40 Pf32
Falher CDN (ALB) 15 Og18
Falkland CDN (BC) 16 Of20
Falkland USA (NC) 31 Qg28
Fall City USA (WA) 16 Oe22
Fallon USA (MT) 18 Pc22
Fallon USA (NV) 32 Of26
Fall River USA (MA) 30 Qk25
Fall River Mills USA (CA) 24 Oe25
Falls City USA (NE) 35 Ph25
Falmouth USA (KY) 28 Qc26
False Bay CDN (BC) 16 Oc21
False Pass USA (AK) 12 Md18
Fannin USA (MS) 36 Qa29
Fanny Bay CDN (BC) 16 Oc21
Fannystelle CDN (MAN) 19 Pg21
Farewell USA (AK) 10 Mj14
Fargo USA (GA) 37 Qd30
Fargo USA (ND) 19 Pg22
Faribault USA (MN) 27 Pj23
Farley USA (NM) 34 Pc27
Farmer USA (WA) 16 Of22
Farmer City USA (IL) 28 Qa25
Farmersville USA (TX) 35 Pg29
Farmerville USA (LA) 36 Pj29
Farmington CDN (BC) 15 Oe18
Farmington USA (IA) 27 Pk25
Farmington USA (IL) 27 Pk25
Farmington USA (ME) 22 Qk23
Farmington USA (MO) 36 Pk27
Farmington USA (NM) 33 Pa27
Farmington USA (UT) 25 Ok25
Farmville USA (NC) 31 Qg28
Farmville USA (VA) 31 Qf27
Farnam USA (NE) 26 Pe25
Farnham CDN (QUE) 30 Qj23
Faro CDN (YT) 14 Nj14
Faro, El MEX (BCN) 33 Oh29
Farrell Creek CDN (BC) 15 Oe17
Farson USA (WY) 25 Pa24
Farwell USA (TX) 34 Pd28
Faserwood CDN (MAN) 19 Pg20
Faucett USA (MO) 35 Ph26
Faulkton USA (SD) 26 Pf23
Fauquier CDN (BC) 16 Of21
Fawcett CDN (ALB) 17 Oh18
Fayette USA (AL) 36 Qb29
Fayette USA (MO) 28 Pj26
Fayette USA (MS) 36 Pk30
Fayette USA (ND) 18 Pd22
Fayette, La USA (GA) 36 Qc28
Fayetteville USA (AR) 35 Ph27
Fayetteville USA (NC) 37 Qf28
Fayetteville USA (OH) 29 Qd26
Fayetteville USA (TN) 36 Qb28
Faywood USA (NM) 33 Pb29
Federalsburg USA (MD) 29 Qh26
Fellers Heights CDN (BC) 15 Oe18
Felps USA (LA) 36 Pk30
Felton USA (MN) 19 Pg22
Fence Lake USA (NM) 33 Pa28
Fenelon Falls CDN (ONT) 29 Qf23
Fennimore USA (WI) 27 Pk24
Fenton USA (LA) 36 Pj30
Fenton USA (MI) 29 Qd24
Ferdinand USA (IN) 28 Qb26
Fergus Falls USA (MN) 27 Pg22
Ferland CDN (ONT) 20 Qa20
Ferland CDN (SAS) 18 Pb21
Fermeuse CDN (NFL) 23 Rj22
Fernandina Beach USA (FL) 37 Qe30
Ferndale USA (CA) 24 Oc25
Ferndale USA (WA) 16 Od21
Fernie CDN (BC) 17 Oh21
Ferriday USA (LA) 36 Pk30
Ferris USA (TX) 35 Pg29
Fertile CDN (SAS) 18 Pe21
Fertile USA (IA) 27 Pj24
Fertile USA (MN) 19 Pg22
Fessenden USA (ND) 19 Pf22
Festus USA (MO) 28 Pk26
F.G. Villarreal MEX (TAM) 40 Pg33
Fiatt USA (IL) 28 Pk25
Field CDN (BC) 17 Og20
Field CDN (ONT) 20 Qe22
Fife USA (WA) 16 Od22
Fife Lake CDN (SAS) 18 Pc21
Filer USA (ID) 25 Oh24
Fillmore CDN (SAS) 18 Pd21
Fillmore USA (CA) 32 Of28
Fillmore USA (ND) 19 Pf21
Findlay USA (OH) 29 Qd25
Fine USA (NY) 29 Qh23
Fingal USA (ND) 19 Pg22
Fink Creek USA (AK) 10 Md13
Finland USA (MN) 19 Pk22
Finlay Forks CDN (BC) 15 Od18
Finlayson USA (MN) 27 Pj22
Finley USA (ND) 19 Pg22
Finmark CDN (ONT) 20 Qa21
Fire Island National Seashore ☆ USA (NY) 30 Qj25
Fir Mountain CDN (SAS) 18 Pb21
Fischell CDN (NFL) 23 Rf21
Fishing Creek USA (MD) 29 Qg26
Fish Springs National Wildlife Refuge ☆ USA (UT) 33 Oj26
Fiske CDN (SAS) 17 Pa20
Fitchburg USA (MA) 30 Qk24
Fitzgerald USA (GA) 37 Qd30
Five Points USA (CA) 32 Oe27
Flagler USA (CO) 34 Pd26
Flagler Beach USA (FL) 37 Qe31
Flagstaff USA (AZ) 33 Ok28
Flaming Gorge National Rercreation Area ☆ USA (WY) 25 Pa25
Flamingo USA (FL) 43 Qe33
Flat USA (AK) 10 Mf14
Flathead CDN (BC) 17 Oh21
Flatonia USA (TX) 40 Pg31
Flat River CDN (PEI) 22 Rd22
Flat River USA (MO) 36 Pk27
Flatrock CDN (BC) 15 Oe17
Flat Top USA (WV) 37 Qe27
Flat Valley CDN (SAS) 17 Pa18
Flatwillow USA (MT) 18 Pa22
Flatwoods USA (KY) 29 Qd26
Flaxcombe CDN (SAS) 17 Pa20
Flaxville USA (MT) 18 Pc21
Fleming CDN (SAS) 18 Pe20
Flemingsburg USA (KY) 29 Qd26
Fleur de Lys CDN (NFL) 23 Rg20
Flin Flon CDN (MAN) 18 Pe18
Flint CDN (ONT) 20 Qa21
Flint USA (MI) 29 Qd24
Flintdale CDN (ONT) 20 Qc20
Flint Hills National Wildlife Refuge ☆ USA (KS) 35 Pg26
Flintoft CDN (SAS) 18 Pb21
Flomaton USA (AL) 36 Qb30
Floods CDN (BC) 16 Oe21
Floodwood USA (MN) 19 Pj22
Flora USA (IL) 28 Qa26
Flora USA (MS) 36 Pk29
Florala USA (AL) 36 Qb30
Florence USA (AL) 36 Qb28
Florence USA (AZ) 33 Ok29
Florence USA (CO) 34 Pc26
Florence USA (KS) 35 Pg26
Florence USA (MN) 27 Pg23
Florence USA (MS) 36 Pk29
Florence USA (OR) 24 Oc24
Florence USA (SC) 37 Qf28
Florence USA (WI) 28 Qa23
Florence Junction USA (AZ) 33 Ok29
Flores García MEX (ZAC) 39 Pd34
Floresville USA (TX) 40 Pf31
Florida C (CG) 43 Qf35
Florida USA (NM) 34 Pb29
Florida, Playa de C (CG) 43 Qf35
Florien USA (LA) 35 Pj30
Florissant USA (MO) 28 Pk26
Floydada USA (TX) 34 Pe29
Foam Lake CDN (SAS) 18 Pd20
Fogo CDN (NFL) 23 Rh21
Foisy CDN (ALB) 17 Ok19
Foley USA (AL) 36 Qb30
Foleyet CDN (ONT) 20 Qd21
Folkston USA (GA) 37 Qd30
Folkstone USA (NC) 31 Qg28
Follett USA (TX) 34 Pe27
Follette, La USA (TN) 36 Qc27
Folsom USA (LA) 36 Pk30
Folsom USA (NM) 34 Pd27
Fomento C (SS) 43 Qf34
Fondale USA (LA) 36 Pj29
Fond du Lac USA (WI) 28 Qa24
Fontas CDN (BC) 15 Oe16
Fontenelle USA (WY) [illegible]
Ford USA (ID) 17 Og22
Fordyce USA (AR) 36 Pj29
Foremost CDN (ALB) 17 Ok21
Forest USA (MS) 36 Qa29
Forest, La CDN (ONT) 20 Qe22
Forestburg CDN (ALB) 17 Oj19
Forest City USA (NC) 37 Qe28
Forest Glen USA (CA) 24 Od25
Forestgrove USA (MT) 18 Pa22
Forest Grove USA (OR) 24 Od23
Forest Lake USA (MN) 27 Pj23
Forest River USA (ND) 19 Pg21
Forestville CDN (QUE) 22 Ra21
Forestville, Parc Provincial de ☆ CDN (QUE) 22 Ra21
Forgan USA (OK) 34 Pe27
Forget CDN (SAS) 18 Pd21
Forillon, Parc Nacional de ☆ CDN (QUE) 22 Rc21
Forked Island USA (LA) 36 Pj31
Fork Lake CDN (ALB) 17 Ok18
Forks USA (WA) 16 Oc22
Forks, The USA (ME) 22 Ra23
Forks of Cacapon USA (WV) 29 Qf26
Fork Union USA (VA) 31 Qf27
Forman USA (ND) 27 Pg22
Forrest USA (IL) 28 Qa25
Forrest City USA (AR) 36 Pk28
Forrest Station CDN (MAN) 19 Pf21
Forsyth USA (MO) 35 Pj27
Forsyth USA (MT) 26 Pb22
Fort Abercrombie State Historical Park ☆ USA (AK) 12 Mj17
Fort Adams USA (MS) 36 Pk30
Fort Albany CDN (ONT) 20 Qe19
Fort Amanda State Memorial ☆ USA (OH) 28 Qc25
Fort Anne National Historic Park ☆ CDN (NS) 22 Rc23
Fort Assiniboine CDN (ALB) 15 Oh18
Fort Atkinson USA (WI) 28 Qa24
Fort Babine CDN (BC) 14 Ob18
Fort Battleford National Historic Park ☆ CDN (SAS) 17 Pa19
Fort Belknap Agency USA (MT) 18 Pa21
Fort Benning USA (GA) 36 Qc29
Fort Benton USA (MT) 17 Ok22
Fort Benton Ruins ☆ USA (MT) 17 Ok22
Fort Black CDN (SAS) 17 Pb18
Fort Bragg USA (NC) 37 Qf28
Fort Branch USA (IN) 28 Qb26
Fort Bridger USA (WY) 25 Ok25
Fort Caroline National Memorial ☆ USA (FL) 37 Qe30
Fort Clark USA (ND) 18 Pe22
Fort Collins USA (CO) 26 Pc25
Fort Coulonge CDN (QUE) 29 Qg23
Fort Davis USA (TX) 39 Pd30
Fort Deposit USA (AL) 36 Qb30
Fort Dodge USA (IA) 27 Ph24
Fort Edward National Historic Site ☆ CDN (NS) 22 Rc23
Fort Edwards State Memorial ☆ USA (IL) 27 Pk25
Fort Erie CDN (ONT) 29 Qf24
Fort Fairfield USA (ME) 22 Rb22
Fort Fisher ☆ USA (NC) 37 Qg29
Fort Frances CDN (ONT) 19 Pj21
Fort Fraser CDN (BC) 16 Oc18
Fort Frederica National Monument ☆ USA (GA) 37 Qe30
Fort Gadsden State Historical Site ☆ USA (FL) 36 Qc31
Fort Gaines ☆ USA (AL) 36 Qa30
Fort Garland USA (CO) 34 Pc27
Fort George CDN (QUE) 21 Qf19
Fort Hancock USA (TX) 39 Pc30
Fort Hope CDN (ONT) 20 Qa20
Fortierville CDN (QUE) 21 Qj22
Fort Irwin CDN (ONT) 29 Qf23
Fort Jackson ☆ USA (LA) 36 Qa31
Fort Kent USA (ME) 22 Ra22
Fort Langley National Historic Park ☆ CDN (BC) 16 Od21
Fort la Reine ☆ CDN (MAN) 19 Pf21
Fort Lauderdale USA (FL) 43 Qe32
Fort Lemhi Monument ☆ USA (ID) 25 Oj23
Fort Liard CDN (NWT) 15 Od15
Fort Macleod CDN (ALB) 17 Oj21
Fort Madison USA (IA) 27 Pk25
Fort Massachusetts ☆ USA (MS) 36 Qa30
Fort Matanzas National Monument ☆ USA (FL) 37 Qe31
Fort McHenry ☆ USA (MD) 29 Qg26
Fort McMurray CDN (ALB) 17 Ok17
Fort McPherson CDN (NWT) 11 Nh12
Fort Morgan ☆ USA (AL) 36 Qb30
Fort Morgan USA (CO) 26 Pd25
Fort Morris State Historic Site ☆ USA (GA) 37 Qe30
Fort Myers USA (FL) 43 Qe32
Fort Nelson CDN (BC) 15 Od16
Fort Payne USA (AL) 36 Qc28
Fort Peck USA (MT) 18 Pb21
Fort Pickens ☆ USA (FL) 36 Qb30
Fort Pickett ☆ USA (VA) 31 Qf27
Fort Pierce USA (FL) 43 Qe32
Fort Pierre USA (SD) 26 Pe23
Fort Pierre Verendrye Monument ☆ USA (SD) 26 Pd23
Fort Pitt Historic Park ☆ CDN (SAS) 17 Pa19
Fort Providence CDN (NWT) 15 Og15
Fort Pulaski National Monument ☆ USA (GA) 37 Qe29
Fort Qu'Appelle CDN (SAS) 18 Pd20
Fort Randall Dam ☆ USA (SD) 26 Pf24
Fort Resolution CDN (NWT) 15 Oj15
Fort Ripley USA (MN) 27 Ph22
Fort-Rupert = Waskaganish CDN (QUE) 21 Qf20
Fort Saint James CDN (BC) 16 Oc18
Fort Saint John CDN (BC) 15 Oe17
Fort Saskatchewan CDN (ALB) 17 Oj19
Fort Scott USA (KS) 35 Ph27
Fort Severn CDN (ONT) 20 Qb17
Fort Sheridan ☆ USA (IL) 28 Qb24
Fort Simpson CDN (NWT) 15 Oe15
Fort Smith USA (AR) 35 Ph28
Fort Smith USA (MT) 25 Pb23
Fort Steele CDN (BC) 17 Oh21
Fort Steele Heritage Town ☆ CDN (BC) 17 Oh21
Fort Stockton USA (TX) 39 Pd30
Fort Sumner USA (NM) 34 Pc28
Fort Sumter National Monument ☆ USA (SC) 37 Qf29
Fort Supply USA (OK) 35 Pf27
Fort Témiscamingue National Historic Park ☆ CDN (QUE) 21 Qf22
Fort Thomas USA (AZ) 33 Pa29
Fort Thompson USA (SD) 26 Pf23
Fort Totten USA (ND) 19 Pf22
Fort Trois Rivières ☆ CDN (QUE) 21 Qj22
Fortuna USA (CA) 24 Oc25
Fortuna USA (ND) 18 Pd21
Fortuna, La MEX (BCS) 39 Pa34
Fortuna Ledge USA (AK) 10 Md15
Fortune CDN (NFL) 23 Rh22
Fortune Harbour CDN (NFL) 23 Rh21
Fort Valley USA (GA) 37 Qd29
Fort Vermilion CDN (ALB) 15 Oh16
Fort Victoria Historic Site ☆ CDN (ALB) 17 Oj19
Fort Walsh National Historic Park ☆ CDN (SAS) 17 Pa21
Fort Walton Beach USA (FL) 36 Qb30
Fort Wayne USA (IN) 28 Qc25
Fort William Historic Park ☆ CDN (ONT) 20 Qa21
Fort Wingate USA (NM) 33 Pa28
Fort Worth USA (TX) 35 Pg29
Fort Yukon USA (AK) 11 Nc12
Foss USA (OK) 35 Pf28
Fosston USA (MN) 19 Ph22
Fostoria USA (OH) 29 Qd25
Fothom Five National Marine Park ☆ CDN (ONT) 29 Qe23
Fountain USA (CO) 34 Pc26
Fourchon, Port USA (LA) 36 Pk31
Four Corners CDN (SAS) 17 Pa18
Four Corners USA (CA) 32 Og28
Four Corners USA (WY) 26 Pc23
Four Forks USA (LA) 35 Pj29
Fourtown USA (MN) 19 Ph21
Fowlerton USA (TX) 40 Pf31
Fox USA (AK) 11 Nb13
Fox Creek CDN (ALB) 17 Og18
Foxcroft, Dover- USA (ME) 22 Ra23
Fox Lake CDN (ALB) 15 Oh16
Fox Valley CDN (SAS) 17 Pa20
Foxworth USA (MS) 36 Qa30
Framingham USA (MA) 30 Qk24
Franchere CDN (ALB) 17 Ok18
Francis CDN (SAS) 18 Pd20
Francisco I. Madero MEX (COA) 39 Pd33
Francisco I. Madero MEX (DGO) 39 Pc33
François CDN (NFL) 23 Rg22
Francois Lake CDN (BC) 16 Oc18
Franconia Notch ☆ USA (NH) 22 Qk23
Frankfort USA (IN) 28 Qb25
Frankfort USA (KY) 28 Qc26
Frankfort USA (MI) 28 Qb23
Franklin USA (GA) 36 Qc29
Franklin USA (IN) 28 Qb26
Franklin USA (KY) 36 Qb27
Franklin USA (LA) 36 Pk31
Franklin USA (NC) 37 Qd28
Franklin USA (NE) 35 Pf25
Franklin USA (NH) 30 Qk24
Franklin USA (PA) 29 Qf25
Franklin USA (TN) 36 Qb28
Franklin USA (TX) 40 Pg30
Franklin USA (VA) 31 Qg27
Franklin USA (WV) 29 Qf26
Franklinton USA (LA) 36 Pk30
Franklinton USA (NC) 31 Qf27
Franklinville USA (NY) 29 Qf24
Frankston USA (TX) 35 Ph29
Franktown USA (CO) 34 Pc26
Frannie USA (WY) 25 Pa23
Franz CDN (ONT) 20 Qc21
Fraserdale CDN (ONT) 20 Qe21
Frater CDN (ONT) 20 Qc22
Fraustro MEX (COA) 40 Pe33
Frazee USA (MN) 19 Ph22
Frazer USA (MT) 18 Pb21
Frederick USA (MD) 29 Qg26
Frederick USA (OK) 35 Pf28
Frederick USA (SD) 26 Pf23
Fredericksburg USA (IA) 27 Pj24
Fredericksburg USA (TX) 40 Pf30
Fredericksburg USA (VA) 29 Qg26
Fredericktown USA (MD) 29 Qh26
Fredericktown USA (MO) 36 Pk27
Fredericton CDN (NB) 22 Rb23
Frederiksted USA (VI) 42 Rc37
Fredonia USA (AZ) 33 Oj27
Fredonia USA (KS) 35 Ph27
Fredonia USA (NY) 29 Qf24
Freeburg USA (MO) 28 Pk26
Freedom USA (WY) 25 Ok24
Freeland USA (WA) 16 Od21
Freeman USA (SD) 27 Pg24
Freeman USA (WA) 17 Og22
Freemont CDN (SAS) 17 Pa19
Freeport BS 43 Qf32
Freeport CDN (NS) 22 Rb23
Freeport USA (FL) 36 Qb30
Freeport USA (IL) 28 Qa24
Freeport USA (PA) 29 Qf25
Freeport USA (TX) 41 Ph31
Freer USA (TX) 40 Pf32
Freewater, Milton- USA (OR) 24 Of23
Fremont USA (CA) 32 Oe27
Fremont USA (NC) 31 Qg28
Fremont USA (NE) 27 Pg25
Fremont USA (OH) 29 Qd25
French Cove CDN (NFL) 23 Rh20
Frenchglen USA (OR) 24 Of24
French Lick USA (IN) 28 Qb26
Frenchman Butte CDN (SAS) 17 Pa19
Frenchville USA (ME) 22 Ra22
Fresnal Canyon USA (AZ) 33 Ok30
Fresnillo de González Echeverría MEX (ZAC) 39 Pd34
Fresno USA (CA) 32 Of27
Friday Harbour USA (WA) 16 Od21
Friend USA (NE) 27 Pg25
Friendship USA (OH) 29 Qd26
Friona USA (TX) 34 Pd28
Frisco USA (CO) 34 Pb26
Frobisher CDN (SAS) 18 Pd21
Froid USA (MT) 18 Pc21
Fronteras MEX (SON) 39 Pa30
Frontier CDN (SAS) 18 Pa21
Front Royal USA (VA) 29 Qf26
Frostburg USA (MD) 29 Qf26
Froude CDN (SAS) 18 Pd21
Fruita USA (CO) 33 Pa26
Fruitland USA (UT) 25 Ok25
Fryeburg USA (LA) 35 Pj29
Fryeburg USA (ME) 22 Qk23
Frys CDN (SAS) 18 Pe21
Fuerte, El MEX (SIN) 39 Pa32
Fulda USA (MN) 27 Ph24
Fulford Harbour CDN (BC) 16 Od21
Fullerton USA (NE) 27 Pg25
Fulton USA (IL) 28 Pk25
Fulton USA (KY) 36 Qa27
Fulton USA (MO) 28 Pk26
Fulton USA (NY) 29 Qg24
Fultondale USA (AL) 36 Qb29
Fundición MEX (SON) 39 Pa32
Fundy National Park ☆ CDN (NB) 22 Rc23
Funiak Springs, De USA (FL) 36 Qb30
Funkley USA (MN) 19 Ph22
Funter USA (AK) 14 Nh16
Furnace Creek USA (CA) 32 Og27
Furness CDN (SAS) 17 Pa19
Fusilier CDN (SAS) 17 Pa20

G

Gabarouse CDN (NS) 23 Re23
Gabarus CDN (NS) 23 Re23
Gabbs USA (NV) 32 Og26
Gabriola CDN (BC) 16 Od21
Gadsden USA (AL) 36 Qb29
Gaffney USA (SC) 37 Qe28
Gage CDN (ALB) 15 Of17
Gage USA (NM) 33 Pa2
Gage USA (OK) 35 Pf2
Gagetown CDN (NB) 22 Rb2
Gagnon CDN (QUE) 22 Ra2
Gahern CDN (ALB) 17 Ok2
Gail USA (TX) 34 Pe2
Gaines, Fort ☆ USA (AL) 36 Qa3
Gainesville USA (FL) 37 Qd3
Gainesville USA (GA) 37 Qd2
Gainesville USA (MO) 35 Pj2
Gainesville USA (TX) 35 Pg2
Gainsborough CDN (SAS) 18 Pe2
Gaithersburg USA (MD) 29 Qg2
Gakona USA (AK) 11 Nc1
Galata USA (MT) 17 Ok2
Galax USA (VA) 37 Qe2
Galbraith CDN (BC) 14 Nj1
Galeana MEX (CHA) 39 Pb3
Galeana MEX (NL) 40 Pe3
Galena USA (AK) 10 Mg1
Galena USA (IL) 27 Pk2
Galena USA (MO) 35 Pj2
Galena Bay CDN (BC) 17 Og2
Galesburg USA (IL) 28 Pk2
Galesburg USA (ND) 19 Pg2
Galesville USA (WI) 27 Pk2
Galeton USA (PA) 29 Qg2
Galiano CDN (BC) 16 Od
Galilee CDN (SAS) 18 Pc
Galion USA (OH) 29 Qd
Gallatin USA (MO) 35 Pj
Gallatin USA (TN) 36 Qb
Gallegos USA (NM) 34 Po
Gallipolis USA (OH) 29 Qd
Galloway CDN (BC) 17 Oh
Gallup USA (NM) 33 Pa
Galva USA (IL) 28 Qa
Galveston USA (TX) 41 Ph
Gambo CDN (NFL) 23 Rh
Ganado USA (AZ) 33 Pa
Gananoque CDN (ONT) 29 Qg
Gander CDN (NFL) 23 Rh
Gander Bay CDN (NFL) 23 Rh
Ganges CDN (BC) 16 Oc
Garberville USA (CA) 24 Oc
García, Villa de MEX (NL) 40 Pe
Garden City USA (AL) 36 Qb
Garden City USA (KS) 34 Pe
Garden City USA (TX) 34 Pe
Gardendale USA (TX) 34 Pc
Garden River CDN (ONT) 20 Q
Gardenton CDN (MAN) 19 Pg
Gardiner CDN (ONT) 20 Q
Gardiner USA (ME) 22 R
Gardiner USA (MT) 25 O
Gardner USA (CO) 34 P
Gardner USA (IL) 28 Q
Gardner USA (LA) 36 P
Gardner USA (ND) 19 P
Gardnerville USA (NV) 32 C
Garibaldi CDN (BC) 16 O
Garibaldi Provincial Park ☆ CDN (BC) 16 O
Garland CDN (MAN) 18 P
Garland USA (NC) 31 C
Garland USA (TX) 35 P
Garland USA (WY) 25 P
Garner USA (IA) 27 P
Garner USA (NC) 31 C
Garnett USA (KS) 35 P
Garrison USA (MN) 27
Garrison USA (MT) 25 C
Garrison USA (ND) 18 F
Garrison USA (TX) 35
Gary USA (IN) 28 C
Garysburg USA (NC) 31 Q
Garza Garcia MEX (NL) 40 P
Gascoigne CDN (SAS) 17 P
Gaspé CDN (QUE) 22 F
Gaspereau Forks CDN (NB) 22 F
Gaspésie, Parc de Cons. de la ☆ CDN (QUE) 22 F
Gassaway USA (WV) 29 C
Gastonia USA (NC) 37 C
Gate City USA (VA) 37 C
Gatesville USA (TX) 35
Gateview USA (CO) 33
Gateway USA (CO) 33
Gatineau CDN (QUE) 29 C
Gatos, Los USA (CA) 32
Gaultois CDN (NFL) 23
Gaviota USA (CA) 32
Gaylord USA (MI) 28
Gaylord USA (VA) 29
Geary CDN (NB) 22
Geary USA (OK) 35
Gebo USA (WY) 25
Gemmell USA (MN) 19
General Arnulfo R. Gómez MEX (DGO) 39
General Bravo MEX (NL) 40
General Cepeda MEX (COA) 40
General Francisco Murguía MEX (ZAC) 39
General Ignacio Zaragoza MEX (NL) 40
General Simón Bolívar MEX (DGO) 39
General Terán MEX (NL) 40
General Treviño MEX (NL) 40
General Trías MEX (CHA) 39
Geneseo USA (IL) 28
Geneseo USA (NY) 29
Geneva USA (ID) 25
Geneva USA (NE) 27
Geneva USA (NY) 29
Geneva USA (OH) 29
Genoa USA (NE) 27
Genoa USA (WI) 27
Gentryville USA (MO) 3
Georges Tavern USA (VA) 31
Georgetown USA (DE) 31
Georgetown USA (GA) 36
Georgetown USA (KY) 28
Georgetown USA (OH) 29
Georgetown USA (SC) 37
George West USA (TX) 4
Georgiana USA (AL) 36
Geraldine USA (MT) 17
Geralton CDN (ONT) 20
Gerlach USA (NV) 24
Germansen Landing CDN (BC) 15
Germantown USA (TN) 36

Gettysburg (USA) (PA) 29 Qg26
Gettysburg (USA) (SD) 26 Pf23
Geyser (USA) (MT) 17 Ok22
Ghost River (CDN) (ONT) 19 Pk20
Giant Forest (USA) (CA) 32 Of27
Giant Yellowknife Mine ☆ (CDN) (NWT) 15 Oh14
Gibbon (USA) (NE) 26 Pf25
Gibbon (USA) (OR) 24 Of23
Gibbons (CDN) (ALB) 17 Oj19
Gibbonsville (USA) (ID) 25 Oj23
Gibbs City (USA) (MI) 20 Qa22
Gibsland (USA) (LA) 35 Pj29
ibson (USA) (LA) 36 Pk31
ibson, Port (USA) (MS) 36 Pk30
ibson City (USA) (IL) 28 Qa25
ibson Island (USA) (MD) 29 Qg26
ibsons (CDN) (BC) 16 Od21
iddings (USA) (TX) 40 Pg30
ifford (USA) (WA) 16 Of21
ift Lake (CDN) (ALB) 15 Oh18
ig Harbor (USA) (WA) 16 Od22
ila Bend (USA) (AZ) 33 Oj29
Gila Cliff Dwellings National Monument ☆ (USA) (NM) 33 Pa29
ilbert (USA) (MN) 19 Pj22
ilby (USA) (ND) 19 Pg21
ildford (USA) (MT) 17 Ok21
illespie (USA) (IL) 28 Qa26
illette (USA) (WY) 26 Pc23
illies Bay (CDN) (BC) 16 Oc21
ills Rock (USA) (MI) 28 Qb23
ilman (USA) (IL) 28 Qb25
lman (USA) (WI) 27 Pk23
lmanton (USA) (WI) 27 Pk23
lmer (USA) (TX) 35 Ph29
lmour (CDN) (ONT) 29 Qg23
lroy (USA) (CA) 32 Oe27
ltner (USA) (NE) 26 Pf25
mli (CDN) (MAN) 19 Pg20
ngko Petrified Forest State Park ☆ (USA) (WA) 24 Oe22
rard (USA) (KS) 35 Ph27
rardville (CDN) (QUE) 21 Qj21
rdwood (USA) (AK) 13 Na15
roux (CDN) (MAN) 19 Pg21
rouxville (CDN) (ALB) 15 Og18
rvin (USA) (TX) 39 Pd30
scome (CDN) (BC) 16 Od18
twinksihlkw (CDN) (BC) 14 Oa18
ace, La (CDN) (ALB) 15 Of18
ace Bay (CDN) (NS) 23 Rf22
acier (USA) (WA) 16 Oe21
acier National Park ☆ (CDN) (BC) 17 Og20
acier National Park = Waterton Glacier International Peace Park ☆ (USA) (MT) 17 Oh21
acier Peak Wilderness Area ☆ (USA) (WA) 16 Oe21
adewater (USA) (TX) 35 Ph29
adstone (CDN) (MAN) 19 Pf20
amis (USA) (CA) 33 Oh29
asgow (USA) (KY) 36 Qc27
asgow (USA) (MO) 28 Pj26
sgow (USA) (MT) 18 Pb21
aslyn (CDN) (SAS) 17 Pa19
snevin (CDN) (SAS) 18 Pc21
assboro (USA) (NJ) 29 Qh26
eson (USA) (AZ) 33 Pa30
ichen (CDN) (ALB) 17 Oj20
n (USA) (NH) 22 Qk23
n Alda (CDN) (ONT) 29 Qg23
nboro (CDN) (MAN) 19 Pf21
nboyle (CDN) (YT) 11 Nf14
nburn (USA) (ND) 18 Pe21
ndale (USA) (AZ) 33 Oj29
ndale (USA) (CA) 32 Of28
ndive (USA) (MT) 18 Pc22
ndo (USA) (WY) 26 Pc24
ndon (CDN) (ALB) 17 Ok18
nfield (USA) (ND) 19 Pf22
holme (CDN) (NS) 22 Rd23
n Hope (USA) (PA) 29 Qf25
Kerr (CDN) (SAS) 18 Pb20
n Leslie (CDN) (ALB) 15 Of18
nmora (USA) (LA) 36 Pj30
nnallen (USA) (AK) 11 Nc14
nns (USA) (VA) 31 Qg27
nns Ferry (USA) (ID) 25 Oh24
nville (USA) (CA) 32 Of28
nville (USA) (GA) 29 Qe26
ora (CDN) (MAN) 19 Pf21
rock (USA) (WY) 26 Pc24
Rose (USA) (TX) 35 Pg29
s Falls (USA) (NY) 30 Qj24
tworth (CDN) (SAS) 18 Pb21
ville (USA) (MN) 27 Pj24
wood (CDN) (ALB) 17 Oj21
wood (USA) (AR) 35 Pj28
wood (USA) (IA) 27 Ph25
wood (USA) (MN) 27 Ph23
wood City (USA) (WI) 27 Pj23
wood Springs (USA) (CO) 33 Pb26
den (CDN) (SAS) 17 Pa20
den (USA) (WI) 20 Pk22
e (USA) (AZ) 33 Ok29
a (MEX) (COA) 40 Pe32
a, La (MEX) (NL) 40 Pf32
as, Las (MEX) (SIN) 39 Pa33
eta (USA) (NM) 34 Pc28
er (USA) (MS) 36 Pk30
cester (USA) (MA) 30 Qk24
cester (USA) (VA) 31 Qg27
ersville (USA) (NY) 30 Qh24
ertown (CDN) (NFL) 23 Rh21
on (USA) (MN) 19 Pg22
enthal (CDN) (MAN) 19 Pg21
Rocks Wilderness ☆ (USA) (WA) 24 Oe22
out (CDN) (QUE) 22 Rb21
rich (CDN) (ONT) 29 Qe24
Lake Narrows (CDN) (MAN) 19 Ph18
ma (CDN) (ONT) 20 Qe22
nda (USA) (IL) 36 Qa27
nda (USA) (NV) 24 Og25
Bar (CDN) (BC) 15 Od17
Beach (USA) (OR) 24 Oc24
Bridge (CDN) (BC) 16 Od20
reek (USA) (MT) 25 Oj22
n (CDN) (BC) 17 Og20
ndale (USA) (WA) 24 Oe23
n Ears Provincial Park ☆ (CDN) (BC) 16 Od21

Golden Gate (USA) (FL) 43 Qe32
Golden Gate Bridge ☆ (USA) (CA) 32 Od27
Golden Meadow (USA) (LA) 36 Pk31
Golden Prairie (CDN) (SAS) 17 Pa20
Golden Valley (USA) (ND) 18 Pd22
Goldfield (USA) (NV) 32 Og27
Gold Hill (USA) (UT) 25 Oj25
Gold River (CDN) (BC) 16 Ob21
Gold Rock (CDN) (ONT) 19 Pj21
Goldsboro (USA) (MD) 29 Qh26
Goldsboro (USA) (NC) 31 Qf28
Goldthwaite (USA) (TX) 35 Pf30
Goldwater (USA) (LA) 35 Pj30
Golfo de Santa Clara, El (MEX) (SON) 33 Oh30
Goliad (USA) (TX) 40 Pg31
Golovin (USA) (AK) 10 Md13
Golovin Mission (USA) (AK) 10 Md13
Golva (USA) (ND) 18 Pd22
Gómez Farías (MEX) (CHA) 39 Pb31
Gómez Farías (MEX) (TAM) 40 Pf34
Gómez Palacio (MEX) (DGO) 39 Pd33
Gonzales (USA) (FL) 36 Qb30
Gonzales (USA) (LA) 36 Pk30
Gonzales (USA) (TX) 40 Pg31
González (MEX) (TAM) 40 Pf34
Goobies (CDN) (NFL) 23 Rj22
Gooderham (CDN) (ONT) 29 Qf23
Goodeve (CDN) (SAS) 18 Pd20
Goodfare (CDN) (ALB) 15 Of18
Gooding (USA) (ID) 25 Oh24
Goodland (USA) (KS) 34 Pe26
Goodland (USA) (MN) 19 Pj22
Goodlands (CDN) (MAN) 18 Pe21
Goodlettsville (USA) (TN) 36 Qb27
Goodlow (CDN) (BC) 15 Oe17
Goodnews Bay = Goodnews Mining Camp (USA) (AK) 12 Me16
Goodnews Mining Camp = Goodnews Bay (USA) (AK) 12 Me16
Goodrich (USA) (CO) 26 Pc25
Goodridge (CDN) (ALB) 17 Ok18
Goodridge (USA) (MN) 19 Ph21
Goodsoil (CDN) (SAS) 17 Pa18
Goodsprings (USA) (NV) 33 Oh28
Goodview (USA) (MN) 27 Pk23
Goodwin (CDN) (ALB) 15 Of18
Goose Bay (CDN) (BC) 16 Ob20
Goose Creek (USA) (SC) 37 Qe29
Goose Lake (USA) (IA) 27 Pk25
Goosport (USA) (LA) 41 Pj30
Gorda Cay (BS) 43 Qg32
Gordon (USA) (AK) 11 Ne11
Gordon (USA) (NE) 26 Pd24
Gordon (USA) (TX) 35 Pf29
Gordondale (CDN) (ALB) 15 Of18
Gordonsville (USA) (VA) 29 Qf26
Gorham (USA) (ME) 22 Qk24
Gorham (USA) (NH) 22 Qk23
Gorman (USA) (CA) 32 Of28
Gorman (USA) (TX) 35 Pf29
Goshen (USA) (CA) 32 Of27
Goshen (USA) (IN) 28 Qc25
Gothenburg (USA) (NE) 26 Pe25
Gould (USA) (OK) 35 Pf28
Gouldsboro (USA) (ME) 22 Ra23
Gouverneur (USA) (NY) 29 Qh23
Govenlock (CDN) (SAS) 17 Pa21
Gowanda (USA) (NY) 29 Qf24
Gowganda (CDN) (ONT) 20 Qe22
Gracefield (CDN) (QUE) 29 Qg22
Graceville (USA) (MN) 27 Pg23
Grady (USA) (AR) 36 Pk28
Grady (USA) (NM) 34 Pd28
Grafton (USA) (IL) 28 Pk26
Grafton (USA) (ND) 19 Pg21
Grafton (USA) (NH) 30 Qk24
Grafton (USA) (WV) 29 Qe26
Graham (CDN) (ONT) 19 Pk21
Graham (USA) (TX) 35 Pf29
Graines, Rivière-aux- (CDN) (QUE) 22 Rc20
Grainfield (USA) (KS) 34 Pe26
Grainton (USA) (NE) 26 Pe25
Granada (USA) (CO) 34 Pd26
Granbury (USA) (TX) 35 Pg29
Granby (CDN) (QUE) 30 Qj23
Granby (USA) (CO) 34 Pc25
Grand Bay (CDN) (NB) 22 Rb23
Grand Bend (CDN) (ONT) 29 Qe24
Grand Bruit (CDN) (NFL) 23 Rf22
Grand Canyon (USA) (AZ) 33 Oj27
Grand Canyon Caverns ☆ (USA) (AZ) 33 Oj28
Grand Canyon National Park ☆ (USA) (AZ) 33 Oj27
Grand Centre (CDN) (ALB) 17 Ok18
Grand Coulee (USA) (WA) 16 Of22
Grand Coulee Dam ☆ (USA) (WA) 16 Of22
Grande, La (USA) (OR) 24 Of23
Grande Cache (CDN) (ALB) 16 Of19
Grande-Entrée (CDN) (QUE) 23 Re22
Grande Pointe (CDN) (MAN) 19 Pg21
Grande Prairie (CDN) (ALB) 15 Of18
Gran Desierto del Pinacate, Parque Natural del ☆ (MEX) (SON) 33 Oh30
Grande-Vallée (CDN) (QUE) 22 Rc21
Grand Falls (CDN) (NB) 22 Rb22
Grand Falls (CDN) (NFL) 23 Rh21
Grandfalls (USA) (TX) 39 Pd30
Grand Forks (CDN) (BC) 16 Of21
Grand Forks (USA) (ND) 19 Pg22
Grand Gulf Military Park ☆ (USA) (MS) 36 Pk29
Grand Harbor (USA) (ND) 19 Pf21
Grand Haven (USA) (MI) 28 Qb24
Grandin (USA) (ND) 19 Pg22
Grand Island (USA) (NE) 26 Pf25
Grand Isle (USA) (LA) 36 Qa31
Grand Isle S.P. ☆ (USA) (LA) 36 Qa31
Grand Junction (USA) (CO) 33 Pa26
Grand le Pierre (CDN) (NFL) 23 Rh22
Grand Marais (USA) (MI) 20 Qc22
Grand Marais (USA) (MN) 19 Pk22
Grand-Mère (CDN) (QUE) 21 Qj22
Grand Portage (USA) (MN) 20 Qa22
Grand Prairie (USA) (TX) 35 Pg29
Grand Quarries Fossils, Le ☆ (USA) (IA) 27 Pj25
Grand Rapids (CDN) (MAN) 19 Pf19
Grand Rapids (USA) (MI) 28 Qc24
Grand Rapids (USA) (MN) 19 Pj22
Grand-Remous (CDN) (QUE) 21 Qh22
Grand River (USA) (IA) 27 Pj25

Grand Ronde (USA) (OR) 24 Od23
Grand Saline (USA) (TX) 35 Ph29
Grands-Jardins, Parc de Conservation des ☆ (CDN) (QUE) 22 Qk22
Grand Staircase - Escalante National Monument ☆ (USA) (UT) 33 Oj27
Grand Teton National Park ☆ (USA) (WY) 25 Ok24
Grandview (CDN) (MAN) 18 Pe20
Grandview (USA) (TX) 35 Pg29
Grange, La (USA) (GA) 36 Qc29
Grange, La (USA) (KY) 28 Qc26
Grange, La (USA) (NC) 31 Qg28
Grange, La (USA) (TX) 40 Pg31
Granger (USA) (WY) 25 Pa25
Grangeville (USA) (ID) 24 Og23
Granisle (CDN) (BC) 14 Ob18
Granite Bay (CDN) (BC) 16 Oc20
Granite Falls (USA) (MN) 27 Ph23
Granjas, Las (MEX) (CHA) 34 Pb30
Grant (USA) (CO) 34 Pc26
Grant (USA) (NE) 26 Pe25
Grant City (USA) (MO) 27 Ph25
Grants (USA) (NM) 33 Pb28
Grantsburg (USA) (WI) 27 Pj23
Grants Pass (USA) (OR) 24 Od24
Grantsville (USA) (UT) 25 Oj25
Granum (CDN) (ALB) 17 Oj21
Granville (USA) (ND) 18 Pe21
Grapeland (USA) (TX) 35 Ph30
Grasmere (CDN) (BC) 17 Oh21
Grassland (CDN) (ALB) 17 Oj18
Grasslands National Park ☆ (CDN) (SAS) 18 Pb21
Grassrange (USA) (MT) 17 Pa22
Grass River Provincial Park ☆ (CDN) (MAN) 18 Pe18
Grass Valley (USA) (CA) 32 Oe26
Grassy Butte (USA) (ND) 18 Pd22
Grassy Lake (CDN) (ALB) 17 Ok21
Grates Cove (CDN) (NFL) 23 Rj21
Gratz (USA) (KY) 28 Qc26
Gravelbourg (CDN) (SAS) 18 Pb21
Gravenhurst (CDN) (ONT) 29 Qf23
Gray (USA) (GA) 37 Qd29
Gray (USA) (ME) 22 Qk24
Gray (USA) (OK) 34 Pe27
Gray Creek (CDN) (BC) 17 Og21
Grayling (USA) (MI) 28 Qc23
Grayson (USA) (KY) 29 Qd26
Graysville (CDN) (MAN) 19 Pf21
Grayville (USA) (IL) 28 Qa26
Great Basin National Park ☆ (USA) (NV) 33 Oh26
Great Bend (USA) (KS) 35 Pf26
Great Central (CDN) (BC) 16 Oc21
Great Dismal Swamp National Wildlife Refuge ☆ (USA) (VA) 31 Qg27
Great Divide (USA) (CO) 25 Pb25
Great Falls ☆ (USA) (MT) 17 Ok22
Great Sand Dunes National Park ☆ (USA) (CO) 34 Pb26
Great Smoky Mountains National Park ☆ (USA) (TN) 37 Qd28
Greeley (USA) (CO) 26 Pc25
Greeley (USA) (NE) 26 Pf25
Green (CDN) (ONT) 20 Qa20
Green Bay (USA) (WI) 28 Qa23
Greenbrier (USA) (AR) 35 Pj28
Greenbush (USA) (MN) 19 Pg21
Greencastle (USA) (IN) 28 Qb26
Greencastle (USA) (PA) 29 Qg26
Green City (USA) (MO) 27 Pj25
Green Cove Springs (USA) (FL) 37 Qe31
Greene (USA) (IA) 27 Pj24
Greene (USA) (ND) 18 Pe21
Greene (USA) (NY) 29 Qh24
Greeneville (USA) (TN) 37 Qd27
Greenfield (USA) (IL) 28 Pk26
Greenfield (USA) (IN) 28 Qc26
Greenfield (USA) (MA) 30 Qj24
Greenfield (USA) (MO) 35 Pj27
Greenfield (USA) (TN) 36 Qa27
Green Forest (USA) (AR) 35 Pj27
Green Lake (CDN) (SAS) 17 Pb18
Greenland (USA) (MI) 20 Qa22
Greenport (USA) (NY) 30 Qj25
Green River (USA) (UT) 33 Ok26
Green River (USA) (WY) 25 Pa25
Greensboro (USA) (AL) 36 Qb29
Greensboro (USA) (GA) 37 Qd29
Greensboro (USA) (NC) 37 Qf27
Greensburg (USA) (IN) 28 Qc26
Greensburg (USA) (KS) 35 Pf27
Greensburg (USA) (LA) 36 Pk30
Greensburg (USA) (PA) 29 Qf25
Greenstreet (CDN) (SAS) 17 Pa19
Greenup (USA) (IL) 28 Qa26
Green Valley (USA) (AZ) 33 Ok30
Greenville (CDN) (BC) 14 Oa18
Greenville (USA) (AL) 36 Qb30
Greenville (USA) (CA) 24 Oe25
Greenville (USA) (FL) 37 Qd30
Greenville (USA) (IL) 28 Qa26
Greenville (USA) (ME) 22 Ra23
Greenville (USA) (MS) 36 Pk29
Greenville (USA) (OH) 28 Qc25
Greenville (USA) (PA) 29 Qe25
Greenville (USA) (SC) 37 Qd28
Greenville (USA) (TN) 31 Qg28
Greenville (USA) (TX) 35 Pg29
Green Water Provincial Park ☆ (CDN) (SAS) 18 Pd19
Greenwich (USA) (OH) 29 Qd25
Greenwood (CDN) (BC) 16 Of21
Greenwood (USA) (FL) 36 Qc30
Greenwood (USA) (IN) 28 Qb26
Greenwood (USA) (LA) 35 Pj29
Greenwood (USA) (MS) 36 Pk29
Greenwood (USA) (SC) 37 Qd28
Greenwood (USA) (WI) 27 Pk23
Greer (USA) (SC) 37 Qd28
Gregory (USA) (SD) 26 Pf24
Grenada (USA) (MS) 36 Qa29
Grenfell (CDN) (SAS) 18 Pd20
Grenora (USA) (ND) 18 Pd21
Grenville (USA) (NM) 34 Pd27
Gresham (USA) (NE) 27 Pg25
Gretna (CDN) (MAN) 19 Pg21
Gretna (USA) (FL) 36 Qc30
Gretna (USA) (LA) 36 Pk31
Greybull (USA) (WY) 25 Pa23
Grey River (CDN) (NFL) 23 Rg22

Gridley (USA) (CA) 32 Oe26
Griffin (CDN) (SAS) 18 Pd21
Griffin (USA) (GA) 36 Qc29
Grifton (USA) (NC) 31 Qg28
Grimsby (CDN) (ONT) 29 Qf24
Grimshaw (CDN) (ALB) 15 Og17
Grindstone Provincial Park ☆ (CDN) (MAN) 19 Pg20
Grinell (USA) (IA) 27 Pj25
Griquet (CDN) (NFL) 23 Rh20
Griswold (CDN) (MAN) 18 Pe21
Groesbeck (USA) (TX) 35 Pg30
Gronlid (CDN) (SAS) 18 Pc19
Gros Cap (CDN) (ONT) 20 Qc22
Gros Morne National Park ☆ (CDN) (NFL) 23 Rg21
Grosse Tete (USA) (LA) 36 Pk30
Groton (USA) (SD) 26 Pf23
Grotto (USA) (WA) 16 Oe22
Grouard (CDN) (ALB) 15 Og18
Grouard Mission (CDN) (ALB) 15 Og18
Groundbirch (CDN) (BC) 15 Oe18
Grouse Creek (USA) (UT) 25 Oj25
Grove City (USA) (OH) 29 Qd26
Grovedale (CDN) (ALB) 15 Of18
Grove Hill (USA) (AL) 36 Qb30
Groveland (USA) (CA) 32 Oe27
Grover (USA) (CO) 26 Pc25
Grover (USA) (WY) 25 Ok24
Groveton (USA) (NH) 22 Qk23
Grullita, La (MEX) (SON) 33 Oh29
Grundy (USA) (VA) 37 Qd27
Grundy Center (USA) (IA) 27 Pj24
Gruver (USA) (TX) 34 Pe27
Gu Achi (USA) (AZ) 33 Oj29
Guachochi (MEX) (BCS) 39 Pb32
Guadalupe (MEX) (BCN) 32 Og30
Guadalupe (MEX) (COA) 40 Pe31
Guadalupe (MEX) (NL) 40 Pe33
Guadalupe (MEX) (ZAC) 40 Pd34
Guadalupe (USA) (CA) 32 Oe28
Guadalupe de Bahues (MEX) (CHA) 39 Pc32
Guadalupe de Bravo (MEX) (CHA) 34 Pb30
Guadalupe Mountains National Park ☆ (USA) (TX) 34 Pc30
Guadalupe Victoria (MEX) (DGO) 39 Pc33
Guadalupe Victoria (MEX) (TAM) 40 Pg33
Guadalupe y Calvo (MEX) (CHA) 39 Pb32
Guadeloupe, La (CDN) (QUE) 22 Qk23
Guáimaro (C) (CG) 43 Qg35
Guaje, El (MEX) (COA) 39 Pd31
Guamúchil (MEX) (SIN) 39 Pa33
Guanabacoa (C) (H) 43 Qd34
Guanabo (C) (H) 43 Qd34
Guanaceví (MEX) (DGO) 39 Pc33
Guanajay (C) (LH) 43 Qd34
Guánica (USA) (PR) 42 Rb37
Guasave (MEX) (SIN) 39 Pa33
Guayama (USA) (PR) 42 Rb37
Guaymas (MEX) (SON) 38 Ok32
Guelph (CDN) (ONT) 29 Qe24
Guerette (USA) (ME) 22 Ra22
Guernsey (USA) (WY) 26 Pc24
Guerrero (MEX) (COA) 40 Pe31
Guerrero (MEX) (TAM) 40 Pf32
Guerrero Negro (MEX) (BCS) 38 Oh32
Gueydan (USA) (LA) 36 Pj30
Guilford (USA) (ME) 22 Ra23
Guimbaleta (MEX) (COA) 39 Pd32
Güines (C) (LH) 43 Qd34
Güira de Melena (C) (LH) 43 Qd34
Gulf Breeze (USA) (FL) 36 Qb30
Gulf Islands National Park Reserve ☆ (CDN) (BC) 16 Od21
Gulf Islands National Seashore ☆ (USA) (MS) 36 Qa30
Gulfport (USA) (FL) 43 Qd32
Gulfport (USA) (MS) 36 Qa30
Gulf Shores (USA) (AL) 36 Qb30
Gulliver (USA) (MI) 28 Qb22
Gull Lake (CDN) (SAS) 17 Pa20
Gunn (CDN) (ALB) 17 Oh19
Gunnison (USA) (CO) 34 Pb26
Gunnison (USA) (UT) 33 Ok26
Gunsight (USA) (AZ) 33 Oj29
Guntersville (USA) (AL) 36 Qb28
Gurdon (USA) (AR) 35 Pj29
Gusher (USA) (UT) 25 Pa25
Gustavus (USA) (AK) 14 Nh16
Gutah (CDN) (BC) 15 Oe17
Guthrie (USA) (AZ) 33 Pa29
Guthrie (USA) (OK) 35 Pg28
Guthrie (USA) (TX) 34 Pe29
Guttenberg (USA) (IA) 27 Pk24
Gu Vo (USA) (AZ) 33 Oj29
Guy (CDN) (ALB) 15 Og18
Guymon (USA) (OK) 34 Pe27
Guynemer (CDN) (MAN) 19 Pf20
Guzmán (MEX) (CHA) 39 Pb30
Gwinn (USA) (MI) 20 Qb22
Gwinner (USA) (ND) 27 Pg22
Gypsumville (CDN) (MAN) 19 Pf20

H

Hachita (USA) (NM) 33 Pa30
Hackberry (USA) (AZ) 33 Oj28
Hackensack (USA) (MN) 19 Ph22
Hadashville (CDN) (MAN) 19 Ph21
Hafford (CDN) (SAS) 18 Pb19
Hagar (CDN) (ONT) 20 Qe22
Hagerman (USA) (ID) 25 Oh24
Hagerman (USA) (NM) 34 Pc29
Hagerstown (USA) (MD) 29 Qg26
Hahira (USA) (GA) 37 Qd30
Hahnville (USA) (LA) 36 Pk31
Haigler (USA) (NE) 34 Pe25
Hailey (USA) (ID) 25 Oh24
Haileybury (CDN) (ONT) 21 Qf22
Haines (USA) (AK) 14 Nh16
Haines (USA) (OR) 24 Og23
Haines Junction (CDN) (NWT) 14 Ng15
Hairy Hill (CDN) (ALB) 17 Ok19
Hakai Provincial Recreation Area ☆ (CDN) (BC) 16 Oa20
Hakalau (USA) (HI) 44 Mh36
Halbrite (CDN) (SAS) 18 Pd21
Haleakalā National Park ☆ (USA) (HI) 44 Mg35
Hale'iwa (USA) (HI) 44 Mf35

Haley Dome (USA) (UT) 33 Pa26
Haleyville (USA) (AL) 36 Qb28
Halfmoon Bay (CDN) (BC) 16 Od21
Haliburton (CDN) (ONT) 29 Qf23
Halifax (CDN) (NS) 22 Rd23
Halifax (USA) (NC) 31 Qg27
Halkirk (CDN) (ALB) 17 Oj19
Hallandale Beach (USA) (FL) 43 Qe33
Hallboro (CDN) (MAN) 19 Pf20
Halleck (USA) (NV) 25 Oh25
Hallersville (USA) (AK) 12 Mg16
Hallettsville (USA) (TX) 40 Pg31
Halliday (USA) (ND) 18 Pd22
Hallock (USA) (MN) 19 Pg21
Hallson (USA) (ND) 19 Pg21
Hallsville (USA) (TX) 35 Ph29
Hallville (CDN) (ONT) 29 Qh23
Halstad (USA) (MN) 19 Pg22
Haltom City (USA) (TX) 35 Pg29
Hamar (USA) (ND) 19 Pf22
Hamberg (USA) (ND) 19 Pf22
Hamburg (USA) (AR) 36 Pk29
Hamburg (USA) (IA) 27 Ph25
Hamburg (USA) (NY) 29 Qf24
Hamilton (CDN) (ONT) 29 Qf24
Hamilton (USA) (AK) 10 Md14
Hamilton (USA) (AL) 36 Qb28
Hamilton (USA) (CO) 25 Pb25
Hamilton (USA) (IL) 27 Pk25
Hamilton (USA) (MO) 35 Ph26
Hamilton (USA) (MT) 25 Oh22
Hamilton (USA) (OH) 28 Qc26
Hamilton (USA) (TX) 35 Pf30
Hamilton (USA) (WA) 16 Oe21
Hamilton Dome (USA) (WY) 25 Pa24
Hamiota (CDN) (MAN) 18 Pe20
Hamlin (CDN) (ALB) 17 Ok19
Hamlin (CDN) (SAS) 17 Pa19
Hamlin (USA) (TX) 34 Pe29
Hammon (USA) (OK) 35 Pf28
Hammond (USA) (IN) 28 Qb25
Hammond (USA) (LA) 36 Pk30
Hammondvale (CDN) (NB) 22 Rc23
Hammonton (USA) (NJ) 31 Qh26
Ham-Nord (CDN) (QUE) 22 Qk23
Hampden (CDN) (NFL) 23 Rg21
Hampden (USA) (ME) 22 Ra23
Hampton (CDN) (NB) 22 Rc23
Hampton (USA) (AR) 36 Pj29
Hampton (USA) (IA) 27 Pj24
Hampton (USA) (NH) 22 Qk24
Hampton (USA) (SC) 37 Qe29
Hampton (USA) (VA) 31 Qg27
Hamtown (CDN) (NB) 22 Rb22
Hāna (USA) (HI) 44 Mh35
Hanabanilla, Presa del ☆ (C) (SS) 43 Qe34
Hanalei (USA) (HI) 44 Mf34
Hanapēpē (USA) (HI) 44 Mf35
Hanceville (CDN) (BC) 16 Od20
Hancock (USA) (ME) 22 Ra23
Hancock (USA) (MI) 20 Qa22
Hancock (USA) (NY) 29 Qh25
Handel (CDN) (SAS) 17 Pa19
Hanford (CDN) (NB) 22 Rc23
Hanford (USA) (CA) 32 Of27
Hanford Reach National Monument ☆ (USA) (WA) 24 Of22
Hankinson (USA) (ND) 27 Pg22
Hanksville (USA) (UT) 33 Ok26
Hanley (CDN) (SAS) 18 Pb20
Hanna (CDN) (ALB) 17 Ok20
Hanna (USA) (UT) 25 Ok25
Hannaford (USA) (ND) 19 Pf22
Hannah (USA) (ND) 19 Pf21
Hannibal (USA) (MO) 28 Pk26
Hanover (CDN) (ONT) 29 Qe23
Hanover (USA) (IL) 27 Pk24
Hanover (USA) (IN) 28 Qc26
Hanover (USA) (PA) 29 Qg26
Hanover (USA) (VA) 31 Qg27
Hansboro (USA) (ND) 19 Pf21
Hansen (USA) (NE) 26 Pf25
Happy (USA) (TX) 34 Pe28
Happy Camp (USA) (CA) 24 Od25
Happy Jack (USA) (AZ) 33 Ok28
Harbor Beach (USA) (MI) 29 Qd24
Harbour Breton (CDN) (NFL) 23 Rh22
Harbour Deep (CDN) (NFL) 23 Rg20
Harcourt (CDN) (NB) 22 Rc22
Hard Bargin (BS) 43 Qg32
Hardeeville (USA) (SC) 37 Qe29
Hardin (USA) (IL) 28 Pk26
Hardin (USA) (MT) 25 Pb23
Hardinsburg (USA) (KY) 36 Qb27
Hardisty (CDN) (ALB) 17 Ok19
Hardwick (USA) (GA) 37 Qd29
Hardwick (USA) (VT) 30 Qj23
Hardy (CDN) (SAS) 18 Pc21
Hardy (USA) (AR) 36 Pk27
Hardy, Port (CDN) (BC) 16 Ob20
Hargrave (CDN) (MAN) 18 Pe21
Harlan (USA) (IA) 27 Ph25
Harlan (USA) (KY) 37 Qd27
Harlem (USA) (MT) 18 Pa21
Harleston (USA) (MS) 36 Qa30
Harleton (USA) (TX) 35 Ph29
Harlingen (USA) (TX) 40 Pg32
Harlow (USA) (ND) 19 Pf21
Harlowton (USA) (MT) 18 Pa22
Harmony (USA) (ME) 22 Ra23
Harmony (USA) (MN) 27 Pj24
Harpe, La (USA) (IL) 27 Pk25
Harper (USA) (KS) 35 Pf27
Harper (USA) (OR) 24 Og24
Harrells (USA) (NC) 31 Qf28
Harriman (USA) (TN) 36 Qc28
Harrington (USA) (DE) 31 Qh26
Harrington (USA) (WA) 16 Of22
Harrington Harbour (CDN) (QUE) 23 Rf20
Harris (CDN) (SAS) 18 Pb20
Harrisburg (USA) (IL) 36 Qa27
Harrisburg (USA) (OR) 24 Od23
Harrisburg (USA) (PA) 29 Qg25
Harris Hill (CDN) (ONT) 19 Ph21
Harrison (USA) (AR) 35 Pj27
Harrison (USA) (ID) 17 Og22
Harrison (USA) (MI) 28 Qc23
Harrison (USA) (NE) 26 Pd24

Harrison (USA) (OH) 28 Qc26
Harrisonburg (USA) (LA) 36 Pk30
Harrisonburg (USA) (VA) 29 Qf26
Harrison Hot Springs (CDN) (BC) 16 Oe21
Harrison Mills (CDN) (BC) 16 Oe21
Harrisonville (USA) (MO) 35 Ph26
Harrisville (USA) (MI) 29 Qd23
Harrisville (USA) (WV) 29 Qe26
Harrodsburg (USA) (KY) 36 Qc27
Harrogate (CDN) (BC) 17 Og20
Harrop (CDN) (BC) 17 Og21
Hart (USA) (TX) 34 Pd28
Hartford (USA) (AL) 36 Qc30
Hartford (USA) (CT) 30 Qj25
Hartford (USA) (KY) 36 Qb27
Hartford City (USA) (IN) 28 Qc25
Hartland (CDN) (NB) 22 Rb22
Hartland (USA) (ME) 22 Ra23
Hartland (USA) (WV) 29 Qe26
Hartley (USA) (IA) 27 Ph24
Hartline (USA) (WA) 16 Of22
Hart Mountain National Antelope Refuge ☆ (USA) (OR) 24 Of24
Hartney (CDN) (MAN) 18 Pe21
Hartsel (USA) (CO) 34 Pc26
Hartselle (USA) (AL) 36 Qb28
Hartsville (USA) (SC) 37 Qe28
Hartville (USA) (MO) 35 Pj27
Hartwell (USA) (GA) 37 Qd28
Hartwood (USA) (VA) 29 Qg26
Harty (CDN) (ONT) 20 Qd21
Harvard (USA) (IL) 28 Qa24
Harvard (USA) (NE) 26 Pf25
Harvey (USA) (ND) 19 Pf22
Harwood (USA) (ND) 19 Pg22
Harwood (USA) (TX) 40 Pg31
Haskell (USA) (TX) 35 Pf29
Hassman (USA) (MN) 19 Pj22
Hastings (CDN) (ONT) 29 Qg23
Hastings (USA) (FL) 37 Qe31
Hastings (USA) (MI) 28 Qc24
Hastings (USA) (MN) 27 Pj23
Hastings (USA) (NE) 26 Pf25
Hastings, Port (CDN) (NS) 23 Re23
Haswell (USA) (CO) 34 Pd26
Hatch (USA) (NM) 34 Pb29
Hatch (USA) (UT) 33 Oj27
Hatchel (USA) (TX) 35 Pf30
Hatfield (CDN) (SAS) 18 Pc20
Hatteras (USA) (NC) 31 Qh28
Hattiesburg (USA) (MS) 36 Qa30
Hatton (CDN) (SAS) 17 Pa20
Hatton (USA) (ND) 19 Pg22
Hauterive (CDN) (QUE) 22 Ra21
Havana (USA) (AR) 35 Pj28
Havana (USA) (FL) 36 Qc30
Havana (USA) (IL) 28 Pk25
Havanna = La Habana (C) (H) 43 Qd34
Havasu National Wildlife Refuge ☆ (USA) (AZ) 33 Oh28
Havelock (CDN) (ONT) 29 Qg23
Havelock (CDN) (QUE) 30 Qj23
Havelock (USA) (NC) 31 Qg28
Haven (USA) (KS) 35 Pg27
Havensville (USA) (KS) 35 Pg26
Haverhill (USA) (NH) 30 Qk24
Havre (USA) (MT) 17 Pa21
Havre-Aubert (CDN) (QUE) 23 Re22
Havre-Saint-Pierre (CDN) (QUE) 22 Rd20
Hawaii Volcanoes National Park ☆ (USA) (HI) 44 Mh36
Hawesville (USA) (KY) 36 Qb27
Hāwī (USA) (HI) 44 Mh35
Hawke's Bay (CDN) (NFL) 23 Rg20
Hawkesbury (CDN) (ONT) 30 Qh23
Hawk Inlet (USA) (AK) 14 Nh16
Hawkins (USA) (TX) 35 Ph29
Hawkins (USA) (WI) 27 Pk23
Hawkinsville (USA) (GA) 37 Qd29
Hawk Junction (CDN) (ONT) 20 Qc21
Hawk Lake (CDN) (ONT) 19 Pj21
Hawk Springs (USA) (WY) 26 Pc25
Hawley (USA) (MN) 19 Pg22
Hawley (USA) (TX) 35 Pf29
Hawthorne (USA) (FL) 37 Qd31
Hawthorne (USA) (NV) 32 Of26
Haxtun (USA) (CO) 26 Pd25
Hayden (USA) (CO) 26 Pb25
Hayden (USA) (ID) 17 Og22
Hayes (USA) (LA) 36 Pj30
Hayes (USA) (SD) 26 Pe23
Hayfield (USA) (MN) 27 Pj24
Hay Lakes (CDN) (ALB) 17 Oj19
Haylow (USA) (GA) 37 Qd30
Haymarket (USA) (VA) 29 Qg26
Haynesville (USA) (LA) 35 Pj29
Haynesville (USA) (ME) 22 Rb23
Hay River (CDN) (NWT) 15 Oh15
Hays (USA) (KS) 35 Pf26
Hays (USA) (MT) 18 Pa22
Hay Springs (USA) (NE) 26 Pd24
Haysville (USA) (KS) 35 Pg27
Hayti (USA) (MO) 36 Qa27
Hayward (USA) (CA) 32 Od27
Hayward (USA) (WI) 27 Pk22
Hazard (USA) (KY) 37 Qd27
Hazard (USA) (NE) 26 Pf25
Hazel (CDN) (MAN) 19 Pg21
Hazel Green (USA) (WI) 27 Pk24
Hazelton (CDN) (BC) 14 Ob18
Hazen (USA) (ND) 18 Pe22
Hazenmore (CDN) (SAS) 18 Pb21
Hazlehurst (USA) (GA) 37 Qd30
Hazlehurst (USA) (MS) 36 Pk30
Hazlet (CDN) (SAS) 18 Pa20
Hazleton (USA) (PA) 29 Qh25
Headingley (CDN) (MAN) 19 Pg21
Headquarters (USA) (ID) 25 Oh22
Head Smashed-In Buffalo Jump ☆ (CDN) (ALB) 17 Oj21
Heafford Junction (USA) (WI) 28 Qa23
Healy (USA) (AK) 11 Na14
Hearne (CDN) (SAS) 18 Pc20
Hearne (USA) (TX) 40 Pg30
Hearst (CDN) (ONT) 20 Qd21
Heart Butte (USA) (MT) 17 Oj21
Heart's Content (CDN) (NFL) 23 Rj22
Heath Steele (CDN) (NB) 22 Rb22
Hebbronville (USA) (TX) 40 Pf32
Heber (USA) (AZ) 33 Ok28
Heber City (USA) (UT) 25 Ok25
Heber Springs (USA) (AR) 36 Pj28
Hebert (USA) (LA) 36 Pk29
Hebo (USA) (OR) 24 Od23
Hebron (USA) (MS) 36 Qa30
Hebron (USA) (ND) 18 Pd22
Hebron (USA) (NE) 35 Pg25
Hecla (CDN) (MAN) 19 Pg20
Hecla Provincial Park ☆ (CDN) (MAN) 19 Pg20
Hectanooga (CDN) (NS) 22 Rb23
Hector (USA) (AR) 35 Pj28
Hector (USA) (MN) 27 Ph23
Hedgesville (USA) (WV) 29 Qg26
Hedley (CDN) (BC) 16 Oe21
Heffley Creek (CDN) (BC) 16 Oe20
Heidelberg (USA) (MS) 36 Qa30
Heiden, Port (USA) (AK) 12 Mf17
Heinsburg (CDN) (ALB) 17 Ok19
Helena (USA) (AR) 36 Pk28
Helena (USA) (MT) 25 Oj22
Hells Canyon National Recreation Area ☆ (USA) (OR) 24 Og23
Hells Gate Airtram ☆ (CDN) (BC) 16 Oe21
Helper (USA) (UT) 33 Ok26
Helvetia (USA) (WV) 29 Qe26
Hemaruka (CDN) (ALB) 17 Ok20
Hemet (USA) (CA) 32 Og29
Hemingford (USA) (NE) 26 Pd24
Heming Lake (CDN) (MAN) 18 Pe18
Hemlo (CDN) (ONT) 20 Qc21
Hemlock Grove (USA) (PA) 30 Qh25
Hemphill (USA) (TX) 35 Pj30
Hempstead (USA) (NY) 30 Qj25
Hempstead (USA) (TX) 40 Pg30
Henderson (USA) (KY) 36 Qb27
Henderson (USA) (LA) 36 Pk30
Henderson (USA) (NC) 31 Qf27
Henderson (USA) (NE) 27 Pg25
Henderson (USA) (NV) 33 Oh27
Henderson (USA) (NY) 29 Qg24
Henderson (USA) (TN) 36 Qa28
Henderson (USA) (TX) 35 Ph29
Hendersonville (USA) (NC) 37 Qd28
Hendersonville (USA) (TN) 36 Qb27
Hendon (CDN) (SAS) 18 Pd19
Hennessey (USA) (OK) 35 Pg27
Henrietta (USA) (TX) 35 Pf29
Henriette (USA) (MN) 27 Pj23
Henry (USA) (IL) 28 Qa25
Henry (USA) (SD) 27 Pg23
Henryetta (USA) (OK) 35 Ph28
Henryville (USA) (IN) 28 Qc26
Hepburn (CDN) (SAS) 18 Pb19
Heppner (USA) (OR) 24 Of23
Herbert (CDN) (SAS) 18 Pb20
Hereford (USA) (CO) 26 Pc25
Hereford (USA) (TX) 34 Pd28
Herington (USA) (KS) 35 Pg26
Heriot Bay (CDN) (BC) 16 Oc20
Hermanas (USA) (NM) 33 Pb30
Hermann (USA) (MO) 28 Pk26
Hermantown (USA) (MN) 19 Pj22
Hermiston (USA) (OR) 24 Of23
Hermitage (USA) (AR) 36 Pj29
Hermitage (USA) (MO) 35 Pj27
Hermleigh (USA) (TX) 34 Pe29
Hermosillo (MEX) (SON) 38 Ok31
Hermoso, Valle (MEX) (TAM) 40 Pg33
Herndon (USA) (VA) 29 Qg26
Heron (USA) (MT) 17 Oh21
Herradura (MEX) (SLP) 40 Pe34
Herreid (USA) (SD) 26 Pe23
Herreras, Las (MEX) (DGO) 39 Pc33
Herreras, Los (MEX) (NL) 40 Pf33
Herrick Center (USA) (PA) 29 Qh25
Herrin (USA) (IL) 36 Qa27
Herschel (CDN) (SAS) 17 Pa20
Herschel (CDN) (YT) 11 Nf11
Hershey (USA) (PA) 29 Qg25
Hervey Junction (CDN) (QUE) 21 Qj22
Hesperia (USA) (CA) 32 Og28
Hesperia (USA) (MI) 28 Qb24
Hettinger (USA) (ND) 26 Pd23
Héva, Rivière- (CDN) (QUE) 21 Qf21
Heward (CDN) (SAS) 18 Pd21
Hewitt (USA) (TX) 35 Pg30
Heyden (CDN) (ONT) 20 Qc22
Hialeah (USA) (FL) 43 Qe33
Hiawatha (USA) (CO) 25 Pa25
Hiawatha (USA) (KS) 35 Ph26
Hibbing (USA) (MN) 19 Pj22
Hickiwan (USA) (AZ) 33 Oj29
Hickman (USA) (KY) 36 Qa27
Hickory (USA) (NC) 37 Qe28
Hico (USA) (WV) 29 Qe26
Hidalgo (MEX) (DGO) 39 Pc33
Hidalgo (MEX) (NL) 40 Pe33
Hidalgo (MEX) (TAM) 40 Pf33
Hidalgo, Villa (MEX) (DGO) 39 Pc32
Hidalgo, Villa (MEX) (SON) 39 Pa30
Hidalgo del Parral (MEX) (CHA) 39 Pc32
Higgins (USA) (TX) 34 Pe27
High Bluff (CDN) (MAN) 19 Pf20
Highgate (CDN) (SAS) 17 Pa19
High Island (USA) (TX) 41 Ph31
Highland Park (CDN) (ALB) 15 Of17
Highland Park (USA) (IL) 28 Qb24
Highland Springs (USA) (VA) 31 Qg27
High Level (CDN) (ALB) 15 Og16
Highmore (USA) (SD) 26 Pf23
High Point (USA) (NC) 37 Qe28
High Prairie (CDN) (ALB) 15 Og18
High River (CDN) (ALB) 17 Oj20
High Rock (BS) 43 Qf32
High Springs (USA) (FL) 37 Qd31
Highwood (USA) (MT) 17 Ok22
Hilda (CDN) (ALB) 17 Ok20
Hildale (USA) (UT) 33 Oj27
Hilger (USA) (MT) 17 Pa22
Hilliardton (CDN) (ONT) 21 Qf22
Hill (USA) (LA) 36 Pj29
Hill City (USA) (ID) 25 Oh24
Hill City (USA) (KS) 35 Pf26
Hill City (USA) (MN) 19 Pj22
Hill City (USA) (SD) 26 Pd24
Hilliard (USA) (FL) 37 Qe30
Hilliards Bay Provincial Park ☆ (CDN) (ALB) 15 Oh18
Hillmond (CDN) (SAS) 17 Pa19
Hills (CDN) (BC) 17 Og20
Hillsboro (USA) (IL) 28 Qa26
Hillsboro (USA) (ND) 19 Pg22
Hillsboro (USA) (NM) 34 Pb29
Hillsboro (USA) (OH) 29 Qd26
Hillsboro (USA) (TX) 35 Pg29
Hillsboro (USA) (WI) 27 Pk24
Hillsborough (USA) (NC) 37 Qf27
Hillside (USA) (AZ) 33 Oj28
Hillsport (CDN) (ONT) 20 Qc21
Hill Spring (CDN) (ALB) 17 Oj21
Hillsville (USA) (VA) 37 Qe27
Hilo (USA) (HI) 44 Mh36
Hilt (USA) (CA) 24 Od25
Hilton (USA) (NY) 29 Qg24
Hilton Head Island (USA) (SC) 37 Qe29
Hinckley (USA) (MN) 27 Pj22
Hines Creek (CDN) (ALB) 15 Of17
Hineston (USA) (LA) 36 Pj30
Hinesville (USA) (GA) 37 Qe30
Hingham (USA) (MT) 17 Ok21
Hinsdale (USA) (MT) 18 Pb21
Hinsdale (USA) (NY) 29 Qf24
Hinton (CDN) (ALB) 17 Og19
Hinton (USA) (WV) 37 Qe27
Hipólito (MEX) (COA) 40 Pe33
Hiram (USA) (ME) 22 Qk24
Hixon (CDN) (BC) 16 Od19
Hoback Junction (USA) (WY) 25 Ok24
Hobart (USA) (OK) 35 Pf28
Hobbs (USA) (NM) 34 Pd29
Hochfield (CDN) (MAN) 19 Pg21
Hockin (CDN) (MAN) 19 Pg18
Hoctún (MEX) (YUC) 42 Qa35
Hodgenville (USA) (KY) 36 Qc27
Hodges Gardens ☆ (USA) (LA) 35 Pj30
Hodgeville (CDN) (SAS) 18 Pb20
Hodgson (CDN) (MAN) 19 Pg20
Hogeland (USA) (MT) 18 Pa21
Hog Landing (USA) (AK) 10 Mh12
Hohenwald (USA) (TN) 36 Qb28
Hoisington (USA) (KS) 35 Pf26
Hola Bend National Wildlife Reserve ☆ (USA) (AR) 35 Pj28
Holbrook (USA) (AZ) 33 Ok28
Holbrook (USA) (ID) 25 Oj24
Holden (CDN) (ALB) 17 Oj19
Holden (USA) (MO) 35 Pj26
Holden (USA) (UT) 33 Oj26
Holdenville (USA) (OK) 35 Pg28
Holdrege (USA) (NE) 26 Pf25
Holland (CDN) (MAN) 19 Pf21
Holland (USA) (MI) 28 Qb24
Hollidaysburg (USA) (PA) 29 Qf25
Hollis (USA) (AK) 14 Nj18
Hollis (USA) (AR) 35 Pj28
Hollis (USA) (OK) 35 Pf28
Hollister (USA) (CA) 32 Oe27
Hollister (USA) (MO) 35 Pj27
Holly (USA) (CO) 34 Pd26
Holly Ridge (USA) (NC) 31 Qg28
Holly Springs (USA) (AR) 35 Pj29
Holly Springs (USA) (MS) 36 Qa28
Hollywood (USA) (AR) 35 Pj28
Hollywood ☆ (USA) (CA) 32 Of28
Hollywood (USA) (FL) 43 Qe32
Holmfield (CDN) (MAN) 19 Pf21
Holstein (USA) (IA) 27 Ph24
Holt (USA) (FL) 36 Qb30
Holton (USA) (KS) 35 Ph26
Holyoke (CDN) (ALB) 17 Ok18
Holyoke (USA) (CO) 26 Pd25
Holyrood (CDN) (NFL) 23 Rj22
Holyrood (USA) (KS) 35 Pf26
Homedale (USA) (ID) 24 Og24
Homer (USA) (AK) 13 Mk16
Homer (USA) (LA) 35 Pj29
Homerville (USA) (GA) 37 Qd30
Homestead (USA) (FL) 43 Qe33
Homewood (USA) (AL) 36 Qb29
Hominy (USA) (OK) 35 Pg27
Hondo (USA) (NM) 34 Pc29
Hondo (USA) (TX) 40 Pf31
Hone (CDN) (MAN) 18 Pe17
Honesdale (USA) (PA) 30 Qh25
Honeymoon Bay (CDN) (BC) 16 Oc21
Honokaa (USA) (HI) 44 Mh35
Honokahua (USA) (HI) 44 Mg35
Honolulu (USA) (HI) 44 Mg35
Hoodsport (USA) (WA) 16 Od22
Hooker (USA) (OK) 34 Pe27
Hoonah (USA) (AK) 14 Nh16
Hooper (USA) (CO) 34 Pc27
Hooper (USA) (NE) 27 Pg25
Hooper Bay (USA) (AK) 10 Mb15
Hoopeston (USA) (IL) 28 Qb25
Hoople (USA) (ND) 19 Pg21
Hoosier (CDN) (SAS) 17 Pa20
Hoover Dam ☆ (USA) (NV) 33 Oh28
Hope (CDN) (BC) 16 Oe21
Hope (USA) (AK) 13 Na15
Hope (USA) (AR) 35 Pj29
Hope (USA) (ID) 17 Og21
Hope (USA) (ND) 19 Pg22
Hope, Port (CDN) (ONT) 29 Qf24
Hope Simpson, Port (CDN) (NFL) 23 Rg19
Hopetown (CDN) (ONT) 29 Qg23
Hopewell (USA) (VA) 31 Qg27
Hopewell Cape (CDN) (NB) 22 Rc23
Hopkins (USA) (MO) 27 Ph25
Hopkinsville (USA) (KY) 36 Qb27
Hopland (USA) (CA) 32 Od26
Hoquiam (USA) (WA) 24 Od22
Hormigas (MEX) (COA) 39 Pd32
Hornby Island (CDN) (BC) 16 Oc21
Horndean (CDN) (MAN) 19 Pg21
Hornell (USA) (NY) 29 Qg24
Hornepayne (CDN) (ONT) 20 Qc21
Horse Creek (USA) (WY) 26 Pc25
Horsefly (CDN) (BC) 16 Oe19
Horseshoe Bay (CDN) (BC) 16 Od21
Horseshoe Beach (USA) (FL) 37 Qd31
Horseshoe Bend (USA) (ID) 24 Og24
Horsham (CDN) (SAS) 17 Pa20
Hoselaw (CDN) (ALB) 17 Ok18
Hosford (USA) (FL) 36 Qc30
Hosmer (CDN) (BC) 17 Oh21
Hospah (USA) (NM) 33 Pb28
Hotchkiss (CDN) (ALB) 15 Og17
Hotchkiss (USA) (CO) 33 Pb26
Hot Springs (USA) (AR) 35 Pj28
Hot Springs (USA) (NC) 37 Qd28
Hot Springs (USA) (SD) 26 Pd24
Hot Springs Cove (CDN) (BC) 16 Ob21
Hot Springs National Park ☆ (USA) (AR) 35 Pj28
Hot Springs Village (USA) (AR) 35 Pj28
Houghton (USA) (NY) 29 Qf24
Houghton (USA) (WI) 20 Qa22
Houghton Lake (USA) (MI) 28 Qc23
Houlton (USA) (ME) 22 Rb22
Houma (USA) (LA) 36 Pk31
Houston (CDN) (BC) 16 Ob18
Houston (USA) (AK) 13 Na15
Houston (USA) (MN) 27 Pk24
Houston (USA) (MO) 36 Pk27
Houston (USA) (MS) 36 Qa29
Houston (USA) (TX) 41 Ph31
Hovland (USA) (MN) 20 Pk22
Howard (USA) (SD) 27 Pg23
Howard (USA) (WI) 28 Qa23
Howard City (USA) (MI) 28 Qc24
Howell (USA) (MI) 29 Qd24
Howes (USA) (SD) 26 Pd23
Howland (USA) (ME) 22 Ra23
Hoxie (USA) (AR) 36 Pk27
Hoxie (USA) (KS) 34 Pe26
Hoyt Lakes (USA) (MN) 19 Pj22
Huachuca City (USA) (AZ) 33 Ok30
Huajuapan (MEX) (DGO) 39 Pc33
Huasabas (MEX) (SON) 39 Pa31
Huatabampo (MEX) (SON) 39 Pa32
Hubbard (USA) (IA) 27 Pj24
Hubbard (USA) (TX) 35 Pg30
Hubbards (CDN) (NS) 22 Rc23
Hubbell Trading Post National Historic Site ☆ (USA) (AZ) 33 Pa28
Hub City (USA) (WI) 27 Pk24
Hudson (USA) (IA) 27 Pj24
Hudson (USA) (MD) 29 Qg26
Hudson (USA) (MI) 28 Qc25
Hudson (USA) (NY) 30 Qj24
Hudson (USA) (WI) 27 Pj23
Hudson Bay (CDN) (SAS) 18 Pd19
Hudson Falls (USA) (NY) 30 Qj24
Hudson's Hope (CDN) (BC) 15 Oe17
Hueco (USA) (TX) 34 Pc30
Huejúcar (MEX) (JAL) 39 Pd34
Huejuquilla El Alto (MEX) (JAL) 39 Pd34
Huerfano Trading Post (USA) (NM) 33 Pb27
Huertecillas (MEX) (SLP) 40 Pe33
Hughenden (CDN) (ALB) 17 Ok19
Hughes (USA) (AK) 10 Mh12
Hughesville (USA) (MD) 29 Qg26
Hughesville (USA) (PA) 29 Qg25
Hugo (USA) (OK) 35 Ph29
Huivulai (MEX) (SON) 39 Pa32
Hulett (USA) (WY) 26 Pc23
Hull (CDN) (QUE) 29 Qh23
Hull (USA) (IL) 28 Pk26
Humble (USA) (TX) 41 Ph31
Humboldt (CDN) (SAS) 18 Pc19
Humboldt (USA) (IA) 27 Ph24
Humboldt (USA) (NV) 24 Of25
Humboldt (USA) (SD) 27 Pg24
Humboldt (USA) (TN) 36 Qa28
Humboldt Redwoods State Park ☆ (USA) (CA) 24 Oc25
Humeston (USA) (IA) 27 Pj25
Humphrey (USA) (ID) 25 Oj23
Humphrey (USA) (NE) 27 Pg25
Humptulips (USA) (WA) 16 Od22
Hungry Horse (USA) (MT) 17 Oh21
Hunt (USA) (AZ) 33 Pa28
Hunter (USA) (ND) 19 Pg22
Hunter River (CDN) (PEI) 22 Rd22
Hunters (USA) (WA) 16 Of21
Huntingburg (USA) (IN) 28 Qb26
Huntingdon (CDN) (QUE) 29 Qh23
Huntingdon (USA) (PA) 29 Qf25
Huntington (USA) (IN) 28 Qc25
Huntington (USA) (OR) 24 Og23
Huntington (USA) (TX) 35 Ph30
Huntington (USA) (UT) 33 Ok26
Huntington (USA) (WV) 29 Qd26
Huntington Beach (USA) (CA) 32 Og29
Huntoon (CDN) (SAS) 18 Pd21
Huntsville (CDN) (ONT) 29 Qf23
Huntsville (USA) (AL) 36 Qb28
Huntsville (USA) (AR) 35 Pj27
Huntsville (USA) (MO) 28 Pj26
Huntsville (USA) (TX) 41 Ph30
Hunucmá (MEX) (YUC) 42 Qa35
Hurdsfield (USA) (ND) 19 Pf22
Hurley (USA) (NM) 33 Pa29
Hurley (USA) (WI) 20 Pk22
Huron (USA) (SD) 26 Pf23
Huron, Port (USA) (MI) 29 Qd24
Hurricane (USA) (UT) 33 Oj27
Hurricane (USA) (WV) 29 Qd26
Hurricane = Chulitna (USA) (AK) 11 Na14
Hurstown (USA) (TX) 35 Pj30
Huslia (USA) (AK) 10 Mg13
Hussar (CDN) (ALB) 17 Oj20
Hutchinson (USA) (KS) 35 Pg26
Hutchinson (USA) (MN) 27 Ph23
Huttonsville (USA) (WV) 29 Qf26
Hyak (USA) (WA) 16 Oe22
Hyannis (USA) (MA) 30 Qk25
Hyannis (USA) (NE) 26 Pe25
Hyattsville (USA) (MD) 29 Qg26
Hyattville (USA) (WY) 25 Pb23
Hydaburg (USA) (AK) 14 Nj18
Hyder (USA) (AK) 14 Nk18
Hyder (USA) (AZ) 33 Oj29
Hylo (CDN) (ALB) 17 Oj18
Hysham (USA) (MT) 25 Pb22
Hythe (CDN) (ALB) 15 Of18

I

Iberia (USA) (MO) 28 Pj26
Ibstone (CDN) (SAS) 17 Pa19
Ice Caves ☆ (USA) (WA) 24 Oe23
Idabel (USA) (OK) 35 Ph29
Ida Grove (USA) (IA) 27 Ph24
Idaho Falls (USA) (ID) 25 Oj24
Idalia (USA) (CO) 34 Pd26
Iffley (CDN) (SAS) 17 Pa19
Igiugig (USA) (AK) 12 Mh16
Ignace (CDN) (ONT) 19 Pk2
Ignacio (USA) (CO) 33 Pb2
Île-à-la-Crosse (CDN) (SAS) 17 Pb1
Ilford (CDN) (MAN) 19 Ph1
Illescas (MEX) (SLP) 40 Pd3
Illgen City (USA) (MN) 19 Pk2
Illinois City (USA) (IL) 27 Pk2
Illmo (USA) (MO) 36 Qa2
Ilnik (USA) (AK) 12 Mf1
Ilwaco (USA) (WA) 24 Oc2
Imlay (USA) (NV) 24 Of2
Imlay City (USA) (MI) 29 Qd2
Immokalee (USA) (FL) 43 Qe3
Imperial (CDN) (SAS) 18 Pc2
Imperial (USA) (NE) 26 Pe2
Imperial (USA) (TX) 39 Pd3
Imperial Mills (CDN) (ALB) 17 Ok1
Imperial National Wildlife Refuge ☆ (USA) (AZ) 33 Oh2
Imuris (MEX) (SON) 38 Ok3
Inadale (USA) (TX) 34 Pe2
Inalik (USA) (AK) 10 Ma1
Indé (MEX) (DGO) 39 Pc3
Independence (USA) (CA) 32 Of
Independence (USA) (IA) 27 Pk
Independence (USA) (KS) 35 Ph
Independence (USA) (LA) 36 Pk
Independence (USA) (MN) 19 Pj
Independence (USA) (MO) 35 Ph
Independence (USA) (VA) 37 Qe
Independence Hall ☆ (USA) (PA) 30 Qh
Index (USA) (WA) 16 Oe
Indiana (USA) (PA) 29 Qf
Indianapolis (USA) (IN) 28 Qb
Indian Bay (CDN) (NFL) 23 Rj
Indian Cabins (CDN) (ALB) 15 Og
Indian Head (CDN) (SAS) 18 Pd
Indian Head (USA) (MD) 29 Qg
Indianola (USA) (IA) 27 Pj
Indianola (USA) (MS) 36 Pk
Indian Springs (USA) (NV) 33 Oh
Indian Wells (USA) (AZ) 33 Ok
Indio (USA) (CA) 32 Og
Industry (USA) (IL) 27 Pk
Inez (USA) (KY) 37 Qd
Ingleside (CDN) (ONT) 29 Qh
Inglis (USA) (FL) 37 Qd
Ingomar (USA) (MT) 18 Pb
Ingonish Beach (CDN) (NS) 23 Re
Inkster (USA) (ND) 19 Pg
Inner Space Caverns ☆ (USA) (TX) 40 Pg
Innisfail (CDN) (ALB) 17 Oj
Innisfree (CDN) (ALB) 17 Ok
Inocentes, Los (MEX) (BCS) 38 Ok
Inster (USA) (ND) 19 Pg
Instow (CDN) (SAS) 18 Pa
Insurgentes, Villa (MEX) (BCS) 38 Ok
Interior (USA) (SD) 26 Pe
Interlachen (USA) (FL) 37 Qd
Interlaken (CDN) (ONT) 29 Q
International Falls (USA) (MN) 19 P
Inuvik (CDN) (NWT) 11 N
Inverness (CDN) (NS) 23 R
Inverness (CDN) (QUE) 22 Q
Inverness (USA) (FL) 43 Q
Inwood (CDN) (MAN) 19 P
Inwood (USA) (IA) 27 P
Inyokern (USA) (CA) 32 O
Iola (USA) (KS) 35 P
Ionesport (USA) (ME) 22 R
Ionia (USA) (MI) 28 Q
Iota (USA) (LA) 36 P
Iowa (USA) (LA) 36 P
Iowa City (USA) (IA) 27 P
Iowa Falls (USA) (IA) 27 P
Iowa Park (USA) (TX) 35 P
Ipswich (USA) (SD) 26
Ira (USA) (TX) 34 P
Iraan (USA) (TX) 39 P
Irasville (USA) (VT) 30
Iredell (USA) (TX) 35 P
Irma (CDN) (ALB) 17 O
Iron Creek (USA) (AK) 10 M
Irondequoit (USA) (NY) 29 Q
Iron Mountain (USA) (MI) 28 Q
Iron River (CDN) (ALB) 17 O
Iron River (USA) (MI) 28 Q
Iron River (USA) (WI) 19
Ironton (USA) (MO) 36
Ironton (USA) (OH) 29
Ironwood (USA) (MI) 20
Ironwood Forest National Monumet ☆ (USA) (AZ) 33
Iroquois (CDN) (ONT) 29
Iroquois (USA) (SD) 27
Iroquois Falls (CDN) (ONT) 20
Irvine (CDN) (ALB) 17
Irvines Landing (CDN) (BC) 16
Irving (USA) (IA) 27
Irving (USA) (TX) 35
Isabel (USA) (SD) 26
Isabel, Port (USA) (TX) 40
Isabela de Sagua (C) (VC) 43
Isabeles, Las (MEX) (BCN) 33
Isabella (USA) (MN) 19
Isabel Rubio (C) (PR) 42
Isham (CDN) (SAS) 17
Ishpeming (USA) (MI) 20
Isla Angel de la Guarda, Parque Natural ☆ (MEX) (BCN) 38
Isla de la Juventud ☆ (C) (JU) 42
Isla de Pinos = Juventud, Isla de la ☆ (C) (JU) 42
Islamorada (USA) (FL) 43
Isla Mujeres ☆ (MEX) (QR) 42
Island Falls (CDN) (ONT) 20
Island Falls (USA) (ME) 22
Island Lake (CDN) (ONT) 20
Island Lake (USA) (MN) 19
Island Pond (USA) (VT) 22
Isla San Pedro Martir ☆ (MEX) (BCN) 38
Islay (CDN) (ALB) 17
Isle (USA) (MN) 2

sle Royale National Park ☆ (USA) (MI) 20 Qa21
sleta (USA) (NM) 34 Pb28
ssaquah (USA) (WA) 16 Od22
taly (USA) (TX) 35 Pg29
tasca (USA) (TX) 35 Pg29
tcha Ilgachuz Provincial Park ☆ (CDN) (BC) 16 Oc19
thaca (USA) (NY) 29 Qg24
tuna (CDN) (SAS) 18 Pd20
turbide (MEX) (NL) 40 Pf33
tzamna ☆ (MEX) (YUC) 42 Qa35
uka (USA) (MS) 36 Qa28
van (USA) (FL) 36 Qc30
vavik National Park ☆ (CDN) (NWT) 11 Nf11
zamal (MEX) (YUC) 42 Qa35

J

ackhead Harbour (CDN) (MAN) 19 Pg20
ackman (USA) (ME) 22 Qk23
acksboro (USA) (TX) 35 Pf29
ackson (USA) (AL) 36 Qb30
ackson (USA) (CA) 32 Oe26
ackson (USA) (GA) 37 Qd29
ackson (USA) (LA) 36 Pk30
ackson (USA) (MI) 28 Qc24
ackson (USA) (MN) 27 Ph24
ackson (USA) (MS) 36 Pk29
ackson (USA) (NC) 31 Qg27
ackson (USA) (OH) 29 Qd26
ackson (USA) (TN) 36 Qa28
ackson (USA) (WY) 25 Ok24
ackson Arm (CDN) (NFL) 23 Rg21
acksonboro (USA) (SC) 37 Qe29
ackson Junction (USA) (IA) 27 Pj24
acksonville (C) (JU) 43 Qd35
acksonville (USA) (AR) 36 Pj28
acksonville (USA) (FL) 37 Qe30
acksonville (USA) (IL) 28 Pk26
acksonville (USA) (NC) 31 Qg28
acksonville (USA) (TX) 35 Ph30
acksonville Beach (USA) (FL) 37 Qe30
ck Wade (USA) (AK) 11 Ne13
cob Lake (USA) (AZ) 33 Oj27
cobson (USA) (MN) 19 Pj22
cques Cartier, Parc de la ☆ (CDN) (QUE) 22 Qk22
cumba (USA) (CA) 32 Og29
gua (C) (CF) 43 Qe34
güey Grande (C) (MZ) 43 Qe34
l (USA) (NM) 34 Pd29
mestown (USA) (MO) 28 Pj26
mestown (USA) (ND) 19 Pf22
mestown (USA) (NY) 29 Qf24
mestown (USA) (PA) 29 Qe25
mestown (USA) (SC) 37 Qf29
mestown (USA) (TN) 36 Qc27
nesville (USA) (WI) 28 Qa24
nice (USA) (MS) 36 Qa30
n Lake (CDN) (SAS) 18 Pd18
nos (MEX) (CHA) 39 Pa30
ns Bay (CDN) (SAS) 17 Pa18
quet River (CDN) (NB) 22 Rb22
rahueca (C) (SS) 43 Qf34
row (CDN) (ALB) 17 Ok19
per (CDN) (ALB) 16 Of19
sper (USA) (AL) 36 Qb29
sper (USA) (AR) 35 Pj27
sper (USA) (FL) 37 Qd30
sper (USA) (GA) 36 Qc28
sper (USA) (IN) 28 Qb26
sper (USA) (NY) 29 Qg24
sper (USA) (TX) 41 Pj30
per National Park ☆ (CDN) (ALB) 16 Of19
bonico (C) (SS) 43 Qf35
mave (MEX) (TAM) 40 Pf34
a Center (USA) (NY) 29 Qf24
(USA) (OK) 35 Pf27
ton (USA) (TX) 34 Pe29
lark Salyer National Wildlife Refuge = Lower Souris National Wildlife Refuge ☆ (USA) (ND) 18 Pe21
n (USA) (NV) 33 Oh28
nerette (USA) (LA) 36 Pk31
ers (USA) (MN) 27 Ph23
erson (USA) (AR) 36 Pj28
erson (USA) (GA) 37 Qd28
erson (USA) (TX) 35 Ph29
erson, Port (USA) (NY) 30 Qj25
erson City (USA) (MO) 28 Pj26
erson City (USA) (MT) 25 Oj22
erson City (USA) (TN) 37 Qd27
ersontown (USA) (KY) 28 Qc26
ersonville (USA) (GA) 37 Qd29
ersonville (USA) (IN) 28 Qc26
ersonville (USA) (VT) 30 Qj23
ey City (USA) (WY) 25 Pb24
co (USA) (TN) 36 Qc27
coe (CDN) (BC) 16 Oe21
ez Pueblo (USA) (NM) 34 Pb28
seg (CDN) (NB) 22 Rb23
(USA) (LA) 36 Pj30
ins (USA) (KY) 37 Qd27
er (CDN) (ALB) 17 Ok20
er (USA) (CA) 32 Od26
ings (USA) (LA) 36 Pj30
sen (USA) (UT) 25 Pa25
z de García Salinas (MEX) (ZAC) 39 Pd34
me (USA) (ID) 25 Oh24
ey City (USA) (NJ) 30 Qh25
ey Shore (USA) (PA) 29 Qg25
eyville (USA) (IL) 28 Pk26
s, Port (USA) (NY) 30 Qh25
yo (MEX) (BCN) 33 Oh29
ond (CDN) (BC) 16 Oe20
(USA) (GA) 37 Qe30
(USA) (IA) 27 Pj24
s Carranza (MEX) (CHA) 34 Pb30
(USA) (OK) 35 Pf27
ore (USA) (KS) 35 Pf26
tt (USA) (TX) 35 Pg30
(USA) (NV) 25 Oh25
nez (MEX) (CHA) 39 Pc32
nez (MEX) (COA) 40 Pe31
nez de Teul (MEX) (ZAC) 39 Pd34
co (MEX) (COA) 39 Pd33
(C) (CG) 43 Qf35
uin (USA) (TX) 35 Ph30
oo (C) (LT) 43 Qg35
Joe Batts Arm (CDN) (NFL) 23 Rh21
Jogues (CDN) (ONT) 20 Qd21
John Day (USA) (OR) 24 Of23
John D'Or Prairie (CDN) (ALB) 15 Oh16
John D. Rockefeller Junior Memorial Parkway ☆ (USA) (WY) 25 Ok23
John Fitzgerald Kennedy Space Center ☆ (USA) (FL) 43 Qe31
Johnson (USA) (KS) 34 Pe27
Johnson City (USA) (TN) 37 Qd27
Johnson City (USA) (TX) 40 Pf30
Johnsons Crossing (CDN) (YT) 14 Nj15
Johnsons Landing (CDN) (BC) 17 Og20
Johnston (USA) (SC) 37 Qe29
Johnstown (USA) (PA) 29 Qf25
Johnstown Flood National Monument ☆ (USA) (PA) 29 Qf25
Joli, Mont- (CDN) (QUE) 22 Ra21
Joliet (USA) (IL) 28 Qa25
Joliette (CDN) (QUE) 30 Qj22
Jones (CDN) (ONT) 19 Ph21
Jonesboro (USA) (AR) 36 Pk28
Jonesboro (USA) (LA) 35 Pj29
Jonesboro (USA) (TX) 35 Pg30
Jonesville (USA) (LA) 36 Pk30
Jonquière (CDN) (QUE) 22 Qk21
Joplin (USA) (MO) 35 Ph27
Joplin (USA) (MT) 17 Ok21
Jordan (USA) (MN) 27 Pj23
Jordan (USA) (MT) 18 Pb22
Jordan, River (CDN) (BC) 16 Oc21
Jordan Valley (USA) (OR) 24 Og24
Joseph (USA) (OR) 24 Og23
Joshua (USA) (TX) 35 Pg29
Joshua Tree (USA) (CA) 32 Og28
Joshua Tree National Park ☆ (USA) (CA) 33 Oh29
Jourdanton (USA) (TX) 40 Pf31
Joussard (CDN) (ALB) 15 Og18
Joutel (CDN) (QUE) 21 Qf21
Jovellanos (C) (MZ) 43 Qe34
Joyce (USA) (WA) 16 Od21
Juan Aldamo (MEX) (ZAC) 39 Pd33
Juárez (MEX) (CHA) 39 Pa30
Juárez (MEX) (COA) 40 Pe32
Juárez, Ciudad (MEX) (CHA) 33 Pb30
Juárez, Villa (MEX) (DGO) 39 Pd33
Judith Gap (USA) (MT) 18 Pa22
Julesburg (USA) (CO) 26 Pd25
Julian (USA) (CA) 32 Og29
Jump River (USA) (WI) 27 Pk23
Junction (USA) (TX) 40 Pf30
Junction City (USA) (AR) 35 Pj29
Junction City (USA) (KS) 35 Pg26
Junction City (USA) (OR) 24 Od23
Junction City (USA) (SD) 27 Pg24
Juneau (USA) (AK) 14 Nh16
June Lake (USA) (CA) 32 Of27
Juniata (CDN) (SAS) 18 Pb19
Juniper (CDN) (NB) 22 Rb22
Juno (USA) (TX) 40 Pe30
Junta, La (MEX) (CHA) 39 Pb31
Junta, La (USA) (CO) 34 Pd27
Juntura (USA) (OR) 24 Of24
Justice (CDN) (MAN) 19 Pf20
Juventud, Isla de la = Isla de Pinos ☆ (C) (JU) 42 Qc35

K

Kadoka (USA) (SD) 26 Pe24
Kaena Point ☆ (USA) (HI) 44 Mf35
Kahoka (USA) (MO) 27 Pk25
Kahului (USA) (HI) 44 Mg35
Kaigani (USA) (AK) 14 Nj18
Kailua (USA) (HI) 44 Mg35
Kailua Kona (USA) (HI) 44 Mh36
Kakabeka Falls (CDN) (ONT) 19 Pk21
Kake (USA) (AK) 14 Nj17
Kaktovik (USA) (AK) 11 Nd10
Kakwa Provincial Recreation Area ☆ (CDN) (BC) 16 Oe18
Kaladar (CDN) (ONT) 29 Qg23
Kalaloch (USA) (WA) 16 Oc22
Kalamazoo (USA) (MI) 28 Qc24
Kalaupapa (USA) (HI) 44 Mg35
Kalb, De (USA) (IL) 28 Qa25
Kalb, De (USA) (TX) 35 Ph29
Kaledon (CDN) (BC) 16 Of21
Kaleida (CDN) (MAN) 19 Pf21
Kalispell (USA) (MT) 17 Oh21
Kalkaska (USA) (MI) 28 Qc23
Kalona (USA) (IA) 27 Pk25
Kalskag (USA) (AK) 12 Me15
Kaltag (USA) (AK) 10 Mf13
Kamas (USA) (UT) 25 Ok25
Kamiah (USA) (ID) 24 Og22
Kamloops (CDN) (BC) 16 Oe20
Kamsack (CDN) (SAS) 18 Pe20
Kanab (USA) (UT) 33 Oj27
Kanata (CDN) (ONT) 29 Qh23
Kanatak (USA) (AK) 12 Mg17
Kane (CDN) (MAN) 19 Pg21
Kane (USA) (PA) 29 Qf25
Kāne'ohe (USA) (HI) 44 Mg35
Kangik (USA) (AK) 10 Mf10
Kankakee (USA) (IL) 28 Qb25
Kannapolis (USA) (NC) 37 Qe28
Kanosh (USA) (UT) 33 Oj26
Kansas (USA) (OK) 35 Ph27
Kansas City (USA) (KS) 35 Ph26
Kansas City (USA) (MO) 35 Ph26
Kantah (CDN) (BC) 15 Oe16
Kantishna (USA) (AK) 10 Mk14
Kanuti National Wildlife Refuge ☆ (USA) (AK) 10 Mj12
Kapa'a (USA) (HI) 44 Mf34
Kaplan (USA) (LA) 36 Pj31
Kapuskasing (CDN) (ONT) 20 Qd21
Karlsruhe (USA) (ND) 18 Pe21
Karlstad (USA) (MN) 19 Pg21
Karluk (USA) (AK) 12 Mh17
Karnes City (USA) (TX) 40 Pg31
Kasabonika (CDN) (ONT) 20 Qa19
Kaseyville (USA) (MO) 28 Pj26
Kashabowie (CDN) (ONT) 19 Pk21
Kasha-Katuwe National Monument ☆ (USA) (NM) 34 Pb28
Kashechewan (CDN) (ONT) 20 Qe19
Kasigluk (USA) (AK) 12 Md15
Kaskaskia River State Fish and Wildlife Area ☆ (USA) (IL) 28 Qa26
Kaslo (CDN) (BC) 17 Og21
Katmai National Park and Preserve ☆ (USA) (AK) 12 Mh16
Katy (USA) (TX) 41 Ph31
Kaufman (USA) (TX) 35 Pg29
Kaukauna (USA) (WI) 28 Qa23
Kaumalapau Harbor (USA) (HI) 44 Mg35
Kaunakakai (USA) (HI) 44 Mg35
Kaupō (USA) (HI) 44 Mg35
Kawa (CDN) (ONT) 19 Qa20
Kawaihae (USA) (HI) 44 Mh35
Kawene (CDN) (ONT) 19 Pk21
Kaycee (USA) (WY) 26 Pb24
Kayenta (USA) (AZ) 33 Ok27
Kayville (CDN) (SAS) 18 Pc21
Kazabazua (CDN) (QUE) 29 Qg23
Kea'au (USA) (HI) 44 Mh36
Kearney (USA) (NE) 26 Pf25
Kearns (USA) (UT) 25 Oj25
Keddie (USA) (CA) 32 Oe26
Kedgwick (CDN) (NB) 22 Rb22
Keene (USA) (NH) 30 Qj24
Keewatin (CDN) (ONT) 19 Ph21
Kegaska (CDN) (QUE) 23 Re20
Kegworth (CDN) (SAS) 18 Pd20
Keithville (USA) (LA) 35 Pj29
Keizer (USA) (OR) 24 Od23
Kejimkujik National Park ☆ (CDN) (NS) 22 Rc23
Kekaha (USA) (HI) 44 Mf35
Kelfield (CDN) (SAS) 17 Pa20
Kelford (USA) (NC) 31 Qg27
Keller (USA) (WA) 16 Of21
Kelliher (USA) (MN) 19 Ph22
Kellogg (USA) (ID) 17 Og22
Kellogg (USA) (MN) 27 Pj23
Kelowna (CDN) (BC) 16 Of21
Kelsey (CDN) (MAN) 19 Pg17
Kelso (CDN) (SAS) 18 Pe21
Kelso (USA) (CA) 33 Oh28
Kelso (USA) (WA) 24 Od22
Kelvington (CDN) (SAS) 18 Pd19
Kemano (CDN) (BC) 16 Ob19
Kemmerer (USA) (WY) 25 Ok25
Kemnay (CDN) (MAN) 18 Pe21
Kemp (USA) (TX) 35 Pg29
Kemps Bay (BS) 43 Qg33
Kemptville (CDN) (NS) 22 Rc23
Kemptville (CDN) (ONT) 29 Qh23
Kenai (USA) (AK) 13 Mk15
Kenai Fjords National Park ☆ (USA) (AK) 13 Mk16
Kenai National Wildlife Refuge ☆ (USA) (AK) 13 Mk15
Kenansville (USA) (FL) 43 Qe32
Kenaston (CDN) (SAS) 18 Pb20
Kenbridge (USA) (VA) 31 Qf27
Kendall (USA) (FL) 43 Qe33
Kendall (USA) (KS) 34 Pe27
Kendall (USA) (WA) 16 Od21
Kendallville (USA) (IN) 28 Qc25
Kenedy (USA) (TX) 40 Pg31
Kenly (USA) (NC) 31 Qf28
Kenmare (USA) (ND) 18 Pd21
Kenna (USA) (WV) 29 Qe26
Kennard (USA) (TX) 35 Ph30
Kennebunk (USA) (ME) 22 Qk24
Kennedy (CDN) (SAS) 18 Pd20
Kennedy (USA) (NY) 29 Qf24
Kenner (USA) (LA) 36 Pk31
Kennett (USA) (MO) 36 Pk27
Kennewick (USA) (WA) 24 Of22
Kennisis Lake (CDN) (ONT) 29 Qf23
Keno Hill (CDN) (YT) 14 Nh14
Kenora (CDN) (ONT) 19 Ph21
Kenosee Park (CDN) (SAS) 18 Pd21
Kenosha (USA) (WI) 28 Qb24
Kensal (USA) (ND) 19 Pf22
Kensington (CDN) (PEI) 22 Rd22
Kent (USA) (OH) 29 Qe25
Kent (USA) (OR) 24 Oe23
Kent (USA) (TX) 39 Pc30
Kent (USA) (WA) 16 Od22
Kent Junction (CDN) (NB) 22 Rc22
Kentland (USA) (IN) 28 Qb25
Kenton (CDN) (MAN) 18 Pe21
Kenton (USA) (MI) 20 Qa22
Kenton (USA) (OH) 29 Qd25
Kentville (CDN) (NS) 22 Rc23
Kentwood (USA) (LA) 36 Pk30
Kenyon (USA) (MN) 27 Pj23
Keokuk (USA) (IA) 27 Pk25
Keosauqua (USA) (IA) 27 Pk25
Keota (USA) (IA) 27 Pk25
Kerby (USA) (OR) 24 Od24
Keremeos (CDN) (BC) 16 Of21
Kerens (USA) (TX) 35 Pg29
Kermit (USA) (TX) 34 Pd30
Kerrobert (CDN) (SAS) 17 Pa20
Kerrville (USA) (TX) 40 Pf30
Kershaw (USA) (SC) 37 Qe28
Kersley (CDN) (BC) 16 Od19
Kesagami Lake Provincial Park ☆ (CDN) (ONT) 20 Qe20
Ketchikan (USA) (AK) 14 Nk18
Kettering (USA) (OH) 28 Qc26
Kettle Falls (USA) (WA) 16 Of21
Kettle Valley (CDN) (BC) 16 Of21
Kewanee (USA) (IL) 28 Qa25
Kewaunee (USA) (WI) 28 Qb23
Keweenaw Bay (USA) (MI) 20 Qa22
Keyaluvik (USA) (AK) 12 Mc15
Keyes (CDN) (MAN) 19 Pf20
Key Largo (USA) (FL) 43 Qe33
Keyser (USA) (WV) 29 Qf26
Keystone (USA) (NE) 26 Pe25
Keystone (USA) (WA) 16 Oe21
Keystone Heights (USA) (FL) 37 Qd31
Keysville (USA) (VA) 31 Qf27
Keytesville (USA) (MO) 28 Pj26
Key West (USA) (FL) 43 Qe33
Kezar Falls (USA) (ME) 22 Qk24
Khedive (CDN) (SAS) 18 Pc21
Kiana (USA) (AK) 10 Me12
Kīhei (USA) (HI) 44 Mg35
Kilauea Crater ☆ (USA) (HI) 44 Mh36
Kīlauea Lighthouse ☆ (USA) (HI) 44 Mf34
Kildonan (CDN) (BC) 16 Oc21
Kilgore (USA) (TX) 35 Ph29
Killaloe Station (CDN) (ONT) 29 Qg23
Killaly (CDN) (SAS) 18 Pd20
Killam (CDN) (ALB) 17 Ok19
Killarney (CDN) (MAN) 19 Pf21
Killarney (CDN) (ONT) 29 Qe23
Killarney Provincial Park ☆ (CDN) (ONT) 29 Qe22
Killdeer (CDN) (SAS) 18 Pb21
Killdeer (USA) (ND) 18 Pd22
Killeen (USA) (TX) 40 Pg30
Kiln (USA) (MS) 36 Qa30
Kim (USA) (CO) 34 Pd27
Kimball (USA) (MN) 27 Ph23
Kimball (USA) (NE) 26 Pd25
Kimball (USA) (SD) 26 Pf24
Kimberley (CDN) (BC) 17 Oh21
Kinard (USA) (FL) 36 Qc30
Kincaid (CDN) (SAS) 18 Pb21
Kincardine (CDN) (ONT) 29 Qe23
Kinchil (MEX) (YUC) 42 Qa35
Kincolith (CDN) (BC) 14 Oa18
Kinder (USA) (LA) 36 Pj30
Kindersley (CDN) (SAS) 17 Pa20
King City (USA) (CA) 32 Oe27
King Cove (USA) (AK) 12 Md18
Kingfisher (USA) (OK) 35 Pg28
Kingfisher Lake (CDN) (ONT) 19 Qa19
Kingman (USA) (AZ) 33 Oh28
Kingman (USA) (KS) 35 Pf27
King Salmon (USA) (AK) 12 Mg16
Kings Canyon National Park ☆ (USA) (CA) 32 Of27
Kings Cove (CDN) (NFL) 23 Rj21
Kingsfield (USA) (ME) 22 Qk23
Kingsgate (CDN) (BC) 17 Og21
Kingsland (USA) (GA) 37 Qe30
Kings Mountain (USA) (NC) 37 Qe28
Kingsport (USA) (TN) 37 Qd27
Kingston (CDN) (NB) 22 Rc23
Kingston (CDN) (ONT) 29 Qg23
Kingston (USA) (NY) 30 Qj25
Kingston (USA) (PA) 29 Qh25
Kingstree (USA) (SC) 37 Qf29
Kingsville (USA) (TX) 40 Pg32
Kingwood (USA) (WV) 29 Qf26
Kinmundy (USA) (IL) 28 Qa26
Kinnear (USA) (WY) 25 Pa24
Kinniconick (USA) (KY) 29 Qd26
Kinsella (CDN) (ALB) 17 Ok19
Kinsey (USA) (MT) 18 Pc22
Kinsley (USA) (KS) 35 Pf27
Kinston (USA) (NC) 31 Qg28
Kinuso (CDN) (ALB) 15 Oh18
Kiosk (CDN) (ONT) 29 Qf22
Kiowa (USA) (CO) 34 Pc26
Kiowa (USA) (KS) 35 Pf27
Kiowa (USA) (MT) 17 Oj21
Kiowa (USA) (OK) 35 Ph28
Kipling (CDN) (SAS) 18 Pd20
Kipnuk (USA) (AK) 12 Mc16
Kirbyville (USA) (TX) 41 Pj30
Kirkella (CDN) (MAN) 18 Pe20
Kirkfield (CDN) (ONT) 29 Qf23
Kirkland (USA) (WA) 16 Od22
Kirkland Lake (CDN) (ONT) 21 Qf21
Kirksville (USA) (MO) 27 Pj25
Kirkwood (USA) (IL) 27 Pk25
Kirkwood (USA) (MO) 28 Pk26
Kirtland (USA) (NM) 33 Pa27
Kisatchie (USA) (LA) 35 Pj30
Kisbey (CDN) (SAS) 18 Pd21
Kismet (USA) (KS) 34 Pe27
Kispiox (CDN) (BC) 14 Ob18
Kit Carson (USA) (CO) 34 Pd26
Kitchener (CDN) (BC) 17 Og21
Kitchener (CDN) (ONT) 29 Qe24
Kitimat (CDN) (BC) 16 Oa18
Kitscoty (CDN) (ALB) 17 Ok19
Kitseguecla (CDN) (BC) 14 Ob18
Kittanning (USA) (PA) 29 Qf25
Kittery (USA) (ME) 22 Qk24
Kitt Peak National Observatory ☆ (USA) (AZ) 33 Ok30
Kitty Hawk (USA) (NC) 31 Qh27
Kitwancool (CDN) (BC) 14 Oa18
Kitwanga (CDN) (BC) 14 Oa18
Kivalina (USA) (AK) 10 Mc12
Kiwalik (USA) (AK) 10 Me12
Klamath (USA) (CA) 24 Oc25
Klamath Falls (USA) (OR) 24 Oe24
Klamath Marsh National Wildlife Refuge ☆ (USA) (OR) 24 Oe24
Klawock (USA) (AK) 14 Nj18
Kleena Kleene (CDN) (BC) 16 Oc20
Klery Creek (USA) (AK) 10 Me12
Kluane National Park ☆ (CDN) (YT) 13 Ne15
Knippa (USA) (TX) 40 Pf31
Knolls (USA) (UT) 25 Oj25
Knox (USA) (IN) 28 Qb25
Knoxville (USA) (IA) 27 Pj25
Knoxville (USA) (PA) 29 Qg25
Knoxville (USA) (TN) 37 Qd28
Kobuk (USA) (AK) 10 Mg12
Kobuk Valley National Park ☆ (USA) (AK) 10 Mf12
Kodiak (USA) (AK) 12 Mj17
Kofa National Wildlife Refuge ☆ (USA) (AZ) 33 Oh29
Koidern (CDN) (YT) 11 Ne15
Kokanee Glacier Provincial Park ☆ (CDN) (BC) 17 Og21
Kokish (CDN) (BC) 16 Ob20
Kokomo (USA) (IN) 28 Qb25
Kokruagarok (USA) (AK) 10 Mj10
Kola (CDN) (MAN) 18 Pe21
Koliganek (USA) (AK) 12 Mg16
Kolin (USA) (MT) 17 Pa22
Kōloa (USA) (HI) 44 Mf35
Koosharem (USA) (UT) 33 Ok26
Kooskia (USA) (ID) 25 Oh22
Kootenay Bay (CDN) (BC) 17 Og21
Kootenay National Park ☆ (CDN) (BC) 17 Oh20
Kormak (CDN) (ONT) 20 Qd22
Kosciusko (USA) (MS) 36 Qa29
Kotlik (USA) (AK) 10 Md14
Kotzebue (USA) (AK) 10 Md12
Kouchibouguac (CDN) (NB) 22 Rc22
Kouchibouguac National Park ☆ (CDN) (NB) 22 Rc22
Kountze (USA) (TX) 41 Ph30
Koyuk (USA) (AK) 10 Me13
Koyukuk (USA) (AK) 10 Mg13
Koyukuk National Wildlife Refuge ☆ (USA) (AK) 10 Mg13
Kremlin (USA) (MT) 17 Ok21
Kremmling (USA) (CO) 33 Pb25
Krotz Springs (USA) (LA) 36 Pk30
'Ksan Indian Village ☆ (CDN) (BC) 14 Ob18
Kuldo (CDN) (BC) 14 Ob18
Kuper Island (CDN) (BC) 16 Od21
Kupk (USA) (AZ) 33 Oj30
Kuroki (CDN) (SAS) 18 Pd20
Kustatan (USA) (AK) 13 Mk15
Kuujjuarapik Whapmagoostui (CDN) (QUE) 21 Qg18
Kwadacha Wilderness Provincial Park ☆ (CDN) (BC) 15 Oc17
Kwigillingok (USA) (AK) 12 Md16
Kwiguk (USA) (AK) 10 Mc14
Kwikpak (USA) (AK) 10 Mc14
Kykotsmovi (USA) (AZ) 33 Ok28
Kyle (CDN) (SAS) 18 Pa20
Kynquot (CDN) (BC) 16 Ob20

L

La Alameda (MEX) (DGO) 39 Pc33
La Ascensión (MEX) (NL) 40 Pf33
La Babia (MEX) (COA) 39 Pd31
La Baie (CDN) (QUE) 22 Qk21
La Bajada (C) (PR) 42 Qc35
Labelle (CDN) (QUE) 21 Qh22
La Belle (USA) (FL) 43 Qe32
La Bocana (MEX) (BCN) 32 Og30
La Bocana (MEX) (BCN) 38 Oh31
La Bolsa (MEX) (SON) 33 Oh29
La Boquilla del Conchos (MEX) (CHA) 39 Pc32
Labrieville (CDN) (QUE) 22 Ra21
La Broquerie (CDN) (MAN) 19 Pg21
La Bufadora (MEX) (BCN) 32 Og30
Lacadena (CDN) (SAS) 17 Pa20
La Carbonera (MEX) (TAM) 40 Pg33
Lac-Bouchette (CDN) (QUE) 21 Qj21
Lac Cardinal (CDN) (ALB) 15 Og17
Lac-Cayamant (CDN) (QUE) 29 Qg22
Lac-des-Aigles (CDN) (QUE) 22 Ra22
Lac-des-Commissaires (CDN) (QUE) 21 Qj21
Lac du Bonnet (CDN) (MAN) 19 Pg20
Lac du Flambeau (USA) (WI) 27 Qa23
Lac-Édouard (CDN) (QUE) 21 Qj22
Lac-Etchemin (CDN) (QUE) 22 Qk22
Lacey (USA) (WA) 24 Od22
Lac-Frontière (CDN) (QUE) 22 Qk22
La Chicharrona (MEX) (ZAC) 39 Pd34
Lac-Humqui (CDN) (QUE) 22 Rb21
Lachute (CDN) (QUE) 30 Qh23
Lac la Biche (CDN) (ALB) 17 Oj18
Nitchequon (CDN) (QUE) 21 Qk19
Lac la Hache (CDN) (BC) 16 Oe20
Lac la Ronge Provincial Park ☆ (CDN) (SAS) 18 Pc18
Laclede (USA) (ID) 17 Og21
Lac-Mégantic (CDN) (QUE) 22 Qk23
La Coma (MEX) (TAM) 40 Pf33
Lacombe (CDN) (ALB) 17 Oj19
Laconia (USA) (NH) 22 Qk24
La Corey (CDN) (ALB) 17 Ok18
La Crescent (USA) (MN) 27 Pk24
Lacrosse (USA) (WA) 24 Og22
La Crosse (USA) (WI) 27 Pk24
La Cruz (MEX) (SIN) 39 Pb34
La Cruz (MEX) (TAM) 40 Pg34
Lac-Saguay (CDN) (QUE) 21 Qh22
Lac Saint-Jean ☆ (CDN) (QUE) 21 Qj21
Lac Seul (CDN) (ONT) 19 Pj20
La Cuesta (MEX) (COA) 39 Pd31
La Cueva (USA) (NM) 34 Pb28
La Doré (CDN) (QUE) 21 Qj21
Lady Evelyn Smoothwater Provincial Park ☆ (CDN) (ONT) 20 Qe22
Ladysmith (CDN) (BC) 16 Od21
Ladysmith (USA) (WI) 27 Pk23
La Escondida (MEX) (NL) 40 Pf33
La Esperanza (C) (PR) 43 Qd34
La Fayette (USA) (GA) 36 Qc28
Lafayette (USA) (IN) 28 Qb25
Lafayette (USA) (LA) 36 Pk30
Lafayette (USA) (TN) 36 Qb27
Lafitte (USA) (LA) 36 Pk31
Lafleche (CDN) (SAS) 18 Pb21
La Follette (USA) (TN) 36 Qc27
Laforce (CDN) (QUE) 21 Qf22
La Forest (CDN) (ONT) 20 Qe22
La Fortuna (MEX) (BCS) 39 Pa34
Lage's (USA) (NV) 33 Oh25
La Glace (CDN) (ALB) 15 Of18
La Gloria (MEX) (NL) 40 Pf32
La Grange (USA) (GA) 36 Qc29
La Grange (USA) (KY) 28 Qc26
La Grange (USA) (NC) 31 Qg28
La Grange (USA) (TX) 40 Pg31
La Grullita (MEX) (SON) 33 Oh29
La Guadeloupe (CDN) (QUE) 22 Qk23
Laguna (USA) (NM) 34 Pb28
Laguna Atascosa N.W.R. ☆ (USA) (TX) 40 Pg32
Laguna del Rey (MEX) (COA) 39 Pd32
Laguna Ojo, Parque Natural ☆ (MEX) (BCN) 38 Oh32
La Habana (C) (H) 43 Qd34
La Habana = Havanna (C) (H) 43 Qd34
Lahaina (USA) (HI) 44 Mg35
La Harpe (USA) (IL) 27 Pk25
Laidlaw (CDN) (BC) 16 Oe21
La Jagua (C) (CG) 43 Qf35
Lajitas (USA) (TX) 39 Pd31
Lajord (CDN) (SAS) 18 Pc20
La Junta (MEX) (CHA) 39 Pb31
La Junta (USA) (CO) 34 Pd27
Lake (USA) (ID) 25 Ok23
Lake (USA) (MS) 36 Qa29
Lake (USA) (WY) 25 Ok23
Lake Alma (CDN) (SAS) 18 Pc21
Lake Arthur (USA) (LA) 36 Pj30
Lake Benton (USA) (MN) 27 Pg23
Lake Bronson (USA) (MN) 19 Pg21
Lake Butler (USA) (FL) 37 Qd30
Lake Charles (USA) (LA) 41 Pj30
Lake City (USA) (CO) 33 Pb27
Lake City (USA) (FL) 37 Qd30
Lake City (USA) (MN) 27 Pj23
Lake City (USA) (SC) 37 Qf29

Lake City USA (SD) 27 Pg23
Lake Clark National Park and Preserve ☆ USA (AK) 12 Mj15
Lake Cowichan CDN (BC) 16 Oc21
Lake Crystal USA (MN) 27 Ph23
Lake Errock CDN (BC) 16 Od21
Lakefield CDN (ONT) 29 Qf23
Lake Geneva USA (WI) 28 Qa24
Lake George USA (MN) 19 Ph22
Lake George USA (NY) 30 Qj24
Lake Havasu City USA (AZ) 33 Oh28
Lake Hughes USA (CA) 32 Of28
Lake Isabella USA (CA) 32 Of28
Lake Itasca USA (MN) 19 Ph22
Lake Jackson USA (TX) 41 Ph31
Lakeland USA (FL) 43 Qe31
Lakeland USA (GA) 37 Qd30
Lake Linden USA (MI) 20 Qa22
Lake Louise CDN (ALB) 17 Og20
Lake McDonald USA (MT) 17 Oj21
Lake Mead National Recreation Area ☆ USA (NV) 33 Oh27
Lake Metigoshe International Peace Garden ☆ USA (ND) 18 Pe21
Lake Mills USA (IA) 27 Pj24
Lake Mills USA (WI) 28 Qa24
Lake Minchumina USA (AK) 10 Mj14
Lakenheath CDN (SAS) 18 Pb21
Lake Ophelia National Wildlife Refuge ☆ USA (LA) 36 Pk30
Lake Park USA (GA) 37 Qd30
Lake Placid USA (FL) 43 Qe32
Lake Placid USA (NY) 30 Qj23
Lakeport USA (NY) 29 Qh24
Lake Providence USA (LA) 36 Pk29
Lakeside USA (NY) 29 Qf24
Lakeside USA (OR) 24 Oc24
Lakeside USA (VA) 31 Qg27
Lakeside, Pinetop- USA (AZ) 33 Pa28
Lake Stevens USA (WA) 16 Od21
Lake Superior Provincial Park ☆ CDN (ONT) 20 Qc22
Lakeview USA (ID) 17 Og22
Lakeview USA (MI) 28 Qc24
Lakeview USA (OR) 24 Oe24
Lakeville USA (MN) 27 Pj23
Lake Wales USA (FL) 43 Qe32
Lakewood USA (CO) 34 Pc26
Lakewood USA (NJ) 30 Qh25
Lakewood USA (NM) 34 Pc29
Lake Worth USA (FL) 43 Qe32
Lakin USA (KS) 34 Pe27
Lakota USA (IA) 27 Ph24
Lakota USA (ND) 19 Pf21
La Linda MEX (COA) 39 Pd31
La Loche CDN (SAS) 17 Pa17
La Mancha MEX (COA) 39 Pd33
La Manche Provincial Park ☆ CDN (NFL) 23 Rj22
Lamar USA (CO) 34 Pd26
Lamar USA (LA) 36 Pk29
Lamar USA (MO) 35 Ph27
La Marque USA (TX) 41 Ph31
Lame Deer USA (MT) 26 Pb23
La Melvis C (JU) 43 Qd35
La Mesa USA (CA) 32 Og29
La Mesa USA (NM) 34 Pb29
Lamesa USA (TX) 34 Pe29
La Misión MEX (BCN) 32 Og29
Lamkin USA (TX) 35 Pf30
Lamoille USA (NV) 25 Oh25
Lamoni USA (IA) 27 Pj25
Lamont CDN (ALB) 17 Oj19
Lamont USA (FL) 37 Qd30
Lamont USA (WY) 25 Pb24
La Mora MEX (COA) 39 Pd32
La Morita MEX (CHA) 39 Pc31
Lampasas USA (TX) 40 Pf30
Lampazos de Naranjo MEX (NL) 40 Pe32
Lampman CDN (SAS) 18 Pd21
Lamy USA (NM) 34 Pc28
Lāna'i City USA (HI) 44 Mg35
Lanark USA (NM) 34 Pb30
Lancaster USA (CA) 32 Of28
Lancaster USA (IL) 28 Qb26
Lancaster USA (MN) 19 Pg21
Lancaster USA (MO) 27 Pj25
Lancaster USA (NH) 22 Qk23
Lancaster USA (OH) 29 Qd26
Lancaster USA (PA) 29 Qg25
Lancaster USA (SC) 37 Qe28
Lancaster USA (TX) 35 Pg29
Lancaster USA (WI) 27 Pk24
Lance Creek USA (WY) 26 Pc24
Lancer CDN (SAS) 17 Pa20
Land, De USA (FL) 37 Qe31
Landa USA (ND) 18 Pe21
Land Between The Lakes National Recreation Area ☆ USA (KY) 36 Qa27
Lander USA (WY) 25 Pa24
Landis CDN (SAS) 17 Pa19
Lanett USA (AL) 36 Qc29
Lang CDN (SAS) 18 Pc21
Langbank CDN (SAS) 18 Pd20
Lang Bay CDN (BC) 16 Oc21
Langdale CDN (BC) 16 Od21
Langdon USA (ND) 19 Pf21
Langenburg CDN (SAS) 18 Pe20
Langford CDN (BC) 16 Od21
Langham CDN (SAS) 18 Pb19
Langlade USA (WI) 28 Qa23
Langley CDN (BC) 16 Od21
Langruth CDN (MAN) 19 Pf20
Langtry USA (TX) 40 Pe31
Laniel CDN (QUE) 21 Qf22
Lanigan CDN (SAS) 18 Pc20
L'Annonciation CDN (QUE) 21 Qh22
La Nona MEX (SIN) 39 Pb34
Lansdale USA (PA) 30 Qh25
Lansdowne House CDN (ONT) 20 Qb19
L'Anse USA (MI) 20 Qa22
L'Anse aux Meadows National Historic Park ☆ CDN (NFL) 23 Rh20
L'Anse-Pleureuse CDN (QUE) 22 Rc21
Lansford USA (ND) 18 Pe21
Lansing USA (IA) 27 Pk24
Lansing USA (MI) 28 Qc24
Lantz Corners USA (PA) 29 Qf25
Lantzville CDN (BC) 16 Oc21
La Ochoa MEX (DGO) 39 Pd34
Laona USA (WI) 28 Qa23
La Palma C (PR) 43 Qd34
La Palmarita C (CG) 43 Qf35
La Patrie CDN (QUE) 22 Qk23
La Paz MEX (BCS) 38 Ok33
La Pérade CDN (QUE) 21 Qj22
La Perla MEX (CHA) 39 Pc31
La Pesca MEX (TAM) 40 Pg34
La Place USA (LA) 36 Pk30
La Plant USA (SD) 26 Pe23
La Plata USA (MD) 29 Qg26
La Plata USA (MO) 28 Pj25
La Pocatière CDN (QUE) 22 Ra22
La Poile CDN (NFL) 23 Rf22
Laporte CDN (SAS) 17 Pa20
La Porte USA (IN) 28 Qb25
Laporte USA (PA) 29 Qg25
La Porte USA (TX) 41 Ph31
La Porte City USA (IA) 27 Pj24
Lappe CDN (ONT) 20 Qa21
La Prele Ranger Station USA (WY) 26 Pc24
La Pryor USA (TX) 40 Pf31
La Purisima MEX (BCS) 38 Oj32
La Push USA (WA) 16 Oc22
Laramie USA (WY) 26 Pc25
La Rana C (SS) 43 Qf34
Larder Lake CDN (ONT) 21 Qf21
Laredo USA (TX) 40 Pf32
La Reforma C (JU) 43 Qd35
La Reine CDN (QUE) 21 Qf21
Largo USA (FL) 43 Qd32
Larimore USA (ND) 19 Pg22
Lark Harbour CDN (NFL) 23 Rf21
Larkspur USA (CO) 34 Pc26
Larned USA (KS) 35 Pf26
La Rochelle CDN (MAN) 19 Pg21
La Romaine CDN (QUE) 23 Re20
La Ronge CDN (SAS) 18 Pc18
Larose USA (LA) 36 Pk31
La Rosita MEX (COA) 39 Pd31
Larry's River CDN (NS) 23 Re23
Larson CDN (ONT) 19 Pk21
La Rue USA (TX) 35 Ph29
La Rumorosa MEX (BCN) 32 Og29
La Sal USA (UT) 33 Pa26
La Salle USA (CO) 26 Pc25
Las Animas USA (CO) 34 Pd26
La Sarre CDN (QUE) 21 Qf21
La Scie CDN (NFL) 23 Rh21
Las Cruces USA (NM) 34 Pb29
La Selva MEX (CHA) 39 Pd31
Las Glorias MEX (SIN) 39 Pa33
Lashburn CDN (SAS) 17 Pa19
Las Herreras MEX (DGO) 39 Pc33
La Sierpe C (SS) 43 Qf35
Las Isabeles MEX (BCN) 33 Oh29
Las Martinas C (PR) 42 Qc35
Las Nieves MEX (DGO) 39 Pc32
Las Norias MEX (COA) 39 Pd31
La Soledad MEX (COA) 39 Pd32
La Soledad MEX (DGO) 39 Pc33
Las Palomas USA (NM) 34 Pb29
Lassen Volcanic National Park ☆ USA (CA) 24 Oe25
Last Chance USA (CO) 34 Pd26
Last Lake CDN (ALB) 15 Of17
Las Varas MEX (CHA) 39 Pb31
Las Vegas USA (NM) 34 Pc28
Las Vegas USA (NV) 33 Oh27
Latchford CDN (ONT) 21 Qf22
La Templadera del Derrumbe MEX (DGO) 39 Pb33
Laterrière CDN (QUE) 22 Qk21
Latouche USA (AK) 13 Nb15
Latrobe USA (PA) 29 Qf25
Latulipe CDN (QUE) 21 Qf22
La Tuque CDN (QUE) 21 Qj22
Lauder CDN (MAN) 18 Pe21
Laupāhoehoe USA (HI) 44 Mh36
Laurel USA (DE) 31 Qh26
Laurel USA (IA) 27 Pj25
Laurel USA (MD) 29 Qg26
Laurel USA (MS) 36 Qa30
Laurel USA (MT) 25 Pa23
Laurens USA (SC) 37 Qd28
Laurentides, Réserve Faunique des ☆ CDN (QUE) 21 Qj22
Laurier USA (WA) 16 Of21
Laurie River CDN (MAN) 18 Pe17
Laurinburg USA (NC) 37 Qf28
Laurium USA (WI) 20 Qa22
Lauzon CDN (QUE) 22 Qk22
Lava Beds National Monument ☆ USA (CA) 24 Od25
Lavaca, Port USA (TX) 40 Pg31
Laval CDN (QUE) 30 Qj23
La Valle USA (WI) 27 Pk24
La Vallita C (CG) 43 Qf35
Lavenham CDN (MAN) 19 Pf21
La Ventana MEX (BCN) 33 Oh30
La Ventana MEX (SLP) 40 Pe34
La Vérendrye, Réserve Faunique ☆ CDN (QUE) 21 Qg22
Laverlochère CDN (QUE) 21 Qf22
La Vernia USA (TX) 40 Pf31
La Veta USA (CO) 34 Pc27
La Víbora MEX (COA) 39 Pd32
Lavillette CDN (NB) 22 Rc22
Lavina USA (MT) 25 Pa22
Lavoy CDN (ALB) 17 Ok19
Lawn USA (TX) 35 Pf29
Lawrence USA (KS) 35 Ph26
Lawrence USA (MA) 30 Qk24
Lawrence USA (NC) 31 Qg27
Lawrenceburg USA (TN) 36 Qb28
Lawrence Station CDN (NB) 22 Rb23
Lawrenceville USA (GA) 37 Qd29
Lawrenceville USA (IL) 28 Qb26
Lawrenceville USA (VA) 31 Qg27
Lawton USA (ND) 19 Pf21
Lawton USA (PA) 29 Qg25
Lawton USA (TX) 35 Pf28
Lay USA (CO) 25 Pb25
Layton USA (UT) 25 Ok25
Lázaro Cárdenas MEX (BCN) 33 Oh30
Lea USA (NM) 34 Pd29
Leader CDN (SAS) 17 Pa20
Lead Hill USA (AR) 35 Pj27
Leading Tickles CDN (NFL) 23 Rh21
Leadore USA (ID) 25 Oj23
Leadpoint USA (WA) 17 Og21
Leadville USA (CO) 34 Pb26
Leahy USA (WA) 16 Of22
Leakey USA (TX) 40 Pf31
Leamington CDN (ONT) 29 Qd24
Leander USA (TX) 40 Pg30
Lea Park CDN (ALB) 17 Ok19
Leavenworth USA (KS) 35 Ph26
Leavenworth USA (WA) 16 Oe22
Leavitt CDN (ALB) 17 Oj21
Lebanon USA (IN) 28 Qb25
Lebanon USA (KS) 35 Pf26
Lebanon USA (KY) 36 Qc27
Lebanon USA (MO) 35 Pj27
Lebanon USA (NH) 30 Qj24
Lebanon USA (OR) 24 Od23
Lebanon USA (PA) 29 Qg25
Lebanon USA (TN) 36 Qb27
Lebanon USA (VA) 37 Qd27
Lebanon Station USA (FL) 37 Qd31
Lebeau USA (LA) 36 Pk30
Lebel-sur-Quévillon CDN (QUE) 21 Qg21
Le Bic CDN (QUE) 22 Ra21
Lebo USA (KS) 35 Ph26
Le Center USA (MN) 27 Pj23
Le Claire USA (IA) 27 Pk25
Lecompte USA (LA) 36 Pj30
Ledge USA (MT) 17 Ok21
Leduc CDN (ALB) 17 Oj19
Lee USA (NV) 25 Oh25
Leeburn CDN (ONT) 20 Qd22
Leech Lake USA (MN) 19 Ph22
Leeds USA (AL) 36 Qb29
Leeds USA (ND) 19 Pf21
Lees USA (TX) 34 Pe29
Leesburg USA (FL) 43 Qe31
Leesburg USA (VA) 29 Qg26
Leesville USA (LA) 41 Pj30
Leffellier CDN (MAN) 19 Pg21
Lefor USA (ND) 18 Pd22
Legend CDN (ALB) 17 Ok21
Leggett USA (CA) 32 Od26
Le Grand Quarries Fossils ☆ USA (IA) 27 Pj25
Lehi USA (UT) 25 Ok25
Lehighton USA (PA) 29 Qh25
Lehman USA (TX) 34 Pd29
Lehr USA (MS) 36 Pk30
Leighton USA (AL) 36 Qb28
Leipzig CDN (SAS) 17 Pa19
Leitchfield USA (KY) 36 Qb27
Leland USA (MS) 36 Pk29
Le Mars USA (IA) 27 Pg24
Lemieux CDN (BC) 14 Nj16
Lemmon USA (SD) 26 Pd23
Lemon Creek CDN (BC) 17 Og21
Lemon Grove USA (CA) 32 Og29
Lemsford CDN (SAS) 17 Pa20
Lena CDN (MAN) 19 Pf21
Lena USA (AR) 35 Pj28
Lena USA (LA) 35 Pj30
Lena USA (MS) 36 Qa29
Lennox USA (SD) 27 Pg24
Lenoir USA (NC) 37 Qe28
Lenoir City USA (TN) 36 Qc28
Lenora USA (KS) 34 Pe26
Lenore CDN (MAN) 18 Pe21
Lenox USA (IA) 27 Ph25
Lenswood CDN (MAN) 18 Pe19
Leo Creek CDN (BC) 15 Oc18
Leola USA (AR) 35 Pj28
Leola USA (SD) 26 Pf23
Leon USA (IA) 27 Pj25
Leonard USA (MN) 19 Ph22
Leonard USA (ND) 19 Pg22
Leonard USA (TX) 35 Pg29
Leonardtown USA (MD) 29 Qg26
León Guzmán MEX (DGO) 39 Pd33
Leonia USA (ID) 17 Og21
Leoti USA (KS) 34 Pe26
Lepreau CDN (NB) 22 Rb23
Lerdo, Ciudad MEX (DGO) 39 Pd33
Leross CDN (SAS) 18 Pc20
Le Roy USA (MN) 27 Pj24
Les Escoumins CDN (QUE) 22 Ra21
Leslie USA (AR) 35 Pj28
Leslie USA (ID) 25 Oj24
Les Méchins CDN (QUE) 22 Rb21
Lesser Slave Lake Provincial Park ☆ CDN (ALB) 15 Oh18
Le Sueur USA (MN) 27 Pj23
Letete CDN (NB) 22 Rb23
Lethbridge CDN (ALB) 17 Oj21
Letohatchee USA (AL) 36 Qb29
Leupp USA (AZ) 33 Ok28
Levack CDN (ONT) 20 Qe22
Levan USA (UT) 33 Ok26
Levelland USA (TX) 34 Pd29
Lévis CDN (QUE) 22 Qk22
Levittown USA (PA) 30 Qh25
Lewellen USA (NE) 26 Pd25
Lewes USA (DE) 31 Qh26
Lewis USA (CO) 33 Pa27
Lewisburg USA (OR) 24 Od23
Lewisburg USA (PA) 29 Qg25
Lewisburg USA (TN) 36 Qb28
Lewisburg USA (WV) 37 Qe27
Lewis Point USA (AK) 12 Mf16
Lewisporte CDN (NFL) 23 Rh21
Lewiston USA (ID) 24 Og22
Lewiston USA (IN) 28 Qb25
Lewiston USA (ME) 22 Qk23
Lewiston USA (MN) 27 Pk24
Lewiston USA (UT) 25 Ok25
Lewistown USA (IL) 27 Pk25
Lewistown USA (MT) 17 Pa22
Lewistown USA (PA) 29 Qg25
Lewvan CDN (SAS) 18 Pc20
Lexington USA (KY) 28 Qc26
Lexington USA (NC) 37 Qe28
Lexington USA (NE) 26 Pf25
Lexington USA (TN) 36 Qa28
Lexington USA (VA) 37 Qf27
Lexington Park USA (MD) 29 Qg26
Libau CDN (MAN) 19 Pg20
Libby USA (MN) 19 Pj22
Libby USA (MT) 17 Oh21
Liberal USA (KS) 34 Pe27
Liberty USA (KY) 36 Qc27
Liberty USA (ME) 22 Ra23
Liberty USA (MS) 36 Pk30
Liberty USA (NY) 30 Qh25
Liberty USA (TX) 41 Ph30
Liberty Lake USA (WA) 17 Og22
Libertytown USA (MD) 29 Qg26
Licking USA (MO) 36 Pk27
Liebenthal CDN (SAS) 17 Pa20
Liebenthal USA (KS) 35 Pf26
Lignite USA (ND) 18 Pd21
Ligonier USA (IN) 28 Qc25
Ligurta USA (AZ) 33 Oh29
Līhu'e USA (HI) 44 Mf35
Likely CDN (BC) 16 Oe19
Likely USA (CA) 24 Oe25
Lilbourn USA (MO) 36 Qa27
L'Île-d'Entrée CDN (QUE) 23 Re22
Lillestrom CDN (SAS) 18 Pc20
Lillie USA (LA) 35 Pj29
Lilliwaup USA (WA) 16 Od22
Lillooet CDN (BC) 16 Oe20
Lima USA (OH) 28 Qc25
Limerick CDN (SAS) 18 Pb21
Limerick USA (ME) 22 Qk24
Limon USA (CO) 34 Pd26
Linares MEX (NL) 40 Pf33
Lincoln USA (IL) 28 Qa25
Lincoln USA (KS) 35 Pf26
Lincoln USA (ME) 22 Ra23
Lincoln USA (NE) 27 Pg25
Lincoln USA (NH) 22 Qk23
Lincoln Caverns ☆ USA (PA) 29 Qf25
Lincoln City USA (OR) 24 Od23
Lincolnton USA (NC) 37 Qe28
Linda, La MEX (COA) 39 Pd31
Lindale USA (TX) 35 Ph29
Lindbergh CDN (ALB) 17 Ok19
Linden CDN (ALB) 17 Oj20
Linden USA (TN) 36 Qb28
Lindsay CDN (ONT) 29 Qf23
Lindsay USA (MT) 18 Pc22
Lindsborg USA (KS) 35 Pg26
Lindstrom USA (MN) 27 Pj23
Lineville USA (IA) 27 Pj25
Lingle USA (WY) 26 Pc24
Linn USA (KS) 35 Pg26
Linn USA (MO) 28 Pk26
Linton USA (IN) 28 Qb26
Linton USA (ND) 26 Pe22
Lions, Port USA (AK) 12 Mj17
Lipton CDN (SAS) 18 Pd20
Lisbon USA (ND) 27 Pg22
Lisbon USA (OH) 29 Qe25
Lisbon Falls USA (ME) 22 Qk23
L'Islet CDN (QUE) 22 Qk22
Lister CDN (BC) 17 Og21
Listowel CDN (ONT) 29 Qe24
Litchfield USA (CA) 24 Oe25
Litchfield USA (MN) 27 Ph23
Litchfield USA (NE) 26 Pf25
Litchfield Beach USA (SC) 37 Qf29
Litchville USA (ND) 19 Pf22
Little Bighorn Battlefield National Monument ☆ USA (MT) 25 Pb23
Little Buffalo CDN (ALB) 15 Og17
Little Current CDN (ONT) 29 Qe23
Little Current River Provincial Park ☆ CDN (ONT) 20 Qb20
Little Falls USA (MN) 27 Ph23
Little Falls USA (NY) 30 Qh24
Littlefield USA (AZ) 33 Oj27
Littlefield USA (TX) 34 Pd29
Little Fork USA (MN) 19 Pj21
Little Fort CDN (BC) 16 Oe20
Little Grand Rapids CDN (MAN) 19 Ph19
Little Harbour BS 43 Qg33
Little Lake USA (CA) 32 Og28
Little Lake USA (MI) 20 Qb22
Little River CDN (BC) 16 Oc21
Little Rock USA (AR) 35 Pj28
Littlerock USA (CA) 32 Og28
Little Smoky CDN (ALB) 15 Og18
Littleton USA (CO) 34 Pc26
Littleton USA (NC) 31 Qg27
Littleton USA (NH) 22 Qk23
Little Valley USA (NY) 29 Qf24
Livelong CDN (SAS) 17 Pa19
Livengood USA (AK) 11 Na13
Live Oak USA (FL) 37 Qd30
Livermore Falls USA (ME) 22 Qk23
Liverpool CDN (NS) 22 Rc23
Livingston USA (AL) 36 Qa29
Livingston USA (KY) 36 Qc27
Livingston USA (LA) 36 Pk30
Livingston USA (MT) 25 Ok23
Livingston USA (TN) 36 Qc27
Livingston USA (TX) 41 Ph30
Livingston USA (WI) 27 Pk24
Livonia USA (MI) 29 Qd24
Lizotte CDN (QUE) 21 Qj21
Llano USA (TX) 40 Pf30
Llera de Canales MEX (TAM) 40 Pf34
Lloyd USA (MT) 17 Pa21
Lloydminster CDN (ALB) 17 Pa19
Loa USA (UT) 33 Ok26
Lobatos MEX (ZAC) 39 Pd34
Locate USA (MT) 26 Pc22
Loche, La CDN (SAS) 17 Pa17
Lochiel USA (AZ) 33 Ok30
Lochloosa USA (FL) 37 Qd31
Locke USA (WA) 17 Og21
Lockeport CDN (NS) 22 Rc24
Lockhart USA (TX) 40 Pg31
Lock Haven USA (PA) 29 Qg25
Lockney USA (TX) 34 Pe28
Lockport CDN (MAN) 19 Pg21
Lockport USA (LA) 36 Pk31
Lockport USA (NY) 29 Qf24
Lockwood USA (CA) 32 Oe28
Lockwood USA (MO) 35 Pj27
Locust USA (MN) 27 Pk24
Lodge Grass USA (MT) 25 Pb23
Lodgepole USA (NE) 26 Pd25
Lodi USA (CA) 32 Oe26
Lodi USA (OH) 29 Qd25
Logan USA (NM) 34 Pd28
Logan USA (OH) 29 Qd26
Logan USA (UT) 25 Ok25
Logan USA (WV) 37 Qd27
Logansport USA (IN) 28 Qb25
Logansport USA (LA) 35 Pj30
Loganton USA (PA) 29 Qg25
Loggieville CDN (NB) 22 Rc22
Loleta USA (CA) 24 Oc25
Lolo USA (MT) 25 Oh22
Lolo Hot Springs USA (MT) 25 Oh22
Loma USA (MT) 17 Ok22
Loma USA (ND) 19 Pf21
Loma Alta USA (TX) 40 Pe31
Lomas de Arena USA (TX) 39 Pc30
Lometa USA (TX) 40 Pf30
Lomond CDN (ALB) 17 Oj20
Lompoc USA (CA) 32 Oe28
London CDN (ONT) 29 Qe2
London USA (KY) 36 Qc2
London USA (MN) 27 Pj2
London USA (OH) 29 Qd2
Lone Butte CDN (BC) 16 Oe2
Lonepine USA (MT) 17 Oh2
Lone Prairie CDN (BC) 15 Oe1
Lone Rock CDN (SAS) 17 Pa1
Lone Rock USA (WI) 27 Pk2
Longbeach CDN (BC) 17 Og2
Long Beach USA (CA) 32 Of29
Long Beach USA (MS) 36 Qa3
Longbow Lake CDN (ONT) 19 Ph2
Long Branch USA (NJ) 30 Qj2
Long Creek CDN (NB) 22 Rb2
Long Creek USA (OR) 24 Of2
Long Harbour CDN (NFL) 23 Rj2
Longlac CDN (ONT) 20 Qb2
Long Lake USA (WA) 17 Og2
Long Lake National Wildlife Refuge ☆ USA (ND) 18 Pe2
Longmont USA (CO) 34 Pc2
Long Pine USA (NE) 26 Pf2
Long Point CDN (ONT) 29 Qe2
Long Prairie USA (MN) 27 Ph2
Longueuil CDN (QUE) 30 Qj2
Long Valley Junction USA (UT) 33 Oj2
Longview CDN (ALB) 17 Oh2
Longview USA (TX) 35 Ph2
Longview USA (WA) 24 Od2
Lono USA (AR) 35 Pj2
Lonsdale USA (MN) 27 Pj2
Loogootee USA (IN) 28 Qb2
Lookout USA (ME) 22 Ra2
Loomis CDN (SAS) 18 Pa2
Loomis USA (WA) 16 Of2
Loon Lake CDN (SAS) 17 Pa1
Loon Lake USA (WA) 17 Og
Loose Creek USA (MO) 28 Pk
Loost River USA (AK) 10 Mb
Lorain USA (OH) 29 Qd
Loraine USA (TX) 34 Pe
Lordsburg USA (NM) 33 Pa
Lorena USA (MS) 36 Qa
Loreto MEX (BCS) 38 Ok
Loretta USA (WI) 27 Pk
Lorette CDN (MAN) 19 Pg
Loretteville CDN (QUE) 22 Qk
Loring USA (MT) 18 Pb
Loring, Port CDN (ONT) 29 Qf
Lorlie CDN (SAS) 18 Pd
Lorneville CDN (NB) 22 Rb
Lorton USA (NE) 27 Pg
Los Alamos USA (NM) 34 Pb
Los Aldamas MEX (NL) 40 Pf
Los Angeles USA (CA) 32 Of
Los Banos USA (CA) 32 Oe
Los Barriles MEX (BCS) 39 Pa
Los Gatos USA (CA) 32 Oe
Los Inocentes MEX (BCS) 38 Ok
Los Lunas USA (NM) 34 Pb
Los Mochis MEX (SIN) 39 Pa
Los Molinos MEX (SON) 33 Ok
Los Picos MEX (COA) 39 Pc
Los Puentes MEX (SIN) 39 Pb
Los Ramones MEX (NL) 40 P
Los Rodríguez MEX (COA) 40 Pe
Lost Hills USA (CA) 32 O
Lostwood USA (ND) 18 Pc
Lothair USA (MT) 17 O
Louisa USA (KY) 29 Q
Louisbourg CDN (NS) 23 R
Louisburg USA (NC) 31 C
Louisdale CDN (NS) 23 R
Louise USA (TX) 40 P
Louiseville CDN (QUE) 21 C
Louisiana USA (MO) 28 P
Louisville USA (GA) 37 Q
Louisville USA (KY) 28 Q
Louisville USA (MS) 36 Q
Louisville USA (NE) 27 P
Loup, Rivière-du- CDN (QUE) 22 R
Loup City USA (NE) 26 P
Louvicourt CDN (QUE) 21 Q
Love CDN (SAS) 18 P
Lovelady USA (TX) 41 P
Loveland USA (CO) 26 P
Lovell USA (WY) 25 P
Lovelock USA (NV) 24 C
Loverna CDN (SAS) 17 P
Loving USA (NM) 34 P
Loving USA (TX) 35 P
Lovington USA (NM) 34 P
Low CDN (QUE) 29 C
Lowe Farm CDN (MAN) 19 P
Lowell USA (ID) 25 C
Lowell USA (MA) 30 C
Lower Fort Garry National Historic Park ☆ CDN (MAN) 19 P
Lower Klamath National Wildlife Refuge ☆ USA (24 C
Lower Lake USA (CA) 32 C
Lower Post CDN (BC) 14 C
Lower Souris National Wildlife Refuge = J. Clark Sa National Wildlife Refuge ☆ USA (ND) 18 P
Lower Suwannee National Wildlife Refuge ☆ USA (FL) 37 C
Lowman USA (ID) 25 C
Lowville USA (NY) 29 C
Loysville USA (PA) 29 C
Lubbock USA (TX) 34
Lubec USA (ME) 22
Lucan CDN (ONT) 29
Lucedale USA (MS) 36
Lucerne USA (MO) 27

ucerne Valley (USA) (CA) 32 Og28
ucero (MEX) (CHA) 39 Pb30
uceville (CDN) (QUE) 22 Ra21
ucien (USA) (MS) 36 Pk30
ucin (USA) (UT) 25 Oj25
uck (USA) (WI) 27 Pj23
ucky (USA) (LA) 35 Pj29
ucky Lake (CDN) (SAS) 18 Pb20
ude (USA) (MN) 19 Ph21
udington (USA) (MI) 28 Qb24
udlow (USA) (CA) 32 Og28
udlow (USA) (CO) 34 Pc27
udowici (USA) (GA) 37 Qe30
ueders (USA) (TX) 35 Pf29
ufkin (USA) (TX) 35 Ph30
ukeville (USA) (AZ) 33 Oj30
ula (USA) (MS) 36 Pk28
umberton (CDN) (BC) 17 Oh21
umberton (USA) (MS) 36 Qa30
umberton (USA) (NC) 37 Qf28
umby (CDN) (BC) 16 Of20
umpkin (USA) (GA) 36 Qc29
umsden (CDN) (SAS) 18 Pc20
una (USA) (NM) 33 Pa29
unas, Los (USA) (NM) 34 Pb28
und (CDN) (BC) 16 Oc21
und (USA) (UT) 33 Oj26
undbreck (CDN) (ALB) 17 Oh21
unenburg (CDN) (NS) 22 Rc23
uray (USA) (KS) 35 Pf26
uray (USA) (VA) 29 Qf26
urton (USA) (AR) 35 Pj28
useland (CDN) (SAS) 17 Pa19
usk (USA) (WY) 26 Pc24
stre (USA) (MT) 18 Pc21
tcher (USA) (LA) 36 Pk30
thersburg (USA) (PA) 29 Qf25
tsen (USA) (MN) 19 Pk22
verne (USA) (AL) 36 Qb30
verne (USA) (MN) 27 Pg24
xemburg (USA) (IA) 27 Pk24
ddal (CDN) (MAN) 19 Pf18
le (USA) (WA) 24 Oe23
leton (CDN) (MAN) 18 Pe21
man (USA) (MS) 36 Qa30
mburn (CDN) (ALB) 15 Of18
nchburg (USA) (VA) 37 Qf27
nden (USA) (WA) 16 Od21
ndonville (USA) (NY) 29 Qf24
ndonville (USA) (VT) 30 Qk23
nn (USA) (IN) 28 Qc25
nn (USA) (MA) 30 Qk24
ndyl (USA) (UT) 33 Oj26
nn Haven (USA) (FL) 36 Qc30
nnwood (USA) (WA) 16 Od22
ons (USA) (CO) 26 Pc25
ons (USA) (GA) 37 Qd29
ons (USA) (KS) 35 Pf26
ons Falls (USA) (NY) 29 Qh24
site (USA) (WY) 25 Pb24
ton (CDN) (BC) 16 Oe20

M

bank (USA) (TX) 35 Pg29
bel (USA) (MN) 27 Pk24
belle (USA) (TX) 35 Pf29
bou (CDN) (NS) 23 Re22
bton (USA) (WA) 24 Oe22
cclenny (USA) (FL) 37 Qd30
cdiarmid (CDN) (ONT) 20 Qa21
cDonald (CDN) (MAN) 19 Pf20
cGregor (CDN) (MAN) 19 Pf21
cGregor (USA) (TX) 35 Pg30
chias (USA) (ME) 22 Rb23
ck (USA) (CO) 33 Pa26
ckenzie (CDN) (BC) 15 Od18
ckenzie Delta ☆ (CDN) (NWT) 11 Nh11
ckinac Bridge ☆ (USA) (MI) 28 Qc23
ckinaw City (USA) (MI) 28 Qc23
cklin (CDN) (SAS) 17 Pa19
cks Inn (USA) (ID) 25 Ok23
leod, Fort (CDN) (ALB) 17 Oj21
comb (USA) (IL) 27 Pk25
con (USA) (GA) 37 Qd29
on (USA) (MO) 28 Pj26
on (USA) (MS) 36 Qa29
on (USA) (OH) 29 Qd26
oun (CDN) (SAS) 18 Pd21
opès (CDN) (QUE) 22 Ra21
rorie (CDN) (SAS) 18 Pb20
wahoc (USA) (ME) 22 Ra23
awaska (CDN) (ONT) 29 Qf23
awaska (USA) (ME) 22 Ra22
dock (USA) (ND) 19 Pf22
eira Park (CDN) (BC) 16 Od21
era (MEX) (CHA) 39 Pa31
era (USA) (CA) 32 Oe27
eras del Carmen, Area Protegida ☆ (MEX) (COA) 39 Pd31
ll (USA) (OK) 35 Pg28
son (CDN) (SAS) 17 Pa20
son (USA) (FL) 37 Qd30
son (USA) (IN) 28 Qc26
son (USA) (KS) 35 Pg26
son (USA) (ME) 22 Ra23
son (USA) (NE) 27 Pg25
son (USA) (SD) 27 Pg24
son (USA) (VA) 29 Qf26
son (USA) (WI) 28 Qa24
son (USA) (WV) 37 Qe26
son Bird Refuge ☆ (USA) (MT) 25 Oj23
son Canyon Earthquake Area (1959) ☆ (USA) (MT) 25 Ok23
sonville (USA) (KY) 36 Qb27
sonville (USA) (LA) 36 Pk30
sonville (USA) (TX) 41 Ph30
as (USA) (OR) 24 Oe23
d (USA) (NE) 26 Pe25
uga (C) (LH) 43 Qe34
alena (USA) (NM) 33 Pb28
alena de Kino (MEX) (SON) 38 Ok30
e (USA) (MS) 36 Qa30
a (USA) (UT) 25 Oj25
olia (USA) (AR) 35 Pj29
olia (USA) (MS) 36 Pk30
Magog (CDN) (QUE) 30 Qj23
Magrath (CDN) (ALB) 17 Oj21
Magueyal, El (MEX) (COA) 39 Pd32
Mahnomen (USA) (MN) 19 Ph22
Mahtowa (USA) (MN) 19 Pj22
Maiden Rock (USA) (WI) 27 Pj23
Maidens (USA) (VA) 31 Qg27
Maidstone (CDN) (SAS) 17 Pa19
Main à Dieu (CDN) (NS) 23 Rf23
Main Brook (CDN) (NFL) 23 Rg20
Mainero, Villa (MEX) (TAM) 40 Pf33
Mainland (CDN) (NFL) 23 Rf21
Maisonnette (CDN) (NB) 22 Rc22
Maitland, Port (CDN) (NS) 22 Rb24
Majagua (C) (CA) 43 Qf35
Majestic (CDN) (ALB) 17 Ok20
Major (CDN) (SAS) 17 Pa20
Mākaha (USA) (HI) 44 Mf35
Makwa Lake Provincial Park ☆ (CDN) (SAS) 17 Pa18
Malachi (CDN) (ONT) 19 Ph21
Malad City (USA) (ID) 25 Oj24
Malaga (USA) (NM) 34 Pc29
Malahat (CDN) (BC) 16 Od21
Malakoff (USA) (TX) 35 Ph29
Malakwa (CDN) (BC) 16 Of20
Malbaie, La (CDN) (QUE) 22 Qk22
Malcolm (USA) (NE) 27 Pg25
Malden (USA) (MO) 36 Qa27
Maleb (CDN) (ALB) 17 Ok21
Malheur National Wildlife Refuge ☆ (USA) (OR) 24 Of24
Maljamar (USA) (NM) 34 Pd29
Mallorytown (CDN) (ONT) 29 Qh23
Malmo (USA) (MN) 27 Pj22
Malone (USA) (NY) 30 Qh23
Malott (USA) (WA) 16 Of21
Malta (USA) (MT) 18 Pb21
Malverick (USA) (TX) 34 Pe30
Malvern (USA) (AR) 35 Pj28
Malvern (USA) (IA) 27 Ph25
Malvern (USA) (TX) 35 Ph30
Ma-Me-O-Beach (CDN) (ALB) 17 Oj19
Mammoth (USA) (AZ) 33 Ok29
Mammoth Cave National Park ☆ (USA) (KY) 36 Qb27
Mammoth Hot Sprimgs (USA) (WY) 25 Ok23
Mamou (USA) (LA) 36 Pj30
Manaffey (USA) (PA) 29 Qf25
Manassas (USA) (VA) 29 Qg26
Manati (C) (CA) 43 Qf35
Mancelona (USA) (MI) 28 Qc23
Mancha, La (MEX) (COA) 39 Pd33
Manchester (USA) (CT) 30 Qj25
Manchester (USA) (GA) 36 Qc29
Manchester (USA) (IA) 27 Pk24
Manchester (USA) (KY) 37 Qd27
Manchester (USA) (NH) 22 Qk24
Manchester (USA) (OH) 29 Qd26
Manchester (USA) (TN) 36 Qb28
Manchester (USA) (VT) 30 Qj24
Mancos (USA) (CO) 33 Pa27
Mandan (USA) (ND) 18 Pe22
Mandarin (USA) (FL) 37 Qe30
Manderson (USA) (WY) 25 Pb23
Mandeville (USA) (LA) 36 Pk30
Maneadero (C) (MZ) 43 Qe34
Maneadero (MEX) (BCN) 32 Og30
Manes (USA) (MO) 35 Pj27
Mangas (USA) (NM) 33 Pa28
Mangham (USA) (LA) 36 Pk29
Manguito (C) (MZ) 43 Qe34
Mangum (USA) (OK) 35 Pf28
Manhattan (USA) (KS) 35 Pg26
Manicaragua (C) (VC) 43 Qf34
Manicouagan (CDN) (QUE) 22 Ra20
Manicouagan, Réservoir ☆ (CDN) (QUE) 22 Ra20
Manigotagan (CDN) (MAN) 19 Pg20
Manila (USA) (UT) 25 Pa25
Manistee (USA) (MI) 28 Qb23
Manistique (USA) (MI) 28 Qb23
Manitou (CDN) (MAN) 19 Pf21
Manitou Springs (USA) (CO) 34 Pc26
Manitouwadge (CDN) (ONT) 20 Qc21
Manitowoc (USA) (WI) 28 Qb23
Maniwaki (CDN) (QUE) 21 Qh22
Mankato (USA) (KS) 35 Pf26
Mankato (USA) (MN) 27 Ph23
Mankins (USA) (TX) 35 Pf29
Mankota (CDN) (SAS) 18 Pb21
Manley Hot Springs (USA) (AK) 10 Mk13
Manlius (USA) (NY) 29 Qh24
Manly (USA) (IA) 27 Pj24
Manning (CDN) (ALB) 15 Og17
Manning (USA) (IA) 27 Ph25
Manning (USA) (ND) 18 Pd22
Manning (USA) (SC) 37 Qe29
Manning Park (CDN) (BC) 16 Oe21
Manning Provincial Park ☆ (CDN) (BC) 16 Oe21
Mannville (CDN) (ALB) 17 Ok19
Manor (CDN) (SAS) 18 Pd21
Manouane (CDN) (QUE) 21 Qh22
Mansfield (USA) (AR) 35 Pj28
Mansfield (USA) (LA) 35 Ph29
Mansfield (USA) (MO) 35 Pj27
Mansfield (USA) (OH) 29 Qd25
Mansfield (USA) (PA) 29 Qg25
Mansfield (USA) (TX) 35 Pg29
Mansfield (USA) (WA) 16 Of22
Manson (CDN) (MAN) 18 Pe20
Manson (USA) (IA) 27 Ph24
Manson (USA) (WA) 16 Oe22
Manson Creek (CDN) (BC) 15 Oc18
Mansons Landing (CDN) (BC) 16 Oc20
Mansura (USA) (LA) 36 Pj30
Mantario (CDN) (SAS) 17 Pa20
Manteca (USA) (CA) 32 Oe27
Manteo (USA) (NC) 31 Qh28
Manton (USA) (MI) 28 Qc23
Mantua (C) (PR) 42 Qc34
Manuel Benavides (MEX) (CHA) 39 Pd31
Manvel (USA) (ND) 19 Pg21
Manville (USA) (WY) 26 Pc24
Many (USA) (LA) 35 Pj30
Manyberries (CDN) (ALB) 17 Ok21
Mapimí (MEX) (DGO) 39 Pd33
Maple Creek (CDN) (SAS) 17 Pa21
Mapleton (USA) (IA) 27 Ph24
Mapleton (USA) (OR) 24 Od23
Maple Valley (USA) (WA) 16 Od22
Mappsville (USA) (VA) 31 Qh27
Maquoketa (USA) (IA) 27 Pk24
Maramec (USA) (OK) 35 Pg27
Marana (USA) (AZ) 33 Ok29
Marathon (CDN) (ONT) 20 Qb21
Marathon (USA) (FL) 43 Qe33
Marathon (USA) (TX) 39 Pd30
Maravillas (MEX) (CHA) 39 Pc32
Marble (USA) (WA) 17 Og21
Marble Falls (USA) (TX) 40 Pf30
Marble Hill (USA) (MO) 36 Qa27
Marcell (USA) (MN) 19 Pj22
Marchand (CDN) (MAN) 19 Pg21
Marco (USA) (FL) 43 Qe33
Marcoux (USA) (MN) 19 Pg22
Marcus (USA) (IA) 27 Ph24
Marengo (CDN) (SAS) 17 Pa20
Marengo (USA) (IA) 27 Pj25
Marenisco (USA) (MI) 20 Qa22
Marfa (USA) (TX) 39 Pc30
Margaree Forks (CDN) (NS) 23 Re22
Margate (USA) (FL) 43 Qe32
Margie (CDN) (ALB) 17 Ok18
Margie (USA) (MN) 19 Pj21
Marguerite (CDN) (BC) 16 Od19
Marianna (USA) (AR) 36 Pk28
Marianna (USA) (FL) 36 Qc30
Mariapolis (CDN) (MAN) 19 Pf21
Maricopa (USA) (AZ) 33 Oj29
Maricopa (USA) (CA) 32 Of28
Mariel (C) (LH) 43 Qd34
Marienthal (CDN) (SAS) 18 Pd21
Marie-Reine (CDN) (ALB) 15 Og17
Marietta (USA) (GA) 36 Qc29
Marietta (USA) (OH) 29 Qe26
Marietta (USA) (OK) 35 Pg29
Marín (MEX) (NL) 40 Pe33
Marineland (USA) (FL) 37 Qe31
Marineland of Florida ☆ (USA) (FL) 37 Qe31
Marine Museum ☆ (USA) (ME) 22 Ra24
Marinette (USA) (WI) 28 Qb23
Maringouin (USA) (LA) 36 Pk30
Marion (USA) (AL) 36 Qb29
Marion (USA) (IA) 27 Pk24
Marion (USA) (IL) 36 Qa27
Marion (USA) (IN) 28 Qc25
Marion (USA) (KS) 35 Pg26
Marion (USA) (KY) 36 Qa27
Marion (USA) (KY) 37 Qe27
Marion (USA) (MT) 17 Oh21
Marion (USA) (OH) 29 Qd25
Marion (USA) (SC) 37 Qf28
Marion (USA) (VA) 37 Qe27
Mariposa (USA) (CA) 32 Of27
Marissa (USA) (IL) 28 Qa26
Marked Tree (USA) (AR) 36 Pk28
Markham (CDN) (ONT) 29 Qf24
Markham (USA) (MN) 19 Pj22
Marksville (USA) (LA) 36 Pj30
Marlborough (USA) (MA) 30 Qk24
Marlin (USA) (TX) 40 Pg30
Marlinton (USA) (WV) 29 Qe26
Marlow (USA) (OK) 35 Pg28
Marmarth (USA) (ND) 26 Pd22
Marmora (CDN) (ONT) 29 Qg23
Marple Hill (USA) (NC) 31 Qg28
Marque, La (USA) (TX) 41 Ph31
Marquette (USA) (IA) 27 Pk24
Marquette (USA) (MI) 20 Qb22
Marquette (USA) (NE) 26 Pf25
Marquez (USA) (NM) 34 Pb28
Marquez (USA) (TX) 40 Pg30
Marrero (USA) (LA) 36 Pk31
Mars, Le (USA) (IA) 27 Pg24
Marsden (CDN) (SAS) 17 Pa19
Marshall (CDN) (SAS) 17 Pa19
Marshall (USA) (AK) 10 Md15
Marshall (USA) (AR) 35 Pj28
Marshall (USA) (IL) 28 Qb26
Marshall (USA) (MI) 28 Qc24
Marshall (USA) (MN) 27 Ph23
Marshall (USA) (MO) 35 Pj26
Marshall (USA) (ND) 18 Pd22
Marshall (USA) (TX) 35 Ph29
Marshalltown (USA) (IA) 27 Pj24
Marshburg (USA) (PA) 29 Qf25
Marshfield (USA) (MO) 35 Pj27
Marshfield (USA) (WI) 27 Pk23
Marsh Harbour (BS) 43 Qg32
Mars Hill (USA) (ME) 22 Rb22
Marsoui (CDN) (QUE) 22 Rb21
Mart (USA) (TX) 35 Pg30
Martell (USA) (WI) 27 Pj23
Marten River (CDN) (ONT) 21 Qf22
Martin (USA) (SD) 26 Pe24
Martin (USA) (TN) 36 Qa27
Martinsburg (USA) (IA) 27 Pj25
Martinsburg (USA) (WV) 29 Qg26
Martinsville (USA) (IN) 28 Qb26
Martinsville (USA) (TX) 35 Ph30
Martinsville (USA) (VA) 37 Qf27
Marvel (USA) (CO) 33 Pa27
Marwayne (CDN) (ALB) 17 Ok19
Maryhill (USA) (WA) 24 Oe23
Maryneal (USA) (TX) 34 Pe29
Marystown (CDN) (NFL) 23 Rh22
Marysvale (USA) (UT) 33 Oj26
Marysville (CDN) (BC) 17 Oh21
Marysville (CDN) (ONT) 29 Qg23
Marysville (USA) (AR) 35 Pj29
Marysville (USA) (CA) 32 Oe26
Marysville (USA) (IN) 28 Qc26
Marysville (USA) (KS) 35 Pg26
Marysville (USA) (OH) 29 Qd25
Marysville (USA) (WA) 16 Od21
Maryville (USA) (MO) 27 Ph25
Maryville (USA) (TN) 37 Qd28
Masefield (CDN) (SAS) 18 Pb21
Mashkode (CDN) (ONT) 20 Qc22
Maskinongé (CDN) (QUE) 21 Qj22
Mason (USA) (MI) 28 Qc24
Mason (USA) (TX) 40 Pf30
Mason City (USA) (IA) 27 Pj24
Massachusetts, Fort ☆ (USA) (MS) 36 Qa30
Massadona (USA) (CO) 25 Pa25
Mass City (USA) (MI) 20 Qa22
Massena (USA) (NY) 29 Qh23
Massey (CDN) (ONT) 29 Qd22
Massillon (USA) (OH) 29 Qe25
Mastic Point (BS) 43 Qg33
Mastigouche, Réserve Faunique ☆ (CDN) (QUE) 21 Qj22
Matachewan (CDN) (ONT) 20 Qe22
Matachic (MEX) (CHA) 39 Pb31
Matador (USA) (TX) 34 Pe28
Matagami (CDN) (QUE) 21 Qg21
Matamoros (MEX) (COA) 39 Pd33
Matamoros (MEX) (TAM) 40 Pg33
Matane (CDN) (QUE) 22 Rb21
Matane, Réserve Faunique de ☆ (CDN) (QUE) 22 Rb21
Matanzas (C) 43 Qe34
Mata Ortiz (MEX) (CHA) 39 Pa30
Matapédia (CDN) (QUE) 22 Rb22
Matehuala (MEX) (SLP) 40 Pe34
Mather (CDN) (MAN) 19 Pf21
Matheson (CDN) (ONT) 20 Qe21
Mathis (USA) (TX) 40 Pg31
Mathiston (USA) (MS) 36 Qa29
Matlock (USA) (WA) 16 Od22
Matrimonio (MEX) (COA) 39 Pd32
Mattawa (CDN) (ONT) 29 Qf22
Mattawamkeag (USA) (ME) 22 Ra23
Mattawa River Provincial Park ☆ (CDN) (ONT) 29 Qf22
Mattice (CDN) (ONT) 20 Qd21
Mattoon (USA) (IL) 28 Qa26
Maumee (USA) (OH) 29 Qd25
Maunaloa (USA) (HI) 44 Mg35
Maurelle Islands Wilderness ☆ (USA) (AK) 14 Nh18
Mauston (USA) (WI) 27 Pk24
Mavillette (CDN) (NS) 22 Rb23
Max (USA) (ND) 18 Pe22
Maxbass (USA) (ND) 18 Pe21
Maxim (CDN) (SAS) 18 Pc21
Máximo Gómez (C) (MZ) 43 Qe34
Maxstone (CDN) (SAS) 18 Pc21
Maxville (USA) (FL) 37 Qd30
Maxwell (USA) (NE) 26 Pe25
May (USA) (TX) 35 Pf30
Mayaca, Port (USA) (FL) 43 Qe32
Mayagüez (USA) (PR) 42 Rb36
Maybell (USA) (CO) 25 Pa25
Mayerthorpe (CDN) (ALB) 17 Oh19
Mayfair (CDN) (SAS) 18 Pb19
Mayfield (CDN) (SAS) 18 Pe21
Mayfield (USA) (ID) 25 Oh24
Mayfield (USA) (KY) 36 Qa27
Mayflower (USA) (AR) 35 Pj28
Mayhill (USA) (NM) 34 Pc29
Maymont (CDN) (SAS) 18 Pb19
Maynooth (CDN) (ONT) 29 Qg23
Mayo (USA) (FL) 37 Qd30
Mayor, El (MEX) (BCN) 33 Oh29
Maysel (USA) (WV) 29 Qe26
Maysville (USA) (KY) 29 Qd26
Maysville (USA) (MO) 35 Ph26
Maysville (USA) (NC) 31 Qg28
Mayville (USA) (ND) 19 Pg22
Maywood (USA) (NE) 26 Pe25
Mazama (USA) (WA) 16 Oe21
Mazatán (MEX) (SON) 38 Ok31
Mazatlán (MEX) (SIN) 39 Pb34
Mazenod (CDN) (SAS) 18 Pb21
Mazocahui (MEX) (SON) 38 Ok31
McAlester (USA) (OK) 35 Ph28
McAllen (USA) (TX) 40 Pf32
McArthur (USA) (OH) 29 Qd26
McBride (CDN) (BC) 16 Oe19
McCallum (CDN) (NFL) 23 Rg22
McCamey (USA) (TX) 39 Pd30
McCammon (USA) (ID) 25 Oj24
McCarthy (USA) (AK) 13 Nd15
McClellanville (USA) (SC) 37 Qf29
McClusky (USA) (ND) 18 Pe22
McComb (USA) (MS) 36 Pk30
McConnellsburg (USA) (PA) 29 Qf26
McConnelsville (USA) (OH) 29 Qe26
McCook (USA) (NE) 34 Pe25
McCool Junction (USA) (NE) 27 Pg25
McCormick (USA) (SC) 37 Qd29
McCreary (CDN) (MAN) 19 Pf20
McCulloch (CDN) (BC) 16 Of21
McDavid (USA) (FL) 36 Qb30
McDermitt (USA) (NV) 24 Og25
McDonald (USA) (KS) 34 Pe26
McDowell (USA) (VA) 29 Qf26
McFaddin National Wildlife Refuge ☆ (USA) (TX) 41 Ph31
McGee (CDN) (SAS) 18 Pa20
McGehee (USA) (AR) 36 Pk29
McGill (USA) (NV) 33 Oh26
McGivney (CDN) (NB) 22 Rb22
McGrath (USA) (AK) 10 Mh14
McGrath (USA) (MN) 27 Pj22
McGregor (USA) (MN) 19 Pj22
McGregor (USA) (ND) 18 Pd21
McIntosh (USA) (SD) 26 Pe23
McKenzie (USA) (TN) 36 Qa27
McKenzie Bridge (USA) (OR) 24 Od23
McKinney (USA) (TX) 35 Pg29
McKittrick (USA) (CA) 32 Of28
McLain (USA) (MS) 36 Qa30
McLaughlin (USA) (SD) 26 Pe23
McLean (USA) (TX) 34 Pe28
McLeansboro (USA) (IL) 28 Qa26
McLean's Town (BS) 43 Qg32
McLennan (CDN) (ALB) 15 Og18
McLeod Lake (CDN) (BC) 15 Od18
McMasterville (CDN) (QUE) 30 Qj23
McMinnville (USA) (OR) 24 Od23
McMinnville (USA) (TN) 36 Qc28
McMorran (CDN) (SAS) 17 Pa20
McMurray (USA) (WA) 16 Od21
McNary (USA) (AZ) 33 Pa28
McNeal (USA) (AZ) 33 Pa30
McNeill (USA) (MS) 36 Qa30
McNeill, Port (CDN) (BC) 16 Ob20
McPherson (USA) (KS) 35 Pg26
McRae (CDN) (ALB) 17 Ok18
McRae (USA) (GA) 37 Qd29
McTaggart (CDN) (SAS) 18 Pc21
McTavish (CDN) (MAN) 19 Pg21
McVille (USA) (ND) 19 Pf22
Meacham (CDN) (SAS) 18 Pc19
Mead (CDN) (ONT) 20 Qd21
Meade (USA) (KS) 34 Pe27
Meadow (USA) (TX) 34 Pd29
Meadow Creek (CDN) (BC) 17 Og20
Meadow Creek (USA) (ID) 17 Og21
Meadow Lake (CDN) (SAS) 17 Pa18
Meadow Lake Provincial Park ☆ (CDN) (SAS) 17 Pa18
Meadowlands (USA) (MN) 19 Pj22
Meadows (CDN) (MAN) 19 Pg20
Meadville (USA) (PA) 29 Qe25
Meander River (CDN) (ALB) 15 Og16
Meath Park (CDN) (SAS) 18 Pc19
Mecca (USA) (CA) 32 Og29
Mechanicville (USA) (NY) 30 Qj24
Méchins, Les (CDN) (QUE) 22 Rb21
Medart (USA) (FL) 36 Qc30
Medford (USA) (OR) 24 Od24
Medford (USA) (WI) 27 Pk23
Mediapolis (USA) (IA) 27 Pk25
Medical Lake (USA) (WA) 17 Og22
Medicine Bow (USA) (WY) 26 Pb25
Medicine Hat (CDN) (ALB) 17 Ok20
Medicine Lake (USA) (MT) 18 Pc21
Medicine Lodge (USA) (KS) 35 Pf27
Medina (USA) (ND) 19 Pf22
Medina (USA) (NY) 29 Qf24
Medina (USA) (OH) 29 Qe25
Medley (CDN) (ALB) 17 Ok18
Medora (CDN) (MAN) 18 Pe21
Medora (USA) (ND) 18 Pd22
Medstead (CDN) (SAS) 17 Pa19
Meeker (USA) (CO) 25 Pb25
Meeteetse (USA) (WY) 25 Pa23
Mekoryuk (USA) (AK) 12 Mb15
Melbourne (USA) (AR) 36 Pk27
Melbourne (USA) (FL) 43 Qe31
Melchor Múzquiz (MEX) (COA) 39 Pd32
Meldrum Bay (CDN) (ONT) 29 Qd23
Melfort (CDN) (SAS) 18 Pc19
Melita (CDN) (MAN) 18 Pe21
Mellen (USA) (WI) 19 Pk22
Mellette (USA) (SD) 26 Pf23
Mellon (CDN) (BC) 16 Od21
Melrose (CDN) (NS) 22 Rd23
Melrose (USA) (MT) 25 Oj23
Melrose (USA) (NM) 34 Pd28
Melrose (USA) (WI) 27 Pk23
Melstone (USA) (MT) 18 Pb22
Melstrand (USA) (MI) 20 Qb22
Melville (CDN) (SAS) 18 Pd20
Melville (USA) (LA) 36 Pk30
Memphis (USA) (MO) 27 Pj25
Memphis (USA) (TN) 36 Pk28
Memphis (USA) (TX) 34 Pe28
Mena (USA) (AR) 35 Ph28
Menahga (USA) (MN) 19 Ph22
Mendenhall (USA) (MS) 36 Qa30
Méndez (MEX) (TAM) 40 Pf33
Mendham (CDN) (SAS) 17 Pa20
Mendon (USA) (IL) 27 Pk25
Mendota (USA) (CA) 32 Oe27
Mendota (USA) (IL) 28 Qa25
Menegers Dam (USA) (AZ) 33 Oj30
Menier, Port (CDN) (QUE) 22 Rc21
Menneval (CDN) (QUE) 22 Rb22
Menoken (USA) (ND) 18 Pe22
Menominee (USA) (MI) 28 Qb23
Menomonee Falls (USA) (WI) 28 Qa24
Menomonie (USA) (WI) 27 Pk23
Mentone (USA) (TX) 34 Pd30
Meoqui (MEX) (CHA) 39 Pc31
Meota (CDN) (SAS) 17 Pa19
Merced (USA) (CA) 32 Oe27
Mercedes (USA) (TX) 40 Pg32
Mercer (USA) (ND) 18 Pe22
Mercer (USA) (PA) 29 Qe25
Mercer (USA) (WI) 20 Pk22
Mercers Bottom (USA) (WV) 29 Qd26
Meredith (USA) (CO) 34 Pb26
Meredith (USA) (NH) 22 Qk24
Meresichic (MEX) (SON) 38 Ok30
Mérida (MEX) (YUC) 42 Qa35
Meriden (USA) (CT) 30 Qj25
Meridian (USA) (MS) 36 Qa29
Meridian (USA) (TX) 35 Pg30
Merkel (USA) (TX) 34 Pe29
Merlin (USA) (OR) 24 Od24
Merrill (USA) (OR) 24 Oe24
Merrill (USA) (WI) 28 Qa23
Merrillan (USA) (WI) 27 Pk23
Merrillville (USA) (CA) 24 Oe25
Merriman (USA) (NE) 26 Pe24
Merritt (CDN) (BC) 16 Oe20
Merritt Island (USA) (FL) 43 Qe31
Mertzon (USA) (TX) 40 Pe30
Merville (CDN) (BC) 16 Oc21
Mervin (CDN) (SAS) 17 Pa19
Mesa (USA) (AZ) 33 Ok29
Mesa (USA) (CO) 33 Pa26
Mesa (USA) (NM) 34 Pc29
Mesa (USA) (WA) 24 Of22
Mesa, La (USA) (CA) 32 Og29
Mesa, La (USA) (NM) 34 Pb29
Mesa de las Tablas (MEX) (COA) 40 Pe33
Mesa Verde National Park ☆ (USA) (CO) 33 Pa27
Mesick (USA) (MI) 28 Qc23
Mesilla (USA) (NM) 34 Pb29
Mesquite (USA) (TX) 35 Pg29
Metagama (CDN) (ONT) 20 Qe22
Metairie (USA) (LA) 36 Pk31
Metaline Falls (USA) (WA) 17 Og21
Metchosin (CDN) (BC) 16 Od21
Meteghan (CDN) (NS) 22 Rb23
Metiskow (CDN) (ALB) 17 Ok19
Metlakatla (USA) (AK) 14 Nk18
Metropolis (USA) (IL) 36 Qa27
Mexia (USA) (TX) 35 Pg30
Mexicali (MEX) (BCN) 33 Oh29
Mexican Hat (USA) (UT) 33 Pa27
Mexican Water (USA) (AZ) 33 Pa27
Mexico (USA) (ME) 22 Qk23
Mexico (USA) (MO) 28 Pk26
Mexico Beach (USA) (FL) 36 Qc31
Mexiko (USA) (NY) 29 Qg24
Meyersdale (USA) (PA) 29 Qf26
Meziadin Junction (CDN) (BC) 14 Oa17
Mezquital (MEX) (DGO) 39 Pc34
Mezquital (MEX) (TAM) 40 Pg33
Mezquite (MEX) (CHA) 34 Pb30
Mezquite, El (MEX) (ZAC) 39 Pd34
Miami (USA) (AZ) 33 Ok29

Miami (USA) (FL) 43 Qe33
Miami (USA) (OK) 35 Ph27
Miami (USA) (TX) 34 Pe28
Miami Beach (USA) (FL) 43 Qe33
Mica Creek (CDN) (BC) 16 Of19
Michel (CDN) (SAS) 17 Pa17
Michigan City (USA) (IN) 28 Qb25
Michigan City (USA) (ND) 19 Pf21
Microondas (MEX) (SON) 33 Oj30
Midale (CDN) (SAS) 18 Pd21
Mid America Air Museum ☆ (USA) (KS) 34 Pe27
Midas (USA) (NV) 24 Og25
Middlebro (CDN) (MAN) 19 Ph21
Middleburg (USA) (PA) 29 Qg25
Middlebury (USA) (VT) 30 Qj23
Middle Gate (USA) (NV) 32 Of26
Middle Lake (CDN) (SAS) 18 Pc19
Middle Sackville (CDN) (NS) 22 Rd23
Middlesboro (USA) (KY) 37 Qd27
Middleton (CDN) (NS) 22 Rc23
Middleton (USA) (TN) 36 Qa28
Middleton (USA) (WI) 27 Pk24
Middletown (USA) (CT) 30 Qj25
Middletown (USA) (IA) 27 Pk25
Middletown (USA) (NY) 30 Qh25
Middletown (USA) (OH) 28 Qc26
Middletown (USA) (PA) 29 Qg25
Midkiff (USA) (TX) 34 Pe30
Midland (CDN) (ONT) 29 Qf23
Midland (USA) (MI) 28 Qc24
Midland (USA) (SD) 26 Pe23
Midland (USA) (TX) 34 Pd30
Midlothian (USA) (TX) 35 Pg29
Midway (USA) (AL) 36 Qc29
Midway (USA) (WA) 16 Of21
Midwest (USA) (WY) 26 Pb24
Midwest City (USA) (OK) 35 Pg28
Mier (MEX) (TAM) 40 Pf32
Mier y Noriega (MEX) (NL) 40 Pe34
Miguasha Park ☆ (CDN) 22 Rb21
Miguel Auza (MEX) (ZAC) 39 Pd33
Milaca (USA) (MN) 27 Pj23
Milagro, El (MEX) (COA) 39 Pd31
Milam (USA) (TX) 35 Pj30
Milan (USA) (MI) 29 Qd24
Milan (USA) (MO) 27 Pj25
Milan (USA) (NM) 33 Pb28
Milan (USA) (TN) 36 Qa28
Milano (USA) (TX) 40 Pg30
Milbank (USA) (SD) 27 Pg23
Milbridge (USA) (ME) 22 Rb23
Milden (CDN) (SAS) 18 Pb20
Mildred (USA) (MT) 18 Pc22
Miles (USA) (TX) 34 Pe30
Miles (USA) (WA) 16 Of22
Miles City (USA) (FL) 43 Qe32
Miles City (USA) (MT) 26 Pc22
Milestone (CDN) (SAS) 18 Pc20
Milford (USA) (CA) 24 Oe25
Milford (USA) (DE) 31 Qh26
Milford (USA) (IA) 27 Ph24
Milford (USA) (MA) 30 Qk24
Milford (USA) (NE) 27 Pg25
Milford (USA) (NH) 30 Qk24
Milford (USA) (PA) 30 Qh25
Milford (USA) (UT) 33 Oj26
Milk River (CDN) (ALB) 17 Oj21
Millboro (USA) (VA) 29 Qf26
Millbrook (CDN) (ONT) 29 Qf23
Mill City (USA) (OR) 24 Od23
Milledgeville (USA) (GA) 37 Qd29
Millen (USA) (GA) 37 Qe29
Miller (USA) (NE) 26 Pf25
Miller (USA) (SD) 26 Pf23
Millerdale (CDN) (SAS) 17 Pa20
Millersburg (USA) (OH) 29 Qe25
Millersburg (USA) (PA) 29 Qg25
Millers Corners (USA) (PA) 29 Qf26
Millerton (CDN) (NB) 22 Rc22
Millertown (CDN) (NFL) 23 Rg21
Millington (USA) (TN) 36 Qa28
Millinocket (USA) (ME) 22 Ra23
Millston (USA) (WI) 27 Pk23
Milltown (CDN) (NFL) 23 Rh22
Milltown (USA) (IN) 28 Qb26
Mill Village (CDN) (NS) 22 Rc23
Millville (CDN) (NB) 22 Rb22
Millville (USA) (NJ) 31 Qh26
Millville (USA) (PA) 29 Qg25
Millwood (USA) (WA) 17 Og22
Milnesand (USA) (NM) 34 Pd29
Milo (USA) (ME) 22 Ra23
Milton (USA) (FL) 36 Qb30
Milton (USA) (IA) 27 Pj25
Milton (USA) (ND) 19 Pf21
Milton (USA) (PA) 29 Qg25
Milton-Freewater (USA) (OR) 24 Of23
Milwaukee (USA) (WI) 28 Qb24
Milwaukie (USA) (OR) 24 Od23
Mina (USA) (NV) 32 Of26
Minaki (CDN) (ONT) 19 Ph21
Minas (C) (CG) 43 Qg35
Minas de Barroterán (MEX) (COA) 40 Pe32
Minas de Hércules (MEX) (COA) 39 Pd32
Minas de Matahambre (C) (PR) 43 Qd34
Minatina Batoche National Historic Park ☆ (CDN) (SAS) 18 Pb19
Minburn (CDN) (ALB) 17 Ok19
Minden (CDN) (ONT) 29 Qf23
Minden (USA) (IA) 27 Ph25
Minden (USA) (LA) 35 Pj29
Minden (USA) (NE) 26 Pf25
Mine Centre (CDN) (ONT) 19 Pj21
Mineola (USA) (TX) 35 Ph29
Mineral (USA) (CA) 24 Oe25
Mineral Point (USA) (WI) 27 Pk24
Mineral Wells (USA) (TX) 35 Pf29
Minersville (USA) (UT) 33 Oj26
Minidoka (USA) (ID) 25 Oj24
Miniota (CDN) (MAN) 18 Pe20
Minneapolis (USA) (KS) 35 Pg26
Minneapolis (USA) (MN) 27 Pj23
Minnedosa (CDN) (MAN) 19 Pf20
Minneola (USA) (KS) 34 Pe27
Minnewaukan (USA) (ND) 19 Pf21
Minong (USA) (WI) 27 Pk22
Minot (USA) (ND) 18 Pe21
Mint Hill (USA) (NC) 37 Qe28
Minto (CDN) (MAN) 19 Pf21
Minto (CDN) (NB) 22 Rb22
Minto (CDN) (YT) 11 Ng14
Minto (USA) (ND) 19 Pg21
Minton (CDN) (SAS) 18 Pc21
Minturn (USA) (CO) 34 Pb26
Miquelon (CDN) (QUE) 21 Qg21
Miquihuana (MEX) (TAM) 40 Pf34
Miramichi, Nelson- (CDN) (NB) 22 Rc22
Miscou Centre (CDN) (NB) 22 Rc22
Misión, La (MEX) (BCN) 32 Og29
Misión de San Fernando (MEX) (BCN) 38 Oh30
Missanabie (CDN) (ONT) 20 Qc21
Missinaibi Provincial Park ☆ (CDN) (ONT) 20 Qd21
Missing (CDN) (SAS) 17 Pa19
Missinipe (CDN) (SAS) 18 Pc18
Mission (CDN) (BC) 16 Od21
Mission (USA) (SD) 26 Pe24
Misión de San Borja (MEX) (BCN) 38 Oj31
Mississauga (CDN) (ONT) 29 Qf24
Missoula (USA) (MT) 25 Oj22
Missouri City (USA) (TX) 41 Ph31
Missouri Valley (USA) (IA) 27 Ph25
Mist (USA) (OR) 24 Od22
Mistassini (CDN) (QUE) 21 Qj21
Mistassini (CDN) (QUE) 21 Qj20
Mistassini, Parc National ☆ (CDN) (QUE) 21 Qj20
Misty Fiords National Monument ☆ (USA) (AK) 14 Nk18
Mitchell (USA) (IN) 28 Qb26
Mitchell (USA) (NE) 26 Pd25
Mitchell (USA) (OR) 24 Oe23
Mitchell (USA) (SD) 26 Pf24
Mitliktavik (USA) (AK) 10 Me10
Mitsue (CDN) (ALB) 15 Oh18
Mittlintown (USA) (PA) 29 Qg25
Moab (USA) (UT) 33 Pa26
Moapa (USA) (NV) 33 Oh27
Moberly (USA) (MO) 28 Pj26
Moberly Lake (CDN) (BC) 15 Oe18
Mobile (USA) (AL) 36 Qa30
Mobridge (USA) (SD) 26 Pe23
Moccasin (USA) (MT) 17 Pa22
Mochis, Los (MEX) (SIN) 39 Pa33
Mocorito (MEX) (SIN) 39 Pb33
Moctezuma (MEX) (CHA) 39 Pb30
Moctezuma (MEX) (SON) 39 Pa31
Modena (USA) (UT) 33 Oj27
Modesto (USA) (CA) 32 Oe27
Moffit (USA) (ND) 26 Pe22
Mohall (USA) (ND) 18 Pe21
Mohawk (USA) (WI) 20 Qa22
Moisie (CDN) (QUE) 22 Rb20
Mojave (USA) (CA) 32 Of28
Mojave National Preserve ☆ (USA) (CA) 33 Oh28
Moline (USA) (IL) 27 Pk25
Moline (USA) (KS) 35 Pg27
Molino (USA) (FL) 36 Qb30
Molinos, Los (MEX) (SON) 33 Oj30
Molinos, Los (USA) (CA) 32 Od25
Moller, Port (USA) (AK) 12 Me18
Mona (USA) (UT) 33 Ok26
Monahans (USA) (TX) 34 Pd30
Monarch (CDN) (ALB) 17 Oj21
Monarch (USA) (MT) 17 Ok22
Monastery (CDN) (NS) 23 Re23
Monchy (CDN) (SAS) 18 Pb21
Moncks Corner (USA) (SC) 37 Qe29
Monclova (MEX) (COA) 40 Pe32
Moncton (CDN) (NB) 22 Rc22
Mondamin (USA) (IA) 27 Pg25
Mondovi (USA) (WI) 27 Pk23
Moneta (USA) (WY) 25 Pb24
Monett (USA) (MO) 35 Pj27
Monico (USA) (WI) 28 Qa23
Monida (USA) (MT) 25 Oj23
Monitor (CDN) (ALB) 17 Ok20
Monkman Provincial Park ☆ (CDN) (BC) 15 Oe18
Monmouth (USA) (IL) 27 Pk25
Monmouth (USA) (OR) 24 Od23
Monona (USA) (IA) 27 Pk24
Monroe (CDN) (NFL) 23 Rj21
Monroe (USA) (GA) 37 Qd29
Monroe (USA) (IA) 27 Pj25
Monroe (USA) (LA) 36 Pj29
Monroe (USA) (MI) 29 Qd25
Monroe (USA) (NC) 37 Qe28
Monroe (USA) (UT) 33 Oj26
Monroe (USA) (WA) 16 Oe22
Monroe (USA) (WI) 28 Qa24
Monroe City (USA) (MO) 28 Pk26
Monroeville (USA) (AL) 36 Qb30
Montague (CDN) (PEI) 22 Rd22
Montauk (USA) (NY) 30 Qk25
Montcerf (CDN) (QUE) 21 Qg22
Montebello (CDN) (QUE) 29 Qh23
Monte Creek (CDN) (BC) 16 Of20
Monte Cristo (USA) (WA) 16 Oe22
Montello (USA) (NV) 25 Oh25
Montello (USA) (WI) 28 Qa24
Monte Mariana (MEX) (ZAC) 39 Pd34
Montemorelos (MEX) (NL) 40 Pf33
Monterey (USA) (CA) 32 Oe27
Monterey (USA) (VA) 29 Qf26
Monterrey (MEX) (NL) 40 Pe33
Montevideo (USA) (MN) 27 Ph23
Monte Vista (USA) (CO) 34 Pb27
Montezuma (USA) (GA) 36 Qc29
Montezuma (USA) (IA) 27 Pj25
Montezuma Creek (USA) (UT) 33 Pa27
Montfort (USA) (WI) 27 Pk24
Montgomery (USA) (AL) 36 Qb29
Montgomery (USA) (LA) 35 Pj30
Montgomery (USA) (MN) 27 Pj23
Montgomery (USA) (WV) 29 Qe26
Montgomery City (USA) (MO) 28 Pk26
Monticello (USA) (AR) 36 Pk29
Monticello (USA) (FL) 37 Qd30
Monticello (USA) (GA) 37 Qd29
Monticello (USA) (IA) 27 Pk24
Monticello (USA) (KY) 36 Qc27
Monticello (USA) (MO) 27 Pk25
Monticello (USA) (MS) 36 Pk30
Monticello (USA) (NM) 34 Pb29
Monticello (USA) (NY) 30 Qh25
Monticello (USA) (UT) 33 Pa27
Monticello ☆ (USA) (VA) 29 Qf27
Mont-Laurier (CDN) (QUE) 21 Qh22
Montmagny (CDN) (QUE) 22 Qk22
Montmartre (CDN) (SAS) 18 Pc20
Montney (CDN) (BC) 15 Oe17
Montpelier (USA) (ID) 25 Ok24
Montpelier (USA) (ND) 19 Pf22
Montpelier (USA) (VA) 31 Qg27
Montpelier (USA) (VT) 30 Qj23
Montréal (CDN) (QUE) 29 Qh23
Montreal Lake (CDN) (SAS) 18 Pc18
Montreal River (CDN) (ONT) 20 Qc22
Montrose (CDN) (BC) 17 Og21
Montrose (USA) (AR) 36 Pk29
Montrose (USA) (CO) 33 Pb26
Montrose (USA) (IA) 27 Pk25
Montrose (USA) (PA) 29 Qh25
Mont Tremblant, Parc du ☆ (CDN) (QUE) 21 Qh22
Monument (USA) (NM) 34 Pd29
Monument Valley Navajo Tribal Park ☆ (USA) (AZ) 33 Ok27
Moody (USA) (TX) 40 Pg30
Moody, Port (CDN) (BC) 16 Od21
Moorcroft (USA) (WY) 26 Pc23
Moore (USA) (MT) 17 Pa22
Moore (USA) (TX) 40 Pf31
Moore Home State Memorial ☆ (USA) (IL) 28 Qa26
Moore Park (CDN) (MAN) 19 Pf20
Moores Creek National Battlefield ☆ (USA) (NC) 31 Qf28
Mooresville (USA) (NC) 37 Qe28
Moorhead (USA) (MN) 19 Pg22
Moose (USA) (WY) 25 Ok24
Moose Hill (CDN) (ONT) 20 Qa21
Moose Jaw (CDN) (SAS) 18 Pc20
Moose Lake (CDN) (MAN) 18 Pe19
Moose Lake (USA) (MN) 19 Pj22
Moose Mount Provincial Park ☆ (CDN) (SAS) 18 Pd21
Moose Pass (USA) (AK) 13 Na15
Moose River (CDN) (ONT) 20 Qe20
Moosomin (CDN) (SAS) 18 Pe20
Moosonee (CDN) (ONT) 20 Qe20
Mora (USA) (MN) 27 Pj23
Mora (USA) (NM) 34 Pc28
Mora, La (MEX) (COA) 39 Pd32
Moraine State Park ☆ (USA) (PA) 29 Qe25
Moran (USA) (KS) 35 Ph27
Moran (USA) (TX) 35 Pf29
Moran (USA) (WY) 25 Ok24
Moravia (USA) (IA) 27 Pj25
Moravia (USA) (NY) 29 Qg24
Morden (CDN) (MAN) 19 Pf21
Morecambe (CDN) (ALB) 17 Ok19
Morehead (USA) (KY) 29 Qd26
Morehead City (USA) (NC) 31 Qg28
Morell (CDN) (PEI) 22 Rd22
Morelos (MEX) (COA) 39 Pd31
Morelos (MEX) (COA) 40 Pe31
Morelos (MEX) (ZAC) 39 Pd34
Morenci (USA) (AZ) 33 Pa29
Morewood (CDN) (ONT) 29 Qh23
Morgan (USA) (TX) 35 Pg29
Morgan City (USA) (LA) 36 Pk31
Morganfield (USA) (KY) 36 Qb27
Morgan Hill (USA) (CA) 32 Oe27
Morgan Mill (USA) (TX) 35 Pf29
Morgan's Corner (USA) (NC) 31 Qg27
Morganton (USA) (NC) 37 Qe28
Morgantown (USA) (KY) 36 Qb27
Morgantown (USA) (WV) 29 Qf26
Moriarty (USA) (NM) 34 Pb28
Moricetown (CDN) (BC) 14 Ob18
Morinville (CDN) (ALB) 17 Oj19
Morita, La (MEX) (CHA) 39 Pc31
Morley (CDN) (ALB) 17 Oh20
Morning Star (USA) (MS) 36 Pk29
Moro (USA) (OR) 24 Oe23
Morón (C) (CA) 43 Qf34
Morrilton (USA) (AR) 35 Pj28
Morrin (CDN) (ALB) 17 Oj20
Morrión, El (MEX) (CHA) 39 Pc31
Morris (CDN) (MAN) 19 Pg21
Morris (USA) (IL) 28 Qa25
Morris (USA) (MN) 27 Ph23
Morris (USA) (NY) 29 Qh24
Morris (USA) (PA) 29 Qg25
Morrisburg (CDN) (ONT) 29 Qh23
Morriston (USA) (FL) 37 Qd31
Morristown (USA) (NY) 29 Qh23
Morristown (USA) (SD) 26 Pe23
Morristown (USA) (TN) 37 Qd27
Morrisville (USA) (NY) 29 Qh24
Morrisville (USA) (VT) 30 Qj23
Morro Bay (USA) (CA) 32 Oe28
Morson (CDN) (ONT) 19 Ph21
Morton (USA) (MN) 27 Ph23
Morton (USA) (MS) 36 Qa29
Morton (USA) (WA) 24 Od22
Morven (USA) (GA) 37 Qd30
Mosby (USA) (MT) 18 Pb22
Mosca (USA) (CO) 34 Pc27
Moscow (USA) (ID) 24 Og22
Moscow (USA) (KS) 34 Pe27
Moselle (USA) (MS) 36 Qa30
Mosers River (CDN) (NS) 22 Rd23
Moses Lake (USA) (WA) 24 Of22
Moses Point (USA) (AK) 10 Md13
Mosquero (USA) (NM) 34 Pd28
Mossbank (CDN) (SAS) 18 Pc21
Moss Point (USA) (MS) 36 Qa30
Motley (USA) (MN) 27 Ph22
Mott (USA) (ND) 26 Pd22
Motul (MEX) (YUC) 42 Qa35
Moulton (USA) (IA) 27 Pj25
Moulton Neel (USA) (AL) 36 Qb28
Moultrie (USA) (GA) 37 Qd30
Mound City Group National Monument ☆ (USA) (OH) 29 Qd26
Moundsville (USA) (WV) 29 Qe26
Mountain (USA) (WI) 28 Qa23
Mountainair (USA) (NM) 34 Pb28
Mountain City (USA) (NV) 25 Oh25
Mountain City (USA) (TN) 37 Qe27
Mountain Grove (USA) (MO) 35 Pj27
Mountain Home (USA) (AR) 35 Pj27
Mountain Home (USA) (ID) 25 Oh24
Mountain Point (USA) (AK) 14 Nk18
Mountainside (CDN) (MAN) 18 Pe21
Mountain Springs (USA) (NV) 33 Oh27
Mountain View (CDN) (ALB) 17 Oj21
Mountain View (USA) (AK) 14 Nk17
Mountain View (USA) (AR) 36 Pj28
Mountain View (USA) (AZ) 33 Ok30
Mountain Village (USA) (AK) 10 Md14
Mount Airy (USA) (VA) 37 Qe27
Mount Ayr (USA) (IA) 27 Ph25
Mount Carleton Provincial Park ☆ (CDN) (NB) 22 Rb22
Mount Carmel (USA) (IL) 28 Qb26
Mount Carmel (USA) (ND) 19 Pf21
Mount Carmel Junction (USA) (UT) 33 Oj27
Mount Carrol (USA) (IL) 28 Qa24
Mount Charleston (USA) (NV) 33 Oh27
Mount Clemens (USA) (MI) 29 Qd24
Mount Dora (USA) (FL) 43 Qe31
Mount Edziza Provincial Park ☆ (CDN) (BC) 14 Nk17
Mount Enterprise (USA) (TX) 35 Ph30
Mount Forest (CDN) (ONT) 29 Qe24
Mount Hebron (USA) (CA) 24 Od25
Mount Holly Springs (USA) (PA) 29 Qg25
Mount Ida (USA) (AR) 35 Pj28
Mount Le Moray (CDN) (BC) 15 Od18
Mount Pleasant (USA) (IA) 27 Pk25
Mount Pleasant (USA) (MI) 28 Qc24
Mount Pleasant (USA) (TX) 35 Ph29
Mount Pleasant (USA) (UT) 33 Ok26
Mount Pocono (USA) (PA) 29 Qh25
Mount Rainier National Park ☆ (USA) (WA) 24 Od22
Mount Revelstoke National Park ☆ (CDN) (BC) 16 Of20
Mount Robson Provincial Park ☆ (CDN) (BC) 16 Of19
Mount Rogers National Recreation Area ☆ (USA) (VA) 37 Qe27
Mount Shasta (USA) (CA) 24 Od25
Mount Spokane State Park ☆ (USA) (WA) 17 Og22
Mount Sterling (USA) (IL) 28 Pk26
Mount Sterling (USA) (OH) 29 Qd26
Mount Sterling (USA) (WI) 27 Pk24
Mount Trumbull (USA) (AZ) 33 Oj27
Mount Union (USA) (PA) 29 Qg25
Mount Vernon (USA) (GA) 37 Qd29
Mount Vernon (USA) (IA) 27 Pk25
Mount Vernon (USA) (IL) 28 Qa26
Mount Vernon (USA) (IN) 36 Qb27
Mount Vernon (USA) (OH) 29 Qd25
Mount Vernon (USA) (OR) 24 Of23
Mount Vernon (USA) (WA) 16 Od21
Mount Zion (USA) (MD) 29 Qg26
Moville (USA) (IA) 27 Pg24
Moweaqua (USA) (IL) 28 Qa26
Moyie (CDN) (BC) 17 Oh21
Moyie Springs (USA) (ID) 17 Og21
Muddy Gap (USA) (WY) 25 Pb24
Mujeres, Isla ☆ (MEX) (QR) 42 Qb35
Mukilteo (USA) (WA) 16 Od22
Mule Creek Junction (USA) (WY) 26 Pc24
Mulegé (MEX) (BCS) 38 Ok32
Muleshoe (USA) (TX) 34 Pd28
Mullan (USA) (MT) 17 Oh22
Mullen (USA) (NE) 26 Pe24
Mullens (USA) (WV) 37 Qe27
Mullins (USA) (SC) 37 Qf28
Muncho Lake (CDN) (BC) 15 Oc16
Muncho Lake Provincial Park ☆ (CDN) (BC) 15 Oc16
Muncie (USA) (IN) 28 Qc25
Mundare (CDN) (ALB) 17 Oj19
Munday (USA) (TX) 34 Pe29
Mundelein (USA) (IL) 28 Qb24
Munfordville (USA) (KY) 36 Qc27
Munising (USA) (MI) 20 Qb22
Munson (USA) (FL) 36 Qb30
Murdale (CDN) (BC) 15 Oe17
Murdo (USA) (SD) 26 Pe24
Murdochville (CDN) (QUE) 22 Rc21
Murdock (USA) (NE) 27 Pg25
Murfreesboro (USA) (AR) 35 Pj28
Murfreesboro (USA) (NC) 31 Qg27
Murfreesboro (USA) (TN) 36 Qb28
Muriel Lake (CDN) (ALB) 17 Ok18
Murillo (CDN) (ONT) 20 Qa21
Murphy (USA) (NC) 36 Qc28
Murphysboro (USA) (IL) 36 Qa27
Murray (USA) (KY) 36 Qa27
Murray (USA) (UT) 25 Ok25
Murray Harbour (CDN) (NS) 22 Rd22
Muscatine (USA) (IA) 27 Pk25
Muscoda (USA) (WI) 27 Pk24
Musgrave (CDN) (BC) 16 Od21
Musidora (CDN) (ALB) 17 Ok19
Muskegon (USA) (MI) 28 Qb24
Musket River (CDN) (ALB) 16 Of19
Muskogee (USA) (OK) 35 Ph28
Muskwa (CDN) (BC) 15 Od16
Musquodoboit (CDN) (NS) 22 Rd23
Musselshell (USA) (MT) 18 Pa22
Mutton Bay (CDN) (QUE) 23 Rf20
Myerstown (USA) (PA) 29 Qg25
Mylo (USA) (ND) 19 Pf21
Myrnam (CDN) (ALB) 17 Ok19
Myrtle (CDN) (ONT) 29 Qf23
Myrtle Beach (USA) (SC) 37 Qf29
Myrtle Grove (USA) (LA) 36 Qa31
Myrtle Point (USA) (OR) 24 Oc24
Mystery Caves ☆ (USA) (MN) 27 Pj24
Myton (USA) (UT) 25 Ok25

N

Na'alehu (USA) (HI) 44 Mh36
Nackawic (CDN) (NB) 22 Rb22
Naco (CDN) (ALB) 17 Ok20
Naco (MEX) (SON) 33 Pa30
Nacogdoches (USA) (TX) 35 Ph30
Nacori Chico (MEX) (SON) 39 Pa31
Nacozari de García (MEX) (SON) 39 Pa30
Nadina River (CDN) (BC) 16 Ob19
Nageezi (USA) (NM) 33 Pb27
Nahanni Butte (CDN) (NWT) 15 Od15
Nahanni National Park ☆ (CDN) (NWT) 15 Oc15
Nahlin (CDN) (BC) 14 Nk16
Nahmint (CDN) (BC) 16 Oc21
Nahunta (USA) (GA) 37 Qe30
Nahwitti (CDN) (BC) 16 Oa20
Naica (MEX) (CHA) 39 Pc32
Naicam (CDN) (SAS) 18 Pc19
Nakina (CDN) (ONT) 20 Qb20
Naknek (USA) (AK) 12 Mg16
Nakusp (CDN) (BC) 17 Og20
Namiquipa (MEX) (CHA) 39 Pb31
Nampa (CDN) (ALB) 15 Og17
Nampa (USA) (ID) 24 Og24
Namu (CDN) (BC) 16 Ob20
Namur (CDN) (QUE) 29 Qh23
Nanafalia (USA) (AL) 36 Qa29
Nanaimo (CDN) (BC) 16 Od21
Nanoose Bay (CDN) (BC) 16 Oc21
Nanton (CDN) (ALB) 17 Oj20
Nantucket (USA) (MA) 30 Qk25
Napa (USA) (CA) 32 Od26
Napadogan (CDN) (NB) 22 Rb2
Napaiskak (USA) (AK) 12 Me15
Napanee (CDN) (ONT) 29 Qg2
Napinka (CDN) (MAN) 18 Pe2
Naples (USA) (FL) 43 Qe3
Naples (USA) (ID) 17 Og2
Naples (USA) (NY) 29 Qg2
Naples (USA) (TX) 35 Ph2
Napoleon (USA) (ND) 26 Pf2
Napoleon (USA) (OH) 28 Qc2
Napoleonville (USA) (LA) 36 Pk3
Naramata (CDN) (BC) 16 Of2
Naranjo (MEX) (SIN) 39 Pa3
Nara Visa (USA) (NM) 34 Pd28
Naschitti (USA) (NM) 33 Pa2
Nash Harbor (USA) (AK) 12 Mb1
Nashua (USA) (IA) 27 Pj2
Nashua (USA) (MT) 18 Pb2
Nashua (USA) (NH) 22 Qk2
Nashville (USA) (IL) 28 Qa2
Nashville (USA) (NC) 31 Qg2
Nashville (USA) (TN) 36 Qb2
Nashwaak (CDN) (NB) 22 Rb2
Nashwaak Bridge (CDN) (NB) 22 Rb2
Nashwauk (USA) (MN) 19 Pj2
Nassau (BS) 43 Qg3
Nass Camp (CDN) (BC) 14 Oa
Natal (CDN) (BC) 17 Oh2
Natalia (USA) (TX) 40 Pf3
Natashquan (CDN) (QUE) 23 Re2
Natchez (USA) (MS) 36 Pk3
Natchitoches (USA) (LA) 35 Pj
Nathrop (USA) (CO) 34 Pb
Nation (USA) (AK) 11 Ne
Natural Bridge ☆ (USA) (AL) 36 Qb
Natural Bridge ☆ (USA) (FL) 36 Qc
Natural Bridges National Monument ☆ (USA) (UT) 33 Ok
Naturita (USA) (CO) 33 Pa
Nava (MEX) (COA) 40 Pe
Navajo City (USA) (NM) 33 Pb
Navarre (USA) (FL) 36 Qb
Navasota (USA) (TX) 40 Pg
Navojoa (MEX) (SON) 39 Pa
Navolato (MEX) (SIN) 39 Pb
Nazko (CDN) (BC) 16 Od
Neah Bay (USA) (WA) 16 Oc
Nebraska City (USA) (NE) 27 Ph
Necedah (USA) (WI) 27 Pk
Neche (USA) (ND) 19 Pg
Neches (USA) (TX) 35 Ph
Nederland (USA) (CO) 34 Pc
Nederland (USA) (TX) 41 P
Neeb (CDN) (SAS) 17 Pb
Needles (CDN) (BC) 16 O
Needles (USA) (CA) 33 Oh
Neelin (CDN) (MAN) 19 P
Neenah (USA) (WI) 28 Qa
Neepawa (CDN) (MAN) 19 P
Negaunee (USA) (MI) 20 Qb
Neguac (CDN) (NB) 22 R
Nehalem (USA) (OR) 24 Oc
Neihart (USA) (MT) 17 Ok
Neilburg (CDN) (SAS) 17 P
Neillsville (USA) (WI) 27 P
Neilton (USA) (WA) 16 O
Neligh (USA) (NE) 26 P
Nelma (USA) (WI) 28 Q
Nelson (CDN) (BC) 17 O
Nelson (USA) (NE) 35 P
Nelson (USA) (WI) 27 P
Nelson House (CDN) (MAN) 19 P
Nelson-Miramichi (CDN) (NB) 22 R
Nelway (CDN) (BC) 17 O
Nemaiah Valley (CDN) (BC) 16 O
Nenana (USA) (AK) 11 N
Neodesha (USA) (KS) 35 P
Neola (USA) (UT) 25 O
Neosho (USA) (MO) 35 P
Nephi (USA) (UT) 33 O
Neptune Beach (USA) (FL) 37 Q
Nesbitt (CDN) (MAN) 19 P
Nespelem (USA) (WA) 16 O
Ness City (USA) (KS) 35 P
Netcong (USA) (NJ) 30 Q
Netherhill (CDN) (SAS) 17 P
Nett Lake (USA) (MN) 19
Nevada (USA) (MO) 35 P
Neville (CDN) (SAS) 18 P
Neville, Port (CDN) (BC) 16 O
New Aiyansh (CDN) (BC) 14 O
New Albany (USA) (IN) 28 Q
New Albany (USA) (MS) 36 Q
New Albin (USA) (IA) 27 P
Newark (USA) (DE) 29 Q
Newark (USA) (NJ) 30 Q
Newark (USA) (NY) 29 Q
Newark (USA) (OH) 29 Q
New Athens (USA) (IL) 28
New Augusta (USA) (MS) 36
Newaygo (USA) (MI) 28
New Bedford (USA) (MA) 30
New Berchtal (CDN) (MAN) 19
Newberg (USA) (OR) 24
New Berlin (USA) (NY) 29
New Bern (USA) (NC) 31
Newbern (USA) (TN) 36
Newberry (USA) (FL) 37
Newberry (USA) (MI) 28
Newberry (USA) (SC) 37
Newberry National Volcanic Monument ☆ (USA) 24
New Boston (USA) (IL) 27
New Boston (USA) (MO) 28
New Boston (USA) (TX) 35
New Bothwell (CDN) (MAN) 19
New Braunfels (USA) (TX) 40
New Brigden (CDN) (ALB) 17

New Britain USA (CT) 30 Qj25
Newbrook CDN (ALB) 17 Oj18
New Buffalo USA (MI) 28 Qb25
Newburgh USA (NY) 30 Qh25
Newburyport USA (MA) 22 Qk24
New Canaan CDN (NB) 22 Rc22
Newcastle CDN (NB) 22 Rc22
Newcastle CDN (ONT) 29 Qf24
New Castle USA (IN) 28 Qc26
New Castle USA (PA) 29 Qe25
Newcastle USA (WY) 26 Pc24
New Cleeves CDN (SAS) 17 Pa19
New Cumberland USA (PA) 29 Qg25
Newdale CDN (MAN) 18 Pe20
New Dayton CDN (ALB) 17 Oj21
New Denver CDN (BC) 17 Og21
Newell USA (SD) 26 Pd23
Newellton USA (LA) 36 Pk29
New England USA (ND) 26 Pd22
Newfolden USA (MN) 19 Pg21
Newgate CDN (BC) 17 Oh21
New Germany CDN (NS) 22 Rc23
New Glasgow CDN (NS) 22 Rd23
Newhalem USA (WA) 16 Oe21
Newhalen USA (AK) 12 Mh16
New Hamilton USA (AK) 10 Md14
New Hampton USA (IA) 27 Pj24
New Harbor USA (ME) 22 Ra24
New Harmony USA (IN) 28 Qb26
New Haven USA (CT) 30 Qj25
New Hazelton CDN (BC) 14 Ob18
New Iberia USA (LA) 36 Pk31
Newkirk USA (NM) 34 Pc28
New Knockhock USA (AK) 10 Mc14
New Leipzig USA (ND) 26 Pe22
New Lexington USA (OH) 29 Qd26
New Lisbon USA (WI) 27 Pk24
New Liskeard CDN (ONT) 21 Qf22
New London USA (CT) 30 Qj25
New London USA (IA) 27 Pk25
New London USA (MO) 28 Pk26
New London USA (WI) 28 Qa23
Newman USA (NM) 34 Pb30
Newmarket CDN (ONT) 29 Qf23
New Market USA (VA) 29 Qf26
New Martinsville USA (WV) 29 Qe26
New Meadows USA (ID) 24 Og23
New Milford USA (CT) 30 Qj25
New Milford USA (PA) 29 Qh25
Newnan USA (GA) 36 Qc29
New Orleans USA (LA) 36 Pk31
New Osnaburgh CDN (ONT) 19 Pk20
New Pekin USA (IN) 28 Qb26
New Philadelphia USA (OH) 29 Qe25
Newport CDN (NS) 22 Rc23
Newport USA (AR) 36 Pk28
Newport USA (ME) 22 Ra23
Newport USA (OH) 28 Qc25
Newport USA (OR) 24 Oc23
Newport USA (RI) 30 Qk25
Newport USA (TN) 37 Qd28
Newport USA (VT) 30 Qj23
Newport USA (WA) 17 Og21
Newport News USA (VA) 31 Qg27
New Port Richey USA (FL) 43 Qd31
New Prague USA (MN) 27 Pj23
New Raymer USA (CO) 26 Pd25
New Richland USA (MN) 27 Pj24
New Richmond CDN (QUE) 22 Rc21
New Richmond USA (WI) 27 Pj23
New Ringold USA (OK) 35 Ph28
New Roads USA (LA) 36 Pk30
lew Rochelle USA (NY) 30 Qj25
lew Rockford USA (ND) 19 Pf22
lewry USA (ME) 22 Qk23
lew Salem USA (ND) 18 Pe22
ew Sharon USA (IA) 27 Pj25
ew Smyrna Beach USA (FL) 37 Qe31
ew Stuyahok USA (AK) 12 Mg16
ew Summerfield USA (TX) 35 Ph30
ewton USA (IA) 27 Pj25
ewton USA (IL) 28 Qa26
ewton USA (KS) 35 Pg26
ewton USA (MS) 36 Qa29
ewton USA (NC) 37 Qe28
ewton Grove USA (NC) 31 Qf28
ewton Mills CDN (NS) 22 Rd23
ew Town USA (ND) 18 Pd22
ew Ulm USA (MN) 27 Ph23
ew Waterford CDN (NS) 23 Re22
ew Westminster CDN (BC) 16 Od21
ew York USA (NY) 30 Qj25
agara USA (ND) 19 Pg22
agara Falls ☆ CDN (ONT) 29 Qf24
agara Falls USA (NY) 29 Qf24
agara on the Lake CDN (ONT) 29 Qf24
ceville USA (FL) 36 Qb30
cholasville USA (KY) 36 Qc27
chols Town BS 43 Qg33
ckel Center CDN (ONT) 20 Qe22
ckerson USA (MN) 19 Pj22
cktown USA (PA) 29 Qf25
cman CDN (QUE) 22 Rb20
colet CDN (QUE) 21 Qj22
tau CDN (NB) 22 Rb22
eves, Las MEX (DGO) 39 Pc32
ghtmote USA (AK) 12 Mc15
and USA (CA) 33 Oh29
es USA (MI) 28 Qb25
nrod USA (MN) 19 Ph22
e Mile Falls USA (WA) 17 Og22
ette CDN (MAN) 19 Pf21
nety Six National Historic Site ☆ USA (SC) 37 Qd28
ga CDN (MAN) 19 Pf21
ilchik USA (AK) 13 Mk15
brara USA (NE) 26 Pf24
awin CDN (SAS) 18 Pd19
awin Provincial Park ☆ CDN (SAS) 18 Pc19
igon CDN (ONT) 20 Qa21
ton USA (CA) 33 Oh28
na CDN (QUE) 21 Qk21
nat CDN (BC) 16 Oc21
o USA (WV) 29 Qe26
erville CDN (MAN) 19 Pg21
on USA (NV) 32 Of26
atak USA (AK) 10 Md12
atak National Preserve ☆ USA (AK) 10 Mf11
oleford CDN (ALB) 17 Oj21

Noel CDN (NS) 22 Rd23
Nogales MEX (CHA) 33 Pa30
Nogales MEX (SON) 33 Ok30
Nogales USA (AZ) 33 Ok30
Nogamut USA (AK) 12 Mg15
Nojack CDN (ALB) 17 Oh19
Nokomis CDN (SAS) 18 Pc20
Nolalu CDN (ONT) 20 Qa21
Nombre de Dios MEX (DGO) 39 Pc34
Nome USA (AK) 10 Mc13
Nona, La MEX (SIN) 39 Pb34
Nondalton USA (AK) 12 Mh15
Nonoava MEX (CHA) 39 Pb32
Noonan USA (ND) 18 Pd21
Noonday USA (TX) 35 Ph29
Noorvik USA (AK) 10 Me12
Nopiming Provincial Park ☆ CDN (MAN) 19 Ph20
Nopoló MEX (BCS) 38 Ok33
Nora Springs USA (IA) 27 Pj24
Norcatur USA (KS) 34 Pe26
Nordegg CDN (ALB) 17 Og19
Nordman USA (ID) 17 Og21
Norembega CDN (ONT) 20 Qe21
Norfolk USA (NE) 27 Pg24
Norfolk USA (VA) 31 Qg27
Norias MEX (ZAC) 39 Pd33
Norias, Las MEX (COA) 39 Pd31
Norland CDN (ONT) 29 Qf23
Norlina USA (NC) 31 Qf27
Normal USA (IL) 28 Qa25
Norman USA (OK) 35 Pg28
Normandeau CDN (ALB) 17 Ok18
Normandin CDN (QUE) 21 Qj21
Normandy USA (TX) 40 Pe31
Normétal CDN (QUE) 21 Qf21
Norquay CDN (SAS) 18 Pd20
Norris USA (MT) 25 Ok23
Norris USA (WY) 25 Ok23
Norris Point CDN (NFL) 23 Rg21
Norristown USA (PA) 30 Qh25
North USA (SC) 37 Qe29
North Adams USA (MA) 30 Qj24
Northampton USA (MA) 30 Qj24
North Augusta CDN (ONT) 29 Qh23
North Augusta USA (SC) 37 Qe29
North Battleford CDN (SAS) 17 Pa19
North Bay CDN (ONT) 29 Qf22
North Bend USA (NE) 27 Pg25
North Bend USA (OR) 24 Oc24
North Bend USA (WA) 16 Oe22
North Berwick USA (ME) 22 Qk24
North Branch USA (MN) 27 Pj23
North Bridge CDN (ONT) 19 Ph21
North Cascades National Park ☆ USA (WA) 16 Oe21
North Charleston USA (SC) 37 Qe29
North Cowden USA (TX) 34 Pd29
North Cowichan CDN (BC) 16 Od21
North East USA (PA) 29 Qf24
North East Carry USA (ME) 22 Ra23
Northern Yukon National Park ☆ CDN (NWT) 11 Nf11
Northfield USA (MN) 27 Pj23
Northgate CDN (SAS) 18 Pd21
North Head CDN (NB) 22 Rb23
Northhome USA (MN) 19 Ph22
North Komelik USA (AZ) 33 Oj29
North Lake CDN (NB) 22 Rb23
North Liberty USA (IA) 27 Pk25
North Limington USA (ME) 22 Qk24
North Little Rock USA (AR) 35 Pj28
North Pine CDN (BC) 15 Oe17
North Platte USA (NE) 26 Pe25
Northport USA (MI) 28 Qc23
Northport USA (WA) 17 Og21
North Portal CDN (SAS) 18 Pd21
North Powder USA (OR) 24 Og23
North Rim USA (AZ) 33 Oj27
North Saanich CDN (BC) 16 Od21
North Sandwich USA (NH) 22 Qk24
North Star CDN (ALB) 15 Og17
North Stratford USA (NH) 22 Qk23
North Sydney CDN (NS) 23 Re22
North Tonawanda USA (NY) 29 Qf24
North Vancouver CDN (BC) 16 Od21
North Waterford USA (ME) 22 Qk23
Northwest Angle Provincial Forest ☆ CDN (MAN) 19 Ph21
Northwest Bay CDN (ONT) 19 Pj21
North Wilkesboro USA (NC) 37 Qe27
Northwood USA (IA) 27 Pj24
Northwood USA (ND) 19 Pg22
North Woodstock USA (NH) 22 Qk23
Norton USA (KS) 35 Pf26
Norton USA (VA) 37 Qd27
Norton USA (VT) 22 Qk23
Norton Shores USA (MI) 28 Qb24
Nortonville USA (KY) 36 Qb27
Nortonville USA (ND) 26 Pf22
Norwalk USA (CA) 32 Of29
Norwalk USA (CT) 30 Qj25
Norwalk USA (IA) 27 Pj25
Norwalk USA (OH) 29 Qd25
Norway House CDN (MAN) 19 Pg19
Norwich USA (CT) 30 Qj25
Norwich USA (NY) 29 Qh24
Norwood CDN (ONT) 29 Qg23
Norwood USA (CO) 33 Pa26
Norwood USA (LA) 36 Pk30
Norwood USA (MN) 27 Pj23
Notre-Dame-de-Lorette CDN (QUE) 21 Qj21
Notre-Dame-du-Lac CDN (QUE) 22 Ra22
Notre-Dame-du-Laus CDN (QUE) 29 Qh22
Notre-Dame-du-Nord CDN (QUE) 21 Qf22
Bégin CDN (QUE) 21 Qk21
Notre Dame Junction CDN (NFL) 23 Rh21
Notrees USA (TX) 34 Pd30
Nouvelle CDN (QUE) 22 Rb21
Novato USA (CA) 32 Od26
Nowitna National Wildlife Refuge ☆ USA (AK) 10 Mj13
Noxon USA (MT) 17 Oh22
Noxubee National Wildlife Refuge ☆ USA (MS) 36 Qa29
Nuangola USA (PA) 29 Qh25
Nubieber USA (CA) 24 Oe25
Nucla USA (CO) 33 Pa26
Nueva Ciudad Guerrero MEX (TAM) 40 Pf32
Nueva Gerona C (JU) 43 Qd35
Nueva Rosita MEX (COA) 40 Pe32

Nuevitas C (CG) 43 Qg35
Nuevo Casas Grandes MEX (CHA) 39 Pb30
Nuevo Laredo MEX (TAM) 40 Pf32
Nuevo Padilla MEX (TAM) 40 Pf33
Nugents Corner USA (WA) 16 Od21
Nuiqsut USA (AK) 10 Mk10
Nulato USA (AK) 10 Mf13
Nunda USA (NY) 29 Qg24
Nunn USA (CO) 26 Pc25
Nuri MEX (SON) 39 Pa31
Nutrioso USA (AZ) 33 Pa29
Nyssa USA (OR) 24 Og24

O

Oak Bluff CDN (MAN) 19 Pg21
Oakburn CDN (MAN) 18 Pe20
Oak City USA (NC) 31 Qg28
Oak Creek USA (CO) 25 Pb25
Oakdale USA (CA) 32 Oe27
Oakdale USA (LA) 36 Pj30
Oakes USA (ND) 26 Pf22
Oak Grove USA (LA) 36 Pk29
Oak Harbor USA (WA) 16 Od21
Oak Hill USA (FL) 43 Qe31
Oak Hill USA (WV) 37 Qe27
Oakhurst USA (CA) 32 Of27
Oak Lake CDN (MAN) 18 Pe21
Oakland CDN (MAN) 19 Pf20
Oakland USA (CA) 32 Od27
Oakland USA (IA) 27 Ph25
Oakland USA (MD) 29 Qf26
Oakland USA (MS) 36 Qa28
Oakland USA (NE) 27 Pg25
Oakland City USA (IN) 28 Qb26
Oak Lawn USA (IL) 28 Qb25
Oakley USA (ID) 25 Oj24
Oakley USA (KS) 34 Pe26
Oak Point CDN (MAN) 19 Pg20
Oak Ridge USA (LA) 36 Pk29
Oakridge USA (OR) 24 Od24
Oak Ridge USA (TN) 36 Qc27
Oak Ridge USA (TX) 41 Ph30
Oak River CDN (MAN) 18 Pe20
Oakview CDN (MAN) 19 Pf20
Oakville CDN (MAN) 19 Pf21
Oakwood USA (OK) 35 Pf28
Oakwood USA (TX) 35 Ph30
Oasis USA (NV) 25 Oh25
Oasis, El MEX (SON) 38 Ok31
Oatman USA (AZ) 33 Oh28
Oba CDN (ONT) 20 Qc21
Obed CDN (ALB) 17 Og19
Oberlin USA (KS) 34 Pe26
Oberlin USA (LA) 36 Pj30
Oberon CDN (MAN) 19 Pf20
Obregón, Ciudad MEX (SON) 39 Pa32
Ocala USA (FL) 37 Qd31
Ocampo MEX (COA) 39 Pd32
Ocampo MEX (TAM) 40 Pf34
Ocampo, Villa MEX (DGO) 39 Pc32
Ocate USA (NM) 34 Pc27
Ocean City USA (MD) 31 Qh26
Ocean City USA (NJ) 31 Qh26
Ocean Falls CDN (BC) 16 Ob19
Ocean Shores USA (WA) 24 Oc22
Ocean Springs USA (MS) 36 Qa30
Ochoa, La MEX (DGO) 39 Pd34
Ochopee USA (FL) 43 Qe33
Ocilla USA (GA) 37 Qd30
Ocmulgee National Monument ☆ USA (GA) 37 Qd29
Oconto USA (NE) 26 Pf25
Oconto USA (WI) 28 Qb23
Ocracoke USA (NC) 31 Qh28
Odenton USA (MD) 29 Qg26
Odessa USA (NJ) 29 Qh26
Odessa USA (TX) 34 Pd30
Odessa USA (WA) 16 Of22
Oelrichs USA (SD) 26 Pd24
Oelwein USA (IA) 27 Pk24
Ogallala USA (NE) 26 Pe25
Ogden USA (IA) 27 Ph24
Ogden USA (UT) 25 Ok25
Ogdensburg USA (NY) 29 Qh23
Ogema CDN (SAS) 18 Pc21
Ogema USA (MN) 19 Ph22
Ogema USA (WI) 27 Pk23
Ogilvie CDN (YT) 11 Nf13
Ogoki CDN (ONT) 20 Qc20
Ohogamuit USA (AK) 10 Me15
Oil City USA (LA) 35 Pj29
Oil City USA (PA) 29 Qf25
Oildale USA (CA) 32 Of28
Oilmont USA (MT) 17 Ok21
Oilton USA (TX) 40 Pf32
Ojibwa USA (WI) 27 Pk23
Ojinaga MEX (CHA) 39 Pc31
Ojo de Carrizo MEX (CHA) 39 Pc31
Ojos Negros MEX (BCN) 32 Og30
Ojuelos, Estado MEX (ZAC) 39 Pd34
Okanagan Centre CDN (BC) 16 Of20
Okanagan Falls CDN (BC) 16 Of21
Okanogan USA (WA) 16 Of21
Okarche USA (OK) 35 Pg28
Okeechobee USA (FL) 43 Qe32
Okefenokee National Wildlife Refuge and Wilderness Area ☆ USA (GA) 37 Qd30
Okemah USA (OK) 35 Pg28
Okla CDN (SAS) 18 Pd19
Oklahoma City USA (OK) 35 Pg28
Okmulgee USA (OK) 35 Ph28
Okotoks CDN (ALB) 17 Oj20
Ola USA (AR) 35 Pj28
Olathe USA (CO) 33 Pa26
Olathe USA (KS) 35 Ph26
Olcott USA (NY) 29 Qf24
Old Crow CDN (YT) 11 Nf12
Old Faithful Geyser ☆ USA (WY) 25 Ok23
Old Ford USA (NC) 31 Qg28
Old Forge USA (NY) 30 Qh24
Old Fort CDN (BC) 14 Ob18
Old Fort Henry ☆ CDN (ONT) 29 Qg23
Old Fort Massachusetts ☆ USA (MS) 36 Qa30
Old Harbor USA (AK) 12 Mj17
Old Hogem CDN (BC) 15 Oc18
Old Horse Springs USA (NM) 33 Pa29

Old Minto USA (AK) 11 Na13
Old Orchard Beach USA (ME) 22 Qk24
Old Perlican CDN (NFL) 23 Rj21
Old Rampart USA (AK) 11 Ne12
Olds CDN (BC) 17 Oh20
Old Sitka USA (AK) 14 Nh17
Old Station USA (CA) 24 Oe25
Old Town USA (FL) 37 Qd31
Old Town USA (ME) 22 Ra23
Old Village USA (AK) 12 Mh15
Olean USA (NY) 29 Qf24
O'Leary CDN (PEI) 22 Rc22
Oletha USA (TX) 35 Pg30
Olin USA (TX) 35 Pf30
Olive Hill USA (KY) 29 Qd26
Oliver CDN (BC) 16 Of21
Olivet USA (SD) 27 Pg24
Olivia USA (MN) 27 Ph23
Olla USA (LA) 36 Pj30
Olney USA (IL) 28 Qa26
Olney USA (MD) 29 Qg26
Olney USA (MT) 17 Oh21
Olney USA (TX) 35 Pf29
Olympia USA (WA) 24 Od22
Oma USA (MS) 36 Pk30
Omaha USA (AR) 35 Pj27
Omaha USA (NE) 27 Ph25
Omak USA (WA) 16 Of21
Omega USA (NM) 33 Pa28
Ompah CDN (ONT) 29 Qg23
Onamia USA (MN) 27 Pj22
Onancock USA (VA) 31 Qh27
Onandaga Cave State Park ☆ USA (MO) 28 Pk26
Onawa USA (IA) 27 Pg24
Onaway USA (MI) 28 Qc23
One Hundred and Fifty Mile House CDN (BC) 16 Oe19
One Hundred Mile House CDN (BC) 16 Oe20
Oneida USA (NY) 29 Qh24
Oneida USA (TN) 36 Qc27
O'Neill USA (NE) 26 Pf24
Oneonta USA (NY) 30 Qh24
Onion Lake CDN (SAS) 17 Pa19
Ontario USA (CA) 32 Og28
Ontario USA (OR) 24 Og23
Ontario USA (WI) 27 Pk24
Ontonagon USA (MI) 20 Qa22
Onyx Cave ☆ USA (AR) 35 Pj27
Ootsa Lake CDN (BC) 16 Ob19
Opasatika CDN (ONT) 20 Qd21
Opelika USA (AL) 36 Qc29
Opelousas USA (LA) 36 Pj30
Openshaw CDN (SAS) 18 Pd21
Opheim USA (MT) 18 Pb21
Ophir CDN (ONT) 20 Qd22
Ophir USA (AK) 10 Mg14
Opitsat CDN (BC) 16 Oc21
Opp USA (AL) 36 Qb30
Opportunity USA (WA) 17 Og22
Optic Lake CDN (MAN) 18 Pe18
Oquawka USA (IL) 27 Pk25
Oquossoc USA (ME) 22 Qk23
Oracle USA (AZ) 33 Ok29
Oracle Junction USA (AZ) 33 Ok29
Orange USA (TX) 41 Pj30
Orange USA (VA) 29 Qf26
Orange, Port USA (FL) 37 Qe31
Orangeburg USA (SC) 37 Qe29
Orange Park USA (FL) 37 Qe30
Orangeville CDN (ONT) 29 Qe24
Orchard, Port USA (WA) 16 Od22
Orchard City USA (CO) 33 Pb26
Orchard Valley USA (WY) 26 Pc25
Orchardville USA (IL) 28 Qa26
Ord USA (NE) 26 Pf25
Orderville USA (UT) 33 Oj27
Ordway USA (CO) 34 Pd26
Ore City USA (TX) 35 Ph29
Oregon USA (MO) 35 Ph26
Oregon USA (WI) 28 Qa24
Orem USA (UT) 25 Ok25
Orestes, Villa de MEX (DGO) 39 Pc32
Orford, Port USA (OR) 24 Oc24
Organ USA (NM) 34 Pb29
Organ Pipe Cactus National Monument ☆ USA (AZ) 33 Oj29
Orick USA (CA) 24 Oc25
Orient USA (WA) 16 Of21
Orillia CDN (ONT) 29 Qf23
Orin USA (WY) 26 Pc24
Orion CDN (ALB) 17 Ok21
Oriska USA (ND) 19 Pg22
Orkney CDN (SAS) 18 Pb21
Orla USA (TX) 34 Pd30
Orland USA (CA) 32 Od26
Orlando USA (FL) 43 Qe31
Orleans USA (IN) 28 Qb26
Ormiston CDN (SAS) 18 Pc21
Ormond Beach USA (FL) 37 Qe31
Ormsby USA (MN) 27 Ph24
Oro, El MEX (COA) 39 Pd32
Oro Blanco USA (AZ) 33 Ok30
Orofino USA (ID) 24 Og22
Orogrande USA (NM) 34 Pb29
Oromocto CDN (NB) 22 Rb23
Orondo USA (WA) 16 Oe22
Orono USA (ME) 22 Ra23
Orono USA (MN) 27 Pj23
Oro Valley USA (AZ) 33 Ok29
Oroville USA (CA) 32 Oe26
Oroville USA (WA) 16 Of21
Orr USA (MN) 19 Pj21
Ortiz MEX (SON) 38 Ok31
Ortonville USA (MN) 27 Pg23
Orwell USA (OH) 29 Qe25
Osage CDN (SAS) 18 Pd21
Osage USA (AR) 35 Pj27
Osage USA (IA) 27 Pj24
Osage Beach USA (MO) 28 Pj26
Osborne CDN (MAN) 19 Pg21
Osborne USA (KS) 35 Pf26
Osburn USA (ID) 17 Og22
Oscar Soto Maynes MEX (CHA) 39 Pb31
Osceola USA (AR) 36 Qa28
Osceola USA (IA) 27 Pj25
Osceola USA (MO) 35 Pj26
Osceola USA (NE) 27 Pg25
Osceola USA (WI) 27 Pj23
Oscoda USA (MI) 29 Qd23

Oshawa CDN (ONT) 29 Qf24
Oshkosh USA (NE) 26 Pd25
Oshkosh USA (WI) 28 Qa23
Oskaloosa USA (IA) 27 Pj25
Oskélanéo CDN (QUE) 21 Qh21
Oslo USA (MN) 19 Pg21
Osnaburgh House CDN (ONT) 19 Pk20
Oso USA (WA) 16 Oe21
Oso, El MEX (COA) 39 Pd32
Osoyoos CDN (BC) 16 Of21
Ospasquia Provincial Park ☆ CDN (ONT) 19 Pj19
Osseo USA (MN) 27 Pj23
Osseo USA (WI) 27 Pk23
Ossining USA (NY) 30 Qj25
Ostenfeld CDN (MAN) 19 Pg21
Osterwick CDN (MAN) 19 Pf21
Oswego USA (KS) 35 Ph27
Oswego USA (NY) 29 Qg24
Othello USA (WA) 24 Of22
Otis USA (NM) 34 Pc29
Chute-des-Passes CDN (QUE) 21 Qk21
Otselic USA (NY) 29 Qh24
Ottawa CDN (ONT) 29 Qh23
Ottawa USA (IL) 28 Qa25
Ottawa USA (KS) 35 Ph26
Ottawa USA (OH) 28 Qc25
Otter USA (MT) 26 Pb23
Otter = Baie-à-la-Loutre CDN (QUE) 22 Rd21
Otterburne CDN (MAN) 19 Pg21
Otter Creek USA (FL) 37 Qd31
Otter Lake CDN (QUE) 29 Qg23
Otter Rapids CDN (ONT) 20 Qe20
Ottumwa USA (IA) 27 Pj25
Ouray USA (CO) 33 Pb26
Ouray USA (UT) 25 Pa25
Outing USA (MN) 19 Pj22
Outlook CDN (SAS) 18 Pb20
Outlook USA (MT) 18 Pc21
Overflowing River CDN (MAN) 18 Pe19
Overland Park USA (KS) 35 Ph26
Overton USA (NV) 33 Oh27
Overton USA (TX) 35 Ph29
Ovid USA (NY) 29 Qg24
Owatonna USA (MN) 27 Pj23
Owego USA (NY) 29 Qg24
Owen USA (WI) 27 Pk23
Owens USA (VA) 29 Qg26
Owensboro USA (KY) 36 Qb27
Owen Sound CDN (ONT) 29 Qe23
Owensville USA (IN) 28 Qb26
Owensville USA (MO) 28 Pk26
Owenton USA (KY) 28 Qc26
Owl River CDN (ALB) 17 Ok18
Owosso USA (MI) 28 Qc24
Oxbow CDN (SAS) 18 Pd21
Oxdrift CDN (ONT) 19 Pj21
Oxford CDN (NS) 22 Rd23
Oxford USA (IN) 28 Qb25
Oxford USA (MS) 36 Qa28
Oxford USA (NC) 31 Qf27
Oxford USA (NE) 35 Pf25
Oxford USA (OH) 28 Qc26
Oxford USA (PA) 29 Qh26
Oxford House CDN (MAN) 19 Ph18
Oxford Junction USA (IA) 27 Pk24
Oxnard USA (CA) 32 Of28
Oxville USA (IL) 28 Pk26
Oyama CDN (BC) 16 Of20
Oyen CDN (ALB) 17 Ok20
Oysterville USA (WA) 24 Oc22
Ozark USA (AL) 36 Qc30
Ozark USA (AR) 35 Pj28
Ozark USA (MO) 35 Pj27
Ozark National Scenic Riverways ☆ USA (MO) 36 Pk27
Ozona USA (TX) 40 Pe30
Ozone USA (AR) 35 Pj28

P

Pablo USA (MT) 17 Oh22
Pacheco MEX (DGO) 39 Pd33
Pachuta USA (MS) 36 Qa29
Pacific CDN (BC) 14 Oa18
Pacific USA (MO) 28 Pk26
Pacific Beach USA (WA) 16 Oc22
Pacific Grove USA (CA) 32 Oe27
Pacific House USA (CA) 32 Oe26
Pacific Rim National Park Reserve ☆ CDN (BC) 16 Oc21
Packington CDN (QUE) 22 Ra22
Packton USA (LA) 36 Pj30
Packwood USA (WA) 24 Oe22
Paden City USA (WV) 29 Qe26
Padre Island National Seashore ☆ USA (TX) 40 Pg32
Paducah USA (KY) 36 Qa27
Paducah USA (TX) 34 Pe28
Page USA (AZ) 33 Ok27
Page USA (ND) 19 Pg22
Page USA (OK) 35 Ph28
Pageland USA (SC) 37 Qe28
Pagosa Springs USA (CO) 34 Pb27
Pagwa River CDN (ONT) 20 Qc20
Pāhala USA (HI) 44 Mh36
Pahaska Tepee USA (WY) 25 Pa23
Pāhoa USA (HI) 44 Mh36
Pahokee USA (FL) 43 Qe32
Pahrump USA (NV) 33 Oh27
Pā'ia USA (HI) 44 Mg35
Paila MEX (COA) 40 Pd33
Painesville USA (OH) 29 Qe25
Paint Lake Provincial Park ☆ CDN (MAN) 19 Pf18
Paint Rock USA (TX) 35 Pf30
Paintsville USA (KY) 37 Qd27
Paisano USA (TX) 39 Pd30
Paisley USA (OR) 24 Oe24
Palacios USA (TX) 40 Pg31
Palatka USA (FL) 37 Qe31
Palau MEX (COA) 40 Pe32
Palermo USA (ND) 18 Pd21
Palestine USA (TX) 35 Ph30
Palisade USA (CO) 33 Pa26
Palisade USA (NE) 26 Pe25
Palmdale USA (CA) 32 Of28
Palmdale USA (FL) 43 Qe32
Palm Desert USA (CA) 32 Og29

A B C D E F G H I J K L M N O P Q R S T U V W X Y Z

Palmer CDN (SAS) 18 Pb21
Palmer USA (AK) 13 Na15
Palmer USA (TX) 35 Pg29
Palmer Lake USA (CO) 34 Pc26
Palmers USA (MN) 19 Pk22
Palmerton USA (PA) 29 Qh25
Palmetto USA (FL) 43 Qd32
Palmillas MEX (TAM) 40 Pf34
Palmito, El MEX (DGO) 39 Pc33
Palm Springs USA (CA) 32 Og29
Palmyra USA (IN) 28 Qb26
Palmyra USA (NY) 29 Qg24
Palmyra USA (VA) 31 Qf27
Palo CDN (SAS) 17 Pa19
Palo USA (IA) 27 Pk24
Palo Alto USA (CA) 32 Od27
Palo Alto USA (PA) 29 Of26
Palomas, Las USA (NM) 34 Pb29
Palo Pinto USA (TX) 35 Pf29
Palos C (LH) 43 Qe34
Palouse USA (WA) 24 Og22
Palo Verde USA (CA) 33 Oh29
Palpite C (MZ) 43 Qe34
Pambrun CDN (SAS) 18 Pb21
Pampa USA (TX) 34 Pe28
Pamplin City USA (VA) 31 Qf27
Pana USA (IL) 28 Qa26
Panabá MEX (YUC) 42 Qa35
Panama City USA (FL) 36 Qc30
Panama City Beach USA (FL) 36 Qc30
Panamint Springs USA (CA) 32 Og27
Pangman CDN (SAS) 18 Pc21
Panhandle USA (TX) 34 Pe28
Panora USA (IA) 27 Ph25
Panther Swamp N.W.R. ☆ USA (MS) 36 Pk29
Paola USA (KS) 35 Ph26
Paoli USA (IN) 28 Qb26
Paonia USA (CO) 33 Pb26
Pāpaʻikou USA (HI) 44 Mh36
Papalote, El MEX (COA) 39 Pd32
Papillion USA (NE) 27 Pg25
Papineau Labelle, Réserve Faunique de ☆ CDN (QUE) 21 Qh22
Parachute USA (CO) 33 Pa26
Paradise USA (CA) 32 Oe26
Paradise USA (MI) 20 Qc22
Paradise USA (MT) 17 Oh22
Paradise USA (NV) 33 Oh27
Paradise Hill CDN (SAS) 17 Pa19
Paradox USA (CO) 33 Pa26
Paragould USA (AR) 36 Pk27
Parás MEX (NL) 40 Pf32
Parc d'Anticosti ☆ CDN (QUE) 22 Rd21
Parc de Cons. de la Gaspésie ☆ CDN (QUE) 22 Rb21
Parc de Conservation des Grands-Jardins ☆ CDN (QUE) 22 Qk22
Parc de la Jacques Cartier ☆ CDN (QUE) 22 Qk22
Parc du Mont Tremblant ☆ CDN (QUE) 21 Qh22
Parc Nacional de Forillon ☆ CDN (QUE) 22 Rc21
Parc National d'Assinica ☆ CDN (QUE) 21 Qh20
Parc National de Mistassini ☆ CDN (QUE) 21 Qj20
Parc provincial Chibougamau ☆ CDN (QUE) 21 Qj21
Parc Provincial de Forestville ☆ CDN (QUE) 22 Ra21
Parent CDN (QUE) 21 Qh22
Paris USA (AR) 35 Pj28
Paris USA (IL) 28 Qb26
Paris USA (KY) 28 Qc26
Paris USA (MO) 28 Pj26
Paris USA (TN) 36 Qa27
Paris USA (TX) 35 Ph29
Parkbeg CDN (SAS) 18 Pb20
Park City USA (KY) 36 Qb27
Parker USA (AZ) 33 Oh28
Parker USA (SD) 27 Pg24
Parkersburg USA (IA) 27 Pj24
Parkersburg USA (WV) 29 Qe26
Parkers Prairie USA (MN) 27 Ph22
Park Falls USA (WI) 27 Pk23
Parkman CDN (SAS) 18 Pe21
Parkman USA (OH) 29 Qe25
Parkman USA (WY) 25 Pb23
Park Rapids USA (MN) 19 Ph22
Park River USA (ND) 19 Pg21
Parkston USA (SD) 27 Pg24
Parksville CDN (BC) 16 Oc21
Parma USA (OH) 29 Qe25
Paron USA (AR) 35 Pj28
Parowan USA (UT) 33 Oj27
Parque Nacional Bahía de Loreto ☆ MEX 38 Ok33
Parque Nacional Balneario de los Novillos ☆ MEX (COA) 40 Pe31
Parque Nacional Constitución de 1857 ☆ MEX (BCN) 32 Og29
Parque Nacional Cumbres De Majalca ☆ MEX (CHA) 39 Pb31
Parque Nacional Cumbres de Monterrey ☆ MEX (NL) 40 Pe33
Parque Nacional del Puerto de los Ángeles ☆ MEX (DGO) 39 Pc34
Parque Nacional de Península de Guanahacabibes ☆ C (PR) 42 Qc34
Parque Nacional Sierra de San Pedro Mártir ☆ MEX (BCN) 38 Og30
Parque Natural Barranca del Cobre ☆ MEX (CHA) 39 Pa32
Parque Natural del Gran Desierto Del Pinacate ☆ MEX (SON) 33 Oh30
Parque Natural Isla Angel de la Guarda ☆ MEX (BCN) 38 Oj31
Parque Natural Laguna Ojo ☆ MEX (BCN) 38 Oh32
Parque Natural Río Lagartos ☆ MEX (YUC) 42 Qa35
Parque Natural San Felipe ☆ MEX (YUC) 42 Qa35
Parras de la Fuente MEX (COA) 40 Pd33
Parrsboro CDN (NS) 22 Rc23
Parry CDN (SAS) 18 Pc21
Parry Sound CDN (ONT) 29 Qe23
Parshall USA (ND) 18 Pd22
Parsons USA (KS) 35 Ph27
Parson's Pond CDN (NFL) 23 Rg20
Pas, The CDN (MAN) 18 Pe19
Pasadena CDN (NFL) 23 Rg21
Pasadena USA (CA) 32 Of28
Pasadena USA (TX) 41 Ph31
Pascagoula USA (MS) 36 Qa30
Pasco USA (WA) 24 Of22
Paskenta USA (CA) 32 Od26
Paso, El USA (IL) 28 Qa25
Paso, El USA (TX) 34 Pb30
Paso de Lesca C (CG) 43 Qg35
Paso Gap, El USA (NM) 34 Pc29
Paso Nacional MEX (DGO) 39 Pd33
Paso Real de San Diego C (PR) 43 Qd34
Paso Robles USA (CA) 32 Oe28
Pasqua CDN (SAS) 18 Pc20
Passayten Wilderness Area ☆ USA (WA) 16 Oe21
Pass Christian USA (MS) 36 Qa30
Pass Island CDN (NFL) 23 Rg22
Passmore CDN (BC) 17 Og21
Pastor, El MEX (CHA) 39 Pc31
Pastura USA (NM) 34 Pc28
Patagonia USA (AZ) 33 Ok30
Patchogue USA (NY) 30 Qj25
Pateros USA (WA) 16 Of21
Paterson USA (NJ) 30 Qh25
Paterson USA (WA) 24 Of23
Patricia CDN (ALB) 17 Ok20
Patricia USA (TX) 34 Pd29
Patrie, La CDN (QUE) 22 Qk23
Patterson USA (GA) 37 Qd30
Patterson USA (LA) 36 Pk31
Pattison USA (MS) 36 Pk30
Patton Junction USA (MO) 36 Pk27
Pattonsburg USA (MO) 35 Ph25
Patuanak CDN (SAS) 17 Pb18
Paul B. Johnson State Park ☆ USA (MS) 36 Qa30
Paul Bunyan & Blue Ox Statue ☆ USA (MN) 19 Ph22
Pauline USA (ID) 25 Oj24
Paul Spur USA (AZ) 33 Pa30
Pauls Valley USA (OK) 35 Pg28
Pavilion CDN (BC) 16 Oe20
Pavilion USA (NY) 29 Qf24
Pavo USA (GA) 37 Qd30
Pawhuska USA (OK) 35 Pg27
Pawnee USA (OK) 35 Pg27
Pawnee City USA (NE) 35 Pg25
Paw Paw USA (MI) 28 Qc24
Pawtucket USA (RI) 30 Qk25
Paxson USA (AK) 11 Nc14
Paxton USA (NE) 26 Pe25
Payette USA (ID) 24 Og23
Paynes Creek USA (CA) 24 Oe25
Paynesville USA (MN) 27 Ph23
Paynton CDN (SAS) 17 Pa19
Payson USA (AZ) 33 Ok28
Payson USA (UT) 33 Ok25
Paz, La MEX (BCS) 38 Ok33
Peace River CDN (ALB) 15 Og17
Peachland CDN (BC) 16 Of21
Peach Springs USA (AZ) 33 Oj28
Peachtree City USA (GA) 36 Qc29
Pearce CDN (ALB) 17 Oj21
Pearce USA (AZ) 33 Pa30
Pearcy USA (AR) 35 Pj28
Pearisburg USA (VA) 37 Qe27
Pearl USA (MS) 36 Pk29
Pearland USA (TX) 41 Ph31
Pearl Harbor ☆ USA (HI) 44 Mg35
Pearsall USA (TX) 40 Pf31
Pearson USA (GA) 37 Qd30
Peawanuck CDN (ONT) 20 Qc18
Pecan Island USA (LA) 36 Pj31
Pecos USA (TX) 39 Pd30
Pedriceña MEX (DGO) 39 Pd33
Pedro Betancourt C (MZ) 43 Qe34
Peebles CDN (SAS) 18 Pd20
Peebles USA (OH) 29 Qd26
Peekskill USA (NY) 30 Qj25
Peerless CDN (SAS) 17 Pa18
Peerless USA (MT) 18 Pc21
Peers CDN (ALB) 17 Oh19
Peetz USA (CO) 26 Pd25
Peggys Cove CDN (NS) 22 Rd23
Pekin USA (IL) 28 Qa25
Pekin USA (ND) 19 Pf22
Pelahatchie USA (MS) 36 Qa29
Pelican USA (AK) 14 Ng17
Pelikan Narrows CDN (SAS) 18 Pd18
Pelikan Rapids USA (MN) 27 Pg22
Pelkie USA (MI) 20 Qa22
Pella USA (IA) 27 Pj25
Pelland USA (MN) 19 Pj21
Pell City USA (AL) 36 Qb29
Pelletier CDN (QUE) 22 Ra22
Pellston USA (MI) 28 Qc23
Pelly Crossing CDN (YT) 11 Ng14
Pemberton CDN (BC) 16 Od20
Pembine USA (WI) 28 Qb23
Pembroke CDN (ONT) 29 Qg23
Pender USA (NE) 27 Pg24
Pender Island CDN (BC) 16 Od21
Pendleton USA (IN) 28 Qc26
Pendleton USA (OR) 24 Of23
Pendroy USA (MT) 17 Oj21
Penetanguishene CDN (ONT) 29 Qf23
Península de Guanahacabibes, Parque Nacional de ☆ C (PR) 42 Qc34
Pennant CDN (SAS) 18 Pa20
Penney Farms USA (FL) 37 Qe31
Penn Hills USA (PA) 29 Qf25
Penny CDN (BC) 16 Oe19
Penn Yan USA (NY) 29 Qg24
Peñón Blanco MEX (DGO) 39 Pd33
Pensacola USA (FL) 36 Qb30
Pentecôte, Rivière CDN (QUE) 22 Rb21
Penticton CDN (BC) 16 Of21
Pentwater USA (MI) 28 Qb24
Penwell USA (TX) 34 Pd30
Peoria USA (AZ) 33 Oj29
Peoria USA (IL) 28 Qa25
Pequot Lakes USA (MN) 19 Ph22
Pérade, La CDN (QUE) 21 Qj22
Percé CDN (QUE) 22 Rc21
Percy Quin State Park ☆ USA (MS) 36 Pk30
Perdue CDN (SAS) 18 Pb19
Perham USA (MN) 19 Ph22
Delisle CDN (QUE) 21 Qk21
Hébertville CDN (QUE) 21 Qk21
Péribonka CDN (QUE) 21 Qj21
L'Ascension CDN (QUE) 21 Qk21
Perico C (MZ) 43 Qe34
Perico USA (TX) 34 Pd27
Pericos MEX (SIN) 39 Pb33
Perkinstown USA (WI) 27 Pk23
Perla, La MEX (CHA) 39 Pc31
Perley USA (MN) 19 Pg22
Perma USA (MT) 17 Oh22
Perow CDN (BC) 16 Ob18
Perrine USA (FL) 43 Qe33
Perry CDN (ONT) 20 Qc22
Perry USA (FL) 37 Qd30
Perry USA (GA) 37 Qd29
Perry USA (IA) 27 Ph25
Perry USA (ME) 22 Rb23
Perry USA (MO) 28 Pk26
Perry USA (OK) 35 Pg27
Perry USA (TX) 35 Pg30
Perry, Port CDN (ONT) 29 Qf23
Perryton USA (TX) 34 Pe27
Perryville USA (AK) 12 Mf18
Perryville USA (AR) 35 Pj28
Perryville USA (MO) 36 Qa27
Perth CDN (ONT) 29 Qg23
Perth Amboy USA (NJ) 30 Qh25
Perth-Andover CDN (NB) 22 Rb22
Perth Road CDN (ONT) 29 Qg23
Peru USA (IL) 28 Qa25
Peru USA (IN) 28 Qb25
Peru USA (NE) 27 Ph25
Pesca, La MEX (TAM) 40 Pg34
Petal USA (MS) 36 Qa30
Petaluma USA (CA) 32 Od26
Petawawa CDN (ONT) 29 Qg23
Peterbell CDN (ONT) 20 Qd21
Peterborough CDN (ONT) 29 Qf23
Petersburg USA (AK) 14 Nj17
Petersburg USA (IL) 28 Qa25
Petersburg USA (IN) 28 Qb26
Petersburg USA (ND) 19 Pg21
Petersburg USA (OK) 35 Pg29
Petersburg USA (VA) 31 Qg27
Petersville USA (AK) 10 Mk14
Petite Forte CDN (NFL) 23 Rh22
Petit Jardin CDN (NFL) 23 Rf21
Petit Jean State Park ☆ USA (AR) 35 Pj28
Petit-Rocher CDN (NB) 22 Rc22
Petit-Saguenay CDN (QUE) 22 Qk21
Petoskey USA (MI) 28 Qc23
Petrified Forest ☆ USA (MS) 36 Pk29
Petrified Forest National Park ☆ USA (AZ) 33 Pa28
Petroglyphs National Park ☆ CDN (ONT) 29 Qf23
Petrolia USA (CA) 24 Oc25
Pharr USA (TX) 40 Pf32
Phenix City USA (AL) 36 Qc29
Philadelphia USA (MS) 36 Qa29
Philadelphia USA (PA) 31 Qh26
Philip USA (SD) 26 Pe23
Philipsburg USA (PA) 29 Qf25
Phillips USA (ME) 22 Qk23
Phillips USA (WI) 27 Pk23
Phillipsburg USA (KS) 35 Pf26
Phillipsburg USA (MO) 35 Pj27
Phippen CDN (SAS) 17 Pa19
Phoenix USA (AZ) 33 Oj29
Phoenix USA (MI) 20 Qa22
Phoenixville USA (PA) 29 Qh25
Piapot CDN (SAS) 17 Pa21
Picayune USA (MS) 36 Qa30
Picher USA (OK) 35 Ph27
Pichilingüe MEX (BCS) 38 Ok33
Pickens, Fort ☆ USA (FL) 36 Qb30
Pickneyville USA (IL) 28 Qa26
Pickstown USA (SD) 26 Pf24
Picos, Los MEX (COA) 39 Pd31
Picton CDN (ONT) 29 Qg23
Pictou CDN (NS) 22 Rd23
Picture Butte CDN (ALB) 17 Oj21
Pictured Rocks National Lakeshore ☆ USA (MI) 20 Qb22
Piedmont USA (AL) 36 Qc29
Piedras Negras MEX (COA) 40 Pe31
Piedritas MEX (COA) 39 Pd31
Pierceland CDN (SAS) 17 Pa18
Pierre USA (SD) 26 Pe23
Pierre, Rivière-à- CDN (QUE) 21 Qj22
Pierson CDN (MAN) 18 Pe21
Pierson USA (FL) 37 Qe31
Pie Town USA (NM) 33 Pa28
Piggott USA (AR) 36 Pk27
Pikangikum CDN (ONT) 19 Pj20
Pike USA (NY) 29 Qf24
Pike Lake CDN (SAS) 18 Pb20
Piketon USA (OH) 29 Qd26
Pikeville USA (KY) 37 Qd27
Pikeville USA (TN) 36 Qc28
Pikmiktalik USA (AK) 10 Md14
Pile Bay Village USA (AK) 12 Mj16
Pilgrim Springs USA (AK) 10 Mc13
Pillsbury USA (ND) 19 Pg22
Pilot Mound CDN (MAN) 19 Pf21
Pilot Point USA (AK) 12 Mg17
Pilot Rock USA (OR) 24 Of23
Pilot Santa USA (AK) 10 Md15
Pinar del Río C (PR) 43 Qd34
Pinawa CDN (MAN) 19 Ph20
Pincher CDN (ALB) 17 Oj21
Pincher Creek CDN (ALB) 17 Oj21
Pine Apple USA (AL) 36 Qb30
Pine Bluff USA (AR) 36 Pk28
Pine Bluffs USA (WY) 26 Pc25
Pine City USA (MN) 27 Pj23
Pinecreek USA (MN) 19 Ph21
Pine Creek Gorge ☆ USA (PA) 29 Qg25
Pine Dock CDN (MAN) 19 Pg20
Pine Falls CDN (MAN) 19 Pg20
Pine Hill CDN (QUE) 29 Qh23
Pinehouse Lake CDN (SAS) 18 Pb18
Pine Island USA (LA) 36 Pj30
Pine Island USA (MN) 27 Pj23
Pineland USA (TX) 35 Pj30
Pinellas Park USA (FL) 43 Qd32
Pine Point CDN (NWT) 15 Oh15
Pine Portage CDN (ONT) 20 Qa21
Pine Ridge USA (CA) 32 Of27
Pine Ridge USA (SD) 26 Pd24
Pine River USA (MN) 19 Ph22
Pine Springs USA (TX) 34 Pc30
Pinetop-Lakeside USA (AZ) 33 Pa28
Pinetops USA (NC) 31 Qg28
Pinetta USA (FL) 37 Qd30
Pine Valley CDN (BC) 15 Od18
Pineview USA (UT) 25 Ok25
Pineville USA (KY) 37 Qd27
Pineville USA (LA) 36 Pj30
Pine Woods USA (MS) 36 Qa29
Piney CDN (MAN) 19 Ph21
Pingree USA (ND) 19 Pf22
Pink Hill USA (NC) 31 Qg28
Pink Mountain CDN (BC) 15 Od17
Pinland USA (FL) 37 Qd31
Pinola USA (MS) 36 Qa30
Pinon USA (NM) 34 Pc29
Pinon Hills USA (CA) 32 Og28
Pinos Altos USA (NM) 33 Pa29
Pioche USA (NV) 33 Oh27
Pipestone CDN (MAN) 18 Pe21
Pipestone USA (MN) 27 Pg24
Métabetchouan CDN (QUE) 21 Qk21
Piqua USA (OH) 28 Qc25
Pirtleville USA (AZ) 33 Pa30
Pisek USA (ND) 19 Pg21
Pistol River USA (OR) 24 Oc24
Pitaga CDN (NFL) 22 Rc19
Pitkas Point USA (AK) 10 Md14
Pitkin USA (LA) 36 Pj30
Pitt Meadows CDN (BC) 16 Od21
Pittsburg USA (KS) 35 Ph27
Pittsburg USA (KY) 36 Qc27
Pittsburgh USA (PA) 29 Qf25
Pittsfield USA (IL) 28 Pk26
Pittsfield USA (MA) 30 Qj24
Pittsfield USA (ME) 22 Ra23
Pittston USA (PA) 29 Qh25
Pittston Farm USA (ME) 22 Ra23
Pittsville USA (WI) 27 Pk23
Pivot CDN (ALB) 17 Ok20
Place, La USA (LA) 36 Pk30
Placentia CDN (NFL) 23 Rj22
Placerville USA (CA) 32 Oe26
Placerville USA (CO) 33 Pa26
Placetas C (VC) 43 Qf34
Placitas USA (NM) 34 Pc27
Plain USA (WA) 16 Oe22
Plain City USA (OH) 29 Qd25
Plainfield USA (IA) 27 Pj24
Plainfield USA (WI) 28 Qa23
Plains USA (MT) 17 Oh22
Plains USA (TX) 34 Pd29
Plainview USA (MN) 27 Pj23
Plainview USA (NE) 27 Pg24
Plainview USA (TX) 34 Pe28
Plainville USA (KS) 35 Pf26
Plainwell USA (MI) 28 Qc24
Plankinton USA (SD) 26 Pf24
Plano USA (TX) 35 Pg29
Plant, La USA (SD) 26 Pe23
Plant City USA (FL) 43 Qd31
Plaquemine USA (LA) 36 Pk30
Plaster City USA (CA) 33 Oh29
Plaster Rock CDN (NB) 22 Rb22
Plata, La USA (MD) 29 Qg26
Plata, La USA (MO) 28 Pj25
Plateros MEX (ZAC) 39 Pd34
Platina USA (CA) 24 Od25
Platinum USA (AK) 12 Me16
Platte USA (SD) 26 Pf24
Platte, Ville USA (LA) 36 Pj30
Platte City USA (MO) 35 Ph26
Platten USA (ME) 22 Ra22
Platteville USA (CO) 26 Pc25
Platteville USA (WI) 27 Pk24
Plattsburgh USA (NY) 30 Qj23
Plattsmouth USA (NE) 27 Ph25
Playa Dayaniguas C (PR) 43 Qd34
Playa de Florida C (CG) 43 Qf35
Playa las Cañas C (PR) 43 Qd34
Playa Lauro Villar MEX (TAM) 40 Pg33
Playa Rosario C (LH) 43 Qd34
Plaza USA (ND) 18 Pe21
Pleasant Hill USA (LA) 35 Pj30
Pleasant Lake USA (ND) 19 Pf21
Pleasanton USA (KS) 35 Ph26
Pleasanton USA (TX) 40 Pf31
Pleasant View USA (CO) 33 Pa27
Plenty CDN (SAS) 17 Pa20
Plentywood USA (MT) 18 Pc21
Plessisville CDN (QUE) 22 Qk22
Notre-Dame-du-Rosaire CDN (QUE) 21 Qk21
Pliny USA (MN) 27 Pj22
Plum Coulee CDN (MAN) 19 Pg21
Plummer USA (ID) 17 Og22
Plummer USA (MN) 19 Pg22
Plunkett CDN (SAS) 18 Pc20
Plymouth USA (IN) 28 Qb25
Plymouth USA (NC) 31 Qg28
Plymouth USA (NE) 27 Pg25
Plymouth USA (NH) 22 Qk24
Plymouth USA (PA) 29 Qh25
Plymouth USA (RI) 30 Qk25
Plymouth USA (WA) 24 Of23
Plymouth USA (WI) 28 Qb24
Pocahontas CDN (ALB) 17 Og19
Pocahontas USA (AR) 36 Pk27
Pocahontas USA (IA) 27 Ph24
Pocatello USA (ID) 25 Oj24
Pocatière, La CDN (QUE) 22 Ra22
Pocomoke City USA (MD) 31 Qh26
Pohénégamook CDN (QUE) 22 Ra22
Poile, La CDN (NFL) 23 Rf22
Point Arena USA (CA) 32 Od26
Point Baker USA (AK) 14 Nj17
Point Bickerton CDN (NS) 23 Re23
Point Comfort USA (TX) 40 Pg31
Pointe au Baril Station CDN (ONT) 29 Qe23
Pointe Parent CDN (QUE) 23 Re20
Point Gamble USA (WA) 16 Od22
Point Harbor USA (NC) 31 Qh27
Point Hope USA (AK) 10 Mb11
Point Lay USA (AK) 10 Md11
Point Lookout USA (MD) 29 Qg26
Point of Rocks USA (MD) 29 Qg26
Point of Rocks USA (WY) 25 Pa25
Point Pelee National Park ☆ CDN (ONT) 29 Qd25
Point Pleasant USA (NJ) 30 Qh25
Point Pleasant USA (WV) 29 Qd26
Point Renfrew CDN (BC) 16 Oc21
Point Reyes National Seashore ☆ USA (CA) 32 Od26
Pokemouche CDN (NB) 22 Rc22
Polar Bear Provincial Park ☆ CDN (ONT) 20 Qb18
Polebridge USA (MT) 17 Oh21
Pollock USA (LA) 36 Pj30
Polo USA (IL) 28 Qa25
Polson USA (MT) 17 Oh22
Pomeroy USA (OH) 29 Qd26
Pomeroy USA (WA) 24 Og22
Pomona USA (KS) 35 Ph26
Pompano Beach USA (FL) 43 Qe32
Pompeys Pillar USA (MT) 25 Pb23
Pompeys Pillar National Monument ☆ USA (MT) 25 Pa22
Ponca USA (NE) 27 Pg24
Ponca City USA (OK) 35 Pg27
Ponce USA (PR) 42 Rb36
Ponce de Leon USA (FL) 36 Qc30
Poncha Springs USA (CO) 34 Pb26
Ponchatoula USA (LA) 36 Pk30
Pond Creek USA (OK) 35 Pg27
Ponderosa USA (CA) 32 Of27
Pondosa USA (CA) 24 Oe25
Ponoka CDN (ALB) 17 Oj19
Ponteix CDN (SAS) 18 Pb21
Pontiac USA (IL) 28 Qa25
Pontiac USA (MI) 29 Qd24
Ponton CDN (MAN) 19 Pf18
Pontotoc USA (MS) 36 Qa28
Pontypool CDN (ONT) 29 Qf23
Poolesville USA (MD) 29 Qg26
Pool's Cove CDN (NFL) 23 Rh22
Poorman USA (AK) 10 Mh13
Popham Beach USA (ME) 22 Ra24
Poplar USA (MN) 19 Ph22
Poplar USA (MT) 18 Pc21
Poplar USA (WI) 19 Pk22
Poplar Bluff USA (MO) 36 Pk27
Poplarfield CDN (MAN) 19 Pg20
Poplar Point CDN (MAN) 19 Pg20
Poplarville USA (MS) 36 Qa30
Popotla MEX (BCN) 32 Og29
Porcupine USA (AK) 14 Ng16
Porcupine Plain CDN (SAS) 18 Pd19
Porcupine Provincial Forest ☆ CDN (MAN) 18 Pe19
Porquis Junction CDN (ONT) 20 Qe21
Portage CDN (PEI) 22 Rc22
Portage USA (AK) 13 Na15
Portage USA (WI) 28 Qa24
Portage la Prairie CDN (MAN) 19 Pf21
Portageville USA (NY) 29 Qf24
Portal USA (ND) 18 Pd21
Portal, El USA (CA) 32 Of27
Port Alberni CDN (BC) 16 Oc21
Port Albion CDN (BC) 16 Oc21
Portales USA (NM) 34 Pd28
Port Alexander USA (AK) 14 Nh17
Port Alice CDN (BC) 16 Ob20
Port Allegany USA (PA) 29 Qf25
Port Allen USA (LA) 36 Pk30
Port Andrew USA (WI) 27 Pk24
Port Angeles USA (WA) 16 Od21
Port Arthur USA (TX) 41 Pj31
Port au Choix CDN (NFL) 23 Rg20
Port Austin USA (MI) 29 Qd23
Port Barre USA (LA) 36 Pk30
Port Blandford CDN (NFL) 23 Rh21
Port Bolivar USA (TX) 41 Ph31
Port Burwell CDN (ONT) 29 Qe24
Port Charlotte USA (FL) 43 Qd32
Port Chilkoot USA (AK) 14 Nh16
Port Clinton USA (OH) 29 Qd25
Port Clyde USA (ME) 22 Ra24
Port Colborne CDN (ONT) 29 Qf24
Port-Daniel CDN (QUE) 22 Rc2
Porte, La USA (IN) 28 Qb25
Porte, La USA (TX) 41 Ph31
Porte City, La USA (IA) 27 Pj24
Porteneuf, Réserve Faunique de ☆ CDN (QUE) 21 Qj2
Porter CDN (SAS) 17 Pa1
Porters Corner USA (MT) 25 Oj2
Porterville USA (CA) 32 Of2
Port Fourchon USA (LA) 36 Pk3
Port Gibson USA (MS) 36 Pk3
Port Hardy CDN (BC) 16 Ob2
Port Heiden USA (AK) 12 Mf1
Porthill USA (ID) 17 Og2
Port Hope CDN (ONT) 29 Qf2
Port Hope Simpson CDN (NFL) 23 Rg1
Port Huron USA (MI) 29 Qd2
Port Isabel USA (TX) 40 Pg3
Port Isabel Lighthouse State Historic Site ☆ USA (TX) 40 Pg3
Port Jefferson USA (NY) 30 Qj
Port Jervis USA (NY) 30 Qh
Portland USA (IN) 28 Qc
Portland USA (ME) 22 Qk
Portland USA (OR) 24 Od
Portland USA (TX) 40 Pg
Port Lavaca USA (TX) 40 Pg
Port Lions USA (AK) 12 Mj
Port Maitland CDN (NS) 22 Rb
Port Mayaca USA (FL) 43 Qe
Port Menier CDN (QUE) 22 Rc
Port Moller USA (AK) 12 Me
Port Moody CDN (BC) 16 Od
Port Neville CDN (BC) 16 Ob
Port Orange USA (FL) 37 Qe
Port Orchard USA (WA) 16 Od
Port Perry CDN (ONT) 29 Qf
Port Rowan CDN (ONT) 29 Qe
Port Royal USA (VA) 29 Qg
Port Saint Joe USA (FL) 36 Qc
Port Sanilac USA (MI) 29 Qd
Port Simpson CDN (BC) 16 Nk
Portsmouth USA (IA) 27 Ph
Portsmouth USA (NH) 22 Qk
Portsmouth USA (OH) 29 Qd
Portsmouth USA (VA) 31 Qg
Port Stanley CDN (ONT) 29 Qe
Port Sulphur USA (LA) 36 Qa
Port Townsend USA (WA) 16 Od
Port Washington USA (WI) 28 Qb
Port Wing USA (WI) 19 Pk
Porvenir, El MEX (CHA) 39 Pc
Post USA (TX) 34 Pe
Poste-de-la-Baleine CDN (QUE) 21 Qg
Post Falls USA (ID) 17 Og
Post Oak USA (MO) 35 Pj
Postville USA (IA) 27 Pk
Poteau USA (OK) 35 Ph
Poteet USA (TX) 40 Pf
Potosi USA (MO) 28 Pk
Potrero de Gallegos MEX (ZAC) 39 Pc

Potrero del Llano MEX (CHA) 39 Pc31
Potsdam USA (NY) 29 Qh23
Potter USA (NE) 26 Pd25
Potters Mills USA (PA) 29 Qg25
Pottstown USA (PA) 29 Qh25
Pottsville USA (PA) 29 Qg25
Pouce Coupe CDN (BC) 15 Oe18
Pouch Cove CDN (NFL) 23 Rj22
Poughkeepsie USA (NY) 30 Qj25
Poularies CDN (QUE) 21 Qf21
Poulsbo USA (WA) 16 Od22
Poultney USA (VT) 30 Qj24
Powassan CDN (ONT) 29 Qf22
Powder River USA (WY) 26 Pb24
Powell USA (WY) 25 Pa23
Powell River CDN (BC) 16 Oc21
Power USA (MT) 17 Ok22
Powers USA (MI) 28 Qb23
Powers Lake USA (ND) 18 Pd21
Powhatan USA (LA) 35 Pj30
Poyen USA (AR) 35 Pj28
Pozo de Gamboa MEX (ZAC) 39 Pd34
Prairie USA (MN) 27 Pj23
Prairie City USA (OR) 24 Of23
Prairie du Chien USA (WI) 27 Pk24
Prairie River CDN (SAS) 18 Pd19
Pratt USA (KS) 35 Pf27
Prattville USA (AL) 36 Qb29
Preeceville CDN (SAS) 18 Pd20
Preemption USA (IL) 27 Pk25
Prehistoric Mounds ☆ CDN (MAN) 18 Pe21
Prehistoric Trackways National Monument ☆ USA (NY) 34 Pb29
Prelate CDN (SAS) 17 Pa20
Prele Ranger Station, La USA (WY) 26 Pc24
Premier CDN (BC) 14 Nk17
Premio CDN (QUE) 22 Rc20
Prentice USA (WI) 27 Pk23
Prentiss USA (MS) 36 Qa30
Presa del Hanabanilla ☆ C (SS) 43 Qe34
Prescott USA (AR) 35 Pj29
Prescott USA (AZ) 33 Oj28
Prescott USA (WA) 24 Of22
Presho USA (SD) 26 Pe24
Presidio USA (TX) 39 Pc31
Prespatou CDN (BC) 15 Oe17
Presque Isle USA (ME) 22 Rb22
Presque Isle USA (WI) 20 Qa22
Preston USA (ID) 25 Ok24
Preston USA (MN) 27 Pj24
Preston USA (MO) 35 Pj27
Price USA (MD) 29 Qh26
Price USA (NC) 37 Qf27
Price USA (UT) 33 Ok26
richard USA (AL) 36 Qa30
richard USA (ID) 17 Oh22
riddis CDN (ALB) 17 Oh20
riddy USA (TX) 35 Pf30
riest River USA (ID) 17 Og21
rimate CDN (SAS) 17 Pa19
rimero de Mayo MEX (COA) 40 Pe32
rince CDN (SAS) 17 Pa19
rince Albert CDN (SAS) 18 Pc19
rince Albert National Park ☆ CDN (SAS) 18 Pb18
rince Edward Island ☆ CDN (PEI) 22 Rd22
rince Edward Island National Park ☆ CDN (PEI) 22 Rd22
rince Frederick USA (MD) 29 Qg26
rince George CDN (BC) 16 Od19
ince George USA (VA) 31 Qg27
incess Anne USA (MD) 29 Qh26
inceton CDN (BC) 16 Oe21
inceton USA (AR) 35 Pj29
inceton USA (IL) 28 Qa25
inceton USA (IN) 28 Qb26
inceton USA (KY) 36 Qb27
inceton USA (MN) 27 Pj23
inceton USA (MO) 27 Pj25
inceton USA (NJ) 30 Qh25
inceton USA (WV) 37 Qe27
indle USA (WA) 24 Od23
neville USA (OR) 24 Oe23
ingle USA (SD) 26 Pd24
tchett USA (CO) 34 Pd27
octer CDN (BC) 17 Og21
octor USA (MN) 19 Pj22
octor USA (TX) 35 Pf30
octorville USA (OH) 29 Qd26
ogreso MEX (COA) 40 Pe32
ogreso MEX (YUC) 42 Qa35
ogress CDN (BC) 15 Oe18
ospector CDN (MAN) 18 Pe19
otection USA (KS) 35 Pf27
otivin USA (IA) 27 Pj24
ovidence USA (KY) 36 Qb27
ovidence USA (RI) 30 Qk25
ovidence Bay CDN (ONT) 29 Qd23
ovincetown USA (MA) 30 Qk24
ovo USA (UT) 25 Ok25
ovost CDN (ALB) 17 Ok19
udhoe Bay USA (AK) 11 Na10
or USA (MT) 25 Pa23
or, La USA (TX) 40 Pf31
or Creek USA (OK) 35 Ph27
nico CDN (NS) 22 Rc24
kett USA (MS) 36 Qa29
eblo USA (CO) 34 Pc26
eblo Pintado USA (NM) 33 Pb28
eblo Taos ☆ USA (NM) 34 Pc27
entes, Los MEX (SIN) 39 Pb33
ertecitos MEX (BCN) 38 Oh30
erto Adolfo López Mateos MEX (BCS) 38 Oj33
rto Chicxulub MEX (YUC) 42 Qa35
erto de los Ángeles, Parque Nacional del ☆ MEX (DGO) 39 Pc34
rto Escondido MEX (BCS) 38 Ok33
erto Juárez MEX (QR) 42 Qb35
rto Libertad MEX (SON) 38 Oj31
rto Magdalena MEX (BCS) 38 Oj33
rto Nuevo MEX (BCN) 32 Og29
rto Padre C (LT) 43 Qg35
rto Peñasco MEX (SON) 33 Oj30
wash CDN (NS) 22 Rd23
alani USA (HI) 44 Mg35
askwa National Park ☆ CDN (ONT) 20 Qb21
atawagan CDN (MAN) 18 Pe18
ski USA (NY) 29 Qg24
ski USA (TN) 36 Qb28
Pulaski USA (VA) 37 Qe27
Pullman USA (WA) 24 Og22
Pulpit Harbor USA (ME) 22 Ra23
Punchaw CDN (BC) 16 Od19
Punkin Center USA (CO) 34 Pd26
Punta Abreojos MEX (BCS) 38 Oj32
Punta Alegre C (CA) 43 Qf34
Punta Cabras MEX (BCN) 32 Og30
Punta del Este C (JU) 43 Qd35
Punta Eugenia MEX (BCS) 38 Oh32
Punta Prieta MEX (BCS) 38 Oh32
Punxsutawney USA (PA) 29 Qf25
Purcell USA (OK) 35 Pg28
Purcell Wilderness Conservancy ☆ CDN (BC) 17 Og20
Purdy USA (WA) 16 Od22
Purisima, La MEX (BCS) 38 Oj32
Purple Springs CDN (ALB) 17 Ok21
Purvis USA (MS) 36 Qa30
Push, La USA (WA) 16 Oc22
Putnam USA (OK) 35 Pf28
Putnam USA (TX) 35 Pf29
Pu'uwai USA (HI) 44 Me35
Puyallup USA (WA) 24 Od22
Pyote USA (TX) 34 Pd30

Q

Quadeville CDN (ONT) 29 Qg23
Quakertown USA (PA) 30 Qh25
Qualicum Beach CDN (BC) 16 Oc21
Quanah USA (TX) 35 Pf28
Qu'Appelle CDN (SAS) 18 Pd20
Quarryville USA (PA) 29 Qg26
Quartzsite USA (AZ) 33 Oh29
Québec CDN (QUE) 22 Qj22
Queen, De USA (AR) 35 Ph28
Queen City USA (MO) 27 Pj25
Queens Bay CDN (BC) 17 Og21
Queets USA (WA) 16 Oc22
Quemado USA (NM) 33 Pa28
Quesnel CDN (BC) 16 Od19
Questa USA (NM) 34 Pc27
Quetico CDN (ONT) 19 Pk21
Quetico Provincial Park ☆ CDN (ONT) 19 Pk21
Quibell CDN (ONT) 19 Pj21
Quicksand USA (KY) 37 Qd27
Quijotoa USA (AZ) 33 Oj29
Quila MEX (SIN) 39 Pb33
Quilcene USA (WA) 16 Od22
Quilchena CDN (BC) 16 Oe20
Quill Lake CDN (SAS) 18 Pc19
Quimet CDN (ONT) 20 Qa21
Quinault USA (WA) 16 Od22
Quincy USA (FL) 36 Qc30
Quincy USA (IL) 28 Pk26
Quincy USA (MA) 30 Qk24
Quinhagak USA (AK) 12 Me16
Quinlan USA (TX) 35 Pg29
Quintín Banderas C (VC) 43 Qe34
Quitman USA (GA) 37 Qd30
Quitman USA (LA) 35 Pj29
Quitman USA (MS) 36 Qa29
Quitman USA (TX) 35 Ph29
Quitovac MEX (SON) 33 Oj30
Quivira National Wildlife Refuge ☆ USA (KS) 35 Pf26
Quoin, Du USA (IL) 28 Qa26

R

Raceland USA (LA) 36 Pk31
Rachal USA (TX) 40 Pf32
Rachel USA (NV) 33 Oh27
Racine USA (WI) 28 Qb24
Radford USA (VA) 37 Qe27
Radisson CDN (QUE) 21 Qg19
Radisson CDN (SAS) 18 Pb19
Radium Hot Springs CDN (BC) 17 Og20
Radium Springs USA (NM) 34 Pb29
Radville CDN (SAS) 18 Pc21
Rae CDN (NWT) 15 Og14
Ragland USA (NM) 34 Pd28
Ragley USA (LA) 41 Pj30
Ragueneau CDN (QUE) 22 Ra21
Raiford USA (FL) 37 Qd30
Rainbow USA (AK) 13 Na15
Rainbow Lake CDN (ALB) 15 Of16
Rainy River CDN (ONT) 19 Ph21
Raith CDN (ONT) 20 Qa21
Raleigh CDN (NFL) 23 Rh20
Raleigh USA (MS) 36 Qa29
Raleigh USA (NC) 31 Qf28
Raley CDN (ALB) 17 Oj21
Ralls USA (TX) 34 Pe29
Ralph CDN (SAS) 18 Pd21
Ramah USA (NM) 33 Pa28
Ramea CDN (NFL) 23 Rg22
Ramon USA (NM) 34 Pc28
Ramona USA (CA) 32 Og29
Ramón Corona MEX (DGO) 39 Pd33
Ramones, Los MEX (NL) 40 Pf33
Ramos Arizpe MEX (COA) 40 Pe33
Rampart USA (AK) 10 Mk13
Ramsey CDN (ONT) 20 Qd22
Ramsey USA (IL) 28 Qa26
Ranchester USA (WY) 25 Pb23
Ranchuelo C (VC) 43 Qe34
Rand USA (CO) 26 Pb25
Randado USA (TX) 40 Pf32
Randolph USA (KS) 35 Pg26
Randolph USA (NE) 27 Pg24
Ranfurly CDN (ALB) 17 Ok19
Rangeley USA (ME) 22 Qk23
Rangely USA (CO) 25 Pa25
Ranger USA (TX) 35 Pf29
Rankin USA (OK) 35 Pe28
Rankin USA (TX) 39 Pe30
Ranoke CDN (ONT) 20 Qe20
Ransom USA (KS) 35 Pf26
Rantoul USA (IL) 28 Qa25
Rapelje USA (MT) 25 Pa23
Rapid City CDN (MAN) 18 Pe20
Rapid City USA (SD) 26 Pd23
Rapide-Blanc-Station CDN (QUE) 21 Qj22
Rapide-Sept CDN (QUE) 21 Qf22
Rapid River USA (MI) 28 Qb23
Rapids USA (AK) 11 Nc14
Rapids City USA (IL) 28 Pk25
Rapid View CDN (SAS) 17 Pa18
Ratcliff USA (TX) 35 Ph30
Ratcliff City USA (OK) 35 Pg28
Rathdrum USA (ID) 17 Og22
Rathwell CDN (MAN) 19 Pf21
Raton USA (NM) 34 Pc27
Rattling Brook CDN (NFL) 23 Rg21
Ravalli USA (MT) 17 Oh22
Ravendale USA (CA) 24 Oe25
Ravenna USA (NE) 26 Pf25
Ravenscrag CDN (SAS) 17 Pa21
Rawlins USA (WY) 26 Pb25
Ray USA (MN) 19 Pj21
Ray USA (ND) 18 Pd21
Raymond CDN (ALB) 17 Oj21
Raymond USA (IL) 28 Qa26
Raymond USA (ME) 22 Qk24
Raymond USA (MS) 36 Pk29
Raymond USA (MT) 18 Pc21
Raymond USA (WA) 24 Od22
Raymore CDN (SAS) 18 Pc20
Rayne USA (LA) 36 Pj30
Raynesford USA (MT) 17 Ok22
Rayón MEX (SON) 38 Ok31
Rayville USA (LA) 36 Pk29
Reading USA (PA) 29 Qh25
Readstown USA (WI) 27 Pk24
Reardan USA (WA) 17 Og22
Rebalse, El MEX (CHA) 39 Pc31
Reco CDN (ALB) 17 Og19
Red Bank CDN (NB) 22 Rc22
Red Bank USA (NJ) 30 Qh25
Red Bank USA (TN) 36 Qc28
Red Bay CDN (NFL) 23 Rg20
Red Bay USA (AL) 36 Qa28
Red Bluff USA (CA) 24 Od25
Redbridge CDN (ONT) 29 Qf22
Red Bud USA (IL) 28 Pk26
Redby USA (MN) 19 Ph22
Redcliff CDN (ALB) 17 Ok20
Red Cloud USA (NE) 35 Pf25
Red Deer CDN (ALB) 17 Oj19
Redding USA (CA) 24 Od25
Redditt CDN (ONT) 19 Ph21
Red Earth CDN (SAS) 18 Pd19
Red Earth Creek CDN (ALB) 15 Oh17
Red Feather Lakes USA (CO) 26 Pc25
Redfield CDN (SAS) 18 Pb19
Redfield USA (NY) 29 Qh24
Redfield USA (SD) 26 Pf23
Redford USA (TX) 39 Pc31
Redington USA (AZ) 33 Ok29
Red Lake CDN (ONT) 19 Pj20
Red Lake Falls USA (MN) 19 Pg22
Red Lake Road CDN (ONT) 19 Pj21
Red Lake Wildlife Management Area ☆ USA (MN) 19 Ph21
Redlands USA (CA) 32 Og28
Red Lion USA (PA) 29 Qg26
Red Lodge USA (MT) 25 Pa23
Redmond USA (OR) 24 Oe23
Redmond USA (WA) 16 Od22
Red Mountain USA (CA) 32 Og28
Red Oak USA (IA) 27 Ph25
Red Pheasant CDN (SAS) 17 Pa19
Red Rock USA (AZ) 33 Pa27
Red Rock USA (OK) 35 Pg27
Red Rock USA (PA) 29 Qg25
Red Spring USA (MO) 35 Pj27
Redvers CDN (SAS) 18 Pe21
Redwater CDN (ALB) 17 Oj19
Red Wing USA (MN) 27 Pj23
Redwood USA (MS) 36 Pk29
Redwood Falls USA (MN) 27 Ph23
Redwood National Park ☆ USA (CA) 24 Oc25
Redwood Valley USA (CA) 32 Od26
Reed City USA (MI) 28 Qc24
Reeder USA (ND) 26 Pd22
Reedpoint USA (MT) 25 Pa23
Reedsburg USA (WI) 28 Pk24
Reedsport USA (OR) 24 Oc24
Reedville USA (VA) 29 Qg27
Reeves USA (LA) 36 Pj30
Reform USA (AL) 36 Qa29
Refugio, El MEX (BCS) 38 Ok33
Refugio de Abreojo, El MEX (ZAC) 39 Pd34
Regent CDN (MAN) 18 Pe21
Reggio USA (LA) 36 Qa31
Regina CDN (SAS) 18 Pc20
Regina Beach CDN (SAS) 18 Pc20
Regocijo MEX (DGO) 39 Pc34
Regway CDN (SAS) 18 Pc21
Reidsville USA (NC) 37 Qf27
Reindeer Depot CDN (NWT) 11 Nh11
Reindeer Station USA (AK) 10 Me12
Reine, La CDN (QUE) 21 Qf21
Reisterstown USA (MD) 29 Qg26
Reliance USA (WY) 25 Pa25
Rellano MEX (CHA) 39 Pc32
Remedios C (VC) 43 Qf34
Remer USA (MN) 19 Pj22
Remolino, El MEX (COA) 40 Pe31
Renard, Rivière-au- CDN (QUE) 22 Rc21
Renata CDN (BC) 16 Of21
Rencontre East CDN (NFL) 23 Rh22
Renfrew CDN (ONT) 29 Qg23
Rennie CDN (MAN) 19 Ph21
Reno CDN (ALB) 15 Og18
Reno USA (MN) 27 Pk24
Reno USA (NV) 32 Of26
Reno, El USA (OK) 35 Pg28
Renous CDN (NB) 22 Rc22
Renovo USA (PA) 29 Qg25
Renton USA (WA) 16 Od22
Repentigny CDN (QUE) 30 Qj23
Republic USA (MI) 20 Qb22
Republic USA (MO) 35 Pj27
Republic USA (WA) 16 Of21
Reserva de la Biósfera Alto Golfo de California y Delta del ☆ MEX (SON) 33 Oh30
Reserva de la Biósfera El Vizcaíno ☆ MEX (BCS) 38 Oh32
Reserve CDN (SAS) 18 Pd19
Reserve USA (MT) 18 Pc21
Réserve de Parc Nacional de L'Archipel-de-Mingan ☆ CDN (QUE) 22 Rd20
Réserve Faunique de Dunière ☆ CDN (QUE) 22 Rb21
Réserve Faunique de Matane ☆ CDN (QUE) 22 Rb21
Réserve Faunique de Papineau Labelle ☆ CDN (QUE) 21 Qh22
Réserve Faunique de Portneuf ☆ CDN (QUE) 21 Qj22
Réserve Faunique des Chic-Chocs ☆ CDN (QUE) 22 Rc21
Réserve Faunique de Sept- Îles-Port Cartier ☆ CDN (QUE) 22 Rb20
Réserve Faunique des Laurentides ☆ CDN (QUE) 21 Qj22
Réserve Faunique du Saint-Maurice ☆ CDN (QUE) 21 Qj22
Réserve Faunique La Vérendrye ☆ CDN (QUE) 21 Qg22
Réserve Faunique Mastigouche ☆ CDN (QUE) 21 Qj22
Réserve Faunique Rouge-Matawin ☆ CDN (QUE) 21 Qh22
Réserve provincial de Rimouski ☆ CDN (QUE) 22 Ra21
Réserve provincial du Duchénier ☆ CDN (QUE) 22 Ra21
Réservoir Mainicouagan ☆ CDN (QUE) 22 Ra20
Reston CDN (MAN) 18 Pe21
Restored Village ☆ USA (IA) 27 Pk25
Retallack CDN (BC) 17 Og20
Reva USA (SD) 26 Pd23
Revelstoke CDN (BC) 16 Of20
Reventon, El MEX (SLP) 40 Pe34
Revenue CDN (SAS) 17 Pa19
Revés, El MEX (COA) 39 Pd32
Reward CDN (SAS) 17 Pa19
Rexburg USA (ID) 25 Ok24
Rexford USA (MT) 17 Oh21
Reynaud CDN (SAS) 18 Pc19
Reynolds USA (ND) 19 Pg22
Reynoldsburg USA (OH) 29 Qd26
Reynosa MEX (TAM) 40 Pf32
Rhea USA (OK) 35 Pf28
Rhinelander USA (WI) 28 Qa23
Ribstone CDN (ALB) 17 Ok19
Ricardo Flores Magón MEX (CHA) 39 Pb31
Rice USA (CA) 33 Oh28
Rice USA (TX) 35 Pg29
Rice USA (WA) 16 Of21
Rice Lake USA (WI) 27 Pk23
Riceton CDN (SAS) 18 Pc20
Richan CDN (ONT) 19 Pj21
Richardson USA (TX) 35 Pg29
Richardton USA (ND) 18 Pd22
Richer CDN (MAN) 19 Pg21
Richey USA (MT) 18 Pc22
Richfield USA (ID) 25 Oh24
Richfield USA (KS) 34 Pe27
Richfield USA (UT) 33 Oj26
Richford USA (NY) 29 Qg24
Richgrove USA (CA) 32 Of28
Richibucto CDN (NB) 22 Rc22
Rich Lake CDN (ALB) 17 Ok18
Richland USA (MO) 28 Pj27
Richland USA (TX) 35 Pg30
Richland USA (WA) 24 Of22
Richland Center USA (WI) 27 Pk24
Richlands USA (VA) 37 Qe27
Richmond CDN (BC) 16 Od21
Richmond CDN (ONT) 29 Qh23
Richmond CDN (QUE) 30 Qj23
Richmond USA (AR) 32 Od27
Richmond USA (IN) 28 Qc26
Richmond USA (KS) 35 Ph26
Richmond USA (KY) 36 Qc27
Richmond USA (VA) 31 Qg27
Richmond Dale USA (OH) 29 Qd26
Richmound CDN (SAS) 17 Pa20
Rich Square USA (NC) 31 Qg27
Richton USA (MS) 36 Qa30
Richwood USA (WV) 29 Qe26
Rico USA (CO) 33 Pa27
Ridder, De USA (LA) 41 Pj30
Riddle USA (ID) 24 Og24
Riddle USA (OR) 24 Od24
Rideau Canal ☆ CDN (ONT) 29 Qg23
Ridge Crest USA (CA) 32 Og28
Ridgeland USA (MS) 36 Pk29
Ridgeville CDN (MAN) 19 Pg21
Ridgeway USA (SC) 37 Qe28
Ridgway USA (CO) 33 Pb26
Ridgway USA (PA) 29 Qf25
Riding Mountain National Park ☆ CDN (MAN) 18 Pe20
Rifle USA (CO) 33 Pb26
Rigby USA (ID) 25 Ok24
Riggins USA (ID) 24 Og23
Riley USA (KS) 35 Pg26
Riley USA (OR) 24 Of24
Rimbey CDN (ALB) 17 Oh19
Rimouski CDN (QUE) 22 Ra21
Rimouski, Réserve provincial de ☆ CDN (QUE) 22 Ra21
Rincon USA (NM) 34 Pb29
Rinconada USA (NM) 34 Pc27
Rincón del Guanal C (JU) 43 Qd35
Ringgold USA (LA) 35 Pj29
Ringgold USA (TX) 35 Pg29
Ringling USA (MT) 25 Ok22
Rio Blanco USA (CO) 33 Pb26
Rio Bravo MEX (TAM) 40 Pf33
Rio Dell USA (CA) 24 Oc25
Rio Grande MEX (ZAC) 39 Pd34
Rio Lagartos MEX (YUC) 42 Qa35
Rio Lagartos, Parque Natural ☆ MEX (YUC) 42 Qa35
Rio Vista USA (TX) 35 Pg29
Ripley USA (KY) 29 Qd26
Ripley USA (MS) 36 Qa28
Ripley USA (WV) 29 Qe26
Rising Star USA (TX) 35 Pf29
Rising Sun USA (IN) 28 Qc26
Riske Creek CDN (ALB) 16 Od20
Ritzville USA (WA) 24 Of22
Rivercourse CDN (ALB) 17 Pa19
Riverdale USA (ND) 18 Pe22
River Falls USA (WI) 27 Pj23
Riverhead USA (NY) 30 Qj25
River Hills CDN (MAN) 19 Ph20
River of No Return Wilderness ☆ USA (ID) 25 Oh23
Rivers CDN (MAN) 18 Pe20
Riversdale CDN (ONT) 29 Qe23
Riverside USA (CA) 32 Og29
Riverside USA (IA) 27 Pk25
Riverside USA (MD) 29 Qg26
Riverside USA (WA) 16 Of21
Riverside USA (WY) 26 Pb25
Riverton CDN (MAN) 19 Pg20
Riverton USA (WY) 25 Pa24
River Valley CDN (ONT) 20 Qe22
Riviera USA (TX) 40 Pg32
Rivière-à-Pierre CDN (QUE) 21 Qj22
Rivière-au-Renard CDN (QUE) 22 Rc21
Rivière-aux-Graines CDN (QUE) 22 Rc20
Rivière-aux-Saumons CDN (QUE) 22 Rd21
Rivière-Bleue CDN (QUE) 22 Ra22
Rivière-Chicotte CDN (QUE) 22 Rd21
Rivière-du-Loup CDN (QUE) 22 Ra22
Rivière-Héva CDN (QUE) 21 Qf21
Rivière Pentecôte CDN (QUE) 22 Rb21
Rivière Saint-Jean CDN (QUE) 22 Rc20
Rivière Veuve CDN (ONT) 20 Qe22
Road Town GB (VI) 42 Rc36
Roanoke USA (AL) 36 Qc29
Roanoke USA (VA) 37 Qf27
Roanoke Rapids USA (NC) 31 Qg27
Roaring Springs USA (TX) 34 Pe29
Robeline USA (LA) 35 Pj30
Robersonville USA (NC) 31 Qg28
Roberta USA (GA) 37 Qd29
Robert Lee USA (TX) 34 Pe30
Robert's Arm CDN (NFL) 23 Rh21
Roberts Creek CDN (BC) 16 Od21
Robertsdale USA (AL) 36 Qb30
Roberval CDN (QUE) 21 Qj21
Robinhood CDN (SAS) 17 Pa19
Robinson USA (IL) 28 Qb26
Robinson USA (ND) 19 Pf22
Robinson USA (TX) 35 Pg30
Robious USA (VA) 31 Qg27
Robles Junction USA (AZ) 33 Ok29
Roblin CDN (MAN) 18 Pe20
Roblin CDN (ONT) 29 Qg23
Robsart CDN (SAS) 17 Pa21
Robson CDN (BC) 17 Og21
Robstown USA (TX) 40 Pg32
Roby USA (MO) 35 Pj27
Roby USA (TX) 34 Pe29
Rocanville CDN (SAS) 18 Pd20
Rochéachic MEX (CHA) 39 Pb32
Rochelle USA (IL) 28 Qa25
Rochelle USA (TX) 40 Pf30
Rochelle, La CDN (MAN) 19 Pg21
Rocher River CDN (NWT) 15 Oj15
Rochester USA (IN) 28 Qb25
Rochester USA (MI) 29 Qd24
Rochester USA (MN) 27 Pj23
Rochester USA (NH) 22 Qk24
Rochester USA (NY) 29 Qg24
Rock Creek CDN (BC) 16 Of21
Rockdale USA (TX) 40 Pg30
Rock Falls USA (IL) 28 Qa25
Rockford USA (AL) 36 Qb29
Rockford USA (IL) 28 Qa24
Rockford USA (WA) 17 Og22
Rockglen CDN (SAS) 18 Pc21
Rock Hall USA (MD) 29 Qg26
Rockhaven CDN (SAS) 17 Pa19
Rock Hill USA (SC) 37 Qe28
Rockingham USA (NC) 37 Qf28
Rock Island CDN (QUE) 30 Qj23
Rocklake USA (ND) 19 Pf21
Rockland CDN (ONT) 29 Qh23
Rockland USA (ME) 22 Ra23
Rock Point USA (MD) 29 Qg26
Rockport USA (IN) 36 Qb27
Rock Port USA (MO) 27 Ph25
Rockport USA (TX) 40 Pg31
Rockport USA (WA) 16 Oe21
Rock Rapids USA (IA) 27 Pg24
Rock River USA (WY) 26 Pc25
Rock Springs USA (AZ) 33 Oj28
Rock Springs USA (MT) 18 Pb22
Rocksprings USA (TX) 40 Pe30
Rock Springs USA (WY) 25 Pa25
Rockville USA (MD) 29 Qg26
Rockville USA (NE) 26 Pf25
Rockwall USA (TX) 35 Pg29
Rockwell City USA (IA) 27 Ph24
Rockwood USA (ME) 22 Ra23
Rockwood USA (TN) 36 Qc28
Rockwood USA (TX) 35 Pf30
Rocky Boy USA (MT) 17 Pa21
Rocky Ford USA (CO) 34 Pd26
Rocky Mount USA (NC) 31 Qg28
Rocky Mount USA (VA) 37 Qf27
Rocky Mountain House CDN (ALB) 17 Oh19
Rocky Mountain House National Historic Park ☆ CDN (ALB) 17 Oh19
Rocky Mountain National Park ☆ USA (CO) 26 Pb25
Rocky Mountains Forest Reserve ☆ CDN (ALB) 17 Og19
Rocky Mountains Forest Reserve ☆ CDN (ALB) 17 Oh20
Roddickton CDN (NFL) 23 Rg20
Rodeo USA (NM) 33 Pa30
Rodney USA (MS) 36 Pk30
Rodrigo M. Quevedo MEX (CHA) 34 Pb30
Rodríguez, Los MEX (COA) 40 Pe32
Rogers USA (AR) 35 Ph27
Rogers USA (ND) 19 Pf22
Rogers City USA (MI) 29 Qd23
Rogerson USA (ID) 25 Oh24
Rogers Pass CDN (BC) 17 Og20
Rogersville CDN (NB) 22 Rc22
Roland CDN (MAN) 19 Pg21
Rolette USA (ND) 19 Pf21
Roll USA (OK) 35 Pf28
Rolla CDN (BC) 15 Oe18
Rolla USA (KS) 34 Pe27
Rolla USA (MO) 28 Pk27
Rolla USA (ND) 19 Pf21
Rolling Fork USA (MS) 36 Pk29
Rolling Hills CDN (ALB) 17 Ok20
Rollins USA (MN) 19 Pk22
Rollins USA (MT) 17 Oh22
Roma USA (TX) 40 Pf32
Romaine, La CDN (QUE) 23 Re20

Romancoke USA (MD) 29 Qg26
Rome USA (GA) 36 Qc28
Rome USA (NY) 29 Qh24
Romero USA (TX) 34 Pd28
Romney USA (IN) 28 Qb25
Romney USA (WV) 29 Qf26
Ronan USA (MT) 17 Oh22
Ronge, La CDN (SAS) 18 Pc18
Roosevelt USA (AZ) 33 Ok29
Roosevelt USA (UT) 25 Ok25
Roosevelt Campobello International Park ☆ CDN (NB) 22 Rb23
Roosville CDN (BC) 17 Oh21
Rosa CDN (MAN) 19 Pg21
Rosa de Castillo MEX (BCN) 32 Og30
Rosales, Culiacán MEX (SIN) 39 Pb33
Rosalia USA (WA) 24 Og22
Rosario MEX (SON) 39 Pa32
Rosario, El MEX (BCN) 38 Oh30
Rosario, El MEX (SIN) 39 Pc34
Rosario, Playa C (LH) 43 Qd34
Rosario, Valle del MEX (CHA) 39 Pb32
Rosarito MEX (BCN) 32 Og29
Rosarito MEX (BCN) 38 Oh31
Rosarito MEX (BCS) 38 Ok32
Rosburg USA (WA) 24 Od22
Roscoe USA (TX) 34 Pe29
Roscommon USA (MI) 28 Qc23
Roseau USA (MN) 19 Ph21
Rosebank CDN (MAN) 19 Pf21
Rose-Blanche CDN (NFL) 23 Rf22
Roseboro USA (NC) 31 Qf28
Rose Bud USA (AR) 35 Pj28
Rosebud USA (SD) 26 Pe24
Rosebud USA (TX) 40 Pg30
Roseburg USA (OR) 24 Od24
Rosedale CDN (BC) 16 Oe21
Rosefield USA (LA) 36 Pk30
Roseglen USA (ND) 18 Pe22
Rose Hill USA (MS) 36 Qa29
Rose Hill USA (NC) 31 Qf28
Roseisle CDN (MAN) 19 Pf21
Rose Lake CDN (BC) 16 Ob18
Rose Lake USA (ID) 17 Og22
Roseland USA (LA) 36 Pk30
Rosemount USA (MN) 27 Pj23
Rosenberg USA (TX) 41 Ph31
Rosenburg CDN (MAN) 19 Pg21
Rosenfeld USA (TX) 39 Pd30
Rosenort CDN (MAN) 19 Pg21
Rose Prairie CDN (BC) 15 Oe17
Roses USA (PA) 29 Qf25
Rosetitla MEX (CHA) 39 Pc31
Rosetown CDN (SAS) 18 Pb20
Rose Valley CDN (SAS) 18 Pd19
Roseville USA (IL) 27 Pk25
Rosiers, Cap-des- CDN (QUE) 22 Rc21
Rosita, La MEX (COA) 39 Pd31
Roslin CDN (ONT) 29 Qg23
Rossburn CDN (MAN) 18 Pe20
Rosser CDN (MAN) 19 Pg20
Rossland CDN (BC) 17 Og21
Rossport CDN (ONT) 20 Qb21
Ross River CDN (NWT) 14 Nj15
Rosston USA (AR) 35 Pj29
Rosston USA (OK) 35 Pf27
Rosswood CDN (BC) 14 Oa18
Rosthern CDN (SAS) 18 Pb19
Rostraver USA (PA) 29 Qf25
Roswell USA (GA) 36 Qc28
Roswell USA (NM) 34 Pc29
Rosyth CDN (ALB) 17 Ok19
Rothsay USA (MN) 27 Pg22
Rouge-Matawin, Réserve Faunique ☆ CDN (QUE) 21 Qh22
Rough Rock USA (AZ) 33 Pa27
Saint-Ambroise CDN (QUE) 21 Qk21
Round Hill CDN (ALB) 17 Oj19
Round Mountain USA (CA) 24 Oe25
Round Mountain USA (NV) 32 Og26
Round Rock USA (AZ) 33 Pa27
Round Rock USA (TX) 40 Pg30
Round Spring USA (MO) 36 Pk27
Roundup USA (MT) 18 Pa22
Rounthwaite CDN (MAN) 19 Pf21
Rouyn-Noranda CDN (QUE) 21 Qf21
Rover USA (AR) 35 Pj28
Rowan, Port CDN (ONT) 29 Qe24
Rowden USA (TX) 35 Pf29
Rowena USA (TX) 34 Pe30
Roxboro USA (NC) 37 Qf27
Roxie USA (MS) 36 Pk30
Roy USA (MT) 18 Pa22
Roy USA (NM) 34 Pc28
Roy USA (UT) 25 Oj25
Roy, Le USA (MN) 27 Pj24
Royal, Port USA (VA) 29 Qg26
Royalton USA (MN) 27 Ph23
Royston USA (GA) 37 Qd28
Ruby USA (AK) 10 Mh13
Ruby USA (AZ) 33 Ok30
Ruby Valley USA (NV) 25 Oh25
Rucio, El MEX (ZAC) 40 Pd34
Ruckersville USA (VA) 29 Qf26
Rudyard USA (MT) 17 Ok21
Rue, La USA (TX) 35 Ph29
Rugby USA (ND) 18 Pe21
Ruidosa USA (TX) 39 Pc30
Ruidoso USA (NM) 34 Pc29
Rule USA (TX) 35 Pf29
Ruleville USA (MS) 36 Pk29
Rumorosa, La MEX (BCN) 32 Og29
Rupert USA (AR) 35 Pj28
Rupert USA (ID) 25 Oj24
Rupert USA (WV) 37 Qe27
Rush Center USA (KS) 35 Pf26
Rush City USA (MN) 27 Pj23
Rushfort USA (MN) 27 Pk24
Rush Springs USA (OK) 35 Pg28
Rushville USA (IL) 27 Pk25
Rushville USA (IN) 28 Qc26
Rusk USA (TX) 35 Ph30
Ruso USA (ND) 18 Pe22
Russel CDN (MAN) 18 Pe20
Russell USA (KS) 35 Pf26
Russell USA (ND) 18 Pe21
Russell USA (NY) 29 Qh23
Russell Fiord Wilderness ☆ USA (AK) 14 Nf16
Russellville USA (AL) 36 Qb28
Russellville USA (AR) 35 Pj28
Russellville USA (KY) 36 Qb27
Russel Springs USA (KS) 34 Pe26
Rustic USA (CO) 26 Pc25
Ruston USA (LA) 35 Pj29
Ruthilda CDN (SAS) 17 Pa20
Ruthville USA (ND) 18 Pe21
Rutland CDN (BC) 16 Of21
Rutland CDN (SAS) 17 Pa19
Rutland USA (VT) 30 Qj24
Ryan USA (OK) 35 Pg29
Rycroft CDN (NFL) 15 Of18
Ryder USA (ND) 18 Pe22
Ryegate USA (MT) 18 Pa22
Ryerson CDN (SAS) 18 Pe21
Rykerts CDN (BC) 17 Og21

S

Saanich CDN (BC) 16 Od21
Sabinal USA (TX) 40 Pf31
Sabinas MEX (COA) 40 Pe32
Sabinas Hidalgo MEX (NL) 40 Pe32
Sabine National Wildlife Refuge ☆ USA (LA) 41 Ph31
Sachigo Lake CDN (ONT) 19 Pj19
Sackville CDN (NB) 22 Rc23
Saco USA (ME) 22 Qk24
Saco USA (MT) 18 Pb21
Sacramento MEX (COA) 39 Pd32
Sacramento USA (CA) 32 Oe26
Saddle Lake CDN (ALB) 17 Ok19
Safford USA (AZ) 33 Pa29
Sage USA (WY) 25 Ok25
Sage Mesa CDN (BC) 16 Of21
Saginaw USA (MI) 29 Qd24
Saguache USA (CO) 34 Pb26
Sagua la Grande C (VC) 43 Qe34
Saguaro National Park ☆ USA (AZ) 33 Ok29
Sahuaral MEX (SON) 38 Ok31
Sahuaripa MEX (SON) 39 Pa31
Sahuarita USA (AZ) 33 Ok30
Sahuaro, El MEX (SON) 38 Oj30
Sain Alto MEX (ZAC) 39 Pd34
Saint Adolphe CDN (MAN) 19 Pg21
Saint Albans CDN (NFL) 23 Rh22
Saint Albans USA (WV) 29 Qe26
Saint Albert CDN (ALB) 17 Oj19
Saint-Alexandre CDN (QUE) 22 Ra22
Saint Alphonse CDN (MAN) 19 Pf21
Saint Ambroise CDN (MAN) 19 Pf20
Saint-Augustine CDN (QUE) 21 Qk21
Saint-André = Andréville CDN (QUE) 22 Ra22
Saint-André-du-Lac-Saint-Jean CDN (QUE) 21 Qj21
Saint Andrews CDN (NB) 22 Rb23
Saint Andrew's CDN (NFL) 23 Rf22
Saint Anne USA (IL) 28 Qb25
Saint Ansgar USA (IA) 27 Pj24
Saint Anthony CDN (NFL) 23 Rh20
Saint Anthony USA (ID) 25 Ok24
Saint Athanase CDN (QUE) 22 Ra22
Saint-Augustin CDN (QUE) 23 Rf20
Saint-Bruno CDN (QUE) 21 Qk21
Saint Augustine USA (FL) 37 Qe31
Saint Augustine USA (IL) 28 Pk25
Saint Barbe CDN (NFL) 23 Rg20
Saint-Barnabe CDN (QUE) 21 Qj22
Saint-Basile CDN (NB) 22 Ra22
Saint Bernard's CDN (NFL) 23 Rh22
Saint Brendan's CDN (NFL) 23 Rj21
Saint Brides CDN (ALB) 17 Ok19
Saint Bride's CDN (NFL) 23 Rh22
Saint Brieux CDN (SAS) 18 Pc19
Sainte-Monique CDN (QUE) 21 Qk21
Saint Catharines CDN (ONT) 29 Qf24
Saint Charles USA (ID) 25 Ok24
Saint Charles USA (MN) 27 Pj24
Saint Charles USA (MO) 28 Pk26
Saint-Charles-Garnier CDN (QUE) 22 Ra21
Saint Clair USA (MO) 28 Pk26
Saint Clairsville USA (OH) 29 Qe25
Saint Claude CDN (MAN) 19 Pf21
Saint Cloud USA (FL) 43 Qe31
Saint Cloud USA (MN) 27 Ph23
Saint Croix CDN (NB) 22 Rb23
Saint Croix Falls USA (WI) 27 Pj23
Saint Croix Island National Monument ☆ CDN (NB) 22 Rb23
Saint Croix State Park ☆ USA (MN) 27 Pj23
Saint David USA (AZ) 33 Ok30
Saint-Donat CDN (QUE) 21 Qh22
Sainte Agathe CDN (MAN) 19 Pg21
Sainte-Agathe-des-Monts CDN (QUE) 30 Qh22
Sainte-Angèle-de-Mérici CDN (QUE) 22 Ra21
Sainte Anne CDN (MAN) 19 Pg21
Sainte-Anne-de-Beaupré CDN (QUE) 22 Qk22
Sainte-Anne-des-Monts CDN (QUE) 22 Rb21
Sainte-Anne-du-Lac CDN (QUE) 21 Qh22
Sainte-Brigitte-de-Laval CDN (QUE) 22 Qk22
Sainte-Catherine CDN (QUE) 22 Qk22
Sainte-Henri-de-Taillon CDN (QUE) 21 Qk21
Sainte Croix USA (IN) 28 Qb26
Sainte Elisabeth CDN (MAN) 19 Pg21
Sainte-Émélie-de-l'Énergie CDN (QUE) 21 Qj22
Sainte-Eulalie CDN (QUE) 21 Qj22
Sainte Genevieve USA (MO) 28 Pk27
Sainte-Gertrude CDN (QUE) 21 Qf21
Sainte-Hedwige-de-Roberval CDN (QUE) 21 Qj21
Sainte-Justine CDN (QUE) 22 Qk22
Saint Eleanors CDN (PEI) 22 Rd22
Saint-Éleuthère CDN (QUE) 22 Ra22
Saint-Elzéar CDN (QUE) 22 Ra22
Sainte-Marie CDN (QUE) 22 Qk22
Sainte-Marie-de-Blandford CDN (QUE) 21 Qj22
Sainte-Ludger-de-Milot CDN (QUE) 21 Qk21
Sainte Rose du Lac CDN (MAN) 19 Pf20
Sainte-Rose-du-Nord CDN (QUE) 22 Qk21
Saint-Esprit CDN (QUE) 30 Qj23
Sainte-Thérese CDN (QUE) 21 Qh22
Sainte-Félicien CDN (QUE) 21 Qj21
Saint-Félix-de-Valois CDN (QUE) 21 Qj22
Saint Francis CDN (ALB) 17 Oh19
Saint Francis USA (KS) 34 Pe26
Saint Francis USA (ME) 22 Ra22
Saint Francis USA (MN) 27 Pj23
Saint Francisville USA (LA) 36 Pk30
Saint François CDN (QUE) 22 Qk22
Saint-Gabriel CDN (QUE) 21 Qj22
Saint George CDN (NB) 22 Rb23
Saint George USA (SC) 37 Qe29
Saint George USA (UT) 33 Oj27
Saint George Island USA (MD) 29 Qg26
Saint George's CDN (NFL) 23 Rf21
Saint-Georges CDN (QUE) 22 Qk22
Saint-Gérard CDN (QUE) 22 Qk23
Saint Helens USA (OR) 24 Od23
Saint-Henri CDN (QUE) 22 Qk22
Saint-Nazaire CDN (QUE) 21 Qk21
Saint-Hyacinthe CDN (QUE) 30 Qj23
Saint Ignace USA (MI) 28 Qc23
Saint-Ignace-du-Lac CDN (QUE) 21 Qj22
Saint Ignatius USA (MT) 17 Oh22
Saint-Jacques CDN (NB) 22 Ra22
Saint James USA (MI) 28 Qc23
Saint James USA (MN) 27 Ph24
Saint James USA (MO) 28 Pk27
Saint-Jean, Lac ☆ CDN (QUE) 21 Qj21
Saint-Jean, Rivière CDN (QUE) 22 Rc20
Saint Jean Baptiste CDN (MAN) 19 Pg21
Saint-Jean-de-Dieu CDN (QUE) 22 Ra21
Saint-Jean-Port-Joli CDN (QUE) 22 Qk22
Saint-Jean-sur-Richelieu CDN (QUE) 30 Qj23
Saint-Jérome CDN (QUE) 30 Qh23
Saint Jo USA (TX) 35 Pg29
Saint Joe USA (AR) 35 Pj27
Saint Joe USA (ID) 17 Og22
Saint Joe, Port USA (FL) 36 Qc31
Saint John CDN (NB) 22 Rb23
Saint John USA (KS) 35 Pf27
Saint John's CDN (NFL) 23 Rj22
Saint Johns USA (AZ) 33 Pa28
Saint Johns USA (MI) 28 Qc24
Saint Johnsbury USA (VT) 30 Qj23
Saint John Station USA (UT) 25 Oj25
Saint Joseph USA (LA) 36 Pk30
Saint Joseph USA (MO) 35 Ph26
Saint Josephs CDN (NFL) 23 Rj22
Saint-Jovite CDN (QUE) 30 Qh22
Saint Labre CDN (MAN) 19 Pg21
Saint-Lambert CDN (QUE) 22 Qk22
Saint Lawrence Island National Park ☆ USA (NY) 29 Qh23
Saint Lazare CDN (MAN) 18 Pe20
Saint Léonard CDN (NB) 22 Rb22
Saint Louis USA (MO) 28 Pk26
Saint-Ludger CDN (QUE) 22 Qk23
Pont-Rouge CDN (QUE) 21 Qk22
Saint Luis CDN (SAS) 18 Pc19
Saint-Malachie CDN (QUE) 22 Qk22
Saint-Malo CDN (QUE) 22 Qk23
Saint-Marc-des-Carrières CDN (QUE) 21 Qj22
Saint-Marcel CDN (QUE) 22 Qk22
Saint Margarets CDN (NB) 22 Rc22
Saint Maries USA (ID) 17 Og22
Saint Marks USA (FL) 36 Qc30
Saint Marks National Wildlife Refuge ☆ USA (FL) 36 Qc30
Saint-Martin CDN (QUE) 22 Qk23
Saint Martins CDN (NB) 22 Rc23
Saint Martinville USA (LA) 36 Pk30
Saint Mary USA (MT) 17 Oj21
Saint Marys USA (GA) 37 Qe30
Saint Marys USA (KS) 35 Pg26
Saint Marys USA (PA) 29 Qf25
Saint Marys USA (WV) 29 Qe26
Saint-Maurice, Réserve Faunique du ☆ CDN (QUE) 21 Qj22
Saint-Méthode CDN (QUE) 21 Qj21
Saint Michael USA (AK) 10 Md14
Saint Michaels USA (AZ) 33 Pa28
Saint-Michel-des-Saints CDN (QUE) 21 Qj22
Sainte-Croix CDN (QUE) 21 Qk22
Saint Norbert CDN (MAN) 19 Pg21
Saint-Pamphile CDN (QUE) 22 Ra22
Saint-Pascal CDN (QUE) 22 Qk22
Saint Paul CDN (ALB) 17 Ok19
Saint Paul USA (AR) 35 Pj28
Saint Paul USA (MN) 27 Pj23
Saint Paul USA (NE) 26 Pf25
Saint Paul USA (VA) 37 Qd27
Saint Pauls CDN (NFL) 23 Rg20
Saint Pauls USA (NC) 37 Qf28
Saint Peter USA (MN) 27 Ph23
Saint Peters CDN (NS) 23 Re23
Saint Peters Bay CDN (PEI) 22 Rd22
Saint Petersburg USA (FL) 43 Qd32
Saint-Philémon CDN (QUE) 22 Qk22
Saint-Philippe-de-Neri CDN (QUE) 22 Ra22
Saint-Pierre CDN (QUE) 22 Qk22
Saint-Pierre CDN (QUE) 29 Qh23
Saint Pierre F (SPM) 23 Rg22
Saint Pierre Jolys CDN (MAN) 19 Pg21
Saint-Prime CDN (QUE) 21 Qj21
Saint-Quentin CDN (NB) 22 Rb22
Saint-Raphaël CDN (QUE) 22 Qk22
Saint-Raymond CDN (QUE) 21 Qk22
Saint Regis USA (MT) 17 Oh22
Saint Robert USA (MO) 35 Pj27
Saint Shott's CDN (NFL) 23 Rj22
Saint-Siméon CDN (QUE) 22 Ra22
Saint-Stanislas CDN (QUE) 21 Qj22
Saint Stephen CDN (NB) 22 Rb23
Saint Teresa USA (FL) 36 Qc31
Saint Theresa Point CDN (MAN) 19 Ph19
Saint Thomas CDN (ONT) 29 Qe24
Saint Thomas USA (ND) 19 Pg21
Saint-Thomas-Dydime CDN (QUE) 21 Qj21
Saint-Tite CDN (QUE) 21 Qj22
Saint-Urbain CDN (QUE) 22 Qk22
Saint Victor CDN (SAS) 18 Pc21
Saint Victor's Petroglyphs Historic Park ☆ CDN (SAS) 18 Pc21
Saint Vincent CDN (ALB) 17 Ok18
Saint Vincent USA (MN) 19 Pg21
Saint Vincent National Wildlife Refuge ☆ USA (FL) 36 Qc31
Saint Walburg CDN (SAS) 17 Pa19
Saint Xavier USA (MT) 25 Pb23
Saint-Zénon CDN (QUE) 21 Qj22
Sal, La USA (UT) 33 Pa26
Salaberry-de-Valleyfield CDN (QUE) 30 Qh23
Salamanca USA (NY) 29 Qf24
Salem USA (AR) 36 Pk27
Salem USA (FL) 37 Qd31
Salem USA (IL) 28 Qa26
Salem USA (IN) 28 Qb26
Salem USA (MO) 36 Pk27
Salem USA (NH) 22 Qk24
Salem USA (NJ) 31 Qh26
Salem USA (OH) 29 Qe25
Salem USA (OR) 24 Od23
Salem USA (SD) 27 Pg24
Salida USA (CO) 34 Pb26
Salina USA (KS) 35 Pg26
Salina USA (UT) 33 Ok26
Salinas USA (CA) 32 Oe27
Salinas Pueblo Missions National Monument (Gran Quivira) ☆ USA (NM) 34 Pb28
Salinas Victoria MEX (NL) 40 Pe33
Saline USA (LA) 35 Pj29
Salisbury CDN (NB) 22 Rc22
Salisbury USA (MD) 31 Qh26
Salisbury USA (MO) 28 Pj26
Salisbury USA (NC) 37 Qe28
Salkum USA (WA) 24 Od22
Salle, La USA (CO) 26 Pc25
Sallisaw USA (OK) 35 Ph28
Sally's Cove CDN (NFL) 23 Rg21
Salmo CDN (BC) 17 Og21
Salmon USA (ID) 25 Oj23
Salmon Arm CDN (BC) 16 Of20
Saltcoats CDN (SAS) 18 Pd20
Saltery Bay CDN (BC) 16 Oc21
Salt Flat USA (TX) 34 Pc30
Saltillo MEX (COA) 40 Pe33
Salt Lake City USA (UT) 25 Ok25
Salto, El MEX (DGO) 39 Pc34
Salton City USA (CA) 33 Oh29
Salt River Bay National Park ☆ USA (VI) 42 Rc37
Salt Springs USA (FL) 37 Qe31
Saluda USA (SC) 37 Qe29
Salus USA (AR) 35 Pj28
Salvador CDN (SAS) 17 Pa19
Salvador, El MEX (ZAC) 40 Pe33
Salvage CDN (NFL) 23 Rj21
Salyersville USA (KY) 37 Qd27
Samachique MEX (CHA) 39 Pb32
Samalayuca MEX (CHA) 34 Pb30
Sambro CDN (NS) 22 Rd23
Sams USA (CO) 33 Pb26
Samuels USA (ID) 17 Og21
Sanak USA (AK) 12 Md18
San Angelo USA (TX) 34 Pe30
San Anselmo USA (CA) 32 Od27
San Antonio MEX (BCS) 38 Ok34
San Antonio USA (NM) 34 Pb29
San Antonio USA (TX) 40 Pf31
San Antonio de los Alazanes MEX (COA) 40 Pe33
San Antonio El Grande MEX (CHA) 39 Pc31
San Augustin MEX (BCN) 38 Oh31
San Augustine USA (TX) 35 Ph30
San Benito USA (TX) 40 Pg32
San Bernardino MEX (SON) 33 Pa30
San Bernardino USA (CA) 32 Og28
San Blas MEX (COA) 39 Pd32
San Blas MEX (SIN) 39 Pa32
San Borja, Missión de MEX (BCN) 38 Oj31
Sanborn USA (MN) 27 Ph23
Sanbornville USA (NH) 22 Qk24
San Buenaventura MEX (COA) 40 Pe32
Sanca CDN (BC) 17 Og21
San Carlos MEX (BCS) 38 Oj33
San Carlos MEX (COA) 40 Pe31
San Carlos MEX (TAM) 40 Pf33
San Carlos USA (AZ) 33 Ok29
San Clara CDN (MAN) 18 Pe20
San Clemente USA (CA) 32 Og29
San Cristóbal C (PR) 43 Qd34
Sancti Spíritus C (SS) 43 Qf35
Sanders USA (AZ) 33 Pa28
Sanderson USA (TX) 39 Pd30
Sandersville USA (GA) 37 Qd29
Sandhill USA (MS) 36 Qa29
Sand Hill USA (MS) 36 Qa30
San Diego USA (CA) 32 Og29
San Diego USA (TX) 40 Pf32
Sandilands Provincial Forest ☆ CDN (MAN) 19 Pg21
Sandino C (PR) 42 Qc34
Sand Lake CDN (ONT) 20 Qc22
Sand Lake CDN (ONT) 29 Qf23
Sand Lake National Wildlife Refuge ☆ USA (SD) 26 Pf23
Sandoval USA (IL) 28 Qa26
Sand Point USA (AK) 12 Me18
Sandpoint USA (ID) 17 Og21
Sand Springs USA (MT) 18 Pb22
Sand Springs USA (OK) 35 Pg27
Sandstone USA (MN) 27 Pj22
Sandusky USA (MI) 29 Qd24
Sandusky USA (OH) 29 Qd25
Sandwith CDN (SAS) 17 Pa19
Sandy USA (UT) 25 Ok25
Sandy Bay CDN (MAN) 18 Pd18
Sandy Cove CDN (NS) 22 Rb23
Sandy Harbor Beach USA (NY) 29 Qg24
Sandy Hook USA (KY) 29 Qd26
Sandy Hook USA (MS) 36 Qa30
Sandy Lake CDN (ALB) 17 Oj18
Sandy Lake CDN (ONT) 19 Pj19
Sandy Point BS 43 Qg32
Sandy Springs USA (OH) 29 Qd26
San Esteban MEX (BCS) 38 Oj32
San Felipe MEX (BCN) 38 Oh30
San Felipe MEX (YUC) 42 Qa35
San Felipe, Parque Natural ☆ MEX (YUC) 42 Qa35
San Felipe Nuevo Mercurio MEX (ZAC) 40 Pd33
San Fernando MEX (TAM) 40 Pf33
San Fernando USA (CA) 32 Of28
Sanford CDN (MAN) 19 Pg21
Sanford USA (FL) 43 Qe31
Sanford USA (ME) 22 Qk24
Sanford USA (NC) 37 Qf28
San Francisco USA (CA) 32 Od27
San Francisco, Sierra de ☆ MEX (BCS) 38 Oj32
San Francisco de Borja MEX (CHA) 39 Pb32
San Francisco de Cabrales MEX (ZAC) 39 Pd33
San Francisco de Horizonte MEX (DGO) 39 Pd33
San Francisco del Oro MEX (CHA) 39 Pc32
San Francisquito MEX (BCN) 38 Oj31
Sanger USA (CA) 32 Of27
San Germán USA (PR) 42 Rb36
San Ignacio MEX (BCS) 38 Oj32
San Ignacio MEX (SIN) 39 Pb34
Sanilac, Port USA (MI) 29 Qd24
San Isidro MEX (CHA) 34 Pb30
San Isidro MEX (COA) 39 Pd32
San Javier MEX (BCS) 38 Ok33
San Jon USA (NM) 34 Pd28
San José MEX (SON) 38 Ok32
San Jose USA (CA) 32 Oe27
San Jose USA (IL) 28 Qa25
San José de Dimas MEX (SON) 38 Ok31
San José de Gracia MEX (SIN) 39 Pb32
San José de las Lajas C (LH) 43 Qd34
San José de la Zorra MEX (BCN) 32 Og29
San José del Cabo MEX (BCS) 39 Pa34
San José de Raíces MEX (NL) 40 Pe33
San Juan USA (AK) 13 Na15
San Juan USA (PR) 42 Rb36
San Juan de Guadalupe MEX (DGO) 39 Pd33
San Juan de la Costa MEX (BCS) 38 Ok33
San Juan de los Planes MEX (BCS) 39 Pa34
San Juan del Río MEX (DGO) 39 Pc33
San Juan de Sabinas MEX (COA) 40 Pe32
San Juanito MEX (CHA) 39 Pb32
San Juan National Historic Park ☆ USA (WA) 16 Od21
San Juan y Martínez C (PR) 43 Qd34
San Lorenzo USA (NM) 33 Pb29
San Lucas USA (CA) 32 Oe27
San Lucas, Cabo ☆ MEX (BCS) 39 Pa34
San Luis MEX (BCN) 38 Oh31
San Luis USA (AZ) 33 Ok29
San Luis USA (CO) 34 Pc27
San Luis del Cordero MEX (DGO) 39 Pc33
San Luis Obispo USA (CA) 32 Oe28
San Luis Río Colorado MEX (SON) 33 Oh29
San Marcos USA (TX) 40 Pg31
San Mateo MEX (ZAC) 39 Pd34
San Mateo USA (CA) 32 Od27
San Mateo USA (NM) 33 Pb28
San Miguel MEX (COA) 39 Pd31
San Miguel USA (AZ) 33 Ok30
San Miguel de Baga C (CG) 43 Qg35
San Miguelito MEX (SON) 39 Pa30
San Nicolás MEX (SON) 39 Pa31
San Nicolás de los Garzas MEX (NL) 40 Pe33
Sanosti USA (NM) 33 Pa27
San Pablo C (CA) 43 Qf35
San Pablo Balleza MEX (CHA) 39 Pb32
San Pedro MEX (BCS) 38 Ok34
San Pedro MEX (CHA) 39 Pc31
San Pedro MEX (SON) 33 Oj30
San Pedro MEX (SON) 38 Ok3…
San Pedro de la Cueva MEX (SON) 39 Pa3…
San Pedro de las Colonias MEX (COA) 39 Pd3…
San Pedro Mártir, Isla ☆ MEX (BCN) 38 Oj3…
San Quintín MEX (BCN) 38 Oh3…
San Rafael MEX (DGO) 39 Pc3…
San Rafael MEX (NL) 40 Pe3…
San Rafael MEX (SON) 33 Ok3…
San Roberto MEX (NL) 40 Pe3…
San Roque MEX (BCS) 38 Oh3…
San Saba USA (TX) 40 Pf3…
San Simeon USA (CA) 32 Oe2…
San Simon USA (AZ) 33 Pa2…
Santa USA (ID) 24 Og2…
Santa Ana C (CA) 43 Qf3…
Santa Ana MEX (SON) 38 Ok3…
Santa Ana USA (CA) 32 Og2…
Santa Anita MEX (COA) 39 Pd3…
Santa Anna USA (TX) 35 Pf3…
Santa Bárbara MEX (CHA) 39 Pc3…
Santa Barbara USA (CA) 32 Of2…
Santa Catarina MEX (BCN) 33 Oh3…
Santa Catarina MEX (NL) 40 Pe3…
Santa Clara C (VC) 43 Qf…
Santa Clara MEX (DGO) 39 Pd3…
Santa Cruz MEX (SON) 33 Ok3…
Santa Cruz USA (AZ) 33 Oj3…
Santa Cruz USA (CA) 32 Od2…
Santa Cruz del Norte C 43 Qe…
Santa Cruz del Oregano MEX (DGO) 39 Pd…
Santa Elena MEX (COA) 39 Pd…
Santa Eulalia MEX (COA) 39 Pd…
Santa Fé C (H) 43 Qd…
Santa Fé C (JU) 43 Qd…
Santa Fe USA (NM) 34 Pc…
Santa Lucía C (PR) 43 Qd…
Santa Maria USA (CA) 32 Oe…
Santa María del Oro MEX (DGO) 39 Pc…
Santa María de Mohovano MEX (COA) 39 Pd…
Santa Marta C (MZ) 43 Qe…
Santa Monica USA (CA) 32 Of…
Santander Jiménez MEX (TAM) 40 Pf…
Santa Paula USA (CA) 32 Of…
Santa Rita USA (BCS) 38 O…
Santa Rosa MEX (BCS) 39 Pa…
Santa Rosa USA (CA) 32 Od…
Santa Rosa USA (NM) 34 Pc…
Santa Rosalía MEX (BCS) 38 O…
Santa Teresa MEX (TAM) 40 Pg…
Santiago MEX (BCS) 38 O…
Santiago MEX (NL) 40 Pe…
Santiago de los Caballeros MEX (SIN) 39 Pb…
Santiago Papasquiaro MEX (DGO) 39 Pc…
San Tiburcio MEX (ZAC) 40 Pe…
Santo USA (TX) 35 P…
Santo Domingo C (VC) 43 Qe…
Santo Domingo MEX (BCS) 38 O…
Santo Domingo MEX (SLP) 40 Pe…
Santo Tomás MEX (BCN) 32 O…
Santo Tomás MEX (CHA) 39 Pb…
San Vicente MEX (BCN) 32 O…
San Ysidro USA (NM) 33 P…
Sapinero USA (CO) 33 P…
Saponac USA (ME) 22 R…
Sappho USA (WA) 16 O…
Sapulpa USA (OK) 35 P…
Saragosa USA (TX) 39 P…
Saraland USA (AL) 36 Q…
Saranac Lake USA (NY) 30 Q…
Sarasota USA (FL) 43 Q…
Saratoga USA (NC) 31 Q…
Saratoga Springs USA (NY) 30 Q…
Sardis CDN (BC) 16 O…
Sari, Villa de MEX (SON) 38 O…
Saric MEX (SON) 33 O…
Sarita CDN (BC) 16 O…
Sarles USA (ND) 19 P…

Sarnia CDN (ONT) 29 Qd24
Sarona USA (WI) 27 Pk23
Sarre, La CDN (QUE) 21 Qf21
Sartinville USA (MS) 36 Pk30
Sasabe USA (MI) 33 Ok30
Sasabe, El MEX (SON) 33 Ok30
Saskatchewan, Fort CDN (ALB) 17 Oj19
Saskatchewan Landing Provincial Park ☆ CDN (SAS) 18 Pb20
Saskatchewan River Crossing CDN (ALB) 17 Og20
Saskatoon CDN (SAS) 18 Pb19
Satartia USA (MS) 36 Pk29
Saturna CDN (BC) 16 Od21
Saucier USA (MS) 36 Qa30
Saucillo MEX (CHA) 39 Pc31
Sauk Centre USA (MN) 27 Ph23
Sauk City USA (WI) 28 Qa24
Sauk Rapids USA (MN) 27 Ph23
Saum USA (MN) 19 Ph22
Saumons, Rivière-aux- CDN (QUE) 22 Rd21
Sausalito USA (CA) 32 Od27
Saúz, El MEX (CHA) 39 Pb31
Sauzal, El MEX (BCN) 32 Og30
Savage USA (MT) 18 Pc22
Savage Cove CDN (NFL) 23 Rg20
Savanna USA (IL) 28 Pk24
Savannah USA (GA) 37 Qe29
Savannah USA (TN) 36 Qa28
Savant Lake CDN (ONT) 19 Pk20
Savona CDN (BC) 16 Oe20
Sawbill Landing USA (MN) 19 Pk22
Sawmill USA (AZ) 33 Pa28
Sawtooth National Recreation Area ☆ USA (ID) 25 Oh24
Sawyer USA (MN) 19 Pj22
Saxon USA (WI) 19 Pk22
Sayabec CDN (QUE) 22 Rb21
Sayre USA (OK) 35 Pf28
Sayre USA (PA) 29 Qg25
Sayward CDN (BC) 16 Oc20
Scales Mound USA (IL) 27 Pk24
Scammon Bay USA (AK) 10 Mc15
Scandia CDN (ALB) 17 Oj20
Scandia USA (KS) 35 Pg26
Scarth CDN (MAN) 18 Pe21
Scenic Narrow Gauge Steam Railroad ☆ USA (CO) 33 Pb27
chenectady USA (NY) 30 Qj24
chreiber CDN (ONT) 20 Qb21
chroeder USA (MN) 19 Pk22
chulenburg USA (TX) 40 Pg31
chuler CDN (ALB) 17 Ok20
chuyler USA (NE) 27 Pg25
cie, La CDN (NFL) 23 Rh21
cipio USA (UT) 33 Oj26
clater CDN (MAN) 18 Pe20
cobey USA (MT) 18 Pc21
cotfield CDN (ALB) 17 Ok20
cotia USA (CA) 24 Oc25
cotia Bay CDN (BC) 14 Nj16
cotland Neck USA (NC) 31 Qg27
cotsguard CDN (SAS) 18 Pa21
cotstown CDN (QUE) 22 Qk23
cott CDN (SAS) 17 Pa19
cott City USA (KS) 34 Pe26
ottsbluff USA (NE) 26 Pd25
otts Bluff National Monument ☆ USA (NE) 26 Pc25
ottsboro USA (AL) 36 Qb28
ottsburg USA (IN) 28 Qc26
ottsdale USA (AZ) 33 Ok29
ottsville USA (KY) 36 Qb27
ottsville USA (VA) 31 Qf27
ottville USA (MI) 28 Qb24
otty's Junction USA (NV) 32 Og27
out Lake CDN (SAS) 18 Pc21
ranton USA (PA) 29 Qh25
aford USA (DE) 31 Qh26
agoville USA (TX) 35 Pg29
al Cove CDN (NB) 22 Rb23
al Cove CDN (NFL) 23 Rg21
ale USA (AL) 36 Qc29
aly USA (TX) 40 Pg31
archlight USA (NV) 33 Oh28
archmont CDN (ONT) 20 Qc22
arcy USA (AR) 36 Pk28
arsport USA (ME) 22 Ra23
aside USA (OR) 24 Od23
aton CDN (BC) 14 Ob18
attle USA (WA) 16 Od22
bastian USA (FL) 43 Qe32
astopol USA (CA) 32 Od26
bec Lake USA (ME) 22 Ra23
bree USA (KY) 36 Qb27
oring USA (FL) 43 Qe32
chelt CDN (BC) 16 Od21
ond Mesa USA (AZ) 33 Ok28
alia USA (MO) 35 Pj26
an USA (KS) 35 Pg27
dons Corner CDN (MAN) 19 Pg20
gewick CDN (ALB) 17 Ok19
gwick USA (CO) 26 Pd25
gwick USA (KS) 35 Pg27
ona USA (AZ) 33 Ok28
ro Woolley USA (WA) 16 Od21
be CDN (ALB) 17 Oh20
ley Lake USA (MT) 17 Oj22
uin USA (TX) 40 Pg31
ert USA (CO) 34 Pd26
ng USA (OK) 35 Pf27
h USA (WA) 24 Oe22
wik USA (AK) 10 Me12
y USA (SD) 26 Pe23
en USA (KS) 34 Pe26
ovia USA (AK) 13 Mk16
man USA (AZ) 33 Oj28
gman USA (MO) 35 Pj27
nsgrove USA (PA) 29 Qg25
rk CDN (MAN) 19 Pg20
ck USA (WA) 16 Oe22
rs USA (MS) 36 Qa30
rsburg USA (IN) 28 Qc26
USA (AZ) 33 Ok30
a USA (AL) 36 Qb29
a USA (CA) 32 Of27
er USA (TN) 36 Qa28
, La MEX (CHA) 39 Pd31
ay-Bitterroot Wilderness ☆ USA (ID) 25 Oh22
nole USA (OK) 35 Pg28

Seminole USA (TX) 34 Pd29
Senate CDN (SAS) 17 Pa21
Senatobia USA (MS) 36 Qa28
Seneca USA (KS) 35 Pg26
Seneca USA (OR) 24 Of23
Seneca USA (SC) 37 Qd28
Seneca USA (SD) 26 Pf23
Seneca Falls USA (NY) 29 Qg24
Seney USA (MI) 20 Qc22
Senneterre CDN (QUE) 21 Qg21
Separ USA (NM) 33 Pa29
Sept-Îles CDN (QUE) 22 Rb20
Sept-Îles-Port Carier, Réserve Faunique de ☆ CDN (QUE) 22 Rb20
Sequim USA (WA) 16 Od21
Sequoia National Park ☆ USA (CA) 32 Of27
Serpentine Hot Springs USA (AK) 10 Mc13
Sesser USA (IL) 28 Qa26
Setters USA (ID) 17 Og22
Seven Lakes USA (NM) 33 Pb28
Seven Persons CDN (ALB) 17 Ok21
Seventy Mile House CDN (BC) 16 Oe20
Severn River Provincial Park ☆ CDN (MAN) 19 Pk18
Severy USA (KS) 35 Pg27
Sevier USA (UT) 33 Oj26
Seville USA (FL) 37 Qe31
Sewanee USA (TN) 36 Qc28
Seward USA (AK) 13 Na15
Seward USA (NE) 27 Pg25
Sexsmith CDN (ALB) 15 Of18
Seymour USA (IA) 27 Pj25
Seymour USA (IN) 28 Qc26
Seymour USA (MO) 35 Pj27
Seymour USA (TX) 35 Pf29
Seymour Arm CDN (BC) 16 Of20
Shabaqua Corners CDN (ONT) 20 Pk21
Shackleton CDN (SAS) 17 Pa20
Shade Gap USA (PA) 29 Qg25
Shaerer Dale CDN (BC) 15 Oe17
Shafter USA (NV) 25 Oh25
Shafter USA (TX) 39 Pc31
Shageluk USA (AK) 10 Mf14
Shag Harbour CDN (NS) 22 Rc24
Shakespeare Ghost Town ☆ USA (NM) 33 Pa29
Shaktoolik USA (AK) 10 Me13
Shalalth CDN (BC) 16 Od20
Shallotte USA (NC) 37 Qf29
Shamokin USA (PA) 29 Qg25
Shamrock USA (TX) 34 Pe28
Sharbot Lake CDN (ONT) 29 Qg23
Sharon USA (PA) 29 Qe25
Sharon Springs USA (KS) 34 Pe26
Sharpsburg USA (KY) 29 Qd26
Shaughnessy CDN (ALB) 17 Oj21
Shaunavon CDN (SAS) 18 Pa21
Shaw USA (LA) 36 Pk30
Shawano USA (WI) 28 Qa23
Shawinigan CDN (QUE) 21 Qj22
Shawmut USA (MT) 18 Pa22
Shawnee USA (OK) 35 Pg28
Shawville CDN (QUE) 29 Qg23
Shebandowan CDN (ONT) 20 Pk21
Sheboygan USA (WI) 28 Qb24
Shediac CDN (NB) 22 Rc22
Sheenboro CDN (QUE) 29 Qg23
Sheep Springs USA (NM) 33 Pa27
Sheet Harbour CDN (NS) 22 Rd23
Sheffield CDN (NB) 22 Rb23
Sheffield USA (AL) 36 Qb28
Sheffield USA (IA) 27 Pj24
Sheffield USA (PA) 29 Qf25
Sheffield USA (TX) 40 Pe30
Sheho CDN (SAS) 18 Pd20
Shelbina USA (MO) 28 Pj26
Shelburne CDN (NS) 22 Rc24
Shelburne CDN (ONT) 29 Qe23
Shelby USA (MT) 17 Ok21
Shelby USA (NC) 37 Qe28
Shelbyville USA (IL) 28 Qa26
Shelbyville USA (IN) 28 Qc26
Shelbyville USA (KY) 28 Qc26
Shelbyville USA (MO) 28 Pj26
Shelbyville USA (TN) 36 Qb28
Sheldon USA (IA) 27 Ph24
Sheldon National Wildlife Refuge ☆ USA (NV) 24 Of25
Shell USA (WY) 25 Pb23
Shellbrook CDN (SAS) 18 Pb19
Shell Lake CDN (SAS) 18 Pb19
Shellmouth CDN (MAN) 18 Pe20
Shelter Bay CDN (BC) 17 Og20
Shelter Cove USA (CA) 24 Oc25
Shelton USA (WA) 24 Od22
Shenandoah USA (IA) 27 Ph25
Shenandoah USA (PA) 29 Qg25
Shenandoah National Park ☆ USA (VA) 29 Qf26
Shepherd of the Hills Farm ☆ USA (MO) 35 Pj27
Sherbrooke CDN (QUE) 22 Qk23
Sheridan USA (AR) 36 Pj28
Sheridan USA (WY) 25 Pb23
Sheridan Lake USA (CO) 34 Pd26
Sherman USA (ME) 22 Ra23
Sherman USA (TX) 35 Pg29
Sherman Mills USA (ME) 22 Ra23
Sherridon CDN (MAN) 18 Pe18
Sherwood USA (ND) 18 Pe21
Sherwood Park CDN (ALB) 17 Oj19
Sheshalik USA (AK) 10 Md12
Sheyenne USA (ND) 19 Pf22
Shilo CDN (MAN) 19 Pf21
Shingleton USA (MI) 20 Qb22
Shingletown USA (CA) 24 Oe25
Shinnston USA (WV) 29 Qe26
Shin Pond USA (ME) 22 Ra22
Ship Bottom USA (NJ) 31 Qh26
Shippegan CDN (NB) 22 Rc22
Shippensburg USA (PA) 29 Qg25
Shiprock USA (NM) 33 Pa27
Shirley USA (AR) 35 Pj28
Shishmaref USA (AK) 10 Mb12
Shivel USA (KY) 28 Qc26
Shoal Lake CDN (MAN) 18 Pe20
Shongaloo USA (LA) 35 Pj29
Shoreacres CDN (BC) 17 Og21
Shoshone USA (CA) 32 Og28
Shoshone USA (ID) 25 Oh24
Shoshoni USA (WY) 25 Pa24
Show Low USA (AZ) 33 Pa28

Shreveport USA (LA) 35 Pj29
Shrewsbury USA (PA) 29 Qg26
Shubuta USA (MS) 36 Qa30
Shullsburg USA (WI) 27 Pk24
Shungnak USA (AK) 10 Mg12
Sibanicú C (CG) 43 Qg35
Sibbald CDN (ALB) 17 Ok20
Sibley USA (IA) 27 Ph24
Sibley USA (LA) 35 Pj29
Sibley USA (ND) 19 Pg22
Sicamous CDN (BC) 16 Of20
Sidewood CDN (SAS) 17 Pa20
Sidney CDN (BC) 16 Od21
Sidney CDN (MAN) 19 Pf21
Sidney USA (IA) 27 Ph25
Sidney USA (MT) 18 Pc22
Sidney USA (NE) 26 Pd25
Sidney USA (NY) 29 Qh24
Sidney USA (OH) 28 Qc25
Sierra Blanca USA (TX) 39 Pc30
Sierra de San Francisco ☆ MEX (BCS) 38 Oj32
Sierra de San Pedro Mártir, Parque Nacional ☆ MEX (BCN) 38 Og30
Sierra Mojada MEX (COA) 39 Pd32
Sierraville USA (CA) 32 Oe26
Sierra Vista USA (AZ) 33 Ok30
Signal Hill National Historic Park ☆ CDN (NFL) 23 Rj22
Sigourney USA (IA) 27 Pj25
Siguanea C (JU) 43 Qd35
Sikeston USA (MO) 36 Qa27
Siler City USA (NC) 37 Qf28
Silesia USA (MT) 25 Pa23
Sil Nakya USA (AZ) 33 Ok29
Siloam Springs USA (AR) 35 Ph27
Silsbee USA (TX) 41 Ph30
Silva USA (MO) 36 Pk27
Silver Bay USA (MN) 19 Pk22
Silver City USA (NM) 33 Pa29
Silver City USA (TX) 35 Pg30
Silver Creek USA (NY) 29 Qf24
Silverdale USA (MN) 19 Pj22
Silverdale USA (WA) 16 Od22
Silver Dollar CDN (ONT) 19 Pk21
Silver Gate USA (MT) 25 Pa23
Silver Islet CDN (ONT) 20 Qa21
Silver Lake USA (OR) 24 Oe24
Silver Park CDN (SAS) 18 Pc19
Silver Springs USA (FL) 37 Qd31
Silverthorne USA (CO) 34 Pb26
Silverton USA (CO) 33 Pb27
Silverton USA (OR) 24 Od23
Silverton USA (TX) 34 Pe28
Silver Valley CDN (ALB) 15 Of17
Sima USA (CO) 34 Pc26
Simcoe CDN (ONT) 29 Qe24
Simi Valley USA (CA) 32 Of28
Simmesport USA (LA) 36 Pk30
Simmie CDN (SAS) 18 Pa21
Simmler USA (CA) 32 Of28
Simms USA (MT) 17 Ok22
Simón, Estación MEX (DGO) 39 Pd33
Simonhouse CDN (MAN) 18 Pe18
Simoon Harbour CDN (BC) 16 Ob20
Simpson USA (MT) 17 Ok21
Simpson, Port CDN (BC) 16 Nk18
Sinaloa de Leyva MEX (SIN) 39 Pa33
Sinclair CDN (MAN) 18 Pe21
Sinclair Mills CDN (BC) 16 Oe18
Singhampton CDN (ONT) 29 Qe23
Sinton USA (TX) 40 Pg31
Sinuk USA (AK) 10 Mb13
Sioux Center USA (IA) 27 Pg24
Sioux City USA (IA) 27 Pg24
Sioux Falls USA (SD) 27 Pg24
Sioux Lookout CDN (ONT) 19 Pk20
Sioux Narrows CDN (ONT) 19 Ph21
Sioux Rapids USA (IA) 27 Ph24
Sipiwesk CDN (MAN) 19 Pg18
Sirdar CDN (BC) 17 Og21
Siren USA (WI) 27 Pj23
Sir R. Squires Memorial Provincial Park ☆ CDN (NFL) 23 Rg21
Sisal MEX (YUC) 42 Pk35
Sisseton USA (SD) 27 Pg23
Sissonville USA (WV) 29 Qe26
Sisters USA (OR) 24 Oe23
Sitiecito C (VC) 43 Qe34
Sitka USA (AK) 14 Nh17
Sitka USA (KS) 35 Pf27
Sitting Bull's Grave ☆ USA (SD) 26 Pe23
Six Lakes USA (MI) 28 Qc24
Skagit Provincial Park ☆ CDN (BC) 16 Oe21
Skagway USA (AK) 14 Nh16
Skead CDN (ONT) 20 Qe22
Skeena CDN (BC) 16 Oa18
Skiff CDN (ALB) 17 Ok21
Skokie USA (IL) 28 Qb24
Skookumchuck CDN (BC) 17 Oh21
Skowhegan USA (ME) 22 Ra23
Skownan CDN (MAN) 19 Pf20
Skykomish USA (WA) 16 Oe22
Skyline Caverns ☆ USA (VA) 29 Qf26
Slana USA (AK) 11 Nd14
Slaton USA (TX) 34 Pe29
Slave Lake CDN (ALB) 15 Oh18
Slayton USA (MN) 27 Ph23
Sleeman CDN (ONT) 19 Ph21
Sleeping Bear Dunes National Lakeshore ☆ USA (MI) 28 Qb23
Sleeping Giant Provincial Park ☆ CDN (ONT) 20 Qa21
Sleepy Eye USA (MN) 27 Ph23
Slidell USA (LA) 36 Qa30
Sloan USA (IA) 27 Pg24
Slocan CDN (BC) 17 Og21
Slocan Park CDN (BC) 17 Og21
Smackover USA (AR) 35 Pj29
Smeaton CDN (SAS) 18 Pc19
Smet, De USA (SD) 27 Pg23
Smethport USA (PA) 29 Qf25
Smiley CDN (SAS) 17 Pa20
Smith CDN (ALB) 17 Oj18
Smith Center USA (KS) 35 Pf26
Smithdale USA (MS) 36 Pk30
Smithers CDN (BC) 14 Ob18
Smithers Landing CDN (BC) 14 Ob18
Smithfield USA (NC) 31 Qf28
Smithland USA (TX) 35 Ph29

Smith River CDN (BC) 14 Ob16
Smith River USA (CA) 24 Oc25
Smiths Falls CDN (ONT) 29 Qh23
Smiths Ferry USA (ID) 24 Og23
Smithville USA (GA) 36 Qc30
Smoky Falls CDN (ONT) 20 Qd20
Smoky Lake CDN (ALB) 17 Oj18
Smoot USA (WY) 25 Ok24
Smooth Rock Falls CDN (ONT) 20 Qe21
Smyrna USA (DE) 29 Qh26
Snake River Canyon ☆ USA (WA) 24 Og22
Snellman USA (MN) 19 Ph22
Snipe Lake CDN (SAS) 17 Pa20
Snohomish USA (WA) 16 Od22
Snoqualmie USA (WA) 16 Oe22
Snowflake CDN (MAN) 19 Pf21
Snowflake USA (AZ) 33 Ok28
Snow Hill USA (NC) 31 Qg28
Snow Lake CDN (MAN) 18 Pe18
Snowville USA (UT) 25 Oj25
Snyder USA (NE) 27 Pg25
Snyder USA (OK) 35 Pf28
Soap Lake USA (WA) 16 Of22
Socorro MEX (COA) 39 Pd32
Socorro USA (NM) 34 Pb28
Socorro USA (TX) 34 Pb30
Soda Creek CDN (BC) 16 Od19
Soda Springs USA (ID) 25 Ok24
Soddy-Daisy USA (TN) 36 Qc28
Sola C (CG) 43 Qg35
Solana Beach USA (CA) 32 Og29
Soldotna USA (AK) 13 Mk15
Soledad USA (CA) 32 Oe27
Soledad, La MEX (COA) 39 Pd32
Soledad, La MEX (DGO) 39 Pc33
Solomon USA (KS) 35 Pg26
Solomons USA (MD) 29 Qg26
Solon Springs USA (WI) 19 Pk22
Solway USA (MN) 19 Ph22
Sombrerete MEX (ZAC) 39 Pd34
Somers USA (MT) 17 Oh21
Somerset CDN (MAN) 19 Pf21
Somerset USA (CO) 33 Pb26
Somerset USA (KY) 36 Qc27
Somerset USA (MI) 28 Qc24
Somerset USA (PA) 29 Qf26
Somerton USA (AZ) 33 Oh29
Somerville USA (PA) 30 Qh25
Somerville USA (TN) 36 Qa28
Somerville USA (TX) 40 Pg30
Somes Bar USA (CA) 24 Od25
Sonoita USA (AZ) 33 Ok30
Sonora MEX (SON) 33 Oh29
Sonora USA (CA) 32 Oe27
Sonora USA (TX) 40 Pe30
Sonoran Desert National Monument ☆ USA (AZ) 33 Oj29
Sonoyta MEX (SON) 33 Oj30
Sooke CDN (BC) 16 Od21
Sopchoppy USA (FL) 36 Qc30
Sorel CDN (QUE) 30 Qj22
Sorrento CDN (BC) 16 Of20
Sorrento USA (LA) 36 Pk30
Soto la Marina MEX (TAM) 40 Pf34
Souris CDN (MAN) 18 Pe21
Souris CDN (PEI) 22 Rd22
Southampton CDN (ONT) 29 Qe23
Southampton USA (NY) 30 Qj25
South Baranof Island Wilderness ☆ USA (AK) 14 Nh17
South Bay CDN (ONT) 19 Pj20
South Baymouth CDN (ONT) 29 Qd23
South Bend USA (IN) 28 Qb25
South Boston USA (VA) 37 Qf27
South Branch CDN (NFL) 23 Rf22
South Brook CDN (NFL) 23 Rg21
South Charleston USA (WV) 29 Qe26
South China USA (ME) 22 Ra23
South Cove USA (NV) 33 Oh27
South East Bight CDN (NFL) 23 Rh22
Southend CDN (SAS) 18 Pd17
Southern Pines USA (NC) 37 Qf28
Southey CDN (SAS) 18 Pc20
South Fork CDN (SAS) 18 Pa21
South Fork USA (CO) 34 Pb27
South Gloucester CDN (ONT) 29 Qh23
South Gut Saint Ann's CDN (NS) 23 Re22
South Harbour CDN (NS) 23 Re22
South Haven USA (MI) 28 Qb24
South Hazelton CDN (BC) 14 Ob18
South Heart USA (ND) 18 Pd22
South Hill USA (VA) 31 Qf27
South Junction CDN (MAN) 19 Ph21
South Lake Tahoe USA (CA) 32 Of26
South Milford CDN (NS) 22 Rc23
South Mountain CDN (ONT) 29 Qh23
South Paris USA (ME) 22 Qk23
South Pender CDN (BC) 16 Od21
South Porcupine CDN (ONT) 20 Qe21
Southport CDN (NFL) 23 Rj21
Southport USA (FL) 36 Qc30
South Prince of Wales Wilderness ☆ USA (AK) 14 Nj18
South River CDN (ONT) 29 Qf23
South Shore USA (KY) 29 Qd26
South Sioux City USA (NE) 27 Pg24
South Slocan CDN (BC) 17 Og21
South Teton Wilderness Area ☆ USA (WY) 25 Ok23
South Tucson USA (AZ) 33 Ok29
South West Harbor USA (ME) 22 Ra23
Southworth USA (WA) 16 Od22
Spangle USA (WA) 17 Og22
Spaniard's Bay CDN (NFL) 23 Rj22
Spanish Fork USA (UT) 25 Ok25
Sparkman USA (AR) 35 Pj29
Sparks USA (NV) 32 Of26
Sparrows Point USA (MD) 29 Qg26
Sparta USA (GA) 37 Qd29
Sparta USA (NC) 37 Qe27
Sparta USA (TN) 36 Qc28
Sparta USA (WI) 27 Pk24
Spartanburg USA (SC) 37 Qe28
Sparwood CDN (BC) 17 Oh21
Spatsizi Plateau Wilderness Provincial Park ☆ CDN (BC) 14 Oa17
Spearfish USA (SD) 26 Pd23
Speculator USA (NY) 30 Qh24
Spedden CDN (ALB) 17 Ok18

Speed USA (WV) 29 Qe26
Spencer USA (IA) 27 Ph24
Spencer USA (IN) 28 Qb26
Spencer USA (WV) 29 Qe26
Spencerville CDN (ONT) 29 Qh23
Spences Bridge CDN (BC) 16 Oe20
Sperling CDN (MAN) 19 Pg21
Sperryville USA (VA) 29 Qf26
Spickard USA (MO) 27 Pj25
Spirit Falls USA (WI) 27 Qa23
Spirit Lake USA (IA) 27 Ph24
Spirit River CDN (ALB) 15 Of18
Spiritwood CDN (SAS) 18 Pb19
Spiritwood Lake USA (ND) 19 Pf22
Spiro USA (OK) 35 Ph28
Split Lake CDN (MAN) 19 Pg17
Spofford USA (TX) 40 Pe31
Spokane USA (MO) 35 Pj27
Spokane USA (WA) 17 Og22
Spooner USA (WI) 27 Pk23
Spotted House USA (WY) 26 Pc23
Sprague USA (WA) 17 Og22
Spray USA (OR) 24 Of23
Springbrook USA (WI) 27 Pk23
Spring Coulee CDN (ALB) 17 Oj21
Springdale CDN (NFL) 23 Rg21
Springdale USA (AR) 35 Ph27
Springdale USA (WA) 17 Og21
Springer USA (NM) 34 Pc27
Springerville USA (AZ) 33 Pa28
Springfield CDN (NB) 22 Rc23
Springfield USA (CO) 34 Pd27
Springfield USA (FL) 36 Qc30
Springfield USA (IL) 28 Qa26
Springfield USA (KY) 36 Qc27
Springfield USA (MA) 30 Qj24
Springfield USA (ME) 22 Ra23
Springfield USA (MO) 35 Pj27
Springfield USA (OH) 29 Qd26
Springfield USA (OR) 24 Od23
Springfield USA (VA) 29 Qg26
Springfield USA (VT) 30 Qj24
Spring Grove USA (VA) 31 Qg27
Springhill CDN (NS) 22 Rc23
Spring Hill USA (FL) 43 Qd31
Springhill USA (LA) 35 Pj29
Spring Lake USA (NC) 37 Qf28
Springlake USA (TX) 34 Pd28
Springvale USA (ME) 22 Qk24
Spring Valley CDN (SAS) 18 Pc21
Spring Valley USA (MN) 27 Pj24
Springview USA (NE) 26 Pf24
Springville USA (AL) 36 Qb29
Springville USA (NY) 29 Qf24
Springville USA (UT) 25 Ok25
Springwater CDN (SAS) 17 Pa20
Sproat Lake CDN (BC) 16 Oc21
Sprouses Corner USA (VA) 31 Qf27
Sprucedale CDN (ONT) 29 Qf23
Spruce Grove CDN (ALB) 17 Oj19
Spruce Home CDN (SAS) 18 Pc19
Spruce Lake CDN (SAS) 17 Pa19
Spruce Pine USA (NC) 37 Qd28
Spruce Woods Provincial Forest ☆ CDN (MAN) 18 Pe21
Spruce Woods Provincial Park ☆ CDN (MAN) 19 Pf21
Spur USA (TX) 34 Pe29
Sputinow CDN (ALB) 17 Ok19
Squamish CDN (BC) 16 Od21
Square Ilands CDN (NFL) 23 Rh19
Squaw Lake USA (MN) 19 Ph22
Squilax CDN (BC) 16 Of20
Stackpool CDN (ONT) 20 Qe22
Stacyville USA (IA) 27 Pj24
Stamford USA (CT) 30 Qj25
Stamping Ground USA (KY) 28 Qc26
Stamps USA (AR) 35 Pj29
Stanberry USA (MO) 27 Ph25
Standish USA (MI) 29 Qd24
Stand Off CDN (ALB) 17 Oj21
Stanford USA (KY) 36 Qc27
Stanford USA (MT) 17 Ok22
Staniard Creek BS 43 Qg33
Stanley CDN (NB) 22 Rb22
Stanley USA (ID) 25 Oh23
Stanley USA (ND) 18 Pd21
Stanley, Port CDN (ONT) 29 Qe24
Stanley Mission CDN (SAS) 18 Pc18
Stanton USA (ND) 18 Pe22
Stanton USA (TX) 34 Pe29
Stanwood USA (WA) 16 Od21
Stapleton USA (NE) 26 Pe25
Star USA (MS) 36 Pk29
Starboard USA (ME) 22 Rb23
Starbuck CDN (MAN) 19 Pg21
Starbuck USA (MN) 27 Ph23
Star City USA (AR) 35 Pj29
Starke USA (FL) 37 Qd31
Starkville USA (MS) 36 Qa29
Starkweather USA (ND) 19 Pf21
Startup USA (WA) 16 Oe22
State College USA (PA) 29 Qg25
State Line USA (MS) 36 Qa30
Statenville USA (GA) 37 Qd30
Statesboro USA (GA) 37 Qe29
Statesville USA (NC) 37 Qe28
Staunton USA (VA) 29 Qf26
Steamboat USA (OR) 24 Od24
Steamboat Springs USA (CO) 26 Pb25
Stebbins USA (AK) 10 Md14
Steele USA (ND) 19 Pf22
Steele, Fort CDN (BC) 17 Oh21
Steelman CDN (SAS) 18 Pd21
Steelville USA (MO) 28 Pk27
Steep Rock CDN (MAN) 19 Pf20
Steinbach CDN (MAN) 19 Pg21
Steinhatchee USA (FL) 37 Qd31
Steins USA (NM) 33 Pa29
Stein Valley Provincial Park ☆ CDN (BC) 16 Od20
Stellarton CDN (NS) 22 Rd23
Stenen CDN (SAS) 18 Pd20
Stephen USA (MN) 19 Pg21
Stephens USA (AR) 35 Pj29
Stephens City USA (VA) 29 Qf26
Stephenville CDN (NFL) 23 Rf21
Stephenville USA (TX) 35 Pf29
Stephenville Crossing CDN (NFL) 23 Rf21
Sterling USA (CO) 26 Pd25

Sterling (USA) (KS) 35 Pf26
Sterling (USA) (ND) 18 Pe22
Sterling City (USA) (TX) 34 Pe30
Sterling Heights (USA) (MI) 29 Qd24
Sterling Landing (USA) (AK) 10 Mh14
Sterlington (USA) (LA) 36 Pj29
Stettler (CDN) (ALB) 17 Oj19
Steubenville (USA) (OH) 29 Qe25
Stevenson (USA) (WA) 24 Oe23
Stevens Point (USA) (WI) 28 Qa23
Stevens Village (USA) (AK) 11 Na12
Stevensville (USA) (MT) 25 Oh22
Stewardson Inlet (CDN) (BC) 16 Ob21
Stewart (CDN) (BC) 14 Oa18
Stewart (USA) (MN) 27 Ph23
Stewartstown (USA) (NH) 22 Qk23
Stewart Valley (CDN) (SAS) 18 Pb20
Stewartville (USA) (MN) 27 Pj24
Stickney Corner (USA) (ME) 22 Ra23
Stigler (USA) (OK) 35 Ph28
Stikine-Leconte Wilderness ☆ (USA) (AK) 14 Nj17
Stillwater (USA) (MN) 27 Pj23
Stillwater (USA) (OK) 35 Pg27
Stinnett (USA) (TX) 34 Pe28
Stirling (CDN) (ALB) 17 Oj21
Stirling (CDN) (ONT) 29 Qg23
Stockbridge (USA) (GA) 36 Qc29
Stockdale (USA) (TX) 40 Pg31
Stockett (USA) (MT) 17 Ok22
Stockholm (CDN) (SAS) 18 Pd20
Stockton (USA) (CA) 32 Oe27
Stockton (USA) (FL) 37 Qd30
Stockton (USA) (IL) 28 Pk24
Stockton (USA) (KS) 35 Pf26
Stockton (USA) (MO) 35 Pj27
Stockville (USA) (NE) 26 Pe25
Stokesdale (USA) (PA) 29 Qg25
Stonecliffe (CDN) (ONT) 29 Qg22
Stoneham (USA) (CO) 26 Pd25
Stone Lake (USA) (WI) 27 Pk23
Stonewall (CDN) (MAN) 19 Pg20
Stonington (USA) (ME) 22 Ra23
Stony Creek (USA) (VA) 31 Qg27
Stony Mountain (CDN) (MAN) 19 Pg20
Stonyridge (CDN) (ONT) 29 Qf23
Stony River (USA) (AK) 12 Mg15
Storm Lake (USA) (IA) 27 Ph24
Stornoway (CDN) (QUE) 22 Qk23
Storthoaks (CDN) (SAS) 18 Pe21
Story City (USA) (IA) 27 Pj24
Stouffville (CDN) (ONT) 29 Qf24
Stoughton (CDN) (SAS) 18 Pd21
Stoughton (USA) (WI) 28 Qa24
Strang (USA) (NE) 27 Pg25
Stranraer (CDN) (SAS) 17 Pa20
Strasbourg (CDN) (SAS) 18 Pc20
Strasburg (USA) (CO) 34 Pc26
Strasburg (USA) (ND) 26 Pe22
Strasburg (USA) (VA) 29 Qf26
Stratford (CDN) (ONT) 29 Qe24
Stratford (USA) (CA) 32 Of27
Stratford (USA) (TX) 34 Pd27
Stratford (USA) (WI) 27 Pk23
Strathcoma Provincial Park ☆ (CDN) (BC) 16 Oc21
Strathcona (USA) (MN) 19 Pg21
Strathmore (CDN) (ALB) 17 Oj20
Strathnaver (CDN) (BC) 16 Od19
Strathroy (CDN) (ONT) 29 Qe24
Stratton (CDN) (ONT) 19 Ph21
Stratton (USA) (ME) 22 Qk23
Stratton (USA) (NE) 34 Pd26
Strawberry Point (USA) (IA) 27 Pk24
Strawn (USA) (TX) 35 Pf29
Streamstown (CDN) (ALB) 17 Ok19
Streator (USA) (IL) 28 Qa25
Streetman (USA) (TX) 35 Pg30
Strevell (USA) (ID) 25 Oj24
Stromsburg (USA) (NE) 27 Pg25
Strong (USA) (AR) 35 Pj29
Strong City (USA) (KS) 35 Pg26
Stronghurst (USA) (IL) 27 Pk25
Stroudsburg (USA) (PA) 30 Qh25
Struan (CDN) (SAS) 18 Pb19
Stryker (USA) (MT) 17 Oh21
Stuart (USA) (FL) 43 Qe32
Stuart (USA) (IA) 27 Ph25
Stuart (USA) (NE) 26 Pf24
Stuart (USA) (VA) 37 Qe27
Stuartburn (CDN) (MAN) 19 Pg21
Stuie (CDN) (BC) 16 Ob19
Sturgeon (CDN) (QUE) 21 Qh22
Sturgeon Bay (USA) (WI) 28 Qb23
Sturgeon Falls (CDN) (ONT) 29 Qf22
Sturgeon Heights (CDN) (ALB) 15 Og18
Sturgis (USA) (MI) 28 Qc25
Sturgis (USA) (SD) 26 Pd23
Stuttgart (USA) (AR) 36 Pk28
Stuyahok (USA) (AK) 10 Me14
Styal (CDN) (ALB) 17 Oh19
Sublett (USA) (ID) 25 Oj24
Sublette (USA) (KS) 34 Pe27
Subway Caves ☆ (USA) (CA) 24 Oe25
Suchil (MEX) (DGO) 39 Pd34
Sudan (USA) (TX) 34 Pd28
Sudbury (CDN) (ONT) 20 Qe22
Sueco, El (MEX) (CHA) 39 Pb31
Sueur, Le (USA) (MN) 27 Pj23
Suffern (USA) (NY) 30 Qh25
Suffield (CDN) (ALB) 17 Ok20
Suffolk (USA) (VA) 31 Qg27
Sugar Land (USA) (TX) 41 Ph31
Sula (USA) (MT) 25 Oj23
Sulligent (USA) (AL) 36 Qa29
Sullivan (USA) (IN) 28 Qb26
Sullivan (USA) (MO) 28 Pk26
Sully (USA) (IA) 27 Pj25
Sulphur (USA) (LA) 41 Pj30
Sulphur (USA) (NV) 24 Of25
Sulphur (USA) (OK) 35 Pg28
Sulphur, Port (USA) (LA) 36 Qa31
Sulphur Springs (USA) (TX) 35 Ph29
Sultan (CDN) (ONT) 20 Qd22
Sumas (USA) (WA) 16 Od21
Sumatra (USA) (FL) 36 Qc30
Sumatra (USA) (MT) 18 Pb22
Summerfield (USA) (KS) 35 Pg26
Summerfield (USA) (LA) 35 Pj29
Summerland (CDN) (BC) 16 Of21
Summerside (CDN) (PEI) 22 Rd22
Summersville (USA) (MO) 35 Pj27
Summersville (USA) (WV) 29 Qe26
Summerville (USA) (GA) 36 Qc28
Summerville (USA) (SC) 37 Qe29
Summit (USA) (MS) 36 Pk30
Summit (USA) (SD) 27 Pg23
Summit Lake (CDN) (BC) 15 Oc16
Summit Lake (CDN) (BC) 16 Od18
Sumner (USA) (IL) 28 Qb26
Sumner (USA) (MO) 35 Pj26
Sumner (USA) (MS) 36 Pk29
Sumrall (USA) (MS) 36 Qa30
Sumter (USA) (SC) 37 Qe29
Sunburst (USA) (MT) 17 Ok21
Sunbury (USA) (PA) 29 Qg25
Sun City (USA) (AZ) 33 Oj29
Suncook (USA) (NH) 22 Qk24
Sundance (USA) (WY) 26 Pc23
Sundown (CDN) (MAN) 19 Pg21
Sundre (CDN) (ALB) 17 Oh20
Sunny Hills (USA) (FL) 36 Qc30
Sunnyside (USA) (WA) 24 Oe22
Sunnyvale (USA) (CA) 32 Od27
Sun Prairie (USA) (WI) 28 Qa24
Sunrise Valley (CDN) (BC) 15 Oe18
Sunset (USA) (LA) 36 Pj30
Sunset Beach (USA) (WA) 16 Oc22
Sunset Crater Volc. National Monument ☆ (USA) (AZ) 33 Ok28
Sunset House (CDN) (ALB) 15 Og18
Sunset Prairie (CDN) (BC) 15 Oe18
Sunstrum (CDN) (ONT) 19 Pj20
Sun Valley (USA) (ID) 25 Oh24
Suomi (CDN) (ONT) 20 Qa21
Superb (CDN) (SAS) 17 Pa20
Superior (USA) (AZ) 33 Ok29
Superior (USA) (MT) 17 Oh22
Superior (USA) (NE) 35 Pf25
Superior (USA) (WI) 19 Pj22
Surf (USA) (CA) 32 Oe28
Surrey (CDN) (BC) 16 Od21
Surrey (USA) (ND) 18 Pe21
Susanville (USA) (CA) 24 Oe25
Susquehanna (USA) (PA) 29 Qh25
Sussex (CDN) (NB) 22 Rc23
Sutherland (USA) (NE) 26 Pe25
Sutherlin (USA) (OR) 24 Od24
Sutton (CDN) (ONT) 29 Qf23
Sutton (USA) (NE) 27 Pg25
Sutton (USA) (WV) 29 Qe26
Suwannee (USA) (FL) 37 Qd31
Swainsboro (USA) (GA) 37 Qd29
Swanburg (USA) (MN) 19 Ph22
Swan Hills (CDN) (ALB) 15 Oh18
Swan Lake (USA) (MT) 17 Oj22
Swan-Pelican Provincial Forest ☆ (CDN) (MAN) 18 Pe19
Swan Plain (CDN) (SAS) 18 Pd19
Swanquarter (USA) (NC) 31 Qg28
Swanquarter National Wildlife Refuge ☆ (USA) (NC) 31 Qg28
Swan River (CDN) (MAN) 18 Pe19
Swan River (USA) (MN) 19 Pj22
Swansboro (USA) (NC) 31 Qg28
Swansea (USA) (SC) 37 Qe29
Swanton (USA) (VT) 30 Qj23
Swan Valley (USA) (ID) 25 Ok24
Swartz Bay (CDN) (BC) 16 Od21
Swedehome (USA) (NE) 27 Pg25
Sweet Grass (CDN) (SAS) 17 Pa19
Sweetgrass (USA) (MT) 17 Ok21
Sweet Home (USA) (OR) 24 Od23
Sweetwater (USA) (OK) 35 Pf28
Sweetwater (USA) (TX) 34 Pe29
Sweetwater Station (USA) (WY) 25 Pa24
Swift Current (CDN) (SAS) 18 Pb20
Sydney (CDN) (NS) 23 Re22
Sylacauga (USA) (AL) 36 Qb29
Sylva (USA) (NC) 37 Qd28
Sylvania (CDN) (SAS) 18 Pd19
Sylvania (USA) (GA) 37 Qe29
Sylvania (USA) (OH) 29 Qd25
Sylvan Lake (CDN) (ALB) 17 Oh19
Sylvester (USA) (GA) 37 Qd30
Sylvester (USA) (TX) 34 Pe29
Sylvia (USA) (KS) 35 Pf27
Synder (USA) (TX) 34 Pe29
Syracuse (USA) (KS) 34 Pe27
Syracuse (USA) (NE) 27 Pg25
Syracuse (USA) (NY) 29 Qg24
Syre (USA) (MN) 19 Pg22

T

Tabala (MEX) (SIN) 39 Pb33
Tabara (C) (H) 43 Qd34
Taber (CDN) (ALB) 17 Oj21
Tabor (USA) (IA) 27 Ph25
Tabor City (USA) (NC) 37 Qf28
Tacoma (USA) (WA) 16 Od22
Taco Taco (C) (PR) 43 Qd34
Tacubaya (MEX) (COA) 39 Pd33
Tadoussac (CDN) (QUE) 22 Ra21
Taghum (CDN) (BC) 17 Og21
Tahlequah (USA) (OK) 35 Ph28
Tahoka (USA) (TX) 34 Pe29
Taholah (USA) (WA) 16 Oc22
Tahquamenon Falls State Park ☆ (USA) (MI) 20 Qc22
Tahsis (CDN) (BC) 16 Ob21
Tajicaringa (MEX) (DGO) 39 Pc34
Takla Landing (CDN) (BC) 15 Oc18
Takoma Park (USA) (MD) 29 Qg26
Talbotton (USA) (GA) 36 Qc29
Talihina (USA) (OK) 35 Ph28
Talkeetna (USA) (AK) 10 Mk14
Talladega (USA) (AL) 36 Qb29
Tallahassee (USA) (FL) 36 Qc30
Tallassee (USA) (AL) 36 Qb29
Talleysville (USA) (VA) 31 Qg27
Tallulah (USA) (LA) 36 Pk29
Talmage (CDN) (SAS) 18 Pd21
Talpa (USA) (TX) 35 Pf30
Tama (USA) (IA) 27 Pj25
Tamaqua (USA) (PA) 29 Qh25
Tamarack (USA) (MN) 19 Pj22
Tamarac National Wildlife Refuge ☆ (USA) (MN) 19 Ph22
Tampa (USA) (FL) 43 Qd32
Tanana (USA) (AK) 10 Mj13
Tanani (USA) (AK) 14 Nh16
Taneytown (USA) (MD) 29 Qg26
Tangent (CDN) (ALB) 15 Og18
Tangier (USA) (VA) 29 Qh27
Tank (USA) (TX) 39 Pd30
Tannin (CDN) (ONT) 19 Pk21
Tanque Nuevo (MEX) (COA) 40 Pd32
Tanque Verde (USA) (AZ) 33 Ok29
Taos (USA) (NM) 34 Pc27
Taos, Pueblo ☆ (USA) (NM) 34 Pc27
Tappahannock (USA) (VA) 29 Qg27
Tarboro (USA) (NC) 31 Qg28
Tarkio (USA) (MO) 27 Ph25
Tarkio (USA) (MT) 25 Oh22
Tarpon Springs (USA) (FL) 43 Qd31
Tarzan (USA) (TX) 34 Pe29
Taschereau (CDN) (QUE) 21 Qf21
Tashota (CDN) (ONT) 20 Qb20
Ta Ta Creek (CDN) (BC) 17 Oh21
Tatamagouche (CDN) (NS) 22 Rd23
Tatitlek (USA) (AK) 13 Nb15
Tatla Lake (CDN) (BC) 16 Oc20
Tatlatui Provincial Park ☆ (CDN) (BC) 14 Ob17
Tatsfield (CDN) (SAS) 17 Pa19
Tatshenshini-Alsek Kluane National Park ☆ (CDN) (YT) 13 Ne15
Tatum (USA) (NM) 34 Pd29
Tatum (USA) (TX) 35 Ph29
Taunton (USA) (MA) 30 Qk25
Tauria (USA) (MO) 35 Pj27
Tawas City (USA) (MI) 29 Qd23
Taylor (CDN) (BC) 15 Oe17
Taylor (USA) (AK) 10 Mc13
Taylor (USA) (NE) 26 Pf25
Taylor (USA) (TX) 40 Pg30
Taylor Park (USA) (CO) 34 Pb26
Taylors Falls (USA) (MN) 27 Pj23
Taylors Island (USA) (MD) 29 Qg26
Taylorsville (USA) (MS) 36 Qa30
Taylorville (USA) (IL) 28 Qa26
Tayoltita (MEX) (DGO) 39 Pc33
Tazewell (USA) (TN) 37 Qd27
Tazewell (USA) (VA) 37 Qe27
Tchula (USA) (MS) 36 Pk29
Teacapán (MEX) (SIN) 39 Pc34
Teague (USA) (TX) 35 Pg30
Tebenkopf Bay Wilderness ☆ (USA) (AK) 14 Nh17
Tecate (MEX) (BCN) 32 Og29
Tecolote, El (MEX) (NL) 40 Pe33
Tecumseh (USA) (NE) 27 Pg25
Teepee (CDN) (BC) 14 Nh16
Teepee Creek (CDN) (ALB) 15 Of18
Tees (CDN) (ALB) 17 Oj19
Tehachapi (USA) (CA) 32 Of28
Tekoa (USA) (WA) 24 Og22
Telchac (MEX) (YUC) 42 Qa35
Telegraph Creek (CDN) (BC) 14 Nk17
Teller (USA) (AK) 10 Mb13
Telluride (USA) (CO) 33 Pb27
Temagami (CDN) (ONT) 21 Qf22
Temascal, El (MEX) (TAM) 40 Pf33
Temax (MEX) (YUC) 42 Qa35
Temecula (USA) (CA) 32 Og29
Témiscamingue (CDN) (QUE) 21 Qf22
Témoris (MEX) (CHA) 39 Pa32
Tempe (USA) (AZ) 33 Ok29
Templadera del Derrumbe, La (MEX) (DGO) 39 Pb33
Temple (USA) (TX) 40 Pg30
Templeman (USA) (VA) 29 Qg26
Tenaha (USA) (TX) 35 Ph30
Tenakee Springs (USA) (AK) 14 Nh17
Tennessee (USA) (TX) 35 Ph30
Tennille (USA) (FL) 37 Qd31
Tennyson (USA) (TX) 34 Pe30
Tensas River National Wildlife Refuge ☆ (USA) (LA) 36 Pk29
Ten Sleep (USA) (WY) 25 Pb23
Tenstrike (USA) (MN) 19 Ph22
Tepehuanes (MEX) (DGO) 39 Pc33
Tepuxtla (MEX) (SIN) 39 Pb34
Terlingua (USA) (TX) 39 Pd31
Terrace (CDN) (BC) 16 Oa18
Terra Nova National Park ☆ (CDN) (NFL) 23 Rj21
Terrebonne (CDN) (QUE) 30 Qj23
Terre Haute (USA) (IN) 28 Qb26
Terrell (USA) (TX) 35 Pg29
Terrenceville (CDN) (NFL) 23 Rh22
Terreton (USA) (ID) 25 Oj24
Terry (USA) (MT) 18 Pc22
Teslin (CDN) (YT) 14 Nj15
Testerazo, El (MEX) (BCN) 32 Og29
Tête Jaune Cache (CDN) (BC) 16 Of19
Tetlin Junction (USA) (AK) 11 Nd14
Tetlin National Wildlife Refuge ☆ (USA) (AK) 11 Nd14
Teulon (CDN) (MAN) 19 Pg20
Texarkana (USA) (AR) 35 Ph29
Texas City (USA) (TX) 41 Ph31
Texhoma (USA) (RI) 34 Pe27
Thamesville (CDN) (ONT) 29 Qe24
Thatcher (USA) (CO) 34 Pc27
Thayer (USA) (KS) 35 Ph27
Thayer (USA) (MO) 36 Pk27
Thayne (USA) (WY) 25 Ok24
The Current (BS) 43 Qg33
The Dalles (USA) (OR) 24 Oe23
Thedford (USA) (NE) 26 Pe25
The Forks (USA) (ME) 22 Ra23
Theodore (CDN) (SAS) 18 Pd20
Theodore (USA) (AL) 36 Qa30
Theodore Roosevelt National Park North Unit ☆ (USA) (ND) 18 Pd22
Theodore Roosevelt National Park South Unit ☆ (USA) (ND) 18 Pc22
Theodosia (USA) (MO) 35 Pj27
The Pas (CDN) (MAN) 18 Pe19
Therien (CDN) (ALB) 17 Ok18
Thermopolis (USA) (WY) 25 Pa24
Thessalon (CDN) (ONT) 29 Qd22
Thetford-Mines (CDN) (QUE) 22 Qk22
Thetis Island (CDN) (BC) 16 Od21
Thibodaux (USA) (LA) 36 Pk31
Thief River Falls (USA) (MN) 19 Pg21
Thomas (USA) (WV) 29 Qf26
Thomaston (USA) (GA) 36 Qc29
Thomaston Corner (CDN) (NB) 22 Rb23
Thomasville (USA) (AL) 36 Qb30
Thomasville (USA) (GA) 37 Qd30
Thomasville (USA) (NC) 37 Qe28
Thompson (CDN) (MAN) 19 Pg18
Thompson (USA) (ND) 19 Pg22
Thompson Falls (USA) (MT) 17 Oh22
Thomson (USA) (GA) 37 Qd29
Thoreau (USA) (NM) 33 Pa28
Thornburg (USA) (IA) 27 Pj25
Thorne (CDN) (ONT) 21 Qf22
Thornloe (CDN) (ONT) 21 Qf22
Thornton (USA) (AR) 35 Pj29
Thornton (USA) (IA) 27 Pj24
Thorp (USA) (WI) 27 Pk23
Thorsby (CDN) (ALB) 17 Oj19
Three Creeks (CDN) (ALB) 15 Og17
Three Creeks (USA) (AR) 35 Pj29
Three Forks (USA) (MT) 25 Ok23
Three Hills (CDN) (ALB) 17 Oj20
Three Rivers (USA) (MI) 28 Qc25
Three Rivers (USA) (NM) 34 Pb29
Three Rivers (USA) (TX) 40 Pf31
Throckmorton (USA) (TX) 35 Pf29
Throne (CDN) (ALB) 17 Ok19
Thunder Bay (CDN) (ONT) 20 Qa21
Thurmont (USA) (MD) 29 Qg26
Tiahualilo de Zaragoza (MEX) (DGO) 39 Pd32
Ticaboo (USA) (UT) 33 Ok27
Ticonderoga (USA) (NY) 30 Qj24
Tidewater (USA) (LA) 36 Qa31
Tierra Amarilla (USA) (NM) 34 Pb27
Tie Siding (USA) (WY) 26 Pc25
Tiffin (USA) (OH) 29 Qd25
Tifton (USA) (GA) 37 Qd30
Tiger (USA) (WA) 17 Og21
Tignish (CDN) (PEI) 22 Rc22
Tijeras (USA) (NM) 34 Pb28
Tijuana (MEX) (BCN) 32 Og29
Tika (CDN) (QUE) 22 Rc20
Tikiklut (USA) (AK) 10 Mg10
Tilbury (CDN) (ONT) 29 Qd24
Tilden (USA) (NE) 27 Pg24
Tilden (USA) (TX) 40 Pf31
Tilden Lake (CDN) (ONT) 21 Qf22
Tillamook (USA) (OR) 24 Od23
Tiller (USA) (OR) 24 Od24
Tillsonburg (CDN) (ONT) 29 Qe24
Tilston (CDN) (MAN) 18 Pe21
Timber (USA) (OR) 24 Od23
Timberville (USA) (VA) 29 Qf26
Timmins (CDN) (ONT) 20 Qe21
Timonium (USA) (MD) 29 Qg26
Timpanogos Cave National Monument ☆ (USA) (UT) 25 Oj25
Timpas (USA) (CO) 34 Pd27
Timpson (USA) (TX) 35 Ph30
Tioga (USA) (ND) 18 Pd21
Tionesta (USA) (PA) 29 Qf25
Tipton (USA) (CA) 32 Of27
Tipton (USA) (IA) 27 Pk25
Tipton (USA) (MO) 28 Pj26
Tiptonville (USA) (TN) 36 Qa27
Tisdale (CDN) (SAS) 18 Pc19
Tishomingo (USA) (OK) 35 Pg28
Titusville (USA) (FL) 43 Qe31
Titusville (USA) (PA) 29 Qf25
Tivoli (USA) (TX) 40 Pg31
Tizimín (MEX) (YUC) 42 Qa35
Toba (CDN) (BC) 16 Oc20
Tobermory (CDN) (ONT) 29 Qd23
Tobin Lake (CDN) (SAS) 18 Pc19
Toccoa (USA) (GA) 37 Qd28
Todos Santos (MEX) (BCS) 38 Ok34
Tofield (CDN) (ALB) 17 Oj19
Tofino (CDN) (BC) 16 Oc21
Togiak (USA) (AK) 12 Me16
Togo (CDN) (SAS) 18 Pe20
Togo (USA) (MN) 19 Pj22
Tohatchi (USA) (NM) 33 Pa28
Tok = Tok Junction (USA) (AK) 11 Nd14
Tok Junction = Tok (USA) (AK) 11 Nd14
Toledo (CDN) (ONT) 29 Qh23
Toledo (USA) (OH) 29 Qd25
Toledo (USA) (OR) 24 Od23
Tolland (CDN) (ALB) 17 Ok19
Tolley (USA) (ND) 18 Pe21
Tolono (USA) (IL) 28 Qa26
Tolstoi (CDN) (MAN) 19 Pg21
Tomah (USA) (WI) 27 Pk24
Tomahawk (USA) (WI) 28 Qa23
Tomatán (MEX) (BCN) 38 Oh31
Tombstone (USA) (AZ) 33 Ok30
Tomiko (CDN) (ONT) 21 Qf22
Tomochic (MEX) (CHA) 39 Pb31
Tompkins (CDN) (SAS) 17 Pa20
Tomslake (CDN) (BC) 15 Oe18
Toms River (USA) (NJ) 31 Qh26
Tonasket (USA) (WA) 16 Of21
Tonichi (MEX) (SON) 39 Pa31
Tonkawa (USA) (OK) 35 Pg27
Tonopah (USA) (NV) 32 Og26
Tonsina (USA) (AK) 13 Nc15
Tooele (USA) (UT) 25 Oj25
Topawa (USA) (AZ) 33 Ok30
Topaz Lake (USA) (NV) 32 Of26
Topeka (USA) (KS) 35 Ph26
Topia (MEX) (DGO) 39 Pb33
Topley Landing (CDN) (BC) 14 Ob18
Topolobampo (MEX) (SIN) 39 Pa33
Toppenish (USA) (WA) 24 Oe22
Topsfield (USA) (ME) 22 Rb23
Toquerville (USA) (UT) 33 Oj27
Torbay (CDN) (NFL) 23 Rj22
Torboy (USA) (WA) 16 Of21
Toronto (CDN) (ONT) 29 Qf24
Toronto (USA) (KS) 35 Ph27
Torquay (CDN) (SAS) 18 Pd21
Torrance (USA) (CA) 32 Of29
Torreón (MEX) (COA) 39 Pd33
Torreon (USA) (NM) 34 Pb28
Torrey (USA) (UT) 33 Ok26
Torrington (USA) (CT) 30 Qj25
Torrington (USA) (WY) 26 Pc24
Tory Hill (CDN) (ONT) 29 Qf23
Toston (USA) (MT) 25 Ok22
Totnes (CDN) (SAS) 17 Pa20
Tour Village, De (USA) (MI) 29 Qd22
Toutes Aides (CDN) (MAN) 19 Pf20
Towanda (USA) (PA) 29 Qg25
Towaoc (USA) (CO) 33 Pa27
Tower (USA) (MN) 19 Pj22
Towner (USA) (ND) 18 Pe21
Townsend (USA) (MT) 25 Ok22
Townsend, Port (USA) (WA) 16 Od21
Towson (USA) (MD) 29 Qg26
Toyah (USA) (TX) 39 Pd30
Toyahvale (USA) (TX) 39 Pd30
Tracadie (CDN) (NB) 22 Rc22
Tracy (CDN) (NB) 22 Rb23
Tracy (USA) (AZ) 33 Oj29
Tracy (USA) (CA) 32 Oe27
Tracy (USA) (MN) 27 Ph23
Traer (USA) (IA) 27 Pj24
Trail (CDN) (BC) 17 Og21
Trail (USA) (MN) 19 Ph22
Tramping Lake (CDN) (SAS) 17 Pa19
Traskwood (USA) (AR) 35 Pj28
Traverse City (USA) (MI) 28 Qc23
Traynor (CDN) (SAS) 17 Pa19
Treelon (CDN) (SAS) 18 Pa21
Treesbank (CDN) (MAN) 19 Pf21
Trego (USA) (MT) 17 Oh21
Trego (USA) (WI) 27 Pk23
Treherne (CDN) (MAN) 19 Pf21
Tremont (USA) (PA) 29 Qg25
Tremonton (USA) (UT) 25 Oj25
Tren, El (MEX) (SON) 33 Oj30
Trenary (USA) (MI) 28 Qb22
Trent (USA) (TX) 34 Pe29
Trenton (CDN) (ONT) 29 Qg23
Trenton (USA) (FL) 37 Qd31
Trenton (USA) (IL) 28 Qa26
Trenton (USA) (MI) 29 Qd24
Trenton (USA) (MO) 35 Pj2
Trenton (USA) (NC) 31 Qg28
Trenton (USA) (NE) 34 Pe25
Trenton (USA) (NJ) 30 Qh25
Trepassey (CDN) (NFL) 23 Rj22
Tres Hermanos (MEX) (BCN) 32 Og3
Tres Piedras (USA) (NM) 34 Pc2
Trewdate (CDN) (SAS) 18 Pb2
Triangle (CDN) (ALB) 15 Og1
Tribune (CDN) (SAS) 18 Pd2
Tribune (USA) (KS) 34 Pe2
Tridell (USA) (UT) 25 Pa2
Trinidad (C) (SS) 43 Qe3
Trinidad (USA) (CO) 34 Pc2
Trinity (CDN) (NFL) 23 Rj2
Trinity (USA) (TX) 41 Ph3
Tripp (USA) (SD) 27 Pg2
Trochu (CDN) (ALB) 17 Oj2
Trois-Pistoles (CDN) (QUE) 22 Ra2
Trois-Rivières (CDN) (QUE) 21 Qj2
Trona (USA) (CA) 32 Og2
Trotters (USA) (ND) 18 Pd2
Troup (USA) (TX) 35 Ph2
Trout Creek (CDN) (ONT) 29 Qf2
Trout Creek (USA) (MT) 17 Oh2
Trout Lake (CDN) (NWT) 15 Oe1
Trout Lake (USA) (MI) 28 Qc2
Trout Lake (USA) (WA) 24 Oe
Trout River (CDN) (NFL) 23 Rf
Troy (USA) (AL) 36 Qc
Troy (USA) (KS) 35 Ph
Troy (USA) (MO) 28 Pk
Troy (USA) (MT) 17 Oh
Troy (USA) (NY) 30 Qj
Troy (USA) (OH) 28 Qc
Troy (USA) (PA) 29 Qg
Truckee (USA) (CA) 32 Oe
Trujillo (USA) (NM) 34 Pc
Truman (CDN) (ALB) 17 Ok
Truro (CDN) (NS) 22 Rd
Trutch (CDN) (BC) 15 Od
Truth or Consequences (USA) (NM) 34 Pb
Tryon (USA) (NE) 26 Pe
Tsawwassen (CDN) (BC) 16 Od
Tsiigehtchic = Arctic Red River (CDN) (NWT) 11 N
Ts'yl-os Provincial Park ☆ (CDN) (BC) 16 Oc
Tubac (USA) (AZ) 33 Ok
Tuba City (USA) (AZ) 33 Ok
Tuchitua (CDN) (YT) 14 Oa
Tucker (USA) (TX) 35 Ph
Tuckerton (USA) (NJ) 31 Qh
Tucson (USA) (AZ) 33 Ok
Tucumcari (USA) (NM) 34 Pd
Tuitán (MEX) (DGO) 39 Pc
Tuktoyaktuk (CDN) (NWT) 11 N
Tula (MEX) (TAM) 40 P
Tulameen (CDN) (BC) 16 O
Tulare (USA) (CA) 32 O
Tularosa (USA) (NM) 34 P
Tule, El (MEX) (COA) 40 P
Tulia (USA) (TX) 34 P
Tullahoma (USA) (TN) 36 Q
Tullos (USA) (LA) 36 P
Tulsa (USA) (OK) 35 P
Tulsequah (CDN) (BC) 14 N
Tuluksak (USA) (AK) 12 M
Tumbler Ridge (CDN) (BC) 15 O
Tunas de Zaza (C) (SS) 43 Q
Tungsten (CDN) (NWT) 14 O
Tunkhannock (USA) (PA) 29 Q
Tuntutuliak (USA) (AK) 12 M
Tununak (USA) (AK) 12 M
Tununuk (CDN) (NWT) 11 N
Tupelo (USA) (MS) 36 Q
Tupper (CDN) (BC) 15 O
Tupper Lake (USA) (NY) 29 Q
Tuque, La (CDN) (QUE) 21
Turin (CDN) (ALB) 17
Turkey (USA) (TX) 34
Turkey Creek (USA) (LA) 36
Turlock (USA) (CA) 32
Turnbull N.W.R. ☆ (USA) (WA) 17
Turner (USA) (ME) 22
Turner (USA) (MT) 18
Turnersville (USA) (TX) 35
Turtleford (CDN) (SAS) 17
Turtle Lake (USA) (ND) 18
Turtle Lake (USA) (WI) 27
Tuscaloosa (USA) (AL) 36
Tuscola (USA) (IL) 28
Tuscola (USA) (TX) 35
Tuscumbia (USA) (MO) 28

Tuskegee USA (AL) 36 Qc29
Tuttle USA (ND) 19 Pf22
Tutuaca MEX (CHA) 39 Pb31
Tuxford CDN (SAS) 18 Pc20
Tuzigoot National Monument ☆ USA (AZ) 33 Oj28
Tweed CDN (ONT) 29 Qg23
Tweedsmuir Provincial Park ☆ CDN (BC) 16 Ob19
Twentynine Palms USA (CA) 33 Oh28
Twillingate CDN (NFL) 23 Rh21
Twin Bridges USA (MT) 25 Oj23
Twin Butte CDN (ALB) 17 Oj21
Twin City CDN (ONT) 20 Qa21
Twin Falls USA (ID) 25 Oh24
Twin Mountain USA (NH) 22 Qk23
Twin Valley USA (MN) 19 Pg22
Twisp USA (WA) 16 Oe21
Two Creeks CDN (MAN) 18 Pe20
Twodot USA (MT) 18 Ok22
Two Harbors USA (MN) 19 Pk22
Two Hills CDN (ALB) 17 Ok19
Two Inlets USA (MN) 19 Ph22
Two Rivers USA (WI) 28 Qb23
Tye CDN (BC) 17 Og21
Tygh Valley USA (OR) 24 Oe23
Tyler USA (TX) 35 Ph29
Tyler USA (WA) 17 Og22
Tylertown USA (MS) 36 Pk30
Tyndall CDN (MAN) 19 Pg20
Tyndall USA (SD) 27 Pg24
Tyner USA (KY) 37 Qd27
Tyrone USA (NM) 33 Pa29
Tyrone USA (PA) 29 Qf25

U

Jcluelet CDN (BC) 16 Oc21
Jcross USA (WY) 26 Pb23
Jhrichsville USA (OH) 29 Qe25
Jkiah USA (CA) 32 Od26
Jkiah USA (OR) 24 Of23
Jlm USA (MT) 17 Ok22
Jlm USA (WY) 26 Pb23
Jlysses USA (KS) 34 Pe27
Jlysses USA (NE) 27 Pg25
Jmán MEX (YUC) 42 Qa35
Jmatilla USA (FL) 37 Qe31
mbarger USA (TX) 34 Pd28
miat USA (AK) 10 Mj11
nadilla USA (GA) 37 Qd29
nalakleet USA (AK) 10 Me14
nderwood USA (ND) 18 Pe22
ngalik USA (AK) 10 Me13
nimak USA (AK) 12 Mc18
nion USA (MO) 28 Pk26
nion USA (MS) 36 Qa29
nion USA (SC) 37 Qe28
nion USA (WV) 37 Qe27
nión, Villa MEX (COA) 40 Pe31
nión, Villa MEX (DGO) 39 Pc34
nión, Villa MEX (SIN) 39 Pb34
nion Bay CDN (BC) 16 Oc21
nion Center USA (SD) 26 Pd23
nion Church USA (MS) 36 Pk30
nion City USA (PA) 29 Qf25
nion City USA (TN) 36 Qa27
ion Creek USA (OR) 24 Od24
ion Springs USA (AL) 36 Qc29
iontown USA (PA) 29 Qf26
ionville USA (MO) 27 Pj25
ionville USA (NV) 24 Of25
ited States Air Force Academy ☆ USA (CO) 34 Pc26
ity CDN (SAS) 17 Pa19
ity USA (ME) 22 Ra23
iversal City USA (TX) 40 Pf31
iversity City USA (MO) 28 Pk26
iversity of Virginia ☆ USA (VA) 29 Qf26
iversity Park USA (NM) 34 Pb29
win CDN (SAS) 17 Pa19
ham USA (ND) 18 Pe21
per Canada Village ☆ CDN (ONT) 29 Qh23
per Gulf of California and Colorado River Delta Biosphere ☆ MEX (SON) 33 Oh30
per Lake USA (CA) 32 Od26
per Missouri River Breaks National Monument ☆ USA (MT) 17 Ok22
per Musquodoboit CDN (NS) 22 Rd23
per Sandusky USA (OH) 29 Qd25
sala CDN (ONT) 19 Pk21
on USA (WY) 26 Pc23
ana USA (IL) 28 Qa25
ana USA (OH) 29 Qd25
andale USA (IA) 27 Pj25
s MEX (SON) 38 Ok31
h USA (MO) 35 Pj26
achic MEX (CHA) 39 Pa32
CDN (BC) 16 Oa18
USA (WA) 17 Og21
a USA (MS) 36 Pk29
a USA (MT) 17 Ok22
a USA (NY) 29 Qh24
a USA (OH) 29 Qd25
rson CDN (ONT) 29 Qf23
de USA (TX) 40 Pf31
idge CDN (ONT) 29 Qf23

V

ville USA (CA) 32 Oe26
erie USA (LA) 36 Pk31
r USA (WA) 24 Od22
USA (CO) 34 Pb26
deces MEX (TAM) 40 Pf32
es-Bois CDN (QUE) 29 Qh23
ez USA (AK) 13 Nb15
'Or CDN (QUE) 21 Qg21
sta USA (GA) 37 Qd30
USA (OR) 24 Og24
mount CDN (BC) 16 Of19
tia CDN (ONT) 29 Qf23
tine USA (NE) 26 Pe24
tine USA (TX) 39 Pc30
tine National Wildlife Refuge ☆ USA (NE) 26 Pe24
Valera USA (TX) 35 Pf30
Valerio MEX (CHA) 39 Pb32
Valhalla Centre CDN (ALB) 15 Of18
Valhalla Provincial Park ☆ CDN (BC) 17 Og21
Valier USA (MT) 17 Oj21
Val-Jalbert CDN (QUE) 21 Qj21
Valle USA (AZ) 33 Oj28
Valle, La USA (WI) 27 Pk24
Vallecillos MEX (NL) 40 Pf32
Valle de Allende MEX (CHA) 39 Pc32
Valle del Rosario MEX (CHA) 39 Pb32
Valle de Viñales ☆ C (PR) 43 Qd34
Valle de Zaragoza MEX (CHA) 39 Pc32
Vallée-Jonction CDN (QUE) 22 Qk22
Valle Hermoso MEX (TAM) 40 Pg33
Vallejo USA (CA) 32 Od26
Valley USA (NE) 27 Pg25
Valley USA (WA) 17 Og21
Valley USA (WY) 25 Pa23
Valley City USA (ND) 19 Pf22
Valley East CDN (ONT) 20 Qe22
Valley Falls USA (KS) 35 Ph26
Valley Falls USA (OR) 24 Oe24
Valley Head USA (WV) 29 Qe26
Valley Mills USA (TX) 35 Pg30
Valley of Willow USA (AK) 10 Mh11
Valley Park USA (MS) 36 Pk29
Valley Station USA (KY) 28 Qc26
Valleyview CDN (ALB) 15 Og18
Valley Wells USA (CA) 33 Oh28
Val Marie CDN (SAS) 18 Pb21
Valmeyer USA (IL) 28 Pk26
Valmy USA (NV) 24 Og25
Valor CDN (SAS) 18 Pb21
Val-Paradis CDN (QUE) 21 Qf21
Valparaíso MEX (ZAC) 39 Pd34
Valparaiso USA (FL) 36 Qb30
Valparaiso USA (IN) 28 Qb25
Valparaiso USA (NE) 27 Pg25
Val Racine CDN (QUE) 22 Qk23
Vamori USA (AZ) 33 Ok30
Van USA (TX) 35 Ph29
Vananda USA (MT) 25 Pb22
Van Buren USA (AR) 35 Ph28
Van Buren USA (ME) 22 Rb22
Van Buren USA (MO) 36 Pk27
Vanceboro USA (ME) 22 Rb23
Vanceburg USA (KY) 29 Qd26
Vancleave USA (MS) 36 Qa30
Vancouver CDN (BC) 16 Od21
Vancouver USA (WA) 24 Od23
Vandalia USA (IL) 28 Qa26
Vanderhoof CDN (BC) 16 Od18
Vanegas, Estación MEX (SLP) 40 Pe34
Van Etten USA (NY) 29 Qg24
Vanguard CDN (SAS) 18 Pb21
Van Horn USA (TX) 39 Pc30
Vantage CDN (SAS) 18 Pb21
Van Vert USA (OH) 28 Qc25
Varadero C (MZ) 43 Qe34
Varas, Las MEX (CHA) 39 Pb31
Varejonal, El MEX (SIN) 39 Pb33
Vassar CDN (MAN) 19 Ph21
Vassar USA (MI) 29 Qd24
Vaughn USA (MT) 17 Ok22
Vaughn USA (NM) 34 Pc28
Vaughn USA (WA) 16 Od22
Vauxhall CDN (ALB) 17 Oj20
Vawn CDN (SAS) 17 Pa19
Vaya Chin USA (AZ) 33 Oj29
Vázquez C (LT) 43 Qg35
Vega USA (TX) 34 Pd28
Vegas, Las USA (NM) 34 Pc28
Vegas, Las USA (NV) 33 Oh27
Vegreville CDN (ALB) 17 Oj19
Velva USA (ND) 18 Pe21
Venango USA (NE) 26 Pd25
Venetie USA (AK) 11 Nb12
Venice USA (FL) 43 Qd32
Venice USA (LA) 36 Qa31
Ventana, La MEX (BCN) 33 Oh30
Ventana, La MEX (SLP) 40 Pe34
Ventura USA (CA) 32 Of28
Vera CDN (SAS) 17 Pa19
Veracruz MEX (BCN) 33 Oh29
Verbena USA (AL) 36 Qb29
Verdigre USA (NE) 27 Pg24
Vergas USA (MN) 19 Ph22
Vergel MEX (DGO) 39 Pd33
Vergel, El MEX (CHA) 39 Pb32
Verhalen USA (TX) 39 Pd30
Vermilion CDN (ALB) 17 Ok19
Vermilion USA (OH) 29 Qd25
Vermilion Bay CDN (ONT) 19 Pj21
Vermillion USA (SD) 27 Pg24
Vernal USA (UT) 25 Pa25
Verner CDN (ONT) 29 Qe22
Vernia, La USA (TX) 40 Pf31
Vernon CDN (BC) 16 Of20
Vernon USA (FL) 36 Qc30
Vernon USA (LA) 36 Pj29
Vernon USA (TX) 35 Pf28
Vernon USA (UT) 33 Oj25
Vernon Center USA (MN) 27 Ph24
Vero Beach USA (FL) 43 Qe32
Verona CDN (ONT) 29 Qg23
Verona USA (ND) 26 Pf22
Versailles USA (KY) 36 Qc26
Versailles USA (MO) 28 Pj26
Versailles USA (OH) 28 Qc26
Vertientes C (CG) 43 Qf35
Verwood CDN (SAS) 18 Pc21
Veta, La USA (CO) 34 Pc27
Veteran CDN (ALB) 17 Ok20
Veuve, Rivière CDN (ONT) 20 Qe22
Vevay USA (IN) 28 Qc26
Veyo USA (UT) 33 Oj27
Víbora, La MEX (COA) 39 Pd32
Vicente Guerrero MEX (DGO) 39 Pd34
Vicente Guerrero MEX (QR) 42 Qb35
Viceroy CDN (SAS) 18 Pc21
Vichy USA (MO) 28 Pk26
Vici USA (OK) 35 Pf27
Vicksburg USA (MS) 36 Pk29
Victor USA (ID) 25 Ok24
Victor USA (NY) 29 Qg24
Victor USA (SD) 27 Pg23
Victoria CDN (BC) 16 Od21
Victoria USA (TX) 40 Pg31
Victoria USA (VA) 31 Qf27
Victoria, Ciudad MEX (TAM) 40 Pf34
Victoria Beach CDN (MAN) 19 Pg20
Victoria Beach CDN (NS) 22 Rc23
Victoria de Durango = Durango MEX (DGO) 39 Pc33
Victoriaville CDN (QUE) 21 Qk22
Víctor Rosales MEX (ZAC) 39 Pd34
Victorville USA (CA) 32 Og28
Vida USA (MT) 18 Pc22
Vidal USA (CA) 33 Oh28
Vidalia USA (GA) 37 Qd29
Vidalia USA (LA) 36 Pk30
Vidor USA (TX) 41 Pj30
Vidora CDN (SAS) 17 Pa21
Vienna USA (IL) 36 Qa27
Vienna USA (MD) 29 Qh26
Vienna USA (MO) 28 Pk26
Vienna USA (VA) 29 Qg26
Vienna USA (WV) 29 Qe26
Viesca MEX (COA) 39 Pd33
View USA (TX) 35 Pf29
Viking CDN (ALB) 17 Ok19
Villa Ahumada MEX (CHA) 39 Pb30
Villa Coronado MEX (CHA) 39 Pc32
Villa de Cos MEX (ZAC) 40 Pd34
Villa de Garcia MEX (NL) 40 Pe33
Villa de Orestes MEX (DGO) 39 Pc32
Villa de Sari MEX (SON) 38 Ok31
Village Cove CDN (NFL) 23 Rh21
Villa Hidalgo MEX (DGO) 39 Pc32
Villa Hidalgo MEX (SON) 39 Pa30
Villa Insurgentes MEX (BCS) 38 Ok33
Villa Juárez MEX (DGO) 39 Pd33
Villaldama MEX (NL) 40 Pe32
Villa Mainero MEX (TAM) 40 Pf33
Villanueva MEX (ZAC) 39 Pd34
Villa Ocampo MEX (DGO) 39 Pc32
Villa Unión MEX (COA) 40 Pe31
Villa Unión MEX (DGO) 39 Pc34
Villa Unión MEX (SIN) 39 Pb34
Ville-Marie CDN (QUE) 21 Qf22
Villeroy CDN (QUE) 21 Qk22
Villisca USA (IA) 27 Ph25
Viñales, Valle de ☆ C (PR) 43 Qd34
Vinalhaven USA (ME) 22 Ra23
Vincennes USA (IN) 28 Qb26
Vincent USA (TX) 34 Pe29
Vineland USA (NJ) 31 Qh26
Vinita USA (OK) 35 Ph27
Vinton USA (IA) 27 Pj24
Viola USA (IL) 27 Pk25
Viola USA (KS) 35 Pg27
Viola USA (WI) 27 Pk24
Virden CDN (MAN) 18 Pe21
Virden USA (IL) 28 Qa26
Virginia USA (MN) 19 Pj22
Virginia Beach USA (VA) 31 Qh27
Virginia Dale USA (CO) 26 Pc25
Viroqua USA (WI) 27 Pk24
Visalia USA (CA) 32 Of27
Vita CDN (MAN) 19 Pg21
Vivian CDN (MAN) 19 Pg21
Vivian USA (SD) 26 Pe24
Volborg USA (MT) 26 Pc23
Volcano USA (HI) 44 Mh36
Voss USA (TX) 35 Pf30
Voyageurs National Park ☆ USA (MN) 19 Pj21
Vuelta Abajo ☆ C (PR) 42 Qc34
Vulcan CDN (ALB) 17 Oj20
Vuntut National Park ☆ CDN (NWT) 11 Ne11

W

Wabakimi Provincial Park ☆ CDN (ONT) 19 Pk20
Wabash USA (IN) 28 Qc25
Wabasha USA (MN) 27 Pj23
Wabowden CDN (MAN) 19 Pf18
Waco CDN (QUE) 22 Rc20
Waco USA (TX) 35 Pg30
Wade USA (MS) 36 Qa30
Wadena CDN (SAS) 18 Pd20
Wadena USA (MN) 27 Ph22
Wadesboro USA (NC) 37 Qe28
Wadhope CDN (MAN) 19 Ph20
Wadley USA (GA) 37 Qd29
Wadsworth USA (NV) 32 Of26
Wagner USA (SD) 26 Pf24
Wagon Mound USA (NM) 34 Pc27
Wagontire USA (OR) 24 Of24
Wahiawa USA (HI) 44 Mf35
Wahoo USA (NE) 27 Pg25
Wahpeton USA (ND) 27 Pg22
Waialua USA (HI) 44 Mf35
Waialua USA (HI) 44 Mg35
Wai'anae USA (HI) 44 Mf35
Wailuku USA (HI) 44 Mg35
Wainwright CDN (ALB) 17 Ok19
Wainwright USA (AK) 10 Mf10
Waite USA (ME) 22 Rb23
Waitsburg USA (WA) 24 Of22
Wakaw CDN (SAS) 18 Pc19
Wa Keeny USA (KS) 35 Pf26
Wakefield CDN (QUE) 29 Qh23
Wakefield USA (MI) 20 Qa22
Wakefield USA (VA) 31 Qg27
Wake Forest USA (NC) 31 Qf28
Waklarok USA (AK) 10 Mc14
Wakopa CDN (MAN) 19 Pf21
Walakpa USA (AK) 10 Mg10
Wálamo, El MEX (SIN) 39 Pb34
Walcott CDN (BC) 16 Ob18
Walcott USA (WY) 26 Pb25
Walden CDN (ONT) 20 Qe22
Walden USA (CO) 26 Pb25
Waldenburg USA (AR) 36 Pk28
Waldersee CDN (MAN) 19 Pf20
Waldo USA (AR) 35 Pj29
Waldo USA (FL) 37 Qd31
Waldorf USA (MD) 29 Qg26
Waldport USA (OR) 24 Oc23
Waldron USA (AR) 35 Ph28
Wales USA (AK) 10 Ma13
Walhalla USA (ND) 19 Pg21
Walker USA (IA) 27 Pk24
Walker USA (MI) 28 Qc24
Walker USA (MN) 19 Ph22
Wall USA (SD) 26 Pd23
Wallace USA (ID) 17 Oh22
Wallace USA (NC) 31 Qg28
Wallace USA (NE) 26 Pe25
Wallaceburg CDN (ONT) 29 Qd24
Walla Walla USA (WA) 24 Of22
Wallula USA (WA) 24 Of22
Walnut USA (MS) 36 Qa28
Walnut Cove USA (NC) 37 Qe27
Walnut Grove USA (MN) 27 Ph23
Walnut Grove USA (MO) 35 Pj27
Walpole CDN (SAS) 18 Pe21
Walrus Islands State Game Sanctuary ☆ USA (AK) 12 Me16
Walsenburg USA (CO) 34 Pc27
Walsh CDN (ALB) 17 Ok21
Walsh USA (CO) 34 Pd27
Walt Disney World ☆ USA (FL) 43 Qe31
Walterboro USA (SC) 37 Qe29
Waltham Station CDN (QUE) 29 Qg23
Walthill USA (NE) 27 Pg24
Waltman USA (WY) 25 Pb24
Walton CDN (NS) 22 Rc23
Walton USA (KY) 28 Qc26
Wamsutter USA (WY) 25 Pb25
Wanapitei CDN (ONT) 20 Qe22
Waneta CDN (BC) 17 Og21
Wanham CDN (ALB) 15 Of18
Wanless CDN (MAN) 18 Pe18
Wannaska USA (MN) 19 Ph21
Wapanucka USA (OK) 35 Pg28
Wapato USA (WA) 24 Oe22
Wapella CDN (SAS) 18 Pe20
Wapello USA (IA) 27 Pk25
Wapiti CDN (ALB) 15 Of18
Wappapello USA (MO) 36 Pk27
Warburg CDN (ALB) 17 Oh19
Ward Cove USA (AK) 14 Nk18
Wardner CDN (BC) 17 Oh21
Ware CDN (BC) 15 Oc17
Ware USA (MA) 30 Qj24
Wares Crossroads USA (VA) 29 Qg26
Warman CDN (SAS) 18 Pb19
Warm Creek Ranch USA (NV) 25 Oh25
Warm Springs USA (NV) 32 Og26
Warm Springs USA (OR) 24 Oe23
Warm Springs USA (VA) 29 Qf26
Warner CDN (ALB) 17 Oj21
Warner USA (OK) 35 Ph28
Warner Robins USA (GA) 37 Qd29
Warnock USA (KY) 29 Qd26
Warren CDN (MAN) 19 Pg20
Warren USA (AR) 35 Pj29
Warren USA (MI) 29 Qd24
Warren USA (MN) 19 Pg21
Warren USA (MT) 25 Pa23
Warren USA (NH) 30 Qk24
Warren USA (OH) 29 Qe25
Warren USA (PA) 29 Qf25
Warrendale USA (PA) 29 Qe25
Warrensburg USA (MO) 35 Pj26
Warrens Landing CDN (MAN) 19 Pg19
Warrenton USA (GA) 37 Qd29
Warrenton USA (VA) 29 Qg26
Warrington USA (FL) 36 Qb30
Warrior USA (AL) 36 Qb29
Warroad USA (MN) 19 Ph21
Warsaw USA (IN) 28 Qc25
Warsaw USA (KY) 28 Qc26
Warsaw USA (MO) 35 Pj26
Warsaw USA (NC) 31 Qf28
Warsaw USA (NY) 29 Qf24
Warwick USA (GA) 37 Qd30
Warwick USA (ND) 19 Pf22
Warwick USA (OK) 35 Pg28
Wasa CDN (BC) 17 Oh21
Wasagaming CDN (MAN) 19 Pf20
Wasco USA (CA) 32 Of28
Waseca CDN (SAS) 17 Pa19
Waseca USA (MN) 27 Pj23
Washackie Wilderness Area ☆ USA (WY) 25 Pa24
Washago CDN (ONT) 29 Qf23
Washburn USA (ME) 22 Ra22
Washburn USA (ND) 18 Pe22
Washburn USA (WI) 19 Pk22
Washington USA (GA) 37 Qd29
Washington USA (IA) 27 Pk25
Washington USA (IN) 28 Qb26
Washington USA (KS) 35 Pg26
Washington USA (MO) 28 Pk26
Washington USA (MS) 36 Pk30
Washington USA (NC) 31 Qg28
Washington USA (PA) 29 Qe25
Washington USA (WI) 28 Qb23
Washington, Port USA (WI) 28 Qb24
Washington Court House USA (OH) 29 Qd26
Washington D.C. USA (DC) 29 Qg26
Washtucna USA (WA) 24 Of22
Wasilla USA (AK) 13 Na15
Waskaganish CDN (QUE) 21 Qf20
Waskaganish = Fort-Rupert CDN (QUE) 21 Qf20
Waskesiu Lake CDN (SAS) 18 Pb19
Waskom USA (TX) 35 Ph29
Wasola USA (MO) 35 Pj27
Wasta USA (SD) 26 Pd23
Waterbury USA (CT) 30 Qj25
Waterhen CDN (MAN) 19 Pf20
Waterloo CDN (ONT) 29 Qe24
Waterloo USA (IA) 27 Pj24
Waterloo USA (IL) 28 Pk26
Waterloo USA (NY) 29 Qg24
Waterproof USA (LA) 36 Pk30
Watersmeet USA (MI) 20 Qa22
Waterton Glacier International Peace Park = Glacier National Park ☆ USA (MT) 17 Oh21
Waterton Park CDN (ALB) 17 Oj21
Watertown USA (NY) 29 Qh24
Watertown USA (SD) 27 Pg23
Watertown USA (WI) 28 Qa24
Water Valley USA (MS) 36 Qa28
Water Valley USA (TX) 34 Pe30
Waterville CDN (QUE) 22 Qk23
Waterville USA (KS) 35 Pg26
Waterville USA (ME) 22 Ra23
Waterville USA (MN) 27 Pj23
Waterville USA (WA) 16 Oe22
Watford City USA (ND) 18 Pd22
Watino CDN (ALB) 15 Og18
Watkins Glen USA (NY) 29 Qg24
Watonga USA (OK) 35 Pf28
Watrous CDN (SAS) 18 Pc20
Watrous USA (NM) 34 Pc28
Watseka USA (IL) 28 Qb25
Watson CDN (SAS) 18 Pc19
Watson Lake CDN (YT) 14 Oa15
Watsonville USA (CA) 32 Oe27
Waubaushene CDN (ONT) 29 Qf23
Wauchope CDN (SAS) 18 Pe21
Wauconda USA (WA) 16 Of21
Waukegan USA (IL) 28 Qb24
Waukesha USA (WI) 28 Qa24
Waukon USA (IA) 27 Pk24
Wauneta USA (NE) 26 Pe25
Waupaca USA (WI) 28 Qa23
Waupun USA (WI) 28 Qa24
Waurika USA (OK) 35 Pg28
Wausau USA (WI) 28 Qa23
Wausaukee USA (WI) 28 Qb23
Wauwatosa USA (WI) 28 Qa24
Waverly USA (IA) 27 Pj24
Waverly USA (MO) 35 Pj26
Waverly USA (NE) 27 Pg25
Waverly USA (NY) 29 Qg24
Waverly USA (TN) 36 Qb27
Waverly USA (VA) 31 Qg27
Wawa CDN (ONT) 20 Qc22
Wawanesa CDN (MAN) 19 Pf21
Wawota CDN (SAS) 18 Pd21
Waxahachie USA (TX) 35 Pg29
Waycross USA (GA) 37 Qd30
Wayerton CDN (NB) 22 Rc22
Wayland USA (NY) 29 Qg24
Wayne USA (NE) 27 Pg24
Wayne USA (WV) 29 Qd26
Wayne City USA (IL) 28 Qa26
Waynesboro USA (GA) 37 Qd29
Waynesboro USA (MS) 36 Qa30
Waynesboro USA (PA) 29 Qf26
Waynesboro USA (TN) 36 Qb28
Waynesburg USA (PA) 29 Qe26
Waynesville USA (MO) 28 Pj27
Waynesville USA (NC) 37 Qd28
Waynoka USA (OK) 35 Pf27
Wayside USA (VA) 31 Qg27
Weagamow Lake CDN (ONT) 19 Pk19
Weatherford USA (OK) 35 Pf28
Weatherford USA (TX) 35 Pg29
Weaton USA (MD) 29 Qg26
Weaver USA (MN) 27 Pk23
Weaverville USA (CA) 24 Od25
Webbville USA (KY) 29 Qd26
Webequie CDN (ONT) 20 Qb19
Webster USA (ND) 19 Pf21
Webster USA (NY) 29 Qg24
Webster USA (SD) 27 Pg23
Webster City USA (IA) 27 Pj24
Webster Springs USA (WV) 29 Qe26
Weches USA (TX) 35 Ph30
Wedge Point CDN (NS) 22 Rc24
Wedowee USA (AL) 36 Qc29
Weed USA (CA) 24 Od25
Weedville USA (PA) 29 Qf25
Weeks USA (LA) 36 Pk31
Weeping Water USA (NE) 27 Pg25
Weirton USA (OH) 29 Qe25
Weiser USA (ID) 24 Og23
Weiss USA (LA) 36 Pk30
Weitchpec USA (CA) 24 Od25
Wekusko CDN (MAN) 19 Pf18
Welch USA (WV) 37 Qe27
Weldon USA (NC) 31 Qg27
Welling CDN (ALB) 17 Oj21
Wellington CDN (ONT) 29 Qg24
Wellington USA (CO) 26 Pc25
Wellington USA (KS) 35 Pg27
Wellington USA (UT) 33 Ok26
Wellman USA (TX) 34 Pd29
Wells USA (NV) 25 Oh25
Wells USA (TX) 35 Ph30
Wells Gray Provincial Park ☆ CDN (BC) 16 Oe19
Wellston USA (OH) 29 Qd26
Wellsville USA (MO) 28 Pk26
Wellsville USA (NY) 29 Qg24
Wellwood CDN (MAN) 19 Pf20
Welsford CDN (NB) 22 Rb23
Welsh USA (LA) 36 Pj30
Welshpool CDN (NB) 22 Rb23
Wembley CDN (ALB) 15 Of18
Wemindji CDN (QUE) 21 Qf19
Wenatchee USA (WA) 16 Oe22
Wenden USA (AZ) 33 Oj29
Wendover USA (UT) 25 Oh25
Wenona USA (MD) 29 Qh26
Wentworth Centre CDN (NS) 22 Rd23
Wentzville USA (MO) 28 Pk26
Weott USA (CA) 24 Od25
Werner Lake CDN (ONT) 19 Ph20
Weslaco USA (TX) 40 Pg32
Weslemkoon CDN (ONT) 29 Qg23
Wesley USA (ME) 22 Rb23
Wesleyville CDN (NFL) 23 Rj21
Wessington Springs USA (SD) 26 Pf23
Wesson USA (MS) 36 Pk30
West USA (TX) 35 Pg30
Westbank CDN (BC) 16 Of21
West Bend CDN (SAS) 18 Pd20
West Bend USA (WI) 28 Qa24
Westboro USA (WI) 27 Pk23
Westbourne CDN (MAN) 19 Pf20
West Branch USA (IA) 27 Pk25
West Branch USA (MI) 28 Qc23
Westbridge CDN (BC) 16 Of21
Westbrook USA (ME) 22 Qk24
Westbrook USA (TX) 34 Pe29
Westby USA (MT) 18 Pc21
Westby USA (WI) 27 Pk24
West Chester USA (PA) 29 Qh26
West Chichagof Yakobi Wilderness ☆ USA (AK) 14 Ng17
Westcliffe USA (CO) 34 Pc26
West Columbia USA (TX) 41 Ph31
West End BS 43 Qf32
Westerly USA (RI) 30 Qk25
Western USA (NE) 27 Pg25
Westerville USA (OH) 29 Qd25

West Fargo USA (ND) 19 Pg22
Westfield CDN (NB) 22 Rb23
Westfield USA (MA) 30 Qj24
Westfield USA (NY) 29 Qf24
West Frankfort USA (IL) 36 Qa27
West Glacier USA (MT) 17 Oj21
West Hamlin USA (WV) 29 Qd26
West Hawk Lake CDN (MAN) 19 Ph21
Westhope USA (ND) 18 Pe21
West Jordan USA (UT) 25 Ok25
West Levant USA (ME) 22 Ra23
West Liberty USA (IA) 27 Pk25
West Liberty USA (KY) 37 Qd27
Westlock CDN (ALB) 17 Oj18
Westmeath CDN (QUE) 29 Qg23
West Memphis USA (AR) 36 Pk28
Westminster USA (MD) 29 Qg26
Westmond USA (ID) 17 Og21
West Monroe USA (LA) 36 Pj29
Westmorland USA (CA) 33 Oh29
Weston USA (ID) 25 Oj24
Weston USA (WV) 29 Qe26
West Ossipee USA (NH) 22 Qk24
West Palm Beach USA (FL) 43 Qe32
West Plains USA (MO) 36 Pk27
West Point CDN (PEI) 22 Rc22
West Point USA (IA) 27 Pk25
West Point USA (NE) 27 Pg25
West Point USA (VA) 31 Qg27
West Poplar CDN (SAS) 18 Pb21
Westport CDN (NFL) 23 Rg21
Westport CDN (ONT) 29 Qg23
Westport USA (OR) 24 Od22
Westport USA (WA) 24 Oc22
Westray CDN (MAN) 18 Pe19
Westree CDN (ONT) 20 Qe22
West Salem USA (IL) 28 Qa26
Westside USA (MS) 36 Pk30
West Springfield USA (PA) 29 Qe25
West Thumb USA (WY) 25 Ok23
West Union USA (IA) 27 Pk24
West Valley City USA (UT) 25 Oj25
West Vancouver CDN (BC) 16 Od21
Westview CDN (BC) 16 Oc21
Westwego USA (LA) 36 Pk31
West Wendover USA (NV) 25 Oh25
Westwood USA (CA) 24 Oe25
West Yellowstone USA (MT) 25 Ok23
Wetaskiwin CDN (ALB) 17 Oj19
Wetmore USA (MI) 20 Qb22
Wevok USA (AK) 10 Mb11
Wewahitchka USA (FL) 36 Qc30
Weyakwin CDN (SAS) 18 Pc18
Weyburn CDN (SAS) 18 Pd21
Weymouth CDN (NS) 22 Rc23
Whalan USA (MN) 27 Pk24
Wharton USA (TX) 40 Pg31
Wha Ti CDN (NWT) 15 Og14
Wheatland CDN (MAN) 18 Pe20
Wheatland USA (CA) 32 Oe26
Wheatland USA (WY) 26 Pc24
Wheaton USA (MN) 27 Pg23
Wheeler USA (TX) 34 Pe28
Wheeler USA (WI) 27 Pk23
Wheeler Ridge USA (CA) 32 Of28
Wheelers Point USA (MN) 19 Ph21
Wheeling USA (WV) 29 Qe25
Whiskey Gap CDN (ALB) 17 Oj21
Whistler CDN (BC) 16 Od20
Whitbourne CDN (NFL) 23 Rj22
Whitby CDN (ONT) 29 Qf24
White Bear Lake USA (MN) 27 Pj23
White Castle USA (LA) 36 Pk30
White City CDN (SAS) 18 Pc20
Whiteclay USA (NE) 26 Pd24
Whitecourt CDN (ALB) 17 Oh18
Whitedog CDN (ONT) 19 Ph20
White Earth USA (MN) 19 Ph22
White Earth USA (ND) 18 Pd21
Whiteface USA (MN) 19 Pj22
Whitefish CDN (ONT) 29 Qe22
Whitefish USA (MT) 17 Oh21
Whitefish Point USA (MI) 20 Qc22
Whitehall USA (MT) 25 Oj23
Whitehall USA (NY) 30 Qj24
Whitehall USA (WI) 27 Pk23
Whitehaven USA (MD) 29 Qh26
White Haven USA (PA) 29 Qh25
Whitehorse CDN (YT) 14 Nh15
Whitehorse USA (SD) 26 Pe23
Whitehouse USA (TX) 35 Ph29
White Lake USA (SD) 26 Pf24
White Lake USA (WI) 28 Qa23
Whitelaw CDN (ALB) 15 Of17
Whitelaw CDN (ALB) 15 Of17
White Mountain USA (AK) 10 Md13
Whitemouth CDN (MAN) 19 Ph21
White Pine USA (MI) 20 Qa22
White River CDN (ONT) 20 Qc21
White River USA (SD) 26 Pe24
White River Junction USA (VT) 30 Qj24
White River National Wildlife Refuge ☆ USA (AR) 36 Pk28
White Rock CDN (BC) 16 Od21
White Salmon USA (WA) 24 Oe23
White Sands National Monument ☆ USA (NM) 34 Pb29
Whitesburg USA (KY) 37 Qd27
Whites City USA (NM) 34 Pc29
White Settlement USA (TX) 35 Pg29
Whiteshell Provincial Park ☆ CDN (MAN) 19 Ph20
White Signal USA (NM) 33 Pa29
White Star USA (MI) 28 Qc24
White Sulphur Springs USA (MT) 25 Ok22
White Sulphur Springs USA (WV) 37 Qe27
Whitetail USA (MT) 18 Pc21
Whiteville USA (NC) 37 Qf28
Whitewater CDN (MAN) 18 Pe21
Whitewater USA (CO) 33 Pa26
Whitewater USA (MT) 18 Pb21
Whitewater USA (WI) 28 Qa24
Whitewood CDN (SAS) 18 Pd20
Whitla CDN (ALB) 17 Ok21
Whitlash USA (MT) 17 Ok21
Whitley City USA (KY) 36 Qc27
Whitman USA (NE) 26 Pe24
Whitney CDN (ONT) 29 Qf23
Whitney USA (TX) 35 Pg30
Whitney Point USA (NY) 29 Qh24
Whittier USA (AK) 13 Na15
Whitworth CDN (QUE) 22 Ra22
Whonnock CDN (BC) 16 Od21
Why USA (AZ) 33 Oj29
Whycocomagh CDN (NS) 23 Re23
Wiarton CDN (ONT) 29 Qe23
Wibaux USA (MT) 18 Pc22
Wichita USA (KS) 35 Pg27
Wichita Falls USA (TX) 35 Pf29
Wickenburg USA (AZ) 33 Oj29
Wickes USA (AR) 35 Ph28
Wickett USA (TX) 34 Pd30
Wickliffe USA (KY) 36 Qa27
Widen USA (WV) 29 Qe26
Widewater CDN (ALB) 15 Oh18
Wiggins USA (CO) 34 Pc25
Wiggins USA (MS) 36 Qa30
Wilber USA (NE) 27 Pg25
Wilberforce CDN (ONT) 29 Qf23
Wilbert CDN (SAS) 17 Pa19
Wilbur USA (WA) 16 Of22
Wilburton USA (OK) 35 Ph28
Wilcox CDN (SAS) 18 Pc20
Wilcox USA (NE) 26 Pf25
Wildcat Hill Provincial Wilderness Park ☆ CDN (SAS) 18 Pd19
Wilde CDN (MAN) 19 Pg18
Wilderness Corner USA (VA) 29 Qg26
Wild Horse CDN (ALB) 17 Ok21
Wildwood USA (NJ) 31 Qh26
Wilgus USA (OH) 29 Qd26
Wilkes-Barre USA (PA) 29 Qh25
Wilkie CDN (SAS) 17 Pa19
Willard USA (MO) 35 Pj27
Willard USA (NM) 34 Pb28
Willcox USA (AZ) 33 Pa29
Willen CDN (MAN) 18 Pe20
Willet USA (NY) 29 Qh24
Williams USA (AZ) 33 Oj28
Williams USA (CA) 32 Od26
Williams USA (MN) 19 Ph21
Williamsburg USA (IA) 27 Pk25
Williamsburg USA (VA) 31 Qg27
Williams Junction USA (AR) 35 Pj28
Williams Lake CDN (BC) 16 Od19
Williamson USA (WV) 37 Qd27
Williamsport USA (AK) 12 Mj16
Williamsport USA (MD) 29 Qg26
Williamsport USA (PA) 29 Qg25
Williamston USA (NC) 31 Qg28
Williamstown USA (KY) 28 Qc26
Williamsville USA (MO) 36 Pk27
Willimantic USA (CT) 30 Qj25
Williston USA (FL) 37 Qd31
Williston USA (ND) 18 Pd21
Williston USA (SC) 37 Qe29
Willmar CDN (SAS) 18 Pd21
Willmar USA (MN) 27 Ph23
Willmore Wilderness Provincial Park ☆ CDN (ALB) 16 Of19
Willow USA (AK) 13 Na15
Willowbrook CDN (SAS) 18 Pd20
Willow Bunch CDN (SAS) 18 Pc21
Willow City USA (ND) 18 Pe21
Willow Creek CDN (SAS) 17 Pa21
Willow Point CDN (BC) 17 Og21
Willow Ranch USA (CA) 24 Oe25
Willow River USA (MN) 27 Pj22
Willows CDN (SAS) 18 Pc21
Willows USA (CA) 32 Od26
Willow Springs USA (MO) 36 Pk27
Willow Valley USA (IN) 28 Qb26
Willsboro USA (NY) 30 Qj23
Wills Point USA (TX) 35 Ph29
Wilma USA (FL) 36 Qc30
Wilmer USA (AL) 36 Qa30
Wilmington USA (DE) 29 Qh26
Wilmington USA (NC) 37 Qg28
Wilmington USA (OH) 29 Qd26
Wilmot USA (OH) 29 Qe25
Wilson CDN (ALB) 17 Oj21
Wilson USA (NC) 31 Qg28
Wilson Creek USA (WA) 16 Of22
Wilson's Creek National Battlefield Park ☆ USA (MO) 35 Pj27
Wilson's Mills CDN (QUE) 22 Qk22
Wilton USA (ME) 22 Qk23
Wilton USA (ND) 18 Pe22
Wilton USA (WI) 27 Pk24
Wiltondale CDN (NFL) 23 Rg21
Wimbledon USA (ND) 19 Pf22
Wimborne CDN (ALB) 17 Oj20
Winagami Lake Provincial Park ☆ CDN (ALB) 15 Og18
Winamac USA (IN) 28 Qb25
Winchester CDN (ONT) 29 Qh23
Winchester USA (ID) 24 Og22
Winchester USA (KY) 36 Qc27
Winchester USA (TN) 36 Qb28
Winchester USA (VA) 29 Qf26
Winchester USA (WI) 20 Qa22
Winchester USA (WY) 25 Pa24
Windber USA (PA) 29 Qf25
Wind Cave National Park ☆ USA (SD) 26 Pc24
Winder USA (GA) 37 Qd29
Windham USA (AK) 14 Nj17
Windom USA (MN) 27 Ph24
Wind River USA (WY) 25 Pa24
Windsor CDN (NFL) 23 Rh21
Windsor CDN (NS) 22 Rc23
Windsor CDN (ONT) 29 Qd24
Windsor CDN (QUE) 22 Qj23
Windsor USA (CO) 26 Pc25
Windsor USA (NC) 31 Qg28
Windsor Ruins ☆ USA (MS) 36 Pk30
Windthorst CDN (SAS) 18 Pd20
Windthorst USA (TX) 35 Pf29
Windygates CDN (MAN) 19 Pf21
Winfield CDN (ALB) 17 Oh19
Winfield CDN (BC) 16 Of21
Winfield USA (IA) 27 Pk25
Winfield USA (KS) 35 Pg27
Wing USA (ND) 18 Pe22
Wing, Port USA (WI) 19 Pk22
Wingate USA (TX) 34 Pe29
Winger USA (MN) 19 Ph22
Wingham CDN (ONT) 29 Qe24
Winifred USA (MT) 17 Pa22
Winisk CDN (ONT) 20 Qc18
Winisk River Provincial Park ☆ CDN (ONT) 20 Qb19
Wink USA (TX) 34 Pd30
Winkelman USA (AZ) 33 Ok29
Winkler CDN (MAN) 19 Pg21
Winnebago USA (MN) 27 Ph24
Winnemucca USA (NV) 24 Og25
Winnepegosis CDN (MAN) 19 Pf20
Winner USA (SD) 26 Pf24
Winnett USA (MT) 18 Pa22
Winnfield USA (LA) 36 Pj30
Winnie USA (TX) 41 Ph31
Winnipeg CDN (MAN) 19 Pg21
Winnipeg Beach CDN (MAN) 19 Pg20
Winnsboro USA (LA) 36 Pk29
Winnsboro USA (TX) 35 Ph29
Winona USA (AZ) 33 Ok28
Winona USA (MI) 20 Qa22
Winona USA (MN) 27 Pk23
Winona USA (MO) 36 Pk27
Winona USA (MS) 36 Qa29
Winslow USA (AR) 35 Ph28
Winslow USA (AZ) 33 Ok28
Winston USA (OR) 24 Od24
Winston-Salem USA (NC) 37 Qe27
Winter CDN (SAS) 17 Pa19
Winter Harbour CDN (BC) 16 Oa20
Winter Haven USA (FL) 43 Qe31
Winter Park USA (FL) 43 Qe31
Winterport USA (ME) 22 Ra23
Winters USA (TX) 35 Pf30
Winterset USA (IA) 27 Ph25
Winterville USA (NC) 31 Qg28
Winthrop USA (ME) 22 Ra23
Winthrop USA (MN) 27 Ph23
Winthrop USA (WA) 16 Oe21
Winton USA (MN) 19 Pk22
Wiscasset USA (ME) 22 Ra23
Wisconsin Dells USA (WI) 28 Qa24
Wisconsin Rapids USA (WI) 28 Qa23
Wisdom USA (MT) 25 Oj23
Wisemen USA (AK) 10 Mk12
Wishart CDN (SAS) 18 Pd20
Wishek USA (ND) 26 Pf22
Wisner USA (LA) 36 Pk30
Wisner USA (NE) 27 Pg25
Witt, De USA (AR) 36 Pk28
Witt, De USA (IA) 27 Pk25
Wittenberg USA (WI) 28 Qa23
Wittman USA (AZ) 33 Oj29
Witts Springs USA (AR) 35 Pj28
Woburn CDN (QUE) 22 Qk23
Woking CDN (ALB) 15 Of18
Wolcott USA (CO) 33 Pb26
Wolcott USA (NY) 29 Qg24
Wolf Creek USA (MT) 25 Oj22
Wolf Creek USA (OR) 24 Od24
Wolfeboro USA (NH) 22 Qk24
Wolford USA (ND) 19 Pf21
Wolf Point USA (MT) 18 Pc21
Wolseley CDN (SAS) 18 Pd20
Wolsey USA (SD) 26 Pf23
Wonowon CDN (BC) 15 Oe17
Woodbine USA (GA) 37 Qe30
Wood Buffalo National Park ☆ CDN (ALB) 15 Oj16
Woodburn USA (OR) 24 Od23
Woodbury USA (GA) 36 Qc29
Woodcock CDN (BC) 14 Oa18
Wood Islands CDN (PEI) 22 Rd23
Wood Lake USA (NE) 26 Pe24
Woodland USA (CA) 32 Oe26
Woodland USA (ME) 22 Rb23
Woodland USA (WA) 24 Od23
Woodland Caribou Provincial Park ☆ CDN (ONT) 19 Ph20
Woodland Park USA (CO) 34 Pc26
Woodlawn CDN (ONT) 29 Qg23
Wood Mountain CDN (SAS) 18 Pb21
Woodnorth CDN (MAN) 18 Pe21
Woodridge CDN (MAN) 19 Pg21
Wood River USA (NE) 26 Pf25
Woodrow CDN (SAS) 18 Pb21
Woodrow USA (AK) 13 Na15
Woodruff USA (WI) 28 Qa23
Woodsboro USA (TX) 40 Pg31
Woodsfield USA (OH) 29 Qe26
Woodside CDN (MAN) 19 Pf20
Woods Landing USA (WY) 26 Pb25
Woodson USA (TX) 35 Pf29
Woodstock CDN (NB) 22 Rb22
Woodstock CDN (ONT) 29 Qe24
Woodstock USA (IL) 28 Qa24
Woodstock USA (NY) 30 Qh24
Woodstock USA (VA) 29 Qf26
Woodsville USA (NH) 30 Qj23
Woodville CDN (ONT) 29 Qf23
Woodville USA (FL) 36 Qc30
Woodville USA (MS) 36 Pk30
Woodville USA (TX) 41 Ph30
Woodward USA (OK) 35 Pf27
Woodworth USA (ND) 19 Pf22
Woody Point CDN (NFL) 23 Rg21
Woonsocket USA (RI) 30 Qk25
Wooster USA (OH) 29 Qe25
Worcester USA (MA) 30 Qk24
Worden USA (MT) 25 Pa23
Worden USA (OR) 24 Oe24
Wordsworth CDN (SAS) 18 Pd21
Worland USA (WY) 25 Pb23
World's Largest Mineral Hot Springs ☆ USA (WY) 25 Pa24
Worsley CDN (ALB) 15 Of17
Wortham USA (TX) 35 Pg30
Worthington USA (MN) 27 Ph24
Worthville USA (KY) 28 Qc26
Wrangell USA (AK) 14 Nj17
Wray USA (CO) 34 Pd25
Wrecks ☆ MEX (YUC) 42 Qa34
Wrens USA (GA) 37 Qd29
Wrentham CDN (ALB) 17 Oj21
Wright USA (WY) 26 Pc24
Wrightsville USA (GA) 37 Qd29
Wrigley CDN (NWT) 15 Od14
Writing Rock ☆ USA (ND) 18 Pd21
Wroxton CDN (SAS) 18 Pe20
Wupatki National Monument ☆ USA (AZ) 33 Ok28
Wyalusing USA (PA) 29 Qg25
Wyandotte Caves ☆ USA (IN) 28 Qb26
Wyeville USA (WI) 27 Pk23
Wymore USA (NE) 35 Pg25
Wyndmere USA (ND) 27 Pg22
Wynndel CDN (BC) 17 Og21
Wynne USA (AR) 36 Pk28
Wyola USA (MT) 25 Pb23
Wyoming USA (MI) 28 Qc24
Wyoming USA (MN) 27 Pj23
Wytheville USA (VA) 37 Qe27

X

Xenia USA (IL) 28 Qa26
Xenia USA (OH) 29 Qd26
Xicoténcatl MEX (TAM) 40 Pf34
Xlacah ☆ MEX (YUC) 42 Qa35

Y

Yaak USA (MT) 17 Oh21
Yaguajay C (SS) 43 Qf34
Yahk CDN (BC) 17 Og21
Yakima USA (WA) 24 Oe22
Yakutat USA (AK) 14 Nf16
Yale CDN (BC) 16 Oe21
Yale USA (WA) 24 Od22
Yampa USA (CO) 26 Pb25
Yankton USA (SD) 27 Pg24
Yaqui MEX (SON) 38 Ok32
Yarmouth CDN (NS) 22 Rb24
Yarmouth USA (ME) 22 Qk24
Yates Center USA (KS) 35 Ph27
Yatesville USA (GA) 36 Qc29
Yávaros MEX (SON) 39 Pa32
Yawkey USA (WV) 29 Qe26
Yazoo City USA (MS) 36 Pk29
Ycliff CDN (ONT) 19 Pk20
Yécora MEX (SON) 39 Pa31
Yellow Creek USA (PA) 29 Qf25
Yellow Grass CDN (SAS) 18 Pc21
Yellowknife CDN (NWT) 15 Oh14
Yellowstone National Park ☆ USA (WY) 25 Ok23
Yellville USA (AR) 35 Pj27
Yelm USA (WA) 24 Od22
Yemassee USA (SC) 37 Qe29
Yerington USA (NV) 32 Of26
Ymir CDN (BC) 17 Og21
Yoakum USA (TX) 40 Pg31
Yoder USA (CO) 34 Pc2
Yoho National Park ☆ CDN (BC) 17 Og2
Yokena USA (MS) 36 Pk29
Yonkers USA (NY) 30 Qj25
York USA (AL) 36 Qa29
York USA (ND) 19 Pf21
York USA (NE) 27 Pg25
York USA (PA) 29 Qg2
York USA (SC) 37 Qe2
York Haven USA (PA) 29 Qg2
Yorkton CDN (SAS) 18 Pd2
Yosemite National Park ☆ USA (CA) 32 Of2
Youbou CDN (BC) 16 Oc2
Young CDN (SAS) 18 Pc2
Youngs Cove CDN (NB) 22 Rc2
Youngstown CDN (ALB) 17 Ok2
Youngstown USA (FL) 36 Qc3
Youngstown USA (NY) 29 Qf2
Youngstown USA (OH) 29 Qe2
Ypsilanti USA (MI) 29 Qd2
Yreka USA (CA) 24 Od2
Yuba City USA (CA) 32 Oe2
Yucatán MEX (YUC) 42 Qb3
Yucca USA (AZ) 33 Oh2
Yucca Valley USA (CA) 32 Og2
Yukon-Charley-Rivers National Preserve ☆ USA (AK) 11 Nd
Yukon Delta National Wildlife Refuge ☆ USA (AK) 10 Mc
Yukon Flats, National Wildlife Refuge ☆ USA (AK) 11 Nc
Yulee USA (FL) 37 Qe
Yuma USA (AZ) 33 Oh
Yuma USA (CO) 34 Pd

Z

Zacatecas MEX (ZAC) 39 Pd
Zacatosa MEX (COA) 39 Pd
Zachary USA (LA) 36 Pk
Zahl USA (ND) 18 Pd
Zanesville USA (OH) 29 Qd
Zapata USA (TX) 40 Pf
Zape MEX (DGO) 39 Pc
Zaragoza MEX (CHA) 34 Pb
Zaragoza MEX (CHA) 39 Pb
Zaragoza MEX (COA) 40 Pe
Zaragoza, Valle de MEX (CHA) 39 Pc
Zealand Station CDN (NB) 22 Rb
Zeballos CDN (BC) 16 Ob
Zebulon USA (NC) 31 Q
Zenia USA (CA) 24 Oe
Zephyr USA (TX) 35 P
Zephyrhills USA (FL) 43 Q
Zerkel USA (MN) 19 P
Zhoda CDN (MAN) 19 P
Zim USA (MN) 19 P
Zimmerman USA (MN) 27 P
Zion USA (IL) 28 Q
Zion National Park ☆ USA (UT) 33 O
Zolfo Springs USA (FL) 43 Q
Zumbro Falls USA (MN) 27
Zumbrota USA (MN) 27
Zuni USA (NM) 33
Zurich USA (MT) 18
Zwolle USA (LA) 35

Bildnachweis: Navajo Tribal Park: getty-images / Andrew Gunners (9); San Francisco Transamerica Bld.; Dumont Bildarchiv / C. Heeb (45); Miami South Beach, G. Haenel / laif (79); Arches NP, R. Harscher / laif (93); Miami Biscayne [B...] M. Malherbe / laif; LOOK-foto: age fotostock (99 l., 2 x 101, 102 r., 2 x 103, 105 l., 106 r., 108, 109 l., 110 r., 111 r., 2 x 112, 113 l., 2 x 114, 2 x 115, 116 l.), TerraVista (100 r.), Wolfgang Ehn (104 l.), Hauke Dressler (105 r.), Michael Boyny (10[...] Thomas Stankiewicz (107 r., 109 r.); picture alliance: dpa / Paul van Gaalen (98 l.), Bildagentur-online / McPhoto-SBA (89 r.), Arco Images / Doerr, C. & R. (99 r.), Arco Images / T.Schaeffer (100 l.), dpa / A.j. Sisco (102 l.), © Bruce Colem[an] Photoshot / Peter French (104 r.), © Bruce Coleman / Photoshot / Lee Rentz (106 l.), Oliver Blum (110 l.), Bildagentur-online / TIPS-Images (111 l.), WILDLIFE / Die Naturfotografen (113 r.), Arco Images / F.Poelking (116 r.)

Design: fpm – factor product münchen (Cover) / Stilradar, Stuttgart

→ 2016 © 2012 MAIRDUMONT, D-73751 Ostfildern (1.) Printed in Germany 01 30 131